# I BEG TO R ...

*Policing in Guernsey during the German Occupation*

William M. Bell

First published 1995

Made and printed in Great Britain by
The Guernsey Press Co, Ltd, Guernsey, Channel Islands.

ISBN 0 9520479 1 8

# CONTENTS

# ILLUSTRATIONS

During the occupation, cameras were confiscated by the Germans and film was unobtainable. Consequently the number of photographs available is extremely limited and their quality often poor. It is regretted that some of the photographs included in this book are not up to usual publication standard.

# ACKNOWLEDGEMENTS

The Author gratefully acknowledges the help, advice and information willingly given by the following persons. Without their assistance the scope and accuracy of the book would have been severely curtailed.

Arthur Bailey.
David Barry.
Stanley Bichard.
Paul Balshaw.
Rex Bonnel.
Peter Bougourd.
Rex Champion.
F.L.Duquemin.
Alec Forty.
Mrs Foster.
Bill Green.
Mrs Queenie Guillemette.
Richard Heaume.
B.B.Hodgson.
Elsie Kenny.
Ronald Langmead.
Francois Le Cocq.
M.Le Moignan.QPM.
Hugh Lenfestey and staff of the Island Archives Service.
Kenneth Lewis.
Mrs P.M.Mauger.
Mrs Mavis Tardif.
Walter Mahy.
Roy Northey.
Jack Salmon.
Alan Sarchet.
Fred W.Short.
Rose Short,
Kenneth Tough.
Frank Tuck.
Peter Vermeulen.

# FOREWORD

by Arthur Bailey

**Arthur Bailey, Chief Officer of Guernsey Police.**

I was honoured when invited by the author to write the foreword to 'I Beg to Report ...', although I must admit when I first heard that this book was to be written I had certain misgivings. However now that I have read the finished product I realise that those reservations were erroneous on my part. I recognise the vast amount of research that has been carried out in the preparation of this book. I congratulate the author for the authenticity of the facts as related and that nowhere does he express his opinion or attempts to draw conclusions, he leaves that to the reader.

I am particularly pleased to note that the book has at last 'laid to rest' the subject of the deportation of Jews from the Island by the German occupying authorities. It has been a subject so often aired in the past by the media, but the truth has never been as clearly defined as it is now in 'I Beg to Report...'.

Many of the facts related have never before been published and they are interesting, because they relate to Police officers carrying out their day to day duties both prior to and during the occupation. Of course the policing during the occupation period is unique to any British Police Force. The five year period of occupation is the only occasion in the history of a British Police Force that they have had to carry out their duties as civilian Police whilst occupied by an enemy.

The Island Police Force has changed dramatically since its formation in 1920. Today we have a force equal to any in the United Kingdom. It is so vastly different to when I joined the service in January 1945. I well recall my night shifts of those early days, carrying out observation duties in stables, greenhouses and open fields and on occasions being 'visited' by German troops, bent on stealing cattle or foodstuffs and wondering what sort of response I was going to get when I challenged them.

I strongly recommend this book, it not only contains the history of the Island Police Force, but covers a period of the Island's history which is both unique and interesting.

*Arthur Bailey joined the Guernsey Police as an Auxiliary Constable in January 1945. He was appointed Chief Officer in 1977 and retired, after 38 years service, in 1983.*

# Chapter 1

## AN INSPECTOR ARRIVES

Inspector William Sculpher, Chief Officer of the Island Police, saluted the newly arrived German officer and handed him a sealed letter from Victor Carey, the Lieutenant Governor and Bailiff of Guernsey.

Earlier the same evening, Sunday 30th June 1940, an air raid warning had sounded and shortly afterwards five German Junkers troopcarriers landed at the Island's airport. The advance party of German troops, on their motorcycle combinations equipped with mounted machine guns, quickly fanned out and secured the immediate area. Road blocks were set up on the approaches to the airport.

At 8.45pm, Inspector Sculpher, together with Deputy Inspector Langmead, Police Sergeant Harper and Constable Plevin, set off for the airport in the Police car. He took with him the sealed envelope addressed to 'The Officer Commanding German Forces, Guernsey' which Victor Carey, the Lieutenant Governor and Bailiff, had personally given him three days previously. He had been instructed to deliver the letter if and when the Island was occupied.

As they approached the airport they were stopped by German soldiers and escorted the rest of the way under armed guard.

Inspector Sculpher handed the letter to a German officer, who passed it to his Commandant, who then asked the Inspector to read the letter to him. It stated:-

"This Island has been declared an Open Island by His Majesty's Government of the United Kingdom. There are in it no armed forces of any description.

The bearer has been directed to hand this communication to you. He does not understand the German language.

Victor Carey
Lieutenant Governor and Bailiff of Guernsey".

The Inspector assured the German Commandant that there were no armed forces in the Island and escorted him and other officers to the Royal Hotel. The Commandant demanded to see the 'Chief Man in the Island'. Mr A.J.Sherwill, His Majesty's Attorney General* and President of the newly created Controlling Committee, was sent for and arrived in the Police car with Victor Carey. Later the Postmaster, Mr Chapell, the Telephone Manager, Mr Bennett and the Harbourmaster, Captain Franklin were also summoned by the Germans. An interpreter was requested and the Inspector sent for the proprietor of the Hotel de Normandie, Mr Isler.

The Commandant announced that the Island was forthwith under German occupation and that the German Headquarters would, for the present, be the Royal Hotel. He directed that a list of Orders and Regulations be published in the two local newspapers the next day and that no charge was to be made for those editions. At 11.30pm the Island officials were permitted to leave the Royal Hotel.

* H.M.Attorney General also known as H.M.Procureur.

At the conclusion of the meeting the German Commandant instructed Inspector Sculpher, "to carry on Police duties as usual". Policing in Guernsey was never to be quite the same again.

The Police Force in Guernsey had only come into being as an Island Force in April 1920. Its first Inspector was Edward Albert Green, who was regarded as the 'father of the Force'.

Inspector Green joined the Metropolitan Police in 1886. He was promoted Sergeant in 1890 and Inspector in 1898. Further promotion to Divisional Inspector and Chief Inspector followed before he retired in 1912.

A well-earned retirement, however, was not to be long enjoyed, as within a week of the outbreak of the Great War Mr Green was recalled to duty, assisting with the enrolment of Special Constables.

In October 1914 the Commissioner of Police sent for him and asked if he would go to Guernsey, which needed a Chief Inspector of Police who would be capable of organising an efficient insular Police body. Mr Green accepted and arrived in Guernsey on October 14th 1914.

Up to that time policing in Guernsey had been the responsibility of the ten Parishes. The elected Constables who were administrators rather than law enforcers, coped adequately with the incidents and crime arising in their parishes. Very little had changed over the centuries and the parochial system was reasonably efficient, though some of the parishes, Vale, St Martin and St Sampson employed uniformed Constables. St Peter Port employed 12 policemen who were known as the Town Police. Recruitment at that time was based on height and weight rather than ability and education. Each Constable, paid or elected, only had jurisdiction in his own parish.

In February 1915 a temporary wartime Island-wide Police Force, with a Station at the Constables Office in Le Marchant Street, was brought into being, with Mr Green as Chief Officer at an annual salary of £218.8.0.

In 1919 the States decided to make the wartime arrangement permanent and the new Force commenced its duties on the 10th April 1920 with an establishment of thirty officers. During Inspector Green's period in command, the force grew to thirty-four and functioned efficiently, despite ever increasing duties, which in the main were due to the advent of the motor car.

In 1930 the States of Guernsey invited applications for the post of Inspector to fill the vacancy occasioned by the retirement of Inspector Green.

**Inspector W. R. Sculpher.**

The advertisement for the post caught the eye of W.R.Sculpher, a 47 year old Metropolitan Sub Divisional Inspector who would soon be due for retirement. The position advertised was tenable to the age of 65. Inspector Sculpher was a dedicated policeman, who enjoyed the life and had no desire to retire. After consulting his wife and superior officer, he applied for the post. It was a simple application, a hand written letter, as there were no application forms supplied. He enclosed a number of testimonials and made sure it arrived before the closing date of the 30th August 1930.

William Robert Sculpher, a married man with no family, was born in Norfolk on

7th February 1883. He joined the Metropolitan Police on 11th July 1904, having previously served 2 years with the Railway Police. He was promoted Sergeant in February 1910, Station Sergeant in February 1917, then Inspector in June 1921, before being appointed sub divisional Inspector on 7th August 1925. He was a tall man of commanding appearance, with blue eyes, hair just turning grey and a mole on his right cheek.

His application, along with 159 others, was received by the Bailiff, Arthur W.Bell, who was also the President of the Appointments Board. A short list was speedily compiled and the candidates invited to attend for interview on the 8th September 1930. Mr Sculpher travelled over from the mainland with his wife and was accommodated at the Grange Lodge Hotel.

At the interview, held at the Royal Court House, the Board were clearly impressed with Inspector Sculpher's record in the Metropolitan Police. The references which had been obtained showed him as a disciplinarian and an officer who always wanted to be sure of his facts before making a decision. His bearing and confidence also influenced the Board which had no hesitation in selecting him as the new Police Inspector. The Press was informed and the news published in *'The Star'* that evening.

The Appointments Board directed that His Majesty's Attorney General prepare an Agreement between the States and Mr Sculpher setting out the conditions of the appointment. The Agreement was dated 28th October 1930 and stipulated that the salary was to be £350 per annum, rising by annual increments of £10 to £400 and that he should be entitled to 28 days holiday leave a year.

The Inspector was required to diligently and faithfully serve the States and:-

"shall be responsible for the performance of the duties assigned to the States Police Force under the Law of the tenth of January Nineteen Hundred and twenty, entitled 'Loi ayant rapport A la Police Salariee pour l'Ile entiere' and any subsequent Law amending or replacing the same and if nominated by the States Supervisor and approved by His Excellency the Lieutenant Governor, he shall also perform the duties of Immigration Officer and Registration Officer under the Law of the twenty ninth day of July Nineteen hundred and twenty two entitled 'Loi portant reglementation sur L'admission et l'enregistrement des Etrangers' and any subsequent law amending or replacing the same.

He shall also perform such duties as may be assigned to him under such laws as may from time to time be enacted. And generally his duties shall also comprise the collection of evidence and attendance at the Magistrate Court on behalf of the Law Officers of the Crown for the prosecution of all punishable offences in which he shall be under the direction of the Law Officers of the Crown or either of them, the command and maintenance of discipline in the Police Force and the training of the members thereof in the execution of their duties, attendance at meetings of the States Police Committee as required by the Committee and the execution of such instructions as the said Committee in the due exercise of its powers may give him."

The Agreement could be determined by either party, giving three months notice. The States could, however, terminate the Agreement at any time in the event of misconduct on the part of the Inspector.

Inspector W.R.Sculpher took up his appointment on the 15th October 1930 and quickly realised that he had exchanged life as a small but important cog in the most famous Police Force in the greatest metropolis on earth, for being Chief of one of the smallest and least known Forces in the world.

Everything was of a different scale, even the Police Station, which had moved from the two rooms in Le Marchant Street to the slightly larger premises at St James' Chambers, was tiny and primitive in comparison to the labyrinth of Scotland Yard.

**St James Chambers, left of centre, before becoming the Police Station in 1920.**

The Station had been enlarged by incorporating the next door Umbrella Shop. Electricity was only installed on the ground floor and access to the first floor, where the Inspector had his office, was by the outside stairs. The Inspector's room was also used by the Police Committee for its meetings. The top floor was let to the Guernsey Operatic and Dramatic Club and was also used by the Santangelo Orchestra for band practices.

On the ground floor was the reception area, the Sergeants' room and a small room, 10 feet x 6 feet, which was used by Dr Bostock, the Police Doctor, for examination of suspected drunks.

The forecourt of the Station was usually crowded with bicycles as there was no cycle shed. There was a total lack of privacy as everything that was said in the reception office could be heard by all and sundry. Whenever someone was arrested and taken to the Station a crowd would gather outside to listen to the proceedings. Often a sergeant or a constable would go outside and 'shoo' the crowd away.

In 1920, when the Force was inaugurated, the Police Committee had set about trying to obtain suitable premises. A scheme for a Station on the Lefebvre Street end of the Royal Court buildings was shelved owing to the cost - estimated at £3,000. Each year the matter of a purpose-built Police Station was raised by the Committee but no progress made. Mr Sculpher was soon to be heard complaining that the building was "totally unsuitable for a Police Station and a disgrace to the community".

One of the duties of the Police Inspector was to conduct all prosecutions before the Magistrate in the Police Court but the Island's Courts, their procedures and traditions were an entirely new and different concept from that with which the Inspector had previously known.

The Magistrate, H.J.Casey Esq., presided over the Police Court and dealt with all cases brought by the Police. The Court had the power to award imprisonment up to two months on any one charge. The Court also sat on Inquests and dealt with Infractions of Ordinances, except in cases in which the possible liability of the defendant exceeded £10. Such cases were referred to the Royal Court.

There was also the Ordinary Court which was presided over by the Bailiff or one of the Lieutenant Bailiffs sitting with two or more Jurats. This Court dealt with Civil actions of all kinds, with the exception of Petty Debts, up to £25, which were dealt with by the Magistrate sitting as the Petty Debts Court.

The Bailiff or a Lieutenant Bailiff presided over the Royal Court, sitting with not less than seven Jurats. In Criminal cases the Court was assisted by the Crown Officers and could award any penalty, including the death penalty. In Civil actions the Court dealt with appeals from the Ordinary Court and it was also the Local Licensing Assembly, dealing with all applications for Hotels, Clubs, Cabarets and Beer and Cider Houses. The Full Royal Court swore in such officials as the Bailiff and the Lieutenant Governor.

The Court of Chief Pleas was composed in the same manner as the Royal Court with the assistance of the Crown Officers and a Constable representing each Parish. This Court promulgated Ordinances and amongst other duties, dealt with the swearing in of Special Constables.

The level of crime in Guernsey was, by Metropolitan standards, almost non existent. In 1929 the number of 'actions' taken by the Guernsey Police under the various Laws and Ordinances was 249, 174 Charges and 75 Summons cases.*

Prior to Mr Sculpher's appointment the Police Committee had set a budget for 1931. It provided for a net expenditure of £6,002**.

The Police Force that Inspector Sculpher commanded in 1930, consisted of 33 Sergeants and Constables.

| | | | | | |
|---|---|---|---|---|---|
| Sergeant. | 1 | F.G.Le Poidevin | Sergeant. | 2 | A.W.Howlett |
| Sergeant. | 3 | J.Langmead | Sergeant. | 4 | E.J.Pill |
| Sergeant. | 5 | F.P.Duquemin | Sergeant. | 6 | A.J.Langmead |
| Sergeant. | 7 | F.J.Banneville | Constable. | 8 | S.Gallienne |
| Constable. | 9 | C.J.Tardif | Constable. | 10 | J.Harper |
| Constable. | 11 | H.J.Bull | Constable. | 12 | E.Banneville |
| Constable. | 13 | G.H.Dyson | Constable. | 14 | A.P.Lamy |
| Constable. | 15 | W.J.Burton | Constable. | 16 | G.Froome |
| Constable. | 17 | M.Jarvis | Constable. | 18 | H.P.Smith |
| Constable. | 19 | D.Browning | Constable. | 20 | F.W.Whare |
| Constable. | 21 | F.A.Le Page | Constable. | 22 | H.F.Chappon |
| Constable. | 23 | W.Quin | Constable. | 24 | H.Brown |
| Constable. | 25 | J.C.Cobley | Constable. | 26 | G.Perry |
| Constable. | 27 | R.Kimber | Constable. | 28 | P.J.F.Bretel |
| Constable. | 29 | J.Grainger | Constable. | 30 | C.Le Lievre |
| Constable. | 31 | Y.H.Mercier | Constable. | 32 | H.T.Pugh |
| Constable. | 33 | T.J.Gaudion | | | |

The Force included five members of the former Town Police. Sergeant Fred Le Poidevin and Constable Sam Gallienne both joined on March 15th 1902, while Sergeant John Langmead, Constables Cliff Tardif and Mark Jarvis were later recruits.

The average age of the force was almost 39, with only 8 men being under thirty. Eight were over fifty, three being over 60 and Constable Emile Banneville 64. The youngest was Constable Frank Le Page who was just 24. Sergeant Langmead and Constable Banneville both had sons in the Force. Sergeant John Langmead's son, Sergeant Arthur J.Langmead had clearly impressed his superiors, because after only two year's service he had been promoted Corporal and two years later Sergeant.

The Inspector made time to get to know all his men. He wanted to command a friendly united team and he wanted to know each man as an individual.

Shortly after taking up his appointment he met the full Police Committee for the first time. He had previously met the President, Mr W.E.Poat, when he was

* See Appendix 1 for details of Charges and Summons cases
**See Appendix 2 for Estimated Police Budget for 1931.

interviewed. The other members were A.H.Brice Vice-President, Col D.C.Le Pelley, Col A.L.Elliott, W.W.Watkin, I.C.Ozanne, Captain L.D.Gosselin, C.E.Agnew and T.Millard.

The relationship between the Inspector of Police and the Island Police Committee, for a time, was going to prove to be progressively more difficult. The Inspector saw his role as being a servant of the Establishment with a professional duty to run an efficient and modern Police Force. He regarded it as his responsibility to recommend and bring about changes, whilst at the same time maintaining a tight control on expenditure.

The Police Committee, on the other hand, quickly saw its role as one of keeping the new Inspector in check. His ambitious plans, although inexpensive, were scrutinised and delayed, much to his annoyance. After being in post for little over a year he wrote to the President, saying :-

"...this subject has been previously discussed in Committee and no action taken. It has again been raised and would give me satisfaction to know exactly where I stand." He concluded by saying "The whole matter is one for the Committee and I merely ask for a plain yes or no."

The Committee at its meeting on 12th October 1931 asked the Inspector to prepare a report "examining the working of the present system", the classic and time honoured way of any Committee wishing to bring about delay.

One success the Inspector had been able to achieve was the appointment of Sergeant Arthur Langmead as Clerk Sergeant on the 1st January 1931. Langmead also became Secretary to the Police Committee. For the previous seven years he had been employed on clerical duties and was an accomplished typist and in his own expression, 'almost an expert in shorthand'.

The Inspector knew that any proposals that he made as a result of the review would be unlikely to be accepted if they involved additional expenditure so he shrewdly drew up a Budget for 1932 which was no more and no less than the one he had inherited.

In his report he reviewed the 'Police Organisation' and defined his duties as :-

"General supervision of all matters, preparation of cases and prosecution of offenders before the Magistrate. Obtaining evidence and conducting Inquests. Attendance at Ordinary and Royal Courts, interviewing complainants and tendering legal advice to the poorer classes etc."

Sergeants, he reported, worked on an overlapping system, one coming on duty every four hours from 6.00am to 10.00pm. They worked the first 4 hours of their tour of duty in the Station and patrolled for the next four hours. The Constables, in the main, paraded at 6.00am, 2.00pm and 10.00pm for beat duty. Each Sergeant and Constable was allowed one day off in ten.

A motorcycle patrol operated from 8.00am to midnight through the parishes of St Martin, Forest, St Peter, Torteval, St Saviour and St Andrew on a route roughly from Town to Pleinmont and via Cobo back to Town, telephoning in periodically to report or receive instructions.

The Beats were :-

No.1 North of a line from the Red Lion, Banques to Grandes Rocques.

No.2 From Grandes Rocques to Richmond, St Saviour and through St Andrew, St Peter and Torteval.

No.3 Forest, St Peter and Torteval.

No.4 From the Station via the Grange, Croutes, Kings Road to Ruettes Brayes, Colborne Road to Pier Steps.

No.5 Pier Steps to Red Lion, Rohais and the Grange.

No.6 White Rock and the Harbour.

The Patrols were :-

No.1 High Street - Town Church to Weighbridge including the Arcade, Quay and Pollet.

No.2 Albert Pier - Town Church to Bathing Places and Castle Emplacement.

No.3 St Sampson - Harbour, north and south.

No.4 Fountain Street - Fountain Street to Trinity Square, Market Square and Place.

The Inspector reported that in his view, "The Country Parishes were poorly policed, many of the roads were not being patrolled simply because it was not possible with the available strength of the Force. There are 300 miles of main roads in the Island and if this was worked out at 2½ miles per hour per PC per day it would require 50 Policemen for these roads alone, which would mean doubling the existing Force."

He continued, "By utilising the foot Patrols mainly in Town, it may be said that St Peter Port has more than its share. On the present strength, this is true, but it must be borne in mind that 75% of the licensed premises and Boarding Houses are in Town. All the main Banks and shops are there. All omnibus traffic emerges from St Peter Port and most of the commerce goes to and from the White Rock and the greater portion of the travelling public make the Town its rendezvous".

The Inspector was happy to report, that in his view there was not much serious crime in the Island, otherwise an increase in the strength of the Force would have had to be seriously considered. He did, however, recommend that instead of a weekly change of beat, it should take place on the first Monday in each calendar month. He believed it would have a beneficial effect on his men and give them a better opportunity of knowing what was taking place around them.

An additional motorcycle would improve policing, but owing to the economic situation he did not feel disposed to recommend such expenditure at that time. However, he recommended that when a vacancy occurred the purchase of an additional motorcycle should be considered, even if it meant that the Force establishment be reduced by one Constable for a period of time.

Mr Sculpher concluded his report by saying that having regard to the need for stringent economy, he did not feel justified in suggesting any further variations in the working of the existing personnel. "However" he added " I would suggest that the whole subject be reviewed in 12 months' time"

In May 1933 two vacancies arose in the Force due to the retirement of Constables 25 J.C.Cobley and 12 Emile Banneville. There was always a considerable number of men interested in making a career in the Police Force. It was regarded as a secure job, with a pension, which, at the time, was the ambition of many young men, particularly if they had served in His Majesty's Forces. From the many applications, the Inspector selected seven local candidates for interview. He wrote requesting each to attend at his office for an examination on the 29th April. One man declined, one did not reply and five duly presented themselves at 8.00pm.

The Inspector tested them with, as he put it, a fairly stiff piece of dictation, reading aloud, a topical essay and some elementary arithmetic.*

Three candidates, H.E.Piesing, C.H.Bougourd and G.H.Gale appeared to be suitable and they were interviewed by the Police Committee. Piesing and Bougourd were appointed and sworn in before the Court on the 25th May 1933. These were the first changes in the Force since the Inspector's appointment. "That fact in itself suggests general satisfaction", Mr Sculpher observed.

* See Appendix 3 for details of the examination.

Harold Edward Piesing, 24, known as 'Snip', who had previously completed six years' service in the 3rd Dragoon Guards as a Musketry Instructor, became PC 25.

Clifford Bougourd, 26, universally known as 'Chipper' was given the Number 12. For the previous eight years he worked for the building firm of J. and S. Rabey. He had served 5 years in the Royal Guernsey Militia, reaching the rank of Sergeant.

The Inspector quickly made his assessment of Constable Bougourd:- "Active, shows aptitude for his work and with more experience should develop into a first class man".

In the summer of 1933 Mr Sculpher felt it appropriate to again raise the matter of re-organisation of the Force with the Committee. He had, in his opinion, been appointed to bring the experience and expertise that he had gained with the Metropolitan Police, to the benefit of the Island and its Force. There were many matters that needed urgent attention if the Force was going to function in a proper and efficient manner.

The Committee, he found to his annoyance, had a built-in resistance to change, or change at too fast a rate. They saw it as their duty and responsibility to supervise and regulate not only the administrative side of the Force, but also the day to day operations. They wished to be involved and have the final say in many of the decisions which had been his prerogative as a Metropolitan Inspector. He accepted that in a small community with a small Force it was inevitable that the Police Committee would get involved in more of the detail than he had been accustomed. However, he sought to minimize their involvement by taking decisions and then, as he put it 'wait and see what happens'.

At the August meeting of the Police Committee, in 1933, he again raised the matter of re-organisation and said that he saw his role as being solely responsible for Police operations, with the Committee dealing with administrative and financial matters.

The Police Committee responded, predictably, by setting up a sub-Committee to:-

'Examine and report on the question of re-organisation of the Island Police Force'.

The Inspector was asked, by the sub-Committee, to submit written reports, which he did, but only on matters of his choosing. In presenting his first report he added:-

"In so doing I recognise that some of my remarks will possibly be criticized, but I wish it to be clearly understood that any statements or suggestions of mine are made solely in the interests of the Island".

He identified Recruiting, Training and Discipline as fundamental matters in the administration of the Force and that priority should be given to recruitment, as everything depends on the type of men joining the Force. When the Island Police Force came into being, many elderly men were drafted from the Old Town Constabulary and the procedure and practices they acquired in their early days still remained. He added "only time will eradicate them". Training had, in his opinion, been neglected and discipline could be improved, but that largely depended on training.

"Police work has undergone and will continue to undergo great changes. Fraud has taken the place of drunkenness as the major crime. Criminals are more mobile, due to the advent of cheap and fast travel. The Force must be trained and prepared to meet these changes. The success or failure of a Police Force depends on the keenness or apathy of a number of individuals working independently and in a large measure without supervision.

We want a Police Force, each member of which is capable of taking the proper action in any case that may arise and be able to submit a full report, concluding with the proper action taken. At present, in many cases the matter is only half completed, being left for my office to issue directions. The men cannot be wholly blamed for this, they have never mastered their job, through lack of teaching."

Although the Force had been in existence for a number of years, no regulations were in force to govern it. There was no code of conduct, so that a man would know when he was committing a breach of discipline.

"For instance" the Inspector explained "supposing on a hot day an officer on duty walks into a public house, purchases and consumes a drink. This would be regarded by me as a breach of discipline. I ask, is there anything laid down for the Officer's guidance, that he should not do what others, in different walks, are permitted to do? This should be remedied, a policeman should know exactly what he can do and be brought to book if he exceeds his duty."

As regards public criticism, the Inspector said that "the only thing we hear is, the Police cost £6,000 a year and what do we get for it". He answered this criticism, by using every Chief Officer's ploy of comparing Guernsey with a series of mainland forces who were costing their communities at least double, while being smaller both in population and size.

He threw caution to the wind by saying that he was "clearly of the opinion that very few people, including some members of the Committee, know but little of the doings of the Police".

Continuing in the same vein:-

"Referring to supervision I must here blame the Police Committee for what I consider to be lack of initiative. The Police are a utility protective Force engaged for the whole 24 hours and as Chief I am available always with no public holidays, indeed these mean extra work. Despite this I am obliged to live where I can, at present in Cognon Road, Vale, two and a half miles from the Station. It is true that I am on the telephone, this many people know and quite a number regard my house as a sub-station, sometimes calling as late as 11.30pm on matters that could be dealt with at the Station."

"The Town is responsible for 75% of the Police work and that is where I should live, or not more than a quarter of a mile from the Station, in a house provided for the purpose. I could then easily attend to unusual matters, liberate detained persons earlier and patrol the Town at unusual and late hours. I am convinced that many illegal acts are taking place during the early hours of the morning, but who can expect me to walk two and a half miles after 1.00 or 2.00am and be back at 9.30am to attend to correspondence and prepare cases for Court. Moreover such supervision would have a beneficial effect on the discipline of the Force."

He reported that he was finding it impossible to give the required time and detailed attention to the investigation of criminal cases. Further, owing to the sensitivity of some people, he felt that many enquiries could be more effectively performed by an officer in plain clothes. He therefore proposed that one of the Sergeants be appointed Detective Sergeant, to be wholly employed in plain clothes, for which he would be given an allowance of 5/- per week. This officer could also enforce some of the Ordinances which were said to be ignored. He could meet the Mail and other boats and make notes of those who arrive and depart, check lodging house registers and make such Alien, firearm and other enquiries as were necessary.

Whilst he made no recommendations as to the deployment of Constables, he did suggest an additional motorcycle patrol to cover the 10.00pm to 6.0am shift, so as to cover the whole 24 hours.

"Occasionally after midnight a motor car is missing, obviously taken for a joy ride. With the whole 24 hours covered we should stand a better chance of dealing with this and give increased attention to the country." He proposed that the Fountain Street beat be abolished and the High Street extended to provide for the additional motorcycle patrolman.

In time he hoped to see the whole of the Island, except for St Peter Port, patrolled by motorcycles. The motorcycle was far more effective, in his opinion, than foot or push bike patrols. There were two factors against motorcycles, the noise that advertises their presence and at night the light which can be seen a long way off, giving wrongdoers the opportunity to hide. However, these, compared with the increased protection, could be regarded as minor drawbacks.

On the matter of leave, the system which he had inherited allowed for each officer one day off in ten. He pointed out that in most employment, employees were given one and a half days off in seven. Police on the mainland received one day each week as a rest day and he recommended that the same should apply in Guernsey.

In order to improve efficiency he proposed that a comprehensive instruction book be issued to every Police officer and every member of the Committee. This would be a confidential document and embrace conditions of service, discipline, street duty, accidents, criminal law, Police powers and, as far as possible, instruct members of the Force what they were expected to do under given circumstances.

As it would take some time to compile and produce, in the meantime he proposed to set aside at least two afternoons each month for lectures on Police work. Although much was required from the men, this should act as an incentive for them to learn their work and to master their chosen occupation.

The Inspector also raised the matter of releasing persons arrested but still untried. There was no legal provision for granting bail to these prisoners, they could only be released on his authority. He suggested that serious consideration should be given to the States enacting a Bail Law.

Summarizing his thoughts on Law and Order, he observed that :-

"I freely admit that there is a certain free and easy attitude and the inhabitants are ready to observe and obey the law, but already I can detect certain traits in the younger element, produced through education, that will cause Police trouble in the future. I suggest that in the main the observance of the law and obedience to the Police is brought about chiefly from ignorance and fear. In time these will disappear and we must be prepared; this can only be done by officers being thoroughly trained in their job."

The Police Committee, after considering a report from its sub-Committee, accepted the need for adequate training, the provision of an Instruction Book and regulations governing the Force. Sergeant Fred Banneville was promoted Detective Sergeant on 16th April 1934 and allowed to wear plain clothes. However, they refused to concede the improvement in leave and deferred a decision on an additional motorcycle patrol.

The Committee were not happy with the pressure being applied by the Inspector and they soon had the opportunity to assert their authority. Sergeant Fred Le Poidevin having reached the age of 65, retired. The Committee agreed to fill the vacancy by promotion and Mr Sculpher was asked for his recommendation.

This was the first occasion since being appointed that there was to be a change in the 'management' of the Force. He believed that the selection should be based on merit and take into consideration the candidate's initiative, energy and self reliance. The latter, he felt, was of paramount importance.

The Inspector selected a short list for the Committee's consideration:-

| | | |
|---|---|---|
| PC 10 Jack Harper | born 16.1.1900 | joined 14.5.22 |
| PC 30 Charles Le Lievre | born 10.6.1895 | joined 16.3.25 |
| PC 20 Frank Whare | born 13.5.1894 | joined 18.1.26 |
| PC 11 Harry Bull | born 7.5.1902 | joined 9.5.27 |

While only giving the most brief supporting information in respect of three of the candidates, he enthused over Constable Harper's qualities. Jack Harper had been employed as the car driver and driving licence tester for the previous five years. In this respect he had been brought into contact with a large number of the public without complaint. His activities as a policeman had made him a number of enemies, particularly among the motoring public. Although appearing in the witness box more than any other officer, he had never had his word successfully disputed. Mr Sculpher, added "Though lacking in polish, he will do the job while many are thinking of it and possesses a good working knowledge of how to do it. Therefore I beg to recommend his appointment as Sergeant."

The Committee exerted its authority by appointing PC C.Le Lievre. Mr Sculpher was furious.

Sergeant Le Lievre was appointed on the 16th April 1934. Two days later all the sergeants and constables submitted a 'Round Robin' requesting the President and Members of the Police Committee 'to grant 1 day per week leave instead of one day in ten as at present'. Some members of the Committee openly suspected the Inspector of 'encouraging' the Round Robin. The Committee was in no mood to consider the request seriously and inevitably the 'Round Robin' was rejected.

# Chapter 2

# PRACTICAL POLICING

In April 1935 Advocate Ambrose Sherwill was appointed His Majesty's Attorney General. As such he and the Inspector worked closely together and developed considerable respect for each others ability. Mr Sherwill took a great deal of interest in Policing matters and was always ready to offer advice, often when it had not even been sought! In the summer of 1937 he raised a number of matters with the Inspector, including the the need for a higher standard of officer and the possible employment of women Police.

Mr Sherwill's view was "that the Force required a type of man in advance of the artisan class". Mr Sculpher agreed that it was essential to improve the calibre of recruits. In his view Guernsey Police officers and their work were not fully recognised, in fact "the public treated them as necessary nuisances, yet the first person required in all cases of trouble or difficulty was the Policeman. Better selection and training was essential if the Force was going to be proper and respected servants of society."

He recognised that there was much that women could do in connection with Police work, but "as this is a young Force I consider that the male side should first be developed. Whilst it may be considered in the future, I do not think the time is yet opportune for the employment of women Police in Guernsey".

On the 23rd November 1936 every Constable signed a 'Round Robin' organised by Constable Bert Lamy. They asked that consideration again be given to:-

1. An increase in pay.
2. A weekly rest day.

The Police Committee, on this occasion, responded by asking the Inspector to prepare a report on the existing conditions and particulars of the likely cost if the request for a weekly rest day was to be granted.

The Inspector was delighted to report on the matter as he was totally supportive of the men's request. In his view, better pay and conditions meant that the Force could attract a better standard of recruit.

In mainland Britain conditions of service were governed by the Desborough Report, which fixed, subject to the approval of the Home Secretary, scales of pay and such matters as the frequency of rest days.

"I beg to report", wrote the Inspector "that pay of Police in this Island bears no comparison with rates of pay existing on the mainland..

| | |
|---|---|
| Constables' pay in Guernsey | 50/- to 55/- a week |
| Constables' pay in England | 70/- to 90/- a week |
| Sergeants' pay in Guernsey | 65/- to 75/- a week |
| Sergeants' pay in England | 100/- to 112/6 a week |

"I am surprised that this subject has not been presented before, being at a loss to understand how the men manage to pay their way on their wages. Indeed I am under the impression that many of them take on supplementary work which is undesirable for Policemen."

On the question of one day's rest in seven, he reported that he did no know of any other Police Force where this did not operate.

The Police Committee realised that they were going to have to concede to the request for increased pay and improved rest days, but it was not until the Spring of 1938 that the changes were implemented.

Constable's pay was increased to 57/- to 62/6 a week and the Sergeant's to 72/6 to 80/- a week.

Due to the improvement in rest days, it was necessary to increase the establishment by two Constables. There were also three vacancies due to retirements and resignations. In January 1938 an advertisement appeared in the local press.

ISLAND POLICE FORCE.

> The States of Guernsey, having recently approved a weekly rest day, as well as an increase in pay for the Force, there are now several vacancies for Police Constables and the Police Committee invite applications for the posts.
>
> Candidates must be well educated, between 21 and 25 years of age (men up to 27 years with special qualifications will be considered), in good health with normal physique.
>
> Applications stating age, height, weight, standard of education and other qualifications to be forwarded to the Inspector, Police Office, not later than 22nd January 1938.

Within a short time a number of appointments had been made. Alf Le Gallez replaced PC 24 Harry Brown and Reg Marsh took over as PC 9. The other new men were PC 34 Eugene Le Lievre and PC 35 Tom Luscombe.

Previously the Police Committee had promoted Jack Harper to the rank of Sergeant to replace John Langmead, who had retired. On this occasion the Inspector made no specific recommendation, he merely submitted a list of seven names "'whom the Committee may care to consider".

Gradually but inevitably the 'Old Brigade' were departing and a new breed of younger, better educated men was taking their place in the Force. Constables Dave Browning, George Froome, Mark Jarvis, Sam Gallienne, Cliff Tardif, all old sweats, and Yves Mercier left the Force and were replaced by PC 8 Francis Gale,

**The Guernsey Police Force in 1936.**
**Back Row: F.W. Short. E.W. Plevin, R.W. Kimber, F.H. Tuck, K.O. Shaw, A.L. Tardif, C. Bougourd, F.T. Gale, H.E. Piesing, W.J.Burton, H.F. Chappon, F.W. Whare.**
**Middle Row: F.A. Le Page, G. Perry, H.P. Smith, G.H.L. Dyson, H.T. Pugh, J. Harper, H. Brown, A.P. Lamy, P.J.F. Bretel, J. Grainger, T.J. Gaudion, H.J. Bull.**
**Front Row: C.J. Tardif, Sgt. A.W. Howlett, Sgt. C. Le Lievre, Sgt. J. Langmead, Inspector W.R. Sculpher, Sgt. E.J. de J. Pill, Sgt. A.J. Langmead, Sgt. F.P. Duquemin. Sgt. F.J. Banneville, W.G. Quin.**

PC 30 Fred Short, PC 19 Archie Tardif, PC 16 Frank Tuck, PC 17 Ernie Plevin, PC 31 Ken Shaw and PC 10 Cyril Eley.

Training of new officers was entirely undertaken within the Island and on only one occasion prior to the war, did any member of the Force, other than the Inspector, go to the mainland on a training course. In 1933 Sergeant A.J.Langmead attended a six weeks course at New Scotland Yard.

The new policemen were put on the beat with a more experienced officer and at the end of each day had to report to the Station Sergeant on what they had learnt. The Sergeant then reported to Mr Sculpher, who at regular intervals called recruits up to his office and questioned them. Men with military background found it comparatively easy to adapt to Police discipline and procedures, others found it more difficult.

The Inspector regularly held lectures at which all Constables, on or off duty, were required to attend. The different laws and how they were to be applied were the principal subjects at these lectures. Mr Sculpher, however, also used the opportunity to deal with other matters.

On one occasion the 'Old Man', as many of the younger men referred to Sculpher, said "It has come to my ears that some policemen are not doing their job. I have had reports that there was a fracas going on in the Truchot, an officer just looked and walked away in the other direction. People who were watching from their windows, saw what happened and they complained to me. As a number of beats cover the area I cannot be certain which officer was failing in his duty. If ever I find out, they will leave their uniform on my office floor."

Another of his well-known sayings was:- "I don't want no Wednesday men here." Wednesday was pay day, when every member of the Force went down to the States office and signed for their pay. Any man whose interest in the Force was largely confined to pay day was labelled by Sculpher as a 'Wednesday man'. He told his men:- "It is not fair to your comrades if you are not seeing this or seeing that and leaving it all to two or three of your colleagues.

If I hear somebody saying about one of my men, 'he's a nice man', then he is not doing his job. If you are doing your job as it should be carried out, politely and courteously, somebody will hate your guts - and that is how it should be!" Sculpher said he wanted 'Proficient Officers'.

At the end of each lecture the Inspector would always ask "Now, any questions?" Inevitably there were. A favourite subject, regularly raised, particularly by the younger men, was:-

"Yes Sir, I would like to know why so and so was taken to court for parking in the Bordage? I booked Colonel so and so in the same place a week before and he never went to court. I want to know why ? The chap who was fined is just an ordinary workman, is it one rule for the rich and another for the poor?"

The Inspector would answer by saying "I have done my job. All the cases for prosecution are sent to the Attorney General and he decides who is to be summoned and who receives a warning." However, he backed his men, saying "Book every car that contravenes the law, you can't pick and choose, otherwise you are going to cause a lot of animosity amongst the public."

The procedure was that if an officer apprehended a motorist, a report was written up in his pocket book. The Station Sergeant then entered the details in the Occurrence Book, which would be inspected every morning by the Inspector. He decided which cases should be passed to the Attorney General, who would pronounce on who should be charged and who should receive a warning. The Sheriff's Sergeant then served the summons on the person concerned. When the case was taken to the Police Court, Mr Sculpher usually conducted the prosecution.

Years later, one of the Constables who joined the Force in the early thirties, commented :-

"Of course in those days the only persons to have cars were the 'toffee nosed' people, the upper crust. It was the Admirals, the Colonels, the Majors or their wives who drove around in cars, while some ordinary working class people couldn't even afford a bicycle.

Very few of the 'establishment' went to court. As soon as you wrote Colonel, or wife of the Admiral in your pocket book, you knew it was a waste of time. The next thing there would be a warning and you would be delivering a letter.

We were trained to be polite and civil, par excellence. No matter how rude anybody was to us, we were always polite. It was 'they' who were going to be rude and 'they' were not going to be able to accuse us of being rude or uncivil. The advice we were continually given, particularly by our Sergeants, was 'Keep your eyes and ears open and your bloody great mouth shut'.

I would go into a shop and enquire,

'Has anybody got a car outside with number so and so,'

'Yes and what about it?' would be the gruff response.

'It should not be parked out there Sir, there is a park at the bottom of the pier steps and I would suggest that you park your car there.'

You would tell them in a polite way, but their reply was often

'Damned lot of rot, damned lot of rot, do you expect me to walk from there, up the steps if I want to go to the Post Office? Are you aware who I am'

'No Sir, I am not. I am afraid I will want your full name sir.'

I would have to put that all in my pocket book.

My army training stood me in good stead. I knew how to take orders and I knew how to use my loaf. Often a member of the public, who perhaps was the worse for wear, would give you some abuse or even physically attack you. In my time I had some bad kicks, mainly on the shins, and received a lot of abuse. If there was a crowd around, you could not kick him back, but when you were back at the station and there was nobody around, that was different. I would say

'There is blood on my leg, see what you have done. Try this one'.

On other occasions someone would screech,

'Why don't you bastard Police get the f...... hell out of it'.

If there was nobody about and it was dark, I would quietly respond in like terms.

I found if you responded to brutality with a degree of brutality you tamed the criminal. Just the same as you would with an animal. If an animal is given a tap for misbehaving, then it does not do it any more. I found it the same with human beings. Did you like that,- wallop - then have another one for luck with the other hand,- wallop ! I would not say that was brutal treatment, it was 'Practical Policing' and you found that they rarely came back for more.

There were occasions when you needed to use your truncheon. To draw it in front of a crowd and then use it on an unarmed man always put the crowd against you. I learnt to slide my truncheon up my sleeve prior to approaching any situation which might call for its use. One punch in the guts, with fist and truncheon, invariably was sufficient to bring the situation under control."

Seven years had elapsed since Mr Sculpher had taken up his appointment as Inspector. His salary had risen by the five yearly increments to £400. The only increase he had received, was in 1935 when the Committee granted him an annual clothing allowance of £15. He now requested that his Contract of Service affecting both pay and leave be reviewed.

In support of his application he followed his favourite approach - presentation of comparative figures applying to Guernsey and other Forces, detailing pay, personnel and work performed.

There had been no increase in the Force establishment since he was appointed. The number of pages filled in the Occurrence Book in 1929 had been 1,268 and by 1936 it had risen to 2,571.

The number of persons arrested or dealt with by charge had risen from 174 to 320, whilst the number of persons summoned was 476 in 1936 compared with 75 in 1929.

On the matter of pay he argued:-

"I know of no Chief of Police in England whose pay is on such a low scale as Guernsey, indeed in City and Borough Forces, with similar populations, the pay and allowances are between £700 and £800 per annum. The Home Office scale of pay for Second Officers of such forces is between £430 and £500.

His case for a review of leave was more direct.

"By my Contract of Service I am allowed 28 days leave each year. I get no other time. I am always available day and night. There is no free time on Sundays or weekdays. The recognised holidays bring extra work. It is appreciated that anyone holding my office must be available for any emergency, but bearing in mind all public officers get at least one day off each week in addition to an annual period, I respectfully submit that an increase in the leave I am allowed is long overdue."

By this time the relationship between the Inspector and the Police Committee had considerably improved. Mr Sculpher had developed a little more tact and also gained considerable experience in dealing with the Committee. Mr W.E.Poat had stood down as President, although still remaining a member of the Committee. Deputy Stephen Rabey had taken over as President and four Committee Members had also changed.

Full and fair consideration was given to Mr Sculpher's application by both the Police Committee and the Board of Administration, who were responsible for all States staffing matters.

A discussion was held with Mr Sculpher and as a result it was agreed that a new position of Deputy Inspector would be created. This allowed for reasonable rest days for the Inspector to be arranged within the general allocation of duties. In those circumstances the Committee did not think that the question of additional leave for the Inspector need be considered. Mr Sculpher agreed.

With regard to salary, a new scale, starting at £400 rising to £500 was agreed. The Committee decided that the Inspector should receive the maximum rate of salary, back dated to the 30th March 1938.

On the 24th October 1938 Sergeant Arthur John Langmead was appointed to the newly created post of Deputy Inspector. He was sworn in and commenced his duties on the 19th November 1938, his salary being £300 per annum, rising by £10 increments to £350. His appointment meant that he was now 'Salaried Staff' and as such officially 'entered' the Guernsey Civil Service.

Deputy Inspector Langmead was born in Guernsey in 1898 and served as a Corporal in the Royal Guernsey Light Infantry during the Great War, being discharged in 1919. He was a total abstainer, discreet, punctual and of smart appearance.

The Inspector was not keen to define the duties of his new Deputy Inspector too precisely, he envisaged a wide role, with his main responsibility being that of dealing with traffic matters. He suggested that his Deputy "can take the place of an English 'Courtesy Cop' and deal, on the spot, with such cases of overtaking at corners, leaving vehicles in dangerous places and such like matters". He added "I shall require a daily entry in the Occurrence Book, with a brief outline of duties performed and an additional entry made of occasional visits at irregular hours".

Constable Bert Lamy was promoted Sergeant to fill the vacancy created by Deputy Inspector Langmead's promotion and in turn Charles Friend joined the Force as PC 14.

Albert Peter Lamy was born in Guernsey in 1902 and before joining the Police in 1928, had worked as a Stonemason. In August 1939 he received further promotion, being appointed Clerk Sergeant.

In the Inspector's office was a large table around which the Police Committee met. It had a drawer, the key of which Mr Sculpher kept in his waistcoat pocket.

The locked drawer contained the Inspector's large collection of anonymous letters. He was very critical of people who did not sign their names. Sculpher's view was that if they didn't have the stomach to sign their names to these letters, then he wasn't interested in reading them and was certainly not going to take any action.

PC Fred Short remembers being in the Inspector's office on one occasion and being shown an anonymous letter. "I was asked for my opinion - did I know the person referred to and was he the type of person who would do what the letter indicated. After reading the letter, which was about somebody I had been at school with, I expressed my opinion. Mr Sculpher took the key from his waistcoat pocket, unlocked the drawer and flicked the letter in with all the others. Then the drawer was locked and the key returned to his waistcoat.

He told me that he received about two or three anonymous letters a week and they all went into the drawer, unactioned. They were never destroyed - but he detested the writers".

In the autumn of 1937 the Police Committee requested the Board of Administration that electric light be installed in the offices on the upper floors of the Station. Year by year the building of a new station was considered and deferred. Alterations to the existing Police Station were also considered - and deferred. Year by year the installation of electricity on the upper floors had been shelved because work was about to commence on a new building or alterations to the existing one. Finally the Committee were prepared to wait no longer and they 'directed' their President, Deputy Stephen Rabey, to inform the Board of Administration 'of the situation'. An electricity supply was installed almost immediately.

On the 13th July 1937 Peter Robin was sentenced to death by the Royal Court for the murder of his 12 year old daughter, Edith. This was only the third murder trial held in Guernsey during the previous hundred years. During the first war Private Humphreys had been sentenced to ten years imprisonment for murdering a fellow soldier in Alderney and Gertie De la Mare was convicted, in 1935, of cutting the throat of her elderly employer. Her death sentence had been accompanied by a recommendation for mercy. She was reprieved and served a life sentence.

His Majesty's Prison, which was directly under the control of the Lieutenant Governor, was not equipped with a gallows to carry out the death sentence on Robin. The officer commanding the Royal Engineers was consulted and informed the Governor that up to six weeks would be required for the construction of a gallows. In view of the fact that no recommendation for mercy had been made, the Governor felt that he had no alternative but to authorise the work to be put in hand immediately.

The gallows were erected within the workshop on the south side of the dividing wall of the prison yard and a new workshop constructed as a replacement. However, Robin was reprieved and the gallows were never used. The account for the work carried out by the Royal Engineers, which amounted to more than £350, was in due course submitted to the States by the War Office. The account was disputed and no one would accept responsibility for its payment. Even the Police Committee had at one stage to deny responsibility for the cost of the gallows. It is not recorded who finally paid the account, but the Inspector made sure that it was not the Police.

One of the best known and most easily recognised cars in Guernsey during the thirties was a yellow Morris Isis. This was the Police car, known as the 'yellow peril'. Early in 1938 it was decided to trade it in for a newer and hopefully more economical vehicle. Quotations were received and on a Police Committee day a number of vehicles were lined up outside the Police Station for inspection and examination by Members.

**The pre-war Police Car, the 'Yellow Peril,' with PC P.J.F. Bretel and the official Police driver PC J. Harper.**

After due consideration and some joy riding, the Committee decided to accept the tender from Le Lacheur's Garage for a 14/56 Wolseley five-seater Salon de Ville motor car for the sum of £280 and the Morris Isis in part exchange. It was the type of vehicle used by Scotland Yard and many English Forces. The manufacturers promised that the car supplied would be to the 'special Scotland Yard specification'.

In October 1938, as a result of a conference held between the Island Authorities and the Military, consideration was given to the possibility of arming the Police in case of war. Mr Sculpher made it quite clear that he was opposed to the suggestion, although he did recognise that in certain circumstances it could be essential. In the Station store there was a collection of weapons which had been handed in or surrendered. These were sent to the Military at Fort George, who examined them and reported that only nine of them were serviceable. It was agreed that these weapons should be held, together with 100 rounds of ammunition, for possible Police use. A lecture on gun handling was given to 24 officers and individual training carried out under the supervision of the Military Authorities at Fort George.

The rising tension in Europe and the talk of war had little apparent effect on Guernsey's slow and leisurely way of life. Tourists came, enjoyed their stay and returned home with happy memories of a peaceful and contented island. However, in the Island, not every one was unaffected - PC 8 Francis Gale, being on the Army reserve, was recalled to the colours in the autumn of 1938. He was replaced, on Boxing Day, by new recruit Ted Sparrow and on the same day Kingston Bailey took over from Henry Chappon as PC 22.

Many of the men in the Force liked their 'lotion' and were regular visitors to licensed premises, both off and on duty. Most publicans welcomed policemen and were only too happy to supply them with a drink. For many years Randall's Vauxlaurens Brewery kept a virtual open house for men going off duty. Their basement premises were regularly visited by the old sweats.

On one occasion a popular constable was seen escaping by a rear window from a well known hostelry when the Sergeant was entering by the front door. The same constable would regularly tell a new recruit, who was accompanying him on his beat, to "bugger off and come back in ten minutes". The recruit then observed the constable disappearing up the steps and around the back of a certain licensed premises.

The Inspector was aware of what was going on and did everything he could to catch any of his men who broke his disciplinary code. In the main he was singularly unsuccessful, largely because some of the sergeants were just as partial to their 'lotion' as the constables. Alf Howlett, when he was Patrolling Sergeant, regularly visited 'The Brighton' public house at the top of Market Street and downed a pint or two. PC Fred Short recalls finding a vantage point at the top of a flight of steps opposite 'The Brighton' from where he obtained a bird's eye view of the sergeant knocking back pints.

Sergeant Howlett was a big burly policeman, an ape of a man, who earned himself the nickname of 'The Prussian Guard' for the way he strutted around with his helmet on the back of his head. Whilst very partial to a pint himself, he was not as keen on constables partaking.

One evening, while on duty, PC 16 Frank Tuck was just about to enjoy a crafty pint in the bar of the Yacht Hotel, when in walked Sergeant Howlett. Tuck believed he had successfully concealed his still full tankard under his cape. Howlett said "Come on Tuck" and walked him up Cornet Street, around Trinity Square and down Fountain Street until there was no beer left in the tankard. Tuck commented afterwards, "He bloody well knew I had a pint under my cape and he deliberately walked hell out of me so that all my beer was spilled."

On one occasion PC 30 Short, who was on motorcycle patrol duties, was asked to give Sergeant Howlett a lift home because he was not in a fit enough condition to make his own way. The Sergeant was on the 6.00pm - 2.00am shift and had been patrolling from 10.00pm. After making a visit to the Brighton and possibly one or two other hostelries, he returned to the Station around 1.30am rolling around and exclaiming "That was a nice one".

"Take him home Fred" was Sergeant Pill's reaction.

"No, not on the motorcycle, the last time he nearly pulled me off with his swaying on the back."

"All right then" Sergeant Pill exclaimed "get the Police car out ".

Some members of the Force were 'chapel' and booze was out completely. Deputy Inspector Langmead was one of those and there were one or two others, but the ordinary policeman, the old sweats, certainly liked their lotion and 'went around the back regularly'.

One of the newer recruits soon earned himself a reputation, for liking more than a drop. PC 35 Luscombe paraded ten minutes late one night, with his face disfigured and his hand cut. He claimed that his injuries were caused through his bicycle skidding. He was examined by Dr Bostock, who certified him unfit for duty through drink and owing to his injuries, placed him on the sick list. The Inspector immediately suspended him. When PC Tom Luscombe, eight days later, was certified fit for duty, the Inspector reinstated him and investigated the complaint of drunkenness. He was 'permitted' to resign.

To fill the vacancy the Police Committee interviewed four candidates, Daniel McKane, Edwin Thoume, Edmund Plevin and Francois Le Cocq. All sat the normal examination with Le Cocq obtaining a mark of 89.74%, which was the highest ever achieved by any candidate. The worst candidate ever must have been the unnamed man who, when asked to read a passage out loud from a book, requested to speak to the Inspector privately. Sculpher took him outside and returned moments later to announce to the other candidates sitting around his large desk "He has failed, you would not believe it, he can't even read."

'Ginger' Le Cocq, as he was known, could speak French fluently, a considerable asset which very few of the Force possessed. He was appointed as PC 35 on 25th May 1939, the last recruit before war was declared.

Two soldiers, both of the 1st Battalion of the Royal Irish Fusiliers, appeared in the Police Court on the 12th June 1939 to face charges of 'feloniously and with premeditated design attempted to commit the crime of murder on the person of Charles Le Lievre, then acting in the exercise of his duties as a Police officer'.

At about 9.00pm on Friday the 9th June 1939 two privates, Frank Stringer and James Brady, in uniform, entered the Mariners Inn at St Sampson and asked for Irish whiskey. The landlady, Mrs Mary Haugh, thought that they had had sufficient to drink and refused to serve them. They used strong language and one of them smashed a large plate glass window in the public house.

The two soldiers then went along Nocq Road smashing the windows of two cars, before turning into Lowlands. They continued to leave a trail of smashed windows in houses and greenhouses as they made their way through various properties to the Braye Road. One of the soldiers took hold of the door handle of a passing car and tried to get into it. The driver, Walter Marquand, drove off and fetched Sergeant C.Le Lievre from his home and together they drove around the district looking for the two soldiers.

They eventually overtook the fusiliers at Grande Rue, Vale. They were being followed by several people at a respectful distance. Both were in shirt sleeves having discarded their tunics and caps, Stringer was carrying a spade and Brady a wooden club. When Sergeant Le Lievre approached them, Stringer said ;-

"If you value your life, you will leave us alone, get out of the way."

Le Lievre told them he was a Police officer and that he had a job to do.

"I don't care who you are, get out, I tell you, or I will murder you."

Brady shouted "Yes, kill him, we've nothing to lose."

Stringer then struck the Sergeant twice with the spade. The first blow, which was aimed at his head, he managed to ward off with his forearm. The second caught him on the ribs under the shoulder blade, breaking the skin and injuring his arm. Sergeant Le Lievre, who was unarmed, closed with Stringer and floored him. Brady repeatedly struck the Sergeant on the head with the wooden club he was carrying, until it broke. He then struck the Sergeant on the ear with his fist. Seeing that the Sergeant was bleeding profusely from a scalp wound, Tom Wyatt, a Special Constable, went to his assistance and helped secure and handcuff Stringer.

Brady in the meantime tried to get away over the hedge and across a field. Walter Marquand and Frank Falla gave chase and detained him. With both men under arrest, Stringer handcuffed to Sergeant Le Lievre and Brady being held by PC Eley, who had arrived on the scene, they were taken by car to the Police Station. During the journey both prisoners were continually chanting "Up De Valera, Up the I.R.A. and F... the King".

Both men pleaded guilty at the subsequent Royal Court trial, Frank Stringer being sentenced to 21 months and James Brady to 18 months, both with hard labour.

Sergeant Le Lievre was on sick leave for six days before returning to duty. The Inspector made a full report of the incident to the Police Committee and suggested that they might consider recommending that the King's Police Medal be awarded to Sergeant Le Lievre. The qualifications, he explained, were:-

'Conspicuous gallantry in saving life and property, or in preventing or arresting criminals, the risks incurred to be estimated with due regard to the obligations and duties of the officer concerned. This medal is awarded to Police officers who perform acts of exceptional courage and risk or exhibit conspicuous devotion to duty'.

The Police Committee felt that Sergeant Le Lievre acted with great courage and bravery in facing the two armed men and instructed the Inspector to submit the facts to the Bailiff for him to forward them through His Excellency the Lieutenant Governor to the Home Office for consideration.

On the 3rd January 1940 the London Gazette announced that Sergeant Charles Le Lievre had been awarded the King's Police Medal. There is no doubt that, but for the war, Sergeant Le Lievre would have received his medal from the hands of the King at Buckingham Palace. Instead he attended a sitting of the States and immediately after the Roll Call, was presented with the King's Police Medal, the Victoria Cross of Police awards, by the Bailiff, who congratulated him and paid tribute to his heroism for which the award had been made.

Just prior to the outbreak of hostilities, four members of the Force, who were reservists, were called up for active service. All four men, PC 8 Sparrow, PC 10 Eley, PC 29 Grainger and PC 31 Shaw left for their various depots on the 1st September and were struck off pay from that date.

The Island Police Force at the outbreak of war was 33 strong.

Inspector William Robert Sculpher
Deputy Inspector Arthur John Langmead

| | |
|---|---|
| | PS 1. Charles Le Lievre |
| PS 2. Alfred William Howlett | PS 3. Jack Harpur |
| PS 4. Edward James de Jersey Pill | PS 5. Frederick Peter Duquemin |
| PS 6. Albert Peter Lamy | PS 7. Frederick James Banneville |
| PC 9. Reginald Percy George Marsh | PC 11. Henry John Bull |
| PC 12. Clifford Henry Bougourd | PC 13. George Henry Dyson |
| PC 14. Charles Albert Friend | PC 15. William J.Burton |
| PC 16. Frank Hubert Tuck | PC 17. Ernest William Plevin |
| PC 18. Herbert Percival Smith | PC 19. Archibald Lloyd Tardif |
| PC 20. Frank William Whare | PC 21. Frank Anthony Le Page |
| PC 22. Kingston George Bailey | PC 23. William George Quin |
| PC 24. Alfred Thomas Le Gallez | PC 25. Harold 'Snip' Piesing |
| PC 26. George Perry | PC 27. Robert William Kimber |
| PC 28. Peter John Francis Bretel | PC 30. Frederick Winzer Short |
| PC 32. Henry Thomas Pugh | PC 33. Thomas John Gaudion |
| PC 34. Eugene Henri Le Lievre | PC 35. Francois Le Cocq. |

# Chapter 3

## THEY CALL ME A SPY

Every Islander realised, deep down, that war was inevitable, when on Friday 1st September 1939 Germany invaded Poland. The next day the British Prime Minister, Neville Chamberlain, dispatched an ultimatum to Adolf Hitler demanding the immediate withdrawal of German forces from Poland. For a while there lingered a faint hope that war could be averted, then the announcement that Chamberlain would broadcast on Sunday morning brought a return to reality.

At the Police Station, Sergeant Howlett was struggling to complete an entry in the Occurrence Book regarding Miss Ida Crossley who had driven the wrong car to Perchard's Garage. She explained that she had mistaken the car, a red Morris 8, for a similar one she was driving on behalf of its owner. Alf Howlett was confused and so was his report, he was far more concerned with what Mr Chamberlain was going to say in his broadcast. He knew what war meant, he had served in France in the Great War and was deeply worried. As Miss Crossley offered to apologise to the owner, he was happy to leave the matter there.

Sergeant Jack Harper was on foot patrol around the town. PC 21 Frank Le Page was on motorcycle patrol. Clerk Sergeant Bert Lamy and PC 17 Ernie Plevin were upstairs in the office. Sunday or not the amount of additional paper work that was required as a result of the emergency was enormous. They were putting on paper the final details of the planned 'Black Out' rehearsal for Monday night.

Inspector Sculpher was at his home, Rose Cottage, in the Rohais, preparing to listen to the Prime Minister speak at 11.15am. He was going over and over in his mind the actions he would have to take if war was declared, when suddenly he realised that Chamberlain was speaking,

"...and I must tell you that no such undertaking has been received and consequently this country is at war with Germany".

Neville Chamberlain continued, "I cannot believe that there is anything more, or anything different, that I could have done.... It is evil things that we shall be fighting against, brute force, bad faith, injustice, oppression and persecution. And against them I am certain that right will prevail."

Inspector Sculpher immediately telephoned the Station and asked for the Police car to be sent to collect him. While he waited, he sat down and rolled himself a cigarette. As soon as PC 11 Bull arrived in the Wolseley, he put his cigarette out, he never permitted himself to smoke in the street, and was driven to the Station.

The first real effect of the declaration of war was the immediate imposition of the blackout. Whilst it had been planned to have an Island-wide test of the effectiveness of the blackout, now a special Sunday edition of The Star newspaper announced that it would be effective immediately. Street lamps were turned off and cars were only permitted to use side lights. The speed limit, during the hours of darkness, was reduced to 15mph. It was also announced that all cinemas and places of entertainment were closed until further notice.

That Sunday evening the Town was a very different place, no street lights and very few people. PC 14 Charlie Friend was on patrol in the High Street and PC 20 Frank Whare in Fountain Street. At about 9.40pm the two men met in Church Square. They were talking over the day's momentous events just prior to making their way back to the Station to go off duty at 10.00pm. Suddenly they heard the sound of raucous singing coming from the direction of the High Street. PC Friend went to investigate and found two eighteen-year-olds and a sixteen-year-old, singing, totally out of tune, "There will always be an England". He requested them to be quiet, but without success. After several further requests had been ignored PC Friend warned them for Court at 10.00am the next morning to answer a charge of disorderly conduct. However, the next morning the Inspector wrote in the Occurrence Book, 'All cautioned, W.Sculpher'.

PC 20 Whare, when he returned to the station, reported that the light in the urinal in the Bordage reflected across the street and that no provision had yet been made for screening the lights in the public urinals in Market Street. These, he reported, throw a light directly towards the sky.

Throughout the first night of the blackout, Wardens and Policemen were out and about, knocking on doors, telling people, politely, "You have got a light showing". Motorists were being stopped to be told that they were showing too much light. By morning the authorities were satisfied that the blackout had worked reasonably well and were confident that it would improve as time went on.

Inevitably there were contraventions of the regulations, but generally the public were co-operative and fewer and fewer lights were visible at night. A.R.P. Wardens patrolled their own districts and were supplemented by Special Constables. One evening Special Constables Baudains and Le Mesurier noticed that light was visible all around the blinds in the windows at the Government Office. The Special Constables spoke to the Government Secretary, Colonel Brousson, who curtly responded "I am too busy to attend to it".

Just prior to the declaration of war, Special Constables had been brought in to assist in patrolling and guarding vulnerable areas in the Island. The oil tanks at Bulwer Avenue, the Shell-Mex facilities at Castle Emplacement and the telegraph cable huts at Jerbourg and Saints were all guarded night and day. The duty Sergeant visited the sites regularly and issued and collected torches as necessary.

The Military Authorities provided and maintained guards at:-

The Waterworks sites at Kings Mills and Forest Road.
The Electricity power stations at North Side and Les Amballes.
The Guernsey Gas Light Company site at the Longstore.
The Telephone Exchange in the Grange.

After a few weeks these 'protection measures' were considerably scaled down. The general public, however, were becoming jittery and prone to over reaction.

One night, just after midnight, the Station Sergeant, Jack Harper received a message from Stafford Ogier, the Area Chief Warden for St Sampson and the Vale, stating that he had seen signalling at Grand Havre, on the beach and from the sea. "I want you to send as many Police officers as you can, as quickly as possible."

In consequence of receiving this message, Sergeant Harper together with PC 23 Quin, PC 24 Le Gallez and Special Constable Pagnier, proceeded in the Police car to Grand Havre where they met Stafford Ogier. He reported, "I have seen a small light on the beach at Grand Havre. Also a steam boat has dropped anchor off Rousse and has been there for about three hours. My men have surrounded the bay".

Sergeant Harpur and his colleagues searched the beach and the vicinity, without result. The steam boat supposed to have been seen was established to be a cottage at Chouet headland and as the Sergeant politely pointed out to the Area Chief Warden, it had been there more than three hours.

Submarines, spies, morse signalling, mysterious boats, real and imaginary, soon became an everyday part of Island life, particularly as far as the Police were concerned.

On the 7th September a telephone call was received in the Station from Mr Ray, of Icart, who reported:- "I have just seen a submarine about 1½ miles off the Pea Stacks, heading south west". After informing the Airport of the report, Sergeant Duquemin went out to Icart and saw Mr Ray, who told him that the submarine had just submerged. A steam boat, the Coudon, soon after passed Icart Point, with all lights ablaze. When it reached St Peter Port harbour, PC 27 Kimber, interviewed the Captain, who said he had not seen any submarine.

Earlier the same day John Queripel, of Paradise, Pleinmont, saw PC 21 Le Page and claimed that, "at 7.15am, I saw three submarines in line appear from the east of Lihou Island, they travelled west, stopped on the inside of the Hanois for a few minutes. One had a red sail up, it was silver grey and bore no identification marks". The occurrence book records 'No action taken'.

The next day the Station received a telephone call from Mr F.Martin, of York House, Candie, stating that his 20 year old daughter, Jean had seen a submarine at Vazon. PC 34 Eugene Le Lievre was immediately sent to verify the call. Miss Martin said:- "I was with my girlfriend Miss Jones at the end of Fort Crocq at about 5.30pm today and I saw a submarine quite close in amongst the rocks. I saw the conning tower, then it went towards the west and dived". The Airport and the Military at Beaucamp were notified.

At 11.00pm the same day, an out of breath James Guille rushed into the Station and between gasps said:- "I have just been asked by Charles Guilbert to notify the Police that signalling is going on at the Longstore beach near the rocks. I saw a light being flashed myself."

PC 19 Tardif, Special Constables Pagnier and W.Mauger immediately went to the beach and detained William Wallbridge and Henry Herring and took them back to the Station.

William Wallbridge said "I used my cycle lamp to see my fishing trots, I am sorry". William Herring, who was only 14, said "I went with my friend Wallbridge to see his trots and we had to flash a light to find them". They were both warned of the seriousness of this offence and allowed to go home.

Late one evening the Station received a call from Fred Hockey, the St Peter Port harbour watchman, asking them to telephone the Dame of Sark. A call was put through and answered by Mrs Briscoe, a daughter of the Dame. Apparently a steam boat, without lights, had dropped anchor in Derrible Bay, on the east of Sark. Mr Hathaway, the Dame's husband, went out to the vessel and later he telephoned Sergeant Harpur and reported that the steam boat was from Holland, with a Dutch flag painted on its side. The Captain had anchored there because he did not wish to travel at night and would be leaving at 5.00am in the morning.

All these real or imagined events had taken place within ten days of the declaration of war. This was to be the pattern for some months to come and it imposed a considerable burden on the Police Force. Inspector Sculpher knew that the vast majority of the incidents reported were imaginary or mistaken identity, but he also realised that one of them might just be the real thing and he could not take the chance of missing or ignoring that possibility. Therefore, every incident reported had to be investigated.

Miss Julia Brichta came to the Island in July 1939, from Hungary, where she was born. The 43 year old obtained employment as a live-in cook with Mr and Mrs Alfred Branch, of Sausmarez Place, Les Gravees. As a result of a telephone call received at the Station on the 10th September, PC Le Lievre called at Sausmarez Place. Julia Brichta was apparently on hunger strike. Mr Branch said:- "My wife engaged her as a cook and she won't do any other work. She wants to go back to Hungary, but she can't just now, so for the past two days she has refused to eat or drink and stopped in bed all day. She complains of a headache. She has caused no trouble before."

The Constable saw Julia Brichta, who complained:- "They call me a spy and do not let me go out at all. I will eat if it is brought in from outside, but I will not eat anything in this house. I won't get out of bed". PC Le Lievre called Dr Bostock who, after examining her, said:- "She is a little weak, but has no illness." He ordered her removal to the Town Hospital.

The strength of the Police Force had been reduced to thirty-three as a result of four officers being recalled to the colours. Inspector Sculpher gave the President of the Police Committee an assurance that he did not require the four replaced, at least for the time being and that he could manage with his Deputy, seven Sergeants and twenty-four Constables. He was, however, able to call on a considerable number of Special Constables.

The Specials were not provided with uniforms but were issued with a badge, Warrant Card, armlet, truncheon, whistle and chain. Inspector Sculpher was keen to train them so that when he needed to call upon them they would be reasonably knowledgeable about their duties and responsibilities.

A series of 'Sculpher' lectures were arranged to which Special Constables were 'invited' to attend. The subjects included:-

Police Law.
Powers of Arrest
Mode of Arrest
Defence Regulations

At 5.50pm on 12th September Deputy Inspector Langmead, together with Sergeant Banneville went to the premises of Hacklander (Mohair Fabrics) Limited, in Rue de Pre and arrested the manager, Herr Berthold Zulauf. Instructions had been received from Government Office ordering the arrest and detention of the German citizen. Zulauf was taken to H.M.Prison and handed over to the goaler at 6.00pm.

A few days later, with the authority of a search warrant signed by John Roussel, a Lieutenant Bailiff, Mr Sculpher accompanied by Sergeant Banneville, searched the home of Berthold Zulauf at Village de Putron. The bungalow, Roemryke, was searched and numerous papers in German were examined, but nothing incriminating found. Possession was taken of a contribution book No.K952181, entitled Dieteutfche Arbeitsfront and a membership card, both bearing the name of Berthold Zulauf. Mrs Zulauf who was present throughout the search, offered every assistance.

Late in November 1939, the Dame of Sark telephoned the Station requesting that the Guernsey lifeboat be sent to the assistance of a French trawler, B.3035, which was in difficulties at Havre Gosselin, Sark. The lifeboat left for Sark and found that the trawler had developed engine trouble and required towing to St Peter Port harbour. The 350 ton vessel proved too much for the lifeboat, so the S.S. New Fawn was sent to tow the trawler to St Peter Port. Captain Franklin, the Harbourmaster, had accompanied the New Fawn and when he came ashore at 4.20am, informed PC Burton, "There is nothing of importance to report".

That was not entirely accurate, but no doubt the Harbourmaster was keen to let as few persons as possible know that the B.3035 was in fact a French Naval vessel. She was a Submarine Chaser, with a crew of forty-three, armed with six guns and carried depth charges. The French Consul in the Island, Baron de Coudenhove, went aboard for a short time before the B.3035 left at 4.30pm the next day.

Christmas and the New Year were celebrated in much the same way as they had been in previous years. The blackout and petrol rationing were new but they did not really spoil the festivities to any noticeable degree. The war had become the 'phoney war' and life, to a very great extent, had almost returned to normal. The mailboats were running, the tomato crop had been planted and bookings were being received for the 1940 holiday season. Soon the wartime regulations, requiring passports or permit cards, for travel to or from England were abolished.

Despite the apparent return to normality, the Force did not forget their colleagues who had been recalled to the Army and the Royal Navy. A small collection was made amongst 'all hands at the Station' and cigarettes were sent to 'You happy reservists' in France and a 5/- postal order to those in England.

One person who welcomed the New Year more than most was Berthold Zulauf who was still being detained as an alien. The authorities felt that he no longer presented any threat to the security of the Island, so on January 12th 1940 he was released and returned home.

Although there was no conscription as such in Guernsey, many Islanders were 'joining up' to play their part in the war against Hitler. Volunteers, from Guernsey, during the first four months of the war exceeded one thousand. There was no doubt that Guernseymen were very loyal to the Crown. A number of the Force sought Inspector Sculpher's permission to join the ranks of the volunteers, but his response was always, "Your duty is to remain in Guernsey and there can be no guarantee of getting your job back if you do go". Sergeant Harper was offered a Commission in the Royal Corps of Military Police, which he reluctantly turned down after consulting Mr Sculpher.

The 'phoney war' brought with it the desire of authorities to rehearse every circumstance imaginable. In February 1940 'An air raid rehearsal' was staged, to which an official gave the label, "You want the best Air Raids - we have them". An unfortunate turn of phrase that he was going to bitterly regret.

Part of the exercise included the 'planting' of two drunks in a telephone kiosk in the Bouet. Ronald Trimble and Douglas Dames performed the roles of the drunks so effectively that when PC Le Cocq and two Specials went with the Police car to the Bouet, they actually arrested these two for being drunk and disorderly. It was only after they had been taken to the Station, that they explained. PC Le Cocq was reported as saying:- "I thought they were docile drunks."

A few days later Francois Le Cocq was married. To mark the occasion his colleagues made a collection and in the Inspector's room Mr Sculpher presented him with a frameless mirror, so "he could see himself as others see him". The Inspector said he was "glad that yet another member of the Force had entered into the mysterious bonds of matrimony. I have always recommended marriage to everyone and a good Police officer should be married. He needs a woman to look after him - especially when he is on night duty".

At 4.25am one morning, early in April, Fred Hockey, the St Peter Port harbour night watchman, received a telephone message from William Browell, an Air Raid Warden, saying:- "I heard motors running below the cliffs near Jerbourg Point and the sound is very similar to that of a submarine".

Shortly after Fred Hockey had informed the Station of the message, Sergeant Harper received a direct call from Mr Browell, who sounded very jittery, saying:- "I phoned the Watch Tower at White Rock and informed them when I heard this submarine coming from Jerbourg Point. I went down on my verandah and with my telescope I could clearly see the submarine making for Jersey or Carteret in France. I am an ex-submarine man and I know the sound of a submarine."

The Sergeant sent PC 9 Marsh and PC 23 Quin to Jerbourg Point where they saw Mr Browell at his home. They quickly formed the opinion that he was on the verge of the D.T.'s. (Delirium tremens).

On the 9th April 1940 German forces invaded Denmark and Norway. While this caused concern in the Island, it did not change Islanders' way of life to any real extent. However, when, in the middle of May, Hitler invaded Holland, Belgium and Luxembourg, bypassing the French Maginot Line and reached the English Channel, Islanders became decidedly uneasy. Many people, particularly those in authority, realised that the war was going to reach the Island and were very concerned for the future.

Military guards were reinstated at the States waterworks, the electricity power stations, the gas installation and at the telephone exchange.

Whilst the enforcement of the 'blackout' had become a little less rigorous, with a warning usually thought to be more appropriate than a prosecution, the dramatic German advances in France and the Low Countries, brought about a change in attitude. Well at least amongst the Air Raid Wardens. Pierre de Putron, the President of the Air Raid Precautions Committee, was soon at loggerheads with Inspector Sculpher over the enforcement of the wartime Lighting Restriction Order.

The case of Mrs Johnston Smith, of Maison Blanche, Queens Road really brought matters to a head between Pierre de Putron and the Inspector. On a Thursday evening in the middle of May an Air Raid Warden noticed an unshaded light at the home of Mrs Johnston Smith. She was seen by the Warden and the offending light put out. The next day Clerk Sergeant Lamy received a telephone call from Captain W.L.Henderson, the Chief Area Warden, reporting the details and asking for action to be taken. He did not specify what action and the Inspector directed that the woman be seen and officially cautioned. This was done by PC 16 Tuck, Mrs Johnston Smith expressed regret and undertook that there would be no further cause for complaint.

The next day Captain Henderson called at the Station and asked the Inspector what action had been taken. When told that a caution had been given, he said:- "We have had a lot of trouble with that woman and she has been insolent to Wardens". Captain Henderson also mentioned that he was having trouble with Mr Williams, the butler at Government House. The Inspector promised that the matter would be dealt with.

Later that day Mr de Putron told the Inspector,"I want Mrs Johnston Smith prosecuted". It was explained that as an official warning had been given it was not possible to prosecute, but if she or Mr Williams offended again, they would be taken to Court. Mr De Putron replied "I do not want you to deal with the Williams case, His Excellency is leaving on Wednesday and I will take the matter up with the new Governor".

Later Mr De Putron handed the Inspector a list of several houses and shops that Wardens had reported and said "I do not want these people prosecuted as they are poor". The Inspector pointed out very firmly that it was not for Mr De Putron to decide who was and who was not to be prosecuted.

On the 21st May Mr de Putron wrote, as President of the Air Raid Precautions Committee, to the Bailiff stating:- "For some time there has been grave dissatisfaction among the Wardens at the inadequate action of the Police to enforce the Regulations and lack of co-operation. This position cannot continue in the present circumstances.

I feel sure that you will appreciate that it is impossible to continue the direction of the A.R.P. unless I have the fullest co-operation of the Police."

The Bailiff passed the letter on to the Attorney General, Mr Sherwill, who wrote to Mr Sculpher requiring a written explanation. The Inspector responded in his usual forthright and vigorous manner, pointing out that the Wardens rarely presented their reports of lighting infractions in writing, making it almost impossible to take those cases to Court. He added:- "I am inclined to think that Mr de Putron is taking too much for granted from his various Wardens, who know little of what is required to present a successful prosecution and they are not prepared to be told by those who do."

Mr Sculpher continued:- "On the 11th May, Mrs Despointes, L'Islet Place, St Sampson, was reported by Wardens for excessive light. The window was screened by brown paper, but not sufficiently. PC 21 Le Page attended and told the Wardens it would be necessary for them to attend Court. A day or so later the Chief Warden of that District reported that his men could not attend Court in such cases and if their attendance was necessary all the A.R.P.Wardens in the Northern District would resign. The Police do not wish to cause friction, but this incident illustrates the difficulties."

A few days later the Bailiff called a conference which was attended by Mr De Putron, a number of his subordinate Officers and the Attorney General. Mr Sculpher was not invited. Later the Attorney General wrote to the Inspector saying:- "The conference discussed at some length the matter of insufficient observance of the Lighting Restriction Order and concluded that it was becoming increasingly apparent that rigid adherence is necessary for the public safety. It was felt that this will only be attained by a series of prosecutions of offenders, repeated if necessary at intervals."

"It was suggested", the Attorney General wrote, "that Police Constables do not take particulars of and report breaches of the Order which may or should come to their notice in the ordinary course of their patrols. It appeared to the conference that the only really effective way of dealing with the matter is for two Police officers to be detailed from time to time to patrol selected districts and to take particulars of every flagrant breach of the Order observed by them and that in all such cases a prosecution should follow. I shall be obliged therefore if you will, from time to time, detail Police officers to this special duty and will also issue general instructions that all Police officers on patrol should henceforth keep a look-out for lighting offences."

Mr Sculpher was furious and replied saying:-

"Mr de Putron has made a direct charge against me and the Police generally, if true, I submit it should be substantiated and if anyone is guilty of neglect, he should be dealt with."

Whilst not directly agreeing to carry out the instructions of the Attorney General, he concluded by adding:- "I will endeavour to put a little ginger into my men and hope for a better understanding."

He commented to a colleague that it was "a classic case of the 'Establishment' closing ranks, at my expense."

# Chapter 4

# THIS TIME THEY HAD COME TO STAY

In view of the deteriorating war situation it was decided that four German nationals, resident in the Island, should be interned. Colonel Brousson, the Government Secretary, signed an Order for the arrest Karl Hacklander, of 2 Les Terres, Euguene Hacklander, of Les Terres Cottage, Hans Hacklander, of Westlecot, Les Vardes, and re-arrest of Berthold Zulauf. The four Germans were arrested by Sergeant Banneville and handed over to H.M.Sheriff at the Prison on the 18th May 1940. The only other male German on the Island was Dr.Hans Frisch, who was considered to be very anti-German. He was to leave for England with his wife Dora before his fellow countrymen arrived.

"Old Dan from the Star says he is a German spy" claimed Percy Le Page when he hurried into the Police Station, after a good lunch-time session, to report an Irishman for sticking up for the Germans. Percy kept repeating to Jack Harper, the Station Sergeant, that this man went to the Star Hotel every day and ran down the English and praised the Germans. The Sergeant gradually coaxed the information from Percy, that the man was about 40, 5'7", wore a striped blue suit, had a trilby hat and went there almost every day between 11.00am and 12.30pm. The Sergeant promised to investigate.

Later that evening PC 12 Bougourd spoke to Matthew McDonald, the landlord of the Star Hotel, about the man. He remembered the Irishman and confirmed that he was a regular, particularly when the Royal Irish Fusiliers were stationed at Fort George. He concluded, "My opinion is that he should be watched".

Colonel Brousson issued a stream of instructions to the Inspector to arrest and detain enemy aliens. In all, Guernsey Police detained 30 aliens in the period up to the 1st June 1940. These included not only German citizens but also former Austrians who had acquired German citizenship as a result of the annexation of their country by Hitler.

The need to provide suitable internment facilities for the enemy aliens was solved when Fort Houmet was taken over for the women and part of the Country Hospital at Castel was adapted and renovated for the men. Mr Frank Le Page, Master of Castel Hospital, was put in charge of the men and Mrs F.Le Page the women.

One of those detained was Frau Annie Wranowsky, a friend of the Dame of Sark. A divorcee, she had arrived in the Island in 1934 and taken a post as companion to retired artist Ernold Mason and his wife. It was believed at the time that she was a German citizen, although later she was listed as Czech. By arrangement she travelled from Sark on the S.S. New Fawn and was met by Deputy Inspector Langmead, who took her to Fort Houmet and handed her over to the Matron.

Further instructions were received from the Government Office on the 4th June and Deputy Inspector Langmead detained the former Austrian citizens Anna Holler, Katherine Proskowitz, Therese Steiner and Augusta Spitz.

On the 7th June Maj-Gen F.R. Minshull-Ford was sworn in as the new Lieutenant Governor in succession to Maj-Gen A.P.D.Telfer-Smollett, who had resigned after only a year in office, because of the death of his wife.

As a consequence of Italy's entry into the war, on the 10th June, Inspector Sculpher received instructions to detain seven Italians resident in Guernsey. Deputy Inspector Langmead took L.Angella, E.Agnelli, G.Polli, F.Biancherie, R.Bonivita, J.Vigezzi and A.Carratu to the Prison. A few days later these Italians, six of whom worked at the Central Cafe in Smith Street, were moved by PC 11 Bull and PC 35 Le Cocq to the Castel Hospital internment camp.

Although the Island was daily becoming more and more embroiled in war measures, the Police were still involved in their day to day duties. Petty crime still occurred and each case was required to be fully investigated.

A schoolgirl and her 11-year-old brother were caught stealing two bottles of mineral water, valued 5d, from Mrs Burt, of the Lower Market. When they appeared in Court the Magistrate told the boy, that past leniency had not had the desired effect. Despite only being eleven, he had several previous convictions and was sentenced to two strokes of the birch. The schoolgirl was put on probation for one year.

Two other boys, aged 12 and 13, also appeared in Court accused of taking half a crown from a basket in a passageway at Dalgairns Road. The thirteen-year-old, who had made several previous appearances in Court, was sentenced to three strokes of the birch. The other boy was put on probation for a year.

News that Paris had fallen to the advancing Germans on the 14th June caused great concern amongst Islanders and many considered whether to abandon their homes and possessions and catch the next available boat. During the weekend a large number of sightseers congregated at White Rock, causing considerable congestion. Some just sat in their cars watching the hurly-burly of the harbour. Many were there because they could not decide whether to go or stay and as all departures from the Island were through the harbour, they felt it was the place to be, the place that would help them to make up their minds.

All this extra activity at White Rock brought with it the need for an additional Police presence. Inspector Sculpher and his depleted Force were fully stretched during these abnormal times with many officers working hours greatly in excess of their normal duties. The Special Constabulary, whose strength was now almost two hundred, provided their full-time colleagues with considerable support.

Deputy Inspector Langmead was regularly working a fourteen-hour day. After spending the day patrolling the Town on foot and parts of the country parishes on a Police motorcycle, he often finished the day by attending to paper work in the office until midnight. He became closely involved with the increasing stream of French refugees who were arriving on fishing boats and motor yachts. Often they were met by Colonel Brousson, the Government Secretary, and the French Consul, who made arrangements for them to be fed and accommodated.

At 9.57pm on Monday 17th June Sergeant Howlett received a telephone call at the Station from PC 25 Piesing who was at the Airport, saying that the siren had sounded and that enemy aircraft were approaching the Island. Sergeant Howlett informed the Inspector, who immediately went to the Station. At 10.00pm the air raid warning sounded in town.

Deputy Inspector Langmead was at White Rock, where a large crowd had assembled to watch troop activity at the harbour. Captain Mack, the officer in command, ordered him to:- "Clear all these people off at once, an air raid is expected". With Inspector Cowley and Constables Smith and Roberts, of the Special Constabulary, Mr Langmead cleared White Rock. The All Clear was sounded at 10.55pm without further incident.

In fact no enemy aircraft had approached the Island, but next day a German reconnaissance aircraft flew over photographing the harbours, the airport and other strategic areas.

The 19th June 1940 was to be a particularly traumatic day in the history of the Island and an exceptionally busy day for the Guernsey Police Force. News came early in the morning that the Germans had entered Cherbourg, not that it was unexpected because explosions had been observed on the Cotentin peninsula for some days. This for many Islanders was the final confirmation that the Germans would soon arrive in Guernsey.

It had been reported to the Attorney General that Herr Karl Hacklander was complaining that the reason for his internment was spite on the part of the authorities and in the event of an invasion of the Island, retaliatory measures would probably be taken by the Germans. Whilst there was no truth in the allegation, it was foreseen that a difficult situation could arise in the event of a German occupation. Mr Sherwill consulted the Home Office and it was decided that the Hacklander and Zulauf families should be transferred to the United Kingdom.

Guernsey-born Mrs Lilian Hacklander, wife of Hans Hacklander, who before her marriage was Miss Rawlins-Duquemin, had not been detained with the rest of her German family. On the orders of the Lieutenant Governor, Sergeant Banneville arrested her and later in the day accompanied her, her husband and other members of the Hacklander and Zulauf families on the Mailboat to Southampton, where he handed them over to the British Military Authorities.

Later that day the Bailiff issued a statement:-

"I am instructed to inform the people of Guernsey that the Government of the United Kingdom has decided that this Bailiwick is to be entirely demilitarized".

As a consequence of that decision, the Royal Court was convened and decreed that the Royal Guernsey Militia be immediately de-mobilised. Arms, uniforms and equipment were to be handed in at the Town Arsenal and all ranks were then to proceed quietly to their homes.

It was announced that all persons in possession of firearms must immediately hand them in to the Constables of their parish or the Police Station. Soon there was a queue outside the Station, with people waiting to surrender their arms and ammunition. Alfred Digard, of the *Guernsey Press*, came with a .32 revolver, Colonel Lawson handed in his Mauser automatic, Mr Rihoy, of Military Road, a service rifle, Mr G.Timmer, a .32 revolver and 18 rounds of ammunition. Ancient and modern, the arsenal of surrendered weapons was enormous. They ranged from an antique Turkish rifle to a 'Spadau' machine gun and even three Mills grenades. All these weapons and ammunition were speedily conveyed to the Town Arsenal.

The Lieutenant Governor was informed by the Home Secretary that if he was recalled, then the Bailiff should discharge the civil duties of the Lieutenant Governor. The Home Secretary also intimated that the Bailiff should stay at his post and administer the government of the Island to the best of his ability, in the interests of the inhabitants, whether or not he was in a position to receive instructions from His Majesty's Government. The Crown Officers should also remain at their posts.

Press notices appeared in the newspapers announcing the evacuation of school children, their teachers and mothers with children under school age. Those wishing to be evacuated had to register with their Parish Constables by 8.00pm that evening.

Almost immediately a queue formed outside the Constable's Office in Lefebvre Street of people waiting to register. Many had to wait for up to two hours, during which time some people became very agitated. Mr Sculpher detailed four officers to control the crowd and St John Ambulance men were called to attend to a number of people who fainted.

Despite all the pressures and different priorities of the previous few days, the exports of Island produce had continued and on the 19th June, over 350,000 chips of tomatoes were shipped to the mainland.

That night a curfew was imposed on cars from 10.30pm. to 5.00am and this helped to facilitate the Military evacuation of the Island. At 4.00am. the S.S.Biarritz docked in St Peter Port harbour and immediately the remaining 1000 troops started embarking. When the S.S.Biarritz left port at 8.00am the Island had been totally demilitarized. The Lieutenant Governor, Maj-Gen F.R.Minshull-Ford, and his wife Dorothy were also on board, having had only two hour's notice to evacuate. The troopship also embarked over one hundred French servicemen and civilians who had recently arrived in the Island.

Guernsey awoke the next morning to find itself de-militarised and defenceless and many Islanders bitterly resented being left to the mercy of Adolf Hitler. Many more made the decision to evacuate if the opportunity occurred. Throughout the day the evacuation of mothers and children continued with shipload after shipload leaving for the mainland.

During the day the Bailiff, Victor Gosselin Carey, was sworn in by Jurat Drake as Lieutenant Governor. One of his first acts was to sign a Requisition Order authorising 'Every Police officer to enter the premises of Hacklander (Mohair Fabrics) Limited, at Rue du Pre, by force if necessary and take possession of the premises and contents, particularly a number of bales or parcels of "Cotine" seeds - and I hereby direct the removal of such bales and parcels and their transmission to England'

Immediately Deputy Inspector Langmead, assisted by PC 17 Plevin and PC 11 Bull and accompanied by Mr F.W.Thomas, the Company's Accountant, entered the Hacklander premises and removed 29 bags of 'Cotine' seeds. Arrangements were made for them to be transported to White Rock and placed on board the S.S.New Fawn. They were consigned to the Controller, Board of Trade (Company Department), Great Smith Street, London S.W.1.

'Strong advice' was given to men aged between 20 and 33 to volunteer for military service and they were told that priority would be given to them in the evacuation plans. A great many saw it as their duty and left the Island to serve in the forces. A considerable number of the younger members of the Police Force also wished to join the armed forces but Sculpher continued to discourage anyone from volunteering.

One evening whilst the evacuation was in progress, Ambrose Sherwill the Attorney General, addressed the Force, which had been assembled in the Inspector's office.

"Should the Germans come", he conjectured, "what they will do is have a look around and see that there is nothing here for them and go off again. There would be nothing for them to stay here for. If the British had stayed they would not have been able to hold on to the Channel Islands, there weren't enough of them and we would have been bombed out of existence. If there is a general evacuation, the Police Force will be the last to leave and you will have the lifeboat at your disposal. Of course, if anybody does go, it will be like a soldier deserting his post in time of a crisis and there will be no job to come back to." Everyone totally believed him and stayed, but many still harboured the desire to serve King and Country.

As there were now no troops available to guard strategic points in the Island, it was decided that twelve full time Special or Auxiliary Constables be appointed to supplement the regular Police Force. Those recruited were:-

| | |
|---|---|
| A/1 | Herbert Frederick Sutherland Champion |
| A/2 | John Nicholas Corbin |
| A/3 | Frank Langford |
| A/4 | George Lewis |
| A/5 | Frederick John Moore |
| A/6 | Cyril William Guilbert Petit |
| A/7 | William Thomas Pealling |
| A/8 | Lennox Roberts |
| A/9 | Walter Arthur Robilliard |
| A/10 | William Kelly Sebire |
| A/11 | Albert James Vanden Bergh |
| A/12 | Herbert Frederick Williams |

All the new recruits, with the exception of Bert Champion, were over forty, 8 of them over fifty and 2 were fifty five. It was anticipated that their appointment would be temporary and they would only be employed during normal working hours, so experienced Special Constables were preferred to younger totally untrained men.

The States of Deliberation, the Guernsey Parliament, met on the 21st June and in order to streamline the government of the Island, decided:-

'To create an Emergency Controlling Committee, to be called 'The Controlling Committee of the States of Guernsey' whose first President shall be Ambrose James Sherwill, which Committee shall have the right and power to do and cause to be done all executive and administrative acts which the States have authorised or could authorise whenever such acts appear to the Committee to require early decision - notwithstanding that the carrying out of such decisions may override or run contrary to decisions taken by the States or by any other Committee, Council or Board of the States and such Committee shall have full power to pledge the credit of the States to any extent and to draw on the Board of Administration for all financial requirements'.

In practice what was created was a new form of government for Guernsey, with Ambrose Sherwill, H.M.Attorney General, taking on the role of Prime Minister. He quickly appointed seven members to the Committee, each with responsibility for a particular Department. The Island was now to be run by a Cabinet of eight Islanders, with the authority and ability to make quick decisions. In the circumstances which prevailed at that time, speed was of the essence.

Ambrose Sherwill's Cabinet consisted of:

| | |
|---|---|
| Jurat A.M. Drake | Horticulture |
| Raymond Falla | Agriculture |
| Deputy R.H. Johns | Employment |
| Jurat John Leale | Economics |
| Dr.A.N. Symons | Medical Services |
| Deputy Stamford Raffles | Information |
| Jurat Sir Abraham Laine | Essential Commodities |

It was a very strong team which was to serve the Island well. Ambrose Sherwill was a man of sound judgement with the ability to make speedy and decisive decisions. With his typical legal approach, he liked twenty-four hours to mull over a matter, before arriving at a decision, but when made, it was sound and solid. In Court he was regarded by many of his colleagues as an actor who never used a single plain word if he could find two outsize ones. He was always immaculately dressed and invariably carried a pencil stump in his waistcoat pocket. He was often referred to, by members of the legal profession as 'His Nibs'. It has been said that the occasion produces the man, certainly Ambrose Sherwill was the man for the occasion.

With the departure of the R.A.F., the Airport was deserted. During the early evening of the 21st June, Deputy Inspector Langmead, accompanied by Mr T.G.Heggs, the Assistant States Engineer and Mr A.Edmonds, States Foreman, examined the Airport buildings, hangars and huts. They found that considerable damage had been done to the main building, probably by R.A.F. personnel prior to their evacuation. Telephones had been forceably disconnected and hurled about, electric light shades and bulbs smashed, furniture overturned and litter strewn about. Cupboards in various offices were opened and books and papers scattered around. In the Control room a fire extinguisher had been set off, the contents of which now covered the floor and the furniture. In the restaurant, the Deputy Inspector found only empty bottles strewn all over the floor. The buildings and huts were made secure and the main hangar doors closed.

About 100 two-gallon petrol cans littered the eastern end of the airport, near Rue des Auberts. These cans had all been punctured in two places with a pickaxe and the contents left to drain away. Mr Langmead managed to save about 2 gallons which he put into the tank of the Police Motorcycle. Special Constable Frank Langford was posted to prevent any person from entering the Airport premises.

The Deputy Inspector also inspected the Happy Landings and Manor Hotels, which has been abandoned by the R.A.F. Both hotels were open but apparently undamaged. He turned off the electricity at the mains and secured both premises.

Later in the week, in the company of Mr Sculpher, he visited Castle Cornet and found that the whole place had been left open by the Military Authorities when they evacuated. In the guard room the beds had been left just as they were when their occupants got out of them. In the cookhouse there were loaves, flour and an assortment of food strewn about. In the scullery, the vile smell, which met them, was clearly caused by a quantity of rotting meat. Mr Langmead reported the matter to the States Supervisor's secretary, who undertook to get the filth cleared up and the place secured.

Fort George, which had also been abandoned by the Military, was deserted and unprotected. The Fort, in the days following the departure of the Military, attracted considerable attention from 'souvenir' hunters, no doubt because of the large quantities of stores which had been left and the existence of a NAAFI. Arrangements were made to transfer as much as possible of the remaining stores to St Paul's Church, with the medical supplies going to the Country Hospital. It was estimated that there was over £2,000 of stock left behind at Fort George by the Military Authorities, including 900 gallons of petrol.

Many people took the view that it was better for them to 'acquire' the goods rather than leave them for the Germans. Police officers detailed to guard Fort George were soon fully occupied apprehending people leaving the Fort, by both official and unofficial routes, carrying items plundered from the NAAFI, the canteen and the sergeant's Mess. One man was caught carrying a sack containing hundreds of items ranging from tins of mansion polish to bottles of ink. His home was searched and a further mass of items were recovered. The accused pleaded guilty in Court and exclaimed "I don't see any harm in it, I don't see why we shouldn't have a share before the Germans come over".

When the troops departed they took with them large quantities of the stores from Fort George, but many items of a non military nature were left behind. The regimental silver of the Royal Irish Fusiliers, worth many thousands of pounds, could not be taken, so arrangements were made for it to be transferred to a vault of one of the Island's banks. Mr Sculpher detailed PC 30 Short to assist in its transfer to Lloyds Bank.

As the transfer and the destination, was considered to be highly secret, PC Short was required to wear civilian clothes. When he reported to the Military

Authorities at Fort George, besides being sworn to secrecy, he was provided with a revolver and 50 rounds of ammunition. Soon after the transfer was completed, the Military left the Island without having collected the revolver and ammunition back from the Constable. He decided that if the Germans were coming, then having a revolver might be an advantage, so he took it home. In order to make sure that the revolver was in working order and to test the recoil, Fred fired one shot into the ground. Then he cleaned and greased the revolver before putting it away in a safe place.

As a result of the evacuation, almost half the population had left the Island. Many had just locked their doors, some had not even done that and caught the next boat, leaving their maids and their pets to fend for themselves. Sergeant Pill was on patrol in the Esplanade when he was approached by Mrs Vaudin, who pointed out a cat locked in No.16. As the owners had left the Island, he released the catch on a window, climbed in and rescued the cat. This act was to be repeated many times, by many people, over the next few days.

Julia Brichta had recovered from her brief stay in hospital and obtained new employment with Miss Francis de.B.Tupper in St Martin. Her new employer decided to evacuate and wrote to the Inspector, informing him that she had paid for seven day's board and lodging for her Hungarian maid, given her £5 and told her to report to the Station the next morning. When she reported, Miss Brichta was merely told to find herself employment as soon as possible.

Many families had to make the difficult decision, whether to go or stay. Constable Fred Short and his wife decided that she and their two children would leave the Island with the general evacuation. Fred, who was on motorcycle patrol, promised them that he would be down at the jetty to see them off. The general public were not allowed on White Rock due to the danger of air raids but Fred as a Police officer was able to be there.

Fred Short later recalled:-"I went up the gangway with my family and spoke to one of the ship's officer's. He was most helpful and said he would put my wife and children in a nice big cabin. It was a big boat, larger than the mail boats running at that time. The officer asked me if I was staying aboard, I said, I wasn't. He told me the Germans were all down the French coast, which, of course I knew. If I stayed aboard he promised to give me a pair of overalls to put on over my uniform. I admit I was tempted".

As Fred Short was contemplating his and his family's future, an announcement over the loud speakers brought him back to reality:- 'Will PC Short please report at the Harbour office on the jetty, immediately.'

"When I heard this call for me, I said to my family, look I had better go, they want me on the phone. So I kissed them all and said farewell. There were a few tears, but I went down the gangway and picked up the telephone. The Station Sergeant wanted me to go up to Fort George as quickly as possible as the NAAFI stores were being raided. I think somebody, probably Arthur Langmead, must have seen me go aboard and thought I was going to slip away with my family. When I look back and think what eventually happened to me, I should have stayed on board. I guess duty called and like Mr Sherwill said, deserting your post wasn't on.

When I arrived at Fort George I learnt that 'the old man' had driven through in the Police car with Sergeant Harper at the wheel and had caught two people in the act of removing goods from the NAAFI. He arrested them and took them to the Station."

Fred Short was to spend quite a considerable time over the next few days patrolling Fort George, ostensibly to prevent equipment and stores being removed by all and sundry. In practice he located items which were removed by himself and other Police officers. One evening he and Chipper Bougourd visited

Fort George on the Police motorcycle and collected a wireless set which Chipper wanted.

In all, the families of seven men in the Force had evacuated, PCs Bailey, Bougourd, Quin, Kimber, Short, Tardif and Sergeant F.P.Duquemin. A few days later a trunk telephone call was received by Sergeant Harper at the Station, from the City of Glasgow Police, saying "Tell PC 19 Tardif that his wife is at Hillington Park, Church of Scotland, Berrytnowes Road, Glasgow." Jack Harper telephoned Archie Tardif with the news.

On the 25th June 1940 an order was signed by Colonel F.W.Brousson, Government Secretary, on behalf of the Lieutenant Governor, directing that all enemy aliens held in internment, were to be released. The twenty-eight held, were immediately freed.

The Island of Alderney had been almost totally evacuated on the 23rd June, with only about twelve residents remaining. The newly appointed Controlling Committee made arrangements for cattle, pigs and some of the abandoned military stores to be shipped to Guernsey. The S.S. New Fawn and the S.S. Courier belonging to Sark Motor Ships Ltd., were plying back and forth between the Islands with cargo. At 7.50am on Thursday 27th June, Alan Mackay went into the Police Station and reported:- "There has been a lot of looting in Alderney. I have just seen an Anchor Laundry basket come ashore on the New Jetty, White Rock, and then it was taken back on board again. It looks suspicious to me."

The statement intrigued and concerned Sergeant Le Lievre. Together they went to the harbour where he saw the Anchor Laundry basket aboard the New Fawn. It was consigned from James Rutter, of Alderney. The Sergeant spoke to Captain Fred Noyon, who said:- "It's no use leaving Rutter's stuff on the Jetty, he is in Alderney and will be coming back with us tonight and bringing the remainder of his stuff then."

The basket was stuffed full with a variety of items from bottles of surgical spirit to tins of condensed milk. The Sergeant took no action, but it was an incident that he was going to have good reason to recall later.

With almost 20,000 people, about half the population, having evacuated and many of those remaining regretting that they had not gone, or still deciding whether to go or stay, there were many cases of individual panic and hysteria.

Chipper Bougourd and Archie Tardif, who were great pals off duty and worked together whenever the opportunity occurred, were walking down Smith Street, past the Press Company shop, when they were called upstairs by Mrs Digard. Her husband, Claude, had collapsed. The two PCs rendered first aid until Dr Wilson arrived. He examined Mr Digard and pronounced "It's hysteria".

Great consternation was caused when a German plane passed low over the Town flying towards St Sampson. The visibility was good and Islanders could clearly see the iron crosses on the fuselage and wings.

During the afternoon the Bailiff asked Mr Sculpher to come and see him in his chambers. The Inspector knew that the matter must be serious as the Bailiff normally communicated his instructions either by telephone or letter. The Bailiff told the Inspector that it was obvious that the Germans would soon arrive in the Island. Whether it would be by sea or air he did not know, but come they would and they must be received courteously and no resistance was to be offered. He handed the Inspector a sealed envelope and instructed him to give it personally to the Commander of any German Force which landed.

Returning to the Station, Mr Sculpher immediately called in Clerk Sergeant Lamy and dictated a memo, addressed to :-

'Sergeants'

"In the event of the occupation of this Island by German forces, it is presumed that application will be made to the Police for assistance and the officer in charge will require to see the persons responsible for the control of the Island.

If at night, I must be fetched to explain the circumstance of how the Island is controlled. All questions are to be courteously answered and such assistance as the Police can render is to be given. All attempts at opposition must be suppressed."

At the meeting of the Controlling Committee on the morning of the 28th June the States Supervisor, H.E.Marquand, expressed the view that:- "The Island is most likely to remain unmolested if exports cease and we would thus be able to maintain communications with England".

After discussing the matter, it was resolved that:-

'The President take this matter up with the Home Office, enquiring whether in the general interest of Guernsey and the Empire we should cease the export of tomatoes to England to avoid possible danger to our harbour and shipping'.

During the meeting the Manager of the Telephone Department, Mr E.H.Bennett, asked for an immediate interview. He reported that he had been instructed, in the case of German occupation, to communicate with England in order that telegraphic communications could be cut. The Committee took a very serious view of this and an Order was immediately issued, that no such steps must be taken without first referring the matter to the President or a Member of the Committee. Inspector Sculpher was informed of the decision.

There were still many people who could not make up their minds whether they should leave or stay in Guernsey. Some actually left the Island and returned. A former Austrian, but now a German citizen, Miss Gertrude Stefan, who was employed by Mr and Mrs F.R.Clarke on the Island of Brecqhou, had left for England, with her employers. Twenty-five-year old Miss Stefan reappeared in the Island at the height of the evacuation and was, on Sherwill's authority, allowed to take up employment and live in the Pollet.

Another who went back and forth was an elderly widow, Mrs Paul King. She and her husband had retired to Guernsey after a career in the Diplomatic Service and for many years had resided in the Royal suite at the Royal Hotel. Just before the outbreak of war he died and Mrs King continued to live there on her own. During the evacuation period she informed Mr Mentha, the manager:- "I am going back to England. It is ridiculous to stop here in Guernsey, I am going to London."

She had not been away for any time at all before she reappeared at the Royal. When the Germans raided London, she decided she would be much safer in Guernsey. She announced, which was her way, to the hotel staff:- "All this talk of the Island being occupied is ridiculous, it is quite alright here in Guernsey." All her luggage, which consisted of about 12 trunks, was put back in the Royal Suite.

At 6.00pm on the 28th June, Sergeant Jack Harper handed over the duties of Station Sergeant to Sergeant Alf Howlett and went into Town to start his four hours of patrolling duty. As he walked down Smith Street, crowds were assembling to listen to Ambrose Sherwill. He was due to speak at 6.15pm from an upstairs window of the Guernsey Press Office. The public wanted to hear from him what the present situation was in regard to possible invasion by the Germans. Jack Harper continued his way down the High Street, meeting and exchanging remarks with many people he knew.

"Still with us then Emile - I thought that you were off to England."

"Perhaps next week Jack - we shall see what happens."

Jack Harper lived in an upstairs flat at 39 High Street and as he passed the entrance, he decided to nip in for a moment to see what his housekeeper, Doris Guilbert, was planning to leave him for supper when he came off duty at 10.00pm. Miss Guilbert was looking after him since his marriage had broken down. His wife had left him and with their two sons had gone to Canada. Back on patrol, he passed the Town Church and when he reached the Quay, saw across the harbour, the Mailboat, the 'Isle of Sark', loading passengers for their journey to England.

At the Ex-servicemen's Club in Victoria Road, Chipper Bougourd and Archie Tardif, were playing snooker. They had been teaching Frank Tuck to play the game, but he had gone home. Frank had completed his duty for the day, guarding the St Saviours Reservoir, while Chipper and Archie were due to go on night duty at 10.00pm.

Chipper Bougourd was a friendly, sociable and universally respected member of the Force. Always meticulous about his appearance, his belt and boots were highly polished, everything about him was always just so. Gloves in hand, he was always the gentleman. Although it must be said that he was not entirely at home with a Police notebook.

Fred Short was in bed, asleep, at his home in Steam Mill Lanes. He was due to go on night duty and as was his normal practice had only retired to bed at lunch time. He planned to get up about 8.00pm, wash, shave, cook himself some breakfast and report at the Station in good time for his 10.00pm shift.

Clerk Sergeant Bert Lamy and PC 35 Francois Le Cocq had both finished work in the Station office and had left to cycle home. Deputy Inspector Arthur Langmead had spent the later part of the afternoon patrolling the L'Eree and Mont Saint area of the Island on a Police motorcycle. On his way back to Town, at about 5.30pm, he called in at his home in Les Cornus, St Martin, for tea. Then just before 6.30pm to set off for Town.

PC 33 Tom Gaudion was at home in bed, with severe stomach pains. The Police Doctor, Dr A.Bisson, had been called but declined to go and see him as he was too busy to undertake Police work.

PC 14 Charlie Friend was patrolling Fort George, he had taken over from PC 20 Frank Whare at the 2.00pm change over. Frank had said to Charlie, "there is nothing doing - its a dead bore". After four hours Frank entirely agreed with him. PC 24 Alf Le Gallez and PC 25 'Snip' Piesing were on their respective beats in Town. As Alf passed the Weighbridge he thought that the Growers were back in business, because there was a double line of lorries, right down White Rock, loaded with tomatoes for export. The cargo boat the S.S.Sheringham, was in harbour ready to take aboard a full consignment of Guernsey tomatoes.

Sergeants Fred Banneville and Fred Duquemin had spent the day on plain clothes duty, but before going home both had decided to go to Smith Street to hear what Ambrose Sherwill had to say.

As soon as Sherwill finished speaking at 6.45pm the crowd broke up and many ran down the North Pier steps and along the front to catch buses to take them home. Others went down to the White Rock to enjoy the evening sunshine and watch the departure of the Mailboat. Ambrose Sherwill returned to his office and was soon on the telephone to C.G.Markbreiter, an Assistant Secretary at the Home Office, bringing him up to date with the situation in the Island.

PC 27 Bob Kimber was on duty in the watch tower at White Rock and was thinking of going home to his empty house at 10.00pm. He was really missing his wife and family who had evacuated. Suddenly the constable heard the throb of aeroplane engines and saw three planes, flying in formation, coming in from the south east. He was reasonably sure that they were German Dornier 215s.

As he watched, the centre plane dropped back and he heard bursts of machine gun fire and saw puffs of smoke coming from the plane. Then he saw bombs released and knew that Guernsey was about to suffer its first air raid. The time was 6.54pm. The bombs hit the Cambridge Sheds, the Information Bureau and tomato lorries in the queue extending from the New Jetty to the

Weighbridge. Soon there was a thick pall of smoke drifting slowly across the sky. The reality of war had come to Guernsey.

PC Kimber immediately telephoned the States Supervisor's office and during the rest of the raid, provided 'leading Island officials' with a running commentary.

After the German planes had flown across the Island they returned and delivered another attack on the harbour. Then they split up and individually attacked different targets. One plane attacked the Vazon area, another the Fruit Export Sheds and the third dropped a bomb at La Vassalerie, St Andrew.

When the raid started Charlie Froome, was on duty at the St John Ambulance Brigade Headquarters. He received calls for immediate assistance and with his colleague Lionel Taylor drove the ambulance down to White Rock and parked it alongside the Weighbridge, facing up the Avenue with its rear doors open.

Joe Way was just about to board the Isle of Sark and leave the Island when the raid started. Joe, a former Ambulance driver, realising that there were casualties, headed back to the Weighbridge where the ambulance was parked. There he joined Lionel Taylor and Charlie Froome in attending to the injured and tried to persuade Charlie to drive the ambulance farther down White Rock, saying:-

"There are many injured down there who need attention."

"I'm sorry" Charlie said, "we can't be everywhere, there are people here who need attention." and added "It is safer for the ambulance to stay where it is, as many of the tomato lorries are ablaze and if we managed to get down, we probably would not be able to get back again."

As the Dorniers roared in for yet another attack Lionel and Charlie sought cover under the ambulance, while Joe lay flat on the ground. Two bombs exploded between the vehicle and the Weighbridge, causing considerable damage to the ambulance and injuring Lionel in the backside. Charlie was concussed although otherwise uninjured. Joe was also injured.

It had previously been arranged that if there was an air raid all off-duty Policemen would report at the Station. Francois Le Cocq, Deputy Inspector Langmead, Chipper Bougourd and Archie Tardif all reported for duty just after 7.00pm. Mr Langmead issued everyone with steel helmets and they all set off on foot down the Forest Lane to the Weighbridge.

**PC 'Chipper' Bougourd.**

On arrival at the harbour, they found William Nicolle at the north west corner of the Weighbridge with a serious leg injury. Constable Bougourd immediately went to his assistance and was seen pulling down a wooden bar from the window of the Weighbridge, to use as a splint. PC Tardif assisted Joe Way who was lying against the upper walk opposite the Weighbridge, near the ambulance. The Deputy Inspector attended to Miss Alice Le Poidevin, who was severely injured in both legs and feet. Francois Le Cocq attended to the injured farther down White Rock.

As the Dorniers came in for another attack, a bomb landed in the roadway near the Weighbridge. Joe Way and William Nicolle received further injuries. Chipper Bougourd, who was only ten yards from where the bomb exploded, received a shrapnel wound in the head. He was unconscious and bleeding from the mouth and nose when the Arthur Langmead went to him. He died soon afterwards. When Francois Le Cocq came back to the Weighbridge, he found Archie Tardif repeating time after time "What about my mate - what about my mate."

Joe Way, Lionel Taylor and two other men were placed in the ambulance and Constable le Cocq was ordered by the Deputy Inspector to drive the ambulance and the casualties to the hospital. As Mr Langmead put it;

"Take all you can and get out of it, in case the Germans come back again".

One of the ambulance's rear tyres was flat, as was the spare but the Constable managed to drive the damaged ambulance up St Julians Avenue as far as the South African War Memorial before the tyre finally came off the rim. Despite that he continued his 'bumpity, bumpity' progress until he reached St James, where he was stopped by Inspector Sculpher. It was obvious that the ambulance was no longer drivable, so a passing coal lorry belonging to Stan Collings and driven by Charlie Fisher, was commandeered. A tarpaulin was laid over the back of the lorry and the injured were transferred from the ambulance. The lorry was turned around and driven by PC Le Cocq to the Country Hospital. The damaged ambulance was abandoned in St James Street, some fifty yards down from the junction with Saumarez Street.

During the last attack a salvo of 10 bombs was dropped around the Weighbridge causing further damage and starting more fires in the queue of lorries. The fires quickly spread owing to some of the petrol tanks in the lorries exploding.

When the bombing raid started PC 16 Frank Tuck was at home in St Martin. It was a beautiful summer evening, with clear blue skies. He was enjoying the silence of the countryside, only to have it shattered by the screeching of bombs and the sound of explosions. Frank raced down to Town to see what was happening. On the way he met one or two people he knew who were clearly frightened and were pedalling like mad in the opposite direction

PC 30 Short was suddenly awakened by the sound of explosions and looking out of the window and saw a German plane. Realising that it was a bombing raid, he quickly put on his uniform and without shaving or washing, rushed out of the house and arrived at the station in next to no time. He was told to get down to the White Rock as fast as he could, so he ran all the way.

The scene which confronted him, momentarily stopped him in his tracks. Dead and injured lay unattended, lorries and their loads were on fire and only a short distance away small groups of dumbstruck civilians watching all that was going on, hardly able to believe that it was an Air Raid.

PC 25 'Snip' Piesing, who was already on duty at White Rock when the air raid started, directed as many people as possible to shelter below the pier. He said later that it was very fortunate that the tide was out because if it had not been, the number of casualties would have been far greater.

Two horses that had recently been shipped from Alderney were stabled in a shed on the White Rock. As a result of the crescendo of noise from the air raid, the horses stampeded. After checking that the injured were being cared for, Fred and 'Snip' Piesing, both being ex-cavalry men, decided to try and quieten the two horses down. They knew the value of sugar, so they went into the White Rock Cafe, which was open and deserted and helped themselves to handfuls of sugar lumps.

They approached the frightened horses, remembering their cavalry training, to 'make much of them'. They soft talked them, saying 'come on my boys' and 'everything is going to be all right my beauties'. The sugar lumps worked wonders and when the horses settled down Fred put sacks over their heads to restrict their vision and a rope round their necks as a halter. Then 'Snip' and Fred led them out of the shed and along the sea front to the Terres field at the bottom of Havelet, where they released them.

As Fred returned, he noticed an abandoned Morris Oxford car with its driver's door wide open, parked near the Weighbridge. Near at hand injured people were lying, desperately in need of medical attention. PC Short pulled the rear seat out of the abandoned car, put in some of the injured and drove them to the Country Hospital. He quickly returned and continued to use the car as an ambulance until all the injured had been removed to hospital.

The all clear sounded at 8.00pm and slowly Guernsey came back to life, though everyone was a little apprehensive and wondered if the raid was over or if it was just another lull. The air raid was concentrated on the White Rock and killed thirty-three people and injured sixty-seven. Lines of tomato vans and lorries waiting with produce for shipment to the mainland were left as smouldering wrecks. Forty-nine vehicles were burnt out or seriously damaged. Bomb craters were everywhere. The Weighbridge was extensively damaged and its clock stopped at a few minutes before seven.

Alf Le Poidevin, who was foreman for W.Head and Sons Ltd., the carters and carriers, of Mont Arrive, later recalled how he and other drivers had the job of clearing up the debris from White Rock. "We had to clear all the broken-down lorries, the bodies and the tomatoes from White Rock. We took all the rubbish to Mont Crevelt. It was like tomato sauce, so in effect there was a trail of tomato sauce from White Rock to St Sampson. There was no road sweeping or cleaning in those days. As a result there were tomato plants growing all the way along Les Banques as far as Richmond Corner."

The whole of the sea front, from the Guernsey Brewery, where over one hundred windows were broken, right along to Les Banques suffered considerable damage, there was hardly an unbroken window to be seen. Well over a hundred windows were broken in the Royal Hotel and in the States Offices every single window was blown out.

In the country a bomb was dropped near the St Saviour's Reservoir and another at the race course at Vazon. A house in St Andrew, at La Vassalerie, suffered considerable structural damage, all the windows and doors being blown in. Fortunately none of the occupants were injured as they had taken cover. In the Strand, Strand Villa, an adjoining cottage and another house received considerable structural damage. The Police Station escaped damage, except for one broken window.

The Germans machined-gunned other areas of the town and haymakers in the fields, without causing any serious injury. The lifeboat, which was at sea during the raid, was machine gunned and Harold Hobbs, the son of the Coxswain, killed.

Just as Bob Kimber put the telephone down after giving his commentary, a bomb dropped close by in the harbour. The blast blew him out of the watch tower, fortunately not seriously injuring him, but it was a narrow escape.

After the air raid Mrs Paul King, who had only that morning re-ensconced herself in the Royal Suite, of the Royal Hotel, summoned Mr Mentha, the manager, and announced that she was returning to London, immediately. Alan Sarchet, the Hotel porter was detailed to drive her the short distance to where the 'Isle of Sark' was berthed.

Alan, who like his father was to be employed by the Royal for over fifty years, recalling the events of that evening, said:- "The Hotel was still running the old 'Hotchkiss', which I used to take Mrs King to the Mailboat. I will never forget it because I had to get special permission from the Police to go. This was immediately after the raid. The area was littered with wreckage and bodies, it was one of the worst journeys I ever made. I managed to get Mrs King up the gangway and literally pushed her on to the deck. The 'old soul' acted as if she was going on a summer holiday. I followed her for a few steps on the deck and I said, 'I am afraid that I shall have to leave you here madam'.

'Oh' she said. 'oh no, just come along, I want to see the purser, I must reserve a cabin'.

'Reserve a cabin' ! I exclaimed and left her to come to terms with the world as it really was, unlike the privileged diplomatic world that had been her life until that moment."

At 10.00pm that evening the 'Isle of Sark' left St Peter Port harbour and headed for England, the last Mailboat the Island was to see until after the occupation.

At about the same time as the mailboat was leaving, PCs Short and Le Cocq were trying to encourage 58-year-old Marshall Taylor, who had obviously over indulged, to move on quietly. Despite repeated requests, he refused and was arrested. When Taylor appeared in Court, Mr Sculpher although prosecuting, was at pains to point out that he had been seen on the night of the air raid assisting the Fire Brigade until 9.00pm. The Court fined him 2/6.

Just after midnight, Deputy Inspector Langmead, who had been on duty for more than 15 hours, noticed a light in the premises of T.N.Wyatt and Co. the gentlemen's outfitters in the Pollet. He instructed Constable Whare, along with Special Constables Isler and Woolnough, to put the light out, if need be, by forcing open the premises. Frank Whare found a ladder and managed to get into the back yard, break a window and climb into the shop. As he could not find the switches he removed light bulbs.

At a meeting of the Police Committee held a few days later, the Inspector reported in glowing terms regarding the Force's performance during the air raid:-

"All the available Police on duty were quickly on the scene and the remainder reported as quickly as possible. In the circumstances the Police behaved splendidly without exception, but I would draw special attention to the conduct of Deputy Inspector Langmead, Sergeants Harper, Duquemin and Banneville and PCs Tardif, Piesing, Le Gallez, Kimber, Dyson and Short, the later two Constables performed very valuable work with the injured.

**The Weighbridge after the German Air Raid.**

While the above named performed their various duties with commendable promptitude, courage and calmness, I beg to draw special attention to the action of PC 35 Le Cocq. This Constable is the youngest member of the Force and he was in the midst of this dastardly attack. When I first noticed him he was alone in charge of an ambulance that had been badly damaged. The tyre came off the wheel and I stopped him with four dead and injured persons in the ambulance. The PC promptly stopped a lorry and took his load to hospital. He then commandeered the Frobel motor brake from the Country Hospital and continued his work until all the injured were in hospital. Later this PC was instrumental in getting all the dead identified, some of which only portions of the body was left and three badly burned.

Doctor Collings has since spoken to me of PC Le Cocq's conduct and wishes to be associated with my remarks to the Police Committee.

PC 17 Plevin had, by previous arrangement, proceeded to the Country Hospital where he performed invaluable work with the dead and injured, being on duty until 2.00am.

While all the Police acted with commendation I beg to ask that the conduct of the officers specially named be noted in the Committee's Minutes and recorded on their Conduct Sheets."

**The burnt out remains of tomato lorries after the German Air Raid.**

The Air Raid siren sounded at 11.00am the morning after the raid and the all clear went half an hour later. A German aircraft was seen, but no bomb was dropped, clearly it was a reconnaissance mission to assess the results of the air raid.

At the 2.00pm shift change PC 27 Kimber failed to parade for duty. Sergeant Harper sent PC21 Le Page, on the Police motorcycle, to his home in Jerbourg Road. After knocking and getting no response, he forced an entry and found Bob Kimber lying in bed suffering from shock as a result of the air raid. The blast that blew Bob out of the watch tower had a greater effect than had at first been realised. Dr Dick Gibson was called. PC Kimber returned to duty two days later.

Later that afternoon the Deputy Inspector put through a trunk call to the Birmingham City Police saying:- "Please inform Mrs Bougourd, of 107 Byron Road, Small Heath, Birmingham, that her husband Constable C.H.Bougourd of this Force, was seriously injured in an air raid on this Island last evening and has since died. Her brother-in-law, Willie Ogier, is willing to undertake the funeral arrangements if necessary. Please telephone instructions as mailboat movements are uncertain."

A reply was received from the Birmingham Police the next day to the effect that Mrs Bougourd had been seen and that she wished her brother-in-law to carry on with the funeral.

The S.S.Courier, which had been plying between Guernsey and Alderney retrieving cattle and stores, was en route to St Peter Port when it was bombed and machine gunned by one of the German planes during the air raid. The Captain beached the ship at the entrance to St Sampson harbour and many of her crew and passengers managed to make their way ashore. The next day the Courier was refloated and Captain James Ingrouille brought his vessel into St Peter Port harbour.

PC 32 Pugh was on duty at the White Rock when the Courier was about to leave for Plymouth with its cargo of pigs. The vessel had untied and left the jetty when the Constable noticed several people sprinting in his direction. Two were in uniform, one R.A.F and the other military, and there were also two civilians. The Captain had also seen them and drew the bow of his ship back towards the jetty, enabling them to make a flying leap on to the ship's deck. They were probably the last persons to leave Guernsey by steamer before the occupation began.

The traumatic events and great activity kept the Police Station and indeed the whole of the Force fully occupied during the Saturday and Sunday following the air raid. Relatives of the dead and injured had to be informed and there was a constant stream of trunk calls from people enquiring about relations and friends. People were also constantly enquiring about every imaginable subject from the possibilities of evacuation, to when the Germans might arrive.

On the Sunday morning, a R.A.F. launch escorted by three Blenheims arrived in the harbour with the intention of picking up some R.A.F. wireless equipment and a number of G.P.O. personnel. The officer in charge of the launch was at the Police Station talking to Sergeant Lamy when the air raid warning sounded. The officer hearing the siren commented to the sergeant that "your wardens are getting a bit jumpy, mistaking our Blenheim escort for the Luftwaffe". Mr Lamy took him to the window and pointed out a large green, grey aircraft carrying a black cross and asked him if he could identify his Blenheim. The officer went off post-haste to the harbour and returned to England.

The siren sounded on Sunday 30th June 1940 at 1.10pm and four German aircraft flew over the Island and after circling low over the Forest, three of them landed at the airport. At 1.45pm the Station Sergeant, Charlie Le Lievre, on hearing the news telephoned the Deputy Inspector at his home in Les Cornus, St Martin, and suggested that he go to the airport. Inspector Sculpher was also informed. As Arthur Langmead reached the Forest Church he saw one aircraft flying in the direction of Jersey. A little farther on, as he turned into the entrance of the airport, three German aircraft left the ground and rose sharply into the air.

The Deputy Inspector went to the airport buildings and found them deserted. He telephoned the Station to report the situation. Then Inspector Sculpher arrived in the Police car with Sergeant Lamy and two other officers. Mr Sculpher had with him the Bailiff's letter, addressed to an unknown, as yet, German Commandant. On this occasion it was not needed. Together they searched the buildings and vicinity and, except for the main door of the airport building, which had been forced, the place was intact. On the edge of the grass near the apron they found a German automatic pistol loaded with eight cartridges. Mr Langmead emptied the magazine and fired the round in the chamber into the ground.

John Ingrouille approached Mr Sculpher and told him that he had been standing in the lane with Alphonse Lajoie and had seen three planes land. "Some of the airmen walked towards the buildings. They only remained on the ground for 10 to 15 minutes. Before they went off they stood beside the machine guns which were by the planes. They started up the aircraft, took the guns aboard and took off sharply without looking for wind direction or anything."

Having assured themselves that the Germans had departed and left no booby traps, Inspector Sculpher, Sergeant Lamy and the two other officers returned to the Police Station. Arthur Langmead remained at the airport until 4.00pm, in case the Germans returned. Everyone now knew that it was not a matter of 'if', only a matter of 'when' the Germans would arrive and they hadn't long to wait.

At 3.00pm Sergeant Harper received a telephone call from Mrs Sibyl Hathaway, the Dame of Sark, who informed him:- "I have just heard a rumour that the Germans have landed in Guernsey. My people are getting panicky".

He informed the Dame that:- "We have received nothing official".

At 7.00pm Langmead reported at the Station and let Mr Sculpher, who was at home, know that he was there.

At 7.30pm Fred Short and his uncle Tom Rees, entered Castel Church to attend the evening service, which was conducted by the Reverend Waterbury. Fred, who was due to go on duty at 10.00pm, sang in the choir and was a regular attender when his duties allowed. As the service ended, the air raid siren sounded and when the congregation came out into the church yard they saw a number of German aircraft circling overhead. Many people were on the point of panic and rushed back into the church for safety. Constable Short and the Reverend Waterbury went around quietly encouraging people to stay calm.

At 7.46pm Sergeant Alf Howlett, the Station Sergeant, put through a trunk call to the Police at Cavendish, Sudbury, Suffolk. He asked the local Police to "Please inform the wife of Gerald Ernest Page, 33, fireman on the S.S.Sheringham, at Peacocks Farm, Cavendish, that her husband is an air raid casualty. Now in Country Hospital, Guernsey. Injury to arm and leg. Condition poorly".

A few minutes later, just after 8.30pm the five Junkers troop carriers which had been circling the Island, finally landed at the airport. This time they had come to stay.

## Chapter 5

# COME ON, THAT'S A BULLET WOUND

As the troop-carrying Junkers were landing at the airport, Ambrose Sherwill was on the telephone to the Home Office and the Bailiff of Jersey, acquainting them with the situation and saying au-revoir. Communications between the Home Office and the Island continued until 10.30pm. when they were finally cut for the duration.

Tom Castle who was on duty at the Telephone Exchange when the Germans arrived and made him disconnect all the lines to England. A guard with a machine gun ensured that no further calls were made. A German officer refused Tom's request that he be allowed to inform England that Guernsey was now occupied. However, when the Germans left the room for a few moments the telephone rang. It was a call from Jersey enquiring why communication with London had ceased. Tom Castle told them to tell London that the Island was now occupied.

The first German Junkers 52 troopcarrier to land did so with some difficulty, because of the cattle that were grazing on and around the grass runway. Two cows were injured when the aircraft landed and were later shot by the Germans. Most of the cattle rescued from Alderney during the days following the evacuation of that island, had been put out to graze on the airport. One of the first orders the Germans issued was for the clearance of the cattle from the runway so that further troopcarriers could land. Inspector Sculpher was instructed to ensure that the cattle were removed by dawn.

At about 9.40pm PC 30 Short was cycling down the Grange on his way to report for duty when he was surprised to see two German soldiers on guard at the entrance to Grange House, the telephone exchange. By the time he reached the Station he had just about recovered from the shock and realised that life was going to be very different from that to which he had been so long accustomed. Sergeant Pill, who had also just come on duty, ordered the whole night shift to stand by and await instructions.

At 3.00am, PC 30 Short, who was the duty motorcyclist, was detailed to go to the airport and do whatever was necessary to remove the cattle and to assist the Germans in any way he could. Fred organised a number of farmers to help and they arrived at the airport at dawn, around 5.00am. As they were debating whether they should drive the cattle into a field on the other side of the Route des Landes, there was a roar of engines and three Junkers troopcarriers landed, miraculously missing the grazing animals.

The planes rapidly disgorged their cargo of fully armed German troops, together with a number of motorcycles and sidecars. The Germans without transport immediately commandeered the farmers' cars and motorcycles. None of the Germans spoke English, but Constable Short clearly understood what they wanted when they kept repeating, 'Benzin, Benzin'. He led them, on his motorcycle, out of the airport and down the road past the Happy Landings Hotel to Snell's petrol pump at Le Bourg. There he broke open the door and started to turn the pump handle, but the tank was dry.

Not knowing quite what to do, he was reminded by a colleague that the Force had 'acquired' a supply of petrol from a damaged Spitfire. When the R.A.F. evacuated, a Spitfire which had crash landed and was damaged beyond repair, had been left in the hangar. Policemen discovered that the fuel tanks in the wings were full and they managed to fill twenty, 5-gallon cans with high octane petrol and secreted them in a store next to the Police garage in Lefebvre Street.

Fred Short decided that there was no alternative but to lead the Germans to that supply of petrol. He headed a 'convoy' of German Military motorcycles, with their mounted machine guns, the commandeered farmers' cars and motorcycles into St Peter Port and stopped outside the Police Station. They arrived, at 6.00am, just as the change-over from night shift to early shift was taking place.

A German officer motioned to the policemen, to line up against the wall outside the Station. Fred said later that he and his colleagues did so, only very reluctantly. "But when you are confronted by fully armed German combat troops, you tend to do as you are told ! We began to wonder if we were going to be mown down in cold blood". Instead the officer produced a camera and took a photograph of 'British' Policemen lined up outside a 'British' Police Station.

Then the Germans drove into the Police yard and seized the entire stock of petrol. It was perhaps fortunate that the aviation fuel was suitable for the vehicles, otherwise the Germans may have suspected PC Short of a deliberate act of sabotage !

Shortly afterwards, two Germans came into the station and drew a sketch of a Nazi flag and indicated that they wanted two large flags made immediately. Because Sergeant Le Lievre could not understand that they wanted them by 9.00am. that morning, one of the Germans climbed up on a chair and changed the hands of the clock to indicate their deadline.

An attempt was made to contact a firm of sailmakers in St Sampson, only for it to be discovered that they had evacuated. Then Sergeant Le Lievre contacted the manager of Creasey's, who undertook to get his dressmakers to run up the two flags required as quickly as possible. At 9.30am PC 15 Bill Burton, delivered the flags to the Island's 'new masters' at the Royal Hotel. One was immediately hoisted on the hotel flagpole and the other over Castle Cornet. Bill Burton, when he handed the flags to a German officer, failed to say 'Heil Hitler' and was slapped across the face with a glove, by the officer.

Probably the first casualty of the Occupation occurred on the evening the Germans landed at the airport. Charlie Froome was on duty at the St John Ambulance station when Harry Ingrouille, came in and asked for a wound in his arm to be dressed. Charlie inspected the wound and asked:-

"Where the hell did you get that from?"

"Never you mind." replied Harry.

"Come on, that is a bullet wound", insisted Charlie, "where did you get that from?"

Apparently when the Germans landed, Harry had been at the top of the Petit Bot valley. He saw them coming down the road on their motorcycles, got scared and ran down the valley. The Germans saw him running away and shot him.

When a special edition of the *Evening Press* was published, gratis, very early on Monday morning, the front page was entirely taken up with the Orders of the German Commandant.

'ORDERS OF THE COMMANDANT OF THE GERMAN FORCES IN OCCUPATION OF THE ISLAND OF GUERNSEY'

1st July 1940.'

(1) All inhabitants must be indoors by 11.00pm and must not leave their homes before 6.00am.
(2) We will respect the population in Guernsey; but, should anyone attempt to cause the least trouble, serious measures will be taken and the town will be bombed.
(3) All orders given by the Military Authority are to be strictly obeyed.
(4) All spirits must be locked up immediately and no spirits may be supplied, obtained or consumed henceforth. This prohibition does not apply to stocks in private houses.
(5) No person shall enter the aerodrome at La Villiaze.
(6) All rifles, airguns, pistols, revolvers, sporting guns, and all other weapons whatsoever, except souvenirs, must, together with all ammunition, be delivered at the Royal Hotel by 12 noon today, 1st July.
(7) All British Sailors, Airmen and Soldiers on leave in this Island must report at the Police Station at 9.00am today and must then report at the Royal Hotel.
(8) No boat or vessel of any description, including any fishing boat, shall leave the harbour or any other place where the same is moored, without an order from the military authority, to be obtained at the Royal Hotel. All boats arriving from Jersey, from Sark or from Herm, or elsewhere, must remain in harbour until permitted by the military to leave. The crews will remain on board. The Master will report to the Harbourmaster, St Peter Port and will obey his instructions.
(9) The sale of motor spirit is prohibited, except for the use on essential services, such as Doctors' vehicles, the delivery of foodstuffs and sanitary services where such vehicles are in possession of a permit from the military authorities to obtain supplies. These vehicles must be brought to the Royal Hotel by 12 noon today to receive the necessary permission. The use of cars for private purposes is forbidden
(10) The black-out regulations already in force must be observed as before.
(11) Banks and shops will open as usual.

(Signed) THE GERMAN COMMANDANT OF THE ISLAND OF GUERNSEY.

As soon as the newspaper was published, British servicemen, on leave in the Island began reporting at the Police Station, in accordance with the German Commandant's Order. By mid-morning 41 men, 34 Army, 4 Navy, 2 R.A.F. and a merchant seaman, had reported and they were marched down to the Royal Hotel. Later the Germans transferred them to Castle Cornet. The German Commandant allowed Aircraftman Jack Robert parole until 4.00pm the following day so that he could attend the funeral of his two sisters, who were killed in the air raid.

Guernsey awoke on 1st July 1940 to find itself occupied by German forces. PC 16 Tuck recalls:-

"They appeared to be everywhere, it seemed as if thousands of them had arrived, they were roaring up and down on motorcycles. Islanders were scared and apprehensive of them, they made so much noise, generated so much activity and created so much officialdom. Their raucous commands, their tendency to be very commanding, they did not ask you something, they told you something. It was alarming, all very alarming. We weren't trained to deal with this new experience and neither were our leaders."

Years later another Police constable recalling the lack of leadership during the period of the evacuation and the first days of the German Occupation, commented:-

"We were young and inexperienced and looked to our superiors, Sculpher, Sherwill and Carey, for leadership. One looked to them, but it was not until later that we realised that they were no better informed or equipped than we were. At the time we thought that they were".

PC 21 Frank Le Page, a motorcycle patrolman, failed to report for duty at 12.00 midnight on the Monday night 1st-2nd July. Station Sergeant Fred Duquemin telephoned the Constable's home, but there was no reply. Later he went up to the house in the Ville au Roi Estate and found everything locked up. The Inspector was informed and immediately suspended the Constable. The next morning he authorised Sergeant Le Lievre to make an entry into PC Le Page's house, but nothing was found. The Inspector wrote to Mr Sherwill, as President of the Controlling Committee, informing him of Frank Le Page's absence. He said that he had seen Le Page on the previous Sunday night and he had appeared very distraught.

Frank Le Page who was a close friend of PC Fred Short and lived not far from him, called at his house on Monday and said:-

"Fred put a few things in a sack, we are off tonight."

"Where ?"

"We are going off to England by boat from around Bordeaux way."

Apparently the Mate from the S.S. 'New Fawn' was going to make a run for it and was prepared to take anyone who wanted a chance to escape.

"Oh I will have to think this one over, Frank."

"Well, you think it over Fred, and if you want to join us, get down there for tenish, it will be dark by then."

This was Fred Short's second opportunity to slip away and again he decided against going. Had he been given more time to think about it, he would have undoubtedly joined the escape party. Frank Le Page and his party arrived safely in Falmouth the next day.

When Fred was questioned by Inspector Sculpher about his colleague's escape, he wisely knew very little. Later he recalled:-

"Had the Germans become aware I knew of the escape and had done nothing to prevent it, I could have been in real trouble."

When the Inspector realised that Constable Le Page had escaped, he felt very bitter and let down. He strongly believed that it was a Policeman's duty to remain in the Island and serve the community, particularly now that the Germans were in occupation. He saw the role of the Force as that of being the buffer between the Germans and the general public. Mr Sculpher made a point in ensuring that neither PC Le Page nor any of his relatives received a penny of the money that was due to him up to the time he escaped.

Frank Le Page obtained a job with Wimpey, the builders, working on the construction of runways and airfields. He never returned to Guernsey, other than for a holiday after the Occupation.

The day after the Germans landed, Major Dr Albrecht Lanz, a Doctor of Law, arrived to take over as 'Insel Kommandantur'. Within days 'Courtesy Visits' between the new German Commandant and the Bailiff, Victor Carey, had taken place.

Mr Sherwill publicly stated, in a letter published in the *Evening Press,* that he had been received by the Commandant and his staff with every consideration and courtesy. He went on:-

> "I felt it my duty at the outset to make the position clear, namely, that as loyal subjects of His Britannic Majesty, we deeply regretted the German Occupation but that in the circumstances imposed upon us the Commandant could rest assured that the attitude of the Civil Authorities and of the population towards himself and the officers and soldiers under his command

would be correct in every respect. I also undertook personally to co-operate in every way towards that end and to behave with the utmost frankness in my relations with the Commandant and his staff. It is my firm intention so to continue during the Occupation.

The German Commandant gave me personal assurances as to the safety of the lives and property of the people of this Island, which he subsequently embodied in his Orders."

While Island officials were publicly praising the behaviour of the German troops, as being perfect, excellent, exemplary and correct, the reality was very different.

Within days of the Occupation the States Gauger, the keeper of the Bonded Store, reported that:-

"On two occasions German Naval and other uniformed men have entered the bonded store on the Jetty and in spite of my protests have helped themselves to the following goods, some of which they shipped aboard a small naval vessel and some transported by lorry."

1 Case of Tobacco
2 Cases of Cigarettes
1 Case of Tea
1 Case of Beer
1 Jar of 5 gallons Whisky
2 Cases of Brandy
1 Case of Gin
6 Cases of Champagne.

Most of the 'plundered' items had been rescued from Alderney and belonged to Bucktrout & Co.Ltd. and Mackay and Co. The Germans never conceded that they should be held responsible, although accounts were repeatedly submitted for payment. It was not until the end of May 1942 that Dr Brosch, of the Feldkommandantur, wrote to the Controlling Committee saying:- "In spite of the long time which has elapsed, we have tried to trace the unit concerned in order to check these allegations. As the goods were stored in the harbour which had been bombed, the troops may have considered them as booty. I therefore request you to inform the firms concerned that these invoices cannot be settled from here."

The wife of one of the British soldiers held as a P.O.W. at Castle Cornet heard that it was possible to obtain a permit to visit her husband who had come home on leave on the 27th June and was still in the Island when the Germans arrived.

At about 7.00pm on the 1st July she went to the Royal Hotel and after she had explained to a member of the staff what she wanted, she was directed to a German soldier.

"I cannot say what rank he held, he was over 6ft tall, fair hair, red face, clean shaven and was dressed in uniform with high boots. He had a belt and something hanging on the left side. I told him I wanted a permit to visit my husband. He spoke fairly good English and said 'I will get one for you if you come this way'. I followed him along the corridor and up the stairs. We went along a passage, he opened a door and pushed me in and came in with me. He put me on the bed and took off my knickers. He said 'if you scream I'll shoot you'. He had relations with me. He pulled up his trousers, put his tunic on and went away and left me. I put my knickers on, straightened my clothing and went downstairs where I saw PC Tardif whom I knew.

PC Tardif spoke to Dr Maass, the German Commandant's Chief of Staff and I heard him say 'we cannot let this go on in the Island'. Shortly afterwards I saw Dr Maass alone and told him what had happened. He said 'I am very sorry, I will try and find the man who did it' and gave me a permit to see my husband."

Some time later the woman, who claimed to be pregnant, saw Dr W.B.Fox who reported the matter of the alleged rape to Inspector Sculpher. The doctor thought that if the pregnancy was due to rape, he would be justified in terminating it. Mr Sculpher differed with the Doctor on that point. He was sceptical of the woman's story which he did not find convincing. She had told him she 'wanted to get rid of this one, as she could not afford to keep another child'. What transpired is not recorded but there is no record of a child being born to the woman during the early part of the Occupation.

On the 4th of July a party of German soldiers went into Laker's wireless shop in Church Square and purchased several items. After they left, Ted Laker noticed that 2 Kodak cameras, valued at £9 were missing. He immediately reported the matter to the German Commandant at the Royal Hotel and also informed Sergeant Banneville. A week later the German Commandant wrote to him saying:-

"I have caused enquiries to be made, but have been unable to trace anything in respect thereof."

D.J.Nicolle, of the Forest, read in the *Evening Press* that anyone wishing to consult the German Commandant or his Chief of Staff, Dr Maass, could do so on any weekday between 11.00am and 1.00pm. He went to the Channel Islands Hotel and was well received by Dr Maass, who listened patiently to his complaint, that his shop at Landes Villa had been forcibly entered on three occasions by German troops. Mr Nicolle was requested to put the complaint in writing, which he did and before long came the standard but courteous reply signed by Dr Maass:-

"I beg to inform you that I have been unable to trace anything with regard to the articles which you state are missing from your grocery shop at the Forest, in spite of the most careful investigation."

All public bus services in the Island had been suspended the day after the Germans arrived. The buses belonging to Guernsey Motors Ltd. were requisitioned for transporting German troops. They were required to be on standby with drivers, in various parts of the Island, for 24 hours a day. The drivers were paid £2.5.0 instead of their normal £4.0.0 a week.

It was obvious that from the very moment that they landed in the Island, the Germans were trying to create good relations between themselves, the civil administration and the local population. The Channel Islands were the only part of the British Empire that they set foot upon and they were well aware that it was important to their international reputation that they refrained from the excesses practised in the rest of occupied Europe. Their occupation was to be the model of correctness as far as the outside world was concerned.

Mr Sherwill discussed with Dr Maass the possibility of sending messages to evacuees in the United Kingdom. On the 6th July he informed the Controlling Committee that the German Commandant had invited them to write a short message of approximately 100 words on behalf of the people of Guernsey for transmission by a German radio station.

The Controlling Committee decided to gratefully avail themselves of the opportunity and wrote:-

"To all who are dear to us from whom we are separated temporarily, we send our loving greetings and good wishes.

The German Occupation took place without a single person being harmed.

As loyal British subjects we do not pretend that we are happy at being in German Occupation but it is a fact that we are being treated with courtesy and consideration.

The Civil Government of the Island functions as before the Occupation and the Churches and Chapels are freely open for public worship. Every

Island Official is at his post, not a single civilian has been deprived of his or her liberty and the utmost correctness characterises the relations between the German forces and the civilian population.

We ask that this message, when received in the United Kingdom, may be re-transmitted by the B.B.C. and published in the English newspapers so that the natural anxiety of our relatives and friends may be relieved. Once again, our love and good wishes.

Signed by Victor G.Carey, Civil Lieutenant Governor and Bailiff of Guernsey. A.J.Sherwill, His Majesty's Attorney General and G.J.P.Ridgway, His Majesty's Solicitor General."*

The Germans were soon requisitioning houses and supplies for their own use. Government House became the residence of their Commandant and the servants, who only a week or so before were serving the Lieutenant Governor, now attended the needs of their new master.

The German Commandant commandeered the Wolseley Police car for his own use and required 3 Police officers, to be available to drive the car as required. PC 24 Le Gallez, PC 19 Tardif and PC 34 Le Lievre, were based at Government House and covered the 24 hours between them. PC 26 Perry acted as reserve driver and covered leave days. Their duty was to last until 15th December 1940 when the Germans finally provided their own driver. In view of the loss of the car to the Police, the President of the Controlling Committee gave approval for the Inspector to hire another vehicle from Le Lacheur's garage.

**PC A.T.H. Le Gallez opening the door of the commandeered police car for the German Commandant, Dr Albrecht Lanz, outside the Little Chapel.**

The Secretary to the President of the Controlling Committee, L.A.Guillemette wrote to H.H.Collins, the managing director of Le Riche's Stores, requiring that each week the following goods should be supplied to the Commandant, at Government House, and stating that the cost would be met by the States:-

500 Cigarettes.
50 Cigars.
10 Bottles of Champagne.
10 Bottles of Whisky.
10 Bottles of White Wine.
10 Bottles of Red Wine.

* H.M.Solicitor General also known as H.M.Comptroller.

The Controlling Committee were not the only suppliers of 'comforts' to the Germans living at Government House. The Commandant's Secretary wrote on the 15th of July to:-

"Messrs Timmer Limited,
The Suntrap,
Forest,
Guernsey.
Gentlemen,

The Commandant has asked me to inform you how much he appreciates the gift of flowers which you are making to him for the adornment of our residence. The gift is greatly appreciated and he has asked me to convey to you his thanks.

Yours truly."

Later in the month, Frank Cochrane, of W.Holmes and Son Ltd., was to receive a similar letter thanking him "for the beautiful grapes which you have again sent us. They have been greatly appreciated in the Mess at Government House".

Soon after the Occupation of the Island, the Germans arranged a Victory March through St Peter Port. PC 30 Short, who, in his father's judgement, was the smartest man in the Force, was instructed by Inspector Sculpher to lead the parade by marching thirty paces in front of the military band.

The parade assembled outside the Royal Hotel, with the military band in front followed by four hundred troops. Batteries of cameramen and news-reel photographers were on hand to record the publicity event for consumption around the world.

**PC F.W.Short leading the German Military Band past Lloyds Bank.**

Fred Short led the parade up the Pollet, past Lloyds Bank where photographers recorded the scene, the photograph of which was to become familiar to generations of Islanders and visitors. Then down the High Street, through Church Square and around the Town Church to the Albert Pier and back along the front to the Weighbridge, where the German Commandant took the salute. PC Short still marching thirty paces in front of the main parade, saluted the Commandant with, as he described it, 'a polished 13/18 Hussars salute'. His salute was returned.

Early on in the Occupation the Germans patrolled the Island with a troop of men in a requisitioned bus. In the early hours of the 15th July the bus was travelling along the Jerbourg Road towards the barracks, which had not yet been taken over by the Germans. When they reached the Jerbourg Tavern the

Germans found the road blocked with large granite boulders. They immediately assumed that it was an act of sabotage and awakened the neighbourhood. Fred Veale was dragged out of bed and accused of the placing boulders across the road near the entrance to the lane that leads down to Petit Port Bay.

Dr Maass, the German Chief of Staff, summoned Mr Sherwill and the Inspector to his office and directed them to investigate this ‘act of sabotage’. With Sergeant Banneville, the Inspector went to Jerbourg and inspected the barricade. The boulders had obviously been taken from Mr Veale’s garden rockery and several would have required two or more men to move.

Tom Jeffreys saw the Inspector talking to Fred Veale and told him that at 10.00am that morning he had found a soldier’s haversack in the parking place opposite the Monument. This contained a towel, shaving utensils, a magazine of live ammunition and two fresh fancy cakes in a paper bag bearing the name and address of a Plymouth baker. The Inspector immediately realised that a landing must have been made by British forces.

A little later, Lilian Luscombe reported finding a bandolier containing 50 rounds of live rifle ammunition in the Jerbourg car park. Charles Thomas, of High Rock, Petit Port told the Inspector that he had heard activity down on Petit Port beach during the night. Mr Sculpher and Sergeant Banneville went down the steep winding concrete steps to the bay and found rifles, ammunition, steel helmets, clothing and other military equipment on the beach. Sergeant Banneville recovered the equipment to prevent it being covered by the rising tide.

Bill Crocker, who lived in a small wooden bungalow Rockcliffe on the Jerbourg Road, complained that, at about 3.00am he was awakened and assaulted by a man carrying a rifle. He showed the Inspector where he had been struck under the left eye.

Opposite Rockcliffe there was a telephone pole and Mr Sculpher noticed that three wires leading to a nearby hotel and fourteen leading to houses to the west had been cut. The owner of the field in which the telephone pole was situated reported that earlier that morning he had found, close by, a new hatchet. The Inspector searched the area and found a further bandolier containing forty rounds of rifle ammunition.

The Inspector also learnt that several residents had heard the noise of an aircraft during the night and others the sound of rifle fire. PC 27 Kimber, who lived in the Jerbourg Road, later confirmed that he had heard what appeared to be rifle shots at around 3.30am.

The Inspector informed Mr Sherwill of the military equipment that had been found. Very soon the Germans were on the scene and they took charge of it.

The next day Dr Maass, the German Chief of Staff asked Inspector Sculpher to go with him to Jerbourg. As they were being driven along the Jerbourg Road they were hailed by Charles Mitchell, who handed the Inspector 20 rounds of rifle ammunition in 4 clips and 10 small red detonators that he had found on the beach at Petit Port earlier in the day

It was later established that a British raiding party, consisting of some forty men, landed at Petit Port at about 1.00am on the 15th July and left about two hours later. While some of the party searched the peninsula and cut telephone wires, others created the barricade outside Vue Des Isles, Fred Veal’s house. The barricade was erected to prevent the Germans cutting off the party’s eventual retreat down to the beach and their boats.

The raiding party found that the Jerbourg Barracks were unoccupied and that there was no sign of any German military presence on the peninsula. They started knocking on doors trying to find someone who could give them information about the Germans and details of the Occupation.

One of the raiding party knocked on Bill Crocker's door. Bill had a stammer, even when he was not nervous and when he was put under pressure he found it almost impossible even to stammer. In the darkness he attempted to remonstrate with the soldier and was stuttering at the top of his voice. In desperation, the British Tommy, fearing that any Germans in the vicinity would hear the noise, knocked Bill out.

Shortly before 3.00am the raiding force withdrew down the steps to Petit Port beach. As they retraced their steps, the officer in command tripped and his revolver went off accidentally. Trying to re-embark, one of their two boats hit the rocks and was holed and the other was unable to get close in to the shore, due to the heavy swell. The Tommies abandoned their equipment and swam to the boat. Four soldiers who could not swim were left behind. What possessed the British military authorities to send men on a raid without them being able to swim is difficult to fathom.

All this information was not known to the Inspector or the Germans. Ambrose Sherwill, as President of the Controlling Committee, wrote to Mr Sculpher the next day, the 16th July, saying:-

"I am directed by the German Commandant to issue instructions to you to the effect that immediate investigation be made as to whether or not there remain in the Island persons who landed at Petit Port on the night of 14th-15th instant.

The German troops have noticed at various places and particularly in the vicinity of Jerbourg Monument and the Gouffre Hotel, groups of men of military age. All these may be Guernseymen who have been continuously in the Island. On the other hand, some may be men who have entered the Island since the German Occupation.

Will you please endeavour to ascertain whether any persons who are British strangers have been noticed in the Island during the last day or so and make a report to me on the subject.

I can foresee all sorts of trouble if people land here clandestinely and are received and housed by our people, for the latter will be liable to very severe military penalties if they receive and assist persons engaged in espionage.

However detestable the duty of reporting the presence in our midst of any such strangers may be, in the present circumstances I can see no way of avoiding it.

In the interest of the whole community, it is essential that the basis of utter frankness between the German Commandant and his Staff on one hand and the Civilian Authorities on the other should be maintained."

In accordance with Mr Sherwill's instructions twenty-five Police and nine Special Constables assembled at 5.00am on the Wednesday morning at the Police Station. The Inspector told them that there was good reason to believe that British soldiers were hiding in the Island and that a careful search was to be made of the south coast.

The men were grouped in threes - two regulars and one Special, and allotted certain areas of the coast from Fort George to Pleinmont. The Inspector took Sergeant Banneville, PCs Bull and Le Cocq and searched the whole of the Pleinmont area. People were stopped and questioned, but none had seen any strangers. PC Le Cocq was then sent on the Police motorcycle to maintain contact with the other parties while the search continued.

PC 30 Fred Short and PC 15 Bill Burton were allocated the area between La Corbiere and Le Creux Mahie caves. At about 5.30am as they approached a cottage at La Corbiere, Fred thought he noticed someone looking over a wall. They went into the cottage and asked the occupant if he had seen any British servicemen. He replied:-

"No, I would not even know what they looked like."

Constable Short found it an interesting reply as he was aware that the man had served in the Hampshire Regiment. He also noticed that there were four cups and saucers on the kitchen table. Fred asked:-

"What have you got four cups and saucers on the table for then?"

"They are for my mother and myself and I have just washed them up."

Fred Short saw a door move and was convinced that there were British servicemen in the cottage, but he had no wish to find them. However, as there were also a considerable number of German troops searching the area he realised the danger to both the occupants of the cottage and to Bill Burton and himself.

When the two constables left the cottage they were met by a party of twenty or so Germans. Fred led them down to Le Creux Mahie caves, where they clambered over the rocks which were black from the fires that had been lit there over the years. When they emerged from the caves the Germans' green uniforms were covered with the filth from the rocks.

Later when the search ended without any British servicemen being discovered, Constable Short reported to Inspector Sculpher his belief that some of the missing 'Tommies' were hiding in the cottage at La Corbiere. Fred told the Inspector that he could find some 'civies' for them and they could be passed off as Irishmen working on the construction of the St Saviour's Dam. Mr Sculpher told the Constable to do nothing until he had consulted the Bailiff. He then walked across to the Royal Court and explained the situation to the Bailiff.

When he returned, he told Fred Short that the Bailiff had 'blown his top', saying that if the British soldiers were not handed over to the Germans immediately he would have PCs Short and Burton arrested and put in prison.

The Inspector asked Fred if he could make contact with the 'Tommies', which he said he could. "Then", said Mr Sculpher, "go and see them and advise them to surrender to the Germans."

Constable Short went back to the cottage, which was demolished later in the Occupation and advised the two Tommies to surrender. They accepted his advice and at 7.00pm that evening, went up to the airport and gave themselves up to a sentry.

Eventually all four men who had been left behind by the raiding party gave themselves up to the Germans. Later the Germans made them rebuild the barricade across the road outside Fred Veal's house, as they had done on the night of the raid. Photographs of the reconstructed barricade were taken and have since been published around the world.

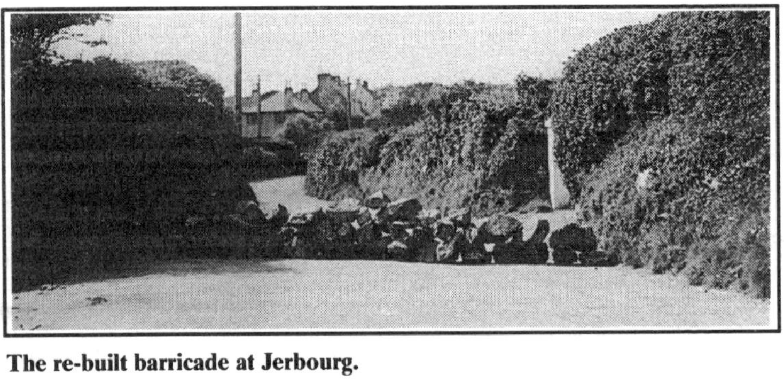

**The re-built barricade at Jerbourg.**

One consequence of the raid was that Ambrose Sherwill attempted to have a letter delivered to C.G.Markbreiter at the Home Office in London. He actually wrote the letter and handed it to the German Commandant with a request that it be delivered through the German Foreign Office channels in a neutral country.

The letter, which was never delivered, demonstrated the extreme naivety of the local administration to the realities of the Island's new situation. It read:-

"On the night of the 14/15th July, an armed British force landed in Guernsey. They assaulted an old man living in the vicinity of the landing place, cut some private telephone wires, erected a barricade across a road and left behind a quantity of arms, ammunition, clothing and accoutrements. Certain of their number became detached from the force and have been taken prisoner. There were no casualties.

I do not know what the object of the landing was but to us it seems senseless.

Until it was definitely established that an armed force landed, the German Military authorities quite naturally suspected a locally staged incident and although the truth soon became apparent, certain restrictions have been imposed as a result of the landing.

The object of this letter is to ask that you will make the strongest representations in the proper quarter to the effect that, it having been decided by the British Government, in the interests of the people of the Channel Islands, to demilitarise them, military activities of the kind referred to above are unwelcome to us and are likely to result in loss of life among the civilian population and generally to make our position much more unpleasant than it is. Please urge this very forcibly. The Bailiff was amazed when he learnt of the landing and in writing you thus I know I am expressing his views and that of many prominent people here.

The local officials have been and are being treated with the greatest courtesy and consideration by the German Military authorities and the general behaviour of the German troops is excellent.

The severance of communications with the United Kingdom has given rise to many problems with which we are grappling to the very best of our ability.

The German authorities have undertaken to provide us with essential supplies and we anticipate that, shortly, seaborne trade with France will begin.

We very much hope that great discrimination will be exercised in regard to offensive action against any ship plying between the Channel Islands and the French coast and between Jersey and Guernsey. Such a ship may well be carrying essential supplies to us or taking our tomatoes in exchange for such supplies.

It would be most helpful if some arrangement could be made between the British and German authorities for the return to us, for trading between Guernsey and Jersey and France, of the steamer 'New Fawn', (Capt. F. Noyon) whose port of registry is Guernsey. She is presumably lying somewhere on the South Coast.

If she could be dispatched with a mixed cargo of flour, salt, margarine, cooking fats, tea and sugar we should be most grateful and payment could be obtained out of the funds belonging to Guernsey in London.

The German Commandant trusts the Island officials and conversely the Island officials trust the German Commandant, who has proved just and humane, and I am satisfied that stores sent here in this way would not be interfered with but would be available for consumption and use by the civilian population.

The Civil Lieutenant Governor and Bailiff is well and carrying on his duties. My kindest personal regards to Sir Alexander Maxwell, yourself and Martin Jones.

Could you, as a personal favour, drop a line to my boy of 15, Richard F.Sherwill, Elizabeth College, c/o Education Office, Oldham, Lancs. and say that his mother and I and Joly and Rollo are quite well and send their love and ask him to so inform his sister Mary Rose and his brother John."

# Chapter 6

## A SERIOUS ERROR OF JUDGEMENT

Ambrose Sherwill was not the only person seeking German assistance in having a letter delivered in London. Mrs Barbara Drummond, an elderly widow, depended upon money received from the mainland to pay her rent and living expenses. She approached the Inspector, who explained that he was unable to help. In desperation she wrote to the German Commandant requesting that he allow a letter to reach her banker in London. He replied personally, in the most courteous terms, saying:-

"Unfortunately, at the present moment, we can see no possibility of communication such as you mention in your letter."

Mrs Walmsley, of Cornet Street, went to the Police Station and complained to Sergeant Jack Harper that Mrs Irene Power, of 32 Cornet Street, was under the influence of drink and shouting 'We are f—ing British'. "She will cause trouble yet. And she is enticing Germans into her house. One was there for about 50 minutes." Jack Harper summarized the complaint in the occurrence book, as 'Riotous conduct alleged'.

Mr Topley, caretaker of Barclays Bank, also complained about Mrs Power's activities.

"I saw a British P.O.W. and a German soldier walking up Cornet Street, they stopped and talked to Mrs Power. I heard the P.O.W. tell the German he would be all right with Mrs Power. The German left his prisoner and went with Mrs Power to her house. The British P.O.W. went to 'Pats' in Fountain Street and had a drink, while he waited."

The British P.O.W.'s held at Castle Cornet were well treated and on occasions were allowed out on their own. It was not until the beginning of August that they were transferred to camps in Germany.

The departure of so many employers from the Island inevitably created problems. Edgar Brache went to Sergeant Le Lievre's house and told him:-

"I cannot get work as my last employer, Mr Frederick Martel, of Capelles, has evacuated and my Insurance card is locked up in his house."

Charlie Le Lievre went with Brache to his employer's house and gained entry through a window. The Insurance card was found and the house was locked and secured.

The owners of O.Dorey and Sons Ltd, coal merchants, had left the Island and the Essential Commodities Committee authorised Bird Bros. Ltd. to take over their stocks of coal for distribution. Mr Sculpher was asked to arrange for a Constable to attend when the premises were opened up and handed over, in accordance with the regulations.

Within hours of arriving in Guernsey, the German Commandant had verbally ordered Mr Sherwill to provide him with a full report on the transfer of the Hacklander and Zulauf families to the United Kingdom. As the Police held files containing a great deal of information regarding these two families and other aliens, this request had been anticipated. After the air raid Clerk Sergeant Lamy had spent the Sunday afternoon burning all these files in case they fell into German hands. It was decided to tell the Commandant that the files had accompanied the Hacklanders and Zulaufs when they left the Island. This explanation was accepted.

Two weeks later the Germans demanded to be supplied immediately with a list of the numbers of aliens of all nationalities in the Island, together with the names and addresses of all Italians. The information was supplied by the Inspector.

On the 17th July an announcement appeared in La Gazette Officielle effectively cutting the salaries and wages of all civil servants, including Policemen. It was described as a 'Revised Rate' by the President of the Controlling Committee. The formula used to calculate the new lower levels of pay was:-

£100 plus half the difference between the existing salary and £100.

The Inspector's salary of £500 per annum, was reduced to £300 and the Deputy Inspector's to £210. A sergeant's weekly wage was reduced from £4.0.0. to £2.19.3 and a constable only received £2.14.3.

There was great resentment at this cut, particularly as many members of the Force were working longer hours without any overtime payment. The Force, which pre war had numbered 37 officers, now effectively had been reduced to 28. Four men had been recalled to the colours, PC Bougourd killed, PC Le Page had escaped and three were acting as drivers for the German Commandant.

The first public dance to be held since the Occupation took place on the 18th July at St Georges Hall. As both Germans and civilians were expected to attend, two Police officers were present in case of trouble. Of over 300 dancers who paid the 1/6 entrance about half were Germans, including some officers. Although there was a shortage of partners, it was noticeable that the Germans shared the honours.

As a consequence of the dance, a call was received at the Station from Mr W.N.Lovell, of Kinmount, Sausmarez Road, who said:-

"My Hungarian maid Elizabeth Kakas was picked up by a German officer at 7 o'clock today and taken to the Bert Williams Orchestra Dance at St George's Hall. It is now 11.05pm and she has still not returned. I am going to dismiss her and will call the Inspector in the morning."

A major difficulty was the German practice of driving on the right hand side of the road. They insisted that they drove on the same side as they had always done in Germany. Locals continued to drive on the left. The matter could have been solved by the Germans issuing another of their many regulations. However, it was almost twelve months before the Germans decreed that everyone had to drive on the right of the road. In the meantime confusion reigned, although in practice very few Islanders drove vehicles and cyclists were able to take the necessary evasive action.

At 11.00pm on the 25th July PC 30 Short was on night motorcycle patrol, driving along Queens Road towards Town. As he passed the entrance to Government House he suddenly saw a car, on the wrong side of the road without lights, coming towards him, Fred had nearly stopped when the car struck his motorcycle and knocked him flying.

He slid along the road, through a newly created gap in the roadside wall and hit a galvanised garage door. The tremendous thud brought a number of Germans running out of Government House to see what had happened.

The Constable received minor injuries, bruises on his right leg and left hip. The Police motorcycle, No 217, had its front wheel and frame buckled. The German driver involved in the accident, pushed the motorcycle up to the entrance of Government House, where it was left. He wanted to take PC Short to the hospital, but Fred insisted on being taken to the Police Station.

Inspector Sculpher reported the accident to Mr Sherwill with the request that representations be made to the German Authorities that their personnel should not drive vehicles unless they were familiar with local traffic rules, otherwise a fatal accident would occur.

Pets left behind by evacuees continually presented the Police with problems. PC 28 Peter Bretel was called to Cornet Street to see Albert Trebert who said:-

"A few minutes ago I was walking down Cornet Street when a large tabby cat, owned by Mrs Rosewell, who has left the Island, jumped at me from behind. When he fell to the ground it started crawling along the footpath and jumping at people as they passed."

Peter Bretel saw the cat, which appeared to be poisoned and was in agony. PC 16 Tuck, who was in the vicinity, destroyed the cat by hitting it on the head with a hammer. The two constables buried the cat in a rough piece of ground in Rosemary Lane.

At 12 noon on the 30th July, Dr Maass marched into the Police Station with another officer and instructed Sergeant Harper and PC 9 Marsh to accompany him to Le Riches in the High Street. There Dr Maass ordered the arrest of sixty five year old Henry Herbert Collins, the managing director of Le Riches and one of the Island leading business men, on the charge of forbidding the use of the German language in his shop.

The Sergeant reluctantly obeyed and Mr Collins was taken to the prison. On his return to the Station he immediately informed the Inspector, who in turn telephoned Mr Sherwill.

Dr Maass notified the Inspector that Mr Collins would be tried later that afternoon at the Channel Islands Hotel. Promptly at 4.30pm Sergeant Harper 'produced' Mr Collins in the Blue Room of the Hotel, where Mr Sherwill and Mr Louis Guillemette, the Secretary to the Controlling Committee, were already present. After hearing evidence, Dr Maass ordered that Mr Collins be remanded in custody until Wednesday 31st July, when his case would be dealt with and witnesses called.

In Mr Sherwill's view, Mr Collins was a sick man and he did not think he could survive a prison sentence. He was sure that if he was tried by the Germans he would be found guilty and probably sentenced to a term of imprisonment, which could well be served on the continent. He suggested to Dr Maass that the Royal Court could immediately pass retrospective legalisation making it an offence to utter speech to the detriment of the German Government or Forces. He suggested that Mr Collins could then be tried by the Royal Court. The Germans surprisingly agreed.

The Royal Court was convened at 11.00am the next morning and passed into Law an Ordinance, which Mr Sherwill had hastily drafted. The legislation read:-

> 1. It shall be and shall be deemed as from the commencement of the Occupation of the Island of Guernsey by the German Forces, always to have been an offence to commit any act or utter any speech inimical to the interests of the German Government or Forces or likely to bring about a deterioration in the relations between German Forces in the Island of Guernsey and the civilian population of that Island or between any part of those Forces and any part of that population.

2. If any person is guilty of any offence under the provisions of the foregoing section, that person shall be liable, on conviction before the Police Court Magistrate, to imprisonment with or without hard labour for a term not exceeding two months or a fine not exceeding ten pounds or to both such imprisonment and or fine, or, on conviction before the Royal Court sitting as a full Court, to imprisonment with or without hard labour, for a term not exceeding twelve months or to a fine not exceeding £500 or to both such imprisonment or fine.

3. The Ordinance shall continue in force until the Chief Pleas after Christmas 1940 and shall be renewed from time to time thereafter during the German Occupation of the Island as may be requisite to prevent this ordinance from lapsing.

As soon as the Ordinance had been passed and approved by the German Commandant, Inspector Sculpher was instructed by H.M.Solicitor General to formally charge Mr H.H. Collins with:-

> 'That you did on or about 29th July 1940, utter speech, such speech being likely to bring about a deterioration in the relations between the German Forces in the Island of Guernsey and the civilian population of that Island or between any part of those Forces and any part of the population at Le Riches Stores Ltd High Street'.

The Inspector went to the Prison and read the charge to Mr Collins, who replied "All right, Sir".

That afternoon a special sitting was held before Magistrate, Quertier Le Pelley, to hear the charge against Mr Collins.

Advocate J.E.L.Martel, who appeared on behalf of Mr Collins, entered a plea of not guilty.

The Solicitor General stated that it was alleged that on the previous Monday, the 29th July, Mr Collins had told an assistant, Mr Cheeseborough:- "You are not to speak German to soldiers in future in this shop. It must be done by the official interpreter."

The Prosecution contended that such statements were likely to cause strained relations between the German garrison and Islanders. Herbert Cheeseborough told the Court that at about 10.00am the previous Monday a German officer had enquired about the non delivery of coffee which had been ordered. The officer was accompanied by an Englishman, although he did not know that at the time. Mr Cheeseborough said that he referred the matter to Mr Collins, who indicated that he would attend to it later. "I do not think that Mr Collins had any intention of causing any misunderstanding or belittling the German Army's rights or privileges. I think he intended that I should not waste time. He said that I was not to waste time by speaking German to the soldiers or to interfere with the assistants who were serving German soldiers."

Crossexamined by Advocate Martel, Mr Cheeseborough said that Mr Collins always wanted the staff to hurry with their work. It took some time to deal with German troops owing to the language difficulties. He admitted that he might have been a little confused as to what Mr Collins had actually said.

"I really don't know that I have a case to answer" said Mr Martel, the defence Counsel. The Magistrate said he wished to hear Mr Collins, who told the Court that he had been 41 years with Le Riches Stores. On Monday morning he had been in his office when Mr Cheeseborough came to him saying that there was a German officer in the shop with a complaint. "I told him that the complaint should be passed to Mr Isler, who handled complaints."

Mr Collins added "in some cases two men were doing one man's work. I therefore instructed Mr Cheeseborough that he should not waste time in interpreting for another assistant, but should carry on with his own work.

Since the Occupation I have enjoyed only pleasant business relations with German officers and troops. I have never forbidden German to be spoken in the shop, in fact I encourage my staff to learn German. Five members of my staff are taking German lessons."

After the evidence had been heard, the Magistrate said :-

"I am sure that Mr Collins did not utter the words inimical to the German Government. In my opinion the case is not proved.

The case is dismissed".

The retrospective legalisation, so hastily enacted, had served its purpose, the Germans were satisfied and Mr Collins avoided a prison sentence. The Law was never invoked again.

Quertier Le Pelley, who had taken over as Magistrate when H.J.Casey evacuated, was kept busy with a continuous stream of black-out infringement cases. The Germans insisted that all cases should be taken to Court, regardless of any extenuating circumstances. Inspector Sculpher, who prosecuted, was always providing possible excuses, by saying it was inadvertent, it was just carelessness or perhaps the accused had not noticed that the window wasn't screened. He was always very sympathetic and it was noticeable that the Magistrate usually 'got the message'.

There were exceptions to this rule of leniency. One such occasion was when Dr Lanz, the German Commandant, saw a light showing in a house in Les Canichers, overlooking the harbour. He detailed a German soldier to attend to the matter. He also summoned the Inspector and instructed him to prosecute the person responsible and stressed the need for stricter enforcement of the black-out regulations. Mr Sculpher reported all the facts to the Court and Mrs Lizzie Frecker, of Clifton Terrace, Les Canichers, was fined the standard £1 for the offence. The Commandant was duly informed of the outcome.

At the same sitting of the Court one of the cases Mr Sculpher presented must have given him a sense of quiet satisfaction, although he was too much of a professional to show it. One of the chief protagonists in his pre Occupation wrangle over the enforcement of black-out regulations, Captain W.L.Henderson, was charged with a black-out infringement. Captain Henderson, the A.R.P. Commandant, pleaded guilty and was fined £1.

Dr Lanz was a regular night owl, as a few days later he again spotted an unscreened light. PC 35 Le Cocq was on duty with PC 18 Smith at the Weighbridge at 1.20am, when the Commandant's car stopped and picked them up. They were taken to the Albert Pier where they were met by the Commandant. He pointed out a pale blue light which was showing from the direction of Hauteville. He ordered:- "Find the light and submit a report to me in the morning."

Francois Le Cocq scaled a telephone pole and from there he counted the number of chimney stacks from the junction of Cliff Street and the Strand, to where the light was showing. As he and PC Smith were going up Hauteville, the blue light went out. They had calculated that it was either No.16 or 18 Hauteville where the light had been showing. No.16 was uninhabited and No.18 let out as flats. In the top flat they spoke to Mrs Ada Parr who said:- "About a quarter of an hour ago, I heard Bob Boyle walking about in his flat."

The Constables knocked up Lt.Colonel Boyle, a 74 year old invalid who said:- "Yes, I was sitting in my room a little while ago. I am blacked out". The Constables examined the curtains of the windows overlooking the harbour, which were pinned together. One window had a slight gap where the curtains should have meet. There was a reading lamp with a light blue shade.

Owing to the lack of evidence that the light seen on Albert Pier came from Lt Colonel Boyle' flat, no action was taken. A report was submitted to the Commandant and nothing further was heard. Generally the Germans chose not to prosecute civilians caught by them for offences which were solely of a civil nature. They handed such cases over to the local Police with a request that they be informed of the outcome. Most of these were of a very minor nature and would probably not have been taken to Court in the normal course of events. The Inspector, when he prosecuted such a case, made sure that the Magistrate was fully aware of the situation, he would say:- "This is a case which the Germans have passed on to me to prosecute." The Germans never queried the sentences passed, all they wanted to know was that the accused had been prosecuted.

A great many of the disturbances the local Police had to deal with involved Germans and their over indulgence. One evening in August, Sergeant Harper received a telephone call from Ernie Thomas, the licensee of the Farmers' Hotel, South Esplanade, requesting assistance. Three German soldiers had been in his public bar for about an hour when they started quarrelling. Other customers left and the Germans started throwing glasses at each other.

Sergeant Harper went to the Farmers Hotel with Special Constable O.Le Lacheur, in his delivery van and sent PC 27 Kimber on foot. When they arrived the Sergeant tried to reason with the three soldiers who were shouting at each other and appeared to be drunk. One, who had his arm in a sling, struck Jack Harper a number of times, knocking his helmet off. Another managed to get between Harper and his assailant and separate them. As all three were wearing side arms the Sergeant withdrew and went to the German Headquarters for assistance.

With two German sergeants, he returned and they tried to persuade the soldiers to leave the premises. The soldier with his arm in a sling picked up a bar stool and aimed a blow at Sergeant Harper's head. He again withdrew and went back to the German Headquarters for further assistance but in the meantime the soldiers had been persuaded to leave, by their sergeants.

PC Kimber arrived at the Hotel on foot just after the German sergeants and Jack Harper had entered the bar. Ernie Thomas, the landlord, asked the Constable to help get the drunken Germans out, but when he entered the bar the soldier with the sling shouted at him in a threatening manner and then repeated it in an even louder voice. The Constable hurriedly withdrew. As a large crowd had gathered to watch the action, he busied himself by moving them away to a safe distance in case the fighting spread outside.

The Inspector wrote a report on the incident, which he sent to Mr Sherwill, requesting a copy be forwarded to the Commandant. However, on this occasion he enclosed a letter, in which he advised Mr Sherwill, "I do not know if you will consider it advisable to send this report forward. Neither Police officer will make a good witness in the case. Both apparently went outside the public house and left the German sergeants to deal with their own men without waiting to find out if they wanted any help."

During the first few months of the Occupation the Germans were extremely successful in establishing what has been called a 'Model Occupation'. In fact they so ingratiated themselves with Ambrose Sherwill that he recorded a talk on the 1st August for transmission by German radio. The text of his broadcast was, at Sherwill's request, published in *The Star* and the *Evening Press*. He added "Anyone interested in hearing it should listen-in to the English broadcast from Bremen over the next few days commencing on Saturday 3rd August."

In the broadcast he said:

"This is His Britannic Majesty's Procureur in Guernsey, Channel Islands, speaking to the people of the United Kingdom and in particular to those who left Guernsey and Alderney during the evacuation which preceded the German Occupation.

I imagine that many of you must be greatly worried as to how we are getting on. Well, let me tell you. Some will fear, I imagine, that I am making this record with a revolver pointed at my head and speaking from a typescript thrust into my hand by a German officer. The actual case is very different.

The Lieutenant Governor and Bailiff, Mr Victor Carey, and every other Island official has been and is being treated with every consideration and with the greatest courtesy by the German Military Authorities. The Island Government is functioning, churches and chapels are open for public worship, banks, shops and places of entertainment are open as usual.

Naturally, the sudden and entire severance of communications with the United Kingdom created innumerable problems with which we have wrestled and are still wrestling. Perhaps the best indication of the measure of our success will be shown by the latest figures of unemployment which are as follows, males unemployed, of whom hardly any are fit for manual labour, 186, females unemployed, 191. Relief by way of public assistance is not above the normal figure.

The States have set up a Controlling Committee to speed up public business. My friends Sir Abraham Laine, A.M. Drake, R.O. Falla, R.H. Johns, John Leale, Stamford Raffles and Dr A.N. Symons are collaborating with me on this Committee and are working like trojans.

The conduct of the German troops is exemplary.

**Constable F.H.Tuck in a 'Propaganda pose' with a German sailor which was published in a German newspaper.**

We have been in German Occupation for 4½ weeks and I am proud of the way my fellow Islanders have behaved and grateful for the correct and kindly attitude towards them, by the German soldiers.

We have always been and we remain intensely loyal subjects of His Majesty and this has been made clear to and is respected by the German Commandant and his staff. On that staff is an officer speaking perfect English, a man of wide experience, with whom I am in daily contact. To him I express my grateful thanks for his courtesy and patience.

And now let me end on a more personal note. To Elizabeth College, the Guernsey Ladies College, the Guernsey Intermediate School, the Guernsey Primary and Voluntary schools, to both Teachers and Scholars, all our love and good wishes.

To all men of military age who left here to join His Majesty's Forces, God speed. To all wives and mothers and sweethearts, God bless you. To all Guernsey children in England, God keep you safe. God bless you all till we meet again.

Will the B.B.C. please re-transmit this message and will the daily papers please publish it."

When Islanders read the text of the speech they were astounded that their leader could fall into the German trap so easily. For a long time Ambrose Sherwill's speech was the local talking point. Some people thought it was right that he should let relations and friends in England know how the Island had fared under the Germans, others thought that he had played into their hands. Another widely-held view was that he was well intentioned, but naive.

When PC Frank Tuck heard the broadcast, which was preceded by skilful propaganda about the conquering of the 'British Channel Islands' he commented to a colleague:- "Sherwill will soon be decorating the Germans for occupying Guernsey."

Over the years, that speech has come to be regarded as a serious error of judgement. It was significant that no one in Jersey volunteered to broadcast in a similar vein.

A notice appeared in *La Gazette Officielle* on the 22nd August:-

> In July last a German aeroplane made a forced landing at La Planque Lane. Police enquiries reveal that many parts of the plane were taken away, believed as souvenirs. These parts are now required and it is desired that they are returned forthwith. Will any person who has any parts of this aeroplane in his possession please return it at once to the Police Station and thus avoid further trouble.

A Heinkel 111 had been severely damaged when it overran the runway, careered across La Planque Lane and came to rest in a field. The Parish Constables closed the road and the Germans were expected to remove the damaged plane. No guard was placed at the site and soon dozens of souvenir hunters were swarming over the plane, tearing off pieces which they triumphantly took home.

Ken Lewis, who was employed by the Controlling Committee as a clerk, kept a diary throughout the Occupation. In it he recalled how he and friends made a number of visits to the scene of the crash.

"On the 18th July we actually went inside that plane for the first time. It was quite a thrill to sit in the pilot's seat of a German plane and work the joy-stick and rudder-bar. On these occasions we brought home many souvenirs."

After a few days all that was left of the Heinkel, was little more than the basic frame.

Inspector Sculpher was ordered by the Germans to retrieve the missing parts. Enquiries were made in the Forest area but with little success. When a Notice was inserted in the local press however the result was spectacular! Soon the Police Station was taking on the appearance of an aviation workshop as souvenir hunters quickly returned their 'trophies'. Among the parts returned were expensive navigation instruments as well as some very large parts which took more than one person to carry.

During the late summer and autumn of 1940 there was great activity at the airport as many German aircraft arrived and departed to play their part in the Battle of Britain. Members of the Force who were on patrol in that part of the Island kept a close watch on the activities at the Airport. On Sunday the 25th August about sixty Messerschmitt 109 fighters landed and refuelled. Later in the afternoon they took off to escort a large formation of bombers that was passing over the Island on their way to raid cities and towns in England.

The first local person to be tried by a German Court was Mrs Ruby Lilian Langlois, a 37-year-old cook employed by the States. She was arrested by the Germans on the 23rd August 1940 at her home in St George's Esplanade. Whilst being held in prison in Guernsey, Mrs Langlois was tried, in her absence, by the Tribunal of Feldkommandantur 515 in Jersey.

Later she was handed a letter dated 26th August 1940, signed by the Chief of the Tribunal, Colonel Schumacher.

INDICTMENT and NOTIFICATION OF SENTENCE.

"You are accused of having since the beginning of July 1940, in Guernsey, publicly and repeatedly abused the German Reich and the German Forces and maliciously and with intent making them an object of contempt, by repeating on several occasions since the Occupation of the Island of Guernsey by the German Forces, in presence of third parties and with reference to members of the German Forces present in Guernsey: 'The Germans are all blackguards, they have occupied the Island, they fill their bellies and the Islanders must starve. The Germans should leave the Island'. And also repeatedly making use, against the Germans, of the expression 'Shit-house'".

Evidence: Denunciation, witnesses, avowal.

"You are therefore sentenced to fourteen days imprisonment. The sentence includes the four days custody before trial.

This sentence will be executed if you do not make an appeal within three days following the Notification.

You can make the appeal either in writing or by word of mouth to the Chief of the Tribunal, to your immediate custodians or to the officer or employee who notified you of the sentence. In the case of a written appeal, the delay is only granted if the written document reaches one of those parties within the three days.

You can renounce the appeal before the expiry of the three days available for appeal."

Mrs Langlois, on advice, renounced her right of appeal and served her sentence in Guernsey Prison.

As H.M.Attorney General, Mr A.J.Sherwill was informed of the sentence and instructed to:- 'Execute the above sentence and report to the Feldkommandantur, Nebenstelle, Guernsey, on the completion and time of release'.

The procedure adopted in the case of Mrs Langlois was to be repeated many times during the Occupation years.

# Chapter 7

# THE TWO LIEUTENANTS

From the day the Germans occupied Guernsey, Islanders perception of the role of the Police Force changed. Gone were the days when they were respected servants of the public, now they were regarded, by many and indeed themselves, as the unwilling servants of the Germans. They were the men who had to implement the German Commandant's orders, they were the men who enforced Hitler's regulations, they were the men who arrested fellow Islanders when German orders were defied or broken and above all they were the men who were making the German subjugation of the Island that much easier.

The Police themselves were disillusioned, many of them were lonely, their families and friends having evacuated. Furthermore they were not doing the type of Police work for which they had been trained, they were disillusioned, dejected and the morale of the Force was low. One constable of the time recalls:-

"Our normal Police work was gone, we did what we were forced to do, we did it reluctantly. As much as I criticised some of the things our leaders did, everybody was in the same boat really. Our morale was completely gone. It is only people who have experienced those times who can really know what it was like."

One of the members of the Force who changed as a result of the Occupation and changed for the better, at least in the Constables' eyes, was Jack Harper. He was a character, always laughing and was everybody's friend when he was a Constable driving the Police car. With three stripes on his arm, he became 'somebody' and he tried to carry it off. With the arrival of the Germans he reverted to being Jack Harper, one of the boys. He liked a drop of drink, but no one ever saw him drunk. During the early days of the Occupation he lived in a flat in the High Street and kept open house for his fellow policemen - they were always welcome and usually there was a glass or cup of something available. Some of his colleagues even stayed with him from time to time, it was better than a long cycle ride home to an empty house.

Policing had become, for the Constable on the beat and the motorcycle patrols, a matter of checking black-out and curfew regulations at night and dealing with reports on break-ins of domestic and business premises during the day. Later when the Germans decreed that no one should cycle two abreast, checking that regulation became a regular part of their duties.

Members of the public complained that the Police were not protecting them and their property. William Le Prevost, of Cauchebree, Vale, saw PC 35 Le Cocq and complained that:- "Mr J.E.Smith the head of Civil Transport and the Manager of Le Lacheur's, has taken my car for the Germans and I don't know where it is now. He has got the registration papers too."

PC Le Cocq explained to him that as he had given Mr Smith permission to take the car, it was a civil matter and could not be dealt with by the Police. Le Prevost said:- "I am a Guernseyman, I pay taxes and that is what we pay the Police for and you won't do anything for me." The Constable, tactfully, advised him to put his case in writing and send it to the Controlling Committee at Elizabeth College.

However, enquiries were made and Special Constable Lewis established that a Wolseley car, number 149, belonging to Mr Le Prevost, was shipped out of the Island, together with a motorcycle, number 605, on the S.S.Holland on the 1st August 1940. The words 'owner notified' were recorded in the Occurrence Book.

On Friday the 24th August 1940 the German Commandant demanded that he be supplied by the following Tuesday with a full list of aliens in the Island, giving details of their name, place and date of birth, present address and nationality.

This proved to be an enormous task and occupied Clerk Sergeant Lamy and many other officers almost until the deadline set by the Germans.

The tally of aliens was:-

| | |
|---|---|
| French | 231 |
| Hungarian | 46 |
| Swiss | 37 |
| Dutch | 36 |
| German | 25 |
| Italian | 11 |
| Spanish | 6 |
| Norwegian | 3 |
| American | 3 |
| Belgian | 3 |
| Yugoslavian | 2 |
| Finish | 1 |
| Polish | 1 |
| Portuguese | 1 |
| Rumanian | 1 |
| Total | 407 |

Frank Stroobant was a successful businessman with an eye for an opportunity. When, as a result of the evacuation, nearly all the Town's cafes and restaurants closed down, Frank saw the gap in the market and quickly opened a cafe on the North Esplanade. He called it the 'Home from Home' and catered for many of the 'grass widowers' who were on their own as a result of their wives being evacuated, as indeed Frank was himself. One night the Station received a call from Frank Stroobant saying:-

"I reported the loss of the cafe key to you earlier today. I have not had time to have the lock changed, so I am unable to lock the cafe." Sergeant Le Lievre, with PC 26 George Perry visited the 'Home from Home' premises at 2.30am. They found 24/- left in a sugar bowl, a £1 note, 3/- in silver, 6d in coppers in a cardboard box, all of which they took back to the Station. The next day, after having the lock changed, Frank Stroobant called at the Station and collected his £2-7-6.

On another occasion Frank Stroobant did not find the Police as co-operative. One of the attractions that Frank provided for his customers was entertainment, usually in the form of a small band, but sometimes just Stan Workman playing on the piano. On occasions Stan would get carried away and his rendition of 'Hang out your washing on the Seigfried Line' inevitably caused trouble amongst the German customers that Frank was forced to admit.

One evening while Stan was rendering his 'provocative' song, a number of Germans started smashing glasses and bottles. Frank telephoned the Police Station and asked Sergeant Harper for immediate assistance. The sergeant declined saying that they tried not to get involved in incidents involving German forces and advised Frank to ask the Germans at the Channel Islands Hotel for assistance.

Bert Ozanne, the owner of the 'White Gables' Hotel, in the Forest, asked Mr H.A.Le Tocq to take charge of the premises when he evacuated. During the first week of the Occupation the hotel was taken over by the German Forces. When they vacated the premises on the 11th September a considerable amount of household and sporting equipment was missing. A maid employed at the hotel said that all the kitchen equipment and utensils had been removed by the Germans for use in the airport kitchen. A Standard and two Singer cars were also missing.

A few days later Mr Le Tocq reported seeing a German sailor and a Hungarian woman named Julia, who had been employed as a maid at the hotel, arrive in an Austin car and force an entry into the premises. When challenged by Mr Le Tocq, the sailor produced a piece of paper which the woman said was authorization for them to go into the hotel. They took away with them an accordion, a silver-plated tray, two rugs a bedspread and bottles from a cupboard. Sergeant Banneville visited the premises with Mr Le Tocq and discovered a civilian gas mask with the name 'Julia Brichta'. The Sergeant concluded that the woman was in fact Julia Brichta, a lady who was becoming well known to the Police.

The R.A.F. paid Guernsey two special visits during September, delivering 'News from England' leaflets. When Islanders pulled back their black-out curtains one morning, they found the countryside littered with leaflets. The Germans inevitably acted swiftly and vigorously, requiring all leaflets to be collected and delivered to the Feldkommandantur at Grange Lodge. The Police collected as many as possible and brought them to the station, where an unofficial system was quickly organised whereby anyone coming into the Station who had not seen a copy was given one.

The leaflets were packed in a cardboard cylinder and in the centre, as a core, was an explosive charge. This mechanism was designed to explode while still in the air and distribute the leaflets over a wide area. The charge in one of the cylinders did not explode and the complete cylinder came down through the roof of a house. The Police collected the cylinder and PC Le Cocq, being of an inquisitive nature, naturally wanted to know why the charge had not exploded, so he took the mechanism to pieces.

"When I reassembled the mechanism, I found, like the little boy with the watch, that I had too many bits and pieces. The cylinder, with a few of the leaflets, was handed over to the Germans.

Amongst the German Police was a man named Kalinna, who was an out and out Nazi. The day after the cylinder was handed over, this Nazi came into the Station and said, 'Things are serious in England, because there is some sabotage'. When asked why, he told the Station Sergeant and the other Constables that 'There were some parts missing from the explosive mechanism and this must have been a deliberate act by British workmen, in order to sabotage the war effort'. I did not dare admit that I was responsible for the missing parts."

Special Constable Smith was instructed by Dr Reffler, a German officer, to inform Mr Sculpher that he had received a letter signed, 'W.A.Collas, St Martin' and that the writer was to be produced at Grange Lodge at 10.00am on the 30th September. Deputy Inspector Langmead was given the task of locating the letter writer. He traced Miss W.Alice Collas, of Havilland Vale, who admitted writing the letter and wished to apologise for her actions. Mr Langmead took her to Grange Lodge where she was seen by a senior officer, who directed him to deal with her. He cautioned her and sent her home.

On the morning of 2nd October, Dr Brosch, of the Feldkommandantur, instructed Mr Sherwill:-

"to make a very early report concerning the internment in this Island of German, former Austrian, and of Italian nationals, the transfer to England of six Germans named Hacklander and three Germans named Zulauf and the requisitioning of certain property belonging to Hacklander (Mohair Fabrics) Limited".

Full lists of the aliens interned, originals of various documents and copies of entries in the Police Occurrence book were supplied to Dr Brosch the same morning. Harry Broughton, manager of the firm of Accountants, Black, Geoghegan & Till, provided a background history of the Hacklanders and their business.

Karl Hacklander had arrived from Germany in 1933 and formed a Limited Liability Company, Hacklander (Mohair) Ltd. He imported a number of specialist sewing machines from Germany and commenced trade. His procedure was to purchase mohair wool and yarn from Yorkshire and have this shipped direct to Germany for weaving and dying. The processed material was then brought to Guernsey where the mohair was turned into rugs, mats and tablecloths. The entire finishing process took place in Guernsey. The sales were mainly to firms in Great Britain.

Later Eugene Hacklander and his son, Hans, joined the business. Mr Zulauf came to the Island and became manager of the company. Factory premises were leased at Rue du Pre and the company developed and expanded. By the time of the declaration of war the company employed around forty Islanders. As it was no longer possible to have the wool and yarn treated in Germany, outstanding orders were fulfilled, the business run down and the local employees dismissed.

The next request by the Germans was for a full list of persons, other than of British nationality, resident in Guernsey on the 1st June 1940. This was clearly the Germans' way of identifying which aliens had left the Island before their arrival.

The Inspector provided the list which showed that besides the Hacklanders and Zulaufs, 28 aliens had left the Island prior to the German Occupation.

The next day Dr Brosch ordered the Inspector to have all German and Italian civilians in the Island notified that they were required to report at the Feldkommandantur, Grange Lodge, at 3.00pm on Monday 21st October. PC 30 Short was given the task of warning all the persons concerned and obtaining their signatures, indicating that they understood the instruction.

The persons instructed to report to Grange Lodge were:-

| | |
|---|---|
| Therese Aicholzer | Rue de Putron. |
| Maria Fuchs | Hermes, Castel. |
| Auguste Gischel | Government House. |
| Anna Holler | Royal Hotel. |
| Marie Hofmaier | Government House. |
| Wilhelmine Hackl | 22 Rouge Val, Rouge Rue. |
| Angela Hanusch | Victoria Hospital |
| Wilhelm F.Lohmeier | 26 Allez Street. |
| Bertha Obermayer | 7 States Houses, Saints Road. |
| Katherine Proskowitz | Government House. |
| Auguste Prandl | The Bungalow, Sausmarez Road. |
| Augusta H.Riderer | 50 Victoria Road. |
| Freda L.Riderer | 50 Victoria Road. |
| Ilse Schlier | Les Fontanelles, Forest. |
| Hermine Schilcher | Victoria Hospital. |
| Auguste Spitz | Country Hospital. |
| Pauline Sommer | Forest Lodge, Forest Lane. |
| Therese Steiner | Country Hospital. |
| Gertrude Stefan | Les Landes, Baissieres. |

| | |
|---|---|
| Vilem C.Traegar | Diamond Farm, Les Hubits. |
| Frederick C.Traegar | Diamond Farm, Les Hubits. |
| Mathilde Torker | Albany House, Les Hubits. |
| Leopoldine Zaccaria | 3 Eaton Place. |
| Josefa Zaccaria | 3 Eaton Place. |
| Ettore Agnelli | Happy Landings Hotel. |
| Livio Angella | 2 Les Canichers. |
| Fulvis Biancherie | Hotel Beaulieu. |
| Raffaell Bonivita | 2 Clifton Terrace. |
| Antonius Carratu | 28 Saumarez Street. |
| Guerina Dobrez | 18 Hauteville. |
| Melania Lanza | Uplands, Uplands Road. |
| Vincenza Peruzzi | Les Granges, Ivy Gates. |
| Guillio Polli | Royal Hotel. |
| Santina Santangelo | Tamar Villa, Elm Grove. |
| Concetta Valdambrini | Ingleside, Croute Havilland. |

The Inspector wrote to Mr Sherwill, saying that all Germans, including Austrians and Italians had been warned to attend Grange Lodge, except for Frau Annie Wranowsky, who was resident in Sark.

At a special sitting of the Royal Court held on the 23rd October 1940, the Bailiff and nine Jurats were presented, by H.M.Solicitor General, with an Order 'Relating to Measures Against Jews' for application in French territory occupied by the Germans and adapted for application in Guernsey. The Order was signed by the Chief of the German Army in France. The Royal Court ordered the registration of the Order in the Island Records and directed that a copy of the Order should be sent to the Seneschal of Sark.

ORDER

Relating to Measures against the Jews.

In virtue of the plenary powers conferred upon me by the Fuhrer and Supreme Chief of the German Army, I make the following Order:-

1. Are recognised as Jews those who belong or have belonged to the Jewish religion, or who have more than two Jewish grandparents. Grandparents who belong or belonged to the Jewish religion are considered as Jews.
2. Jews who fled from occupied zone are forbidden to return thereto.
3. Every Jewish person must appear by the 20th October 1940 (a) before the sub prefect of the arrondissements (b) in which the domicile or usual residence of that person is situated, for the purpose of being inscribed on a special register. The declaration of the head of a family shall be valid on behalf of the whole family.
4. Every business, of which the proprietor or the holder is a Jew must be indicated as a 'Jewish Undertaking' by means of a special notice in the German and French (c) languages by the 31st October 1940.
5. The directors of Israelite communities are required to furnish on demand to the French Authorities (d) all information both documentary and otherwise necessary for the application of the present Order.
6. Contraventions of the present Order shall be punishable with imprisonment or fine or one or other of these penalties, Confiscation of property may also be ordered.
7. This Order shall come into force on the day of its publication.

For the Commander in Chief of the Army.

The Chief of the Military Administration in France.

(a) In the Bailiwick of Guernsey, by the 26th October 1940
(b) In Guernsey, before the Inspector of Police, in Sark before the Seneschal.
(c) In the Bailiwick of Guernsey, in the German and English Languages.
(d) In the Bailiwick of Guernsey, the authorities of the appropriate Island.

14

Elizabeth College,

Guernsey.

18th October, 1940.

Sir,

I am directed by Dr. Brosch to ask you to be so good as to inform all Germans (including Austrians) and Italians to attend at the Feldkommandantur, Grange Lodge, at 3 p.m. on Monday next, 21st instant.

I am, Sir,

Yours obediently,

Secretary to the President, Controlling Committee of the States of Guernsey.

The Police Inspector,
St. James' Chambers,
Guernsey.

15

ISLAND POLICE,
ST. JAMES' CHAMBERS,
GUERNSEY.

TEL. 570.

YOUR REF. ..........
OUR REF. Pr/2/3
W. R. SCULPHER.
CH. OFFICER.

19th October, 1940

Sir,

Referring to your letter dated 18th October, 1940.

I beg to inform you that all Germans, (including Austrians) andItalians have been warned to attend the Feldkommandantur, Grange Lodge, at 3 p.m. 21st October,1940, except WRANOWSKY, Annie who is resident in SArk.

I am,

Sir,

Your obedient servant,

W. R. Sculpher

Inspector.

A.J.Sherwill Esq.,
Elizabeth College.

**Letters dated 18th and 19th October 1940 referring to Dr Brosch's instruction that all German and Italian civilians attend the Feldkommandantur on 21st October. These included Therese Steiner and Auguste Spitz.**

The Bailiff wrote to the Inspector on the 23rd October saying:-

"I beg to inform you that an Order of the Commander in Chief of the German Army of Occupation in France regarding measures against Jews was registered by the Royal Court today and has force of Law in this Bailiwick. Under section 3 of the Order, Jews have to register by the 26th October, giving the following particulars:-

1. Serial number.
2. Name.
3. First name.
4. Date of birth.
5. Place of birth.
6. Sex.
7. Family status.
8. Occupation.
9. Religion.
10. Time of uninterrupted residence on the Island.

Where Jews carry on any business in the Island, - public shops, hotels and the like, - posters printed in black print on yellow paper, 20 x 40 cm. must be posted on the inner side of all shop windows or in the absence of same in other conspicuous places.

Businesses are considered as Jewish businesses when they are owned to the extent of more than 50 per cent by Jews within the meaning of para.1 of the order.

As your office in Guernsey has been designated by the local Feldkommandantur as taking the place of the 'Sous-Prefecture' in France, all registration returns will be made at your office.

You will report on or before the 29th instant the names and addresses of all Jews who have registered as well as the names and addresses of those businesses carried on by Jews and also that the posters mentioned above are being exhibited in such business premises."

The next day the Order relating to measures against the Jews was published in the Press.

The Inspector was relieved that the Order put the obligation on individuals to come forward and "identify" themselves. The Police had never previously kept any register or list of Jews, his responsibilities before the Occupation had been solely with aliens. The whole process of registration of a particular religious sect was repulsive to him.

Within hours of the publication, the Inspector received the first registration and also had a number of enquiries as to the interpretation of the Order.

By the 28th he was in a position to reply to the Bailiff's letter:-

"Registration of Jews.

Averting to your letter dated 23rd October, I have the honour to report that a total of four persons have registered as being of the Jewish persuasion.

Mrs Brouard knows that her mother was a Jewess, but cannot say anything about her father, whom she has not seen since she was a young girl and is now said to be dead.

There are no places registered as Jewish businesses but the managers of Messrs Hipps Ltd., 47 High Street, and Montague Burton Ltd., 38 High Street, both gents' outfitters, have given information that they are not Jews but they are unable to say whether over 50% of the firm's capital is in Jewish hands. Both are branch shops of firms carrying on business in England.

As the managers are not in a position to know, I have not directed them to exhibit notices as required for Jewish businesses.

A copy of the return is attached."

## LIST OF JEWS RESIDENT IN GUERNSEY

| *Name.* | *First Name.* | *Date of birth.* | *Place of birth.* | *Sex.* | *Family status.* | *Occupation.* | *Religion.* | *Time of uninterrupted Residence.* | *Address.* |
|---|---|---|---|---|---|---|---|---|---|
| Duquemin nee Fink | Elisabet | 21.7.99 | Vienna | Female | Married wife of Harry Duquemin. | Housewife | Church of England | Since 23.10.37 | Cobo Post Office. Castel |
| Brouard nee Bauer | Elda | 27.4.84 | Florence | Female | Widow | Housekeeper | Church of England | Since Aug.1938 | 109 Victoria Road |
| Spitz | Auguste | 28.8.01 | Vienna | Female | Single | Domestic | Jewish | Since 10.9.37 | Country Hospital |
| Steiner | Therese | 22.4.16 | Vienna | Female | Single | Nurse | Jewish | Since 4.9.39 | Country Hospital |

The Bailiff passed copies of the letter and return on to Dr Brosch who was not satisfied that it was a comprehensive list of Jews within the Bailiwick. He required the Inspector to make further enquiries in respect of Julia Brichta. She was interviewed and Dr Brosch informed that:-

"Julia Brichta has been seen. She was born on 28.11.95 at Mako, Hungary, and states that her parents are now dead. She is at present employed as a cook by the German Authorities at 'The Thatched House', Rue de Putron. She states she is of the Protestant religion, attending Church of England. A further perusal of her passport will not reveal whether she is of pure aryan birth. She was not asked the direct question."

Dr Brosch was still not satisfied with what he regarded as an evasive answer and directed that Julia Brichta be questioned as to whether she was a Jew. He also required that Sark resident Frau Annie Wranowsky be investigated. The Inspector personally interviewed Julia Brichta and cross questioned her about her parents and grandparents. She told him that as far as she was aware her parents were not Jewish and that she was not related to Jews.

The Seneschal of Sark questioned Annie Wranowsky who stated that neither her parents nor grandparents were Jews and that she could trace back five generations without encountering Jewish blood. However, the Inspector noted that her passport, which he had retained from the time she had been interned, was issued at the German Embassy in London on 13th February 1939 and was stamped with a 'J', indicating that she was a Jew.

The Germans also required the Bailiff to supply the names of all persons, formerly of German nationality, who had acquired Guernsey Nationality or Citizenship since 1933. This was to be done before the 4th November 1940.

At the same time every Islander over fourteen years of age, was required to complete two copies of a 'Registration and Identification of Persons' form, to which personal photographs were later attached.

One night late in September PC 30 Short was on motorcycle patrol, with PC 15 Bill Burton riding pillion. As they approached the L'Islet cross roads they were stopped by a German sentry who ordered them to accompany him to their local headquarters at Summerland, Route Carre. There they were questioned by a lieutenant who spoke very little English. The Constables when asked for their pass to be out after curfew, pointed out that it was not necessary as they were in uniform.

After putting through numerous telephone calls, the lieutenant instructed the two Constables:- "No patrol - go Police Station - sleep". Fred Short and Bill Burton did just that- willingly.

The next night PC 17 Plevin was stopped by a sentry as he passed the Houmets du Nord. He was allowed to continue his motorcycle patrol, but when he reached the L'Islet cross roads, he was again stopped. The Constable produced his warrant card and driving permit and after they had been examined he was ordered to walk to 'Summerland'. There he was questioned on the where he had been on patrol and maps were produced so that he could explain his route. He was told that there were to be no night patrols that night and taken to the Police Station. He was instructed to return the next morning to collect his motorcycle and warrant card.

Sergeant Le Lievre, after hearing PC Plevin's report, telephoned the German Headquarters at the Channel Islands Hotel and was informed that the Commandant had ordered that all Police were to stay indoors that night.

The problems being encountered with night patrols was referred to the President of the Controlling Committee, who immediately raised the matter with the Commandant. Later Mr Sherwill informed the Inspector:- "I have been in communication with the German Commandant and he advises me to tell you that the Police should be kept in St Peter Port for tonight and that permits will be issued shortly and then only in special circumstances will Police go near the coast. In all cases when your men are stopped or hailed by Germans, they are to reply 'Police'".

On 7th October PC 27 Kimber went to the German Headquarters at the Channel Islands Hotel and collected three night duty permits and three maps. He was instructed that no Police were allowed, during curfew hours, to enter those parts of the Island marked green on the maps, which were mainly the coastal areas. All Police patrolling, during curfew hours, areas not marked in green must each carry a permit and a map.

The maps were large and when rolled up were even longer than a Policeman's truncheon and were therefore difficult to carry. Neither the Inspector or his Deputy were issued with a night pass. With the restrictions on the areas that could be patrolled and the limit of three night passes, this, in practice, meant that the Island was virtually unpoliced during the hours of curfew. It also meant that German troops had the unrestricted run of the Island for not only military purposes, but also their other illegal nocturnal activities.

Clearly the Germans had become sensitive and were concerned at what might be taking place during the hours of darkness. On the night of September 4/5th, two British officers, both Guernseymen, landed from a Royal Navy motor torpedo boat at Petit Port, the same bay used by the earlier raiding party. For Lt. Hubert Nicolle it was his second clandestine visit since the Occupation. A week after the Germans arrived he landed from a submarine and stayed for three days, during which time he obtained information regarding their strength, their whereabouts and the restrictions that they had imposed on the local population.

His second visit, in the company of Lt.James Symes was to obtain information about how the Civil Administration, under Mr Sherwill, was coping with the Germans. They were in civilian clothes and knew that under international law, if they were caught they would be treated as spies. They expected to be picked up a few nights later by the Royal Navy, but for one reason or another this did not happen. They were stranded.

The two Lieutenants contacted relatives and some friends who provided them with food and shelter. Gradually more and more locals became aware of their presence in the Island. Ambrose Sherwill certainly knew, he was asked if he had any message for the Home Office, and was very concerned as to the consequences, both to them and the local community. Inevitably the Germans heard rumours that British Servicemen were at large in the Island.

Major Bandelow, who had taken over as the German Military Commandant, expressed his concern to Ambrose Sherwill, about the possibility of British servicemen being on the Island. Sherwill realised the danger and wrote to the Commandant saying:-

"I have given much thought to the subject of our conversation on Tuesday evening last and it has occurred to me that it is possible that the best method of making known to the people of this Island their duties and responsibilities might be by an exchange of letters which, if you approve, would be published.

They would indicate your attitude and that of the Island Administration and would give a lead to the whole population. I enclose draft letters for your consideration, for such amendment as you may see fit. I attach to them German translations which I hope convey the exact shade of meaning which I intend. Should my suggestion meet with your approval, I would wait on you at any time convenient to you to discuss the matter."

In the draft letter which Sherwill suggested that Major Bandelow might sign, he included "Further, I am not wholly satisfied that there are not still hidden and assisted in this Island British soldiers left behind at the time of the evacuation or who have since infiltrated into the Island."

Clearly Sherwill had the two British lieutenants in mind when he composed that paragraph and later in the same letter he added:-

"If at the present time, there are in this Island any of the British armed forces, they must be delivered up forthwith and will become prisoners of war and entitled to treatment as such".

This was the escape clause that Sherwill was trying to provide for the two lieutenants who had arrived in the Island wearing civilian clothes.

Major Bandelow agreed to an exchange of letters and to them being published but required considerable changes to the text. Sherwill took advantage of the rewrite and suggested that the 'escape clause' passage be changed to:- "I intend to arrange with you a certain date by which all members of the British armed forces still in hiding here will have to report. Those reporting up to that date will be treated as prisoners of war, also no measures will be taken against their relatives who had assisted in hiding them". If agreed, that was going to extend the immunity to the relatives of the two lieutenants.

The exchange of letters was duly published and the many people who were now aware of the presence in the Island of the two lieutenants, were delighted. However one Islander who was not so enthusiastic, wrote to Mr Sherwill.

"Dear Mr Sherwill,

I was somewhat surprised to see in the '*Evening Press*' of Saturday last the 12th instant correspondence which had passed between you and Major Bandelow, the German Commandant, with reference to the fact that a certain number of soldiers belonging to the British Army might be still in the Island unknown to the German Authorities and harboured by relations and friends.

I do not in the least wish to interfere with your interviews with the German Commandant, but I am strongly of the opinion that the Commandant should have been invited to address his letter to me as Bailiff of Guernsey and I, with the assistance of the Crown Officers would have sent him a reply on behalf of the people of Guernsey .

I feel that, perhaps quite unconsciously, you and your Committee are taking over my prerogatives and that you will realize I cannot permit and it is resented, I believe, by the inhabitants at large.

I do think I might have been consulted about the matter and the very excellent letter that you drafted in reply should have been under my signature.

I request, therefore that any further correspondence on this matter or notice to be published in the press will be submitted to me and if I am of opinion I will sign all notices regarding this very grave and important subject concerning as it does possible penalties against the people of this Island.

Yours sincerely,
Victor G. Carey.
Bailiff."

On the 19th October a statement from the German Commandant appeared in the press giving the deadline for surrender as 6.00pm on Monday the 21st October and stating that 'Members of the British Armed Forces obeying this Order will be treated as Prisoners of War and no measures will be taken against persons who have assisted them'.

At 4.15pm on the 21st October, Emile Nicolle and Louis Symes went to the Police Station and reported that their sons were at their homes. Mr Symes told Deputy Inspector Langmead:- "My son and Hubert Nicolle came to my house on the night of the 17th October. On Sunday morning I informed Mr Nicolle about his son. In view of the notice in the papers I thought it was my duty to report that my son is at home." Mr Nicolle added:- "At about 11.00am on the 20th October Mr Symes told me my son was in the Island, I saw him and took him home for the night".

The Deputy Inspector, accompanied by Sergeant Le Lievre, went first to Rouge Huis Avenue and collected Lt Hubert Nicolle and then to Clarke's Estate, Grand Bouet, and collected Lt James Symes. Both men, wearing uniforms that Nicolle's uncle had obtained from stocks left behind by the British Military Machine Gun School, were taken to the Police Station. They gave their rank and number but declined to give the name of their unit or make a statement.

At 5.30pm, half an hour before the deadline, the Deputy Inspector informed Ambrose Sherwill of their surrender. The two Lieutenants, after they had been 'lectured' by Inspector Sculphur to only give the Germans their name, rank and number, were placed in prison and the Inspector informed Dr Brosch of their surrender and requested further instructions.

There was considerable activity at the Police Station in the minutes leading up to the deadline of 6.00pm. and as a result five other servicemen surrendered themselves and were transferred to the prison to await German instructions.

The Germans did not honour their undertaking, which had been so well publicised. Hubert Nicolle and James Symes were taken to Fort George and interrogated for long periods before being brought before a Court Martial. They were found guilty of being spies.

Their relatives, including Nicolle's parents, his aunt and uncle, his one time young lady, Jessie Marriette, Symes's parents, his girl friend, Mary Bird, and some of her relatives were all detained. Ambrose Sherwill and H.E.Marquand, the States Supervisor were arrested and relieved of their Offices. Mr Marquand, like Mr Sherwill, had known of the presence of the two British lieutenants. All those arrested were shipped or flown to France, where they were imprisoned in the Cherche Midi Prison, in Paris.

The Secretary to the Controlling Committee, Louis Guillemette, spent a number of sleepless nights after the States Supervisor was arrested, expecting a knock on the door. He too had also known of, and had been involved in, the plan to protect the two young lieutenants. Fortunately the feared knock never came.

The Germans announced that the 'favouring of espionage' by Islanders required further disciplinary measures and on the 12th November they decreed that all wireless sets had to be surrendered. Collecting depots were established and owners had to deliver their sets, suitably labelled. Many sets were not surrendered despite the threat of six weeks' imprisonment and a 30,000Rm fine.

Despite the imposition of more restrictions by the Germans and the tightening of their grip, 'normal' Police activities continued. Miss Irene De La Mare was found in the Grange after curfew by PCs Whare and Bailey. She claimed that she had been in the company of a German soldier who had left her when the air raid siren sounded. She was kept in custody overnight and released at 10.00am the next morning pending further instructions from the German Authorities.

The Germans decreed that all owners of motor vehicles had, when notified, to present their vehicles before a Commission of the German Military Authorities, who would examine them and determine a purchase price. The owner would receive a written voucher which would be redeemed by the States of Guernsey.

The Inspector was notified to present the Wolseley Police car No 5350, at St Peter Port Garage for examination on the 23rd October. He wrote back indignantly stating that the car, the property of the Police Committee, had been commandeered by the Military Commandant for his personal use on the 1st July. "In these circumstances" he wrote "I think an error has been made and I accordingly return the four documents not completed."

The German Military Tribunal had only dealt with five cases of local persons when, in October the Inspector was ordered to keep a 'Register of Persons convicted of Offences by a German Court'. The Register, the Germans instructed, was to contain the name and address of each person convicted and the particulars of the offence, including the date of conviction, the sentence and wherever possible, the date from which it took effect. The Register was to be available for perusal by both German and Civil Authorities. The Register was started, maintained and kept in the Inspector's office.

The annual task of formulating a Police Budget for the ensuing year still had to be carried out despite the German occupation. Whilst the cost of wages of regular members of the Force had been cut, so too had the number of men employed. This had the effect of reducing the wage bill from the 1940 estimate of £6,878 to £4,682 in 1941. However the employment of 12 Specials for daytime duties, at the basic wage of £2.4.3 a week, added £1,410 to the budget. The total cost of the Police Force for 1941 was estimated as £7,164, in comparison with the previous year's figure of £7,781. By any standard a remarkably inexpensive way to run a Police Force !

# Chapter 8

# WHAT ANY POLICEMAN WOULD HAVE DONE IN THE CIRCUMSTANCES.

On the 22nd November 1940 the Feldkommandant 'requested' the Acting President of the Controlling Committee, Jurat John Leale, to 'ascertain the nationality of the Jews residing in the Bailiwick of Guernsey and whether they include Jews of American nationality'.

The letter was passed to the Bailiff who in turn asked the Inspector to provide the details of the nationality of the Jews already known to the Germans. The only new information required being the Jew's nationality and whether there were any American Jews in the Bailiwick.

The Inspector replied to the Bailiff on the 25th November:-

"Nationality of Jews.

I have the honour to report that the Jews resident in the Bailiwick of Guernsey are of the following nationalities:-

| | |
|---|---|
| British | Duquemin, Elisabet nee Fink, Cobo Post Office. |
| | Brouard, Elda nee Bauer, 109 Victoria Road. |
| German | Steiner, Therese, Castel Hospital. |
| | Spitz, Auguste, Castel Hospital. |
| Czech | Wranowsky, Annie, Clos de Ville, Sark. |

There are no Jews of American nationality resident in the Bailiwick of Guernsey."

The Bailiff forwarded three copies of the letter to the Acting President of the Controlling Committee.

On the 26th November the Acting President of the Controlling Committee wrote to the Feldkommandant:-

"In reply to your letter of the 22nd instant regarding the nationality of Jews residing in the Bailiwick of Guernsey, I have the honour to enclose herewith a report from the Inspector of Police on the subject".

The unwritten rule of the Establishment and Civil Service, was that the recipient of a letter was always the one to reply. The Bailiff was a stickler for etiquette, tradition and status, especially his own, which he guarded zealously. The ornate official language, such as 'I have the honour' and 'your obedient Servant' were standard phrases of the day.

One morning, while on Town patrol, Sergeant Duquemin was approached by sixteen-year-old Herbert Hurford, who said:- "My father, Bert Hurford, has not been home since 8.30pm last night. I left him at the Victoria Hotel, Glategny Esplanade, last night and he was alright then. He had his cycle with him, number B.1863".

Sergeant Fred Duquemin went to the Victoria Hotel and spoke to the licensee, Steve Duquemin, who remembered Bert Hurford leaving at about

8.40pm. "He was sober, perhaps a little bit chatty and should have had no trouble in getting home."

At 2.45pm the same afternoon fifty year old Bert Hurford was brought to the Station by a soldier who declared:-

"This man has been sentenced to three days in prison for having being found out after curfew, near the Victoria Hotel at 9.35pm last night. He wishes to see a doctor, will you please arrange and will you give me a paper to say I have handed this man over to you." A receipt for the 'body' of Hurford was given to the German by PC 17 Plevin and the Gaoler was told about Hurford's request for a doctor.

Sir Charles Gill, of Maryland, Cobo, telephoned the Station and reported:-

"There is a balloon about 25 feet in length drifting towards Cobo from the direction of Grandes Rocques." Sergeant Harper, PC 14 Friend and PC 23 Quin immediately went to Port Soif Vineries and saw a deflated barrage balloon with British markings, lying at the foot of a windmill. While in flight the balloon had apparently become entangled with the blades of the windmill and now had a large hole in its silk fabric. The German authorities were informed and they removed the balloon.

It was not long before the Germans were seeking more information from the Island Authorities, this time they required:-

1. A list of all women of German birth at present residing in the Bailiwick who have attained British nationality since January 1914 through marrying a British subject.

2. A list of all children born of German parents who are residing in the Bailiwick at present and who under law, possess British nationality. If on attaining their majority, any such children have declared their nationality, this fact was to be noted against the names concerned.

Mr Sculpher submitted returns as directed. He was surprised how many people were listed. Twenty-two women, German and Austrian by birth, had married British subjects and were living in Guernsey. There were also nine children listed in the return.

At 9.40pm on 3rd December Sergeant Le Lievre received a telephone call from Thomas J.Ozanne, of St Vincent, Castel, saying:-

"I want a policeman out here".

The Sergeant enquired "What for?".

"Never mind what for, I want a Policeman".

"Is there any trouble?".

"No there is no trouble, only there is a German here untidy".

The Sergeant could not get any sense out of the caller. Then a German came on the line and tried to speak to the Sergeant but could not make himself understood. PCs Le Cocq and Smith were sent to see Mr Ozanne at his home near Castel Church. Also present were a German soldier and a civilian, Richard Angell, who appeared to be drunk. There were abrasions on his face, which was smeared with blood. A raincoat he was wearing was also covered in blood.

The soldier who had an abrasion on his chin, claimed that at 9.15pm he approached and attempted to question three men, Angell being one of them, for being out after curfew. Angell struck him and there was a rough and tumble in the road. He took Angell to the house and tried to telephone his headquarters, for assistance, but was unable to get through. Mr Ozanne had then telephone the Police station.

The German soldier said that he had lost his forage cap and bayonet. PC Smith went out with him and found them in the road.

Richard Angell told PC Le Cocq:-

"My mate, I won't tell you his name, and I were walking up the Castel Hill, at about a quarter to nine and were followed by a German. We were talking about the Americans sending over some planes, when the German came up and said something about nine o'clock and that he was taking us to Beaucamp. I struck the soldier and ran away but he caught me and tripped me up. There was then an argument and a fight and here I am,"

The constables took the German to Grange Lodge, where the officer in charge instructed PC Le Cocq to detain Angell until the morning, when telephone instructions would be sent to the Station. He also ordered that the persons involved in the fight must be found.

Later that night PC Smith went to 2 Bellevue, St Andrew where he tried to knock up John Catoroche. He hammered on the door but was unable to awaken him. However, he managed to gain entry through an unlocked window. The Constable shook Catoroche, who had obviously been drinking, and tried to speak to him about the incident, but he had difficulty in speaking. The Constable noticed that a pair of flannel trousers, which Catoroche spent some time trying to put on, had blood on them as did his raincoat. When he was told that he was being arrested he said:-

"This German soldier came up to us, looked at his watch and said 'It is nine o'clock'. My mate started arguing with the soldier and would not listen to me, so I left him, as did a Dutchman who had joined us." Catoroche was taken to the Station.

The Dutchman mentioned by John Catoroche was later traced as a British subject of Dutch ancestry, Conrad Bouwmeester, of Castel Hill. When interviewed he explained that he left St Peter Port at 8.30pm and as he was walking home, met the other two walking up Castel Hill. The last he saw of them was when they were stopped by a German soldier. He claimed that he left them a few minutes before the curfew hour of 9.00pm. His timing was confirmed by his landlord, Edmund Le Page.

The Inspector made a full report to the Acting President of the Controlling Committee, with a request that the papers to be passed on to the German Authorities.

The Germans naturally treated the assault on a soldier as a serious offence and Richard Angell was taken to Jersey and tried by a Military Tribunal for 'resistance to executive authority'. He was sentenced to three months' imprisonment.

One Sunday in December as result of a request for the attendance of a Police officer at Fort George, PC 28 Bretel reported to Oberleutnant Scharp. He had with him a sixteen-year-old local girl, who gave her name as Marjorie. The Oberleutnant said that the girl had been trying to enter the Fort and would not go home. She told the Constable that her father would not allow her to go out at night so she had been sleeping in the fields since the previous Friday. PC Peter Bretel took Marjorie to her home in Cornet Street and placed her in the care of her father. She later appeared in Court charged with being out on the streets after curfew and was fined 10/- and put on probation for a year and a day.

Drunkenness, which between the two world wars had probably been the major crime in Guernsey, came under the spotlight towards the end of December 1940. Previously Mr Sherwill had been given an undertaking by the licensed victuallers that they would try to ensure that drunkenness did not occur and if it did, it would be dealt with very severely. The Inspector sent a return to the Acting President of the Controlling Committee detailing the cases of drunkenness for the six months up to the 18th December 1940 and comparative figures for the two previous years.

1938 45 Cases all male
1939 57 Cases all male
1940 23 Cases 21 male 2 female.

Jurat John Leale then asked if the Inspector considered the undertaking given by the licensed victuallers had been kept. Mr Sculpher said, that taking into consideration the reduction in the population, he did not think that drunkenness was on the increase. On average there was less than one case a week, which, he believed, to be negligible. He added:- "I am satisfied that as a whole, the licensees are doing their best, but since the Occupation there are two who have caused the Police some trouble. They know what it will mean if I can procure the necessary evidence."

One 'statistic' the Inspector did not include in his return was 60 year old Thomas Le Sauvage. In fact Tom nearly missed being included in the full 1940 return. On the 27th December the Police Court had risen after only sitting for twenty minutes, due to lack of business. A few minutes later Tom presented himself to the Station Sergeant and announced that he was due to appear in Court on a charge of drunkenness. His late arrival was, he explained, because he had to make the long journey from Pleinmont.

The sergeant, not wishing to make Tom return the following week, went to the Royal Court and found Mr Sculpher talking to the Magistrate in the lobby. He explained to them that Mr Le Sauvage had just arrived from Pleinmont for the Court sitting. Quertier Le Pelley and Mr Sculpher, who had just left Court, exchanged glances.

"Well, we'll have to have another," said the Magistrate.

So, at a moment's notice, a Court sitting was convened and Le Sauvage was fined 2/6d for being being drunk. No doubt that was better for Tom, because if he had had to return from Pleinmont the following week, he would most likely have been fined another 2/6 for failing to attend Court.

On the 24th December, a Proclamation was published in the *Evening Press* announcing that all persons involved in the affair of the two lieutenants would be exempt from punishment. Those Islanders held in Cherche Midi Prison in Paris would be returned to the Island and Lieutenants Nicolle and Symes were to be treated as Prisoners of War.

Ambrose Sherwill was released, but the Germans decreed that he could no longer hold the office of H.M.Attorney General or be reinstated as President of the Controlling Committee, 'As co-operation with the German Authorities is no longer possible'. The States Supervisor, Mr H.E.Marquand, was, however, allowed to return to his post. All the wireless sets confiscated were also to be returned to their owners, 'for use until further notice'.

The Proclamation concluded:-

'All the above measures have been taken in the expectation and under the condition of a perfect loyalty on the part of the Island Authorities and population in the future. Any disloyal or illegal behaviour will result in immediate counter measures. The whole community would bear the consequences of individual misconduct.'

As a result of the Proclamation the States immediately set about returning the confiscated wireless sets to their owners. Louis Guillemette, the Secretary to the President of the Controlling Committee, James Smith and Ted Laker of the Civil Transport Department and the Postmaster Harry Chapell, together with all the Parish Constables and many others, worked on Christmas day and Boxing day so that Islanders could once again enjoy the pleasure of their wireless sets. Forty-eight lorries were used to deliver them.

PC Harry Bull, the Police driver, was at home in Victoria Terrace, enjoying his Christmas dinner with his family when there was a knock on the door. It was George Torode, of the Civil Transport Department returning his wireless set. Harry Bull thanked him and returned to his dinner. Suddenly there was a loud crash and going outside Harry Bull found that the lorry being used to deliver the wireless sets had backed into the Police car which was parked outside his house.

George Torode apologetically said:- "I am very sorry, I was looking out of my offside window as I was reversing, I had just passed your car and had forgotten it was there. I am very sorry Mr Bull". The Police car suffered damage to the offside front wing, the running board and the offside headlamp was smashed. George Torode appeared in the Police Court charged with driving a motor lorry with want of care. The Inspector, prosecuting, described it as "a case with unfortunate circumstances". The defendant pleaded guilty and was fined 10/- with costs.

It was the practice of the Inspector that he or his deputy should visit many, if not all the licensed premises in Town on Christmas Eve and New Year's Eve. In the occurrence book for the 24th December Sculpher reported, "I beg to report that at 9.00pm I visited Caves de Bordeaux, at 9.10pm West End Bar, 9.20pm Brighton Hotel and at 9.30pm the Albion Hotel. All quite and no disorder." On New Year's eve Deputy Inspector Langmead recorded "I beg to report that between 10.30 and 11.30pm with Sergeant Duquemin I visited all licensed premises in Town and by 11.15 all were closed except for the Hotel de Normandie. Nothing to report."

From the very early days of the Occupation licensed premises were forbidden to sell spirits to locals . They were, however, allowed to supply Germans. Civilians were permitted to drink spirits at home, but only from their pre-Occupation stocks. All stocks of spirits at wholesalers were reserved for the Germans, although some exceptions were made. On the 27th December Dr Reffler signed an authorization, addressed to Mackay and Company, with a copy to the Police Inspector, stating:-

"Madame de Sark is authorised to buy weekly 1 case of whisky and 1 case of gin or the equivalent in jars by intervention of your firm."

This superseded the permit granted to the Dame's husband, Mr R.W.Hathaway, on the 30th July which also granted a weekly supply of whisky and gin.

Mr A.Isler, a Swiss citizen and owner of the Hotel de Normandie, was a respected licensee and a friend of the Force. Since the Germans arrived, he had on many occasions acted as an interpreter. On Christmas Eve, when he was walking through Town, he met a Constable and said:- "Tell the boys that if any of them are passing, to pop in and have a drink with me." This message was passed on and a number of off duty members of the Force took up Mr Isler's invitation.

At about 8.00pm on Christmas day PC 15 Bill Burton was on patrol when he met PC 16 Frank Tuck inside Boots entrance. This was a notorious meeting place for Policemen, because it was possible to keep out of sight in the recessed entrance behind the central window. Many a policeman had enjoyed a crafty cigarette in Boots doorway. They decided to walk up and see if the Hotel de Normandie was quiet.

As they were standing outside the hotel, two German officers came down the Street and stopped.

"Had a good Christmas? "enquired one of the Germans.

"Not too bad," replied Bill.

"You will have drink with us" said the other German officer.

Bill responded disappointedly "It is not allowed."

"Come in, we must keep on friendly relations."

Bill Burton and Frank Tuck were easily persuaded and the Germans paid for the drinks.

After quickly downing their drinks, they were on their way out of the hotel when James Smith, the head of the Civil Transport Department, came in and offered to buy them a drink. They accepted.

Then Frank Tuck bought a round.

Inevitably their presence that night in the hotel became known and word soon reached the ears of the Deputy Inspector. James Smith and his brother, who had also been present, gave detailed statements. They described Frank Tuck as the "tall one" and Bill Burton as the "short one", and their statements included such phrases as, "The short one was worse for drink" and "the short one wanted to get the tall one out".

**Constables W.J.Burton and F.H.Tuck.**

The two constables were charged:-

'They did while on duty enter licensed premises when their presence was not required in the execution of their duty between 8pm and 9pm on the 25th December 1940 at the Hotel de Normandie.'

PCs Burton and Tuck were each fined two days' pay and severely reprimanded and cautioned.

Three days later Bill Burton was again in trouble for 'drinking' whilst on duty, this time for accepting a lemonade. Deputy Inspector Langmead was in Fountain Street when he observed the Constable leaving 'Pat's Bar'. Bill admitted to Mr Langmead that he had been in the premises and had a drink. The barman, Walter Tanguy, said that he had only supplied the Constable with a lemonade. The matter was reported to the Inspector, as a disciplinary offence.

PC 15 W.J.Burton was charged with:-

1. Rendering yourself unfit for duty through drinking when on duty in Fountain Street.

2. Drinking on duty or soliciting drink without the consent of a superior officer. Did drink or receive from another person, intoxicating liquor whilst on duty between 2.00pm and 9.05pm, on the 28th December 1940

3. Entering licensed premises whilst on duty, when your presence was not required in the execution of your duty.

4. Did fail to work your beat in accordance with orders and did leave your beat number 5 to which you had been ordered without permission or with sufficient cause.

PC Burton was found not guilty on the 1st charge, fined one day's pay on the second and severely reprimanded and cautioned on the third and fourth.

The licensee of 'Pat's', Mr P.E.M. Greville, was summonsed for supplying refreshment whether by sale, gift or otherwise to a Police officer while on duty.

Mr Greville pleaded not guilty. Inspector Sculpher read the Ordinance, which stated ....'a licensee should not provide any liquid or refreshment',..... he emphasised the 'or refreshment'... 'to any Police officer'.

Mr Langmead told the Court that he had seen PC Burton leave the premises at 9.05pm and that he admitted that he had consumed a lemonade. The Deputy Inspector said that he went into "Pat's" and saw a barman who admitted that the Constable had been on the premises and that he had given him a lemonade.

Mr Greville, in the witness box, explained that he had left his premises at 8.45pm and had not seen the Constable. He claimed that the translation of the summons read like a personal accusation against him, while he knew nothing about the alleged offence. The Inspector pointed out to the Court that the licensee was deemed responsible for anything that was supplied over the counter.

He added that this summons had been brought to impress upon licensees that Police officers must not be served whilst on duty and that he was not asking for a heavy fine. The Magistrate, Quertier le Pelley, agreed with the Inspector and fined Mr Greville 10/- with costs.

With the removal, by the Germans, of Ambrose Sherwill from office, Jurat John Leale was appointed to replace him as President of the Controlling Committee. Whilst it was constitutionally not possible to replace H.M.Attorney General, G.J.P.Ridgway, H.M. Solicitor General became a member of the Controlling Committee and took over the legal responsibilities of the office.

The Police Committee's President, Deputy Stephen Rabey, died on the 19th July. He was replaced by W.E.Poat, who had previously given up the Presidency due to ill health. He was still not a fit man, but saw it as his duty to resume office. C.E.Agnew was elected Vice-President and John Griffiths joined the Committee for the first time.

Mr Poat's attitude was that the less the Police Inspector bothered him the better. Since the formation of the Controlling Committee Mr Sculpher had referred virtually all matters of Police business to Mr Sherwill. This suited Mr Poat and consequently very few Committee meetings were held. He was grateful to the President of the Controlling Committee for taking over much of the responsibility.

**W.E.Poat.**

Mr Sculpher, in practise, was able to almost ignore the existence of the Police Committee. This arrangement had suited him, as he enjoyed working with Mr Sherwill who always gave him sound advice and answers rather than the procrastination that was the hallmark of many States Committees.

With the removal from office of Mr Sherwill, the Inspector now had the alternatives of either working with John Leale, or reverting to dealing with the Police Committee. It was not a choice as far as the Inspector was concerned, he preferred to work with virtually anybody rather than the Police Committee.

Mr Sculpher, like everyone else, had an immense respect for the Rev Leale. He was a very open man, who was always approachable and had a reputation of total honesty and integrity. Part of his life had been spent as a Methodist Minister in England, before returning to the Island to re-enter the family business of Leale's on the Bridge. He was a tall, slim, white haired man of great modesty, who very rarely, if ever, raised his soft voice. He had an inner strength which, together with his quiet persistence, made him a very formidable and effective negotiator. The Inspector saw in him the ideal man to be dealing with the Germans on behalf of the Island and the ideal man for him to deal with from a Police point of view.

In order to 'see in' the New Year the German Commandant extended the normal curfew hour of 9.00pm to 2.30am. As far as the Police were concerned there was no trouble, although PC 30 Short spent New Year's morning at the Country Hospital taking statements from people who had accidents riding their bicycles the previous evening.

Very soon in the New Year the Germans were again 'requesting' details of Jews resident in Guernsey. This time they approached the Inspector directly and he again listed the four who had 'identified' themselves previously. He added "Included in the return is Annie Wranowsky, a resident in Sark, who is the only person of Jewish extraction living within the Bailiwick, outside Guernsey." He also stated "There are no known male Jews resident in Guernsey. There are no known Jewish children under the age of 16 years resident in Guernsey." The only new information was that Mrs Elda Brouard had taken up employment as housekeeper to Mr A.E.Nicolle, a Special Constable, at 'Electra', Belmont Road.

Sergeant Jack Harper lived in a flat at 39 High Street and he and his neighbour, Mr J.H.Villar, did not get on and regularly exchanged cross words. One night when Frank Tuck called on Jack Harper for a warming drink, he found the two neighbours fighting on the landing. He separated them and Sergeant Harper promptly arrested Villar.

Tuck and Harper dragged him down the stairs, along High Street and up Smith Street as far as the Gas Office, where they released him. Sergeant Harper told Villar that he would be let off if he promised to behave himself. Villar refused to shake Harper's hand.

The next morning Mr Villar, after first making sure that Sergeant Harper was not on duty, made a verbal complaint against Harper and Tuck to the Inspector.

The complainant had a bruise on his right wrist and his jacket was torn. Mr Sculpher requested him to submit his complaint in writing, which he initially agreed to do. Later however he refused to make a statement and withdrew his complaint. Instead he left the matter in the hands of the Inspector.

The Inspector charged both men with:-

'Failing to report a matter that it was your duty to report viz - Having at about 12.30pm on 12th January 1941 at High Street arrested a man on a charge, did improperly release that man and failed to report the occurrence.'

Mr Sculpher reported the matter to the President of the Police Committee stating:- "This case arose out of a domestic quarrel between Sergeant Harper and another tenant of the same premises. PC Tuck was drawn into the matter. As there was obviously wrong on both sides, I verbally cautioned both Police officers."

Sergeant Alf Howlett and three Constables, Le Cocq, Smith and Tuck were in the Station at about 10.45pm one Monday evening in January. It was well past curfew hour and absolutely nothing was happening. Except for the occasional jocular remark there was total silence. Suddenly they heard a noise outside the Station and, led by Sergeant Howlett, the four of them rushed outside to see a German soldier riding off down Le Marchant Street, on the Sergeant's bicycle.

The Constables gave chase and caught up with the thief when he fell off the bicycle at the bottom of the street. The soldier draw his revolver but was prevented from using it by Frank Tuck who grabbed his wrist. The soldier, who was under the influence of drink, kept repeating:-"Nichts, nichts!"

The soldier and the Sergeant's bicycle were taken back to the Station where he gave his name as:- "Adams, Beaucamps".

The German Authorities were informed and an officer from the Weighbridge, arrived and took the soldier away.

But for Frank Tuck's prompt action in tackling the drunken armed soldier, the situation could have turned out to be far more serious. In normal peacetime conditions such action would undoubtedly have been recognised but in the situation of the Occupation it was just, as Frank put it many years later, "what any policeman would have done in the circumstances."

# Chapter 9

# I HAVE A BRITISH AIRMAN AT MY HOUSE

Soon after Ambrose Sherwill's return to the Island, the Bailiff wrote to Dr Brosch acknowledging that he could not return to his former positions, but requesting that Mr Sherwill be appointed Legal Draftsman. After some time a reply was received from Dr Brosch on the 18th January 1941:-

"To the Bailiff of Guernsey.

Re: Mr Sherwill.

Ref: Your letter of 4.1.41.

The decision with regard to the above letter is now forthcoming.

1. It is not possible to allow Mr Sherwill to perform any duty having any public character. The proposal to appoint him draftsman cannot therefore be accepted.

2. Frank Nicolle, Emile Nicolle and Alfred Bird must also be excluded from public duties. It is pointed out that this measure should not be attributed to the fact of having given shelter to the Lieutenants Nicolle and Symes. Exemption from punishment has been guaranteed to them in this respect. However, in the course of the enquiry after the reporting of the two spies, they have endeavoured to mislead the German Authorities. Further co-operation with them is therefore impossible.

3. There is nothing against Henry Marquand.

The assistance given by Mary Bird is insignificant.

Jessie Marriette has given truthful evidence.

They may be further employed.

The dismissal of the persons mentioned in paragraph 2. is to be reported here without delay."

So H.M.Attorney General reverted to being Advocate Sherwill.

Bill Green, the Island's pre-war champion racing motorcyclist, was finding life a little tedious and slow now that he was restricted to a pedal cycle. Being inquisitive by nature he had to content himself with the use of his binoculars from his vantage point at Seaplane Bungalow, at Jerbourg Point. One Saturday evening, just as it was beginning to get dark, he spotted through his binoculars what he thought to be a rubber dingy with two men, adrift off St Martin's Point.

Bill telephoned the Police Station and PCs Perry and Burton were sent to investigate. Because St Martin's Point was a restricted military area, they first went to the Royal Hotel to pick up two German officers.

They were met by Bill Green who pointed out that the Corbiere Lighthouse light had just started flashing for the first time since the Occupation. He said:- "I was looking towards Jersey when I saw what appeared to me to be a rubber boat with 2 men in it. Looking again after I had telephoned the Station, I realised it was the conning tower of a submarine."

The constables and the German officers walked along to St Martin's Point and saw what seemed to be a flare burning on the surface of the water towards Les Rocque Douvres. The Corbiere light which had been flashing for about five minutes, stopped. The two Constables were ordered to return to the Station, leaving the Germans to continue their investigation.

By this time in the Occupation queuing had become part of the daily life of Islanders, particularly for women. Special Constables were often given the job of controlling a queue of Islanders waiting patiently for their turn to be served. One Special later recalled that he learnt more from listening to the banter of a queue than he ever did from any other source. And so too did the Germans since there was always the possibility of some of the chatter being repeated to them. One local to suffer for being too free with her criticism of the Germans was Mrs Mabel Gale. She was reported to the Germans, arrested, tried in her absence and sentenced to five days' imprisonment for 'Spreading anti-German news'.

**Queue control in the Pollet.**

"I am sorry I am late, Sergeant." was PC Frank Tuck's first words when he reported for duty at 10.10pm one Friday night in February. Sergeant Le Lievre thought the Constable looked ill and smelt of drink and not fit for duty. Doctor B.S.Collings, the Police doctor, was sent for and examined the Constable. Frank volunteered "I had some whisky as I did not feel well." The Doctor diagnosed gastric flu and ordered him to be taken to the Emergency Hospital where he remained for six days before being discharged. Sergeant Le Lievre entered a report in the Occurrence Book and the Inspector added, in his standard red pencil, "Friends informed?" Underneath that was written - 'Yes' - with Sergeant Le Lievre's initials. Jack Harper, when he saw the entry, commented "A touch of humanity by the Inspector".

Early in 1941 an Ordinance was introduced directing that all dogs in public places must be kept on a lead and that the Police were to seize and dispose of dogs found wandering in the streets. Mr Sculpher, a dog owner himself, was concerned as he did not think that dogs collected by the Police should have to be destroyed immediately. He told the States Supervisor:- "This may be in order with unwanted animals, but others are valuable and could have easily escaped from their owners' premises unknown and without a collar."

He said that since the Dogs Home had closed there was no temporary accommodation for strays. He had heard that Mr Goubert, a States employee, had some kennels at his house. The Inspector suggested that Mr Goubert be allowed time off his States duties to feed and tend any dogs the Police might send to him. The States Supervisor agreed and requested the Inspector to make the necessary arrangements with Mr Goubert.

The Police often found dogs just walking alongside their owners who claimed that the animal was under control and exclaimed, "So what is the problem!" When James Falla, of Les Baissieres, was caught walking his dog without a lead, the Inspector prosecuted him as a warning to others. He told the Court that he had given instructions that this Order was to be strictly enforced. The Inspector merely asked for the costs of the summons, 4/6d, to be imposed.

The Guernsey Aero Club in the early thirties purchased an Avro Avian MK IV two-seater bi-plane which was regularly used by members of the Club and hired out to other flyers. In 1935 when the plane was parked out in the open, at L'Eree aerodrome, a gust of wind picked it up and hurled it over on its back. The plane was so badly damaged that it was not considered worth repairing. Cecil Noel, who was one of the directors of the Flying Club, carefully collected all the parts and dumped them in a heap outside his home.

A couple of years later Cecil did a deal with the Motor House Garage whereby he was provided with a second-hand car in exchange for the remains of the plane. All the parts were taken up to the loft of the Motor House Garage on the corner of St Julian's Avenue and Ann's Place. After more than two years' work, the garage's manager, Harold Le Parmentier, had fully restored the plane and it was ready to fly. However, prior to the Occupation, Harold left the Island. The loft in which the assembled plane was stored was locked up and he entrusted the keys to an employee, William Gilson, with instructions to keep it clean and well oiled.

The Germans on arrival in the Island requisitioned the Motor House Garage for the repair of their military vehicles. Kenny Bell, who previously worked for Bougourd Brothers, was put in charge by the Germans. Kenny was unaware there was a plane in the loft, the door was locked and he didn't bother to investigate. One day William Gilson broke the news of the existence of the plane to Kenny, but even then he took the view that it was not his responsibility.

When the Germans issued an order that all inflammable material stored in the upper floors of property in the town was to be removed, Kenny Bell was concerned. After considerable thought he decided to report the existence of the plane to the Germans. So early in March 1941, he went up to the Feldgendarmerie Headquarters at Grange Lodge and reported the plane's presence.

The Germans immediately arrested Kenny. He was taken back to the Motor House Garage where the plane was inspected by officers of the Luftwaffe and photographed from every possible angle. Kenny was questioned by the Feldkommandant, Fuerst Von Oettingen. The Germans noticed that the engine had been freshly oiled and said that proved that Kenny had repaired the plane and was planning to escape.

The Motor House Garage was guarded at first by two fully armed Germans, then on the 9th March instructions were received, from the Commandant, that the Police Force were to be responsible for mounting a 24-hour guard.

The round-the-clock guard was maintained until the 27th March when the Secretary of the Controlling Committee, telephoned the Inspector to say that it could be withdrawn from 6.00pm that evening. Clearly this was a community punishment for there being a plane right under the noses of the Germans for eight months, without them finding out.

The Avro Avian had in the meantime been put on board a transporter and taken to the airport prior to being shipped to the continent.

As a direct result of the discovery of the Avro Avian there appeared on the 5th March, in the *Evening Press*, a proclamation from the German Commandant.

"There is occasion to again call attention of the population to the fact that the retention of weapons, including hunting guns, or of implements of war of every description is punishable according to martial law.

The population is herewith requested to search every nook and corner of their premises for weapons and implements of war. They are to be delivered to the Controlling Committee at once."

Private individuals searched and came up with a multitude of items, almost all of which were souvenirs. Many had been declared to the Germans when they first arrived. Then islanders had been allowed to keep the Zulu stabbing assegais, the Turkish cutlass, the dirk and the many swords and hunting knives. Now they were collected and handed over to the Germans.

Mr J.L.Hocart of the Vale surrendered a bow and arrow. Quertier Le Pelley, the Magistrate handed in two obsolete guns and a number of museum swords. G.J.P.Ridgway, the Solicitor General personally delivered a set of fire irons made up from old swords. The Guille-Alles Library passed over their collection of 9 old muskets and pistols and 15 swords and daggers.

Not only were vintage implements of war being surrendered, but suggestions were made where firearms could be found. Mrs P.Gallienne called at the Police Station and told Sergeant Harper that she was certain that there were old Service uniforms and firearms hidden at Bartlett's Palace Theatre premises. Deputy Inspector Langmead and Sergeant Harper searched the premises but only found civilian clothes which had previously been used in theatrical performances.

It was all part of the German response to any act of defiance or minor resistance. They sought to inconvenience and penalise the community and so deter further acts of hostility.

At lunchtime on the 7th March Miss Julia Brichta called at the Station and asked to see 'her friend', Sergeant Lamy. She presented him with six silver dessert spoons and eight silver tea spoons, which, she said, belonged to Harold Ozanne, of the White Gables Hotel, who had evacuated. They were put in the Police Station safe, where they remained until claimed in September 1945.

A few days later a report was received that a car had landed on the pathway leading from Les Val des Terres to the bathing places. PC 17 Ernie Plevin investigated and found the badly damaged car, a Swift 9 hp, on its roof and blocking the footpath. It had obviously fallen over the cliff from Belvedere Field and several small trees and a wall had been damaged. The constable made arrangements for the car, owned by R.A.F officer Joseph M.Smart to be removed. Whether the absent owner ever learnt of the demise of his car is not recorded.

There were many cases of Germans forcing their way into private houses, despite the objections of the families concerned. On the 13th March a schoolboy arrived at the Station in an agitated state, saying that two German soldiers had forced their way into his house and that his mother had sent him to get the Police.

PCs Reg Marsh and Archie Tardif went with the boy to Lyndhurst, 23 Vauvert, and saw Mrs May Raleigh, who said:-

"At about 8.30pm last Tuesday I was standing on my doorstep when two German soldiers came up to me and asked the way to the Intermediate Schools. Last night, Wednesday, at about the same time, the same two German soldiers came to the house and one asked me if he could come in. I refused, but he forced his way in. His pal kept telling him 'come home', but he would not. So his pal left and went away.

The one who forced his way in was under the influence of drink. He laid down on the couch and went to sleep. It was then gone curfew, so neither I nor my son could leave the house. I woke the German up at midnight, as he had been sick, but even then he would not go home. He sat by the fire and eventually went away at about 1.30am. Tonight at about 8.30pm the same two soldiers came to the house and the one who came in last night, again forced his way in. I sent my boy to the Police Station, but now you have arrived they have gone. The one who came in is called George by his pal. He is short, stout, dark and has a high forehead. He speaks very little English and says he is a bus driver. I think he is only a private. He was dressed in a green uniform and was wearing laced boots, not the high boots."

There was little that the Constable could do other than advise Mrs Raleigh to let the Station know if the two soldiers called again.

In the middle of March 1941, a telephone cable in Les Moulipieds, near the airport, was cut in two places. The Germans reacted violently. The Feldkommandant, Colonel Schumacher, issued an Order further restricting the curfew from 9.00pm until 7.00am and requiring the States to supply sixty men between the ages of eighteen and forty-five for patrol and guard duties every night.

The Bailiff called an emergency meeting of the States to hear details of the act of sabotage. He told the States:

"A few days ago an ill-disposed person or persons deliberately and maliciously cut a telephone cable in two places, in the neighbourhood of the airport, which belonged to German Military Authorities, and thus performed an act of grave sabotage. Such an act was not only stupid but criminal, as it involved those who were participating in it with the death penalty and it also brought the population of the whole Island under grave displeasure of the German Authorities and in danger of the loss of their liberties.

Since the Occupation the German Authorities, both Military and Civil, have treated us with humanity and consideration and have gone out of their way on several occasions to help us in these difficult times. It is our duty and obligation to co-operate with them in carrying out their Orders and Regulations.

It is the duty of any individual who has any information with regard to the perpetration of this act of sabotage to inform the Police immediately, as unless the culprit is brought to justice, we do not know what further penalties the population may incur."

In a matter of days the Royal Court passed the 'Compulsory Civil Duties Law' which empowered that any man, who was eighteen or over, could be called upon by the States to do guard or other duties. Every night sixty men from the five parishes closest to the airport had to perform guard duty from 8.30pm until 8.30am the following morning.

The Constables of each Parish were required to supply the States Labour Office with a list of men from their parish who were able to perform the guard duties. Each person 'selected' had to report for duty at Ashmore, a vinery opposite the water tower in Forest Road.

At 8.30pm on the first night, the 19th March 1941, the Guard Party was assembled and addressed by Mr Sculpher, Then they were allocated their posts by a German N.C.O, assisted by PCs Kimber, Piesing and Le Cocq. The three reliefs of twenty men performed duty for 2 hours, with 4 hours off, until 8.30am the next morning. At 8.45am Pc Le Cocq returned the list of the 60 men to the

Deputy Inspector at the Station and reported everything correct. The Guard had been visited by a German officer twice during the night.

At 11.30am on the 5th April, a German officer informed the Station Sergeant that the cable Guard was to cease as from that time and date. The Sergeant informed the Labour Officer, Mr Johns, who said that he would communicate with the German Authorities for confirmation.

Colonel Schumacher confirmed the rescission of the measures and restored the curfew hours to 10.00pm to 7.00am. and added:- "I expressly draw attention to the fact that in case of repetition of such acts of sabotage, considerably stricter measures will be taken."

A few days later Mr Morley, of Grande Rue, St Martin, reported that a German telephone wire was down across his gateway. A few minutes later PC 27 Kimber telephoned, saying that a German telephone wire near his house in the Jerbourg Road appeared to have been damaged by the wind. The two incidents were immediately reported to Grange Lodge, who upon investigation agreed that both wires had been damaged accidentally.

On the 17th March the German Authorities introduced a further measure against Jews. Dr Reffler wrote to the Bailiff instructing that the index cards of all Jews, in the Foreigners Card Index, were to bear distinguishing marks.

"The cards of Jewish persons shall be marked, in a conspicuous place, with a capital 'J' in red and should in addition bear a red line across. This distinctive marking is to be carried out by the 23rd March 1941.

The number of Jews residing in the Bailiwick of Guernsey and to be included in the Foreigners Card Index, is to be communicated to me with an indication of their respective nationalities.

At the same time as the Jews, the persons without nationality and persons emigrated from Germany are to be reported."

The Bailiff wrote to the Inspector enclosing a copy of Dr Reffler's letter and added:- "Will you be so good as to carry out the instructions in the above quoted letter and report to me when this has been done, so that I may transmit it to the German Authorities."

On the 21st March the Inspector replied to the Bailiff stating:-

> "There are four known persons of the Jewish persuasion resident in the Bailiwick of Guernsey, two by marriage, of British nationality and two of German nationality. The latter, Therese Steiner, born Vienna 22nd April 1916 and Auguste Spitz, born Vienna 25th August 1901, both residing at the States Emergency Hospital, Castel, appear in the Foreigners Card Index and their cards have been marked with a capital 'J' in red with a line across in accordance with the instructions contained in the letter.
>
> There are no known persons without nationality, resident in the Bailiwick. Attached please find a list containing the names and addresses of persons at present resident in the Bailiwick who have emigrated from Germany and Austria since 1st January 1933."

The Bailiff passed a copy of the Inspector's letter and list, on to Dr Reffler.

The residents of Fort Road regularly suffered considerable aggravation from inebriated German soldiers on their way home from Town late in the evening. On reaching the top of Les Val des Terres, having lost their bearings, they knocked on doors and asked the way to the Jerbourg Barracks or even wanted to stay the night.

Robert Chilcott, of 'Croyland', Fort Road, was in bed, one night at around 10.20pm, when he heard the noise of breaking glass. He went down to investigate and found that a large pane in his back door had been smashed. He heard footsteps going away from the house but saw no one. Later he found that a window in his lounge had also been broken. On the wooden panel below the broken window was the heel mark of a boot. Also a section of his garden fence had been pulled down.

When he telephoned the Police Station, PC 34 Le Lievre and PC 26 Perry were sent to investigate. As they were leaving the house after seeing Mr Chilcott, a German officer and a woman ran past and entered the front garden of a nearby house. The Constables followed and searched the vicinity, but could find no trace of the officer. They saw John Le Poidevin, of 'The Moat House', who said:- "At 10.30pm I was in my sitting room when the door bell rang. I answered the door and saw a German officer, about 6ft tall, his belt around his neck, no bayonet and no hat. He was drunk and forced his way into my house. He wanted to stop the night. I told him to go away and he struggled with me. My wife went to 'Au Sommet' which has been taken over by the Germans and fetched an officer and soldier. In the meantime I had managed to get away from the officer and leave my house. He followed me out and disappeared."

Harry Mignot was asleep in bed at home in Rue De Putron, when he was awoken by a loud knocking on his door. "I went to see who was there and before opening the door asked 'Who is it?' All I could hear was someone saying 'Open, open'. I opened the door and saw a German soldier leaning against the door post, he was drunk. He asked me the way to Jerbourg Barracks, that was all I could understand, then he forced his way into the house.

He was talking German but I could not understand what he was saying. He asked me for a cigarette, but I told him I hadn't any. He put his gloves on and then drew his bayonet and pushed it inside his glove. I got rather frightened and went out the back door and called him, he followed. I went all the way around to the front of the house and in the front door. As I was pushing the door shut he hit the the glass panel with his bayonet and smashed the glass. He remained outside the house for about ten minutes, shouting and bawling, before I heard him pull the front gate shut."

The next morning Harry Mignot examined his front door and found blood on the step and on the side of the door. He later described the German as being 6ft in height, fair to ginger hair, clean shaven, with high cheek bones, green uniform, no overcoat, black gloves and in possession of a small silver cigarette case. He added "I think I could identify him again."

At Malburt, in Fort Road, at about 12.30am, Cecil Ferguson and his wife Alice, were awakened by a violent banging on the front door accompanied by a man shouting. Cecil put his dressing gown on and went downstairs. As he reached the bottom of the stairs, the glass panel in the door was smashed by a bayonet. When he opened the door he found a German soldier, who was obviously drunk, wanting to know the way to Jerbourg. After a lot of talking, the German was pointed in the right direction and he went upon his way.

Over a period of time virtually all the residents in the Fort Road area received late night visits from Jerbourg-bound Germans.

At 7.30am on the 12th April 1941 Thomas W. Brouard, of Les Bordes, St Saviour telephoned the Station and told the Sergeant:- "I have a British Airman at my house. He came here about 1.00am, I did not go out on account of the curfew and phoned you as soon as I could this morning."

Twenty-three year old, Flight Sergeant Robert Taylor Glen Sterling had been on night patrol in a Hawker Hurricane when he ran out of fuel. He abandoned his plane, which he believed, crashed into the sea some distance from land and parachuted down onto Lihou Island. He then made his way across the causeway and walked along the road until he found Mr Brouard's house.

After receiving Mr Brouard's telephone call, Sergeant Le Lievre went to Mon Plaisir, St Jacques and collected a German officer and two NCOs. Together they drove to St Saviour, where the Germans arrested Flight Sergeant Sterling.

In the meantime PC 13 Harry Dyson had managed to arrive at the Brouard Cottage some time before the 'official' party. Whilst they waited he arranged with Robert Sterling that he would be a link between the Constable and his wife, who had evacuated to England. As soon as he was in a prisoner of war camp Sterling contacted Harry Dyson, who wrote back. Then a letter went from Sterling to Dyson's wife in England, who replied and that was passed on to the Constable. This system lasted for the rest of the Occupation and after the war both men and their families became firm friends.

Inspector Sculpher received a copy of a letter from Dr Reffler addressed to the President of the Controlling Committee, dated 15th April, stating:-

"By order of the Commandant, the Victoria Hotel, Esplanade, has been closed on the 13th April 1941 for members of the forces and civilians, owing to the objectionable behaviour on the part of the occupier. I request you to have a notice regarding the closing of the Hotel published in the newspapers. The Island Police is to be instructed to see to strict compliance with the regulations issued for public houses, hotels etc."

Two days earlier, Sergeant Major Oeser, of the German Feldgendarmerie, arrived at Mr Sculpher's Office and informed him that intoxicating liqueur was not to be supplied to troops or civilians at the Victoria Hotel. No explanation was given. The Inspector informed all members of the Force and gave instructions that the premises were to be kept under observation.

The 69-year-old licensee of the Victoria Hotel, Stephen J.C.Duquemin was also the owner of the Racecourse at Vazon and a farmer. During his life he had earned himself various reputations. At one time it was acknowledged that he could lay bricks faster than any other bricklayer in the Island and he had been a champion cyclist. As far as the Police were concerned he was usually on the extremities of the law, but always managed to avoid being prosecuted. There had been a number of fires at his properties, which very fortunately for him, had always been well insured. The Police had a view on these fires, which they had never been able to test in a Court of law.

**Steve Duquemin.**

On one occasion he had been reported for cruelty to animals that he grazed on Lihou Island but no prosecution had been brought through of lack of evidence. There were three occasions when prosecutions were considered for not providing cattle on Lihou Island with water. On another occasion two steers were lost at sea and a prosecution was considered.

Since the Occupation Steve Duquemin had been very successful in playing the local Police off against the Germans, but obviously had now been too clever and had offended the Germans sufficiently to have the Victoria Hotel closed. The Inspector was not informed of the actual offence which Duquemin was alleged to have committed.

Two weeks later a member of the Feldgendarmerie came to the Station and reported that the Victoria Hotel would be re-opened as from noon on the 26th April. Again no reason was given for the German action, but it was typical of their approach to impose punishments for what they considered crimes, but without involving themselves in any recognised form of trial.

One of the three BSA Police motorcycles was in need of repair and parts were no longer available. Inspector Sculpher learned that a similar model, owned by evacuee Robert Mahy, was in the care of Green's, of Smith Street. He wrote to Mr Ridgway, H.M.Solicitor General, requesting the requisition of the motorcycle for Police use. The parts of the BSA now idle could, he suggested, be used as spares.

Mr Ridgway approached the Bailiff requesting him to use his powers under the Defence Regulations (Guernsey) 1939. On the 19th April 1941 Victor Carey, as Lieutenant Governor, signed a Requisition.

The motorcycle was duly collected and put into use.

While on duty in the High Street, PC 30 Short was approached by a very distressed elderly lady.

"Oh!" she said, "I have lost my dog, its a Pekinese dog."

She had been shopping in Le Riches, when her dog, which had a lead on, disappeared.

This lady had heard the rumour that the Germans were going to eat all cats and dogs in the Island and she was convinced that was to be the fate of her pet. The Constable assured her that he would do his best to try and find her pekinese.

Before Dr Oliver Bostock evacuated, he had employed two Hungarian maids. Being the Police Doctor, many of the Force, including Constable Short, were acquainted with the maids.

After the doctor evacuated and the Germans arrived the two maids found domestic employment at Les Divettes, Jerbourg. The house, owned by Lt Col.Byam, had been requisitioned for use by German Naval officers.

A few days after the Pekinese dog went missing, Fred Short met one of the two Hungarian maids who was out for a walk. Fred later recalled:-

"I said, 'Hello' and she told me that she and her friend were working for the Germans. I looked at her dog, which was a Pekinese, it seemed to be very much like the one that the old lady had lost. I asked where she had got the dog from and she said that one of the officers had brought it home and given it to her.

I told her I thought I knew who the owner of the dog was, but I told her I could not take it away from her if a German officer had given it to her. She told me that the German officer worked in an office at the Crown Hotel.

I went down to the Crown Hotel and spoke to an officer, who confirmed that he had found a small Pekinese dog, which had a lead on, in the High Street. I told him that I thought the dog belonged to a very old lady who was heartbroken about losing it.

He said he took the dog home to Jerbourg and gave it to one of his maids. When I told him how distressed the old lady was at losing her pet, he told me I must take it back to her. I asked him if he would like another dog as I knew where there were some pups. He said he was sure that his maids would like another dog. He gave me permission to go and fetch the dog and take it back to its owner. I thanked him and we shook hands.

When I took the dog back to its owner she was so delighted that she put her arms around me and she started to cry.

I went to see my farmer friend who gave me a little fox terrier puppy which I took up to Jerbourg. The two maids gave me a cup of tea, a cake and offered me some cigarettes.

They made a fuss of me and told me to come and see them any time. I took them up on their offer, particularly when I was on early turn. I made a habit of going up Le Val Des Terres and along the Fort Road when the Naval officers were on their way to the Crown Hotel. They would come flying by with a Nazi flag on the front of their car. I gave them a salute and then make straight for Jerbourg. I would be welcomed with a couple of hugs and kisses and the next thing I am sitting down to fried eggs, ham, bacon, toast and marmalade. That was how I got to know the Hungarian maids and I was well in there, in more ways than one."

On the 26th April 1941 the Germans issued their 'Third Order Relating to Measures Against Jews'. The new Order toughened the definition of a Jew and decreed that in doubtful cases, any person who belongs or has belonged to the Jewish religious community should be deemed to be a Jew.

On and after the 20th May 1941 Jewish undertakings were prohibited from carrying on virtually any economic activity. The Order further stipulated that 'In no undertaking shall a Jew be engaged as a higher official or as an employee who comes into contact with customers' and 'On the order of the Military Authorities, Jewish employees shall be dismissed and replaced by non-Jewish employees'.

It was further decreed that there should be no compensation paid in any circumstance to Jews for the loss of their businesses or jobs.

As no businesses had been identified as being Jewish the Order had no effect and no additional persons were categorized as Jews.

Alan Mackay held the licence of the Caves de Bordeaux in Upper Mansell Street. Towards the end of April he suspected that he was losing bottles of spirits from his store and reported his suspicions to the Inspector. It was arranged that the Deputy Inspector should keep observation on the premises and while watching on the 30th April he saw PC 26 Perry enter the store. The Constable was on duty and in uniform. Mr Langmead waited patiently for George Perry to come out. For a time he thought that he may have left by another exit, but when he emerged he was wearing his cape.

The Deputy Inspector stopped him in the Bordage and asked where he had been since 5.00pm. "Down Mill Street and around" replied the Constable. Mr Langmead then tapped the PCs trouser pockets and enquired:- "What have you got there?"

"A bottle". PC Perry replied.

They returned to the Caves des Bordeaux, where the Constable produced from his trouser pocket a flask of whisky and when questioned said:- "I just took it."

Mr Langmead took the Constable back to the Station where he told Inspector Sculpher:- "I just took it, that's all".

Mr Sculpher and Mr Langmead went to the Constable's home at the Brown House, Les Vardes, and found two bottles partly filled with rum and seven empty rum bottles. Perry told the Inspector that his wife had bought rum from Mr Mackay. This statement was checked and it was found that his wife had purchased rum, but not since the Occupation.

The Inspector suspended PC 26 George Perry and charged the him with stealing whisky to the value of 3/3d.

On the 2nd May, forty year old Perry, who was born in Manchester and joined the force in 1928, appeared in Court and pleaded guilty. He offered no explanation.

"This case is very unfortunate and rather grievous to me." said the Inspector "but I have a duty to perform and I must do it."

The accused was given a good character, but the Inspector added that it would be impossible for him to retain his position in the force.

"Your position, to prevent crime, aggravates this infraction, I cannot pass this off lightly, I shall send you to prison for one month with hard labour." said the Magistrate, Quertier Le Pelley.

The Constable was dismissed from the Force and his clothing and other equipment collected. The Inspector wrote to Mr Poat, the President of the Police Committee, reporting the matter and suggesting that it was not necessary for a special meeting of the Committee to be held. Mr Poat concurred.

On Easter Sunday, the 13th April 1941, Mrs Alice Savident, of Bon Port, telephoned the Police Station and said that a boat with five men had capsized in Saints Bay and that the men were calling for help. PC 30 Short was sent to see Mrs Savident. At 4.40pm Mrs Savident again telephoned to say that the Germans had rescued two of the men but the others had drowned. Just as she was putting the telephone down, PC Short arrived. After listening to her, he walked along the cliff path but could see nothing. Then he went to Jerbourg Point and saw a German fishing patrol boat going towards the Town Harbour. The Constable drove to the harbour and was there when the boat arrived with the two rescued men aboard.

**Constable Fred W.Short on a Police Motorcycle.**

The men, Nicholas Le Page and Frederick Rouget, were taken by a German officer in his car, to the Emergency Hospital. PC Short took a statement from Le Page but Rouget was not in a fit enough condition to make one.

It transpired that a party of five men left the Town Harbour at 1.30pm to go ormering in Saints Bay in John Bougeard's boat. They landed near the moorings at Saints, with all their equipment and a 9ft punt. At about 3.20pm John Bougeard with Arthur Falla, sailed off to inspect his crab pots, leaving the five other men on shore. Despite the shore being out of bounds to all civilians, the party started to walk across the bay to the other side. Suddenly a shot rang out and a bullet hit the sand about 20ft from the party.

They took no notice and continued to cross the beach towards a hut in the prohibited area. Suddenly 4 or 5 more shots rang out and this time the men went back to the punt and took to sea. When they reached the middle of the bay the boat capsized and they were all thrown into the water. Fred Rouget clung to the upturned punt and Nicholas Le Page supported himself with a empty petrol can. As soon as the Germans saw what had happened they sent a patrol boat out in an attempt to save the men in the water.

At this point John Bougeard arrived back on the scene and picked up Le Page and Rouget and searched for the other three men without success. The two survivors were transferred to the German patrol boat and taken to the Town Harbour where they were met by PC Short.

John Leale, President of the Controlling Committee, wrote to the Feldkommandantur thanking the German sailors who helped in the rescue of Le Page and Rouget, enclosing a bottle of brandy and 100 cigarettes as a mark of appreciation.

On the 10th April 1941 the Guernsey Police Force 'celebrated' its coming of age. After 21 years, three of its founder members were still in the Force, Sergeants Ted Pill, Frederick Duquemin and Alf Howlett. As far as the Police Committee were concerned the date passed unnoticed, only the Press somewhat belatedly mentioning the anniversary.

Station Sergeant Alf Howlett received a telephone call on the 6th May from the German Headquarters saying that their Strassburg gun at Jerbourg was to be test fired the next day. The Tarbour Strassburg battery, just south of the Doyle monument, consisted of four 22.0 centimetre French guns which the Germans had captured during the early part of the war.

Sergeant Howlett was instructed to see that all householders within one mile of the Doyle monument were told to open their windows by 10.00am the next morning. PC Bob Kimber, who lived only a short distance from the battery, was sent to inform people in Sausmarez Road, Le Varclin, Calais and the Jerbourg Road. Special Constables were detailed to call on other people within the area.

The gun, which was test fired, turned out to have been sabotaged by the French before it was brought to the Island. It blew the breech out and two Germans were killed. Part of the breach was hurled a considerable distance, landing in a field where some civilians were watching the test firing. Despite the sabotage, the gun, which had a range of about 21 miles, was quickly repaired and used fairly frequently against allied warships.

# Chapter 10

# JUST HOLD HIM UP A BIT

It was almost a year after the Island had been occupied that the Germans began to take a detailed interest in the operation of the Police Force. Early in July 1941 the Inspector was asked to supply details of the strength of the Force and a description of their duties. Mr Sculpher immediately prepared a report.

"The Force", the report recorded, "is now down to thirty men, from the pre-war strength of 37. Four had been recalled to the colours, one had been killed, one escaped by boat and one dismissed. Besides the Inspector and Deputy Inspector, there were seven sergeants and twenty-one constables".

Mr Sculpher described his job, as Inspector, as being in charge, preparing cases for the Courts, prosecuting offenders and generally supervising all Police matters.

"The Deputy Inspector acts in the absence of the Inspector, supervises traffic arrangements and the Force generally. He also makes such enquiries as directed by the Inspector.

One Sergeant, the Detective Sergeant, makes enquiries in criminal cases and such other matters as directed. Another acts as Clerk and is generally employed in the office, keeping records and attending to all clerical duties.

The hours of duty for the other Sergeants and Constables are eight each day and the station is manned for the whole of the 24 hours. One sergeant is always on duty to deal with callers and enter reports. The constables are employed:-

1 as Police car driver.
3 on motorcycle patrols.
1 as a reserve at the Station for emergency enquiries.
3 for relieving during weekly and annual leave.
2 on duty at White Rock.
1 patrolling St Sampsons Harbour and district.
10 for beat duties, traffic control and general enquiries."

"In addition," he reported, "there are twelve paid Special Constables employed by day in patrolling, controlling traffic and attendance in the markets."

Late one afternoon, on a beautiful June day, PC 14 Charlie Friend was on patrol along the West coast. As he passed the beach near Grandes Rocques a party of about forty German soldiers were marched on to the sands. About half of them stripped stark naked and frolicked about on the beach and in the sea. It was high water at the time and there were a number of women and children on the beach and others on the main road. Two of the women suggested to the constable that he should take action to stop 'the performance'. PC Friend did not consider it wise for him to intervene, but told the complainants that he would report the incident to the Inspector. Mr Sculpher, on hearing the details, decided that no further action could or should be taken.

On the 24th June 1941 the *Evening Press* contained a notice signed by Colonel Schumacher, introducing driving on the right of the road. As from midnight all traffic, including lorries, cars, cycles and even wheelbarrows, had to proceed on the right of the road. As the majority of cars and lorries were German driven, the change-over went well, without any serious accidents. The biggest problem concerned horses, that were accustomed to keeping to the left, but even they soon conformed to Colonel Schumacher's order.

Further Road Traffic Regulations were issued by the Germans on the 28th of June, concerning speed limits, the identification of main roads and priority at road crossings.

A speed limit of 40 km an hour (25mph) was imposed in closely built up localities and 80 km an hour (50mph)in other areas, except for lorries and buses which were restricted to 60 km an hour (37mph). During the hours of darkness a speed limit of 20 km an hour (12½mph) was imposed for the whole Island.

Main roads were distinguished by a sign depicting a red diamond on a white background. Side roads leading into a main road were identified by a red triangle standing on its point on a white background.

Main roads were identified as:-

1. The Esplanades, Les Banques, Grandes Maisons Road.
2. Vale Road, Route Militaire.
3. St Julian's Avenue, Grange, Rohais, Cobo Road.
4. Queen's Road, Mount Row, Ville au Roi, Carmel, Forest Road.

At junctions, the main road traffic always had priority, except where a German vehicle was concerned. The German forces always had priority over all other traffic.

On the 2nd July 1941 the Germans discovered that some of their signposts, between Cobo Post Office and the Grandes Rocques Hotel had been marked with the capital letter 'V'. PC 15 Burton was detailed to accompany two members of the Feldgendarmerie to Grandes Rocques where they saw five German signposts marked with several 'V's, in thick blue pencil. It appeared to the Constable that the 'V's had been drawn by children.

The German Police removed the 'V' by washing the signposts and informed local people that if it occurred again they would be held responsible. They made it clear that they took an extremely serious view of the matter.

The next evening further 'V' signs were discovered, this time in St Martin's. PCs Tuck and Bailey were sent to Sausmarez Road, where 'V' signs had been put on the pillar of a house called 'Redleaf'. These were obliterated and a 'V' mark on the side door of Luff's shop was also rubbed out. The Constables then returned to Town and went to Rue des Freres, where they obliterated two 'V' marks. Other 'V' marks were discovered and rubbed out in the gents' lavatory in St Julian's Avenue, also in Bosq Lane, Glategny Esplanade, and on the corner of Sam's Restaurant. All 'V' marks had been written with white chalk.

No doubt because of the effect of the 'V' for victory campaign in occupied Europe, the Germans reacted vigorously to what they must have seen as an extension of the campaign to Guernsey. Fuerst von Oettingen wrote to the Bailiff on the 4th July:-

"During the last days the known mark 'V' has been found on various street signs between the Grandes Rocques Hotel and the Cobo Bay Post Office as well as along the coast road between L'Eree Hotel and the tower at Vazon Bay.

This mark, which the Feldgendarmerie caused to be removed at once by the Island Police, represents in its significance a provocation which the Occupying Forces cannot tolerate.

By order of the Feldkommandant, Colonel Schumacher, I have therefore to request you to inform the population of this Island in a notice to be published in today's newspapers, that such action is punishable and will be considered as an act of sabotage.

If within 72 hours from the first publication of this notice the authors could not be identified, severe reprisals against all the inhabitants of the respective parishes may be expected.

Kindly report about the action taken."

Literally within minutes, the Bailiff reacted to the letter and arranged for an insertion in La Gazette Officielle.

Warning

"I have been informed that the letter 'V' has appeared written in public places in the Island. This matter is regarded very seriously by the German authorities and that the person or persons who have done this are breaking a military order and are rendering themselves liable to severe punishment. Moreover should the culprit not be discovered, the population may be penalised in the same way as in the case of acts of sabotage. The culprit or culprits must be discovered within seventy-two hours of the publication of this warning. May I warm my fellow Islanders against committing these foolish acts which accomplish nothing but merely bring grave consequences in their train."

Deputy Inspector Langmead was given the task of investigating the proliferation of 'V' signs. As a result of information he received from Mr A.R.Winterflood, the Secretary of the Education Council, he went to King's Mills and Cobo and interviewed Leonard Carre, aged 12, with his mother. Leonard said:- "I was with Donald Le Noury and Maurice Le Huray at Vazon. Near the Tower I found an empty tin which had contained red paint. I rubbed the inside of the tin, which was still wet, with paper and made a 'V' on the post of the notice board".

The next morning at the Castel School, Mr Langmead saw, in the presence of the Headmaster:-

William Earl aged 10
Edward Corbin aged 8
David Corbin aged 6.
Donald Le Noury aged 10.
Maurice Le Huray aged 10.
Eric Mechem aged 8.

William Earl and Edward Corbin admitted placing 'V's on the notice boards at La Houguette with a blue pencil. David Corbin was present when this was done but he did not do any writing himself. The other two boys admitted that they were with Leonard Carre when he painted the post at Vazon, but denied placing any 'V's there or anywhere else. Eric Mechem said he watched a boy, who he did not know, place a 'V' in chalk near Cobo Post Office.

Mr Langmead cautioned the boys against doing anything of the kind again and also impressed on the parents, the necessity of controlling their children.

PC 30 Short was on motorcycle patrol along the West coast during the early evening of the 4th July, when he was flagged down by Wilfred Le Page. Wilf had seen the Bailiff's announcement in the *Evening Press* and said:-

"One evening, at 6.30pm about a week ago, I was riding my bicycle along the Cobo coast road, when I passed Mr De Guillebon's house, La Maisonette. He was in his gateway and called me. I got off my bicycle and he asked me if I had caught any more fish. Whilst speaking to him he pulled out a blue pencil from his pocket and marked a blue 'V' on the right sleeve of my sports coat. He also marked a blue 'V' on the saddle cover of my bicycle. He did not pass any remark and I did not think anything of it, but I have since heard that people in France are using 'V' as a sign. I have also read about it in the paper today. If he is responsible for the 'V' signs in the district, he deserves to be punished otherwise all the Island will suffer."

The Constable took possession of Mr Le Page's saddle cover as evidence and reported the incident to the Station Sergeant.

Mr Langmead had, in the meantime, continued his investigation in the Cobo district and Mrs Mabel Guille, of the Cobo Motor Works told him that just over a week previously she had seen her neighbour, Mr De Guillebon place a 'V' on her wall with a blue crayon pencil. She found 'V's on both sides of her gateway and rubbed them out immediately, but did not say anything to Mr de Guillebon.

The next day, the Deputy Inspector saw 57-year-old de Guillebon in Town and took him to the Station, where the Inspector questioned him about the marking of 'V's on Mrs Guille's wall and on Mr Le Page's bicycle. He fervently denied any involvement, saying:- "I have not done anything of the sort, I have not marked any 'V's on anywhere, but I have seen some about the district." Mr Sculpher searched de Guillebon's pockets and found two pieces of black lead pencil, but no blue pencil.

Mr De Guillebon, a Frenchman by birth, who had lived in the Island since 1907, was arrested by the Germans and convicted on 17th July 1941 for 'V' propaganda and anti German manifestations. He was sentenced, by the German Court, to 12 months' imprisonment. On the 25th July he was taken to Jersey, under military escort, before being transferred to Caen Prison. On the 7th March 1942 his sentence was suspended 'under the provision that he shall not make himself liable to punishment for actions against the German Occupation Forces'. He was released on the 17th March and returned to Guernsey.

On the 7th July the Deputy Inspector saw Stanley Osborne, aged 11, at Castel School. Stanley admitted:- "I put a 'V' on the board at Saumarez cross roads, it was a board with a 'D' on it. I did it with a blue pencil. I am very sorry."

Mr Sculpher wrote to the President of the Controlling Committee asking him to pass on a copy to the German authorities.

Fuerst von Oettingen wrote to the Bailiff on the 8th July:-

"A report has been received, ........that an inscription was found on a closed garden door in Rue des Freres reading 'Deutschland unter alles' (Germany below everything) The Feldgendarmerie is able to give the exact location. Although the inscription was removed forthwith, the appearance of the same and the letter 'V' is a provocation of the Occupying Forces and moreover a degradation of Germany so that adequate punishment cannot be foregone.

Before taking further steps, the Feldkommandantur requests you have the perpetrator or perpetrators identified without delay."

What Fuerst von Oettingen did not know was that Sergeant Bert Lamy had seen the chalked message when he had walked down the lane with a member of the Feldgendarmerie. The words were originally 'Deutschland uber alles', which Bert Lamy assumed had been written by a German soldier but some local wag had crossed out 'Uber' and substituted 'Unter'. Not understanding the significance, he innocently asked the German what 'Deutschland uber alles' meant. "Germany over all" was the reply.

Bert commented:- "'You over Us' - You've got a bloody sauce, haven't you." Then he realised what he had said but it was too late. A strong argument ensued, but fortunately the German took the matter no further.

The Inspector went through the motions of trying to detect the culprits and in due course reported to the Bailiff that he had been unsuccessful.

As a result of receiving Fuerst von Oettingen's letter the Bailiff inserted a notice in La Gazette Officielle, which was to cause unprecedented resentment amongst the civilian population.

Reward of £25

"A reward of £25 will be given to the person who first gives the Inspector of Police information leading to the conviction of anyone not already discovered for the offence of marking on any gate, wall or other place whatsoever visible to the public the letter 'V', or any other sign or any word or words calculated to offend the German authorities or soldiers."

Victor Carey
Bailiff

The reward was never claimed, but the thought of selling out fellow Islanders to a ruthless enemy was repulsive to all, particularly to members of the Police Force. It was possible that this pronouncement by the Bailiff did more than anything else to bring about the desire of certain members of the Force to take more positive action against the Germans.

The Germans kept up the pressure, demanding reports, issuing threats and generally making life unpleasant for the Guernsey authorities and the civilian population. They required detailed reports on the parents of the seven children from the Castel school who had admitted involvement in the writing of 'V' signs. Then they required the children, their parents, Peter Girard, the Headmaster, and all the teachers, to attend at Castel School at 1.30pm on Saturday the 19th July. When assembled they were severely reprimanded by German officers, who also threatened severe punishments if the offences were repeated.

It was not long before there was a further 'outbreak' of 'V' for victory signs in the Island, this time in the Parish of St Martin.

On 23rd July 1941, the Feldkommandant complained that the letters 'EV' and 'V' had been found in four places. Inspector Sculpher went to St Martin and found the letters 'EV' on a German sign post at the corner of Rue Maze and Les Caches, on the granite wall in front of Beaulieu Hotel and on the road surface, 60 yards west of the hotel. On the gate pillar of Chertsey House, the letter 'V' had been written in black tar or bitumen. All the letters were, in the Inspector's opinion, very crudely done. While there he and the Deputy Inspector made enquiries around the district but without result.

After further enquiries the Deputy Inspector spoke to Osmond Queripel, of La Bellieuse, a States road employee, who told Mr Langmead:-

"I start work at 6.00am to light the tar boiler for the men to commence work at 7.00am. I left home immediately after the curfew at 6.00am and noticed that the marks were on the road and wall then. I saw no other person and I don't know whether anything has been touched at the road depot."

The States depot was situated at La Villette, about 300 yards to the west of the Beaulieu Hotel. Bitumen was prepared there for use on the roads. At night the depot was left open and the bitumen readily available to anyone.

The Deputy Inspector also spoke to William Vining, of Les Caches Terrace, which adjoins the Beaulieu Hotel, who said that he returned home at 10.45pm the previous night and that he saw no marking at that time.

Mr Sculpher consulted the States Road Engineer, Mr W.H.Broadhurst, and as a result came to the conclusion that the substance used to make the 'V' marks, was bitumen and that it came from the Depot.

Dr Reffler wrote to the Bailiff saying:-

"In one case a number sign of the German Army has been covered by the letters 'EV', what is considered as damaging an accessory of the German Army, which clearly corresponds to sabotage."

He added "The Island Police has not reported the perpetrator within the time limit of 24 hours. The population living in the district concerned and against whom suspicion falls in the first place, has to suffer for these deeds.

I request you to publish in the newspapers appearing tomorrow a notice to the population of the Island regarding the recent event and the way it is judged by the German army. It shall further be ordered, on behalf of the Feldkommandantur, that the wireless receiving sets of all persons living within a radius of 1,000 metres from the Beaulieu Hotel shall be given up to a place to be fixed by you by 6.00pm on the 26th July. I request you to submit the draft of the notice to me before sending same to the press. And also to take the necessary measures for the giving up of the sets.

I request you to report to me by noon on the 27th July on the completed taking over of the sets, the number of same and their place of storage."

The Bailiff immediately prepared a Notice and submitted it to Dr Reffler for approval. On the 25th July 1941 in La Gazette Officielle the Notice appeared, signed by Victor Carey.

"It has come to my notice that 'V' and 'EV' signs have been drawn in black at certain points along the Forest Road in the neighbourhood of the Beaulieu Hotel, on walls and on roadway and on a signboard of the German army. This matter is regarded very seriously and as an Act of Sabotage by the German Authorities. As the person or persons responsible for such acts have not given themselves up to the authorities the people in the vicinity of this district must be held responsible for these acts.

It is ordered by the German Feldkommandantur that the wireless receiving sets of all persons living within a radius of 1000 metres from the Beaulieu Hotel shall be surrendered not later than 6.00pm. on the 26th July, at the St Martin Air Rifle Club, Rue Maze."

461 Wireless sets were handed in and stored at the Club.

On the 25th the Germans also published a notice in the Press, restating the order to surrender wireless sets and additionally requiring men from St Martin to stand guard duty from 10.00pm to 6.00am at the 'besmirched' sign at the junction of Les Caches and Rue Maze and also at two other signs, at Les Cornus and the corner of La Villette and Forest Road.

Each sign was to be guarded by two men on a two-hour rota. Each man was issued with a pass which had to be returned to the St Martin Parish Hall the first thing on the morning following the duty. This procedure was another example of the German way of inconveniencing the local population in order to discourage other similar acts of defiance or as they viewed it - 'sabotage'.

Whilst the 'culprits' were never identified at the time, there is evidence that members of the Police Force were well aware of the availability of bitumen at the States Depot and were on patrol in the area during the night of 22/23rd July.

The Germans had acted predictably and when on the 29th July they discovered two apparently anti-German drawings pinned to a signpost at the junction of Maurepas Road and Fosse Andre. They demanded that the perpetrators be caught and identified by 10.00am on the 3rd of August. The deadline was later extended until the 5th August.

The drawings were of a British Tommy holding a flag with a plain 'V' on it and underneath was written - 'We don't want laurel leaves' - signifying that a plain 'V' stood for an English victory. The Germans had countered the Allied 'V' for victory campaign, with their own 'V' signs to which they had added laurel leaves.

The other drawing was of a Spitfire chasing a Messerschmitt 109 and in the corner was another Messerschmitt going down in flames. The pilot of the M.E.109 was saying 'Mein Gott another Victoria for the German Luftwaffe' and at the top of the drawing were the words 'German Air Squadron scores 700th Air Victory' Above the M.E.109, going down in flames was written 699th. This was, presumably, to show how the German communiques reversed their losses.

After the President of the Controlling Committee reported that the search for the culprits had been unsuccessful, Inspector Zachau, of the Feldgendarmerie, replied that "Although the intention of the unknown perpetrator was obviously to disparage the German army, the particular circumstances of this case do not call for punitive measures which would affect a large proportion of persons who had nothing to do with it. In order to prevent any recurrence of such a case the Feldkommandant has ordered that two inhabitants of St Peter Port should mount a guard of the sign post in question and two further sign posts from 10.00pm to 6.00am."

Whilst the identity of the artist was never officially established, Inspector Sculpher and the German Authorities were inclined to the view that he could have been a German prankster. The ink used was uncommon and not available locally. The word 'Victory' had been written as 'Victoria' and the letters in the word 'Luftwaffe' were written in the German style. Perhaps Inspector Zachau had doubts and that is why he did not carry out his threats of imposing punitive measures against the local population.

The guards were continued, both in St Peter Port and St Martin until the 18th August 1941, when the Germans cancelled their orders.

Within days of the Occupation the Germans had banned the holding of open air meetings and the wearing of uniforms by the Salvation Army. On the 26th July 1941 Mr Sculpher was called to Grange Lodge to see Inspector Zachau, who produced two letters from a Miss Ozanne of the Vale. In the letters she stated that the work of the Salvation Army must be continued and that a service would be held at the Salvation Army hall, Nocq Road, at 11.00am on the 27th July.

Miss Ozanne, who was present at Grange Lodge, was wearing a Salvation Army tunic with badges. Inspector Zachau requested her to refrain from wearing the uniform, but she refused. She asked to be placed in prison. Inspector Zachau asked Mr Sculpher to take her home and hand her over to her relatives. Her uniform, he instructed, was to be handed in to Grange Lodge immediately.

Miss Ozanne was taken home and her mother gave the Inspector two tunics and a Salvation Army bonnet which had been hidden. He took the articles to Grange Lodge and was given a receipt for them.

Mrs Ozanne told the Inspector that her daughter had been a Salvation Army officer in Belgium, but when the Island was occupied, she was at home suffering from influenza. Periodically she had stated that she was determined to ignore German orders and continue her work for the Salvation Army. It was clear to the Inspector that Miss Ozanne had strong convictions but was unwell. He advised her parents to take her for medical treatment.

It was well known to colleagues that PC 15 Bill Burton was having difficulty with his home life and that his wife, Lily, was un-supportive. Bill was a 'Copper' of the old school, who liked his lotion, often to excess.

At 6.25pm on the 5th August a call was received at the Station from Mrs Burton, who claimed that her husband was drunk and creating a disturbance in the house. Deputy Inspector Langmead and PC 16 Tuck went to Sandy Lane, L'Islet, where they were met by Mrs Burton. She complained about her husband and took them up to the bedroom where Bill Burton was in bed. Frank Tuck later commented:- "Bill was totally pickled, stripped to the waist and prattling away. His wife was panicking. There was a lot of domestic trouble due to drink."

Mr Langmead told him that in his opinion he was drunk and unfit for duty. He suspended him there and then and instructed him to report to Inspector Sculpher at noon the next day. Bill replied "Not me".

PC Burton was charged as a defaulter and fined 4 day's pay to be deducted from his wages over a period of four weeks, severely reprimanded and cautioned. In Frank Tuck's view "The 'old man' was very compassionate really and only fined him, it could so easily have been dismissal."

It was not long before Bill Burton was in further trouble. The following October he was fined two day's pay for striking Thomas Bougourd, his 72-year-old father-in-law, in the face. Mr Sculpher wrote to the President of the Police Committee and said that in his opinion PC Burton had been cautioned for the last time, next time it would be dismissal or resignation. However, he added "Domestic trouble - his wife is difficult". Mr W.E.Poat wrote on the bottom of the letter,"I fear that Burton will have to go."

Just after Christmas 1941 Bill Burton left home and went to live at Rougemont, St John's.

Bill Burton, was 45 and very much resented that he had not been allowed to join up to fight the Germans as he had done in the first war. He had been a bombardier in the Royal Artillery, serving in France and Belgium. He was demobilized in 1919 and joined the Police Force in March 1924. In many ways, he was the unofficial leader of the constables, in so much that he would encourage them to chivvy and hassle the Germans.

One night, well after curfew, Bill Burton was on duty with Fred Short. They were 'resting' out of sight, in the doorway of Boots when a German came up the Pollet, staggering all over the place. They were used to inebriated Germans coming out of the Royal Hotel and making their way through the town to their billets. In their condition, their boots striking the cobbles would cause sparks to fly all over the place, so that they would often be seen before they were heard.

This particular German was no exception and as he past them, Bill crept up behind the soldier and shoulder butted him straight down the North Pier Steps.

"Christ!" Fred exclaimed, "what do you think you are doing, there is blood coming out of his ears, what have you done Bill?"

"I would have killed the bastard if I could get away with it."

Bill and Fred went to the Station and told the Sergeant:-

"There is a German laying drunk in the North Pier Steps."

The Sergeant telephoned the Feldgendarmerie who sent two men to meet PCs Burton and Short where the German was lying. Then a German ambulance arrived and took the injured man to hospital.

The Germans gave the Constables a packet of cigarettes each, to thank them for helping their comrade. As the ambulance left, Fred Short turned to Bill Burton and said:- "Be careful Bill, that can't happen too many times before they rumble it."

The Old Government House Hotel, known locally as the O.G.H., had been taken over by the Germans and was used as a Soldatenheime, a type of residential military club. On one occasion a party of German Naval men, who were staying there, attended a celebration party at the Hotel de Normandie.

When they left the party at around midnight to return to the O.G.H. many of them were so drunk that they had difficulty in standing up, far less walking.

Their way back to the O.G.H. was past the Police Station. After enjoying the spectacle for a time the Station Sergeant instructed three or four Constables to assist those Germans who were obviously incapable, to get back to the O.G.H. One of the entrances to the hotel was by way of a steep flight of marble steps. PC 15 Burton and PC 30 Short and two other Constables set about dragging those Germans who were out for the count, along the road and up the flight of steps.

When one of the Germans had been dragged to the top of the steps, Bill Burton said to his colleagues:- "Just hold him up a bit". Then he punched him in the face and the German fell right down the steps again. Bill Burton said as he hit him:- "There, take that one for my son who is in the Royal Artillery."

Then together they carried another victim to the top of the steps and Bill repeated the procedure. "This is for my nephew in Cameron Highlanders" and then another for a nephew in the Hampshire Regiment. Each time they would fall back down the steep marble steps and by the time they were finally 'delivered' to the O.G.H. the Germans were all covered in blood.

Fred Short later recalled the incident:- "The German nurses in the Hotel made a fuss of us for bringing them in and made a collection for us. They gave us a pile of Reichmarks, two or three bottles of Aniseed Brandy and we finished up with cartons of cigarettes. All for taking back these drunks after we had already thrown them down the marble stairs. On going back to the station, the Sergeant, spying our booty, asked - what the hell have you got there?"

For some reason the Germans were getting very touchy towards the end of July 1941, in respect of the possible presence of escaped prisoners of war and parachutists. Inspector Zachau wrote to the Bailiff on the 31st July in respect of the Order regarding 'Protection against Acts of Sabotage' dated 10th October 1940.

"In view of the possibility of the landing of enemy aircraft and parachutists, it is necessary to remind the population of the Order as well as of the punishments provided therein.

I am enclosing the draft of an Important Notice, which you are requested to publish over your own signature in the daily press.

In this connection, I request you to instruct the Police to the following effect:-

It is the duty of all Police officials to report at once to the Standortkommandantur at the Albion Hotel, whenever the presence of escaped prisoners of war or the landing of enemy aircraft or parachutists come to their notice. In the later case, the landing place, time and number of the landing force are to be reported. Failure to report will lead to punishment under the Order in question."

The enclosed draft of the 'Important Notice' read:-

'Important Notice'.

Attention is called to the fact that, under the Order relative to Protection against Acts of Sabotage, dated October 10th 1940, any person who hides or shelters escaped prisoners of war shall be punished with death. The same applies for the hiding or sheltering of members of enemy Forces (for instance crews of landing aircraft, parachutists etc.) Anyone lending assistance to such persons in their escape is also liable to the death sentence.

(signature of Bailiff)

The Bailiff informed Mr Sculpher immediately of the section of the letter which concerned the Police Force. Normally the Bailiff would have ensured that the Press Notice would have been inserted in the next edition of the *Star* or the *Evening Press*. In this instance it is significant that the 'Important Notice' did not appear until the 11th August, eleven days later. When the notice appeared it caused a flood of criticism to be levelled against the Bailiff for putting his signature to a notice describing the British as 'enemy Forces'.

The unusually long delay in publication almost certainly indicated that the Bailiff was reluctant to put his name to the proposed text supplied by Inspector Zachau and that he only did so in the end as a result of an ultimatum or very strong pressure. The judgement made over the years of meek acquiescence by the Bailiff, is clearly wrong.

When the 'Important Notice' finally appeared, it read:-

"I am requested by the Feldkommandant to draw attention to the fact that under the Order relative to Protection against Acts of Sabotage, dated October 10th 1940, any person who hides or shelters escaped prisoners of war shall be punished with death. The same applies for the hiding or sheltering of members of enemy Forces (for instance crews of landing aircraft, parachutists etc.) Anyone lending assistance to such persons in their escape is also liable to the death sentence.

Victor G.Carey,
Bailiff
Royal Court House
August 9th 1941"

# Chapter 11

# ALDERNEY PLUNDER

Ever since a token force of Germans landed in Alderney on the 2nd July 1940, there had been persistent rumours of looting and plundering having taken place in that Island. Apparently looting started within hours of the Island being evacuated and continued up to and after the Germans arrived. The Germans denied that their forces were in any way to blame, but locals, both in Alderney and Guernsey, preferred to put the responsibility on the invaders.

On the 23rd June 1940, between 7.00am and noon, the greater part of the population of Alderney left the Island and sailed to England leaving only about a dozen civilians on the Island. At about 4.00pm the same day, a lifeboat from Cap de Hague arrived in the harbour with 5 or 6 French and 1 Alderney fishermen. One of the civilians who remained, was Mrs Elizabeth Pope, was told by the fisherman that the party was going to stay over night and leave the next morning for England.

During their overnight stay the French fishermen smashed the glass door of Bucktrouts, in Victoria Street, and 'provided' themselves with tobacco and cigarettes for their journey to England.

Mrs Pope, later recalling the events, said:-

"On the following day, the 25th June, at about 11.00am, a party of Guernsey workmen arrived in Alderney. They had with them ropes and hunting guns. About one hour later 10 or twelve men in Red Cross uniforms came to my house and told me that they wanted to take me to Guernsey. I told them I did not wish to leave the Island, whereupon one of the men told me that if I did not, they would force me to do so. The same man, I cannot tell you his name, told me that he had orders to take all the cattle, or kill them.

Some time later I saw several men from the Red Cross in a clothing shop, choosing things for themselves to take away from the Island. I asked them whether they had permission to do so, they replied that if they did not appropriate the things, the Germans would. I saw the men from the Red Cross in Martin's clothes shop and Bichard's, the gold and silversmiths. In these shops the men had thrown everything that was of no use or interest to them, topsy-turvy.

In the afternoon of the 26th June, at about 4.00pm I left the Island with some of the Red Cross men. They had several large parcels and trunks with them in which I believe were linen, clothes and other goods they appropriated while pilfering.

On the 24th July I returned to Alderney with my husband, my mother and my children. Before I left the Island I had locked my house but when we returned the kitchen window was open, the window of the sitting room was broken and the back entrance door had been forced open. In the house everything was thrown about and acid had been poured over the furniture. Almost all the houses which I saw had their windows broken and all the shops were forced open and their contents were strewn about the streets."

After the evacuation of Alderney and prior to the Germans arriving, a Guernsey pioneer party under the command of Peter Mahy, a member of the Royal Guernsey Agricultural and Horticultural Society, was sent to the Island to rescue the remaining inhabitants and round up cattle for shipment to Guernsey. A Red Cross unit of about 10 or 12 men led by Fredrick Bush also arrived from Guernsey. These were the men referred to by Mrs Pope.

Peter Mahy had been given a list of eight persons who were said to have remained in the Island, but they actually found 12, including 4 children.

During the two and a half days the party were on the Island 400 head of cattle, 21 horses and a number of pigs were shipped to Guernsey. Besides the calves, most of the dogs, a few of the cats and a number of horses, which were too old to be of any use or were diseased, were also shot.

Peter Mahy later acknowledged that some pillaging may have taken place, but that it could not have been on any great scale as his men were kept busy from morning till night.

When the last of the Guernsey pioneer party left Alderney on the 28th June 1940, James Rutter and Frank Oselton accompanied them. Rutter, who had married late in life, went to 'Capon Farm' Castel Hill, where his wife Annetta lived and took with him three large trunks.

On the 20th July, almost three weeks after the Germans arrived, a party of 20 specially selected Guernseymen travelled to Alderney, in the motor yacht, White Heather. Their job was to recover the early potato crop, salvage stores and generally clean up the Island.

Frank Oselton also returned to Alderney with the party and a few days later Mr and Mrs George Pope, their children and James Rutter joined them.

James Rutter, on his return from Guernsey, greeted German soldiers very affably. He claimed that his name was Ritter, meaning Knight, a name commonly found in Germany. Rutter, the recipient of a 30/- a week pension from H.M. Government in respect of his service in the Royal Navy, informed the Germans that he disliked the British to such an extent that he would personally cut the throats of any Englishman who attempted to land in Alderney.

By the following April, Charles Hutchesson had taken over as Civil Commandant in Alderney. He kept in contact with members of the Controlling Committee, by letter, and on the 15th April informed them:- "Sonderfuehrer Herzog found fit whilst he was here to walk into the Grand Hotel and go into all the men's bedrooms, also my downstairs rooms and going through the drawers. He did not ask anyone for permission. I consider that this rather jeopardises my position and was taken badly by the men."

Clearly this was the incident referred to later by the Germans when they claimed that the lodgings of the Guernsey party were searched and a number of workmen were found to have goods which they could not account for and that those goods were confiscated.

Whether it was that search or the fact that rumour was rife about looting and plundering in Alderney, that caused an investigation to be undertaken, is unclear. What is clear, however, is that Sergeant Major Oeser was given the task of investigating the allegations of looting and plundering and as a result ten civilians were charged on the 30th April, two more on the 5th May and a thirteenth on May 8th 1941.

In an effort to establish the facts Sergeant Major Oeser thoroughly questioned those inhabitants who had chosen to remain in Alderney and their houses were rigorously searched.

The home of James Rutter, in Victoria Street, was found to be crammed with allegedly stolen and looted property. He told the searchers that they had surprised him on his spring cleaning day. In the house and adjoining shed the

Germans found amazing quantities of foodstuff, cleaning material, dishes, cutlery, clothing, linen, furniture, utensils and electrical goods, all in a total state of confusion. In some parts of the house it was almost impossible to move because of the vast quantity of goods.

A large proportion of the goods were useless as far as Rutter's personal needs were concerned. There was a tailor's dummy, ladies' clothing, ladies' underwear, 69 shirts, 29 waistcoats, 99 ties, 99 pillow cases, 44 chairs, 20 tables, 77 carpets, 13 clocks and 176 curtains. Coffee, tea, jam and soap were hidden between linen. Parts of the vast stock of items had been affected by rats and mice. Numerous carpets had been laid one over the other on the floor with the consequence that doors could not be opened. Despite the obvious conclusion, Rutter claimed that each and every item belonged to him.

Naturally, Rutter became a prime suspect and was soon arrested and transferred to prison in Guernsey. The twelve other men charged with stealing and plundering in Alderney between 23rd June 1940 and April 1941 were:-

Charles F.Hutchesson.
William Thomas Oliver.
Douglas George Rihoy.
Arthur Torode.
Walter John Guille.
Clifford Julias Bichard.
Alfred John de Jersey.
Graham Walter Buckingham.
Neville John Brouard.
Brian Hugh O'Hurley.
Sidney Herbert Batchelor.
Ernest Vincent Clark.

Sergeant Major Oeser systematically carried out interviews and collected evidence. James Rutter was later to complain to Mr Sculpher that "The German Sergeant Major questioned and bullied me. He told me I was a liar and I said, so are you."

As the alleged pilfering was carried out by civilians to the prejudice of British subjects, the Germans decided that the case should be handed over to the Guernsey authorities to prosecute. On the May 20th 1941 Mr Sculpher was asked by H.M.Solicitor General to take over the investigation. He read all the papers and interviewed James Rutter who was still being held in prison.

**James Rutter.**

Rutter, a elderly man with snowy white hair, a voluminous beard and a healthy pinkish complexion, which fitted his alert appearance, stoutly denied any accusation of plundering or stealing. Born at Sudbury in England, he spent some time in India before going to Jersey to pursue his profession as a foot specialist. In 1939 he arrived in Alderney and set up a chiropodist practice in Victoria Street.

The Inspector felt that it would be difficult to prove a charge of stealing and receiving, as Rutter claimed that he had been given a permit by the German Commandant to enter other people's houses. When he returned to Alderney in July, he told the Commandant that a good many of his possessions were missing and asked if he could replace them. The Commandant, according to Rutter, had said "I do not see why not" and gave him a permit. He admitted that he went to a few houses with his wheelbarrow and collected a few things.

The Inspector did, however, advise the Solicitor General that he thought that a charge of plundering under the German Orders of 10th December 1940 would be more likely to succeed.

When the Inspector visited Mrs Rutter at her home, she did not know that her husband was held in prison. She explained that their life was not normal and that he said very little about his business. She had, she said, heard a rumour that he was in trouble with the Germans.

At the house the Inspector found the three large trunks which James Rutter had brought back from Alderney on the night of the German air raid. He found that they contained a large quantity of clothing and medical supplies.

Two shop assistants, Mr Luscombe and Miss D.M.Riley, who were employed by James Mourant at his High Street shop in Guernsey, were requested by the Inspector to inspect the goods found at Rutter's home. They identified a large number of the articles as belonging to Mr Mourant and coming from his Alderney shop which had been forcibly entered.

The Inspector and Sergeant Banneville again interviewed Rutter in prison and produced a list of articles found at his Guernsey house. Certain items were read out and Rutter was asked if he could explain them. He said:-

"I bought the cotton wool and bandages at different places. The eau de Cologne I bought in Jersey, I cannot say the price. I bought the two mincers, about 4/6d. The finger stalls I got from Miss Taylor. Miss de Feu, from Jersey, gave me two table cloths. The white coat is mine. The ladies' handbags must have belonged to people who stayed at my house. A lady visitor must have left the mackintosh. I picked up the brushes on the battlefield during the last war. I bought the batteries in London. I bought the trousers, some in Jersey, some in Guernsey, for my own use. I cannot say the date, about 10/- a pair."

The Inspector pointed out that the trousers would fit a man 6 feet tall.

Rutter replied:- "The trousers are too long, I used to turn them up."

In view of this new evidence Mr Sculpher wrote to Mr Ridgway, H.M.Solicitor General, suggesting that James Rutter be charged with shopbreaking, stealing and receiving stolen property. Sergeant Major Oeser also continued the search of Rutter's house in Alderney. A number of lists of the goods were produced, running to hundreds of items. Oeser wrote:-

"In the house of Rutter, Victoria Street, such large quantities of linen, clothes, curtains and similar goods were heaped up, that it could be assumed that these goods cannot all be his property. Not only the quantity of the things, but also the manner in which they were taken care of, pointed clearly to the fact. Carpets, for instance, were heaped two or three on top of the other, men's suits and linen lay in heaps on the beds and silver articles were hidden in the beds. For this reason an accurate inventory was made of Rutter's house."

The other twelve accused were charged with stealing from various shops and plundering goods in Alderney between the 23rd June and April 1941. They all pleaded Not Guilty.

The Germans made two lists, the first of property, such as clothing, linen and general articles and the other of items of food and perishable goods. The food was sequestrated and the house and contents was put in order by members of the civilian working party and then sealed by the Feldgendarmerie. Eventually on the 23rd September 1941, Rutter and the 12 other accused came before the Magistrate in the Police Court.

James Alfred Rutter, born on 9th March 1875, a foot specialist of Victoria Street, Alderney, was charged with:-

'Breaking and entering a shop in Victoria Street, Alderney, between 23rd and 29th June 1940 and stealing therein a quantity of goods mostly of men's wear valued together at £22, this being the property of James Mourant, of High Street, Guernsey. Also with feloniously receiving the property, well knowing it to have been stolen.'

He was further charged with 'breaking and entering a number of shops and houses in Alderney between 23rd June 1940 and May 1941 and stealing therein a vast quantity of goods, value unknown, the property of persons unknown'. He was also 'charged with plundering in Alderney contrary to orders issued by the German Commandant'.

The full list of the alleged stolen goods filled 13 typed pages and contained over 320 articles.

"False" was the way Rutter described the first charge.

"I had permission to go into the other houses, I was to feed fowls and cats left behind." He pleaded not guilty.

The third set of charges he denied,

"I had permission in writing to go in." he said. He also denied the plundering charge.

On Friday 10th October when the Court assembled the well of the Court was cluttered with goods. The Inspector and the Solicitor General were seated behind a barricade of wood and cardboard boxes topped by a large radio set. On the press reporter's table were two large bales of clothing, new and second hand.

Proceedings had just commenced when Fuerst von Oettingen and Lieutenant Goettmann, the German press censor, entered the Court. Sergeant Major Oeser was also present.

Soon after, the Court was cleared and the cases continued in camera.

The following week James Rutter made an application to the Magistrate, for his release from prison where he had been held since the end of April. Rutter failed to appear when called and H.M.Sheriff was despatched to the prison to ascertain the cause of the delay. He returned 10 minutes latter to announce that Rutter would be along shortly. When he eventually appeared he said:- "Very sorry I have been detaining you, I was taking a bath." In making his apology, Rutter added:- "Why should I be kept in prison, I have done nothing wrong. Why have I been kept locked up for 6 months. I could have been gardening, I have got a large garden."

When asked by the Magistrate where he lived in Guernsey, he replied "Castel Hill, I am on the telephone, call me any time you like." The application, for Rutter's release, was not opposed. He was sworn not to leave the Island and to report to the Police on Tuesdays, Thursdays and Saturdays.

After the Court had adjourned on the 10th October, the Germans, without informing the Guernsey Authorities, held a sitting of the Military Tribunal of the Feldkommandantur 515. Sergeant Major Oeser gave evidence to the Judge, Dr Gunkel in the form of a written statement, about enquiries that he had made in relation to the cases:-

"The evidence of the accused comes from me. Except for the workmen Guille, Rihoy, Batchelor, Clark and Rutter, all the accused have admitted having taken the goods, included in the lists, from abandoned houses of Alderney to their hotel. Except Rihoy, all have admitted that they knew it was forbidden to take any objects from abandoned houses. I have taken the evidence with special care and completeness. At the end of each questioning, each workman was asked whether he had understood everything and whether he wished to add or alter anything. They only had to sign after they had been thoroughly warned. None of them availed themselves of the opportunity of altering their declarations. Should any of them happen to declare that he did not know where the goods came from, it would certainly be an untruth, as all of them, with the above mentioned exceptions, admitted that they had taken the objects away themselves.

The accused cannot maintain either that they did not know that they were not allowed to take the goods from the houses, for according to their own statements the prohibition to take the goods away was known to them. After the report of the 30th April 1941 had been sent, one of the workmen gave me the notice which I now submit to the Court. This notice originates from the Grand Hotel, Alderney, and contains the prohibition to enter houses and to take any civilian property.

The workman, Douglas George Rihoy, on being questioned, stated that he had known nothing of the prohibition to enter houses and take goods from them. It can be objected that the workmen must have talked about these measures between themselves. It is practically impossible that Rihoy could have acted unwittingly. The notice produced is also a contradiction with this statement.

Although Rihoy refused to sign the statement, I can assert on oath that he has stated everything that is contained in the recorded evidence. He only refused to sign because the record was written only in German.

I can assure that the accused Batchelor, Clark and Rutter have stated exactly what I have recorded. In the event of further questions arising in the course of the proceedings, I am ready to make further declarations and request that any further questions are put to me.

Read, approved and signed by,
Franz Heinrich Oeser."

The Germans had become totally dissatisfied with the slow progress the Guernsey Authorities had made in bringing the trial to a conclusion. The cases had been handed over by them to H.M.Solicitor General on the 21st May and the matter had not been pursued, in their view, with the necessary energy and speed. Practically nothing had happened during the period from June to September, so they therefore considered it appropriate that the German Judicial Authority should take the matter into its hands and proceed with the trial.

The Germans were concerned that they would be trying persons for offences which had been committed before they had occupied Alderney. They were advised that under Article 41 of the Hague Convention, the occupying power had not only the right, but was under the obligation of maintaining law and order, regardless of whether the crimes had been committed before or after the date of occupation. Accordingly the Germans deemed that the Military Tribunal was competent to adjudicate on the cases.

**G.J.P.Ridgway.**

On the 24th October 1941 G.J.P.Ridgway, the Solicitor General, was informed that as no guarantees could be given by the Guernsey Authorities that the trial would be quickly concluded, the Germans had decided to take over the prosecution and had set up a Military Tribunal.

When Mr Sculpher heard that the Germans were taking over the prosecution, he commented to a colleague:- "They are more concerned with the honour of the German army than with justice. Their aim is to 'prove' that the German troops had nothing to do with the plundering in Alderney - which is blatantly untrue."

In order to publicly 'expose' the inefficiency of the Guernsey Authorities and emphasise their competence, the trial before the Military Tribunal of the Feldkommandantur 515, was set for the following day the 25th October 1941.

The case against Rutter was commenced on the Saturday, at 9.30am and continued on Monday and Tuesday until 1.30pm. The verdict and sentence of 12 months imprisonment was announced by the Judge at 4.00pm that afternoon.

Of the rest of the accused, six of the men were found guilty and six acquitted. The sentences ranged from 3 weeks to 2 months.

| | |
|---|---|
| Charles F.Hutchesson | 2 months. |
| William Thomas Oliver | 2 months. |
| Douglas George Rihoy | 1 month. |
| Walter John Guille | 1 month. |
| Clifford Julias Bichard | 1 month. |
| Arthur Torode | 1 month. |

Those acquitted were:-
Alfred John de Jersey.
Graham Walter Buckingham.
Neville John Brouard.
Brian Hugh O'Hurley.
Sidney Herbert Batchelor.
Ernest Vincent Clark.

Rutter's sentence was reduced by Colonel Knackfuss, to 9 months due to the time he had been held in prison awaiting trial and Arthur Torode's reduced to 3 weeks as he had freely admitted his part in the thefts.

During his trial Rutter adopted an air of absolute innocence and was adamant in his not guilty plea. Even towards the end of the trial when his case was clearly hopeless, he still persisted in his denials. Evidence was given by Sergeant Major Oeser, Inspector Sculpher, Sergeant Banneville, Constable Plevin, Alfred Erich Roseman, a custom official, Frank Oselton, George Pope, Daphne Pope, Violet Gordon, Frederick W. Bush, Mrs Rutter and Peter Mahy.

The Tribunal was held under the presidency of Dr Peyrer Von Heimstaedt. Advocate J E L Martel, who had appeared in the initial proceedings, appeared again for the men in the German Court. He spent a considerable time trying to explain aspects of the English and local law to the German judiciary.

Some of the accused men were not convicted of plundering but were found guilty of theft. The German Court realised that the order concerning plundering issued by the Military Commander in France did not come into force until 15th November 1940 and the alleged plundering had taken place 3 months previously. The men were then alternatively charged with persistent theft and convicted of that charge.

One of the most telling pieces of evidence concerned a pair of ladies' shoes. 20 pairs had been found in Rutter's procession, he claimed they were used for orthopaedic purposes. Expert evidence was given by Charles Purdy, a partner in the firm of Purdy Bros, of the Pollet. They also had a shop in Alderney. Mr Purdy told the Tribunal that the shoes found on Rutter's premises were only ordinary ladies' shoes, among them were two shoes which only fitted a left foot.

He told the Tribunal that stock from their Alderney shop had been returned to Guernsey. From this stock he had sold a pair of ladies' shoes to a German soldier. Some time later the soldier returned the shoes saying he had sent the shoes to Germany where it was discovered the shoes were both for the right foot. The conclusion was obvious.

James Rutter, if anything, was an obstinate opportunist, who was unable to tell the truth and in many ways a nuisance even to himself. After the evacuation of Alderney took place in June 1940, he witnessed the crews of visiting ships, both French and local, helping themselves to stocks of every description from shops and the contents of abandoned houses. Like everyone else he realised that what they did not take was going to be readily available to the Germans when they arrived.

James Rutter saw it as a 'me or them' situation and he certainly did not want the Germans to have the benefits. Inevitably he was swept along by the wave of pilfering that was taking place and was greedy to an extreme. He did not have sufficient time to transport his spoils to his home in Guernsey. The twelve other men probably did no more than anyone would have done in the circumstances, but they were caught and six of them convicted.

The Germans, with their control of the local press, were extremely successful in pinning the blame for the undoubted wave of looting and plundering which took place both before and after they occupied Alderney, on Rutter and the other civilians. Their objective was to show, as they put it, 'That it was thus indisputably proved that the German troops had nothing to do with the plundering in Alderney.'

# Chapter 12

## CAN YOU MAKE IT 12/6

On the 12th August 1941 Mrs Beer, of Doyle Terrace, reported to Station Sergeant that two old ladies were locked in Candie Cemetery. Sergeant Le Lievre after failing to contact the caretaker of the Cemetery, who was responsible for padlocking the gates at closing time, approached Mr A.C.Bird, a builder and general maintenance man and together they went to Candie Cemetery. The Sergeant spoke through the railings to the two ladies, one of whom was in a wheel chair. Realising that there was no alternative, Sergeant Le Lievre authorised Mr Bird to cut through the padlock and in a truly gentlemanly manner saw the two ladies home.

From time to time the Germans at Grange Lodge showed the Inspector letters they had received from civilians, usually anonymous, either informing on a fellow Islander or on occasions praising the occupying forces. One letter, signed by 'Well-Wisher', particularly annoyed him.

"Dear Dr Reffler,

Just a few lines to tell you what I think of German soldiers. They are a wonderful lot of men and I admire them - so well behaved and so very happy; when I go to the German pictures I always feel I would like to say to them, 'Gute Nacht lieber Deutsche Soldat etc etc'.

Also it is a good thing to have them billeted on private people, make civilians realize that the German soldier is a fine fellow, worthy of love and respect. From Well-Wisher."

The German military Commandant in France issued an Order on the 13th August 1941 regarding the confiscation of wireless sets belonging to Jews. Fuerst von Oettingen wrote to the Bailiff stating the Order must either be published in German and English and registered, or communicated to all Jews by individual notification. The Bailiff chose to notify the four Jews in the Island individually.

Auguste Spitz and Therese Steiner were seen at the Emergency Hospital, Mrs Brouard, at 'Electra', Belmont Road, and Mrs Duquemin, at the Cobo Post Office. The Inspector reported to the Bailiff that each had assured him that they did not possess a wireless set. The Bailiff in turn informed Fuerst von Oettingen.

During the war Switzerland acted as the British Protecting Power and conveyed messages between the two belligerent Governments. In mid September 1941 the Germans informed the Swiss Minister that the British Foreign Office should be aware that they intended to deport and intern a number of British subjects residing in the Channel Islands if German nationals in Iran were interned.

On the 16th September the British Secretary of State for Foreign Affairs informed the Swiss Minister that the two cases were in no way parallel. 'On one hand a number of male Germans, with specialised knowledge and qualifications, had left Germany to take up temporary residence in neutral Iran, with the object of carrying out illegal activities directly calculated to undermine the integrity and independence of a neutral country and further the war aims of the German Government. The British Government had therefore taken such legitimate steps as were open to them to prevent the continuance of the flagrant abuse of neutral territory. No men over military age were interned, women and children were allowed to return to Germany unless they wished to stay with their men.

On the other hand the Germans were proposing to deport innocent and non-combatant British subjects from their permanent homes. The Hague Regulations conferred no right to deport or intern inhabitants of a territory which was under temporary military occupation. There had been no suggestion that the presence of these British subjects living in their own homes constituted any danger to the German military forces, nor that they had in any way been engaged in activities which would justify deportation or internment'. The Swiss Minister was further informed that the British Government could only regard any deportations as unjustifiable and illegal.

The German Authorities required a list to be supplied to them by the end of September, of men between the ages of 18 and 45. John Leale, knowing nothing of the arms length 'discussions' between the British and German Governments, reported to the Controlling Committee that according to the German Commandant it was possible that 1,200 men could be deported to Germany.

Then the Germans required further lists to be prepared, of persons who were considered essential or key persons. The Inspector listed four members of the Force, as 'key' men, essential for the maintenance of law and order;

Inspector W.R.Sculpher
Deputy Inspector A.J.Langmead
Detective Sergeant F.J.Banneville
Clerk Sergeant A.P.Lamy.

John Leale also submitted a list of names of aliens who were considered 'key' persons. The list included Therese Steiner, a nurse, who had previously identified herself as a Jew and Marianne Grunfeld, a Polish agriculture worker. Whether Miss Grunfeld had been identified as a Jew at that time, is unclear.

Whilst the Germans spent some time checking and rechecking the various lists, no further orders were issued and the deportation of Islanders was apparently shelved.

In September the Tribunal of Feldkommandantur sentenced Mrs Winifred Green to 6 months imprisonment 'for spreading anti German information'. Thirty-six-year-old Mrs Green lived at 'Psycho' in the Canichers and worked at the nearby Royal Hotel. A feud developed between her and and the hotel's Swiss chef, who was very pro German. He would greet her with;- "Good morning Mrs Green, Heil Hitler."

"Good morning Chef, Heil Churchill" was her response.

Eventually the Swiss chef reported Mrs Green to the German authorities and she was arrested, convicted and deported to France where she served her sentence in Caen jail. Inspector Sculpher was, as usual, notified and required to enter the conviction and sentence in the Police Register.

When Mrs Green had served four months of her sentence the Germans reviewed her case and announced:-

"In the case of Mrs Winifred Elizabeth Green, the further execution of the sentence is postponed, in amendment of the execution decision of the 16th September 1941, until the end of the state of hostilities, provided that the prisoner behaves in a perfect manner in relation to troops of occupation and gives no rise to prosecution in future.

The suspension of sentence comes into effect on the 31st January 1942 at 12 o'clock midnight."

Mrs Green was released and returned to the Island.

Fuerst von Oettingen issued an Order that the members of the Police Force were required to salute all German officers. Failure to do so would result in the Police officer being punished. This directive was very much resented by the Force and they all determined to avoid saluting Germans if at all possible, although they realised that at times the distasteful chore could not be escaped. Fuerst von Oettingen took pleasure in causing the Force as much embarrassment as possible. He was strongly anti British and took a delight in making things difficult.

On the 23rd September he wrote to the President of the Controlling Committee complaining that a Constable failed to salute a German officer in the High Street. The Inspector investigated and reported:-

"I beg to report that I have seen Policeman PC 34 E.Le Lievre, who states that there were several German soldiers in High Street at this time and he did not see the German officer until addressed by him - this is possible. The question that arises is why did not the Policeman see the German officer? The only answer seems to be that he was day dreaming, seeing that he had been out since 5.15am that morning. This I must regard as inattention to duty.

This Policeman was one of the men detailed to drive Dr Lanz from the commencement of the occupation for about six months. He is familiar with German officers and would not wilfully ignore one. I have severely reprimanded and cautioned him for inattention. I have also instructed all Police respecting their duty on this question."

It was not long before Fuerst von Oettingen was once more complaining to the President of the Controlling Committee that "Again another English Policeman failed to salute two officers of the Luftwaffe as prescribed. I repeat that such a behaviour towards German officers and German officials ranking as officers, will not be tolerated. In case of recurrence you can expect strong measures. The Policeman is not merely to be warned, but actually punished, the action taken being reported to me without delay."

Again Mr Sculpher carried out a sympathetic investigation. This time he replied:-

"Police Discipline.

Referring to the letter dated 13th October 1941, from Fuerst von Oettingen, Rittmeister, complaining of a Police officer failing to salute German officers on 5th October.

I beg to report that I have interrogated PC 32 Pugh, who states that at 3.10pm Sunday 5th October he was on duty at the Weighbridge and standing about four feet from the German guard. The Constable was looking away from the harbour, when he heard the guard click his heels and on looking round a small saloon car containing two German officers was passing at about 15 mph. The car stopped outside the guard room on the opposite side of the road, it was then that the Constable saw that the car contained officers. One of the officers walked towards the Constable, who went to him and saluted. The officer asked why he had not saluted him. The Constable explained that he had not seen who it was in the car, but this was not accepted.

I am satisfied that the Constable did not see the officers, but he should have done. If the guard can, the Policeman should, therefore he was not paying the attention demanded of his position. In these circumstance, I have fined the

Constable 2/6 and severely reprimanded and cautioned him. I have also again drawn the attention of all Police to their obligation in this respect."

The Inspector wrote to Mr Poat, the President of the Police Committee, enclosing a copy of his report to the President of the Controlling Committee, commenting that in view of the complaint from Fuerst von Oettingen, his decision to only fine PC Pugh 2/6 may not be accepted. Mr Poat wrote on the bottom of the Inspector's letter:-

"I fear that the German Authorities will not be satisfied with a 2/6 fine, can you make it 12/6 ?"

PC Harry Pugh paid his 2/6 fine, which was no doubt quietly reimbursed.

The twelve Special Constables who were employed on full time day duties were, from time to time, allocated the duty of checking cyclists and their lights. By this time in the occupation replacement batteries were unobtainable. Cyclists with dynamo lighting had no problem, but there were comparatively few of these sets in use. Despite the difficulties the Police regularly carried out checks on cyclists on the main roads. These purges inevitably led to appearances in Court for those unlucky enough to be caught.

One evening, just before curfew, Special Constables A3 Frank Langford, A1 Herbert Champion and A6 Cyril Petit were detailed to carry our checks on cyclists at Glategny Esplanade and the Longstore. They had a good haul and each offending cyclist was fined 5/- by the Magistrate. One cyclist, Henry G.Ingrouille, told Cyril Petit, who had stopped him, "I'll have you for this, I'll see you after Court". When Inspector Sculpher addressed the Magistrate he mentioned the threat, to which Henry Ingrouille muttered "I might have said something". The Magistrate, Quertier Le Pelley, advised him to "Control yourself".

PC 22 Kingston Bailey took a morbid delight in the discovery of the body of a German N.C.O. washed up at Portelet Bay, Torteval, on the 27th October 1941. He was naturally sad to see anyone lose their life, but was delighted that it was an airman with his parachute harness still strapped to his body. That meant that another German aircraft had been destroyed and one of their pilots lost. The body, which had obviously been in the sea for about two months, still displayed two Iron Crosses. With the Constable's help, the body was removed to the Victoria Hospital by the St John Ambulance.

As a result of the evacuation in 1940, so many children had left the Island that the infants' school room at Les Adams, St Peter, was unused. The Rev B.J.R.Guille offered the room to Police, for use as a sub Station for the Special Constabulary, at a rent of £1 a year. The Deputy Inspector from time to time called at the sub station as part of his patrol. On the 29th October 1941 he found that the premises had been entered and the anthracite stove and fittings were missing. The thieves had had also taken the iron coal scuttle. An attempt had been made to remove the telephone and in consequence it was out of order.

Mr Langmead made enquiries in the neighbourhood and Miss Florence Sarre, told him that she had seen German soldiers at the sub Station the previous evening. Inspector Sculpher made a report, a copy of which went to the German authorities. As usual the Germans were unconcerned and the stove no doubt provided some of their troops with warmth while the supplies of fuel held out.

Former Parish Constable and Douzenier, Ernest A.Brouard was standing by his kitchen window reading a letter, when a shot rang out and Ernest fell to the floor mortally wounded. A German under officer, Philipp Kuhn, who was billeted with the Brouards, was in his room above the kitchen cleaning his automatic pistol. As he removed the magazine, which was stiff, the pistol accidentally fired. The bullet went through the sofa, the floorboards and the ceiling, into the kitchen, hitting Mr Brouard in the shoulder and passed down through his body into his chest.

Sergeant Le Lievre received the telephone call reporting the tragedy and went to the Brouard farmhouse at Le Carrefour, St Andrew. He saw the body, which had been bleeding from the mouth. Dr Sutcliffe arrived and after certifying death, ordered the removal of the body to the Town mortuary. German officers of the Feldgendarmerie arrived and 'took charge' of Unteroffizier Kuhn.

An Inquest was held in the Coroner's Court on the 5th November 1941 and concluded that Mr Brouard's death was a 'pure accident.'

The German troops were, particularly early in the occupation, well disciplined. There were however, incidents which caused the local population concern and distress. On the 20th November 1941 Mr Sculpher reported to the President of the Controlling Committee incidents of alleged assault which took place at Rectory Hill.

A 22-year-old woman, Miriam was walking alone up Rectory Hill at about 4.50pm on Sunday 16th November when a German soldier ran past her. He stopped near Hospital Lane and as Miriam walked past, he caught hold of her right thigh and waist. Miriam later recounted:- "I turned around and he let go and went into the field. I turned around to see if he was following, he then exposed himself to me. I could see his 'person' quite distinctly. He had both hands on his 'person'. When he caught hold of my thigh, his hand was under my dress and between my legs. He did not speak, neither did I. I later reported the incident to the Rector. A Mr White, who lives in Foote's Lane, was behind me. I was not injured."

Miriam gave a description, age about 25, height 5'2", complexion and fair hair, rather red face, thick eyebrows, green uniform with cap.

Harold White confirmed the incident and described how he had seen the soldier put his hand up her clothes. "I shouted at him, I was about 50 yards away. He then ran back into the field. I went to Miriam, who seemed very distressed."

Another young lady, Daphne, was at about the same time walking up Rectory Hill with her friend Gwen. They had just passed the Rectory, when a German soldier stopped in front of them. "I stepped aside to permit him to pass, instead he caught hold of my left thigh, but I wrenched myself away. He did not say anything, I turned around and then saw him exposing himself. He was then 10 or 15 yards away. He did not injure me. He was in green uniform, a short man, red face and clean shaven".

Her friend Gwen added, "At about 4.45pm on Sunday, I was walking up Rectory Hill and had just passed the Rectory, when I saw a German soldier, he grabbed hold of my friend Daphne by the legs. She tried to hit him, he let go and ran away. I turned around to see if he had gone, he was about 10 or 12 yards away and he exposed himself. He was short with a red face. It was all over so quickly."

The Inspector asked the President of the Controlling Committee to forward a copy of his report to the German Authorities for their action. He heard nothing further.

Late one evening farmer Fred Le Huequet, of Les Huriaux, St Martin, heard a noise in his yard, went out and found the pigsty door open. As he looked into the sty, a German soldier sprang on him from behind and threatened him with a revolver. The soldier then ran away still pointing the revolver at Fred.

Fred found that seven of his pigs were missing and there was only one left in the sty. He went to the nearby home of PC 16 Tuck, who was off duty, and told him of his loss. Together they went to see a German officer, living in the Naftiaux Lane, who was in charge of the troops in the district. While the German officer was making enquiries amongst his men, PC Tuck returned to Le Huequet's premises and found the seven missing pigs, loose in the field opposite. The German officer later called on Fred Le Huequet and promised he would make further enquiries in the morning. Again nothing further was heard from the German Authorities but Farmer Fred was lucky, he did not lose his pigs on that occasion. Farmers, however, were becoming accustomed to night time raids on their livestock.

# Chapter 13

## IT WAS A HELL OF A NIGHT SIR

Christmas 1941 passed without any real problems as far as the Police Force was concerned. The New Year, however, was an entirely different matter. The curfew hour had been extended to 1.00am and both the Germans and Islanders were celebrating the New Year, but for very different reasons. Many of the German troops had been drinking heavily and by the approach of the witching hour were pie eyed.

At Mahaut Gardens, where there are two blocks of States houses, the front block was occupied by German troops, while civilians were still living in the rear block. Forty-two-year-old, George Fisher lived in the rear block, with his wife, Mabel, son and two daughters.

The Fisher family were holding their customary party, when at around midnight a group of six Germans walked in through the front door. One of the girls at the party had been friendly with a German sergeant, and had thrown him over for another soldier. The sergeant was one of the Germans who had joined the party. He brought a bottle of wine and some glasses with him and offered his former girlfriend a drink to celebrate the New Year. She took the glass and when the sergeant filled it with wine, she threw the contents in his face.

The German sergeant, who had obviously over indulged, opened the back door and started firing his revolver into the air. George Fisher followed him and attempted to push him outside but almost immediately stumbled back into the room, exclaiming "He has shot me" and then collapsed on the floor.

The sergeant attempted to put the revolver to his head but was restrained by his comrades. Mr Fisher's daughter Ruth, realising that her father was seriously injured, telephoned the St John Ambulance, who arrived soon afterwards.

At 12.10am the Police Station received a call from the St John Ambulance informing them of the shooting. PC 30 Short, was sent to investigate.

Fred Short later recalling the incident:-

"I arrived at the house and George Fisher was semi-conscious. I could see a hole in his chest. I helped the St John Ambulance men and he was taken to the Emergency Hospital at Castel. I then went to Grange Lodge to report the matter to the Germans and obtain their assistance. They were 'having a do' and many of them were two-thirds drunk. I saw Sergeant Major Heindrich Oeser, the Police chief, and told him that a civilian had been shot by a German soldier. He immediately 'barked' out an order and together with a member of the Feldgendarmerie, went to the German Police car parked on the forecourt. He turned to me and said 'You take', 'Right, okay !' I replied.

I drove to the Fisher house, where Sergeant Major Oeser inspected the scene of the shooting. Then he went to a nearby house and arrested the German Sergeant who was lying on a bed in the front room of one of the States houses which they occupied. He was placed in the back of the German Police car and I drove to the Prison.

Sergeant Major Oeser took possession of the revolver which was used in the shooting. Next thing, Oeser turned to me and snapped 'You now take me to the hospital'. It was about 2.00am when we arrived at the Emergency Hospital. We saw a nurse, who said 'Mr Fisher is in that ward'. Off we go and Dr Dick Gibson, who was in charge, was in the doorway and we could see Fisher propped up in bed. I believe he was unconscious.

Oeser said 'I want to speak to that man'. Dr Gibson said 'No'. You should have seen Oeser's face, he shouted all sorts of threats, demanded to know the doctor's name and said that 'You have insulted the third Reich'. Doctor Gibson, who had been a Major in the first war, stood his ground and merely said 'No, I forbid you to go near that man'.

So that was that, Oeser was in a hell of a state. I said to him, did he want to go and see the other people concerned at Collings Road. 'Nein, Nein' he said, he just wanted to go back to his headquarters at Grange Lodge.

It didn't end there, it was a beautiful moonlit night, just like daylight, you could see as plain as day. We were driving up Les Gravees, passing St Stephen's Church, when we met a German sentry. All the big houses in that area of Town were occupied by troops. I was driving the car with Oeser besides me and the other German in the rear. As we reached Les Gravees Post Office, I noticed a German sentry standing on the footpath opposite the house called Hautlieu.

The standard drill, at night, was that if a sentry wanted to stop anybody, they rotated their torch in a clockwise circle. But there was none of that on this occasion, the sentry unslung his rifle from his shoulder and took aim at the car and fired. I saw the flash and instinctively pulled on the handbrake. I thought, by Christ I have I been hit, but fortunately he missed. The sentry was obviously drunk and came staggering towards the car. I went to open the door, 'Nein' shouts Oeser, so I sat still. When the sentry reached the car, Oeser jumped out and bellowed a one word command, which must have been heard right down in St Sampson. The sentry almost dropped dead, Oeser grabbed him and threw him into the back of the car, then he turned to me and said 'You can see that he has had plenty to drink'.

Within minutes there were over three hundred sleepy Germans lined up in Les Gravees, in their underpants and with their uniform over their arms. Sergeant Major Oeser spat out orders at them, as he strutted up and down the road.

After that escapade, I drove the arrested sentry to the prison and returned Oeser and the German police car to Grange Lodge. The Germans there had continued to celebrate the New Year and were singing at the top of their voices when we arrived at nearly 3.00am.

I knew a few of the German Police and one of them greeted me in his guttural accent, with,'Hello Fredrick'. He invited me inside and I exclaimed 'By Christ, what a ruddy night!, have you got a cigarette'. 'Yes', he said and he handed me a full packet. At that moment Oeser came through the door and saw me taking the cigarettes. He didn't half yell,'You give them back'. With that I left and returned to the Police Station."

At 3.30am a telephone call was received from the Emergency Hospital saying that George Fisher's condition was serious. PC Short was sent to Collings Road to take Mrs Fisher to the hospital. At 4.00am another call was received to say that George Fisher had just died. The Station Sergeant notified Grange Lodge, who said they would let Sergeant Major Oeser know at once. Regretfully George Fisher died before his wife arrived.

PC Short asked Dr Gibson if he had recovered the bullet from the body. "No" he said "it passed right through him. He was shot in the right side of the back, the bullet went through the shoulder blade and came out through his right breast".

Fred then went back to the scene of the shooting, to look for the bullet. He searched the area around the door where Fisher had been standing when he was shot and found the bullet embedded in the door frame. Fred dug it out with a knife.

The Constable spent the rest of the night at the Station writing out his report. He gave the bullet to the Station Sergeant. The next day when he came on duty the Sergeant said the 'old man' wanted to see him. Mr Sculpher said:-

"You have done everything fine."

"It wasn't very nice, sir, especially with the sentry shooting off with his rifle."

"No" said Mr Sculpher, who was a man of few words "it couldn't have been, I don't suppose it was."

"It was a hell of a night, sir."

The Germans put the Sergeant on trial for the murder of George Fisher. It was held at 1 Ross Place, Mount Row, the house of Major Marshall Jones, known locally as 'Soapy' Jones, because he owned the soap factory in the Truchot. Constable Short was required as a witness and ordered to report at 7.00am. When he arrived he was confronted by three armed guards who marched him down the corridor into a small kitchenette. Also in there was the accused Sergeant and his escort. All the burners on the gas cooker were lit and there was only one small window, which was closed. Despite it being cold outside, the small room was overpoweringly warm. Fred Short needed some air and opened the door, only to be told "Nein" by the guard who pushed him back into the room and shut the door.

About a quarter of an hour later Dr Gibson arrived and was also put into the kitchenette to wait.

"What the hell is going on in here Short." he said. "We will bloody well die of suffocation, I'll open up the window."

One of the German guards barked "Nein!" and pushed him away from the window.

Fred responded "We can't breath."

"Nein" repeated the German who grabbed hold of Fred and threatened him.

Dr Gibson exclaimed "I am not stopping in here" and opened the door and went out, Fred followed him.

The doctor spoke to the guard in German and as a result they were allowed to walk up and down the corridor.

The trial finally started at 9.00am when the three Judges arrived. The Swastika flag was draped over the bench. Dr Gibson was called as the first witness and instructed to take the oath by "Putting your hand and arm up like that" in a demonstration of the Nazi's salute.

"No", Dr Gibson said "We take the oath, the English way with the Bible." The Judges conferred for a time and allowed him to swear the oath on the Bible. PC Short did the same when he gave his evidence.

Some days after the trial, one of the German policemen at Grange Lodge told Fred Short that the sergeant had been sentenced to fifteen years' imprisonment, but he would probably be sent to the Russian front. "To the Russian front, Frederick, that is a death sentence."

As a result of the Jersey Lending Library issuing the book 'Some other Beauty' by I.A.R.Wylie to a member of the German Forces, a clamp-down on 'Anti German' books took place in Guernsey. Dr Brosch informed the President of the Controlling Committee that:-

"This book contains a number of passages violently directed against Germany and amounting to outrageous hate propaganda. The immediate seizure of the book has been ordered. The owners of all libraries in the Island of Guernsey are required to examine their stocks of books in order to ascertain whether they still possess books of such anti-German nature. Such books are to be handed in by the 5th January 1942 at latest."

The Inspector was advised that he should make sure that the various Libraries were aware of their responsibilities in respect of the German censorship requirements.

The Chief Librarian of the Guille-Alles Library wrote to Dr Brosch stating that they had examined their stock of 70,000 books and were "handing over a number of books which contain or may contain passages of an anti-German nature". Mr Leslie Althorp, of the Old Gate House, which ran The Home Circle Library, handed in 7 books to Dr Brosch, "which may be those, which you are asking". The Germans appeared satisfied with the action taken.

One day Inspector Sculpher left his office at 5.00pm and walked down to his hairdresser, Charles Dubras, in the High Street. There were several customers already there so he sat down and waited his turn. While sitting there he noticed a Police officer's helmet and gloves on the floor. After he had his hair cut, which in all took about thirty minutes, he asked the assistant what the helmet and gloves were doing on the floor and requested him to fetch the Policeman. After a minute or so Constable Friend came out of the lavatory and said to the Inspector "I am sorry, I came in for a shave".

PC 14 Charles Albert Friend was charged with:-

1. Failing to work your beat, No 6 Beat, in accordance with Orders, for 30 minutes, from 5.05pm to 5.35pm on January 12th 1942.

2. Leaving the beat to which you had been ordered without permission or sufficient cause and found at 5.35pm 12th January, 1942 in a shop at 22 High Street, when your presence was not required there in the execution of your duty.

No record exists of the punishment imposed.

On the 13th January the Feldkommandantur required information to be supplied by the following day relating to the financial status of persons registered as Jews.

1. Present income.
2. Property owned.
3. Details of investments.
4. Money in bank.

Deputy Inspector Langmead was deputed to make the necessary enquiries and that evening he interviewed Mrs Elisabet Duquemin and Mrs Elda Brouard. Mrs Duquemin had no income, owned no property and had no investments. She did, however, have £83 in the Post Office Savings Bank which she had saved for the education of her daughter. Mrs Brouard owned no property, but had £250 of British War Loan Stock and £60 in a Barclay's Bank account.

Mr Sculpher passed the information on to the President of the Controlling Committee, adding that details in respect of Miss Auguste Spitz and Miss Therese Steiner were being supplied by the Secretary of the Emergency Hospital, where they were employed. The Secretary in due course reported that neither owned property, held investments or possessed any savings. Miss Spitz was a housemaid earning 15/- a week and board and lodgings, while Miss Steiner, a nurse, received an annual salary of £48.10.0 and board and lodgings.

The emergence of the Black Market did not really become apparent as far as the Police Force was concerned until the early winter of 1941/2. In January 1942 Fuerst von Oettingen required a report on:-

"the activity of the Price Control Authorities as regards the following points:
1. General
2. Price development for the most important commodities.
3. Measures taken.
4. Black Market.
5. Number and nature of penalised contraventions in December 1941.
In future, such a report is to be sent to me at the end of each month."

Mr Sculpher replied on the 30th January 1942:-

Black Market.-

"I beg to report that in November 1941 it came to the knowledge of the Police that cattle were being illegally slaughtered. Enquiries were made and on the 19th December, Police were able to trace a case to premises known as Vazon Cottage, Vazon, occupied by Stanley du Flocq Lihou. Four quarters of beef were found in a greenhouse and German soldiers were in the act of taking some of the meat away.

Beyond saying that the meat was for the Germans forces, Lihou declined to give any information. As German Forces were involved, the facts were at once communicated to the Feldgendarmerie who went there and arrested Lihou and his wife.

This case was then taken over by the German Police. Several other persons were later arrested, but the results have not yet been officially notified to the Police.

The proceedings taken in this case have for the time being, stopped the illegal slaughter of cattle.

Attached is a return of proceedings taken by Police in December 1941."

The list showed that eight people had been taken to Court and that six had been fined, one had the charged dismissed, although the goods were confiscated and one case was adjourned as the defendant was in German custody. Lists of Black Market prosecutions were submitted monthly to the German Authorities, up to the end of the Occupation.

One morning, PC 30 Short was on motorcycle patrol coming down Le Coudre Hill towards Rocquaine Bay when he noticed a man sitting on a roadside wall.

"When he saw me coming," Fred Short recalled, "he gets off the wall and runs, across the road and goes into a yard. Well I think, what is he on about, so I swung into the yard. There was about 20 farmers there. Christ, I thought, what's going on here. There is this steer up on hooks, which they had knocked over and cut in two. I said to them, 'You are going to get shot for this'.

One bloke said 'You're not going to do anything about this are you Fred?'

'Oh yes, I am going to get the Germans down for this,' joking to them.

'Seriously, I suggest you get rid of your look-out man, because he is going to put you all in bloody prison, he gave the game away'.

I told them that as soon as I saw him run, I knew.

Well, they started to have a go at him in Patois. I said 'Now don't go shouting around the place that you knocked over a steer and Fred Short, didn't do anything about it.'

They gave me half of the liver and wrapped it up in brown paper. I got on my motorcycle and put it on my lap, but the blood hadn't properly drained away and things were getting wet, it soaked right through my trousers and underpants. I made a bee-line for home and changed my trousers. I took a bit of liver around to different people, because I had 3-4lb of it.

One of the farmers I had surprised at the bottom of the Coudre Hill was Tommy Sarre, a well-know horseman and carter, of St Peter. He drove a horse and van with seats and on Fridays brought people into town as there was no bus service. He also brought parcels of meat into town, which he regularly supplied to various people including the Magistrate, Quertier Le Pelley. Tommy used the Wellington Pub in Fountain Street, run by William Symes, as a distribution centre with the meat wrapped in brown paper parcels. One day I saw a package with a name on and I said to Tommy Sarre, 'you are chancing things by putting the names on'. The names he had on were Le P and Jimmy and the like."

On many occasions members of the Force had to dissuade Islanders from making accusations against Germans which could not be substantiated. Fred Short often found himself in a difficult position.

"Somebody would come to me and say,

'The Germans have stolen my water pump, they have got it over there in the gun battery.'

I would tell him 'I can't go over there and see if it is yours. The procedure is, I take your statement and then I will go to the German Police with it and they will come out and see you.'

'First, however, they would go to the gun battery and find out if your pump was there. If they found it, then they would lock the Germans up. But if the pump wasn't found, then I would advise you to watch it, because you have signed a statement making an accusation against Germans. You know what will happen if it is not true, because they could have obtained that pump from somewhere else.'

One chap told me that he had lost his wireless and could hear one playing in the German bunker. I said 'Oh yes, I can hear a radio but I can't see it.' He was grumbling and said that they did not have one yesterday.

'If I had your bloody uniform on, I would be in there.'

I told him, 'Just a minute, I am not allowed to go into any German place, I have to go down to the German police, but I have to take a statement from you first'.

However, on that occasion, as the bunker was near the airport and near the road, I said, 'I will go and see the Germans and have a chat with them and see what they say.'

As I walked past the bunker, I made out as if I had been called. I told a white lie. I said 'Do you want me?'

A German said, 'Nein, nein, nein'.

'Sorry' I said, 'I thought he called me,' pointing to another soldier.

The German said something I did not understand, then another Jerry comes out, who speaks English and we have a conversation. As the wireless is still playing, I said 'Good music.'

'Come look' he said.

'Good, yes very good', I responded, noting that the wireless was a German army issue. The Germans were very friendly and I remember that one of them gave me a cigarette.

I went back to the chap who had made the allegation and said 'By Christ you are a lucky chap, if I had gone in there and said that you had made a complaint, you would have been inside by midday. 'God' he said.

'Yes' I said 'it was a German army issue. Don't you ever make an accusation like that again, because if you do I will lock you up for you own safety'.

Another area where it was necessary to be doubly careful was in respect of footprints. I would always say to our people who made accusations,

'You say it is the Germans, are you sure ?'

'Well you can see it is, Mr Short, there are the footprints'.

The German boots had studs which were easily recognisable but they could have been stolen.

Civilians could have got hold of a pair of these boots and used them to steal from greenhouses so I told complainants that if they made an accusation, then I would take a signed statement from them. I warned them to watch out because when Sergeant Major Oeser gets your statement and you are wrong, woe betide you. So I would say it is up to you, do you wish to make a statement. They would say, 'Oh forget it'."

On the 31st January 1942, a thirty-four-year-old Mrs Evelyn ......, of La Fosse, St Martin, called at the Station and complained that she had been molested by a German soldier in her home. She told Mr Sculpher:-

"At about 2.45 pm, on the 31st January 1942 a German soldier who I know by sight, came to my house and asked me if I would like some bread. Naturally, I said yes and he said he would bring some tomorrow. We were standing in the hallway of my bungalow and the soldier then poked me on the chest with his fingers and pointed to the bedroom door. He placed his thumb between his fingers and pushed me towards the bedroom, he did that twice.

The manner on which he pushed me on the chest and the sign he made, left no doubt in my mind what he wanted. I got frightened and called my sister and when she appeared the soldier stopped molesting me. My sister asked what he wanted and he told her about the bread and she said alright and went back into the dining room. When she went, the soldier again pushed me and made the sign with his fingers. He appeared very agitated and said something about Commandant. My sister came back and the soldier went off, saying he would come tomorrow. I have never given the soldier any encouragement for him to make suggestions like that to me."

The Inspector instructed the Deputy Inspector to accompany Evelyn and her husband to the headquarters of the Feldgendarmerie at Grange Lodge, where she made a formal complaint of molestation by a German soldier.

As an interpreter was not available and Evelyn ...... did not know the address of the soldier, the Germans arranged that officers of the Feldgendarmerie would call at her house the next afternoon. The Inspector heard nothing further of the incident from the German authorities.

Although it must have been a frightening experience for Evelyn, other incidents had more serious consequences. The following afternoon, a seventeen-year-old girl, Elfreda, was making her way home through Le Tertre Lane, to the States Houses in Braye Road, when she noticed a number of German soldiers standing in the roadway. They nodded to her and she did likewise. As she passed the group, one of them grabbed her and dragged her towards a house occupied by German soldiers. She struggled and screamed, but the only people about were the other soldiers, who did nothing to help or prevent her from being forceably dragged into the house.

Elfreda later recalled that:-

"The German soldier, who I had never seen before, was too strong, he carried me into the room and put me on a bed and then started to undress me.

I screamed and kicked, you will find a mark in the wall which I did with my shoes when I was struggling on the bed. The soldier took my knickers off and kept me down on the bed by leaning across me. He took his coat off and unslung his braces and took his trousers down and put his person between my legs and I struggled the whole of the time. After he had finished, he took me into another room, a sitting room. When he went out I ran away."

Elfreda went home and told her guardian, who immediately telephoned the Station. PC 18 Smith was sent to Mon Plaisir to inform the Germans and ask for one of their men to accompany him to see Elfreda. The Germans told the Constable that they would see about it in the morning. PC 24 Le Gallez collected

Elfreda in the Police car and took her to the Town Hospital where she was examined by Doctors Bisson and Golding.

They confirmed that intercourse had taken place and kept Elfreda in hospital overnight. The following day Sergeant Banneville took a statement from her and also took possession of a pair of bloodstained knickers which she stated she had been wearing at the time of the assault. The Inspector gave details of the case to the President of the Controlling Committee and the Feldgendarmerie.

One of the continuing problems the Police Force encountered, was communicating with the German authorities. None of the Force spoke any German and none wished to learn, at least officially. The Force had no interpreter and made no attempt to provide one. It was the Germans who provided one in the early days of the Occupation. Then a number of English-speaking Germans arrived and the language problem lessened. However the Germans later issued a regulation, in German and English, requiring that a German translation must accompany all communications.

Whilst the Bailiff and the President of the Controlling Committee adhered to the regulation, other departments took as little notice as they felt they dare. Inevitably the Germans reacted and in February 1942 Colonel Knackfuss, who had replaced Colonel Schumacher in October 1941 as Feldkommandant, issued an Order:-

'NOTICE.

Applications and communications to the German Authorities have lately been submitted in increasing numbers without the necessary German translation. Attention is therefore again drawn to the regulation specifying the use of the German language for all such communications either in writing or in person.'

PC 35 Francois Le Cocq was one of three members of the Force assigned to motorcycle patrol duties. At 1.30pm on Monday 9th February, he was travelling at 20 to 25 m.p.h. in the direction of Town, along the Ville au Roi towards the junction with Ruette Braye. Coming up the Ruette Braye was an empty German ambulance driven by Herbert Warlther.

John Wilson, of Doyle Road, was driving up the Ruette Braye and as he approached the bend near the Alexandra Nursing Home, he saw the ambulance cut the corner and collide with the motorcycle.

George Torode, a Special Constable, was in his shop, the Sarnian Bakery, looking through the window when he saw the ambulance coming up Ruette Braye at what he described "A very moderate speed. It was turning left at the top and next thing I saw, was a man flung into the road and heard a crash at the same time, I rushed out and helped to put him in the ambulance." Later he told Mrs Le Cocq that he had seen things like that at the pictures and in comic cuts, but he had never actually seen anybody go over the top like that.

Cyril de la Mare, was cycling up the Ville au Roi towards St Martin when the accident happened. "The ambulance driver seemed to ignore the rules of the road entirely. I saw the motorcyclist swerve to his left to avoid the collision but the ambulance struck him practically head on. The motorcyclist was flung back up the road."

PC 20 Whare arrived on the scene about fifteen minutes after the accident occurred. Le Cocq, who had been seriously injured, had been removed by the ambulance to the Victoria Hospital. The motorcycle was lying on its side near the footpath. There was a scrape mark on the road, 6ft in length, and a quantity of mud, oil and broken glass. There were also spots of blood on the road. Both headlights of the ambulance were smashed and the lower left-hand side of the bonnet was damaged. The front wheel, mudguard, forks, handlebars and the frame of the motorcycle, were all damaged. The Police motorcycle was taken to Green's of Smith Street, for repair.

PC Le Cocq sustained injuries to his head, face, body and legs and was unconscious when he arrived at the hospital. Later he was transferred to the Emergency Hospital. Mrs Le Cocq, as soon as she heard of the accident, set off for the hospital on her bicycle.

Four days later George Torode was seeking help from the Police. He told PC Short, who had responded to a telephone call at the Station:-

"In the middle of the afternoon three Dutchmen walked into my shop at the Ville au Roi and asked for a lemonade. I served them and they then asked if I could spare them a little salt. I went to the other side of the counter and while I was getting the salt, these men must have taken 3lb of Guernsey butter from a shelf. I did not notice that it was missing until five minutes after they had left. While they were drinking the lemonade, they told me they were Dutch and living at Pleinmont."

In consequence of what George Torode had told him, PC Fred Short took him, on the back of his motorcycle, to the Imperial Hotel, at Pleinmont which was then occupied by Dutch workmen. The Constable told the officer in charge at the hotel of the theft and he immediately paraded all the men in the hotel Yard. Despite carefully inspecting every man George Torode could not identify any of them as being the ones in his shop. Whilst Fred Short was starting his motorcycle and preparing to leave, three men entered the yard and were immediately recognised by George.

The German officer searched the men in the presence of the Constable and not only was the Guernsey butter found, but also:-

2lb loin of pork,
5lb potatoes,
2lb beans,
5 cartons of tomato jam
2 tins of peas,
2 loaves of bread,
2 bags of salt,
1 knife with the name Maison le Noury,
1 electric clock with price ticket 43/6.

All the goods were left in the charge of the officer, who said that he would hand them and the men over to the Feldgendarmerie the next morning. What happened to the soldiers or the goods is unknown.

Special Constable Herbert Champion, who had served full time with the Force since May 1940, was receiving a weekly wage of £2.4.3. His family had not been able to get away during the evacuation because, at the time, three of his seven children had chicken pox. Another child, Rex, had been born in November 1941. The family, the largest in Guernsey during the Occupation, found it very difficult to survive on the small wage.

Champion explained to Dr Symons, the Health Service Officer and a member of the Controlling Committee his difficulty in obtaining sufficient food for his family. He told the doctor that his family consumed approximately 1 lb of potatoes per person per day. Dr Symons said that since it was not possible to increase the family's bread ration they should increase the consumption of potatoes to alleviate the difficulty.

Sir Abraham Laine, who was President of the Essential Commodities Committee, also did what he could to obtain supplies of un-rationed food for the Champion family.

The matter was considered by the Controlling Committee, and they decided that his wages should be increased by 9d to £2.5.0 a week. They also resolved that no Police officer or Special Constable should be paid at a rate below the minimum scale of wages specified for employees of the Glasshouse Utilisation Board.

Early on Friday evening, the 20th February, a woman telephoned the Station reporting that there was a serious fire at the Clarence Hotel in Cornet Street. PC 20 Whare was sent to the scene. When he arrived the Fire Brigade was already there and a senior German officer was in attendance.

More than ninety foreign labourers were billeted in the Hotel. Three Spanish labourers, living on the top floor, had been trying to light a petrol lamp which exploded and caught fire. When the Fire Brigade arrived they found the top floor of the four-storey hotel and the smaller house next door, well alight. A strong easterly wind was blowing and fanning the flames down through the buildings.

As the fire engulfed the hotel and the neighbouring buildings other Police officers arrived on the scene and were employed controlling the ever-growing crowd. Watchers on the Mignot Plateau could feel the heat of the fire, as could the crowd at the South Esplanade Plantation. At one time it was estimated by Deputy Inspector Langmead that the crowds numbered two thousand or more. Nothing as exciting had been seen since the Occupation.

As a precaution all the tenants of the neighbouring properties were evacuated. Special Constables Pealling, Petit, Williams, Le Lacheur and Falla all helped to ensure that everyone was clear of the danger area. No one was injured, but many of the foreign workers lost all their possessions.

The following morning revealed that the affected buildings were completely gutted and still smouldering. Only the outer walls of the Clarence Hotel remained standing. Number 6 Cornet Street, owned by Deputy C.H.Cross, was seriously damaged. The roof of Bucktrout's Waterloo House, was damaged and the rest of building seriously affected by heat, water and smoke.

Sergeant Jack Harper was taken ill on the 28th February and his housekeeper, Miss Guilbert, telephoned the Station to say that he was unfit and would not be able to report for duty for a few days. Sergeant Pill took the call and asked Miss Guilbert to pass on his hope that Jack would soon feel better. He recorded the call in the Occurrence Book.

# Chapter 14

# SHOUTS OF POLIZEI, POLIZEI

Listeners to the B.B.C. at 10.15pm on the 5th December 1941 heard the announcer say,

"Now here is Colonel Britton to give his weekly talk to the people of occupied territories...."

"This is Colonel Britton speaking to the V Army. Every one of you can find something to do which is anti-Nazi. Try to do something anti-Nazi every day."

Douglas Ritchie was a member of the staff of the British Broadcasting Corporation and during the war was the speaker in the 'Colonel Britton' broadcasts to occupied Europe. Many people in Guernsey listened to the weekly broadcasts and re-broadcasts, including members of the Police Force.

From the time Mr Sherwill and Mr Sculpher had actively discouraged members of the Force from joining the armed forces, many had bitterly regretted not going. They now found themselves at the beck and call of the Germans but the Colonel Britton broadcasts gave them encouragement to initiate some form of resistance.

Bill Burton, as one of the older, more experienced and immensely patriotic members of the Force, became the unofficial leader of the younger Constables. He always reminded them that "We owe allegiance to His Majesty the King and should fight back and hinder the Germans in any way possible." Many, like Frank Tuck and Kingston Bailey, needed little encouragement.

These able-bodied and intelligent young policemen in the prime of life, resolved to cause as much disruption to the Germans as possible without putting themselves or their colleagues at unnecessary risk. To start with, it was the little things that gave them satisfaction and caused the Germans aggravation. The request for directions often resulted in considerable additional and unnecessary mileage being covered.

Constables on patrol at night found it comparatively easy to put German vehicles out of action by various means. Plug leads were pulled off or relocated, water found its way into petrol tanks, nails were hammered into tyres and petrol was siphoned from vehicle tanks. At other times telephone wires were cut and 'V' signs appeared where they were bound to be noticed by the Germans. All this was calculated to offend and annoy the German authorities and troops.

Members of the Force went to extreme lengths to avoid saluting German officers. The best way of avoiding a salute, without being pulled up by the Germans, was to be engaged in directing traffic. Later in the Occupation a Policeman was required to be stationed outside Government House to ensure that the Military Commandant always had priority when he left the House. Often when a German officer was in the vicinity the duty Policeman could be observed directing non existing traffic.

Sometimes it was not possible to avoid saluting German officers and then all they received was a very grudging salute. Inevitably the Germans complained that members of the Force still failed to salute and the Inspector had to 'award' more and higher fines. On occasions the Germans dispensed punishment.

PC 30 Short recalled being stopped by a German when he was on motorcycle patrol:-

"Apparently I passed a German officer outside the Royal Hotel, without saluting him. Well he turned around and caught me up at the Salerie corner. I got off the motorcycle and saluted him. I told him that the sun was in my eyes and that I had not seen him. I had to report to Grange Lodge where I told Sergeant Major Oeser that I had not seen the officer. He said 'A Police officer sees all - sees all.' I said I was very sorry. He fined me £2 and I was given a lecture.

Another occasion when I fell foul of the Germans was when the Sergeant said to me 'Fred, see if you can get hold of the High Street man for me'. Instead of taking the motorcycle, I walked down Smith Street. When I got by Boots the Chemist, I heard the sound of boots with spurs coming up the Pollet. Then I saw this German officer coming and turned my back on him and made a show of looking down the High Street. The next thing, I heard a 'bark' and turned around and saw this officer obviously very annoyed at being ignored.

I saluted him and said I was sorry and that I had being looking for another Policeman. He sounded off about Hitler and that I had insulted the Third Reich. Anyway he takes my number and sure enough down comes a letter to the Inspector from the Feldgendarmerie, - I am to go to Grange Lodge and Mr Sculpher told me that I had better take my shaving stuff as I would be locked up this time.

So up I go, this time I was lucky, Oeser had gone on leave. I was up before one of the other officers who I knew and who used to call me Frederick. I told him what had happened and explained how I was looking for another Policeman and that I was doing my work. I said I was sorry and that I hadn't seen the officer until I heard him shout.

This officer did not know that I had been up before, I don't know if they kept a record, they didn't ask me. He gave me a severe reprimand and a fine of £5. Mr Sculpher and the Station Sergeant were quite surprised when I returned to the station and told them that I had had a bit of luck because Oeser was on leave."

The Germans installed a mass of communication wires from the Telephone Exchange in St John's Street, leading down College Street, St James Street and St Julians Avenue to the White Rock. They hung the wires on batons of wood screwed to window frames. In the Avenue the wires were strung through the branches of the trees. When a strong wind blew it was easy for a Constable to grab hold of the wires and pull them down. They were not cut, but stretched until they frayed and broke, or the batons were pulled from the windows. The Station Sergeant regularly had the pleasure of informing the Germans that their lines were in need of repair. It was surprising how often the Germans were called out at 2.00 or 3.00am for this purpose.

PC 14 Charlie Friend was particularly keen on sabotaging German communication lines. He would even don his uniform on nights when he was off duty to do it. Where their lines ran along the hedge of a field with cows, he was an expert in making it look as if the wire had been bitten through.

PC 22 Kingston Bailey years later recalled a night when he and Frank Tuck particularly enjoyed themselves at the Germans' expense. Having met in the vicinity of the Weighbridge, Frank Tuck set off on foot patrol to the north and Kingston Bailey to the south. When they were some distance apart, Kingston started flashing his torch in the direction of the German sentry at the Weighbridge.

Within a very short time the silence of the night was broken by Germans shouting and the noise of cars dashing towards the scene of the flashing light. By this time Kingston was back patrolling in the area of the Weighbridge. Then Frank's light went into action and the Germans were soon to be observed rushing off in the opposite direction. Naturally the two Constables returned to the Weighbridge and enquired what all the activity was about.

Inevitably some members of the Force were keen to take further action against the Germans. As the shortage of food became more apparent, as the black market activities became more prevalent and as applications by members of the Force for heavy worker rations had been turned down on a number of occasions, it was almost inevitable that their attention would turn to German food stores.

Charlie Friend later recalled:-

"At about this time Mr Burton got us all together, the younger policemen, and told us that if we couldn't defeat the enemy in our own country, it was about time we tried to do something. From that time onward we decided that we would mount a series of raids on German food stores.

Meetings were, of course, forbidden and it would have been difficult to arrange them in any event, but we managed between us to make a pretty thorough habit of obtaining German stores. We took a good deal of food one way and another and distributed it amongst various people in the Town. Parcels of food were left at 'Jas' Harris, in Church Square. If we saw needy people in queues, which it was often our duty to regulate, then we told them to call into 'Jas' and pick up some of these goods. I did give food to Mr J.Le Page, of 7 Ville au Roi. I also gave food to their next door neighbour, Mrs Sipley, consisting of corn etc., for the chickens."

Bill Burton also recalled:-

"I, in common with other Police officers entered German stores in order to take foodstuffs and to distribute it amongst people in need. About 75% or 80% of the stuff we took was from German Stores. The remainder was taken from people who were dealing directly with the Germans and distributing it on their behalf.

Colonel Britton, in his broadcasts, made no differentiation between civil or military stores.

I personally distributed food to a lodging house which contained eleven people, situated at Rouge Rue, St Peter Port, and the man running it was Fred Wallbridge. I also gave food to Reginald Brazure, of Blancs Bois, Castel. On two or three occasions I gave Ted Zabiela, of the White Hart Hotel, and Mr and Mrs Hatch, German meat and butter. In addition three or four of my relatives received food from me at various intervals."

Kingston Bailey claimed that Bill Burton and Frank Tuck were the prime movers in the quest for German food, but other members of the Force believed that he, himself was also very considerably involved. Later Kingston was to recall:-

"We distributed a great deal of food to various people. I distributed food to, amongst other people, Mrs Hawke, of Les Croutes, Mr Lihou, of Foulon Farm and Mr Lanyon, of the Bordage.

We had started our operation one beautiful moonlight night, when we very quietly removed the entire lock of a Organisation Todt* store in the Truchot. We entered very slowly, not really knowing what to expect. We climbed up a small stairway and by the light of our torches, saw thousands of neatly stacked tins of meat, butter, sugar and coffee. We thought, all this and our people so short of food, and indeed the French from whom it was taken. We did not take any on that occasion as we were on duty and had to report back to the Station.

*The Organisation Todt was a German civilian undertaking developed pre war by Dr Todt which provided German contractors with foreign labour for military construction work.

During the night, Frank and I discussed our future plans for this store. We decided that the store was not visited by the Germans at all, the tins were covered in dust and the store was completely full. We decided to remove as much of the food as possible, but this would be quite a problem as most of the tins weighed about 4 lb each.

During the following days we made many enquiries and found that as far as the Germans were concerned it was a closed store. We also found other stores, containing corn, potatoes, tinned tomatoes, oil and many other items.

We were indeed very pleased, now we could really hit the Germans and at the same time benefit the poor people who could not afford to buy black market goods.

Frank and I decided one night in December 1941 to start our operation. We were on early turn, 6.00am to 2.00pm, so we were able to sleep in the afternoon. At about midnight we put on our uniforms and proceeded to the store in the Truchot. We carried some empty sacks under our capes. It was with great excitement that we removed the lock from the door. We entered and found everything as it had been on the previous occasion. We filled the two sacks about half full, which was quite enough to carry, as we had to go about a mile to my house. We put back the lock and started on our first of what was going to be six journeys that night. As daylight broke we surveyed our haul, about 120 tins of assorted food. During the following weeks we went to that store many times and distributed hundreds of tins of food."

The activities against the German food stores was not only confined to the Constables on the beat. Sergeant Harper also became involved. He later recalled:-

"Much German foodstuffs were distributed by me from my home at 39 High Street, to all manner of people and right under the noses of the Germans. My housekeeper, Doris Guilbert, took home quantities of food and fats to her mother living at Cobo to help feed two orphaned children whose father, Fred Gilmore, was killed in the German air raid on the Island.

I personally conveyed to my uncle and aunt, Mrs and Mrs Alfred Torode, of 4 Roland Road, St Sampson, quantities of canned meats, fats and coffee. These were buried in the back garden and subsequently dug up by the Germans."

PC 30 Fred Short, on beat duty early one morning, spotted a trail of beans from a German store in the Truchot, leading to Frank Stroobant's 'Home from Home' Restaurant in the Pollet. A sack full of beans had been dragged right down the road. Fred quickly removed the evidence. The restaurant was obviously benefiting from supplies obtained from German stores.

By the middle of February 1942 the 'liberating' of food from German stores had become almost a regular pastime for a majority of members of the Force. Not only German stores, but some civilian premises inadvertently became the target for night time raids. There was a list of civilian stores displayed in the Station and any store not listed was considered to be a military or Organisation Todt store and a potential target. Furthermore the Germans had helpfully left a key to the States Market at the Station and this was used to gain access to military and civilian stores.

When Sergeant Fred Duquemin's wife and four children evacuated, he moved into 3 Park Lane, Trinity Square, with the Prigent family. Across the road from where he was living was the former Groceteria store. Fred noticed stocks of tinned food being unloaded and stored there, by the same local workmen who transported food stocks for the Germans.

Its location was not added to the list of local stores at the Station so he naturally assumed that it was another German store and informed some of his colleagues of its existence. It was not long before the store was 'visited' and some of the tinned food transferred across the road to where Fred Duquemin was living. Fred and his colleagues were to discover, to their cost, that it was in fact a civilian store.

When in June 1940, the Island was demilitarized, large stocks of food and other stores were abandoned by the NAAFI at Fort George. The States took over these stocks and removed them to the old St Paul's church, just across the road from the Police Station. The key to the store was kept at the Station and not once were the premises entered or one solitary item of stock stolen. The stores were later commandeered by the Germans.

While nearly all the foot patrol Constables and some of the Sergeants became involved in the 'supply and distribution' of German food, the men on motorcycle patrol and office duties were not as readily available to take part. Whilst supposedly patrolling their beats, the night shift could usually be found in the Station, either playing cards or sleeping. It was during these night time sessions that many of the 'raids' on German stores were planned.

Whilst not all members of the Force were involved, most benefited to a greater or lesser extent. Not everyone was aware of the clandestine operations, certainly not Inspector Sculpher. Not having a night pass he was unable to check on the activities of his men. The Inspector was however, aware that certain civilian stores, including the States Dairy and stalls in the market were being broken into at night. A member of the Force, on night shift, had seen Sergeant Harper pass the market key to PC 23 Bill Quin, without a word being said between them. He reported the incident to Mr Sculpher. Later he recalled:-

"When I was on night shift and I used to read a lot, I was driving, I must have been the car driver at the time. Bill Quin came into the Station after midnight. I was reading at the back. Sergeant Harper got up off of his seat, climbed on a chair, took the keys for the market down and gave them to Bill, who then went out. Not a word was said between them.

Later there was another 'hoo-ha' when the market was raided again. I went to see Sculpher and reminded him of what I had previously told him. He just sat there rolling a cigarette and humming a tune to himself. Apparently he had it all worked out. The next time Sergeant Harper was on night shift, Sergeant Banneville and Deputy Inspector Langmead would keep special observation on him and the activities of the night shift. Sergeant Harper, however, reported sick."

Whether Sergeant Harper was made aware of the surveillance that was going to be kept on him, or whether he was genuinely ill can only be a matter of speculation. Certainly Deputy Inspector Langmead and Sergeant Banneville were aware of the situation. Did Mr Sculpher take anyone else into his confidence? Was Jack Harper warned?

After a number of 'raids' had been carried out on German food stores, the 'raiders' established a modus operandi to reduce the risk of being caught. The procedure was to break or open the lock, go inside and shout:- "Anybody there!" If there was, then they would say they found the door open and had come inside to see if everything was in order.

During the first few days of March 1942, Fred Short warned Frank Tuck that the Germans had changed all the locks on the doors on their Organisation Todt food store in the Truchot and that everyone should be particularly careful. By this time PC 22 Bailey's cousin, J.A.Bournazel, who was the projectionist at the Gaumont cinema in St Julian's Avenue, had arranged that some of the food could be stored in the basement of the cinema. Kingston Bailey was given a key for the back gate which was only 20 yards from the food store.

On the night of 4th/5th March 1941 PCs Bailey and Tuck decided to transfer a further quantity of tins from the Truchot store, to the basement of the Gaumont Cinema. When Frank had finished his break for refreshment in the Station, he met Kingston and together they walked down to the Truchot. On this occasion they found the door of the store open and entered. Once inside the building they had to climb a small flight of stairs.

As Kingston Bailey neared the top of the stairs, there was suddenly a blinding light with shouts of "Polizei, Polizei". The Germans had been laying in wait for them. Kingston Bailey fell backwards down the stairs knocking Frank Tuck back into the street. O.T. Meister Austen and O.T. Kameradschaftsfuhrer Schuster, who had been keeping watch on the orders of Obertruppfuhrer Wild, arrested PCs.Tuck and Bailey and marched them under armed escort to the Channel Islands Hotel on Glategny Esplanade.

O.T. Meister Austen later explained:-

"I was sent to Guernsey to keep watch and noticed that the locks were being tampered with. My colleague and I were put in the store to keep guard and watch and the lock was left. At 1.50am we heard a noise and hid behind bean sacks. Then the accused, Bailey and Tuck, entered. On seeing that the intruders were Guernsey Police, they were arrested. We had orders to shoot at sight, but did not do so on finding that the intruders were members of the Guernsey Police."

**PC Kingston Bailey.**

**PC Frank Tuck.**

Years later, Frank Tuck surmised, "Our best bet would have been when we found the door open, to have beaten a hasty retreat. I had a torch, I should have lit it and shouted out 'Is anybody there'? We hadn't picked anything up, we had not touched anything, we had nothing, we did not have time to. We were only half way up the stairs when they made a grab for us.

They marched us down to the Channel Islands Hotel where we were held for hours on end. Bailey had in his pocket a note book in which he had recorded all sorts of details of our activities. When he went to the toilet, under guard, he managed to put the book in the lavatory cistern. It was a very dangerous book, I would never have carried it with me. It is easy to be wise after the event, he wasn't really all that clever, to be honest. I have often wondered if that note book was ever found and if so, by whom."

At the Police Station, Sergeant Duquemin became concerned when PCs Tuck and Bailey did not report off duty at 6.00am. Enquiries were made, without result. At 9.20am the two PCs were brought to the station by a member of the Feldgendarmerie, who told the Station Sergeant that he would be informed later of the reason for their arrest.

After being held at the Channel Islands Hotel for hours without anything happening, Tuck and Bailey were thoroughly searched and all their personal belongings taken from them.

They were then taken outside to a waiting car and driven, in turn, to their homes, which were searched. Inevitably the Germans, led by Sergeant Major Oeser, found what they were looking for, food from their stores. In Frank Tuck's house they found:-

43 tins of tomatoes
3 3kg tins of butter
9 tins of meat
9 pieces of sausage.

In Kingston Bailey's home they discovered:-
3 3kg tins of butter
9 tins of meat.

At 11.20am on the 5th March 1942 a member of the Feldgendarmerie arrived at the Station and demanded to see the Inspector immediately. The German officer, after asking for a complete list of the names and addresses of all Police officers, instructed the Inspector to close the Police Station and accompany him, with all available members of the Force to the Feldgendarmerie Headquarters at Grange Lodge. A German N.C.O was left in charge of the Station.

On arrival at Grange Lodge the Inspector was informed that a quantity of butter, sausage and tins of tomatoes had been stolen from the German Forces by PC 16 Tuck and PC 22 Bailey and consequently they were under arrest. All Police officers not already at Grange Lodge, with the exception of PC 35 Le Cocq and PC 9 Marsh, who were in hospital, were rounded up by the Germans and brought to the Feldgendarmerie Headquarters. Sergeant Jack Harper, who had been off sick for five days, was collected by the Germans, from his flat.

PC 30 Fred Short, on motorcycle patrol, was stopped by an armed German as he passed Sergeant Le Lievre's house at L'Islet. He was informed that he was being arrested. As he was on the Police motorcycle, he was instructed to drive in front of the German police car. The Constable led the way along the sea front and as he turned up St Julians Avenue he accelerated and turned into Hospital Lane, without the Germans following him.

Fred knew that the Germans were bound to search his house, so he drove straight to his home at St Davids, in Steam Mill Lanes and collected the revolver and forty nine rounds of ammunition that were hidden under his steel helmet on the top of a wardrobe. He went to see his friend and neighbour, Douglas Ozanne, and asked him to look after them for him. Then he drove to Grange Lodge and reported to the Germans. When he arrived he was put in a room with some of his colleagues and in the middle was a long table stacked with all the food discovered at Frank Tuck's and Kingston Bailey's homes.

All the Police officers were taken, one by one, to their homes where a thorough search was carried out in their presence. Then they were returned to Grange Lodge. At Bill Burton's home the Germans found 11 tins of meat, two packets of coffee and a bag of tea. At PC 18 Smith's house, in La Rue Flere, they found a piece of sausage. Perhaps the most unfortunate member of the Force was Charlie Friend, who was arrested at home eating German food. The Feldgendarmerie also discovered 3 tins of butter in his home where he lived with his parents. PC 27 Bob Kimber was more fortunate, he hid his share of the food up his living room chimney. It remained undiscovered.

When it came Fred Short's turn to have his house searched, he was accompanied by three Feldgendarmerie officers whom he knew reasonably well

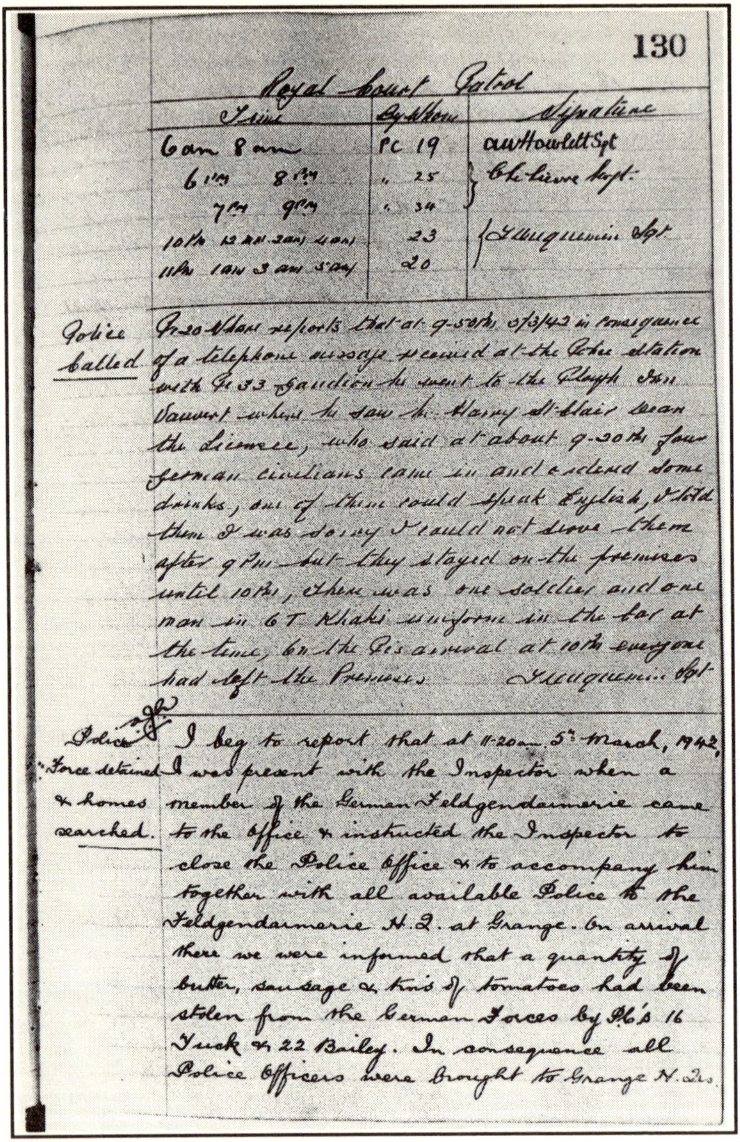

130

Royal Court Patrol

| Time | By whom | Signature |
|---|---|---|
| 6am 8am | PC 19 | AWHowlett Sgt |
| 6pm 8pm | " 25 | C Le Lievre Sgt |
| 7pm 9pm | " 34 | |
| 10pm 12 AM 2am 4am | 23 | F Le Quesne Sgt |
| 11pm 1am 3am 5am | 20 | |

Police called. PC 20 Sloan reports that at 9-50pm 5/3/42 in consequence of a telephone message received at the Police station with PC 33 Gaudion he went to the Plough Inn Sauvert where he saw Mr Harry St Clair Sean the Licensee, who said at about 9-30pm four German civilians came in and ordered some drinks, one of them could speak English, I told them I was sorry I could not serve them after 9pm but they stayed on the premises until 10pm, there was one soldier and one man in O.T. Khaki uniform in the bar at the time, on the PCs arrival at 10pm everyone had left the Premises. F Le Quesne Sgt

Police Force detained & homes searched. I beg to report that at 11-20am 5th March, 1942, I was present with the Inspector when a member of the German Feldgendarmerie came to the office & instructed the Inspector to close the Police Office & to accompany him together with all available Police to the Feldgendarmerie H.Q. at Grange. On arrival there we were informed that a quantity of butter, sausage & tins of tomatoes had been stolen from the German Forces by PC's 16 Tuck & 22 Bailey. In consequence all Police Officers were brought to Grange H.Qs.

**A page from the Occurrence Book of 5th march 1942 recording the closure of the Station by the Feldgendarmerie and PCs Tuck and Bailey's arrest.**

because he had worked with them. That was of no advantage, as they still carried out a thorough search but fortunately found nothing. One of the Germans picked up a magazine about the Royal Family which was lying on the table. Fred suddenly remembered that folded inside the front cover, were three of the propaganda leaflets, which had been dropped by the R.A.F. The German looked at the picture of the King on the cover, made a comment and then threw it back on the table.

At 4.30pm the Germans announced that PCs Friend, Burton, Tuck, Smith and Bailey were being detained and that the remainder of the Force was 'provisionally allowed their freedom' and could resume their duties. Inspector Sculpher was, however, required to remain behind. At 4.45 pm the five detained Constables were transferred to the Prison under German guard, 'pending further enquiries'.

Later that day Fuerst von Oettingen, in a hand delivered letter, informed the President of the Controlling Committee:-

"Since in these circumstances the collaboration of the German Police with the Island Police in the present conjunction is clearly impossible, Inspector Sculpher who is responsible for the Island Police, must forthwith be provisionally removed from office."

Deputy Inspector Langmead later recalled:-

"I returned to the Station, opened up and posted Police on duty. At 6.45pm at my house, I received a telephone call from John Leale, President of the Controlling Committee, notifying me that Inspector Sculpher had been suspended from duty and my name had been submitted to the German Authorities to be responsible to carry on the duties of the Inspector of Police. At 7.00pm I received a message from Grange Lodge, Headquarters of the Feldgendarmerie, to report there at 10.00am the next day. At 10.00am on the 6th March I attended Grange Lodge, when my full name, telephone number and address were verified and I was instructed to carry on as Inspector of Police."

After receiving the telephone call from John Leale, Mr Langmead returned to the Station. As he was going in, he met Mr Sculpher, who was understandably dejected. He handed over the keys of his desk, his notebook and informed his Deputy of the outstanding cases. Mr Langmead worked on in the office until 9.00pm before going home.

It quickly became clear, by the speed of the German reaction, that the operation to catch PCs Tuck and Bailey had been carefully planned well in advance and the removal of Inspector Sculpher was one of their prime aims. The chief 'architect' was, without doubt, Fuerst von Oettingen, Island Chief of the Feldkommandantur.

The Police Station had reopened at 4.30pm. with Sergeant Pill as Station Sergeant. Sergeant Harper, after going home to his flat and changing into uniform, reported for duty at 5.30pm and took charge of the Station.

The much depleted Police Force tried desperately to maintain an air of normality, although nothing could be further from reality. Constables Harry Pugh and Eugene Le Lievre set off on their beats, Harry Dyson went out on motorcycle patrol, but all the time they were reflecting on the events which were enveloping them and their colleagues. Would they be the next to be arrested. They could only wait.

However, sanity and reality quickly returned, when Sergeant Harper was notified by John Langdon, Master of the Country Asylum, that a lunatic had absconded. The inmate had apparently escaped through a section of broken railings. Constables on patrol were notified of the escape but the Station was soon informed that the inmate had returned voluntarily at tea time!

During the next day, March 6th, the Germans interrogated Constable Frank Tuck and later in the day took a statement from him. At 8.15pm that evening the Germans arrested Sergeant Jack Harper at his flat in the High Street.

The next morning the Germans left a message at the Station for PC Short to report at Grange Lodge at 9.15am. The Constable, who was on motorcycle patrol, early turn, returned to the Station at 9.00am, parked the Police motorcycle and slowly and thoughtfully walked up to the Feldgendarmerie Headquarters. He was unsure what to expect. If they were going to arrest him, surely, he thought, they would have just done so. To ask him to report, could mean that they merely wanted him to answer some questions. He was not sure, but he was worried. Had one of the other men, already in custody spilt the beans?

He stood on the other side of the road and looked across at the Feldgendarmerie Headquarters. He had been there on Police business many times, but this visit was different. Was it the end of the road? Fred Short looked at his watch, it was almost 9.15am. He had no intention of being late, so he quickly crossed the road, walked across the forecourt, up the steps into the foyer and reported. He was questioned for some time before being taken down to the prison and locked up.

Sergeant Alf Howlett was in charge of the Station when the Germans arrived at 9.30am and detained him. The Germans waited while Mr Langmead came down from his office to take charge of the Station. They then drove Sergeant Howlett to his home at Edom Villa, Houmet Lane, and despite having found nothing on the previous visit, carried out a second search of his house. This time the Germans found eight tins of meat and two of butter.

Two days after Fred Short was arrested his interrogation began in earnest - a period that he later described as "a nightmare of pain and torture".

Between 12.30pm and 2.00pm on the 10th March Sergeant Duquemin, PC 33 Gaudion, PC 23 Quin, PC 20 Whare, PC 25 Piesing, PC 27 Kimber and Mrs Marguerite Torode, Jack Harper's aunt, were all arrested. PCs Piesing and Kimber were released later that evening and immediately returned to duty.

On the same day the Controlling Committee agreed that a number of Auxiliary Policemen should be recruited and that an advertisement be placed in the Press. The next day the advertisement for recruits appeared.

> 'Applications are invited for employment as full time Auxiliary Police. Preference will be given to men aged between 20 and 50 in possession of a bicycle or have performed duties as Special Constables. Apply in own hand writing giving full name, year of birth, address, occupation and qualifications and knowledge of French, to reach this office by 6.00pm on the 14th March. Signed A.J.Langmead Deputy Inspector.'

One hundred and seventy applications were received.

Other matters also claimed the Deputy Inspector's attention. Frau, or Mrs as she described herself, Annie Wranowsky wrote from Clos de la Ville, Sark, on the 10th March, saying:-

"I require my passport for the German Authorities. Kindly send it soon as possible. The passport has been left with you, after I left the internment camp."

Mr Langmead replied immediately, enclosing her Passport and Certificate of Identity.

Mr Langmead wrote to the President of the Police Committee on the 12th March stating that twelve members of the Force had been arrested and reporting that:-

"In consequence of the arrest I have considered them as suspended from duty as from the day of arrest. I have stopped their pay accordingly and recorded the facts in the records."

Two days later he again wrote to the President of the Police Committee on the subject of vacancies in the Police Force.

"I beg to report that on 10th March, I was called to Grange Lodge, where I was interviewed by Fuerst von Oettingen and Inspector Zachau. The former was very concerned with the amount of stealing of growing crops from fields, which had to be stopped. He asked for an explanation of the operation of Police on country patrols and instructed me to submit to him for approval, a scheme for patrolling the country districts by Police, with adequate supervision of the men, particularly at night. I pointed out the difficulty of passes when Fuerst von Oettingen promised to take the matter up to secure passes for Police and Auxiliaries. Up to the present only three passes have been allowed for the Police at night.

I have considered this matter and beg to submit that in view of the large increase in stealing from fields, houses and stores, that very full patrols will be needed. I have revised existing beats and patrols accordingly to provide for Town and Country beats and submitted a separate report thereon.

With the loss of experienced men, particularly Sergeants, the difficulty is increased. I am left with two duty Sergeants and twelve regular Constables with two in hospital, Marsh and Le Cocq. The regulars will be employed in Town with the uniformed Auxiliaries who have had 20 months' experience. The Country patrols will have to be formed from the new men to be appointed as Auxiliaries. To enable Country men to get Town experience, each week three will be given a week in Town and so on in rotation.

This raises the point of filling vacancies in the regular Force. It is not advisable to do this at the moment for several reasons, but if likely men are engaged as Auxiliaries now, this will enable the Committee to form an opinion as to their ability and adaptability for Police work and this will act as a probationary period. If satisfactory they can be permanently engaged when recruiting opens, or their employment terminated if found unsatisfactory.

The question will be one of adequate supervision and to do this it will be necessary to appoint Acting Sergeants, here the choice is limited. Further, if the full scheme is approved and put into operation, full outside supervision should be provided by appointment of an Acting Deputy Inspector.

The appointments then would be,
One Acting Deputy Inspector.
One Sergeant,
Four Acting Sergeants.

This means one Acting Sergeant more than we had before the suspensions, but this is accounted for by the increased Country patrols.

I beg to ask that this be considered and if approved that the following appointments be made, one Acting Deputy Inspector, one Sergeant, four Acting Sergeants. All Acting ranks to understand that the appointments are for the duration of the war only."

In an accompanying letter Mr Langmead raised the question of Police pay and allowances. He reported that the regular Sergeants had expressed concern at their level of pay in relation to that of Constables.

On the 16th March the Police Committee met to consider the situation in respect of the Police Force. Attending the meeting for the first time was Colonel R.W.Randall, who had been appointed by the Controlling Committee to take the place of Deputy Stamford Raffles, who had died. The President, Mr W.E.Poat, was ill and the Vice-President C.E.Agnew, who took the chair, said he regretted that the serious charges now pending against members of the Force had placed the Committee in a very difficult position with the German Authorities on the question of thieving.

The Police Committee appointed Mr A.J.Langmead as Acting Inspector and he became the first locally-born officer to take command of the Island Police

Force. He was granted a pay increase of £5 a month. Sergeant/Clerk A.P.Lamy became Acting Deputy Inspector and PC 17 Plevin was promoted Sergeant, taking over the clerical and office duties. PC 11 Bull and PC 13 Dyson were appointed Acting Sergeants. It was agreed that two further Acting Sergeants would be selected later.

With his promotion to full Sergeant, Ernie Plevin put up the three stripes on both arms, while Acting Sergeants Bull and Dyson, only displayed the stripes on their right arms.

The Police Committee appointed the twelve uniformed Special Constables, who had been employed on a full day-time basis since the 20th May 1940, as Auxiliary Policemen. A sub-committee, consisting of three members, was formed to select and appoint Auxiliary Police officers.

Another item on the agenda was an application by Bert Lamy and Harry Pugh for the cost to be paid by the Committee, of having all their teeth extracted. The expenditure was agreed. Bert Lamy had all his teeth extracted, but Harry Pugh only had his upper teeth extracted, before his dentist, Mr S.H.Godfrey, of Victoria Road, was deported to Germany. As the rest of his teeth caused him no problem, Harry did nothing about having them removed until after the Occupation when they again gave trouble. He then enquired if the agreement that the Committee should foot the bill still held good - apparently it did.

Fuerst von Oettingen wrote to Colonel Knackfuss on the 16th March, reporting:-

"If the further course of enquiry does not lead to the arrest of Sculpher, the previous Police Inspector, I must reserve the right as I have reported over the telephone, to recommend his being put in a Police detention camp. Sculpher's provisional successor Deputy Inspector Langmead makes an extremely simple impression.

From his verbal descriptions, I have been able to conclude that the Island Police, who had left their pre-war schemes of duties as good as unchanged had, from the point of view of organisation, as well as distribution of duties, completely failed. The members of the Force had not known how to use the generous measure of freedom of action accorded to them. There was no question at all of strict discipline.

The question of pay will come in the present reorganisation of the Police, for I have the impression that the remuneration of the men was inadequate, moreover the Controlling Committee had refused them supplementary rations for night duty."

On the 17th March PC 27 R.W.Kimber was arrested for the second time. PC 24 Alf Le Gallez and Sergeant Ted Pill were also detained and placed in the Prison. Three days later PC 25 'Snip' Piesing was rearrested and PC 34 Eugene Le Lievre, PC 19 Archie Tardif and PC 28 Peter Bretel were also arrested. There were now nineteen Police officers under arrest and Inspector Sculpher under suspension.

The Occurrence Book was the one document which recorded the daily 'happenings' of the Force. Pre Occupation it was really the shortened version of all reports submitted by Constables, the details of all callers, or telephone calls at the Station. Matters relating to individual Policemen were recorded as well as the daily disposition of every man in the Force. To many Policemen the Occurrence Book was the Bible and Doomsday book combined. To many a new recruit, over the years, past Occurrence Books have provided them with a fascinating insight into the workings of the Force. Every morning the ritual was for the Duty Sergeant to take the book up to the Inspector, who read the reports and added his comments and initials. Then the book was returned to the downstairs cupboard, to await the next entry.

Since the Occupation the Sergeants, who made the entries, had become a little more selective in what was entered and more importantly what was omitted. Nothing which was critical of the Germans, nothing which might help the Germans in their investigations was entered.

An entry by Sergeant Plevin, on page 200 of the Occurrence Book on Tuesday the 17th March, suddenly stops in mid sentence:-

'I beg to report that at 3.10 pm on the 17/3/42 Mr William Wrixton, Bader-Idris, St John's, St Peter Port, reported to me at the Police station saying, On Saturday last 14/3/42 I visited my daughter's house at St Clair, everything was in order, I went there today 17/3/42 and found it had been broken into and everything in the house is ......'

The Sergeant was literally interrupted in mid sentence by a member of the Feldgendarmerie, who insisted on taking the book. to Grange Lodge. When the book was returned Mr Langmead wrote, in red ink:-

'This book was taken to Grange Lodge by Feldgendarmerie and kept for 10 days, in the meanwhile a new Occurrence book was commenced and reports continued therein. This book is now considered as full for record purposes.

16th April 1942 A J Langmead'.

The rest of the 150 pages are blank. The report, which Sergeant Plevin was in the middle of writing, was rewritten in the new book and concluded:-

'I beg to report that at 4.10 pm on the 17/3/42 Mr William Wrixton, Bader-Idris, St John's, St Peter Port, reported to me at the Police station saying, I went to my daughter's house at St Clair, St Sampson, on Saturday last (14/3/42) everything was in order. I visited the place this morning (17/3/42) and found all the doors forced open and the furniture scattered around the rooms. Signed E W Plevin, Sergeant'

From then on the Occurrence Book had to be taken to Grange Lodge at 9.00am each day for inspection by the Feldgendarmerie. Some of the handwriting by certain Sergeants was a little difficult to read even by their colleagues, so how the Germans faired it is difficult to imagine. Each day when the Book was returned it carried the initials of the inspecting German officer in red ink. Within two months the practice had been discontinued on German instructions, perhaps the writing had beaten them!

The new Police Appointment sub-Committee was kept busy interviewing many of the 170 applicants wishing to become Auxiliary Policemen. The first eight appointed were passed fit for service by Dr B S Collings on 20th March and commenced duty on 23rd March 1942:-

| | |
|---|---|
| A/13 Henry Brouard, 49. | 83 Mount Durand. |
| A/14 Reginald W Ferbrache, 33. | Rockleaze, Albecq. |
| A/15 William George Ferbrache, 44. | 2 Bouverie Cottages, Cobo. |
| A/16 Harold Hall, 38. | 18 States Houses, Saints. |
| A/17 Albert H Henry, 48. | Hillside, Foulon. |
| A/18 Frank H C Pill, 38. | 5 Marine Terrace, Les Banques. |
| A/19 Charles E Stewart, 31. | La Fontaine, Vale Road. |
| A/20 William A Strickland, 41. | Mare de Carteret, Castel. |

They were sworn in, taking the oath as Auxiliary Constables, in the Royal Court on Saturday 28th March 1942, before the Bailiff. Addressing them, he said:-

"Having been selected as members of the Guernsey Police Force I am about to administer to you the oath of office, before doing so I take this opportunity of impressing upon you that you are undertaking a very important duty in our Island life. You may be called upon to discharge arduous and dangerous duties and I would ask you at all times to remember the honour for the community depends largely upon the behaviour and integrity of its' Police Force.

You must always perform your duties without fear or favour and as model citizens, whilst you do this you can rest assured that I and other Island authorities will do all in our power to support you. I regret it is not possible at the present to provide you with uniforms but they will be provided as soon as possible."

In the meantime, on the 11th March, PC 18 Smith's mother-in-law, Mrs Alice Falla, of Cocagne-Bordeaux, Vale, was arrested by the Germans. Then on the 21st, Stephen J.C.Duquemin, the 70-year-old licensee of the Victoria Hotel, was detained on suspicion of receiving some of the stolen German supplies. Duquemin's wife Edith, was also taken into custody two days later. On the 25th March the Germans again released Constable Kimber.

Up to that time the only members of the Force who had not been questioned were Francois Le Cocq, who was recovering from his motorcycle accident, and Reg Marsh, who was also in hospital suffering from internal bleeding. The Germans interviewed PC Le Cocq in hospital regarding his accident, but he could not remember anything of the incident and no statement was taken. Reg Marsh was interviewed on the 26th March regarding the raiding of German stores and made a statement, but was not arrested. He did not return to duty until the 13th April.

Statements were also taken on the 26th from O.T. Meister Austen and O.T. Kameradschaftsfuhrer Schuster, the two Germans who had lain in wait for PCs Bailey and Tuck. The next day statements were taken from R.W.Randall, of Randalls Brewery, T.E.G. McCathie of Bucktrouts, C.A.Ford, States Superintendent of Imports, H.F.Le Lievre, A.E.Littlefield, of Littlefield and Snell, W.F.Adams, States Market Superintendent, F.H.Best and R.E.Chilcott, the Manager of the States Dairy.

The Controlling Committee met on the 26th and approved the Police Committee's recommendations:-

1. That the suspension of Inspector Sculpher be noted as from 6th March 1942, the Inspector receiving two thirds of pay i.e. £200.00 per annum during suspension.
2. That the members of the Island Police now in prison be considered suspended until the enquiry is completed, their respective wives and dependants receive two thirds of their pay in the meantime.

The Committee also decided to exercise the special powers given it by the States and approve the Police Force numbers being increased to 55 officers.

On the 28th March, the Germans took a statement from Inspector Sculpher and three days later they took him into custody and detained him in prison, without any charge being preferred.

The same day Fuerst von Oettingen received a letter from Colonel Knackfuss, in Jersey, stating:- "I request the earliest possible appointment of a suitable person to the post of Police Inspector in Guernsey since the reinstatement of Police Inspector Sculpher, after the occurrences there, is impossible."

Fuerst von Oettingen replied on the 31st March:-

"For head of the Police I request that Inspector Langmead, who has been officiating, may be allowed provisionally to remain. I am trying to find a suitable person for the post of head. The previous head, Inspector Sculpher, as reported by telegraph, is being provisionally detained in order to exclude the possibility of the new recruits being influenced."

The same day Fuerst von Oettingen also wrote to the President of Controlling Committee, taking direct control of the Police Force:-

"Re Reorganisation of the Island Police.

The scandalous incidents which have occurred among the Island Police have shown that the controlling organs have utterly failed. In future, therefore, the whole of the Island Police will be placed under the direct supervision of the Feldkommandantur. The Chief of the Police will be directly responsible to me for the proper functioning of the Police duties.

The division of the Island into four patrol districts with the provision of check points, undertaken under our order, is hereby approved together with the proposed distribution of duties. For the Town district of St Peter Port, a beat and patrol plan is to be submitted to me at once.

Various recent incidents make it necessary to point out once more that the Police should show marks of respect towards all members of the forces of officer rank. In addition all Police servants have to report (stating name, number and beat) to:

The Commander of the Island,

The Feldkommandant,

The Chief of the Nebenstelle of Feldkommandantur,

The Feldgendarmerie officer in charge of the supervision, or his representative.

The newly appointed Police servants shall as far as possible be provided with uniforms. The uniforms taken from the Policemen in custody may be used for this purpose. Please report to me immediately on the carrying out of this measure.

In the Police Station a guard book is to be kept, in which the distribution of duty for the day and other events are to be entered. This book is to be submitted at 9.00am to the Chief of the Gendarmerie of Nebenstelle.

While the behaviour of the arrested Policeman are without excuse, it nevertheless appears to me that the low wages of the staff may have to a certain extent obliterated the notion of honesty and faithfulness towards the population placed under their protection. I therefore request you to consider the question of the remuneration of the Police and submit to me proposals in view of an improvement."

The Acting Inspector was furnished with a copy of Fuerst von Oettingen's letter and asked by the President of the Controlling Committee for his comments.

Mr Langmead replied on the 2nd of April, commenting:-

"With reference to the copy letter dated 31/3/42 on the subject of the reorganisation of the Island Police.

Para.1 It is noted that the Island Police will be placed under the supervision of the Feldkommandantur and that I am to be responsible to the Rittmeister Fuerst von Oettingen for the proper functioning of all Police duties.

Para.2 The approval of the country patrol scheme is noted and will be put into operation as quickly as possible. The Town district, beat and patrol plan is being submitted. All Police have been instructed in their duties respecting saluting officers.

A list of all Police officers has been prepared and is attached for forwarding to the officer named.

Para.4 Every effort is being made to equip the new men with uniforms, but the garments collected from the men in prison are not fit to issue to new men, they are old, well worn, dirty and were made to measure for the men wearing them.

A number of caps have been obtained and are being prepared for issue. A cape and serge jacket for each man are being cleaned and renovated and will be issued as soon as ready. No trousers, leggings or boots are available.

Para.5 The Guard Book will be available for inspection daily as required.

Para.6 The question of pay is receiving the attention of the Police Committee who suggest that the standard operating before the war should be reverted to. As soon as a decision is reached a report will be sent with full details."

On the 1st of April Fuerst von Oettingen again wrote to the President of the Controlling Committee, this time on a different subject:-

"In the course of the enquiry of the thefts committed by the Police, it has been found that Constable Le Cocq had taken part in house breaking on the premises of the States Dairy at the end of 1939. I request you discharge him immediately and report to me on action taken."

The President of the Controlling Committee, was extremely concerned at receiving such an instruction and sought to have it rescinded. Having failed, he reluctantly passed the letter on to Mr Langmead, for action. The Acting Inspector, in turn wrote to the President of the Police Committee saying:-

"I beg to report that on the 4th April 1942, I received the attached letter from the President of the Controlling Committee concerning PC 35 Le Cocq. This letter requests the immediate dismissal of the PC for alleged complicity in a case of shop breaking which occurred in 1939. As a result of the letter I have suspended the PC as from 5th April.

This PC was appointed in May 1939 and latterly was employed as a motor cyclist where he performed very useful work. In February 1942, he met with a serious accident when on duty and as a result was seven weeks in hospital and is yet unable to move about freely as his leg is still in plaster of paris.

I have seen the PC, who denied the allegation and has signed the attached statement. If the allegation can be proved he should be proceeded against in the public interest.

As he is still unable to work, I beg to suggest that he remain suspended until he is passed fit for work by the doctor. In the meantime the matter can be taken up with the German Authorities with a view to the Constable being given an opportunity to refute the allegation before a competent authority.

So far as I can ascertain a statement by PC 18 Smith was made involving PC Le Cocq, who has not had an opportunity to challenge the allegation before any Court or Tribunal. The PC has performed his duties in a creditable manner and has taken a keen interest in his job."

PC Le Cocq even though his leg was still in plaster, had insisted on returning to duty in the Police Office. Whenever possible, until his suspension, he presented himself for duty. When told of the allegation he made a statement.

"I have been informed that PC 18 Smith has made a statement alleging that I have been concerned with him in breaking and entering the States Dairy during the latter part of 1939.

This I emphatically deny. Smith was a man who because of his morose temperament I never mixed with. I joined the Police Force in May 1939. I was interested in Police work and wanted to be in a position with some prospects before getting married and certainly would not have started by stealing. I was employed on outside duties until December of that year when I was put on office duties and remained in that position until after the Occupation when PC Plevin returned to office duties and I was put on motorcycle patrol and remained in that position until I met with my accident in February of this year.

I have never stolen anything and before joining the Police Force held positions of trust for a number of years. Any statement made by Smith or any other person to the effect that I have stolen anything would be a deliberate lie."

As the President was still ill, the Vice-President, Mr A.E.Agnew, wrote to the President of the Controlling Committee, supporting the recommendation of the Acting Inspector. He added that his sub-Committee felt that before being dismissed PC Le Cocq should be given time to regain his health and strength to enable him to take up civil employment, as he was injured whilst on duty.

The accusation by Constable Smith arose from a statement he signed for his German interrogators on the 20th March 1942. In respect of 'Theft in the States Dairy' he declared:-

"The first time I broke in with PC Le Cocq before the Occupation of the Island by German troops, was towards the end of 1939. The first time each of us stole one lb of butter. The second time I was in the above business at the end of 1940 or at the beginning of 1941, in the company of PC Tuck. We entered the business in the following manner: First we removed the wooden shutters, then Tuck took a thin piece of wood, opened with it the window and reached out his arm to open the lock from within. Both of us went into the business. On that occasion I took one lb of butter, but I do not know how much Tuck took for himself. Before leaving the business we have properly locked up again."

On the 1st of May 1942, the President of the Police Committee again wrote to the President of the Controlling Committee in respect of PC 35 Le Cocq.:-

"Further to my letter of 8th April, re PC Le Cocq. I beg to inform you that the allegation, reported to be made by PC Smith that he, Le Cocq, was concerned in breaking and entering the States Dairy in 1939.

During the week, Mrs Smith, wife of the PC, has received a letter from her husband which she handed to PC Le Cocq. A paragraph of the letter, which is at this Office is as follows:-

When you see Ginger, tell him it is not true that I went to the Dairy with him in 1939, as when I said it, I was in a confused state of mind, but tell him it is not true. 'Ginger' is the nickname by which Le Cocq is known."

The Germans were given a copy of the letter and later that day Dr Brosch informed John Leale that the charges against PC Le Cocq have "failed to be confirmed and he may therefore resume his duties as a member of the Island Police".

Francois Le Cocq returned to duty immediately and received full back pay from the time of his suspension.

At 11.20pm on the 29th March, Acting Sergeant Bull, who was in charge of the Station, received a telephone call from Albert J.Spurdle, the Chief Inspector of Telephones. He reported:- "At 11.00pm the Castel Exchange suddenly cut out, we cannot get any communication with them. It is very important that we should, as the Emergency hospital is on this circuit. Would it be possible for the Police to get out and see what is wrong as we have no one with a night permit."

Acting Sergeant Bull went in the Police car, to the Castel exchange but on arrival two armed sentries prevented him from entering the building. He managed, however, to attract the attention of Mr E.H.Bennett, the Manager of the Telephone Department, who lived at the official manager's residence next door. He explained:-

"There is a general alarm on and the Germans will not allow the exchange to be used until further notice. Would you kindly convey this message to the Town exchange".

Acting Sergeant Bull returned to the Station and telephoned Mr Spurdle and explained the situation.

The sub-Committee of the Police Committee had been kept fully occupied since they were appointed on the 16th March, interviewing applicants. Of the large number of men who responded to the advertisement, 112 were interviewed.

Those who passed the interview were required to submit two references and pass a medical examination. Three applicants failed the medical and one failed to supply the necessary references - they were not appointed.

On the 30th March eight recruits commenced duty. They had been passed fit by Dr Collings and were sworn in by the Bailiff in the Royal Court.

| | |
|---|---|
| A/21 Arthur W.Falla, 55. | 2 Cliff Terrace, The Strand. |
| A/22 George H.Gale, 28. | Victoria House, Les Hubits. |
| A/23 Clifford C.Langlois, 28. | The Willows, L'Aumone. |
| A/24 Basil Le Page, 29. | Portinfer Lodge, Vale. |
| A/25 Ernest Le Prevost, 36. | Downsview, Marais Lane. |
| A/26 Reginald A.Parlett, 29. | La Tourelle Bungalow, Saints. |
| A/27 Geoffrey P.Scraton, 31. | Quarry Cottage, St Andrew. |
| A/28 Edwin J.Thoume, 23. | Saete Place, Capelles. |

Four more Auxiliary Policemen were appointed on the 6th April.

| | |
|---|---|
| A/29 Frank Henry Falla, 44. | Westminister Bank Flat, The Bridge. |
| A/30 Daniel George De Carteret, 32. | Summerfield Road, Vale. |
| A/31 Wilfred John Mansfield, 22. | Le Villocq, Castel. |
| A/32 John William Salmon, 22. | 14 Burnt Lane, St Peter Port. |

One Auxiliary, A/PC 9 Walter A.Robilliard, who had served as a full time Special since May 1940, found the night duties too much for him at his age, he was fifty, and tendered his resignation. He was permitted by the Police Committee to leave as from the 12th April. He quickly found new employment as a carpenter with G.S.Robilliard of the Rohais.

Fuerst von Oettingen, exercising his control over the Police Force, wrote to the President of the Controlling Committee on the 11th April stating that A/PC 2 John Corbin, A/PC 4 George Lewis, A/PC 12 Herbert Williams and A/PC 14 Reginald Ferbrache were not suitable as they were too short for Police duties and were to be discharged immediately.

**A/PC George Lewis.**

Acting Inspector Langmead accepted that three of the men were not be suitable for Police work, but felt that George Lewis had shown, in the twenty-two months he had served as a full time Special Constable, that he was a keen and conscientious Police officer. He wrote to Fuerst von Oettingen:-

"He has an aptitude for controlling queues and has proved one of the best Auxiliaries appointed in the emergency. His height is not up to usual standards, but he is physically fit and strong. He attained the rank of Sergeant Major in the last war and bears an excellent character. I beg to ask that the case of this man be reviewed with a view to him retaining his appointment."

Mr Langmead went to see George Lewis at his home at La Bellieuse, St Martin and told him that he was putting up a fight to retain him. He told him that 'height should not be taken into account under the present circumstances'.

Fuerst von Oettingen was adamant, Lewis had to be discharged along with the other three Auxiliaries. George soon obtained employment as the States

Bootmaker, at the boot factory in the High Street. His wage of 45/- a week, was less than he had been paid as a policeman, but he had every Sunday and one half day a week off, as well as regular hours. John Corbin went to work for Timmer Ltd., Bert Williams, who already had part time employment as a band leader, became an electrician at the Lyric Theatre and Reginald Ferbrache returned to growing.

The training of the new Auxiliary Policemen proved difficult. Some of the recruits had served with the Special Constabulary and that experience ensured that they had at least an outline of what their new career entailed. Mr Langmead arranged a class each week at which he, Acting Deputy Inspector Lamy or Sergeant Banneville instructed the men on an aspect of policing and Police law.

As a result of Fuerst von Oettingen's request for a review of Police wages, the Police Committee passed their views and recommendations on to the Controlling Committee, which considered them on the 14th April.

The President, John Leale, said:- "I have made enquiries with a view to discovering whether there is any basis in fact for the Feldkommandant's impression that low rates of pay might have prompted stealing on the part of the members of the Force now in prison. My enquiries reveal that, of the 19 now in prison or suspended, 8 have no dependants and 7 have only one dependant in the Island. From this, it does not appear reasonable to attribute their dishonesty to any financial hardship."

Dr Symons said that he had always felt that the responsibility resting on policemen justified their receiving better pay than an ordinary worker and he was in favour of an increase. Deputy R.H. Johns pointed out that the pay of policemen, prior to the recent incidents, meant that they were appreciably better off than a labourer and in addition they could rely on holidays with pay, uniform, allowances and a pension.

Mr Percy Dorey was strongly in favour of higher rates, especially for the new men now being taken into the force. The few remaining members of the permanent Force were having to bear added burdens. Mr Dorey contended that the right type of man was not likely to come forward as Auxiliaries for the 45/- per week which was being offered. The pay should be raised and unsuitable men weeded out, if a reliable Force was to be produced.

Sir Abraham Laine supported the contention that the present rates of pay were inadequate, considering the added responsibility imposed by present day conditions. In particular the Acting Inspector and Acting Deputy Inspector were deserving of recognition for this reason.

The States Supervisor, H.E.Marquand, said he felt constrained to say that, if granted, the proposed restoration of cuts in the pay of the Police Force would cause dissatisfaction among employees in other departments, which he thought would be justified. After a lengthy discussion, the Committee approved new rates of pay to operate immediately.

| | |
|---|---|
| Acting Inspector | £350 per annum |
| Acting Deputy Inspector | £260 per annum plus 1/- per week boot allowance |
| Detective Sergeant | 92/- per week plus 6/- per week boot and clothing allowance. |
| Sergeants | 70/- to 80/- plus 1/- boot allowance |
| Acting Sergeants | 68/- to 78/- " " " |
| Police Constables | 55/- to 65/- " " " |
| Auxiliaries Constables | 50/- to 60/- " " " |

The next day John Leale wrote to the Feldkommandantur informing him of the details of the review of Police wages, stating that the additional cost would be £1,100 per annum.

Mr Langmead wished to release Acting Deputy Inspector Lamy from his office duties, so that he could undertake the outside supervision of the increased country patrols. He felt that if PC 35 Le Cocq was allowed to retain his position in the Force, he could fill the vacancy, "although he has admitted to me that he would prefer outside duties and I could well utilize him on a motorcycle".

In Mr Langmead's view there was no one amongst the new recruits capable of doing the clerical job. As an alternative he suggested that a young man be employed as a civilian clerk at 35/- to 40/- a week. "If a suitable youth of good physique could be obtained, a good opportunity would be given to him to obtain experience in Police procedure, which would be of service when he reached an age at which he could transfer to the Force as a Constable, or move to an English Force."

It was agreed that a civilian be appointed and nineteen-year-old Raymond W.P.Ozanne was in due course selected and started work on the 25th May 1942, at a salary of £2.0.0 a week.

Another position Mr Langmead wished to have approved by the Police Committee, was the appointment of a Police tailor. The previous tailor had died over a year previously and there was now an urgent need for a replacement.

"I have spoken", reported Mr Langmead, "to Mr A.B.Pugh, of Mansell Street, who is employed as a tailor by James Mourant, of 8 High Street. He would be prepared to act as Police tailor in his spare time on the same conditions as the previous tailor, that is £10 per annum. The fixed sum basis was for fitting and measuring all Police twice a year and doing all repairs during the year. There will be certain alterations required for serge jackets to fit the new men in addition to minor repairs." Mr Pugh was appointed.

The health of the President of the Police Committee, W.E.Poat, had deteriorated to such an extent that at the meeting of the Committee on the 13th April 1942 he submitted his resignation. It was not as if the Presidency had been a very heavy burden, in respect of the number of meetings held. The meeting of the Committee on the 16th March 1942 had been the first held since the 23rd June 1941. The only other meeting held in 1941 had been on 10th February.

The Committee reluctantly accepted the President's resignation and was replaced by Mr C.E.Agnew, with Mr H.C.Brock being elected Vice-President.

Inspector Sculpher had increasingly ignored the President of the Police Committee ever since the formation of the Controlling Committee. He had worked closely with, first Mr Sherwill and laterally John Leale. Virtually all correspondence with the Germans had been through the President of the Controlling Committee, without even a copy going to the President of the Police Committee.

Mr Poat, whilst being pleased that he had not had too heavy a workload as President, had on occasions, complained about being ignored by the Inspector but with little effect. After the Occupation he wrote:-

"Inspector Sculpher, from the time of the Occupation seemed to me to wish to ignore the Committee to a very considerable extent and when I put questions to him from time to time regarding the work of the Police, I generally received a reply to the effect that he had spoken either to Mr Leale or Mr Sherwill or Mr Ridgway on the subject and that was all I could get out of him."

Mr Langmead, immediately upon his appointment as Acting Inspector, sought to keep the President and Members of the Police Committee better informed of the activities of the Force than had his predecessor. He and Mr Agnew quickly struck up a good working relationship.

# Chapter 15

# A REVOLVER WAS THRUST INTO MY RIBS AND I SIGNED

After PCs Bailey, Tuck, Burton, Smith and Friend were arrested they were held in the prison in St James Street. One by one they were taken, sometimes by car and other times marched with four armed guards, to the Feldgendarmerie Headquarters at Grange Lodge. Each was interrogated for hours on end, generally by three Germans, including Sergeant Major Oeser, an officer named Wolff, who spoke fluent English, and a lieutenant who manned a typewriter.

There can be little doubt that as a result of information gained from the interrogation of these Constables other members of the Force were arrested. First Sergeant Harper, then PC Short and Sergeant Howlett. Some days elapsed before Sergeant Duquemin, PCs Whare, Gaudion and Quin were detained. Finally eighteen Police officers and four civilians were held in the prison.

Frank Tuck was the first man to make a statement, on the 6th March. Kingston Bailey quickly followed, signing a statement the next day. On the 9th Fred Short and on the 10th Sergeant Fred Duquemin and Constable Tom Gaudion made statements. From then on there was a constant stream of statements being signed:-

| | |
|---|---|
| 11th March | PC 18 Smith, |
| 14th | PC 23 Quin, |
| 16th | PC 23 Quin (2nd), Sergeant Harper, |
| 17th | PC 22 Bailey (2nd), PC 16 Tuck (2nd), Sergeant Howlett, |
| 18th | PC 15 Burton, PC 30 Short (2nd), |
| 20th | PC 15 Burton (2nd), PC 23 Quin (3rd), PC 33 Gaudion (2nd), PC 14 Friend, PC 18 Smith (2nd). |
| 21st | Sergeant Duquemin (2nd) PC 18 Smith (3rd) |
| 22nd | Stephen J.C.Duquemin. |
| 23rd | PC 23 Quin (4th), Stephen J.C.Duquemin (2nd) |
| 24th | PC 20 Whare, PC 16 Tuck (3rd) |
| 25th | PC 14 Friend (2nd), PC 25 Piesing, |
| 26th | Sergeant Harper (2nd), PC 15 Burton (3rd) PC 30 Short (3rd), PC 23 Quin (5th), PC 20 Whare (2nd), PC 9 Marsh. |

Frank Tuck, who signed three statements, later recalled:-

"During their interrogation the German Police beat me up with various objects, punched me and kicked me when I was lying on the floor.

They lugged me up again and repeated the process. They then threw me into a bare cell and left me there for several days without being able to wash or shave and with only bread and water.

When this process had been repeated on several occasions, they presented me with documents written in German which they told me were statements from my colleagues, implicating me.

They then told me what was supposed to be in the documents. I disagreed and they invited me to sign under the threat of a repetition of the former treatment. A revolver was thrust into my ribs and I signed. I cannot remember now how many times I signed or if it was only once.

After I had signed they cursed me for not having signed before and for not being what they called 'helpful' and said I'd probably be charged with sabotage anyway and proceeded to give me a bashing-up."

Kingston Bailey some fifteen years after the events of 1942, wrote his version of the affair. He recalled:-

"I was put in a separate cell, the food was terrible, consisting of a small plate of vegetable soup, with one slice of bread for dinner; for breakfast and tea we had the same quantity of bread with a piece of margarine and ersatz coffee without milk or sugar. The cells were terribly cold and one had to sleep fully dressed to keep warm.

On the second day of my imprisonment I was called by one of the gaolers to the guard room. There I was handed over to a German Military Policeman, who had to sign the book kept by the guards, to say that he had taken me from prison. I was taken up to Grange Lodge, to Sergeant Major Oeser. With him was a German in plain clothes, called Wolff. He spoke perfect English. We found him to be a first class liar in the days to come. He questioned me concerning other alleged robberies of foodstuffs. I replied that I knew nothing of the robberies. Oeser flew into a rage and struck me across the face. Several times I was asked the same question and each time I stuck to my first reply.

All day and every day, different Police were being taken to Grange Lodge. We caught a few words when they returned, but otherwise were completely in the dark as to what was happening. One day when Frank Tuck returned, his cell was next to mine, he told me that he had been shown a confession alleged to have been made by one of the Police, involving him in robberies from three stores. Frank assured me that he had still denied this and had received a beating up for his denial.

A favourite trick of Oeser's was to give you a cigarette, offer you a light and at the same time, smack you across the face, knocking the cigarette flying. Then he would say 'Tell us the truth, then you will be able to smoke'.

We were all getting utterly confused. Wolff was so good at his slimy job that we could not tell what was truth and what was lies. So through lack of sleep, bad food, beatings, lies and alleged self-made confessions the Germans gained their object. On the second and third occasions that I was taken to their Headquarters, I was read a list of confessions that were, I was told, made by my comrades, involving myself in robberies from German stores and one civilian store.

I knew I had been to these stores, so I admitted the charges. I thought that if my comrades had made confessions, it was useless for me to deny the fact. But when I spoke at a later date to my comrades, I was amazed to hear that they had had a confession read to them, supposed to have been made by me and that they had made no confessions and had never mentioned my name by word or deed.

By this cross questioning and through continual brutality, the Germans obtained sufficient evidence to stage a first class propaganda trial. They laid stress on the civilian stores so that our acts would not appear as acts against the military but against the civilian population. For months we had sabotaged their food stores and according to Oeser, four thousand tins of food were still not accounted for."

In April 1947 Bill Burton wrote to the Rev Waterbury, Vice-President of the Police Committee.

"On the 5th March 1942 I was arrested by the German Police and put in the local prison. On the 12th I was taken to Grange Lodge where an offer was put before me. 'You know quite a lot of what is going on against us. We are willing to release you and send you back to the Force if you will keep us informed.' My reply was 'My Country is at war with yours, I refuse to accept any offers, I am prepared to accept what is in store for me.' For that reply I received a blow in the mouth, whereby I lost five bottom teeth. Wolff, the interpreter, told me that I was a fool to reject such an offer and that I would be sorry."

**PC Bill Burton.**

Bill Burton further recalled his experiences of the interrogation in a sworn statement he made in 1951.

"After spending a week in a dark cell, I was taken to Grange Lodge, locked in a back room with a German lieutenant and an interpreter asked me questions concerning sabotage and plundering of German stores. Being a loyal British subject, I denied all knowledge of acts against the German forces, which I know they did not believe.

After three hours of this, I was taken back to the prison. Two days after I was taken to Grange Lodge again, but this time the lieutenant, two other officers and a different interpreter by the name of Wolff were there. The door was locked and I was told to sit down. Wolff said to me

'You know what you are here for?'

I said 'No'.

He said 'You are head of a gang of saboteurs, both Police and civilians. We have been told about you, what have you to say?'

'I know nothing about it' I said.

I was asked if I had served with the British forces in France during the last war. I said 'Yes and proud of it'.

The lieutenant left his typing and came by me and started striking me on the side of the head. I ended up on the floor, got to my feet and was going to have a go at him, when others pointed revolvers at me.

Wolff said 'If you strike him, that will be the last thing you do'.

Having enough sense to know that I could not fight against revolvers, I stopped. I was bashed all over the room until I fell exhausted on the floor.

When I came round there was only Wolff left in the room and he offered me a glass of cognac, which I refused. I could have done with it.

He said 'You're a fool, why don't you tell us everything you know'.

I was determined, however, never to betray anyone or divulge information to them. I told him again 'I know nothing'.

Shortly afterwards the others came in and glared at me. They conversed in German.

Wolff left the room and returned with two German soldiers. He said 'You can go back to prison and think over things'.

I was taken there in a German car, so that the public could not see the state I was in.

Shortly after that, in the early hours of the morning, my cell door was flung open and in walked Wolff, who triumphantly said

'We have got you now. I have a letter which you have written to someone outside. Who did you give it to?'

I replied 'I have not written any letters. I can prove that'.

I showed him a specimen of my handwriting and then they left.

I was in peace, but not for long.

A few days after, I was taken to Grange Lodge, again into the same room, where there was a high German officer, four other officers, the lieutenant and Wolff. I said to him 'Your staff has increased'

He said 'You know who that is, he is the chief and he has told me to tell you that this is your last chance to tell us all you know'.

I replied 'I can only repeat what I have already told you, I know nothing about anyone else. I am not the head of the saboteurs or any other movement'.

He spoke to the crowd in the room and they beat me up. I was in a dazed condition and shown a document written in German and told to sign it. I told Wolff that I did not know German and he said

'It is only to say that you have been questioned by the German Police and can tell them nothing'.

I knew he was lying, but I signed and that was to get me three years."

Bill Quin was more concise in regard to his recollections of the events following his arrest.

"With regard to the treatment before the trial, I can only say that I, too, was hit about, knocked about and threatened generally before I signed the statement, in German, that was put before me."

Charlie Friend later recalled:-

**PC Charlie Friend.**

"For about a month I was continually being questioned at Grange Lodge, which was the Feldgendarmerie headquarters.

I was taken to the top floor and made to sit down in the centre of three chairs. I was offered cigarettes etc. and I was hit severely about the head and face and I spent a great deal of time on the floor. They questioned me and accused me of sabotaging the German Occupation forces.

Wolff was the interpreter and he spoke fluent English. There was a man at a typewriter in the room as well. I was threatened by them with revolvers and they stated that it would be easy for them to kill me accidentally. They also said that if I did not plead guilty and give them a full admission to these various charges, they would fetch my mother and those nearest and dearest to me and torture them as well. It was in these circumstances that I made a full confession.

On one occasion I was taken back to the Guernsey prison with my face unrecognisable from the beating I had taken."

Frank Whare, after the occupation, recalled his experiences at the hands of the Germans following his arrest:-

"When I was first arrested I was asked questions about the underground movement in Guernsey, about which I protested my ignorance. On a later occasion Oeser hit me on the face twice when I was more or less stunned. On another occasion he spat in my face and on the spur of the moment I spat back.

I was knocked to the ground, but before I reached the floor I was grabbed by the arms by two men standing by and I was kicked in the back, abdomen and thighs until I began to vomit.

I was informed that Gaudion had informed about my part in the affair. I was then confronted with Gaudion and I was then hit again. They then stated that they would fetch my wife and question her. I could not then stand any more and I confessed that I had been with Gaudion etc. A statement was typed in German and I signed it."

Some years after the liberation of the Island, Jack Harper, who was then a patient in the J.N.Adam Memorial Hospital, in Perryburg, New York State, swore an affidavit in which he said:-

"I was arrested at my flat at 39 High Street, St Peter Port, on the 6th March 1942 and placed in German custody and held until the last for questioning. When I refused to sign statements already prepared, I was brutally bashed about and almost lost my senses.

This went on for some time and then a fat Nazi officer pulled out a revolver and pushed it into my ribs and threatened to shoot. The perspiration poured out of me and I signed. I think I signed four times. I had no idea what was in the statements as they were written in German. I was then a physical and mental wreck and could neither eat nor sleep. When PC Smith, who had been disarranged the whole time, tried to commit suicide, I felt like doing the same."

Another Constable who suffered at the hands of his interrogators was Fred Short. He later recalled the events following his arrest:-

"They didn't take me to Grange Lodge for interrogation, they took me to Ash House, the house next door. I was taken up to a room at the top of the house and they battered hell out of me. They ripped my uniform, kicked me in the face, splitting my lip and smashing my false teeth.

The first thing Sergeant Major Oeser did was to take his revolver out of it's holster and place it on the table in front of him and say, pointedly, in broken English 'Now, these have been known to go off accidentally'.

I was sat on a stool and three Germans fired question after question at me in rapid succession. That continued for hours on end. When I would not admit to one of their accusations, a chap on my left would hit me on the head with his clenched fist. His signet ring kept finding its mark just behind my left ear.

The questioning went on for several days. I kept repeating, 'No I don't know anything about it'. One of the Germans lost his temper and clubbed me with a bootjack. I was beaten with a rifle butt. On one occasion I was grabbed by the hair and my head smashed against the wall. I was unconscious and when I came round blood was streaming down my face. I was made to stand up until I collapsed again. When I was asleep in my cell at 2.00 o'clock one morning, three Jerry policemen arrived and gave me another beating, I was too weak to try and resist and in any case I would only have been bashed about more if I had tried to do so.

I was told that other men had confessed and implicated me. Three times a German stuck a revolver against my side and threatened to press the trigger accidentally if I didn't say 'Yes' to something they wanted me to admit. In the end, like everyone else, I confessed to theft, but the details of the so called confessions were written, not by me, but by the Germans, in German. I was told to sign my name at the bottom. At first I refused, but I was beaten again about the head and body. Finally I signed the document."

Archie Tardif later recalled how he signed his statement.

"After my arrest, I spent about a week in prison and was then eventually questioned. On arrival at the questioning, a glass of cognac was placed just out of my reach and an unlit cigarette was given to me. I had not smoked for about a fortnight. I said I knew nothing and the cognac was thrown in my face and the cigarette thrown into the waste paper basket.

The following day I was questioned for about an hour and punched, kicked, hit with a wooden ruler and questioned further. I was stretched over a stool and my head bashed against a wall. I was shown signed statements by other men and was eventually told that if I did not sign I would be shot, so I eventually signed.

All these statements were typed in German. After I had signed my alleged statement, it was returned to the typewriter and additions made."

On the 31st March 1942 the Germans presented the case they had prepared against the eighteen Guernsey Police officers, to a Military Court in Jersey. As a result permission was given for charges to be preferred against the four Sergeants, fourteen Constables and the four civilians allegedly involved. They were all charged on the 10th April 1942 with various offences in connection with thefts from Military stores.

The civilians charged by the Germans, Stephen Duquemin, Mrs Edith Duquemin, Mrs Alice Falla, and Mrs Marguerite Torode were sentenced by judgement of the Tribunal of the Feldkommandantur 515, in Jersey, on the 20th April 1942, without any of the accused being present.

The Guernsey Authorities were officially informed that:-

Stephen John Christopher Duquemin, proprietor of the Victoria Hotel, Esplanade, was sentenced to four months' imprisonment. The facts were given as:-

'In February 1942, in Guernsey the prisoner had received and concealed for his own use objects which he must have known had been procured by punishable acts.

During the night of 22nd/23rd February 1942 the Police Constables Smith and Quin broke into the O.T.depot in the Truchot Street, St Peter Port and stole 2 boxes containing 48 tins of meat preserves. They brought these cases during the night to the prisoner, who took them under his care. Later the prisoner took 36 tins to his farm at Vazon. He consumed about 20 tins in his household. It appeared that part of the tins were stolen. Smith and Quin obtained a few tins back. The prisoner did not give any cheque to the Police Constables.

Evidence: Admission and statements made by Smith and Quin.'

Mrs Edith Duquemin, wife of S.J.C.Duquemin, born in Norwich, England, was sentenced to six weeks' imprisonment.

The facts were given as:-

'In February 1942, the prisoner has received, in Guernsey goods which she knew had been acquired by punishable acts. In February 1942 she received from Police Constable Quin 2 sausages, which the latter had stolen from the meat store in the Market Hall in St Peter Port. The prisoner knew where the sausages came from.'

Mrs Alice Falla, married, of Cocagne-Bordeaux, Vale. Sentenced to six weeks imprisonment.

Mrs Marguerite Maria Torode, married, of 4 Roland Road, St Sampson. Sentenced to six weeks imprisonment.

Once the eighteen Policemen had been interrogated and charged, they were moved from the prison, to Fort George, where conditions were much better. One of the buildings had been specially prepared for their arrival. Each room was clean and contained two beds, with several blankets and new straw mattresses. The rooms themselves were about twelve feet square and had a large window without bars. The men were allowed to receive cigarettes, letters, food and anything that they needed from their relatives and friends.

After the battering many of the men had received during their interrogation, the contrast which Fort George presented was almost inconceivable. Sergeant Major Oeser, who had treated the accused so brutally, had the audacity to visit them and ask if they were quite comfortable. The Germans clearly planned that the accused were going to be in a good physical condition when they appeared before the Military Court.

The trial, held in the Police Court, started on the 22nd April. The men were brought from Fort George, in two coaches. Gone was the pushing and brutality, now they were, as Kingston Bailey commented:- "Treated like tourists in the good old days". As they entered the Court House, the large crowd that had gathered, gave them the thumbs up and the 'V' sign. Yells of "keep your chins up" helped to encourage the men.

In the Police Court, the gallery was crowded with the men's wives, relatives and other Islanders, many who had queued since early morning to be sure of obtaining a seat when the Trial opened at 9.00am. A large swastika flag covered the Royal Coat of Arms. This was all part of the German propaganda exercise.

The Court was composed of Dr Biel, the Presiding Judge, Fuerst von Oettingen and Uffz Kraft as Assessors. The prosecution was in the hands of the German Attorney-General Dr Graf Trauttmansdorff. Mr Ambrose Sherwill, who had been removed by the Germans from office, appeared on behalf of the accused.

The choice of Fuerst von Oettingen as an Assessor, in view of his very firmly held views, clearly expressed in a number of letters to both his superior in Jersey and to the President of the Controlling Committee, was considered 'interesting' by many people including a number of Germans. Also he had recently decreed that the Island Police Force would, in future, be placed under his direct supervision. Actions which could hardly be viewed as conducive to him being regarded as impartial, detached and independent.

The accused Policemen were brought into Court and sat on chairs in the well of the Court.

THE ACCUSED.

| | |
|---|---|
| Sergeant Frederick Duquemin 46, | 3 Park Lane, St Peter Port. |
| Sergeant Jack Harper 42, | 39 High Street, St Peter Port. |
| Sergeant Edward Pill 48, | Spadina, Rocquettes, St Peter Port. |
| Sergeant Alfred Howlett 50, | Houmet Lane, L'Islet. |
| Constable Kingston Bailey 26, | Les Croutes, St Peter Port. |
| Constable Frank Tuck 27, | Les Huriaux, St Martin. |
| Constable Charles Friend 27, | Veronica, Braye Road, Vale. |
| Constable William Burton 46, | Rougemont, Rouge Rue, St Peter Port. |
| Constable Herbert Smith 38, | Rue Flere, Vale. |
| Constable William Quin 45, | Dracena Way, St Martin. |
| Constable Frederick Short 31, | St David's, Steam Mill Lane, St Martin. |
| Constable Frank Whare 46, | 4 Old Mill, St Martin. |
| Constable Thomas Gaudion 45. | Columbia Villa, St Sampson. |
| Constable Archibald Tardif 31, | Chyebassa, La Ramee, St Peter Port. |
| Constable Eugene Le Lievre 26, | Les Landes, Vale. |
| Constable Alfred Le Gallez 28, | Rougeval, Rouge Rue, St Peter Port. |
| Constable Harold Piesing 33, | Carabyn, Forest Road, St Martin. |
| Constable Peter Bretel 45, | Mont Morin, St Sampson. |

They were all charged, with the exception of Sergeant Pill, with larceny on a grand or small scale as well as receiving stolen goods. Sergeant Harper was also charged with being the instigator of the various robberies of German Military and Organisation Todt foodstuffs. Sergeant Pill was charged with being aware of the thefts of wood from the Military timber yard committed by his subordinates and with not attempting to interfere in any way, thus becoming an accessory to the crime.

The proceedings started with the Presiding Judge questioning the accused on a series of personal matters. This took a considerable time and included questions on family, religion, salary, military service, ownership of property, debts and their Police career.

The Prosecutor then read the charges against each of the accused, detailing contravention of the various sections, articles and paragraphs of the German Criminal Law.

The trial proceeded with the reading of the 'sworn' statements made by each of the accused. As individual defendants were cross examined about the detail of their statements, conflict quickly arose between them and their colleagues, as statements and stories differed and varied. The Prosecutor sought to make the most of these differences.

Many of the men only realised what they had signed when their translated statements were read out in Court. Their main concern, as Fred Short later recalled, was:- "...that we should avoid being charged and convicted of sabotage, which was punishable by death. Therefore we had to admit stealing from their stores, making the excuse that we were hungary - which of course we were".

The trial was 'fully' reported in both the *Evening Press* and *The Star*. The local press, which was not only censored by the Germans, but many of the stories and features were contributed by them. The front pages were virtually without exception reserved for propaganda, contributed by the Germans. Sonderfuehrer Kurt Goettmann was the German censor and it was he who saw that the most effective use was made of the propaganda opportunity presented by the trial.

Goettmann decreed that the front page of *The Star* should be used to report the trial with the headline proclaiming 'Amazing Disclosures at Police Trial'. The clever use of phrases and emphasis were clearly designed to ensure that the general Guernsey public was influenced against the Police. The reports were carefully vetted by the German censor to provide the maximum propaganda advantage.

Frank Falla, who was at that time acting editor of *The Star*, fell foul of the Germans as a result of his inclusion in a limited number of copies of the paper, of part of Mr Sherwill's plea of mitigation on behalf of some of the defendants. Frank had allowed some copies to be printed before it was finally passed by the German censor. One copy with the offending report was read by Fuerst von Oettingen and as a consequence *The Star's* acting editor was fined 100 Reichmarks or alternatively serve 10 days imprisonment. The directors of *The Star* paid the fine.

The trial before the German Military Tribunal lasted for two and a half days, just over 12 hours in total, and resulted in seventeen of the eighteen Police officers charged being found guilty. Sergeant Pill was found not guilty, or in the words of the Presiding Judge "In regard to Pill the Court did not find any guilt".

Ambrose Sherwill, who represented the men at the trial, later commented:-

"I received a message through the German Feldgendarmerie that the accused wished me to represent them at their trial. I then obtained permission to visit them and saw them all in the absence of any German.

A number of them had been beaten up to secure admissions of guilt but it was clear that, however much I deplored the method of obtaining such admissions, those admissions were in accordance with the truth.

In these circumstances, I felt it useless, in all but one case, to do other than concentrate on attempting to secure mitigation of punishment.

No German suggestion or threat was made to me concerning the conduct of the defence, the German prosecutor treated me as a professional colleague and the President* of the Court, Fuerst von Oettingen, allowed me every facility to conduct the defence in my own way."

The only case where Mr Sherwill chose to defend any of the accused was in respect to Sergeant Pill, who was charged with being aware of the theft of firewood by his subordinates. He cross examined a number of the other defendants, seeking to show that other members of the Force had such regard for Sergeant Pill's high reputation for honesty and integrity, that they would in no circumstances have disclosed to him any of their activities. All the men denied that Sergeant Pill had in any way been involved in any of their activities.

Addressing the Court on behalf of the men, Ambrose Sherwill said:-

"Had I been the prosecutor in this case, I might have asked for sentences perhaps not differing from those suggested by the German Prosecutor.

Facts were stubborn things and a large percentage of the Guernsey Police had betrayed the trust reposed in them and facilities accorded to them as guardians of the public had been misused.

I am pleased that Sergeant Pill has been acquitted. As to the others they have lost their pensions, their work and lost their character. So I ask the Court to take their sacrifice into consideration. What they have lost would go on for many years. And there was the relative ages of the accused and the consideration of those who had yielded to sudden temptation made by suggestion."

He added:- "The trial has brought a sense of shame and disgrace to the Island and which has profoundly shocked and disturbed the people".

Then Mr Sherwill gave, at some length, the reasons why he felt the Court might consider mitigation of the sentences asked for by the Prosecutor. However, he added:- "Frankly I was glad at the reasonable sentences asked for by the Prosecutor."

He concluded, by admitting that the sentences represented the law.

While being successful in the case of Sergeant Pill, Ambrose Sherwill had, in the other men's eyes, done little to help their cause. Some of the men were unhappy with the way Mr Sherwill had represented them and rejected his services at a later trial.

Kingston Bailey and Frank Tuck jointly signed a statement in 1950, stating:-

"We were tried by a German Court Martial and sentenced to varying terms in the name of the German people, at which the unseated H.M.Attorney General, Mr A.J.Sherwill, appeared in our defence and made a feeble plea of mitigation, quite inappropriate to the brilliant lawyer that he is."

Just before 11.00am on the third day of the trial, the three members of the Tribunal retired to consider their verdicts and the sentences to be imposed on those found guilty. They returned just before 2.00pm and announced their decision in the name of the German people.

| | |
|---|---|
| Sergeant F.Duquemin | 2 years 6 months hard labour. |
| Sergeant J.Harper | 4 years 6 months hard labour. |
| Sergeant A.Howlett | 2 years imprisonment. |
| PC K.G.Bailey | 2 years 8 months hard labour. |
| PC F.Tuck | 3 years 6 months hard labour. |
| PC C.Friend | 3 years 6 months hard labour. |
| PC W.Burton | 3 years hard labour. |
| PC H.Smith | 4 years hard labour. |
| PC W.Quin | 4 years hard labour. |
| PC F.W.Short | 3 years 3 months hard labour. |
| PC F.Whare | 2 years 6 months hard labour. |

* Fuerst Von Oettingen was an Assessor and not the President of the Court.

| | |
|---|---|
| PC T.Gaudion | 2 years 4 months hard labour |
| PC A.L.Tardif | 1 year 6 months imprisonment. |
| PC E.Le Lievre | 8 months imprisonment. |
| PC A.T.Le Gallez | 8 months imprisonment. |
| PC H.Piesing | 1 year imprisonment. |
| PC P.Bretel | 4 weeks imprisonment. |
| Sergeant E.Pill | Acquitted. |

Sergeant Ted Pill and PC Peter Bretel, who had already spent over four weeks in custody, were released immediately.

The convicted men were then told that their sentences were subject to the confirmation of the Feldkommandantur and after that there could be no appeal. "But" added the Judge "you have the right, if you want to say anything about your sentence, to say it now and it will be placed before the Commandant for consideration."

Only four of the men chose to avail themselves of the opportunity. Sergeant Harper asked for consideration to be given to his length of service. "I think the sentences are severe", he added. Sergeant Howlett, on the grounds of his age, made application to serve his time in Guernsey prison. Constable Bailey asked to see his relations and was told he could do that. Constable Piesing made a plea that his sentence was too heavy.

It had, earlier in the proceedings, been suggested by Mr Sherwill that PC Smith was on the verge of a mental breakdown and the Judge said that if Smith made an application for medical treatment, he would be examined at once.

As soon as the Court rose the convicted men were taken under escort, back to Fort George. They were seen off by a crowd of friends and relations, many of whom were in tears.

The Swastika flag, which had hung behind the Judge throughout the trial, was removed and by 2.15pm the Court was empty.

On the 25th April Fuerst von Oettingen wrote to Colonel Knackfuss, possibly for the last time before he was posted away from the Channel Islands:-

"The trial produced no new developments of the case, nor does the statement of Sculpher, the late Inspector of Police - apart from the known attitude of careless indifference with which Sculpher without apparently bothering himself much about his officers, exercised his office - offer any proof of the complicity of the man with the derelictions of his subordinates.

It now becomes necessary to come to a decision on my recommendation of 30th March 1942 that Sculpher should be put in a Police detention camp. I may say that in my opinion Sculpher deserves some appreciable punishment for in the last resort he must answer for the acts of his subordinates: I do not propose to say whether the 4 weeks he has served in the prison here is to be regarded as sufficient punishment.

The case has not produced any sensations or new developments, it was impressive to find what a complete want of any sort of consciousness of duty and responsibility emerged from the statements of the defendants. This impression would have found much stronger and clearer expression if the trial before the Military Court had been able to take account of the thefts and burglaries of civilian stores and businesses.

It would then have been apparent that the perpetrators had laid hands on the stocks of their own compatriots with the same lack of scruple as they did on Army stocks."

An interesting letter from a German officer who on the previous day, was supposedly acting as an independent and unbiased Assessor at the trial of eighteen Guernsey Policemen!

The letter clearly shows Fuerst Von Oettingen's conviction that Inspector Sculpher was guilty and deserved further punishment, before he had been charged with any offence or even being given a chance to defend himself. It was reminiscent of the way he had demanded the sacking of PC Le Cocq before a chance allegation had time to be checked. His disappointment that the 'trial' produced no new developments was indicative of his desire to maximize its propaganda value.

On the 29th April there appeared in the *Evening Press*, an article, obviously written by the Germans themselves, headed:-

"Departure of Fuerst von Oettingen - The Prince leaves this weekend.

This week Guernsey is to bid farewell to one of the most popular German officers to be stationed here, Rittmeister Fuerst von Oettingen, Commandant of Feldkommandantur 515, Grange Lodge.

Arriving here to take command in March 1941, the Prince as he is known to his officers and to many Sarnians, rapidly became a familiar figure. His personality and distinctive military appearance impressed themselves on local people and those who had business matters to place before him found that their problems were met with sympathetic understanding.

The Prince served in the Great War, having a distinguished career and is married to the Princess Hohenlohe. He is a profound and learned advocate of National Socialism and many local officials have found deeper comprehension of German ideology through the force of his arguments.

We would wish the Prince every fortune and success, trusting that his farewell will be, in actuality, au revoir."

## Chapter 16

# I AM AFRAID, SHE ENGINEERED HER OWN TROUBLES

The day before the trial of the eighteen Guernsey Policemen opened, three Jewish girls were transported from the Island, to St Malo. This was the first stage of their final journey which ended with their deaths in the gas chambers at Auschwitz.

Therese Steiner and Auguste Spitz were both born in Vienna, Austria, and became German citizens on Hitler's take-over of their country. Marianne Grunfeld was born in Katowice, in Poland. Each of them had been notified a few days earlier that they were to be deported from the Island on the 21st of April 1942.

Marianne Grunfeld, who was born on December 5th 1912, travelled to England in 1937 to attend Reading University. In 1939 she graduated with a diploma in Horticulture but was unable to return home when the Germans overran Poland. Instead she responded to an advertisement in an agricultural magazine and obtained a position at Duvaux Farm in St Sampson. Marianne lived at the farm with the Ogier family and was well liked. At the time of the evacuation she was encouraged to leave the Island, but stayed on to help with the cattle rescued from Alderney.

**Miss Marianne Grunfeld.**

When she first arrived in the Island she had registered as an alien at the Police Station and her name was amongst the list of over 400 aliens supplied to the Germans in August 1940. At the end of October 1940 all civilians living in the Island had been required to complete registration forms and attend their Parish Douzaine Room to be photographed. At the same time all Jews were required, by German decree, to identify themselves by registering with the Inspector of Police.

Marianne Grunfeld, when she completed the registration form on the 29th October gave her address as Duvaux Farm and her occupation as 'Landworker, attending cattle'. She did not, however, report to the Police Station, thereby choosing not to identify herself as a Jew.

Marianne continued to work for Ted Ogier at Duvaux Farm until the spring of 1942, when she was informed that she was to be deported to the continent on the 21st April. Ted Ogier and the rest of the family were extremely upset at the prospect of her departure and he approached John Leale to see if anything could be done to reverse the German decision.

On the 18th April, John Leale furnished Ted with a 'Letter of introduction' to the Feldkommandantur:-

"The bearer, Mr E.H.Ogier (Duvaux Farm, St Sampson) is a well known and respected Guernseyman. He was a member of the States for a considerable time and is at present doing most useful work as a farmer producing foodstuffs. He wishes to discuss the possibility of retaining in his employ Miss Marianne Grunfeld. I would be obliged if you would grant him an interview on this subject."

There is no record to show whether the interview took place, but the records do register the fact that Marianne Grunfeld was deported from the Island to France on the 21st April.

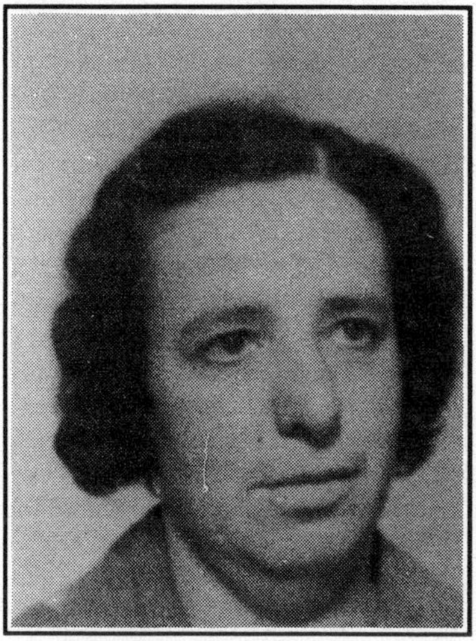

**Miss Auguste Spitz.**

Auguste Spitz was a 41-year old Austrian, born in Vienna. 'Gustie' as she was known to her friends, came to the Island as a nanny in September 1937. In June 1940 she was interned for three weeks as an enemy alien and when released obtained employment at the Castel Hospital as a domestic. When the notice appeared in the *Evening Press* on the 24th October 1940, requiring all Jews to report their presence to the Inspector of Police, she did so. At the time she apparently treated registration as a routine matter, not knowing anything of the treatment that Jews were suffering at the hands of the Germans.

Also employed at the hospital was Therese Steiner, who like her colleague was born in Vienna. She too had identified herself as a Jew in October 1940.

Therese left her home in Vienna in 1937, travelling to England to find a job and earn a living. The family, who had been constantly harassed for being Jewish, were, as a result, poor. Her brother Karl later described Therese as, ' a financial refugee, rather than a political one'. In London she trained as a dental nurse and obtained employment, as a nanny, with the Potts family in Kent. In the late summer of 1939 the Potts family took a lease on Rosebud Cottage, in Sark, and arrived in the Island the day after war was declared. Mrs Marjorie Potts, her two daughters and Miss Steiner remained in Sark, while Edgar Potts returned to England to look after his dental practice. In the early summer of 1940 Mrs Potts moved the family to Guernsey so that her eldest daughter could attend the Ladies' College. Miss Steiner moved with them.

As a former Austrian and now a German citizen, Miss Steiner was treated as an enemy alien. On the 4th June 1940, along with other German citizens, she was interned at Fort Houmet. While she was detained, Mrs Potts and her two daughters left the Island and returned to England. On the 25th June, when the arrival of the Germans appeared imminent, Therese was released and obtained employment at the Castel hospital as a nurse. Before long she was involved in the reception and treatment of the casualties from the German air raid.

Nurses and staff who worked with Therese at that time described her as a very intelligent, highly cultured and lovely person. They welcomed her into their homes, went for cycle rides and accompanied her to concerts at St James the Less Church. They remembered her as a very accomplished pianist, who enjoyed nothing better than relaxing at the piano.

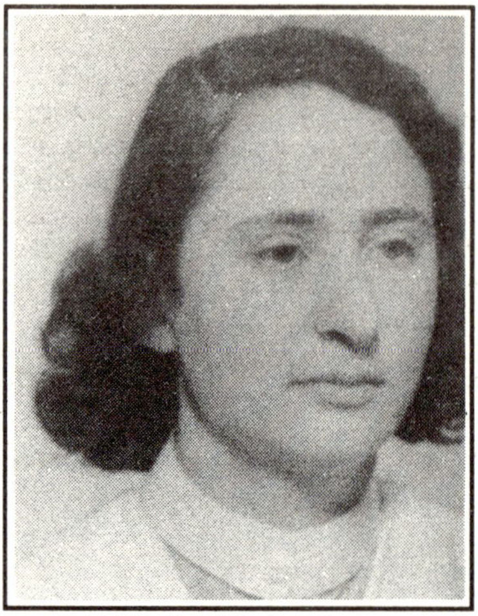
**Miss Therese Steiner.**

Her brother Karl later recalled having taught his sister to play the piano. "She was a very kind and nice person who shared my deep love of music. The last time I saw her was when she left Austria for London in 1937."

After Therese left Vienna, her parents went to live in Leipzig. As a result of the Allied bombing raids on that city, she became very concerned about their safety. She confided to the assistant matron at the hospital, that she had heard nothing from her parents for months and was getting desperately worried. She contacted the Red Cross, but without success.

Then she told friends at the hospital that she was going to approach the Germans to see if they could find out anything about her parents. Everyone, including Doctor A.W.Rose, Doctor R.B.Sutcliffe, Matron Rabey and other members of the staff, warned her against making such an approach. Despite that advice, she didn't believe that she was in any danger. All she wanted was to join her parents in Leipzig or bring them to Guernsey.

Genuinely believing that the Germans would help her, Therese went to Grange Lodge and enquired about the wellbeing of her parents. Not long after, the hospital authorities were telephoned and informed that Miss Steiner and Miss Spitz were to be deported the following day and that they should immediately pack up their possessions. At the time most people at the hospital believed that she was deported only because she had approached the Germans. Dr Alistair Rose commented to Mrs Whale, the assistant matron:- "I am afraid she engineered her own troubles."

There is no evidence to support that contention. The evidence more likely suggests that Therese Steiner and Auguste Spitz, sealed their own fate when they responded to the German decree published in October 1940 and identified themselves as Jews. There is certainly no evidence that they were betrayed. On the other hand, Marianne Grunfeld, who had chosen not to identify herself as a Jew, was also deported to the Continent on the same day. Someone must have informed the Germans that she was a Jew, but there exists no clear evidence of who might have betrayed her. The situation was summed up after the Occupation by an Islander, who commented:- "There was dirty work done there."

The assistant matron, Mrs Whale, packed food for the two girls' journey and told Therese that she would see her after the war.

She replied:- "Don't worry, I will write and I will come and see you after the war, don't worry about me." Apparently she thought that she was being sent back to join her parents in Leipzig.

Nothing further was heard from any of the girls deported to St Malo on the 21st of April 1942.

After the Island was liberated, Mrs Whale commented to her daughter:- "It is very funny, something terrible must have happened to those girls because we have heard nothing and not only that, we have heard nothing from the family, which is very strange."

In 1947 Mrs Whale and her family went on a motoring holiday in France. When they were in St Malo they made enquiries about the girls and were told that two of them had been taken by train to Avranches, the large rail centre in Normandy. Mrs Whale, who could speak fluent French, went there and spoke to some townspeople who remember the two girls. She was taken to the house where the girls had been billeted and spoke to the woman who looked after them. Apparently Therese Steiner and Auguste Spitz stayed there for two or three weeks, under guard. Then, in the middle of the night, two SS guards came and took the girls away and that was all they knew about them.

Later Mrs Whale learnt that Therese and Auguste had been taken to Drancy Concentration camp, north of Paris. On the 20th July 1942 they and Miss Grunfeld, who had arrived there by another but unknown route, were among 824 Jews who left by train for Auschwitz. They arrived there on the 23rd July and were believed to have perished in the gas chambers the same day.

# Chapter 17

# SHOOT COMRADE, SHOOT

Whilst in custody awaiting trial, PC 16 Frank Tuck was sued by his landlord, who claimed that he was £17.0.0 in arrears with his £3.10.0 a month rent in respect of the house and land he rented at Les Huriaux, St Martin. Like many other members of the Force, Frank had run a smallholding prior to the Occupation, growing mainly tomatoes and the income had been sufficient to financially keep his head above water. At the time of the Occupation his crop was almost ready for shipment to the markets on the mainland. Instead it had to be dumped and his financial loss was considerable. Also Police wages had been substantially reduced and the price of food and other essentials had risen. Frank Tuck found it impossible to meet all his obligations.

In the Royal Court on the 18th April, Advocate J.E.L.Martel, who was deputising for the seriously ill G.J.P.Ridgway, explained Frank Tuck's absence. by saying:- "He is one of the Policemen who is now in prison."

The Bailiff commented:- "Tuck could not very well get to Court as I understand that he is at Fort George. I cannot advise the Court of any action when the man is unable to attend and put forward whatever defence he has. The only possible thing to do", added the Bailiff, "pending proceedings being taken in another place is to adjourn this matter. Tuck may possibly at some future date be able to appear, I suggest we postpone the hearing for at least a week and then see what the position is. We cannot evict him from this property, although he may be very much in arrears, because we don't know all the facts from his point of view." The court agreed to an adjournment.

The outcome of the case is not recorded, but the rest of his family soon left their home and Frank Tuck was never to live at Les Huriaux again. On the 13th May an auction sale was held at the house and on the instructions of his brother, furniture, poultry, rabbits, a gentleman's cycle and other effects were sold under the hammer.

Five applicants selected by the Police sub-committee were passed fit by Dr Collings and commencing duty, as Auxiliary Constables, on the 20th April:-

| | |
|---|---|
| A/33 Oswald Harry Brackley, 35, | Oakdene, Collings Road, St Peter Port. |
| A/34 Lacey James Hamon, 39, | Varclin End Cottage, St Martin. |
| A/35 Cyril Percy Royston Northey, 24, | Hillside, Nocq Road, St Sampson. |
| A/36 Henry Thomas Solway, 33, | 13 Summerfield Road, Vale. |
| A/37 Leonard George Tucker, 20, | Grace Dieu, Rue des Croutes, St Martin |

The five new Auxiliaries spent the mornings of their first week in the upper office being instructed by Mr Langmead on the details of Police work and procedure. In the afternoons they patrolled around the Town with more experienced Constables. On the Saturday morning they were sworn in as Police officers, by the Royal Court.

After being sworn in A/PC 35 Roy Northey returned to the Station, where Sergeant Plevin enquired:-

"Are you going home for dinner ?"

"Yes"

"Then, I have got a job for you - call on Dr Billy Fox, at Grandes Maisons Road, he has a breaking and entry to report to you."

The newly sworn in Auxiliary Constable, equipped with his brand new pocket book, called on the doctor, only to discover that the breaking and entry concerned his rabbit hutch and that all his rabbits had been stolen !

"Initially", A/PC Northey recalls:- "the new Auxiliary Constables wore red and white armbands, the same as the Specials. The regular Police had blue and white ones. The Specials were issued with a badge but not the Auxiliaries. As soon as the uniforms of the suspended members of the Force had been recovered and cleaned they were issued to the new recruits.

Our main duty as Auxiliaries, was queue control, especially in the markets. We would have had our breakfast at 7.00am and then go down to the market. They would say 'I was here before you' and so on. I used to end up by telling them 'Now look, I was here before any of you, so if anyone should have it, I should.' They would see my point and generally, they were quite good natured about it. I never had any real problems.

When we paraded, we were inspected to see that we were fit to go out on patrol and the Station Sergeant give us various instructions. On one occasion we were told to look out for a man named Conrad Bouwmeester, who was wanted for arson. He was having trouble with his wife and had burnt her clothing.

I was on No 6 beat as it was then, I was walking down the High Street when I saw another of the new Auxiliary Policeman, Jack Salmon, coming up the Street with a prisoner, whom I recognised as Bouwmeester. Well if I had done my job properly, I should have immediately left my beat and accompanied Jack and his prisoner to the Station. I didn't because I did not want to pinch his glory of arresting his first prisoner.

As they were walking up towards the Station, quietly enough, I carried on down to the bottom of Cornet Street. There I was able to get a good view of the Quay and harbour. Suddenly I saw the figure of a Policeman running towards me along the Quay. I thought, hello Jack's prisoner has done a runner and sure enough there was the prisoner running along in front of Jack.

I immediately ran towards the absconding prisoner and managed to stop him. When Jack joined me, we took the prisoner, my first arrest, to the Police Station making sure that he did not escape again. I held him while he was charged and then we took him to the prison and handed him over to a Warder."

On the 25th April, Mr Ralph Chilcott, the manager of the States Dairy, reported to Sergeant Banneville that the butter store had been forcibly entered during the night of 23/24th April by the use of a key and 45 lb of butter stolen.

The Sergeant established that the head dairy maid, Elizabeth Tulley, had checked her stock of butter the previous night. She made the store secure by locking the two locks and the keys remained in her possession. At 7.00am the next morning Miss Tulley found the door of the store closed, but not locked. On checking the stock, she discovered that 45 lb of butter was missing from one crate, with only 3 lb remaining.

Mr Chilcott told the Sergeant that butter had been taken on two previous occasions, although the matter had not been reported to the Police. On 13th March 1942, 10 lb of butter was missing and on the 3rd April 30 lb stolen. On each occasion entry was made with a key.

He found no sign that the bolts or the two common type locks had been forced or tampered with and interviewed a number of the staff without result. In the time-honoured way, he concluded his written report with "Further enquiries in hand".

The next day Mr Miller, foreman of the States Dairy, caught Gordon ........., aged 16, with ½lb of butter inside his apron. Sergeant Banneville interviewed Gordon, who declared, "There is no butter at home, I was going to take it home."

Mr Chilcott said that he did not want any prosecution and he would dismiss Gordon.

A/PC 10 Sebire was on duty in the Market halls on the 25th April when Mrs Le Moignan, of Paris Street told him that she had just purchased a lettuce from the stall of Edward H.Ogier, Duvaux Farm, for 6d. She said that in yesterday's paper she had read that the controlled retail price, set by the Glasshouse Utilisation Board, was 2½d. Furthermore, she added, the price should have been marked.

The lettuce she'd bought was re-purchased from her by the Constable as evidence. A/PC Sebire then told Miss Edwards, the assistant who served Mrs Le Moignan, that she was exceeding the price laid down by the GUB. She replied:- "Its my boss's orders". The Constable telephoned Mr Ogier, and told him that he would be reported. He replied, "Carry on, I will fight the case."

A/PC Sebire's report was entered in the Occurrence Book and written in the margin was:- "A/PC should have purchased direct from the stall. Mrs Le Moignan could give evidence as an additional witness. A/PC phoned Ogier - quite irregular".

Two days later the Constable went to see Mr Ogier, at Duvaux Farm and he told him:- "I did give orders to my shop assistants in the market to offer for sale lettuce at 6d each, contrary to the price laid down by the GUB, it should have been 2½d each. I know officer, that I failed to display the price of the goods." When informed that he would most probably be charged, he said "The GUB has taken the matter up and they agreed that they should be sold by weight."

The case did not go to Court.

The German decision that the Acting Inspector should be responsible to Feldkommandantur meant that they became more involved in the day-to-day activities of the Force. Acting Sergeant Dyson reported that on the 25th April, when he was checking on the country patrols, he was accompanied, in the Police car, by two members of the Feldgendarmerie. He also reported that A/PC 13 Brouard failed to meet his point at 11.00pm at Vale Rectory. Sergeant Dyson waited with the two Germans at the Ville Baudu and Sohier cross roads from 10.50 to 11.10pm and saw no sign of the Constable. "We circled from the point to Vale Chapel, down Rue des Couture, along Braye Road, but saw no one." A/PC Brouard's duty was on No 1 beat, from 4.00pm to 12 midnight. He reported to the Station at 11.45pm saying "All correct".

Sergeant Dyson's report was entered in the Occurrence Book and alongside Mr Langmead wrote, 'A/PC seen and cautioned'. Also written alongside was 'Explanation accepted by Feldgendarmerie'.

As a result of the conviction of seventeen members of the Force, Mr Langmead wrote to the nine wives who were still in the Island:-

"Dear Madam,

I am instructed by the President of the Police Committee, to inform you that in view of the decision of the Military Court, held on 24th April 1942, the period of suspension of your husband is terminated and his pay is therefore stopped as from that date.

This means that no further payment will be made from the Police Committee to you through the States Office."

Mr Langmead also wrote to Louis Guillemette, the Secretary to the Controlling Committee, advising him of the Police Committee's decision to cease payment of the two thirds pay which was made during their period of suspension. He also added "The hard cases would appear to be Quin, Le Gallez and Smith".

Bill Quin's wife and one child were still in the Island, his other two children having been evacuated. Alf Le Gallez and Bert Smith's wives and three children were also in the Island.

On the 27th April a further three Auxiliary Policemen commenced duty.

| | |
|---|---|
| A/PC 9 Alfred John Bisson, 43, | 26 Norman Terrace, Amherst. |
| A/PC 12 John Frederick Wood Lovell, 22, | 4 College Terrace, The Grange. |
| A/PC 14 Harry Read, 44, | Deepdene, Vazon. |

The next day Mr Langmead accepted the resignation of A/PC 20 Bill Strickland and A/PC Arthur Falla on the grounds of ill health. He agreed that their appointments should terminate on May 10th.

A/PC 6 Cyril Petit was on queue control duty outside the Gaumont, in St Julians Avenue, early one evening, when German soldiers rushed the doors. He reported:-

"I was on duty at the Gaumont at 6.05pm and got the civilians into a queue. By 6.15pm some 200 German soldiers had gathered and were mixing in the queue that I had formed. There were no German Police in attendance at the time.

By 6.25pm, when the doors were opened, there was a further 300 German soldiers, who rushed the doors forcing them away from the bolts, smashing the glass panels and woodwork of the doors."

The report was entered in the Occurrence Book and in the margin is 'reported to Grange Lodge 28/4/42'.

On the same day another entry in the Occurrence Book relates to a woman being taken to the Emergency Hospital. It starts:- 'A/PC 34 Hamon', - 'Hamon' is clearly written over another word which has been erased. In the margin is written:- " Never erase in OB, strike out and write above or below. A J Langmead."

The author of the entry was Acting Sergeant Bull, who presumably did the erasing.

On the 29th April 1942 the Acting Inspector wrote to the President of the Controlling Committee:-

"Report on Island Police.

With reference to the letter of the 16th April from the Feldkommandantur asking for a report on the re-organisation of the Island Police.

I beg to report that the re-organisation is completed, but owing to the resignations there are vacancies for two PCs and one Sergeant yet to be filled. This is receiving immediate attention.

The Force now totals 44 men and comprises:-

One Acting Inspector
One Acting Deputy Inspector
Three Sergeants (One Detective and one Clerk)
Two Acting Sergeants
Three Police Constables
34 Auxiliary PCs.

AGES.The ages of the Police are:-
1 is 59 years
1 is 57 years
4 are 54 years
2 are 50 years
2 are 47 years
6 are 44 years
2 are 42 years
3 are 40 years
3 are 39 years
5 are 36 years
6 are 31 years
4 are 27 years
5 are 23 years

TRAINING. The regular Police have had training and experience in Police duties.

Eight Auxiliaries have had 22 months experience, but very little training. The remaining 26 men have only had a limited training and experience of one month and under, of Police work. The training will be continued weekly and the men encouraged to study Police law and procedure.

DUTIES. The Acting Inspector is responsible for supervision, conduct and discipline of the Force, compiling records and reports, preparation of and presentation of cases before the Police Court. Accounts and correspondence and checking duties of all officers and visiting points as often as possible.

Acting Deputy Inspector is responsible for daily duty sheets, supervising Sergeants and men reporting on and off duty, visiting Beats and Patrols in Town and Country at all times and special enquiries as required.

Detective Sergeant works in plain clothes on enquiries relating to the detection of all crime reported as instructed by the Inspector.

Clerk Sergeant. All office routine, records, reports, charge sheets, correspondence and files.

Sergeants and Acting Sergeants in charge of the office in turn and responsible for parading and instructing men when reporting for duty. Entering reports in daily record book, answering telephone and despatching men where required for accidents, traffic control and complaints in crime reports.

PREMISES. In good state of repair, but facilities for parading men and meals are inadequate.

EQUIPMENT. This consists of a truncheon, whistle, armlet, no firearms are authorised and none are in possession of the Police. Uniform is becoming worn and where possible is being adapted for new men. An enquiry is being made with a view to obtaining cloth for Police trousers from France.

SUPERVISION and DISCIPLINE. The Inspector controls the Force and supervises duties of all ranks. All matters of discipline are dealt with by him, with right of appeal by the defaulter to the Police Committee.

The Deputy Inspector supervises duties of Sergeants in office and all men on beats and patrols at all hours of day and night.

Sergeants parade men reporting on and off duty, visiting points where possible, detailing men to patrol regular beats and checking to see they do so. Supplemented by visits by the Inspector and Deputy Inspector.

A man reported for a disciplinary offence can be fined by deducting one or more days pay or depriving a man of an annual increment for minor cases, or dismissal in serious cases.

Disciplinary punishment during the past month has been two men failing to meet a fixed point. Both were cautioned and the reports recorded with their papers. Both were new and explanations given were reasonable.

DISTRIBUTION. The patrols are arranged so that the hours of duty overlap. The Country commence at 8.00am. to 4.00pm., 4.00pm to 12.00 midnight, 8.00pm to 4.00am. and 12.00 midnight to 8.00am.

The Town 6.00am. to 2.00pm., 2.00pm to 10.00pm. and 10.00pm to 6.00am.

The Country is divided into four districts with double patrol from 8.00pm to daylight. The Town has five beats with a double night patrol from 10.00pm. to 6.00am. Each duty period has one relief man to provide for men on daily leave. A Sergeant is in charge of each relief."

The President of the Controlling Committee forwarded a copy of the Acting Inspector's report to the Feldkommandantur.

The following day Mr Langmead wrote to the President of the Police Committee, detailing the outcome of the trial before the German Military Court. He reported that the Germans had informed him that the re-employment of PC 28 Peter Bretel would not be sanctioned. Mr Langmead added "He is being given employment in another States Department by the States Supervisor."

The Acting Inspector also wrote "Owing to the shortage of Police boots, when collecting uniforms, a pair of boots were taken from the homes of PCs 15 Burton, 20 Whare, and 30 Short. These boots were issued in 1940 and are legally the property of the men. I have to ask whether we shall retain them and pay the men concerned an approved amount for the boots, or whether the boots shall be returned to the men."

No record exists of the decision taken in regard to the boots.

Colonel Knackfuss, Feldkommandantur in Jersey, gave notice that as from the 1st May, the curfew for the civilian population, in the Channel Islands, was fixed at 11.00pm to 5.00am. He also decreed that licensed premises must close half an hour before the curfew. The curfew for Jews was fixed as 9.00pm to 5.00am.

Mr Langmead regarded the filling of the vacancy for an Acting Sergeant as urgent. A Police Committee meeting had been called for the 4th May and he hoped that an appointment would be made then. In anticipation he wrote to Mr Agnew:-

"For the position of Acting Sergeant there are only three regular Police available, PCs Kimber, Pugh and Marsh. I cannot recommend any of these for the position. An application has been received from Mr John F.Robson, the former licensee of the Imperial Hotel, Torteval, and I would suggest that he be appointed as an Auxiliary Constable and after being sworn in, that he be appointed as an Acting Sergeant. This is somewhat unorthodox, but the duties must be carried on and the best man available, appointed.

Mr Robson has proved very keen and reliable during the period he has acted as Inspector of the Special Constabulary in the Western Parishes. He is a man of ability, able to control men, which is of great importance in the present state of the Force, where 75% of the men are new. His records and the Occurrence Book kept for the Special Constabulary are of a high standard."

The Police Committee did not share their Acting Inspector's view of Mr Robson, they felt that, at 48, he was too old. The matter of the appointment of an Acting Sergeant was deferred until a future meeting.

The three new Auxiliary Policemen, A/PCs Bisson, Lovell and Read, who had commenced duty on the 27th April 1942, took the oath in the Royal Court before the Bailiff and three Jurats on Saturday morning, the 2nd May.

**A/PC Harry Read.**

On the following Monday morning the Acting Inspector called A/PC 14 Harry Read to his office and dismissed him with immediate effect, as being unsuitable for employment in the Police Force.

Harry Read had successfully slipped through the administrative net. He completed an application form and had been interviewed by the three-man Sub Committee. It is not recorded how his past caught up with him, but it was probably as a result of his appearance in the Royal Court. It was just over nine years since he had last appeared in Court, but at that time it was in the Police Court, as a defendant.

When Harry Read arrived in the Island in 1932, he already had a long list of previous convictions. On the 13th March 1933 he appeared in the Police Court, before the Magistrate H.J.Casey Esq., charged with fraudulently obtaining the sum of £7 by false pretences from the Rev.E.L.Frossard, attempting to obtain by false pretences, a car valued at £225 from George Thompson and fraudulently obtaining credit from landlady, Mrs Eva Howlett. The Magistrate said it was quite clear from his record that he made a practice of living in this way and sentenced Read to six months imprisonment with hard labour.

The standard of recruit was causing concern. One Police officer who was in the Force at the time commented later:- "They would have done better if they had just taken the next six men walking down the street."

Mr Langmead told the President of the Police Committee:- "It is essential that a better educated type of man should be aimed at in order to get a good foundation for the Force so that a good nucleus is available to carry over the period until recruiting can commence in peacetime."

A few days later an advertisement appeared in the *Evening Press.*

"Island Police.

Applications are invited for the position of Auxiliary Police Constables from men born between 1913 and 1923, of good physique, education and appearance, minimum height 5 feet 8 inches, in possession of cycle with dynamo, a knowledge of French an asset. Pay 50/- to 60/- weekly, plus allowances. Applicants to state date and place of birth, height, qualifications etc.

Apply A.J.Langmead Police Office."

That was probably the only time that the possession of a cycle dynamo was a necessary 'qualification' to join a Police Force.

Peter Tostevin, of Les Menages, St Peters, called at the Police Station on Saturday, 2nd May and told Acting Sergeant Dyson:-

"I had my suspicions that my cows have been milked at night, so last night I decided to keep watch in my stable in company with my father.

About 12.30am this morning two German soldiers came into my stable, had a look around and started to milk a cow. When I stepped out from where I was hiding and said 'What's the game?', one pointed a revolver at me and said 'Hands up or I will shoot' and went to push me aside. I caught hold of him and he shouted to his friend, 'Shoot comrade, shoot'.

When we got outside they ran away, but one had dropped his cap and cook tin with 'KF' scratched on it. About half an hour later they returned with two other men with steel helmets and they banged on the stable door and shouted, 'Comrade I shoot'. Three or four shots were fired, I believe blanks. Two windows were broken with the butts of their rifles, also the door was damaged. They went off after I had returned the cap and tin. The number of one of the soldiers is L04672.

This morning one of the men came to the farm, it was about 9.00am, he begged me not to report it, 'if you do, my comrade will come and burn your farm down'."

The Sergeant accompanied Peter Tostevin to Grange Lodge, where they reported the matter to the Feldgendarmerie, but no action was taken by the Germans.

The Germans were keen to achieve the maximum impact from their prosecution of over half the Guernsey Police Force. The statements they had 'obtained' from some of the men contained apparent confessions in the respect of raids on civilian stores. Twenty six extracts from the men's statements were selected by the Germans.

On the 5th May 1942 Advocate J.E.L.Martel, the Acting Attorney General, received a letter dated the 29th April and 26 enclosures from the Tribunal of Feldkommandantur 515.

"I am enclosing the statements made by the accused Policemen, to serve as a basis for the prosecution to be undertaken by you.

As regards the accused hotel proprietor Duquemin, I am sending you an extract from the record of the main trial, from which it is apparent that Duquemin has been guilty of inciting others to commit theft.

As the statements are confessions on the part of the accused I assume that no difficulty will stand in the way of a speedy judgement. I am therefore expecting your report on the outcome of the proceedings within a period of one month."

Mr Martel responded the same day saying:-

"I have today received your letter of the 29th ultimo with enclosures. I am having the statements translated. As soon as this has been done I shall give them my immediate consideration.

You say these statements constitute confessions, but I would remind you that if they are denied it will not be possible to use them in view of the fact that your officers before whom they were made would not be available to give evidence before our Court.

I presume that instructions have been given to the Feldgendarmerie to allow my department access to these men whenever required and also that they may be easily available for production before the Court both for Committal and for Trial."

Three days later, on the 8th May, Dr Biel replied to the Acting Attorney General.

"Re: Prosecution of Police Servants.

In reply to your letter of the 5th May 1942, I have noted that the proceedings against the accused policemen will be started as soon as the statements have been translated.

In the event of the accused denying the admissions made by them to the Feldgendarmerie, please advise me immediately, as in this case the Chief of Tribunal (Gerichtsherr) will take up the proceedings even as regards the thefts committed at the expense of the English traders."

The message was clear and was underlined by the release from prison on the 8th May 1942 of James Rutter the sixty-nine-year-old chiropodist who had been sentenced by a German Military tribunal to nine months' imprisonment for his part in the plundering of Alderney.

James Rutter's release served to remind everyone of the reasons why the Germans had 'take over' the Alderney plunder trial - the protracted delay by the civil authorities in commencing the proceedings. Dr Biel's letter of the 8th May again raised the possibility of the Germans taking over a civil trial.

On the same day as Rutter was released, fifty-seven-year-old, A/PC 7 Bill Pealling submitted his resignation as a Police officer and was appointed a Prison warder. He had served as a full time Special since May 1940 and became an Auxiliary in March 1942. During his period of Police service he had become known to the public as 'PC Peeler'

At the meeting of the Police Committee on the 4th May, sixteen out of the seventeen Police officers convicted by the German Tribunal were dismissed as from the date of their conviction, the 24th April 1942. The Committee also considered the future of PC 28 Peter Bretel who had been found guilty of having on two occasions, stolen wood from the dump at St Paul's for use on the Station fire. The Committee were divided as to whether he should be reinstated in his position as a Police Constable, so they decided to write to Advocate Sherwill, who was now back in practice and seek his view.

Mr Agnew, the President of the Police Committee, wrote:-

"As you were present in Court when he was tried and sentenced, my Committee would appreciate your opinion, if having regard to all the circumstances whether PC Bretel could be re-instated as a Police Constable after the war. A decision by the Committee has to be made to safeguard the public interest and at the same time, if the charge is not considered serious to enable the man to continue in States employment so that he will not lose his pension rights. The whole course depending on whether the charge against him was of a serious civil character or purely a military offence."

Mr Sherwill replied from his home, in a handwritten letter:-

**Ambrose Sherwill.**

"The German Court inflicted a term of one month's imprisonment as a suitable penalty and this - in view of the fact that he had been in custody for that period - meant his immediate release.

The offences in question could not be described as being of a purely military character. On the other hand they were treated by the German Court as minor offences. In all the circumstances, in my opinion, PC Bretel's offences were not of such a serious character as to preclude his eventual re-instatement in the Police Force."

A few days later it was reported in the *Evening Press* that Mr P.Bretel of Mont Morin, St Sampson was to replace Mr W.F.Adams as States Market attendant. Peter Bretel's pension entitlement had been preserved.

# Chapter 18

## THE STATEMENTS I MADE TO THE GERMAN POLICE ARE UNTRUE

Despite having written to Dr Biel on the 5th May 1942 giving him the impression that it would take some time to translate the statements 'obtained' by the Germans from the Policemen, Mr Martel, the Acting Attorney General, sent Mr Langmead the translations of the statements the same day.

The Acting Inspector was instructed by Mr Martel to prepare cases against the ten Police officers and Stephen Duquemin. Mr Langmead found his task distasteful in the extreme, but realised that if the local Police did not prepare the cases against their former colleagues and friends, it would be done by the Germans. That he wanted to avoid at all costs.

He carefully, but reluctantly, examined the statements and concluded that they appeared to reveal a series of offences, either by the admission of the man concerned, or statements by other men naming their accomplice in particular crimes.

Mr Langmead, Acting Deputy Inspector Lamy and Sergeant Banneville spent Sunday the 10th May at Fort George, interviewing the men concerned. Although they were in military custody, the Police officers were allowed to see the men in private without any German being present. The response they received was far from what they expected.

Bill Burton's riposte was clear, concise and explicit:-

"Littlefield and Snell. I have never been in the markets at all to steal.

Bucktrout. I have never been in the place.

I have never been in the States Dairy.

I have never been in Le Lievre's, on the Pier.

The statements I made to the German Police are untrue."

Jack Harper, interviewed by Mr Langmead, said:-

"I have read the statements alleged to have been made by me. I have nothing to say. I plead Not Guilty and reserve my defence."

Bill Quin, also interviewed by Mr Langmead, responded:-

"The statement about the States Dairy is not true. I have never been in there. It is not correct that I have been into Bucktrout's store at any time, day or night. I have never received anything from there.

I also deny the statement about Best's stall and Littlefield and Snell. I went in the market for a German stall but not any civilian store.

I am not guilty regarding the Lievre's premises, Quay. I did not go in there and I had no stuff from there. I am not guilty of the Essential Commodities Committee store on Trinity Square."

Sergeant Banneville interviewed Frank Whare, who said:-

"I have been shown a statement, I have read it and I plead Not Guilty. This statement refers to breaking and entering premises known as Bucktrouts, Waterloo House, High Street, St Peter Port."

Sergeant Banneville also took a statement from Charlie Friend:-

"I have never been inside the States Dairy at the French Halles, I have never been with anyone else, I have not received anything from the States Dairy, French Halles. I know nothing about the States Dairy at all.

With regards to anything being taken from 'Best' Meat Market, I know nothing about it, nothing at all."

**Sergeant Fred Banneville.**

Fred Short stated in a interview with Mr Lamy:-

"Bucktrout, I have never been in Bucktrout's store on the Pier to steal, I have never been in the markets at all, neither Best or Littlefield. I have never been in the States Dairy in the Market nor have I had anything from it."

Alfred Howlett was interviewed by Mr Langmead and signed a very short statement:-

"I have read the statement I am alleged to have made and wish to plead not guilty. I have nothing further to add."

Mr Langmead interviewed Bert Smith who stated:-

"On Page 12, I deny the statement I made concerning Littlefield and Snell's butcher shop. I was very upset at the time I am supposed to have said that.

About the Essential Commodities Store Trinity Square. I remember going on one occasion only with PCs Tuck and Short. I did not know it was an Essential Commodities Store and I did not receive anything from there. So far as I know Tuck and Short each had a cardboard box full of tins of tomatoes. I cannot swear to the car being used. I don't remember going to their flat. It was somewhere about Christmas time.

There is no truth in the statement about Howlett, I only went to the store once. With respect to Le Lievre's store, Quin did tell me that he had been to Le Lievre's store with Burton and Friend and they had had some stuff. I don't remember him saying Harper's name. The statement on page 13 concerning the Dairy is not true, I have never entered the States Dairy."

The last sentence of Bert Smith's statement referred to the statement he made to the Germans on the 20th March, in which he accused PC 35 Francois Le Cocq of being involved in a break-in at the States Dairy towards the end of 1939. How Bert Smith was induced to make that statement to the German interrogators is unknown, although it appears likely that the same type of 'physical encouragement' was applied to him as was applied to his fellow Police officers. Also, according to Mr Sherwill, when Smith appeared at the Military Tribunal trial, he seemed to be on the verge of a nervous breakdown and many of his conflicting statements appear to confirm this view.

Frank Tuck's later assessment of Bert Smith, was:- "He lost his head and went mental. Somebody took a knife away from him at Fort George. He tried to cut his wrists, he did stupid things. Perhaps he wanted to get rid of himself."

As a result of the interviews carried out by the Acting Inspector and Sergeant Banneville and the statements made by the men, charges were preferred:-

PC 22 K.G.Bailey.

Concerned with Tuck in stealing 6lb butter from States Dairy.

PC 15 W.Burton

1. Concerned with Quin and Friend in stealing 20 bottle of spirits from Alliance Club

2. Concerned with Friend and Whare in stealing 12 bottles of wine and spirits from Bucktrouts & Co.Ltd.

3. Concerned with Friend, Quin and Short in stealing 8 bottles of wine and spirits from Bucktrouts & Co. Ltd.

PC 14 C.A.Friend

1. Concerned with Quin in stealing 4 tins of tomatoes from Essential Commodities Store.

2. Concerned with Burton and Quin in stealing 20 bottles of spirits from Alliance Club.

3. Concerned with Burton, Quin and Short in stealing 8 bottles of wine and spirits from Bucktrouts & Co.Ltd.

4. Concerned with Burton and Whare in stealing 12 bottles of wine and spirits from Bucktrout & Co. Ltd.

Sergeant J.Harper

1. Receiving 5 bottles of spirits stolen from the Alliance Club by Burton, Quin and Friend.

2. Receiving 4 bottles of wine and spirits stolen from Bucktrouts & Co.Ltd. by Burton, Whare and Friend.

Sergeant Howlett

Concerned with Smith in stealing 6 tins of beans from Essential Commodities store.

PC 23 W.G.Quin

1. Concerned with Friend in stealing 4 tins tomatoes from Essential Commodities store.

2. Concerned with Smith in stealing 86 bottles of wine from R.W.Randall Ltd's store.

3. Concerned with Burton and Friend in stealing 20 bottles from the Alliance Club.

4. Concerned with Burton, Friend and Short in stealing 8 bottles of wine and spirits from Bucktrouts & Co.Ltd.

PC 30 F.W.Short

1. Concerned with others (not before Court) in stealing 1 tin of beans and 1 tin of tomatoes from Essential Commodities store.

2. Concerned with Tuck and Smith in stealing 4 cases of tomatoes and cooking oil from Essential Commodities store.

3. Concerned with Burton, Friend and Quin in stealing 8 bottles of wine and spirits from Bucktrouts & Co.Ltd.

PC 18 H.P.Smith

1. Concerned with Short and Tuck in stealing 4 cases of tomatoes and cooking oil from Essential Commodities Store.

2. Concerned with Howlett in stealing 6 tins of beans from Essential Commodities store.

3. Concerned with Quin in stealing 86 bottles of wine from R.W.Randall Ltd's store.

PC 16 F.H.Tuck

1. Concerned with Bailey in stealing 6 lb of butter from States Dairy.

2. Concerned with Short and Smith in stealing 4 cases of tomatoes and cooking oil from Essential Commodities store.

PC 20 F.W.Whare

Concerned with Burton and Friend in stealing 12 bottles of wine and spirits from Bucktrouts & Co.Ltd.

S.J.C.Duquemin

Receiving 86 bottles of wine stolen from R.W.Randall Ltd by Smith and Quin.

Where the Alliance Club is referred to in the charges, the spirits were stolen from Le Lievre's store, where the bottles had been transferred for storage, as the Germans had banned the sale of spirits to civilians.

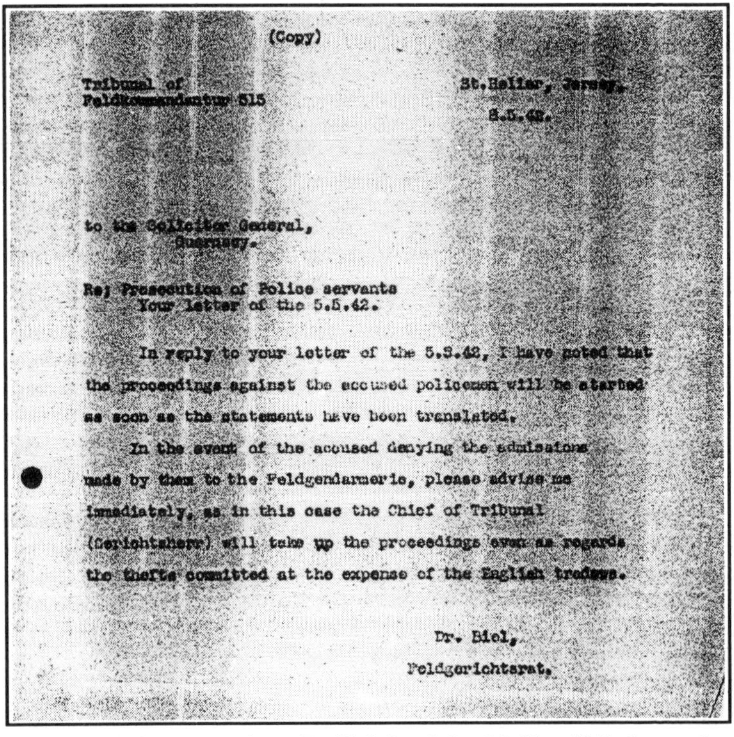

(Copy)

Tribunal of
Feldkommandantur 515

St.Helier, Jersey.
8.5.42.

to the Solicitor General,
Guernsey.

Re; Prosecution of Police servants
Your letter of the 5.5.42.

In reply to your letter of the 5.5.42, I have noted that the proceedings against the accused policemen will be started as soon as the statements have been translated.

In the event of the accused denying the admissions made by them to the Feldgendarmerie, please advise me immediately, as in this case the Chief of Tribunal (Gerichtsherr) will take up the proceedings even as regards the thefts committed at the expense of the English traders.

Dr. Biel,
Feldgerichtsrat.

**A file copy of the letter from Dr Biel dated the 8th May 1942 threatening action if the accused Policemen deny their 'admissions' made to the Feldgendarmerie.**

Acting Inspector Langmead later recalled that he had difficulty in establishing dates and quantities because of the conflicting statements by the men concerned and as a result, a number of possible charges were not proceeded with. In PC Short's case only three out of a possible six charges were proceeded with.

PC Quin 4 charges out of 7.
PC Smith 3 charges out of 6.
PC Tuck 2 charges out of 3.

"In PC Friend's case", Mr Langmead said:- "he admitted one more than was on the papers. No case was taken of stealing from the Markets owing to conflicting statements and lack of evidence, Littlefield and Snell for instance, could only trace the loss of 4 lb of butter, whereas the papers revealed 24 lb."

The Trial in the Police Court was due to open on the 15th May 1942, before Magistrate Quertier Le Pelley. Just before the Trial began, in the waiting room, Mr Langmead showed the defendants the letter from Dr Biel, dated 8th May 1942, which included the statement:-

"In the event of the accused denying the admissions made by them to the Feldgendarmerie, .......... the Chief of Tribunal will take up the proceedings ...... ."

The letter was passed around amongst the defendants. Each of the men reacted in different ways to the threat which was clearly being made.

Whether the letter was shown to the men on the instructions of the Acting Attorney General, or whether it was on Mr Langmead's own initiative is not clear.

Mr Langmead was later to comment:- "I was greatly influenced in my handling of the matter by the desire to save the men, if possible, from further interviews with the German Police and the addition of further penalties which might be added to their German sentences."

Charlie Friend later recalled the letter being passed around and commented:- "It was to the effect that, if we did not corroborate what we had already said to the Germans in our confessions, then the Germans would deal with us personally."

Bill Burton also recalled the letter. "Whilst awaiting our trial a letter from the German High Command was read to us. I listened carefully to the reading and knew that it was another dirty Nazis trick to cause a sensation and turn our people against us.

I personally was not impressed with the letter at all and I was very stubborn at this time and nothing would have shifted me. The other men were more affected by the letter and it generally seemed that they thought the best course was to plead guilty at this trial and admit the offences, as otherwise they would be dealt with by the Germans again and they did not relish the prospect of that."

Frank Tuck commented:- "The letter was in fact shown or the contents mentioned to all the appellants before the Civil Trial and their attitude to their own defence was conditioned accordingly. The letter clearly constituted a threat. That some mentioned this letter at the trial as the reason for changing their plea is in itself remarkable."

Frank Whare also recalled:- "Inspector Langmead showed me the letter before the trial, stating that I would be dealt with by the Germans personally unless we corroborated what we had already said in our confessions to the Germans."

Kingston Bailey commented:- "I pleaded guilty at the Civil Trial, having heard all the evidence and having been shown, prior to the trial, the letter which threatened us with very grave penalties if we did not corroborate what we had already said in our admissions to the Germans.

Mr Martel advised us that the best course was to plead guilty throughout the Civil Trial. He assured us as well that it would all count for nothing after the war and would be washed out."

Fred Short recalled similar advice:- "Jack Martel said to me 'Short, I would advise you to plead guilty, the war is going well, the Russians are advancing in the East and the African war is over. Give it another six months, Short, and you will be back on the beat again. It will all be washed out after the war, it just does not mean a thing.' We all knew Martel and trusted him, he was well known, if he said so - it must be so."

The Court was packed to capacity with relatives and friends of the accused when the hearing commenced at 10.30am on the 15th May 1942. However, they were to be disappointed, as on hearing the first charge - that against Tuck and Bailey - the Magistrate decided that it was of such a grave nature that evidence would be taken in camera and the Court was cleared of public and press. Jurat Le Pelley said that the evidence would be taken in writing and the cases would go before the Royal Court. The Court sat for four days before the Magistrate committed the ten policemen and S.J.C.Duquemin for trial in the Royal Court.

On Saturday the 23rd May, the eleven defendants appeared before the Bailiff and ten Jurats in the Upper Division of the Royal Court when pleas were taken.

**Sergeant A.W.Howlett**

Alfred Howlett, when asked how he pleaded to the charge against him, said that he must make a plea of Guilty, "as he had no option". Bill Burton pleaded Not Guilty to the charges against him. Bill Quin pleaded Guilty to two charges and Not Guilty to two others. Jack Harper also pleaded Not Guilty. All the other defendants pleaded Guilty. Jack Harper and Stephen Duquemin chose Advocate Langlois to represent them, the rest of the defendants declined the assistance of Counsel.

The Civil Trial finally began in the Royal Court at 10.00am on Monday 1st June 1942, before Victor Carey and eight Jurats. Again the public gallery was filled to capacity with relations and friends. Mr J.E.L.Martel prosecuted and Advocate W.H.Langlois represented Jack Harper and Stephen Duquemin. Acting Inspector A.J.Langmead, Acting Deputy Inspector A.P.Lamy and Detective Sergeant F.J.Banneville were also present. The two Germans who had acted as interpreters at the German Military Tribunal were also in attendance.

The first case heard was that against Tuck and Bailey, accused of stealing 6 lb of butter from the States Dairy during the night of the 17-18th November 1941. They both pleaded guilty and a formal verdict was passed. Frank Tuck then made a statement to the Court. Addressing the Bailiff he said:-

"It must occur to you Sir, that there is some fundamental cause, some basic reason for my downfall. It is a public concern and they should know and you should know the reasons for our humiliating position in which we now find ourselves and the stigma which it has placed on the Police Service.

.....Every States employee and shopkeepers etc. under existing conditions had their hours of work reduced and their holidays increased in many cases. Our hours of duty were the same as before the war and irregular and it was necessary to take a meal whilst on duty and which had to be provided out of our rations.

Collective representation and individual request for more food was turned down. The result, Sir, was dissatisfaction and murmuring among the men. The Police have varied duties and have to go out at all hours of the night in the cold and rain. These facts are not generally recognized.

... We have felt that we have not been properly considered. This has had a demoralising effect on the Force. May I point out that it has now been felt necessary to increase substantially the rations for policemen and also to increase their pay."

Kingston Bailey also made a statement to the Court in which he corroborated what Frank Tuck had said in his statement. He added:-

"It became obvious that the rich could live and the poor could starve. We applied for extra bread firstly on an official form and secondly to Mr de Putron in person. I went with Le Gallez, one of my colleagues. I was informed to see Inspector Sculpher. I mentioned to Mr de Putron that Inspector Sculpher would do nothing for us. I reported to Sergeant Lamy the facts and asked to see the Inspector. He replied 'It is no good seeing him: he has already put in an application for more bread and it has been turned down.'

We had nobody to turn to for advice. Our Inspector had no interest in his men. He obviously had sufficient. We did not. We had to go out in all kinds of weather, with wet feet and very little food: when we returned to the Station there was no fire. We had to steal wood from the German Authorities, to have a bit of fire. Compare our position to States workers, regular hours and meals and nights in bed. This brought about the complete demoralization of the Police Force and there was lack of interest by our Inspector and complete lack of discipline.

With regard to the States Dairy, we kept observation and noticed that there was always a surplus of butter. Some people had all the butter they wanted and butter was bartered for meat etc. We have stated in our previous statements that Mr R.Chilcott could take butter when he wanted and without stating for what. This is only one example. When, through lack of food we gave way to temptation and took butter, we knew that everybody had had their rations and would not go short.

I think you will agree Sir, that complete lack of interest by the responsible Authorities coupled with the most trying conditions, has been responsible for the position in which I find myself today. My character, my work, my home, have suffered much, both mentally and physically. It has been said that we have betrayed a public trust. I think it is the Guernsey Police Force that has been betrayed."

Frank Tuck then said:- "Can I ask a question, Sir ?"

The Bailiff:- "No, the question of your sentence will come up later."

The case against Fred Short for stealing goods from the Essential Commodities store in Trinity Square was then heard and the defendant pleaded that he had no knowledge that it was a local store. The Bailiff commented:- "I must confess you make a plea that you did not know it was an Essential Commodities store or a local store. I do not see that it has any bearing on the matter; you went and stole things from a store."

When the case in which Alfred Howlett and Herbert Smith were charged with stealing six tins of beans from the Essential Commodities store, Acting Inspector Langmead was called to give the prosecution evidence.

J.E.L.Martel:- "Will you tell the Court about the statements you took ?"

A.J.Langmead:- "On the 16th May at the local prison I saw Howlett, I told him I was making enquiries concerning a statement he was alleged to have made with reference to a store in Trinity Square. I cautioned him and he made a statement which I took down."

A.W.Howlett interrupted:- "What about the first one Sir ?"

Langmead:- "On the 10th May at Fort George, I saw the prisoner, told him I was making an enquiry concerning breaking and entering in consequence of a statement he had made. He said 'I have read the story of my alleged confession, to that may I add'...."

Howlett again interrupted:- "I would like the Inspector to say what caused me to change my statement. Will you read the second statement."

Langmead:- "That will follow. First of all on the Sunday, 10th May, I saw him at Fort George when he said 'I have read the statement I am alleged to have made and I wish to plead not guilty. I have nothing further to add'.

On Friday 15th May at the Police Court room in company with two other men, I saw the prisoner, I told him that I had received a letter and that I would read a paragraph of the letter. I read it, but Howlett started to say something. 'I will leave the matter over, I will go into Police Court'. Therefore on Saturday 16th that was the reason why I saw him at the prison when he made this statement which he signed."

Martel:-"Did he make it quite voluntarily ?"

Langmead:- "Yes. I told him he need not say anything. He said 'I have read the translation of my statement and wish to state that this case of entering the Essential Commodities store at Trinity Square is true, it is the only time I did go there and I would not have done so had I known it was a civilian store. I only had three tins of beans. Smith was with me and he opened the door, but in what manner, whether by a key or if it was already open, I don't know' That was signed A.W.Howlett."

Bailiff:- "Howlett, are there any questions you would like to ask ?"

Howlett:- "The only thing Sir, is that in the first instance when I was confronted with my alleged statement I pleaded not guilty. During the week I was shown this letter saying that if we did not plead guilty and admit the offence, that we would be tried elsewhere. That is why I changed my plea from, Not Guilty, to Guilty."

Bailiff:- "You pleaded not guilty ?"

Howlett:- "I did not know it was an Essential Commodities store. When Inspector Langmead showed me the statement by the German Authorities, I pleaded not guilty. That was on the Sunday. During the week, I can't say exactly which day, Inspector Langmead came to the prison and showed me this letter that if we did not plead guilty and admit this statement, that we would be tried elsewhere. Therefore that is the reason why I changed my statement. All I have to say is that we are denied the right to plead not guilty. I have nothing else to say."

Bailiff, addressing the Jurats:- "Well Gentlemen, in this case the confession was made voluntarily, although in the case of Howlett he says first of all that he pleaded not guilty. As to whether he was guilty or not guilty I do not know, but afterwards he pleaded guilty on account of a letter he was shown, the contents of which we know nothing about. To understand the mentality of this man Howlett is quite impossible. A man is either guilty or not guilty. If you are guilty you should plead guilty, if you are not guilty, a Policeman should know that, then he should plead not guilty. He pretends that because he has read a letter - of which we know nothing about - he alters his plea quite apart from the fact that he is either guilty or not guilty. He has a mentality I cannot fathom, more especially in a Sergeant of the Police. Smith states he is guilty and he pleads guilty. In both cases both these men have pleaded quilty and the only thing the Court is to do is to confirm this by entering a formal sentence of guilty. In this case, are you all of the same opinion ?"

The Court unanimously agreed.

Had Alf Howlett and Herbert Smith or indeed the other defendants, been represented by Counsel, the subject of the letter from Dr Biel, of the 8th May 1942, might have played a more significant role in the proceedings. Ambrose Sherwill, who was available, but was not chosen by any of the defendants because they felt he had not adequately represented them at the Military Tribunal Trial, could well have used the letter effectively in their defence.

The Bailiff highlighted the absence of the letter when he addressed the Jurats, '... the contents of which we know nothing about.' Mr Sherwill would have surely pointed out that it was the Prosecution's duty to produce the letter to the Court. Moreover he would, most likely, have advised his clients to maintain their pleas of Not Guilty. In those circumstances it would have been difficult to envisage any British Court maintaining a conviction. But the defendants chose not to be represented, other than Jack Harper and Stephen Duquemin. They both chose Advocate W.H.Langlois, the only other practising Advocate, whose long but limited experience did not equip him for such a major trial.

Bill Quin, who had pleaded not guilty on the 23rd May to two charges, now changed his plea and pleaded guilty to all the four charges against him.

Bill Burton persisted with his Not Guilty pleas, despite his fellow accused pleas of Guilty. In defending himself on the charge of being concerned in the stealing of 20 bottles of spirits from the Le Lievre store, he vigorously cross examined his colleagues Charlie Friend, Jack Harper and Bill Quin when they were called to give evidence against him. When asked by the Bailiff:- "Burton, have you anything to say to the Court ?" responded:-

"I have only this to say, I have never entered Le Lievre's store, or stolen any bottles, or taken any to Harper's flat. I have been a Police officer for eighteen years and I have never, alone or with others, broken into any store and stolen from my own people. That is all, Sir."

After all the Jurats had expressed doubt or were dissatisfied with the evidence, the Bailiff addressed Bill Burton:- "The Court gives you the benefit of the doubt and acquits you."

When the case regarding stealing 8 bottles of wine and spirits from Bucktrouts & Co.Ltd, was heard, Bill Burton again vigorously asserted his innocence. "I am not guilty, Sir. I have never entered Bucktrout's store in my life."

When Bill Quin was called to give evidence for the prosecution, he was asked by Mr Martel:-

"Now will you tell the Court what you know about this robbery of eight bottles of spirits from Bucktrout's during November 1941 ?"

Quin:- "Well, except for what is in my statement to the German Authorities I know nothing about it. ......, I know nothing about Bucktrout's store, although I have made a confession."

Fred Short was asked by Mr Martel:- "Will you tell the Court what you know of this robbery during November 1941 ?"

Short:- "I cannot tell the Court anything."

Martel:- "You made a statement to Acting Deputy Inspector Lamy on the 16th May ?"

Short:- "Yes, that was similar to another we made in a certain quarter, which I am alleged to have made. I was in a state of confusion when I made that statement and at that time discretion was the better part of valour, so I made a statement."

Before asking the judgement of the Court, the Bailiff commented:- "I have never heard such an unsatisfactory case before the Court. The most unsatisfactory part of it is the evidence given by the witnesses, ex-constables of our Police Force and I have never seen men come forward here and repudiate what they have said voluntarily. They apparently have not got the first inclination of speaking the truth or anything to do with it. They are foreign to it and I wonder if those men who have brought people in the Courts, were men to be trusted in the Police Force at all and these are the men who were in charge of property for all of us in the Island. I cannot see that there is enough evidence. No doubt he (Burton) has been trading on that. No doubt he knows that he has taken part in this crime. The other three men have come forward and pleaded guilty. They seem to be shielding each other in every possible way. In this particular case I cannot ask you to find this man Burton guilty because we have not sufficient evidence."

The Court was unanimous in deciding that the case had not been proved.

The Bailiff addressing Burton:- "The evidence is not sufficient to prove you guilty but at the same time we all have our opinion about it."

Burton was also given the benefit of the doubt in the third case against him and was acquitted.

Advocate Langlois:- "Mr Bailiff and Gentlemen. On May 10th the accused Harper chose me to defend him. Those instructions have subsequently been withdrawn and it has been decided that Harper will conduct his own defence."

Jack Harper was accused on two counts of receiving. First in respect of five bottles stolen from Le Lievre's store and secondly in respect of four bottles stolen from Bucktrouts.

Harper:- "I plead not guilty Sir."

The only witness called was Acting Inspector Langmead who detailed the statements alleged to have been made by Harper.

Jack Harper challenged the Acting Inspector as to the accuracy of the statement he made at the prison on May 16th.

Harper to Langmead:- "I put it to you that it was not true that I ever mentioned that I knew it was stolen from Le Lievre ?"

Langmead:- "I took down the statement as made by you, read it over to you, which was signed by you."

Harper:- "I did not know it was stolen from Le Lievre. Those are the actual words I used. I put it to you that it was a mistake ?"

Langmead:- "That statement was taken, it was given by you, I read it over to you before you signed it and you said it was quite correct."

Harper:- "I deny that I said it was. I did not know."

Martel:- "If the Court desires, I can put in the other witnesses, but if the Court is satisfied with those confessions I do not think it necessary to do so."

The Court unanimously decided not to hear any further evidence.

After Jack Harper had again denied knowing where the bottles had come from, the Bailiff announced:-

"The Court unanimously finds you guilty of this crime."

Harper:- " I would like to make a statement now, Sir."

Bailiff:- "No, certainly not."

All the charges having been dealt with, Mr Langmead was asked to tell the Court the antecedents of the men convicted.

"Alfred William Howlett, born Guernsey 1891, is married, wife in Guernsey, four grown-up children away. He joined the Police Force in April 1920, was promoted Sergeant in 1928, has once been reprimanded for a disciplinary offence. He has performed his duties satisfactorily.

Jack Harper, born Plymouth 1900, was brought up in Guernsey, is married - wife and two boys away. He joined the Police Force in May 1922, was appointed Sergeant in 1937. From 1928 to 1937 he acted as Official Tester examining persons for driving licences and public vehicles. He has been commended and rewarded by the Police Committee on ten occasions for conspicuous Police work. He has four disciplinary offences recorded against him. Has been regarded as an industrious Police officer.

Charles Alfred Friend, born Guernsey 1914, is single. He joined the Police Force in January 1939, but has not shown any particular initiative. He is easily led and has undoubtedly been led away by older men.

Frank Hubert Tuck, born Guernsey 1914, is single and joined the Police Force in January 1936. He is inclined to be obstinate, had he put his mind to Police work would have made progress in the Force. Has five disciplinary reports against him.

Herbert P.Smith, born South Wales 1904, is married with a wife and 3 young children here. He joined the Police Force in November 1927. He cannot be said to have been particularly successful as a Police officer but has no disciplinary reports against him.

Frank William Whare, born Guernsey 1894, is married, his wife and two children at work, are in the Island. He first joined the Police Force in May 1918, but left and went to Alderney in 1922. He re-joined in January 1926, has been commended and was regarded as a reliable painstaking officer.

Kingston G.Bailey, born in Norfolk 1916, is married with one child, both in England. He joined the Police Force in December 1938. He has not shown any conspicuous ability as a Police Officer.

William G.Quin, born Guernsey 1896. married with wife and one child here and two children away. He joined the Police Force in February 1921. Has been once commended. Has performed his duties satisfactorily without showing any great keenness. Has two disciplinary reports against him.

Frederick W.Short, born Guernsey 1910, married with wife and child in England. He joined the Police Force in April 1934 and two years ago was appointed as motorcycle patrol. Has shown great aptitude as a Police officer and under normal conditions would undoubtedly have made great progress. Abnormal conditions are no doubt responsible for his present position.

Stephen John C.Duquemin, born November 1872, was licensee of the Victoria Hotel, Esplanade, from 16th July 1932 to date of his arrest in March. He has four convictions for motoring offences and one for selling intoxicating liquor after hours, but no criminal offence is recorded against him."

Mr Langmead's choice of words in the case of Stephen Duquemin is interesting. 'No criminal offence is recorded against him'. The Police were very familiar with Steve Duquemin, he was well known for making claims regarding fires and stolen milk. Later in the occupation A/PC 21 R.Le Tissier was told by Bert Lamy not to take any notice of any claim that Duquemin made and that he would back him up. Duquemin was, according to Roland Le Tissier, fly enough to get around that by reporting supposed losses to the Germans.

The Bailiff, before sentencing the men, had them assembled in a row in front of him and addressed them.

"As Police officers ...... you must realise and understand that you have brought shame and humiliation on every single soul in the Island from the Royal Court downwards. We reposed in you, we who swear you in, we reposed in you our confidence and our certainly that by your integrity you would be an example to the people in this Island. And how have you repaid it ?

Clothed in the uniform of the Police, you were given certain privileges by the German Army of occupation in being allowed out after curfew. No one else was allowed out after curfew, you alone and what have you done clothed in the uniform, you have broken into our own property, you have stolen and carried on with the most terrible way and you deserve everything that you can possibly get and you will be looked upon with contempt by the whole of your fellow Islanders.

I can assure you that I am filled with shame and I only regret that we have not been able to inflict greater punishment on you as we have done today. It is revolting that you have used the privileges given to you as members of the Police Force to act in this way and to think what the people, the foreigners here, the workmen, the French, the Germans, the Dutch are thinking of you and of the Police Force, of the British Police Force whom they look upon and proud to look upon.

I am filled with shame that such a thing should have occurred in this Island of Guernsey. I have nothing further to say except to say how much I regret having to speak to you all in this way."

Then the Bailiff announced the sentences.

| | |
|---|---|
| Kingston George Bailey | 3 months hard labour |
| Charles Albert Friend | 12 months hard labour |
| Jack Harper | 15 months hard labour |
| Alfred William Howlett | 9 months hard labour |
| William George Quin | 16 months hard labour |
| Frederick Winzer Short | 9 months hard labour. |
| Herbert Percival Smith | 15 months hard labour |
| Frank Hubert Tuck | 9 months hard labour |
| Frank William Whare | 3 months hard labour |
| Stephen J.C.Duquemin | 9 months hard labour |

The Court rose at 4.30pm. The Bailiff gave permission for the men to see their relatives before being taken back to Fort George.

The sixteen convicted Policemen were held at Fort George for two weeks before being shipped out of the Island on 13th June 1942. In the meantime they were allowed visitors on one or two occasions. Fred Short's brother visited him and brought a tablet of soap, which by then was unobtainable. A German Policeman, who had lived a great part of his life in Canada and who had become friendly with Fred, managed to secretly bring him a pound packet of tobacco and cigarette papers. The German, with his Canadian accent, told Fred:- "You bloody fool, what you get caught for ?"

Fred hid the gifts in his mattress.

They were guarded by two sets of guards, one set locked their prisoners up all day and if anyone wanted to go to the toilet, or the wash house, then it was at the double, under armed guard. The other set of guards, however, allowed the men much greater freedom of movement. They were free to walk about the Fort and even around the Fort Field.

Fred Short later recalled:- "As I walked the Fort Field, I wondered would I make a run for it. All I had to do was to cut across the road and run for it to my brother's place at Saints. But I knew the first thing they would do, would be to rope in my two brothers, so no, I used my loaf and stayed."

When the time came for the sixteen Guernsey Police officers to be deported to France, they were handcuffed in pairs and taken down to the harbour. Kingston Bailey later wrote of his departure:- "On our arrival at the dockside, we were un-handcuffed and told to get on board a small ship lying there. Naturally we all stood together on the deck. Then suddenly one of the guards started yelling 'Get down into the hold, what do you think you're doing, going on a pleasure trip.' He pushed and shoved several of us, until we were all in the hold, which was filthy and had only just been emptied of coal. It was not until 4.00pm that we left Guernsey en route for Caen prison."

# Chapter 19

# FALSE ACCUSATION

Seventy-seven-year-old Doctor Arderne Wilson called at the Police Station and reported to Acting Inspector Langmead that he had given medical attention to a girl suffering from haemorrhage who alleged that she had been raped by a German soldier.

Sergeant Banneville went to see the eighteen-year-old girl and reported:- "This girl is frail, she appeared ill and has an impediment in her speech. She appears to be truthful and of good morals. I questioned her aunt regarding the occurrence and the girl's character. She has given her aunt no trouble."

The girl's Aunt Alice made a statement saying:-

"I keep house for my brother and his children, his wife is dead. On Sunday 3rd May 1942, my niece Doreen told me that a German officer had assaulted her. I did not consider this serious and took no further action.

On Wednesday 13th May, I was home and in bed at about 10.45pm. My niece said she was bleeding and thinking it was her monthly period, I told her to lie down. I did not realise that an assault had been committed. But the following morning she was still bleeding and I sent for Doctor Wilson. He examined her and and questioned her in my presence, she told him that a German soldier had raped her."

Sergeant Banneville also took a statement from Doreen ......:-

"At about 7.30pm on Wednesday the 13th May 1942, I was walking in the Choffins lanes when I met a German soldier. In German, he said 'Good Night, where are you going.' I said 'I am going home'. He got hold of me, took me in a field nearby and threw me on the ground. After he had taken his belt off, he knelt down over me and unbuttoned his trousers. He took my knickers off, right off. I shouted and kicked while he was doing this. He then got on top of me, ......... . When he was finished he got up and put his belt on.

I bled on my way home, I told my auntie that I was bleeding. On the following morning I again complained to my aunt that I was bleeding profusely. Dr Wilson was sent for. Dr Wilson examined me on Thursday morning, 14th May. I told him that a German soldier had had relations with me. I have not had sexual relations with anyone else. I did not consent in any way, he took me by force. I can identify him. I did not give him any encouragement at all. I have never spoken to him before. I have never been with anyone else. This is the first man who has interfered with me".

Mr Langmead was concerned about this alleged rape and immediately sent copies of all the statements to the Feldgendarmerie. He also informed the President of the Controlling Committee.

Dr Arderne Wilson provided the Acting Inspector with a certificate dated the 18th May 1942:-

"I certify,

That I visited a young woman called Doreen..., aged 18, who lives near......Castel. She was suffering from excessive haemorrhage from the vagina. She stated that she had been forcibly seduced by a German soldier.

Upon examination I found that the hymen had been severely ruptured and that haemorrhage was caused by this rupture.

In my opinion the carnal connection she had with the soldier was the first penetration of her person

There were no bruises but both cheeks of the buttocks bore evidence of small excoriations.

Considerable force must have been used, but it is difficult to estimate the degree of force because that will depend upon the man's anatomy, his weight and sexual energy.

E.Arderne Wilson M.B.C.M, E.D.M"

The next day Dr Wilson addressed a further letter to the Acting Inspector.

"I hereby wish to unconditionally withdraw the report I sent to you in regard to an alleged forcible carnal assault upon Miss .... . Upon further enquiry today at her home (from her aunt) I found out that both the girl and aunt had grossly deceived me as regards the alleged assault and the haemorrhage. From the diapens which had been kept and the blood retained in a pail there was clear evidence of the girl having had a miscarriage."

Sergeant Banneville again went to interview Miss Doreen ..... and took another statement.:-

"The statement I made to you on Saturday 16th May was false, it was all lies. I now wish to make a statement telling you the truth. In November 1941, I was working for the German Authorities at the Mont Saint, kitchen work. I worked there for about one month and left in December 1941. Whilst I was working there I became friendly with a German soldier I knew him as Paul, he lived at Mont Saint. During the time I worked there I went out with him twice. Nothing happened between us during this period.

I next saw him in March 1942, at Mont Saint, this was during the latter part of March. We went out together, went for a walk and with my consent went into a field and he had sexual relations with me. I again saw him on the 3rd May 1942. We went out together and we again had sexual relations, with my consent. On Wednesday 13th May, I saw this soldier again and went out with him and with my consent he had sexual relations with me. After he had had relations with me I became unwell and had haemorrhage and told my auntie about it.

The next morning I became worse and Doctor Wilson was sent for. I told Dr Wilson a number of lies and I did not know I had had a miscarriage. On Saturday 16th May, I accompanied the German Police to Mont Saint and there saw the man who had had relations with me. I told the Police after being questioned that I was a consenting party. I am sorry that I told the Doctor and Police lies. The three times that this soldier had connections with me, was with my consent."

As a result, of the new statements Mr Langmead passed the matter over to the Acting Attorney General, to see what action could be taken.

On the 27th May 'Miss Doreen ...... a domestic worker, of Castel was bound over to be of good behaviour for 12 months under the First Offender's Law'. She pleaded guilty to a charge of 'effecting a Public Mischief by making a Statement to a Police officer on May 16th, knowing it to be false, thereby causing Police officers to devote their time and services to the investigation of false allegations'. The Magistrate, after hearing details of the statements made, bound her over and spoke to her severely.

On the 24th May Dr Brosch wrote to the President of the Controlling Committee, saying that A/PC 33 Brackley had been found unsuitable for Police duty and must be dismissed. Mr Langmead reluctantly gave him a week's notice. Thirty-six-year-old, Ossie Brackley was however to wear the uniform of the Guernsey Police again. In the meantime he obtained work with R.G.Froome, at Douit Farm, St Martin, as a farm worker.

"We have had a lot of potatoes stolen, 5 greenhouses have been broken into altogether, 2 this time and 3 before, it is the German soldiers who have done it." That is how A/PC 27 Scraton was greeted by James Tostevin, of Les Maris, La Houguette Lane, late one afternoon in May 1942.

Mr Tostevin went on:-

"Mr Payne, the Glasshouse Utilisation Board organiser, and I traced the foot marks in the dew this morning up to within 50 yards of their gun position. They had dropped a potato on the way. I have left it where I found it. Last Wednesday, during the night, they came and broke the glass of the greenhouse at about 11.10pm. My father heard the glass breaking and shouted. We saw a couple of German soldiers running up the field. It is the soldiers who are looking after the anti-aircraft gun up the Houguette Lane.

We have not reported any of the previous thefts, but Mr Payne has advised us to report this one. I had a final look around the greenhouses just before 11 o'clock last night, everything was alright. I discovered it this morning about 7.15am when I was taking the horse out."

The Constable examined the greenhouses and found that in all five cases, access had been gained by breaking three window panes and a sash bar. In every case the break-in was at the end of the greenhouse, the furthest from the family house. There were footprints visible and these showed a heavily nailed boot with toe plates and heel plates. A/PC Scraton wrote in his notebook:- "The accomplices had also excreted at the rear end of the greenhouses, there being 2 heaps."

A/PC Scraton was shown the tracks found earlier in the day where there were footprints of boots on the damp grass. The trail led to a gun position occupied by German soldiers. The Constable followed the footprints to within 30ft of the gun position, which he felt that was near enough for safety.

The quantity of potatoes stolen on the two nights was estimated by Mr Tostevin as about nine barrels, valued at 21/- per barrel. A/PC Scraton noted that the greenhouses could be approached from the direction of the gun position and that gorse bushes offered splendid cover.

Mr Langmead reported the matter to the Germans but they never informed him of the outcome of their investigations.

On the 23rd May 1942, a locked suitcase and a locked wooden trunk, each containing French currency, were handed in at the Police Station by Mr Roland Barnett. He was one of a small team of Islanders, led by R.O.Falla, who regularly travelled to Granville, in France, to purchase urgently needed supplies on behalf of the Island.

The next morning Mr Barnett returned for the money and signed for it in the Occurrence Book. He and the money were escorted to the Granville boat by Mr Lamy.

The Sub-Committee of the Police Committee met on the 18th May and appointed a further seven men as Auxiliary Constables, to commence duty on the 25th May, subject to medical examination.

| | | |
|---|---|---|
| A/PC 4 | Alexander C.O'Donovan, 38, | Connemara, Braye Road. |
| A/PC 7 | Clifford W Falla, 24, | St Edith, Friquet, Castel |

A/PC 14 Ronald William Le Page, 20, Rue Queripel, St Sampson.
A/PC 20 Denzil A.Le Farge, 25, Pen-y-Bryn, Les Gravees.
A/PC 21 Roland W.Le Tissier, 25, La Villiaze, Mon Plaisir, Forest.
A/PC 33 Roy Le Page, 22, Ewloe, Portinfer.
A/PC 38 Edwal A Robilliard, 19, La Villette, St Martin.

On this occasion the medical was not a formality. A/PC O'Donovan, who had recently undergone a hernia operation, was passed fit, with reservation, by Dr B.S.Collings. He was required to sign a certificate absolving the Police Committee from liability within three years of a recurrence of his hernia. His appointment was delayed until the 1st June

The Police Committee at their meeting on the 4th May, resolved to approach the German Authorities with a view to securing Mr Sculpher's release on the ground that he had not been charged with any offence. However Inspector Sculpher, who had been held in prison since the 31st March 1942, was not released until the 3rd June after the civil trial had been completed.

Sergeant Le Lievre was on duty at the Station, when twenty-year-old Miss Ivy Gallienne, of Clifton Court, reported that:- "Miss Phyllis Hamon, aged 19, came from Sark some months ago and stayed with me, she left on Saturday 30th May and has not returned, I have been ill in bed myself and have been told she is somewhere in St Sampson district, all her clothes are at Clifton Court. I have spoken to a German officer, who told me she had been seen around St Sampson every day." She gave a description of Phyllis Hamon as, dark brown hair, red and white summer dress, no hat, short.

The next afternoon A/PC Lennox Roberts saw Miss Hamon on the Bridge and questioned her. She explained she had been staying with her German boy friend in St Sampson, from 30th May to 7th June, without permission. Her identity card was at Grange Lodge, as she had applied for a permit to return to Sark. The Constable warned her for Court at 10.15am on the 10th June.

At the meeting of the States of Deliberation held on the 10th June 1942, Deputy C W Arnold asked the President of the Police Committee questions regarding the functioning of the Committee. The answers revealed that notices convening meetings of the Committee were signed by Mr Sculpher and not, as had been assumed, by the States Committee Clerk. The minutes of the meetings were taken by the Clerk Sergeant.

The President was asked on how many occasions recently, had the Committee examined the charge book. Mr Agnew told Deputy Arnold that:- "The Committee never examines the charge book, it is not part of our duty."

Deputy Arnold:- "What payment or allowances have been paid to suspended members of the force or their dependants during the period awaiting trial and by whom were such payments authorised?"

Mr Agnew:- "Pay at suspension rate, ie two thirds of their regular pay, was paid to all Police officers pending their trial, the Committee authorised that payment."

The next question concerned the strength and composition of the Force. Mr Agnew replied:- "The strength and composition of the Force is regulated by Orders in Council No 11 of 1920 and No 10 of 1938. States approval has been obtained for such establishment."

Colonel Knackfuss, the Feldkommandantur in Jersey issued a decree dated the 4th June requisitioning all wireless sets.

"By superior orders, the wireless sets of the civilian population are to be requisitioned and placed under the custody of the Feldkommandantur. Sets used by subjects of the Reich and of countries allied to Germany are excepted; for these, special permits will be issued on application.

The sets are to be delivered by the 17th June 1942. In the case of battery sets, the batteries may be retained by the owner. The retaining of any other component parts of sets or their alteration is forbidden. The person concerned shall attach a label on each set, showing the name and exact address of the owner.

Contraventions of the Order, .....shall be punished ...... with imprisonment up to six weeks and a fine up to 30,000 RM."

The Germans were becoming very concerned at B.B.C. broadcasts, that were transmitting messages to the resistance movement in France and other occupied countries. They no doubt felt that the same might happen in Guernsey.

8705 wireless sets were surrendered and an unknown number, probably considerable, were retained by the civilian population. Those surrendered were stored at the Town Arsenal or the Victoria Road Chapel.

A considerable number of the surrendered sets were later 'borrowed' by the Germans. J.H.Audio, J.Munro and a clerk from the Civil Transport Services had the responsibility of selecting, testing and listing all radio sets taken from the Town Arsenal or Victoria Road Chapel and 'loaned' to the German forces.

Acting Inspector Langmead was asked to keep a watch on the Victoria Road Chapel during the night as no caretaker was available. A/PC La Farge, who was on patrol in that area, was instructed to pay attention to the Chapel.

At 11.45pm the Constable found a window broken on the Chapel's ground floor. He telephoned the Station and A/PCs Le Page and Falla were sent to assist him. Two of them entered the building through the window and found the room empty. They came out and were trying to secure the window when an Organisation Todt man arrived and detained the three Constables until the arrival of a Feldgendarmerie officer. They were questioned and their particulars taken and informed that the Chapel was a German store.

The Force, from time to time, became involved in the collection of fines which had not been paid. At 8.35 am on the 16th June A/PC 32 Salmon saw John Torode at Bailiffs Cross in connection with a fine of £1 which had not been paid. Mr Torode said:- "I have been totally cleared out for a few days and have not had enough money, I only had 8/- but I think I can pay it now." He was warned to be at the Sheriff's office, with the money, by 10am the next day. The fine was paid.

On the 15th June the Police Committee met to confirm the appointments made by the sub Committee and to select a new Sergeant. Mr Langmead had again tried to 'guide' the Committee in the direction of his choice. He had written to the President a few days previously in hopeful anticipation.

"I beg to report that a vacancy still exists for a Sergeant. On the 5th May 1942, notice was received from Grange Lodge that Sergeant E.Pill and PC 35 Le Cocq would be permitted to resume duty and in accordance with the minute of the Committee of 4th May, both were re-instated forthwith. This eased the situation and enabled the other Sergeants to have a day off.

The available regular Police Constables on duty from which promotions can be made are PCs 27 R.Kimber, 32 H.Pugh, 9 R.Marsh and 35 F.Le Cocq, of these Kimber and Marsh are unsuitable for promotion, which leaves Pugh and Le Cocq.

PC H.Pugh is aged 42 and joined the force on 18th April 1927. He is married with a wife and two children in England. For several years he was employed on Harbour duties. He has not shown any special aptitude, nor keenness in Police work.

PC F.Le Cocq is aged 27 and joined the Force on 24th May 1939. He is married, his wife remaining in the Island. For about a year he was employed in the office as assistant clerk and for sixteen months was employed as a motorcycle patrol. He has therefore had a varied experience in Police work. This PC has shown great keenness as a Police officer, he is of good education and address, with a knowledge of French, typing and office routine. He is able to drive a car and ride a motorcycle.

I have no hesitation in recommending Le Cocq for the vacancy. I suggest that the Committee should interview both men and that the appointment should be as Acting Sergeant. This will enable the Committee to watch the progress and work of the three acting Sergeants so that when full appointments are made, after the war, the best man will be selected."

The Police Committee appointed PC 32 H.T.Pugh as Acting Sergeant as from the 15th June 1942.

As an Acting Sergeant, Harry Pugh was only able to display his newly awarded three stripes on his right arm. Many of his colleagues quickly noticed that he had developed a habit of throwing his cape over his left arm !

Mr Langmead reported to the Committee that, at 9.45pm on Sunday 17th May the Station Sergeant received an instruction from the Feldgendarmerie to assemble the whole Force at the Station within one hour. This was achieved, except for two men on country beats who later rang in and were brought to Town and one man who was on his way into Town at the expiry of the hour.

The officer in charge of the Feldgendarmerie arrived at the Station at 10.45pm and expressed himself satisfied with the test and dismissed the men. The officer then asked the Sergeant how long it would take in the early hours of the morning and on being told, about three hours owing to the difficulty of telephoning, he said :- Every Police officer must be on the telephone."

The Acting Inspector told the Committee:-

"In the past the practice has been for each man to find out his nearest telephone and keep that number recorded at the Station. If the man is required urgently the Sergeant in charge of the Station would telephone the number and ask the householder to call the policeman. There has been no point in having all Police on the phone. Conditions are somewhat different at the moment, but are only temporary. I have ascertained from the telephone department that an alarm bell similar to that used for the Fire Brigade is not a practical idea for country districts where new installations cannot be made.

I suggest that the calling up of Police might be arranged by dividing the Force into groups in accordance with their respective addresses. A key man, preferably a regular, would be on the telephone and he would be responsible for calling up the men in his area. The difficulty when a key man is on duty will have to be provided for, but the onus will rest on the Station Sergeant to check up duty men and send a patrol man to the area for any other man who must be called.

On enquiry at Grange Lodge I was informed that this system would be acceptable to the German authorities. The number of new telephones would be eight and men who are on the phone would be transferred to Police charge, adding four rentals which would make a total of 12, costing £30 a year."

The Police Committee agreed.

Mr Walter Baker lived at 72 Victoria Road and let furnished rooms to Miss Chazel. Her friend, Miss Mabel Maber, a 37-year-old chambermaid, also slept there occasionally. On the 17th June they had both been to a party at 26 Saumarez Street and returned at about 10.30pm.

Mr Baker later recalling the events, said:- "At about 12.30am I heard the front door bell ring, I went and answered the door. When I opened it, I saw a German soldier, he pushed me aside and said, 'I live here, this is my house, get out.' I told him he was wrong and went to close the door. He caught hold of me by the throat. Then the two women showed themselves. He let go of me and caught hold of one of them. He kicked a door, also broke a jug which was in the passage and a small picture frame."

Mr Baker telephoned the Station and Sergeant Dyson immediately went to Victoria Road where he saw a woman being held around the waist by a German sergeant. The woman, in his view, was making a poor attempt to struggle.

Miss Maber told Sergeant Dyson:- "I sleep here with my friend Miss Chazel. Tonight we went to a party at 26 Saumarez Street and came back at about 10.30pm accompanied by a German soldier. I went to bed, later I heard the front door bell ring and a noise in the passage. Then someone called me. I went to see who it was and saw the Sergeant who is in charge of 26 Saumarez Street. He caught me around the waist and was a bit troublesome. He had had too much to drink."

The German sergeant was taken to his billet in Saumarez Street in the Police car. The two Constables who were on patrol in that part of the Town, were instructed to keep an eye out for trouble. The German sergeant later returned to Victoria Road, but on being told to leave, did so without causing any further trouble.

At about 12.30am on the 19th June A/PC 36 Solway reported that he had just caught a German soldier milking a cow owned by Gerald Brache, in a field behind Vale Castle. A/PCs Solway and A/PC 34 Hamon had been on observation duty as a result of previous complaints by Mr Brache that his cows were being milked at night.

They had watched the soldier start milking the cow. When the two Constables approached, he drew his bayonet and threatened them. A/PC Solway responded by drawing his truncheon but no blows were struck. The German went with the Constables to Brache's house where they telephoned the Station. Later a German officer arrived and took charge of the soldier and the Constables returned to the Station. In the margin, against the report of the incident in the Occurrence Book, the Acting Inspector wrote "Good Work !"

A/PC27 Scraton and A/PC 38 Robilliard were on patrol at Les Blicqs, St Andrew, at about 1.20am on the 27th June when they saw three German soldiers coming towards them along Chemin du Roi from the direction of the water tower. Two of them were carrying sacks which the Constables suspected contained potatoes. The other soldier was carrying what appeared to be a long handled weeder. A/PC Scraton asked them where they had obtained the potatoes but they evaded the question, saying that they were for their comrades in the battery.

A/PC Robilliard went to telephone the Station while Geoffrey Scraton walked with the soldiers. When they came to an earth bank they put down the two sacks of potatoes. The Constable thought they were going to pick the sacks up again after they had climbed over the bank, but instead ran away, leaving the potatoes behind.

In response to A/PC Robilliard's telephone call, Acting Sergeant Harry Bull set off to obtain assistance from the Feldgendarmerie at Mon Plaisir. He rang the door bell repeatedly and shouted several times but could not get any response, so he carried on to where the two Constables were guarding the two sacks of potatoes. The three officers searched the vicinity for the German soldiers, without result. They then went to the local German guard room, which was about 200 yards away and saw the N.C.O in charge, who was un-cooperative.

Sergeant Bull returned to the Station about 2.30am taking the potatoes with him. Although it was suspected that the potatoes had probably been stolen from a field next to the Forest Cemetery owned by Mr William Guilbert, of Bellieuse, St Martin, they were collected from the Station by a Feldgendarmerie officer.

In early March 1942 H.M.Comptroller. G.P.J.Ridgway, had been taken seriously ill and was not able to undertake his duties or those of deputising as H.M.Attorney General. The Bailiff had written to the Feldkommandantur on the 16th March informing him of the situation and requesting that Mr A.J.Sherwill be reinstated. Fuerst von Oettingen refused the request.

At the end of June 1942 Victor Carey became concerned at the possible difficulties that would arise if Advocate J.E.L.Martel's health was to fail. On the 30th he again wrote to the Feldkommandantur pointing out that the Guernsey Bar was reduced to only two Advocates, Mr Martel and W.H.Langlois.

"Should anything happen to Mr Martel or to the other remaining Advocate, Mr W.H.Langlois, the position would be that the Authorities would have no qualified person to act for them or the public would have no one to plead their causes. As presumably Mr Langlois would take Mr Martel's place should he break down, the general public would be the sufferers.

I feel it to be my duty again to bring this matter to your notice and again to request that the ban be lifted from Mr Sherwill's activities as Attorney General.

May I emphasise that although expressing his willingness to serve as Attorney General, on being asked by me, Mr Sherwill has made no move whatever for his own re-instatement. My action in requesting it is made solely in the public interest, in that a position of grave difficulty might arise at any moment in our public administration."

The matter was passed to Colonel Knackfuss, the overall Feldkommandantur for the Channel Islands, and on the 22nd the Bailiff received a reply agreeing to the reinstatement of Mr A.J.Sherwill as Attorney General. Mr Carey immediately informed Ambrose Sherwill and congratulated him.

## Chapter 20

# FOUR STROKES OF THE BIRCH

Arthur Johns, the Glasshouse Utilisation Board Supervisor, reported to A/PC 27 Scraton that the Board's Queux Manor Vinery in Castel had been broken into overnight, on the 28th/29th June and a quantity of tomatoes stolen. The Constable found that access had been gained by the removal of two panes of glass and that later an attempt had been made to replace them. There were imprints of hobnailed boots with heel and toe plates. Arthur Johns suggested:- "We will be picking from the greenhouse soon, so if a watch could be kept for one or two nights, results might be obtained."

The suggestion was acted upon and on the 3rd July A/PC Geoffrey Scraton kept observation with A/PC38 Robilliard at the Vinery. It was not long before they heard a pane of glass being removed and saw a man enter a greenhouse and start to pick tomatoes. A/PC Scraton challenged the intruder, a German soldier and asked him what he was doing. He replied in sign language, "picking tomatoes."

When Constable Robilliard went to telephone the Station for assistance, the soldier made a dash to get away and broke two more panes of glass in getting out of the vinery. When outside he threw away his sack of tomatoes and ran away. Constable Scraton gave chase and caught him. The soldier after making signs to be let go, suddenly made another dash for freedom and again the Constable chased and caught him. The German kept repeating:- "Alles fur eine tomato." .

The soldier made yet another attempt to escape, dashing around a corner and sprinting away. After another chase, he finally gave up saying, "Ich habe twzei kleine kindere." Then he walked with the Constable to the German command post at Hillcrest, where he confessed to the Under officer.

As a result of the telephone call made to the Station by A/PC Robilliard, Acting Sergeant Bull and A/PC 11.Vanden Burgh arrived at Queux Manor Vineries accompanied by Sergeant Major Oeser. The Sergeant Major walked around the vinery and inspected the broken glass where the entry was made. Then they all went to Hillcrest where the soldier concerned was vigorously 'interviewed' by the Sergeant Major.

When the Police Committee met on the 7th July 1942 they received reports from the Acting Inspector regarding A/PC 27 Scraton's courage and initiative in dealing with the German soldiers stealing potatoes and tomatoes on the 27th of June and the 3rd July. He was commended and awarded 5/-. Constable Robilliard was also commended for assisting Constable Scraton on both occasions. A/PC 36 Henry Solway was awarded 5/- for courage and initiative in dealing with the German soldier caught milking a cow on the night of the 18/19th June. A/PC 34 'Pat' Hamon was commended for assisting him.

The activities of German soldiers and foreign workers were causing both the military and civil authorities considerable problems and concern. Jurat John

Leale telephoned the Station at 9.00pm on the 10th July complaining that some German soldiers had been seen in his mother's potato patch, at the Hawthorns, Bulwer Avenue.

PC Le Cocq was sent to investigate. Mrs Leale's maid, Miss Olive le Cras, told him:-

"I was at the top of the house at about 8.00pm this evening, when I saw two German soldiers dressed in blue, one was a big fellow, the other shorter. They came through the hedge going into the potato patch and started raking with their hands. I went down and spoke to them, then the other maid came and said the Police had been phoned for. When they heard this they ran along the wall bordering Bulwer Avenue and jumped over the sea wall towards the gun battery south of 'Gorselea'. They had a double handful of potatoes. One threw his back on the potato patch, the other threw his in the hedge. I would know them again."

Mr Langmead, as usual, sent John Leale a report on the incident, with the usual request for "a copy to be forwarded to the German Authorities for the favour of their enquiry." Despite the President of the Controlling Committee's more than usual interest in this matter, nothing further was heard from the German Authorities.

Acting Sergeant Harry Dyson lived at Mont Mado, in Les Hubits. He rented a field, near by, in Blanche Pierre Lane, in which he had planted a crop of potatoes. He suffered, like many others, from the activities of potato thieves. He estimated that he had lost about 300 lb of potatoes. Whenever he could, he visited his field, only to find still more of the potatoes missing.

At 7.30pm on the 11th July 1942 he found two foreign labourers pulling up his potatoes and putting them in the haversacks they were carrying. He detained one man, but the other managed to escape. The Feldgendarmerie arrived, accompanied by the Lager Fuhrer from the Organisation Todt prison. They visited the field and inspected the damage. The man who ran away left his haversack behind containing about 30 lb of potatoes.

The prisoner was placed in the 'O.T.' prison in George Road. At least on that occasion one of the thieves had been caught, although Harry Dyson never learnt what punishment, if any, was exacted.

The Germans had decreed in October 1940 that shops could not open after 4.00pm, so A/PC 34 Hamon was suspicious when he observed two men entering Arthur Machon's jewellery shop in the Pollet at 5.00pm on the 16th July. The Constable had noticed two foreigners inspecting the window display before entering the shop. While watching, he observed a tray of brooches being taken out of the window.

Later, when the two men came out of the shop, the Constable asked them what they had bought. They replied "a brooch". A/PC Hamon then took them back into the shop where he saw the proprietor, Arthur Alfred Machon, who admitted selling them the brooch for 4 marks. The Constable told Mr Machon to return the money to the men and he took possession of the brooch.

In the Police Court on the 17th July Mr Machon pleaded not guilty denying that he had sold the brooch to the men, but had exchanged it for one they had purchased previously. He said that he was aware that the Policeman was watching him and would have been very foolish to have broken the law under those circumstances.

The Magistrate asked to hear the evidence from the purchaser of the brooch, but was informed that he had left the Island. The case was adjourned until the following Monday for the possible appearance of the purchaser.

On the Monday the Court was informed that the purchaser had in fact left the Island. However, PC Reg Marsh was called to give evidence of how the defendant had approached him and admitted selling the brooch to two young Frenchmen. Mr Machon then refused to give evidence under oath in his own defence. The Magistrate found him guilty and he was fined 10/-.

Mr W.J.Rawlings-Duquemin, who was farm manager for Steve Duquemin, telephoned the Station on the 21st July 1942 and reported that someone had forceably entered a store used by him as a workshop at La Grand Mare.

Detective Sergeant Fred Banneville, accompanied by a member of the Feldgendarmerie, went to the La Grande Mare and was told by Mr Rawlings-Duquemin that approximately 10 gallons of linseed oil and 10 tins of house paint, 3 chairs, 2 cushions, 1 dining gong and 2 blankets had been stolen.

They all went to a nearby hut occupied by German troops where Mr Rawlings-Duquemin identified 3 chairs, 2 cushions and a gong, as his property. Two tins of paint were found which the Germans admitted stealing, but not the quantity stated by Mr Rawlings-Duquemin. When asked by the Feldgendarmerie officer whether he would accept payment for the stolen property, Mr Rawlings-Duquemin agreed and was requested to attend Grange Lodge at 3.00pm that afternoon.

At 4.00pm the same day, a telephone message was received at the Station from Grange Lodge informing Detective Sergeant Banneville that a report was not required, as the matter had been settled.

As a result of another telephone call, A/PC 29 Frank Falla called on Henry Robilliard at Grandes Rocques, on the 23rd July. He complained that:- "At 11.00am yesterday I caught John Mahy, an eleven-year-old local boy, stealing my potatoes from my field bordering my house. When I caught him he started to cry. I took him by the arm to his mother and questioned him. He told me that his mother had told him to do it, but later said it was not true. The quantity of potatoes he had, was about 3½lb, valued at 10d. Within the last two weeks, on two or three occasions, I have lost 10 lb of potatoes, but I cannot say who did it."

The Constable then went to see Mrs Mahy, the boy's mother, who said:-

"I am absolutely fed up with the boy, I have been to Court twice before. I did not tell him to steal the potatoes, he is such a liar and a rogue that I cannot control him. Three weeks ago I bought my potato ration of 14 lb and when I went to get them they were gone. I questioned the boy and gave him a thrashing, then he would not admit he had taken them, but later two boys told me that he had sold them to the O.T's on Cobo Road. When I asked him what he had done with the money, he said he had forgotten. I hope they will do something for me at Court. I cannot control him at all. My husband is away in the navy."

In the Police Court, John Mahy admitted stealing potatoes and exchanging them for bread. The Probation officer told the Court that he was 'hopeless' and a 'bad'un'. The Magistrate described the boy as wicked and sentenced him to be detained until 5.00pm that day and in the meantime ordered that he receive four strokes of the birch. John Mahy was led out of Court in tears.

On the 27th July, Colonel Knackfuss issued a 'Notice' which caused a great concern to relatives of Islanders held in prison by the German authorities. The wives and relatives of the Guernsey policemen serving their sentences on the continent were particularly worried.

NOTICE.

"As from August 1941, all inhabitants of the Channel Islands who are held in custody for any reason by the German authorities, either in the Channel Islands or in France, are liable to the DEATH PENALTY if any attacks or acts of sabotage are made against the Occupying Power in the occupied territory.

In addition, I declare that henceforth I reserve to myself the right to nominate certain members of any parish, who will be liable to the DEATH PENALTY in the event of any attacks against communications, as for instance, harbours, cranes, bridges, cables and wires, if these are made with the assistance or with the knowledge of the inhabitants of the parish concerned.

In their own interest I call upon the population for an increased activity and watchfulness in combatting all suspicious elements and to co-operate in the discovery of the guilty persons.

The population of the Island are once more reminded that, in accordance with the German Military Law and in agreement with the Hague convention, penalties are as follows:-

| | |
|---|---|
| Espionage: | The death penalty. |
| Sabotage: | The death penalty. |
| High Treason: | The death penalty or penal servitude for life." |

Mrs Anna ...., a widow, of Hougue du Moullin, Vale, telephoned the Station on the 28th July and asked that a Constable call to see her on a matter pertaining to her daughter and daughter-in-law. Later that afternoon A/PC 30 De Carteret visited Mrs ...., who complained:-

"I locked my door last night and was awakened at 4.30am this morning to find that my daughter and my daughter-in-law, Mrs Mary ..... and their friend Miss Phyllis ....... were knocking at the door. I said Phyllis must go home, she can't come in here.

They came in and went out again so I locked the door and they slept in the lavatory until 7.00am this morning. This is not the first time they have stayed out after curfew. Last Wednesday they came home at 12.45am. About a fortnight ago an 'O.T.' staying at Dorset Villa, Petit Hougues, came to my house on two nights at 3.30am and 12.30am to try and see my daughter-in-law.

I answered the door on one occasion and told him to go home. Instead he got my little hand cart and tried to get in her bedroom window. People blame me for her going with the Germans. I want my daughter-in-law to leave the house, but she refuses to go. She says as long as my daughter says it is alright she will stay, but I am the head of the house, my husband being dead."

The Constable advised Mrs ...... to give her daughter-in-law a week's notice to leave.

During the morning of the 30th July 1942, a hand delivered letter was received by the President of the Controlling Committee from Dr Brosch.

"Penal proceedings are in course against Police Inspector Langmead. He is to be immediately relieved from his duties. His duties shall be taken up, until further notice, by Acting Deputy Inspector Lamy. A suitable successor is to be suggested to me by return."

The previous day Mr Langmead had been required to report at Grange Lodge where he was confronted with a sheaf of papers purporting to be statements of witnesses to the effect that he had received a quantity of stolen goods and foodstuffs from Sergeant Harper. He was required to make a statement, which he did, repudiating the allegations. Mr Langmead was accused of being friendly with Jack Harper and that, in the Germans' view, it was only reasonable that he would have passed on food to his friends. He strenuously denied receiving anything whatsoever. He was then warned that extensive enquiries were being made and that it would be the worse for him if it was found that he was telling lies.

Mr Langmead recalled:- "I was then asked if I had had any wood. I admitted having received one piece which had been placed in the Police car by PC Short one night in January 1942, when visiting Special Constables in the country. Having made that statement I was told I could go."

Later he commented:- "I was suspended because of an anonymous letter received by them (the Germans) making allegations against me which were untrue."

Jurat John Leale passed Dr Brosch's letter to the President of the Police Committee, who showed it to Acting Inspector A.J.Langmead, explaining that he had no alternative but to suspend him from duty forthwith.

Mr Langmead immediately saw his deputy, Mr A.P.Lamy, and handed him the keys of his desk and the safe, his warrant card, night pass and note book. He left the Station at 11.15am, having served as a Police officer for more than twenty years. He had held every rank in the Guernsey Police and was the first locally born man to command the Force.

Fred Short years later recalled the wood pile incident which Mr Langmead had admitted to the Germans:-

"One night in January 1942, outside the Police Station, in company with Captain Ernest Cowley, an Inspector of the Special Constabulary, and Arthur Langmead, I put some wood, about eight pieces, in the boot and on the back seat of the Police car. The wood came from the German wood pile around St Pauls church. The only other person present when I fetched the wood and put it in the Police car was the Station Sergeant, Ted Pill.

With the Deputy Inspector sitting on the wood in the back seat and Captain Cowley in the front, I drove to Mr Langmead's place in Les Cornus, St Martin. I was taking the wood out of the car, when I stopped and said to Mr Langmead, 'what about a few pieces for the Captain, Sir.' Captain Cowley said he would appreciate it.

So having left half the wood at Mr Langmead's house, I drove back into town and dropped Captain Cowley off at his tobacco shop in Mill Street. There was a side door and steps that went up the back of his place. I took the rest of the wood up there."

Arthur Langmead commenting on the 'wood' incident, later told Mr Agnew, the President of the Police Committee:- "On looking back one can see how foolish it was to have received the wood but you may remember how at the time it was piled so high around St Paul's church that it was overflowing into the road. That it was being freely given by soldiers and others, to drivers, labourers and anyone asking for it. Also two German plain clothes Police said to me, - since you are so short of fuel there is no need for you to go cold as you know where the wood is."

An emergency meeting of the Police Committee was held on the 30th July 1942, when Acting Deputy Inspector A.Lamy was appointed Acting Inspector and Detective Sergeant F.Banneville was appointed Acting Deputy Inspector. Sergeant E.Pill was appointed Detective Sergeant. All three appointments were made subject to confirmation.

On the 7th August Dr Brosch wrote to the President of the Controlling Committee stating:- "There is no objection to A.P.Lamy's leadership for the time being. Before the post is finally filled it should be ascertained whether other suitable persons are available. Technical knowledge, the guarantee for proper leadership and public opinion are to be taken into consideration. I request you to submit your proposal."

When the Police Committee met on the 14th August to consider Dr Brosch's letter, Mr Sherwill, H.M.Attorney General, was in attendance and offered advice and guidance on how to respond to the letter. Two candidates, Mr Lamy and Mr Banneville, were considered for the vacancy and after what was described as 'a full discussion', Mr Lamy was again appointed as Acting Inspector, on a probationary period of three months. Dr Brosch was officially informed.

Also at that meeting, PC 27 R.W.Kimber was appointed Acting Sergeant, to take effect from the 17th of August, five days before his fifty-ninth birthday. He filled the vacancy caused by Sergeant Pill's promotion.

The Committee also confirmed the action of Mr Lamy in dealing with a disciplinary matter. A/PC 6 Petit. was charged with:-

'1. Being insubordinate by word, act or demeanour.

2. Using obscene, abusive or insulting language to another member of the Force.'

**A/PC Cyril Petit.**

Petit was fined one day's pay for each offence and cautioned on the second charge.

The matter had been reported by Acting Sergeant Bull.

The rebuilding of the Force which was necessary as a result of the removal of Inspector Sculpher and seventeen other officers, was, in Mr Langmead view, almost complete when he was suspended. The regular training sessions which he had instigated, were continued by Mr Lamy. The day after Mr Langmead's suspension, a 'mock trial' which he had arranged for the newer recruits, went ahead.

The Police Court was the scene of an unusual sitting, with the recently reinstated Attorney General, Ambrose Sherwill, taking the role of the Magistrate. Mr Lamy and the newly promoted Mr Banneville were the prosecutors. A number of the newer recruits to the Force acted as prosecution witnesses.

The mock trial was staged so that Auxiliary Policemen could gain experience in the art of giving evidence. For two hours the Court 'sat' and many interesting cases were fought out. There were two interested spectators in the public gallery, listening to every word, Advocates J.E.L.Martel and W.H.Langlois.

A/PC Roy Northey years later recalled, with an element of embarrassment, the part he played in the mock trial.

"The day the mock trial took place I was on early turn. I had a German pocket watch, with an alarm, which I used to sleep with under my pillow, so that it did not wake the kids when I got up a 5.00am. That particular day I had not wound my watch the night before and the alarm had not gone off. So when I got up I had a rush to report for duty on time. During the day I wound my watch up, put it in my pocket and blow me if it didn't go off during the mock trial, just when Mr Sherwill was in full flow."

Another occasion which Roy Northey recalls being embarrassed, but in a different way, was when he was applauded by civilians for making Germans get off their bicycles in the High Street. "No one was allowed to ride a bike down the High Street, so I made two Germans get off their bikes. I requested them to get off and they did, no argument. The people watching applauded and were quite chuffed to think that a local Policeman had made the Germans conform to our rule of the road."

Early in August 1942 the Feldkommandantur required the States Controller of Petroleum Supplies, Mr A.C.Richings, to review the number of authorised motor vehicles on the roads, with a view to saving petrol and reducing their number to below 165. This number included cars, vans, lorries, motorcycles and autocycles. Users ranged from the Fire Brigade to the States Dairy, from the nine doctors to the Bailiff, from the Water Board to St John Ambulance.

The Police Force were allowed a total of six gallons a week for the 14 hp. Wolseley car and the three roadworthy motorcycles. As a result of the review and no doubt because the Force was now under the control of the Feldkommandantur, they were granted an extra two gallons a week.

It was not long, however, before Mr Richings and Acting Inspector Lamy were called to Grange Lodge and told by the Germans that the Wolseley car had to be taken off the road, as it used too much petrol. Mr Lamy explained that it was impossible to run the Force without a car and gave various reason which were accepted. As a compromise it was agreed that the car would be taken off the road and replaced by a smaller vehicle.

The Germans issued a permit for the Police to take over a Commer van, No 1947, belonging to F.C.Ware of the Meat Market. The van was available because all home deliveries by butchers had been stopped. However, the Germans omitted to withdraw the permit for the Wolseley Police car and it remained in use, right up to the end of the Occupation.

Shortly after the van was acquired, PC Le Cocq was driving it, still with the original owner's name painted on the sides, across the Bridge, when he collided with an obstruction. He hit the excavations for the new railway line the Germans were constructing. The van only had side lights and the visibility was poor. The Constable inspected the vehicle with his torch and the only damage he could find was to the front number plate. It was ironic that the Constable had only a few moments before left Acting Deputy Inspector Banneville, after complaining to him about the poor lighting on the van.

On the 20th August the Germans advanced the curfew hour from 11.00pm to 10.00pm. The inevitable result was that with the fine summer evenings, more people were caught out on the streets after curfew, particularly girls out with their German boyfriends.

A/PC Bill Sebire, like every other member of the Force, bitterly resented Guernsey girls openly associating with Germans. When he found them out with their Jerry boyfriends after curfew, he took particular delight in identifying them and warning them for Court. At 11.55pm on the 22nd August he stopped thirty-three-year-old Mrs Elizabeth Wareham near the Grand Bouet cross roads and told her she would be charged. She replied:- "I have only been down to see my mother, I thought it would be alright as I had my friend with me." The friend, was a German Under officer. In Court she claimed that she was attending a birthday party. The Magistrate fined her £1.

The next evening, at about 10.35pm A/PC 27 Scraton saw a local girl in the company of two German officers. in Grande Rue, St Martin. As she was walking past, the Constable enquired:-

"Excuse me, but do you have a pass permitting you to be out after curfew ?"

She answered "No".

PC Scraton then said "I must see your identity card please."

One of the officers with her then interjected "Aren't you a little mad."

The Constable replied "No sir, I am merely doing my duty, as she is a local girl and has no pass."

The German officer then said to the girl "Come."

As a parting shot, the Constable said:- “I am really sorry but I am afraid I shall have to report it because she is a local girl.”

A/PC Scraton reported the incident to the Station Sergeant and told him that the girl lived in the Carmel district and although he knew her well by sight, he did not know her name.

On this occasion it appears that the young lady escaped prosecution.

At their meeting on the 28th August the Controlling Committee considered the question of Mr Sculpher’s and Mr Langmead’s pay. Mr Leale said that both Inspector Sculpher and Acting Inspector Langmead were receiving two thirds pay while suspended, but the latter was receiving two thirds of the increased rate recently authorised and this meant that he was receiving more than Mr Sculpher. The Police Committee, he said, were inclined to the view that this was inequitable and had requested the Controlling Committee to decide the matter.

Mr Johns said it appeared that Inspector Sculpher was the more innocent. The President said that if the charge against the Acting Inspector were proved, he would doubtless be discharged while the suspension of Inspector Sculpher might continue indefinitely. The Supervisor said he thought the material point was the date on which the offences were committed. Mr Langmead was at an advantage merely because of the accident of the date of discovery of the alleged offence.

The Committee agreed with this point of view and it was resolved that the pay of both of the suspended men should be placed on the same basis, that of two thirds of their respective “cut” rate of pay as at the 5th of March 1942.

On the 4th September as a result of a telephone call from Mrs Dorey, the caretaker of Luff’s Stores in Back Street, A/PC 19 Stewart was sent to investigate a possible attempted break-in. He arrived at 9.40pm and saw two French foreign labourers, Jean Binet, aged 18, and Louis Jean Walrin, aged 20.

Mrs Dorey said that she had seen these two men climbing up the drain pipes and attempting to break in. A/PC Charles Stewart took the two men to the Station where they were questioned by the Acting Deputy Inspector. They explained that they had been playing with a ball and had knocked it into the gutter of Luff's premises and climbed on the roof to retrieve it. This explanation was accepted by Mr Banneville and they were allowed to go, but this was going to turn out to be an embarrassing mistake.

A report was received that two German soldiers were drunk and molesting nurses from the emergency hospital as they were going on duty. PC 9 Marsh was sent to investigate and when he arrived he saw two Germans, one of whom stopped him and said in fairly good English:- “What is the time ?”

He was told that it was 9.45pm.

The soldier then announced:- “The frauleins must be inside by 10 o'clock.”

PC Marsh asked them to go home but every time a nurse came around the corner, to go into the hospital the soldiers pulled them off their cycles and put an arm around their waists. The Constable tried to pacify the soldiers, but without success, so he telephoned the Station and asked for help. The Station Sergeant contacted the Feldgendarmerie but before they arrived the soldiers said that they were going home and told PC Marsh:- “You are a good comrade. Tomorrow at 10.00pm, you come to the Castle Post near the church and we will give you 20 cigarettes.” They then went up the road towards the Castel Church.

Then the shortest one of the two came back and said to the PC, “It is past 10 o'clock.” The PC replied that it was 9.55pm. The first soldier then called out to the other soldier, who came running back. As they were trying to tell PC Marsh something in German, a nurse came along on her cycle. One of the soldiers went to pull her off and the Constable caught hold of his arm to stop him. The German swung around and punched him, knocking him to the ground. As the PC got up, the soldier grabbed hold of his hair and at the same time pushed him across the road against the wall opposite to the entrance of hospital.

The other soldier then came over and tried to hit the Constable, but missed. The PC then drew his truncheon and hit the hand that was holding his hair, but the truncheon was pulled from his grasp and thrown into the road. Reg Marsh was hit in the face several times. The soldiers went off towards the Castel Church, leaving their hats on the ground.

Shortly after, A/PC 25 Le Prevost arrived accompanied by Sergeant Major Oeser, who directed PC Marsh to show him the way the soldiers had gone. They were found near the Chaumiere and 'seen' by the Sergeant Major. Reg Marsh received a swollen upper lip, his nose was scratched and swollen, a bruise on the left check bone and a bruise near his kidney.

Sergeant Major Oeser told the Constable that he wanted a report on the incident by 9.00am the next morning, the 7th September. This was duly provided, but what action was taken by the Germans in respect of the two soldiers is not recorded.

On the 11th September 1942 thirty-three auxiliary members of the Force signed a 'Round Robin' requesting an increase in pay. The petition was presented to Acting Inspector Lamy and read:-

"Dear Sir,

I beg to draw your attention to a matter which is causing the resignation of several of the new Force. The point is we do not consider the standard wage sufficient for the present cost of living, for the duties we do. We all consider that nothing less than £3.0.0. as a standard wage is fair, as, though we are not able to obtain sufficient food, we have to pay exorbitant prices. May I suggest that a meeting be called so that each individual policeman may state their particular grievances.

Hoping to hear further, we are, yours respectfully.

Signed by thirty three Auxiliary Policemen."

The Acting Inspector was concerned at receiving the 'Round Robin' and did not consider that there was any evidence to support the allegation that men had resigned from the Force due to the level of pay. He asked fifteen of the signatories into his office, one at a time, to ascertain their opinions on the petition.

A/PC 35 Roy Northey recalls being summoned into Mr Lamy's office:-

"I said I thought that the job was worth it. We were doing awkward hours, inconvenient hours and out in all weather and I thought that we were worth a bit more than that. Mr Lamy told me that half the Force are only on for the money, they are not really interested in the job. I quickly flew up at that and said he might think I was one of them, because I was not putting in many reports. Well, I said, as far as I am concerned I do not intend to do what the Germans want me to do, I said, I will do my job to prevent anything from happening. 'No', he said, 'you are one of the few', which pleased me."

Having talked to many of the signatories and establishing who was the author of the 'Round Robin', Mr Lamy reported to the President of the Controlling Committee that in his view it was "only a storm in a teacup and that no notice need be taken of it."

At 1.00am on the 13th September, A/PC 12 John Lovell reported to Acting Sergeant Bull that his cycle was out of commission because the front wheel had collapsed. As a result he was posted to duty in the High Street.

Acting Sergeant Harry Bull reported:- "At 2.40am on the 13th September 1942, I was patrolling the High Street with A/PC38 Robilliard, to visit A/PC12 Lovell whom I had posted on that beat. Half way down the High Street, I heard someone snoring and when I got to Madame Eve's shop, I found A/PC12 Lovell stretched out on his back fast asleep, I tried to wake him by flashing my torch on his face, but could not, I had to make a noise with a dustbin lid to wake him up. I warned A/PC12 Lovell to see the Inspector in the morning."

A/PC John Lovell resigned the same day. He soon obtained employment as a greenhouse worker with Mr Gosselin at the D'Aval Vineries.

At the meeting of the Police Committee on the 14th September Acting Sergeants Bull and Dyson were promoted full Sergeants on twelve months' probation. Also at the meeting, Acting Deputy Inspector Banneville, presented a report on the progress of Police officers since his appointment.

"I beg to report that on the 30th July 1942 I was appointed Acting Deputy Inspector. Shortly after the appointment an interview with Acting Inspector Lamy took place and it was agreed that the standard of discipline was very low, in fact there was very little discipline. The conduct of the Police officers in the Police Station and on their beats was far from good. The saluting of the German officers, Bailiff, members of the Royal Court and members of the Police Committee was poor, in fact some of the members of the Force had no idea who they had to salute and when they did, they did not know how to.

During the period ending the 12th September 1942 the following lectures have been given:- discipline, fire, given by Mr Oliver, first aid, given by Mr Dear, mock Court, conducted by Inspector Lamy, street duty with particular attention to pocket books and how to make notes and write reports, fires, accidents and illness in the streets etc.

In each of the lectures on Police work, discipline, street duty, fires, accidents, illness etc. were carefully selected from the instruction book for the guidance of the Metropolitan Police, taking particular care that only what really effected the local force was used.

The lecture on discipline and the mock Court were well attended but the other lectures were only attended by a few.

In the discipline lecture, code of offences were read out to the men, therefore every man now knows whether he is committing an offence against Police discipline. A lecture was given to the Sergeants and in the lecture they were informed of what was expected from them and what we expected from the men.

**Occupation Regulars 12th September 1942, Back row; PC F.Le Cocq, Sgt. R.E. Kimber, Sgt. H.T. Pugh, Sgt. G.H.L.Dyson, PC R.P.G.Marsh, Sgt. H.J. Bull, Sgt. E.J.de.J.Pill, A/Inspector A.P. Lamy, Sgt. C. Le Lievre, Sgt. E.W.Plevin.**

Since these lectures, the discipline of the men has greatly improved, although there is room for a good deal of improvement in the way the men walk about, stand and salute. Unfortunately some of the men very rarely attend lectures and only rely on what the others say after the lecture. There are a number of men, now in the Force, who are obviously only to remain until the end of the Occupation and these make no progress, which makes it really bad for the men that are keen and try.

During this period a number of good arrests have been made by the members of the Force. A large number of foreigners have been arrested and a number of local charges preferred against the local population for various offences.

On the whole there has been an improvement and progress made with the exception of the undermentioned. These men appear to have made very little progress. A/PCs Moore, Roberts, 29 Falla, Vanden Bergh, Langford, Parlett and Petit. These men appear to take very little interest in the work. Lectures are not attended with regularity of men who are really keen, about one dozen men never miss. These men have shown a marked improvement.

I have visited the Station at various hours, by night and early morning. I have always found the Sergeant alert and nothing to report. I have seen night shifts being dismissed and early turn men paraded for early turn duty, everything was correct."

# Chapter 21

# ONE OF THE FINEST CAT BURGLARS YOU COULD WISH TO FIND

The whole population of the Island and virtually all the German Army of Occupation were mystified when, on Tuesday the 15th September 1942, a Notice signed by Colonel Knackfuss, Feldkommandantur, Jersey, appeared in *The Star* newspaper. It read:-

"By order of higher authorities the following British subjects will be evacuated and transferred to Germany.

a. Persons who have their permanent residence not on the Channel Islands, for instance, those who have been caught here by the outbreak of the war.

b. All those men not born in the Channel Islands and 16 to 70 years of age who belong to the English people, together with their families."

There was no explanation given, no reason for the enforced evacuation of so many people. Every one covered by the order had to complete a form and return it to the Greffe office by the following Friday.

The approaching deportation of what was to turn out to be more than eight hundred Islanders was a great shock and a matter of major concern, not only to the individuals concerned, but also to the Island Authorities. No one could explain why it was happening, even the Germans openly questioned the action. The Island had been under German rule for more than two years and no serious act of sabotage had occurred, so the deportations were not a community punishment.

It was not until some time after the Island had been liberated that the reason for the deportations was finally revealed. In the late summer of 1941, Hitler learnt that Iran was contemplating interning, at the request of the British Government, Germans in that country. Looking for a means of reprisal the Germans realised that there were a considerable number of British-born civilians living in the Channel Islands.

Hitler gave an order that for every German detained in Iran, ten British subjects should be deported from the Channel Islands. For some reason that order was not implemented in the autumn of 1941. It was only when Hitler, almost a year later, queried whether his order had been carried out, that the deportations actually took place.

In September 1941 the Germans had required lists to be compiled by the Island Authorities of all men between the ages of 18 and 45. It had been realised then that as many as 1200 Islanders could have been deported. Whilst the Germans checked and rechecked the lists, no further order was issued and it was assumed that any deportation had been shelved.

The impact of the deportation order was not only devastating for individuals and families, but also seriously affected businesses and organisations. Acting Inspector Lamy quickly realised that the order would, if implemented, reduce the Police Force by ten men, two Sergeants and eight Auxiliary Constables. He immediately informed his President, who wrote to the President of the Controlling Committee on the 16th September:-

"Removal of English born persons from the Island.

I beg to report that the above Order dated 15th September 1942 affects the following 10 members of the Police Force:-

| | |
|---|---|
| Detective Sergeant | E.Pill. |
| Sergeant | H.Bull. |
| Constable | H.Champion, |
| Constable | F.Moore |
| Constable | A.Vanden Bergh, |
| Constable | H.Hall, |
| Constable | R.Parlett, |
| Constable | G.Scraton, |
| Constable | W.Mansfield, |
| Constable | C.Northey. |

If these men are taken, it will cause a serious dislocation in the running of the Police Force, which at this time, is very busily engaged in protecting the food supply of the Island.

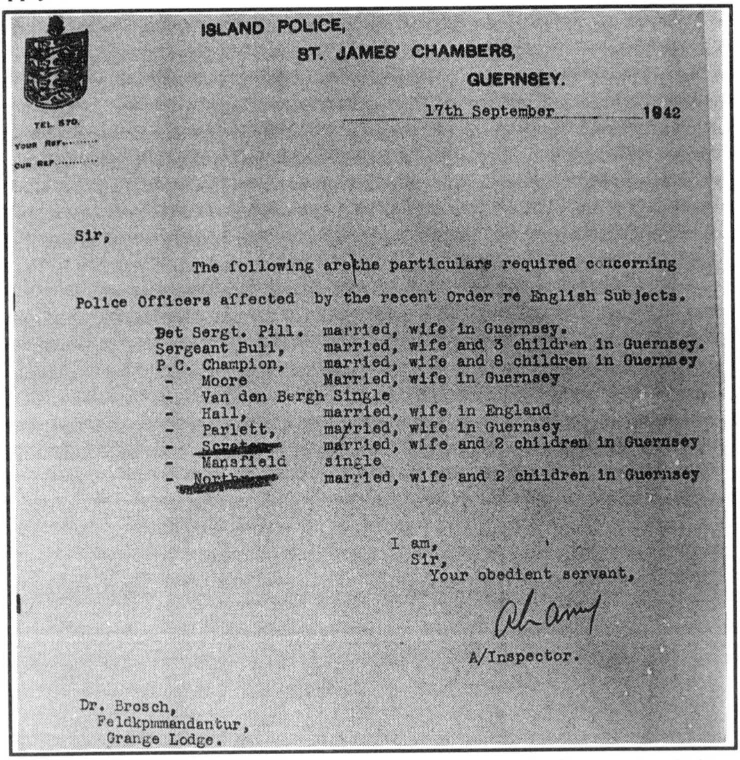

ISLAND POLICE,
ST. JAMES' CHAMBERS,
GUERNSEY.

TEL. 870.
YOUR REF.........
OUR REF.........

17th September 1942

Sir,

The following are the particulars required concerning Police Officers affected by the recent Order re English Subjects.

| | |
|---|---|
| Det Sergt. Pill. | married, wife in Guernsey. |
| Sergeant Bull, | married, wife and 3 children in Guernsey. |
| P.C. Champion, | married, wife and 8 children in Guernsey |
| - Moore | Married, wife in Guernsey |
| - Van den Bergh | Single |
| - Hall, | married, wife in England |
| - Parlett, | married, wife in Guernsey |
| - [redacted] | married, wife and 2 children in Guernsey |
| - Mansfield | single |
| - [redacted] | married, wife and 2 children in Guernsey |

I am,
Sir,
Your obedient servant,

A/Inspector.

Dr. Brosch,
Feldkpmmandantur,
Grange Lodge.

**Letter detailing the members of the Force affected by the deportation Order. The names of the two men and their families crossed out by Dr Brosch were deported.**

I would be pleased if you would make representation to the German Authorities for the retention of these men, especially the Sergeants."

Jurat John Leale passed on the letter to Dr Brosch, who asked Mr Lamy for further details of the men affected. He replied:-

"The following are the particulars required concerning Police officers affected by the recent Order re English subjects.

| | |
|---|---|
| Det.Sergeant Pill | Married, wife in Guernsey. |
| Sergeant Bull | Married, wife and 3 children in Guernsey. |
| A/PC Champion | Married, wife and eight children in Guernsey. |
| A/PC Moore | Married, wife in Guernsey. |
| A/PC Vanden Bergh | Single. |
| A/PC Hall | Married, wife in England. |
| A/PC Parlett | Married, wife in Guernsey. |
| A/PC Scraton | Married, wife and 2 children in Guernsey. |
| A/PC Mansfield | Single. |
| A/PC Northey | Married, wife and 2 children in Guernsey." |

The Germans were also supplied with a complete list of 'States key men', listing the Departments and the names of the men affected. The list was used by the Germans, who wrote against each name 'Ja' or 'Nein', yes they were or no they were not exempted. Eight of the ten Police officers had 'Ja' against their name. Geoffrey Scraton and Roy Northey had 'Nein'. Sergeant Harry Bull was fortunate as 'Nein' had been written against his name, then crossed out and replaced with 'Ja'.

Roy Northey years later recalled his anger at his selection for deportation by the Germans. "But what really upset me was that my colleague PC Francois Le Cocq personally came to my home, with a German and handed me my Deportation Order. He had to do it. I was most upset, but there it was."

Former Policeman W.T.Pealling, who had transferred to the Prison service as a warder, had a 'Nein' written against his name. Other former policemen who were deported included George Perry, who was born in Manchester, and William Strickland, a Londoner by birth. Suspended Inspector W.R.Sculpher, who was born in Norfolk, and Mrs Sarah Sculpher were also deported.

As each deportee received their 'Evacuation' notice, decisions had to be made regarding the future wellbeing of their homes, pets and many other matters. Many persons sought exemption by personally writing to the Feldkommandantur.

Roy Northey wrote on the 19th September to the Feldkommandant:-

"I beg to ask you for an exemption of the Order of Sept 15th re evacuation to Germany.

I am a Police Constable and food grower. In my Police off duty hours I grow food crops for the Island. I have a wife and two young children, one 6 months old and one 18 months old.

My wife and her parents are Guernsey born and I myself have been in Guernsey ever since I can remember and have not been away from Guernsey since brought here to the Island. This is why I ask for an exemption of the Order. Hoping you will consider my case.

I am Sir, yours truly, C.P.R.Northey."

That plea being unsuccessful, Roy Northey made a second attempt to obtain exemption for his wife and family.

"With reference to the Feldkommandant's notice referring to the transfer of British subjects.

I have been in Guernsey since a child, some 20 years or so. I married a Guernsey girl and have two babies under the age of two years. I am employed as a Police Constable by the Island Police.

May I submit this as an appeal against my wife and children being evacuated."

That appeal was also unsuccessful, Roy Northey, his wife and two young children were deported to Germany.

Other potential deportees wrote claiming exemption for a multitude of reasons - D.G.C.Giffard claimed, although being born in Lincolnshire, "I am a Channel Islander and do not belong to the English people." He enclosed copies of his father's and grandfather's birth certificates. He gave his employment as Private Secretary to his father who was the Dean of Guernsey. He was exempted.

The Rev. Edwin Foley, a Baptist Minister who was born in London, wrote privately and confidentially to Colonel Knackfuss, saying "Though I am English born, I am very very sorry for all the wrong which I believe England has done to Germany. I was not in favour of England declaring war on Germany in 1914 and got into trouble for saying so. .....and was not in favour of England declaring war on Germany in 1939."

The German granted Rev. Foley exemption from deportation.

Others took a more patriotic stance. Major F.Rowan Ward, of Grey Towers, Jerbourg, wrote to Dr Brosch:-

"May I take this opportunity of thanking you for your kindness in giving my case so much consideration and for the great trouble you went to on my behalf. I feel, however, I cannot take advantage of your kindness and have therefore decided to leave for Germany tomorrow."

There were those who could not come to terms with the thought of being deported and chose to take their own life. Mr John W.Sibley, a sixty-three-year-old butcher, who was born in Somerset, was found dead at his home of coal-gas poisoning. An inquest recorded that he took his own life whilst in a state of temporary insanity. The German Censor refused to allow a report of the Inquest to be published in the *Press.*

Jurat John Leale was called upon to write many letters urging exemption from deportation. Frank Stroobant wrote to him asking for his help in his claim for exemption. A letter was prepared but before the President of the Controlling Committee was able to sign it, Frank told him that he did not want it sent and that he wished to leave with the other deportees. Frank was destined to become 'Camp Senior' at Laufen, one of the internment camps in Germany.

Whilst most deportees dreaded leaving Guernsey, there were some who apparently went voluntarily. A/PC 1 Champion reported that he was approached by Wilfred Hobbs, of 2 States Houses, Bouet, who informed him that:-

"James Woodruff, of 44 Pedvin Street, has his wife and four children in England. He is my brother-in-law. My mother-in-law Mrs June Cook, of 24 Pedvin Street, wants it reported that Mr Woodruff is proceeding to the Continent with a Miss Lucy Carre, as his wife."

James Woodruff was born in London in 1904 and worked in Guernsey as a stevedore. Miss Lucy Carre was a thirty-year-old 'Sarkie' by birth and employed as a general maid by Mrs H.O.Greener, of Colona, Village de Putron. Acting Sergeant R.Kimber recorded in the Occurrence Book that it was not known if bigamy has taken place. Enquiries were also made at Grange Lodge to ascertain whether they were aware of the situation. There was no requirement for Miss Carre to leave the Island, but she chose to do so voluntarily and left with James Woodruff.

The first party of deportees were due to depart on the 21st September 1942, but rough weather delayed the sailing until the 26th, when the M.V. Minotaur took them to St Malo. The rest of the deportees left two days later.

Roy Northey later recalled his deportation:-

"We were due to go on the first boat on the 21st September. We spent the night on the boat and the weather turned that rough that we did not sail. We were sent back home, with instructions to report the next day and so on. Eventually we left on the Friday. During the delay all our luggage was left on the boat and the Police were sent down to guard it. Two of my colleagues wrote me a note and put it in my luggage."

The note was dated 22nd September 1942.

"You have mates. Tucker 37. and Parlett 26. have been aboard this ship on guard for eight hours. We are both very sorry to lose you and we wish you a pleasant journey and a safe return. We take this opportunity of conveying the same feeling to Geoff Scraton and if you see him, tell him. We cannot write much because we do not know who is watching. Hoping to see you in the near future, we remain your pals, Jim and Reg."

Then added afterwards were the signatures of Frank Falla 29. and Solly 36. and "All the best - cheer up."

As the M.V. Minotaur slowly edged away from the dockside, the deportees were heard singing, 'There'll always be an England' and 'Rule Britannia'. As a Police officer present later commented, "It was a very moving and sad moment."

The feeling of the deportees was well expressed by Mr W.R.Sculpher, when he wrote to the Bailiff:-

"On behalf of my fellow evacuees, may I express to you and through you to the President of the Controlling Committee and Essential Commodities Committee, the local Red Cross Officials, Police and Special Constables for their manifest kindness to us on our departure from Guernsey. None of us wish to leave under the existing circumstance, but we are indeed grateful to the Island Authorities for their help and consideration in these trying times.

It is at such times when forethought and consideration are appreciated and this was shown in the abundant supply of provisions for each evacuee. On all sides I heard appreciative remarks for the great kindness shown to us and on behalf of all I feel it my duty to express our thanks to all concerned."

In all 850 Islanders were warned for deportation to Germany and of those 23 were exempted.

Sergeant Charles Le Lievre received a telephone call from F.J.Ogier, one of the Constables of Torteval, who said:-

"Mr Gallienne, of Landes Hues, Torteval reported to me that a cable owned by the German Forces had been cut. The Germans were working there today outside Gallienne's place where the cable is cut."

As a result A/PC 21 Roland Le Tissier was sent to inform the German Secret Police at Havelet and he then accompanied a German Policeman to the scene to inspect the damage. The Germans considered it to be an act of sabotage and Colonel Knackfuss issued another 'Notice' from his headquarters in Jersey.

"NOTICE.

During the night of the 30th September to 1st October 1942, unknown persons wilfully cut through a cable of the German Forces laid in the south-west part of the Island. Once again I warn the people of Guernsey strongly against committing any act directed against the security of the German Occupation Forces.

Every single inhabitant of the Island must both co-operate in the prevention of such acts and in the discovery of the persons committing the same. In the event of a repetition of acts of sabotage, the population will have to suffer reprisals."

Walter F.Robin lived at 'La Houguette,' St Peter, with his sister Maude. At about 10.45pm on the 8th October Miss Robin was in her bedroom, with the lights out, looking out of the window, watching a nearby gun firing and the flares which were lighting up the sky.

"Then" she told Sergeant Pill later, "I looked down at our garage, which is near the rear of our house, and I saw something in white moving inside. I immediately called my brother Walter and we both went down to our garage. I looked in the garage and saw a German soldier, I then struck a match and saw another German soldier in the garage.

My brother asked them what they were doing there. One of the soldiers said, 'Shoot'. Walter then said 'You can shoot if you like, but you have no right to be there'. With that the one in white ran away, but I gave chase and caught him by our big gates. I clutched him by the hair as he had no hat on and I did not let him go until my brother Walter called out that he had been hit. I immediately went to my brother's assistance and saw he was bleeding badly from a wound over his left eye.

I took him into the house and telephoned for the ambulance. On their arrival I went with one of the ambulance men to the German camp and there I saw an officer. I explained to him what had happened and he came with us to the house, where he saw my brother. The officer then went to the garage and there found German soldiers inside, who ran away, although the officer told them to halt and that he would shoot. The officer then called the guards and a lot of firing took place. At about 1.05am on the 9th October the officer came again to the house and said that he had arrested three men."

Walter Robin was taken to the Emergency Hospital, where he received treatment for his injury. Later he recalled:-

"At about 10.45pm on Thursday I was downstairs when my sister Maud called out to me and said there was someone in our shed. .... I went outside and said to the soldier 'What are you doing here?' He replied 'Stop I shoot' and pointed his finger at me. I then saw him putting some apples in his pocket and I noticed that he had no firearms so I knocked his arm downwards and tried to get his hat. He went a few paces backwards, took of his hat off and put it in his pocket and started to make off. At that moment my sister saw him and gave chase.

..... I noticed another German soldier who walked towards me, but only a few paces as he was already quite close to me. Then suddenly, he struck me on the forehead, above the left eye, with what I thought was a piece of steel which appeared smooth and heavy. I then called out to my sister to come quickly. I was afraid she might get hit also."

No doubt the three Germans were severely punished, not only for the attack on a civilian but also for disobeying the orders of an officer. However, no record exists detailing the punishment.

In October a further five recruits joined the ranks of the Auxiliary Police.

| | |
|---|---|
| A/PC 28 William James Boalch, 24. | 35 States Houses, Sausmarez Mill. |
| A/PC 12 Henry William Mahy, 31. | Les Pecqueries, St Sampson. |
| A/PC 34 Claude Arthur Le Huray, 21. | Les Roches, Forest Road, St Martin. |
| A/PC 20 Emile Edgar Julou, 21. | Passe, St Sampson. |
| A/PC 42 Walter John Le Sauvage, 24. | Glendale, Les Marais Lane, Vale. |

In the meantime A/PC 24 Hamon and A/PC 28 E.J.Thoume had resigned on the 20th September. 'Pat' Hamon became a self-employed grower and Ted Thoume quickly obtained employment as a storeman with Maison Blicq, of the Bordage. Another Auxiliary Constable who resigned to become a self-employed grower was A/PC 7 Cliff Falla. On the 28th September A/PC 6 Cyril Petit gave in his notice and took employment as caretaker for Westminster Bank.

Sergeant Ernie Plevin was on duty at the Police Station on the 16th October 1942 when John de Jersey, a grower, of Le Villocq Lane, Castel, came in and told him about a shooting incident at his home.

"I have had two O.T. men billeted on me since last February, the chief of the two is away at present. On several occasions they have held parties, during which time they have made a lot of noise and fired revolver shots about the house. They have broken glass several times. Last night the O.T. man came home and brought a party with him, I think 2 men and 3 women.

Between 4-5 o'clock this morning I heard a revolver shot being fired downstairs and a lot of noise going on. I didn't go down to see what it was. At 6.30am when I went downstairs I found that several shots had been fired through the window, hitting the house opposite. Some time ago when they fired through the window it went through two sides of the greenhouse and hit the boiler chimney."

Sergeant Plevin went to Le Villocq where he found several bullet holes in the lounge window. There was a bullet hole in the plaster over the window and another in the ceiling. In the room used by one of the O.T. men, he found a bullet hole in a cupboard and another in the mantelpiece. The landing window was also smashed, Mr de Jersey said that it had been done with a bottle which then fell into the greenhouse.

The Sergeant spoke to Mrs Dora Queripel, who lived across the road:-

"I was in bed at about 4.45 this morning when I heard 5 shots fired. When I came down this morning I found a window broken, bullet holes through the doors and a glass dish smashed. One bullet hit the house, chipped the cement, passed through the window and a door before embedding itself in the wall. Another bullet went through the front window, through the kitchen and sitting room doors before smashing a cut glass dish on the china cabinet. Glass was strewn all about the room."

In the lane, about 100 yards from the house, Sergeant Plevin was shown a pile of broken wine glasses, parts of an electric lamp fitting, plaster and broken bottles, apparently thrown there by someone clearing up after the party. At Mr de Jersey's house he spoke to a German sergeant who admitted that he had fired the shots which had done the damage. Sergeant Plevin was not able to estimate the cost of the damage and failed to find any of the bullets. He was told that the Germans had returned after the party and removed one bullet which was found on the floor. What action was subsequently taken by the German Authorities is again not recorded.

Jean Binet, the young Frenchman, whose explanation for being on to the roof of Luff's store, in Back Street, had been accepted by Acting Deputy Inspector Banneville, was subsequently arrested by the Germans. He had quickly earned himself a reputation of being one of the finest cat burglars either the local or German police had come across.

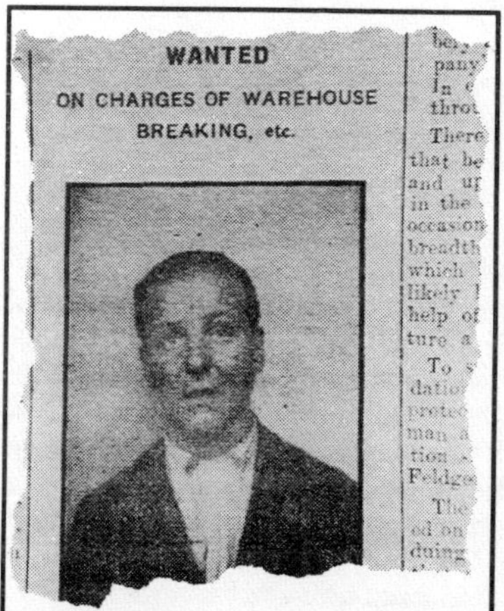

**Jean Binet, Master Cat Burglar.**

Eighteen-year-old Binet had been held in the O.T. prison, at 'Paradis', Vale, but escaped. He was recaptured and then detained at the other O.T. prison at Rosemaire, St Peter Port. He again escaped, only to be recaptured and locked up in the Guernsey prison.

At about 9.40pm on the 16th October, Mr A.E.Pike, H.M.Gaoler at the prison in St James Street, reported to Mr Banneville that Binet had escaped earlier that evening.

Acting Inspector Lamy after the Occupation described Binet as:-

"One of the finest cat burglars you could wish to find. His 'modus operandi' was always the same, up the side of the building, through a skylight or removing slates or tiles from the roof. On many occasions there were easier ways of access, but he just couldn't leave his usual 'modus operandi' alone. He first came to our notice after a series of breaks into German stores and on one isolated case in a local store."

Jean Binet, whilst on the run, managed to exchange identity with another Frenchman, Pierre Nalli. Later the Germans arrested Nalli and were convinced that they had Binet. They informed Mr Lamy that Binet had been arrested and deported to France. He was, however, sceptical about the capture of the ace cat burglar. The robberies continued and it was not long before the Germans admitted that Binet was still at large in the Island.

Sergeant Harry Bull was on patrol in the High Street on the 25th October, when at 1.20am he saw A/PC 4 O'Donovan standing outside Madam Eve's shop. The Sergeant was, from personal experience, well aware of the attraction of Madam Eve's shop, where it was possible to get out of sight and out of the wind and rain. Another enticement was the wooden floor, which provided a much better and warmer surface that the concrete and marble available elsewhere.

When he reached Madam Eve's he found A/PC 22 Gale asleep in the doorway and had to shout to wake him up. When Sergeant Bull returned to the Station he entered a report in the Occurrence Book. Later that morning, Mr Lamy wrote in the margin -'A/PC 4 to see me at 3.30pm 26/10/42 and A/PC 22, at 4.00pm.

The Acting Inspector took no action as far as Alec O'Donovan was concerned, but told George Gale that he would recommend to the Police Committee that he be dismissed. The Committee concurred and A/PC 22 Gale left the service. He obtained a job as a general labourer with the Gas Company.

Later that month A/PC 22 Reginald George Le Gallez, 21, of Little Houmet Lane, L'Islet, was recruited to replace George Gale.

Mr Lamy wanted to prevent confusion with the apparent duplication of numbers between the regular and auxiliary members of the Force. Sergeant Le Lievre was PS1 and Auxiliary Constable Champion was A/PC 1. This sometimes tended to cause difficulties. It was decided that the numbers 1-9 should be kept for the regular members of the Force and 10 upwards for the auxiliary Constables. The changes involved:-

| | | |
|---|---|---|
| PC 35 | F.Le Cocq | becoming PC 8. |
| A/PC 1 | H.Champion | becoming A/PC 27. |
| A/PC 3 | F.Langford | becoming A/PC 35. |
| A/PC 4 | A.O'Donovan | becoming A/PC 40. |
| A/PC 5 | F.Moore | becoming A/PC 39. |
| A/PC 8 | A.Bisson | becoming A/PC 41. |

On the 2nd November Acting Sergeant R.Kimber waited in vain for A/PC Le Huray to arrive at two patrol points. The Constable was seen by Mr Lamy and gave the excuse that he did not have a lamp for his bicycle. On the 6th November he failed to report for duty on the 2.00pm shift. Later that afternoon Claude Le Huray was seen by Sergeant Dyson wearing civilian clothes in the Pollet. He told the Sergeant, "I am looking for a job." He was immediately suspended and on the 9th November the Committee confirmed that he was indeed looking for a job. A few weeks later Mr Lamy learnt that he was working for the Germans at Ashmore Vinery in the Forest Road.

At the same meeting the Committee considered a report from Mr Lamy on the difficulties of obtaining the right type of recruits. The Acting Inspector wrote:-

"Recently it has been found increasingly difficult to obtain the right type of recruit for the Police Force. Men over 5'9" either do not apply or those who do are half witted or medically unfit. I have weeded out some of the useless ones and with your support hope to do more. My aim is to get a really efficient Force with each man pulling his weight. Recently there has been a marked improvement in the work and bearing of the Force. Discipline has been tightened and will be maintained.

At present, Police are working under extremely difficult conditions, these have to be seen to be appreciated. On the evening of the 3rd November, whilst on observation duty at Balmoral Vineries, Vrangue, A/PC Stewart accosted several soldiers in a greenhouse. They had several sacks and a long handled 7 prong fork for the purpose of digging potatoes. All ran away with the exception of the soldier with the fork, who struck at the Constable with the fork and knocked his helmet off. Stewart was able to wrench the fork away and later obtained the man's name from an Under officer. A report has been submitted to the German Police and the soldier will be punished.

In all cases involving members of the Forces, Police are unable to lay hands on the offenders, they are to take what is coming and not hit back. Some Constables have been threatened with a drawn bayonet, one PC was assaulted by two soldiers who knocked his helmet off and struck the PC several times in the face, inflicting minor injuries. So far nothing serious has happened, but we can reasonably expect something will one day.

The foreign labourers are becoming more truculent, we have had several cases where Police have had to resort to the use of truncheons. These cases we are able to deal with.

We are at present eight men short and taking into consideration the increased risks run, I respectfully suggest that to enable the Committee to retain the services of the good PCs at present in the Force and as an inducement to obtain the right type of candidate, the rate of pay should be increased."

One man, the Police Sub Committee considered suitable for appointment as a Auxiliary was Alfred Williams, of Les Cornus Farm, St Martin. He was employed by the Germans at the Airport. Mr Lamy wrote to the Labour officer, Mr R.H.Johns requesting that he make arrangements for Williams's release so that he could commence duty on the 18th November. A request was made to Captain Fehr at the airport for the man's release. On the 17th a response was received:-

"In reply to your letter of the 13th November we regret to express our disagreement with you. Alfred Williams is one of our most qualified workers and we therefore are compelled to insist upon his further employment with us and refrain from his release. We kindly ask you to be guided accordingly."

On the 28th November Mr Lamy received notification that the 14/56 Wolseley Police car, No 5350, which had been requisitioned by the Germans for use by the Military Commandant, had been purchased by them. He received notification from the States Supervisor, H.E.Marquand, that the price set by Stan Noel, the St Peter Port garage owner, could only be paid if a declaration was signed and returned stating that the vehicle was not subject to any hire purchase agreement. Mr Lamy reluctantly signed the declaration and the Police Committee eventually received £155 for the car, for which they had paid £280 in 1938.

The possibility of a German evacuation of the Island was a constant subject of thought and planning, particularly amongst members of the Controlling Committee. After almost two and a half years of Occupation, with the conduct of the war beginning to turn in the Allies' favour it was inevitable that plans were forming in the minds of certain members. Sir Abraham Laine, the Vice-President of the Controlling Committee, had given the matter detailed consideration and on the 30th November 1942 he put his ideas into writing for the benefit of Jurat John Leale.

"We may at any moment be faced by problems arising out of the sudden evacuation from Guernsey of the Occupying German Forces. ..... Should the evacuation take place before the cessation of hostilities, we are certain to be faced with problems of a very difficult nature, to the solution of which it would be prudent for us to devote some thought in advance..... Our first problem will probably be to re-establish communications, in some form or another, with the British mainland. As the fact of evacuation is not likely to be known to the British Authorities as soon as it takes place, the initial onus of attempting to restore communications will rest on us."

Sir Abraham listed three possible methods of re-establishing contact, by telegraphic cable, if still in commission, by wireless transmission, which was likely to be picked up by the Germans, "thereby possibly leading to retaliatory bombing attacks on the Island" and by "some seaworthy steam, motor or sailing craft." He added that "the drawback with the use of a seaborne craft is that the waters separating us from Great Britain may have been extensively mined by one or other, or both of the belligerents.

Simultaneously with the need of restoring communications with the mainland, there will face us the problem of maintaining law and order in the Island, pending the restoration of full communications. As an inevitable reaction from the state of duress under which all inhabitants have been forced to live, we may expect an ebullition of spirits resulting possibly in a certain amount of 'mafficking'.

This should not be difficult to control if we are left to ourselves, but our difficulties will be enormously accentuated if, at the time of the evacuation, there remain on the Island considerable bodies of foreign workmen or imported civilians of various types. These workmen will possibly be half starved and will, like the indigenous inhabitants, inevitably react violently on the sudden disappearance of forced labour, the cessation of payment of wages and of arrangements for their feeding and the equally sudden relaxation of the stringent discipline to which they have hitherto been subjected.

Their first tendency will be to loot food and drink and it will be incumbent upon us to doubly, or trebly, safeguard our stores of food and especially any stores of spirituous liquids that may still remain in the Island. Our Police will have their work cut out and it may prove necessary to enrol forthwith, without the formality of taking an oath before the Royal Court, the entire able bodied male adult population of the Island, as Special Constables."

Sir Abraham covered every conceivable aspect of a possible German withdrawal in his five closely-typed foolscap pages. It was marked, 'Highly Confidential' and as such was not discussed by the Controlling Committee. It really was an exercise in forward thinking, almost at the halfway mark of the Occupation of the Island by the Germans.

At the meeting of the Police Committee on the 7th December Acting Sergeant Harry Pugh was confirmed as a full Sergeant. The Committee also agreed to the appointment of a further recruit, A/PC 34 Raymond Philip Gaudion, 21, of Columbia Villa, Maladerie Road, St Sampson. Raymond was the youngest son of PC 33 Tom Gaudion, who had been convicted by the Germans and deported to France.

The Germans were well aware that a number of Islanders had retained their wireless sets despite the well-publicised orders for their surrender. Colonel Knackfuss decided to issue a further Order 'Concerning the surrender of wireless receiving sets'.

NOTICE.

"Notwithstanding the notice of the Feldkommandantur 515 concerning the surrender of wireless receiving sets, dated the 6th June 1942, there are still such sets in the possession of inhabitants of the Channel Isles.

Contraventions of the above mentioned order after 1st January 1943 will be punished by imprisonment with or without hard labour, or fines, in serious cases by the death penalty as authorised by the Militarbefehlshaber in Frankreich under the Order concerning the performance of service and requisitions in kind, dated 31st January 1942, which order is repeated hereunder.

No proceedings will be taken against any person who of his own free will surrenders his wireless receiving set by the 31st December 1942, to the Feldkommandantur 515 in St Helier or its branch office in St Peter Port."

The Frenchman Jean Binet, the master cat burglar, who had escaped from prison, was still free and various stores were receiving his expert attention. When William Camp opened up Bucktrout's Tobacco Factory in Cornet Street on the 4th December, he discovered that a forcible entry had been made by removing a vent from a window on the third floor of the building. It was apparent that every floor had been searched and several cases of tobacco and cigarettes ransacked. The thieves had made their exit, with their haul of tobacco and German cigarettes, by the main double doors on to Cornet Street.

Sergeant Pill went to the premises and carried out a full investigation. He concluded that it was the work of Jean Binet.

Sergeant Harry Pugh was instructed by Acting Deputy Inspector Banneville to visit two Constables, A/PC 26 Parlett and A/PC 27 Champion, who were on observation duty at the Pleinheaume potato depot. As there had been complaints of cows being milked at Gilroy's cow stable, which was situated close to the road below the shop at Pleinheaume cross-roads, he called in there on his way. Harry Pugh later recalled:-

"I tried the door but could not open it. I then went and looked around the other buildings. On returning I again tried the stable door, this was at exactly 3.00am and suddenly the door was opened and A/PC26 Parlett, who had been in the stable all the time, asked in a sleepy voice 'what I wanted?', I asked him what he was doing in the stable he said, 'I have just been having my grub, Sergeant.' I then entered the stable, all the cows were lying down, behind the door was a heap of hay where the Constable had been lying. He was wearing a civilian mackintosh, his cape was lying on the top of the heap of hay, he was without his helmet which was also lying on the hay. A/PC 17 Henry was with me and heard and saw everything.

I then went on to Pleinheaume potato depot and saw A/PC 27 Champion. I asked where his mate was and he told me, 'He left here half an hour ago to go and have his meal.' Before I left A/PC Parlett came back to their point of observation."

It is not recorded what, if any, disciplinary action was taken against Constable Reg Parlett, but he certainly continued as a member of the Force.

The Germans were so concerned about the spread of Venereal Disease in the Island that they made it compulsory for all local women suffering or suspected of suffering from the disease to be detained in the Town Hospital or at the V.D.Clinic in Hauteville. From time to time the Germans required the Police to detain women and deliver them to the Hospital or the Clinic at 33 Hauteville.

On the 18th December PC 9 Marsh was required to take Miss Irene ...., aged 20, of Cobo, Castel, to the Town Hospital, for examination as a V.D. suspect. This was as a result of information supplied by the Feldgendarmerie.

Later that evening a telephone call was received at the Station from the Town Hospital, stating that Miss Irene .... had not returned to the hospital from the clinic after being examined and would the Police pick her up again and return her to the hospital. As a result the Acting Deputy Inspector accompanied by PC 8 Le Cocq, went in the Police van to Cobo and found Irene .... at her home. They returned her to the hospital at 11.50pm.

She did not remain in the Hospital for very long, because on Boxing morning A/PC 17 Albert Henry was on patrol when an Organisation Todt officer approached him. The Constable was taken to 9 Bouillon Lane, St Peter Port, by the O.T. officer, where they found the front door locked. The O.T. officer said, "There is an O.T. in there with an English woman." They knocked on the door and as no one answered, the O.T. officer forced it open.

In a bedroom at the back, the Constable found Miss Irene ...., who volunteered, "I did not sleep in this house last night, the O.T. officer told me not to. Last night I slept in a house up the road. I do not know the name of the people." She was taken to the Station where Mr Lamy after questioning her ordered that further enquiries be made to establish just where she had slept.

Irene took the Constable to 11 Victoria Terrace, where they saw William Ogier who said, "At about 10.50pm on Christmas Day Miss Irene .... accompanied by a foreigner and an O.T. in civilian clothes, came to my house. The O.T. knocked on the front door and asked if he could come in with his wife and the foreigner.

I let them in and she said they had been married a week ago. They danced a little and then went to bed in number 12 Victoria Terrace."

Irene then admitted that she told Mr Lamy a lie, she had slept at number 12 Victoria Terrace, an O.T. house.

Probably the largest single arrest by the Force during the Occupation occurred on New Year's Eve 1942. A French national by the name of Kutter escaped, on Boxing Day, from the O.T.Prison in Rue Sauvage. At 4.45pm on the 31st December a call was received at the Station from A/PC 19 Stewart reporting that he had detained Kutter and required assistance. Acting Inspector Lamy and PC Le Cocq then went to L'Islet and collected Constable Stewart and his prisoner and took him to the 'O.T.' prison.

Whilst interrogating Kutter, Mr Lamy received information which led him to go, accompanied by the two Constables and a member of the O.T. prison staff, first to a stable near the Vale Pond, then to a military flour store at L'Islet and finally to an O.T. billet at Ville Baudu. They arrested 26 foreign labourers for stealing flour from the military store and vegetables, bread, groceries, rabbits and clothing from local houses. In view of the number of men arrested, a coach had to be obtained from the Civil Transport depot to convey them to the O.T. Prison. The Police Committee later received an invoice for the hire of the coach.

# Chapter 22

# BY THE TIME THEY HAD FINISHED HE WAS JUST A CRYING WRECK

Acting Inspector Arthur Langmead, who had been suspended for almost exactly five months, was requested to report at Grange Lodge on the 30th December 1942.

"On arrival, I was shown a form in German which, on translation, stated that a German Court in Jersey had considered my case and had sentenced me to one month's imprisonment. I was given two days in which to appeal, but on the advice of Advocate Martel, I decided against an appeal. On the 8th January 1943 I was placed in prison and remained there until 8th February."

The Germans had spent the five months since his suspension, trying to obtain evidence to support the allegations contained in the anonymous letter they received. They made extensive enquiries amongst the former Police officers who were in prison in France and Germany, but without success. In the end they relied on the admission that he made at his interview with them on the 29th July 1942, that he had received a piece of wood from the German wood store.

Arthur Langmead knew nothing of the charge, trial or sentence, until he was shown the 'Certified copy of Judgement'

"CERTIFIED COPY OF JUDGEMENT.
Tribunal of St Helier,
Feldkommandantur 515. Jersey.
St L. Nr. 318 1942 23rd December 1942
Against the British subject, Police Inspector,
Arthur John LANGMEAD.
Same particulars as above, plus the following:-
Facts.

In the course of the winter 1941/42 in Guernsey, the accused took for his own use objects which he knew had been illegally obtained. He took a large piece of wood which ex-Police Constable Short had stolen from a German timber store, loaded it in his car, brought it to his house and used it there as fuel.

Offence; Paragraph 259 RStGB.
Evidence; Own admission.
This sentence is to be executed."

Acting Inspector Lamy was told to ensure that Mr Langmead reported to Grange Lodge at 2.00pm. on the 8th January 1943. The former Acting Inspector did so and was immediately placed in the Guernsey prison by the Germans. His term of sentence began officially at 2.30pm that day.

Mr Sherwill received notification of the sentence and the standard request that the sentence be entered in the Police Register. Later he was again notified of the sentence and informed that he was required to 'supervise the execution of the sentence in the States prison' and release the accused at 2.30pm on

February 8th 1943. He was also requested "to acknowledge receipt of this letter and to notify release at the expiration of the term."

At its meeting on the 11th January, the Police Committee resolved that Mr Langmead suspended pay should cease from 9th January 1943. The question of his resignation or dismissal was deferred until the February meeting.

Jean Binet and his accomplices had a busy Christmas and New Year, concentrating their attentions on the Tobacco Factory in Cornet Street. On the 30th December it was discovered that the premises had been entered by forcing a window shutter on the roof and over 20,000 cigarettes and 40 kilos of tobacco had been stolen. On the 5th January the Tobacco Factory was again forcibly entered and a further large quantity of cigarettes and tobacco stolen. On this occasion the thieves were apparently interrupted and left a carton of tobacco in the road.

The manager of the Civil Transport Department, a German appointee, James E.Smith, was driving down Cornet Street, accompanied by Mr Isler, the Swiss interpreter, at about 1.25am when he noticed a brown paper carton in the road. He pulled up and found the carton contained 50 packets of tobacco. As they inspected the carton a bullet struck the wall near them. They quickly left the area.

When they reached Mr Isler's flat in Lefebvre Street, Mr Smith, telephoned the Feldgendarmerie, who immediately sent two men to investigate. Mr Smith, who had a night pass supplied by the Germans, accompanied the two members of the Feldgendarmerie to Cornet Street and pointed out the carton of tobacco.

A few days later many of the stolen cigarettes were discovered in a large derelict house near the tobacco Factory. As it was considered certain that Jean Binet would return to collect his spoils, a number of men were placed in various parts of the house. Eventually a noise was heard and it was assumed that Binet had returned. Despite a thorough search of the house, with the use of German torches, no sign of him was found. The noise that the Police had heard was not of him entering the building, but of him leaving it. Whilst the Police were combing the building for him, he was on the peak of the roof, no doubt watching the search.

A few days later, at 5.45pm on the 11th January PC Le Cocq was cycling along the North Esplanade on his way home when he saw a person whom he believed to be Jean Binet. He stopped him and inspected his papers, which showed that he was Pierre Nalli. The Constable was not satisfied and took him to the Police Station where he admitted his real identity.

Jean Binet, who offered little resistance when arrested, was then taken to the prison by Acting Inspector Lamy and a number of other Policemen and handed over to the Feldgendarmerie.

Mr Lamy years later recalled how after they had handed over Binet to the Feldgendarmerie, he had been present when the Frenchman was interrogated.

"I was the unfortunate witness of the German third degree methods at this time. Binet had been taken to prison and three German Police officers came to interrogate him. They came armed with a rubber hose about half an inch - very flexible and in turn the three of them got at him. By the time they had finished he was just a crying wreck."

Had Binet not been arrested, the Authorities were about to offer a reward of £50 for his capture. A newspaper advertisement had already been prepared for the capture of 'One of the biggest criminals to whom these shores have offered temporary shelter'. However, the Police Committee were generous, they awarded PC Le Cocq, a reward of £3.3.0.

The German Authorities were so pleased that Jean Binet had been recaptured that they gave each member of the Force 2ozs of cigarette tobacco. As one policeman commented, "Cigarette tobacco was like gold to us."

Acting Inspector Lamy, as a result of his enforced relationship with the German Police, had frequently observed the interrogation methods they used when they 'required' a statement from a prisoner. He later recalled:-

"One of their methods was to leave a man in the cells all night with the lights on. A couple of nights later the lights would be turned off and they would come along in the early hours of the morning, wake him up and question him. Of course it was quite obvious that waking under these conditions it was easy to extract a statement, just the kind of statement they wanted. Often statements were taken from accomplices incriminating another, the statement would then be prepared, brought along to the accused, told to read it, that it was true and he had to sign it. These statements were often signed just for the sake of peace and quietness; the prison sentence being the lesser of two evils."

On Christmas Eve Dr Brosch required the President of the Controlling Committee to submit a list showing:-

A. All persons previously convicted.

B. Persons to be considered as unwilling to work,

C. Young males without fixed occupation.

The lists were to be submitted by 5th January 1943.

Jurat John Leale asked Deputy R.H.Johns of the Labour Department, to supply lists dealing with questions B and C. Mr Lamy was required to supply a list in respect of persons previously convicted. It was agreed that only persons convicted during the last ten years should be included. This proved to be a very considerable undertaking and required a great deal of research of Police and Court records. Mr Lamy quickly realised that he would have to supply two lists, one of persons convicted by a Guernsey Court and another of persons sentenced by the Germans.

The list of persons convicted of crime in Guernsey during the previous ten years ran to 305 Islanders. 139 persons appeared on the list of German convictions, of which 38 had been deported to France and Germany to serve their sentences.

At 2.45pm on January 8th 1943, PC Le Cocq was on cycle patrol at Les Delisles, Castel, when he passed a German Lieutenant standing in the road, being brushed down by a soldier. Nearby was a car in the middle of the road, with a long skid mark stretching out behind. The Constable rode on for about 100 yards before stopping. He looked over the hedge in the direction of Albecq and saw a group of children running away.

The Constable returned to where the officer, who was obviously furious, was still being brushed down and asked him what had happened. Apparently while driving down Les Delisles, a lump of turf was thrown into the car striking the officer. PC Le Cocq told the officer that he had seen some children running away and that he would try to find them. This appeared to pacify the officer.

The children that had been seen running away were three Bichard brothers. Leslie, 11, Stanley, 8 and Leonard, 6; two Le Noury brothers, Douglas, 12 and Alec, 7; and Lewis Ogier, 11.

They had been playing skirmishing, throwing lumps of turf at each other and at people cycling up and down the road. Years later Stanley Bichard recalled the incident:-

"This black car, I think it was a Hillman, was coming down the road and I had a lovely turf and 'wham', it was a beauty. The window was open and it hit the German officer in the face. The car skidded into the hedge and bounced off and finished up in the middle of the road. Of course we bolted straight down to the bottom field. My brother, Leslie, spotted a policeman pushing his cycle up the hill and Doug Le Noury checked and said yes let's go, so we ran straight down to the bottom of the hill, right down to St George. We stayed there hiding for about an hour, we were petrified."

The Constable and the German soldier jumped over the hedge and gave chase to the children but failed to find them. Francois Le Cocq then went to see the Headmaster of Castel School, Peter Girard, and together they visited various houses in the Kings Mills, Vazon and Albecq district. Later that afternoon the Constable, Peter Girard and a member of the Feldgendarmerie saw the Bichard children at their home at Bouillon Cottage, Les Delisles, and after a time they admitted that it was them who had been throwing lumps of turf. Although Stanley Bichard had thrown the turf that hit the German officer, the children agreed between themselves that Leslie Bichard and Douglas Le Noury would take responsibility.

The children were required to write letters of apology to the German Commandant and the officer concerned. They and their parents were cautioned. Fortunately the Germans did not take any further action and the incident was closed.

One of the loathsome products of the Occupation was the anonymous letter. In peace time Inspector Sculpher had employed a policy of largely ignoring this type of nauseating mail. Mr Lamy, regretfully, felt that he had to take note of these letters, as often copies were also sent to the Germans.

However, Harry Chapell, the Head Postmaster, operated a completely unofficial system of censoring these treacherous letters. He steamed open any addressed to the Feldkommandantur at Grange Lodge, which he thought suspicious. The bone-fide ones were resealed and delivered, but over two hundred letters were intercepted and destroyed during the Occupation, letters which might otherwise have caused many Islanders to lose their freedom and possibly their lives.

Mr Lamy was able to 'lose' some of the letters but others he felt obliged to follow up and investigate. One anonymous letter led to Peter Le Cheminant, a farmer, of Les Fourgettes, Castel, being charged with:- 'Permitting slaughter of livestock, to wit, a pig between 10th and 12th January 1943, further without authority to supplying rationed food, to wit, meat, for household consumption between 10th and 12th January 1943 at the above address'.

The Acting Inspector told the Court that as the result of an anonymous letter, two Police officers had called on the defendant who refused to show them the pig. Later they searched the premises and found half the pig. They were then told the animal had broken its leg or perhaps badly strained it. The Magistrate, Jurat Le Pelley, fined Mr Le Cheminant a total of £65.

Many members of the public had a secret chuckle, although outwardly maintaining an air of sympathy, when they read the headline and story in *'The Star'* on the 12th January.

"The Policeman's Lot.

Now belongs to someone else.

Have you seen a practically new James bicycle, licence No 952. If you have recently seen this vehicle in the charge of anyone but its rightful owner, you are asked to communicate with the Island Police, for - at the moment - due to its loss, Acting Deputy Inspector F.Banneville has, in the course of his duties, to go around borrowing their cycles in turn !

The sad state of affairs - a case of 'physician cure thyself' - has been brought about by one of the most impudent thefts that have recently come to our notice. It happened like this; Acting Deputy Inspector Banneville, being a Police officer, is ultra careful with his bicycle and takes the precaution of padlocking the rear wheel whenever he parks it. He did this on Friday evening when he left his machine at the Station.

Then he unlocked it, preparatory to going off duty, but was called back to the office for five minutes. During that short time the bicycle was stolen right from under the nose of the Police - outside the Police Station - as an audacious a piece of thieving as possible.

If you can help restore Acting Deputy Inspector Banneville to the seat of his own cycle, please do it now."

Mı Banneville no doubt made suitable alternative arrangements in regard to his personal transport, but it is not recorded whether or not he recovered his cycle.

When forty one year old Albert Pike, the prison Gaoler, died suddenly members of the Police Force formed a guard of honour at his funeral at Foulon Cemetery He had been in the Prison Service for 18 years and had succeeded his father as Gaoler. Auxiliary Police Constable William Ferbrache was appointed to fill the position as Gaoler and resigned from the Police Force on the 12th February.

Acting Inspector Lamy had, since his appointment some six months previously, run a series of lectures on 'Police Duties' for the new recruits. Some of the Auxiliaries had been very diligent in their attendance, but others had shown less dedication. Mr Lamy decided to test the new recruits' knowledge with a set examination. On the 2nd February he issued a memo which was pinned to the Notice Board.

'An examination in Police Duties will be held in the Police Office on Friday 5th February. All Auxiliary Police officers are required to attend. Anyone failing to attend will be considered as failing to report for duty. A minimum of 60% marks is required. Please bring your pencils.'

Whilst the details of the examination are not recorded the results were listed in correspondence to one of the former Policeman, who had been deported to Germany.

99% A/PC 17 Henry.
87% A/PC 40 O'Donovan.
86% A/PC 23 Langlois.
82% A/PC 27 Champion and A/PC 16 Hall.
79% A/PC 19 Stewart.
78% A/PC 26 Parlett.
77% A/PC 24 Basil Le Page and A/PC 33 Roy Le Page.
76% A/PC 25 Le Prevost.
75% A/PC 18 Pill and A/PC 30 De Carteret.
74% A/PC 36 Solway.
72% A/PC 22 Le Gallez.
71% A/PC 38 Robilliard.
68% A/PC 21 Le Tissier.
64% A/PC 14 Ron Le Page and A/PC 32 Salmon.
61% A/PC 35 Langford.
60% A/PC 20 Julou and A/PC 42 Le Sauvage.
59% A/PC 41 Bisson.
58% A/PC 31 Mansfield.
57% A/PC 34 Gaudion.
53% A/PC 29 Falla.
50% A/PC 28 Boalch.
48% A/PC 10 Sebire.
47% A/PC 37 Tucker.

43% A/PC 39 Moore.

42% A/PC 11 Vanden Bergh and A/PC 12 Mahy.

37% A/PC 13 Brouard.

Mr Lamy, who marked the papers, told Bert Henry:- "You are worthy of 100%, but 100% means you know everything in the book, so I can't give you that." So he gave him 99%.

Early in February, Acting Inspector Lamy wrote to Inspector Zachau, at Grange Lodge, informing him that former PC 25 Harold Piesing had arrived back in Guernsey on the 4th February after serving his term of imprisonment in France.

Towards the end of January 1943 the Guernsey Authorities learned that further deportations were likely to take place. A British Commando raid on Sark had taken place in early October and the Germans used this as a reason to deport 130 more Islanders on the 13th February. Unlike the deportations that had taken place in the previous September these took place without any publicity. No notice or announcement of the 'evacuation' appeared in the Press and the German Censor allowed no report of the departure to be published.

The Bailiff was 'required' to write to every Islander who had been selected by the Germans for deportation. On the 3rd February he wrote:-

"Dear Sir/Madam,

I regret to have to inform you that we have been notified that you are likely to be removed to an internment camp in Germany. You are therefore advised to be ready to go at very short notice.

Yours faithfully

Victor Carey,

Bailiff."

Amongst those selected for deportation was H.M.Attorney General, Ambrose Sherwill and as soon as the Bailiff was aware of this he wrote to Colonel Knackfuss:-

"I would be greatly obliged if you would be good enough to place before the General the great difficulties which will arise with reference to the administration of justice in this Island if Mr A.J.Sherwill is taken away from his duties as H.M.Attorney General and removed from the Island. Mr Sherwill has been H.M.Comptroller and later H.M.Attorney General for about 15 years and has therefore had great experience in carrying out the duties of Public Prosecutor in criminal proceedings as well as considerable experience in drafting Laws and Ordinances, besides being legal adviser to various public bodies and States Committees.

There are only two other Advocates or Lawyers in this Island, neither of whom are experienced in these matters. Mr Martel is a lawyer with a large private practice and it would be a great hardship to the public to deprive them of his services. Mr Langlois, the other Advocate, is unfortunately far from strong and could not undertake the arduous work of H.M.Attorney General. Mr Ridgway, H.M.Solicitor General, died last year, so the Royal Court is absolutely dependent on Mr Sherwill to carry out his duties, as otherwise it will only be able to function under the greatest difficulties.

I might also point out that the two above mentioned Advocates are required to defend prisoners who have to undergo Trial. Might I also add that I, as Bailiff, am responsible for the due and proper Administration of Justice in this Island and will find the load of responsibility on my shoulders greatly increased if Mr Sherwill is removed from his duties - a load which as I am not a young man, is not easy to bear."

The letter had no effect, Mr Sherwill was deported and Advocate J.E.L.Martel again became Acting Attorney General.

Others deported included the wives and children of some of the Police officers who were convicted by the Royal Court in June 1942.

Mrs Wilhilmina Quin and her son Francis,
Mrs Eva Whare and her eighteen-year-old son William,
Mrs Irene Smith and her 3 children
Mrs Amy Gaudion and her daughter Margaret,
Mrs Annie Howlett.

The wives and children of those Police officers only convicted by the German Military Court in April 1942 escaped deportation. Ex-PC Harold 'Snip' Piesing, who had only a matter of days previously returned to the Island was deported with his wife Eileen.

Also selected for deportation were the remaining three Jews in the Bailiwick, Mrs Elda Brouard, Frau Annie Wranowsky, and Mrs Elisabet Duquemin, her husband Henry and their daughter Janet. Whilst Annie Wranowsky was served with a deportation notice, she was excused, probably because she was not a British subject.

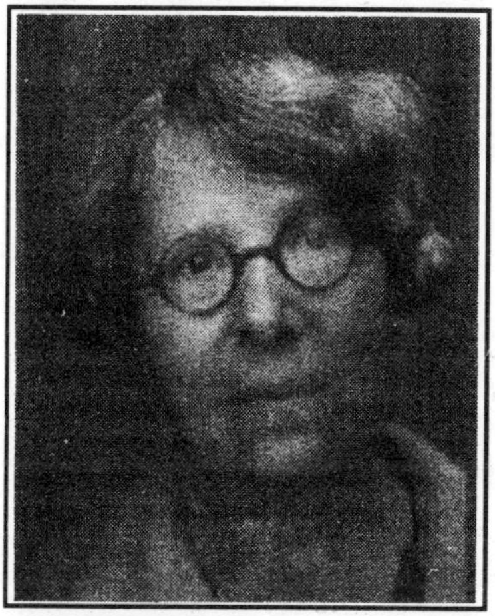

**Mrs Elda Brouard.**

**Mrs Elisabet Duquemin.**

Arthur Langmead, who had been released from prison on the 8th February, had been due to go with the party which left the Island on the 13th February. Whilst serving his sentence he had been held in the condemned cell, a wooden building in the prison yard. He was more comfortable there than his family because he had the unrestricted use of an electric fire. The result was that when he was released he caught a severe chill and was immediately confined to bed. Dr. Richard Gibson certified, on the 11th February, that he was in bed with a temperature of 102. This won him a reprieve, but it was short lived, as he and his wife were included in the second batch of thirteen deportees who left the Island on the 25th February 1942.

Also included in the second party were two former Policemen, Alfred Le Gallez, his wife Nora and their four children; and Eugene Le Lievre and his wife Suzanne. Both men had served their eight-month prison sentences on the continent and were then interned in France for a time, before returning to Guernsey on the 16th February. Nine days later they were again deported.

Prior to his deportation Arthur Langmead wrote to Mr Agnew, the President of the Police Committee:-

"I beg to ask that, in considering my case. the Committee will do so in the light of my past service and with the full assurance that the measure of confidence they may repose in me, I will strive to fully maintain. From the States Office I learn that my pay has been stopped but as I have received no notification from the Committee I can only hope that a final decision has not been reached.

I beg to suggest sir, that I might be suspended without pay until after the Occupation, before a final decision is taken. In suggesting this I have in mind a precedent in the case of PC Bretel."

The President, after he had received the letter scribbled on the bottom, "Please inform him that his letter is under consideration, so nothing definite at present".

Arthur Langmead received his second deportation notice on 21st February and was required to report with his wife, to Vauquiedor Hospital for medical examination the next day. Finally he and his wife had to present themselves, with their luggage, at the Gaumont Cinema at 3.00pm on the 24th. They were instructed to take with them, warm clothing, solid boots, some food for the journey, meal dishes, a drinking bowl and a blanket. They were also allowed to take a trunk packed with clothes, which had to be locked for shipment. A maximum of 50 Reichmarks were allowed to be taken.

When the party of thirteen from Guernsey reached St Malo they were joined by a party of 25 from Jersey. They travelled overnight to Paris, with men and women in separate carriages. The men's carriages went to a internment camp, Ilag VIII, Kreuzburg, near Breslau in Upper Silesia and the women and children, to Compiegne, near Paris.

# Chapter 23

# NOT FOR PRESS

Guernseymen have long considered that their right to go ormering was God given and no one, not even the Germans, or their minefields, had the right to prevent them gathering their favourite delicacy. So thought John Gallienne and his three colleagues when they set out to go ormering during the early afternoon of the 8th February 1943.

The four, John Gallienne, Alfred John Gallienne, his father Alfred Gallienne and Charles Dowington climbed over two barbed wire fences at Pleinmont and then trespassed through a prohibited area of the cliffs, so that they could get to the beach. After descending about 60 or 70 feet, eighteen-year-old Alfred John Gallienne trod on a mine and was killed instantly. John Gallienne was the only member of the party uninjured. He carefully retraced his steps and telephoned Sergeant Dyson at the Police Station.

The Sergeant immediately set off in the Police van and collected the Police doctor, Dr Collings, on the way. The St John Ambulance were also alerted. They were met at the Imperial Hotel by John Gallienne. The Military Authorities were called and they took about threequarters of an hour to clear a path through the mined area so the rescue party could reach the scene of the accident.

The Ambulance men, R.H.Blanchford, C.Froome and T.Sauvarin assisted by Sergeant Dyson worked for five hours rescuing the two injured men and recovering the body of Alfred John Gallienne. The dead man's father received a slight wound to his neck and Charles Dowington suffered a serious wound to his foot.

The next day in the Coroner's Court, Jurat Le Pelley recorded a verdict of 'Death from misadventure'. However, before returning his verdict, he censured the men for their foolhardy venture into the minefield and said that they were entirely to blame.

The Police Committee at its meeting on the 15th February appointed Acting Sergeant R.Kimber, as full Sergeant, on 12 months probation, to date from the 17th February 1943.

During the Occupation there was not space for a regular 'Letters Column' in either the *Evening Press* or *The Star*. However, both papers did on occasions publish letters, often under a pseudonym. One letter was headed:-

"A word for our Policemen to the Editor of the Star.

This morning on my way to business I passed a Police Constable. He was having a tussle with the wind and rain. I stopped him and asked for a match which he willingly produced. I asked him where he was going. He replied 'As far as the coast'. He was soaking wet and no doubt cold. When I suggested that he should be wearing an overcoat and leggings he replied, 'I think the same as you and one or two of my mates do also'. The more I thought about it the more sorry I felt for him and his fellow officers, they must be cold these days.

I, with many others, pay rates and taxes and I wonder why the powers that be do not allow the men who are doing a good job to be warmly clothed. There is no A.R.P. now and there are plenty of waterproofs stored somewhere belonging to this one-time organisation. Why not pass them on to these men doing essential work, who are out night and day."

Signed "Help one another."

This letter must have been taken to heart by 'the powers that be' referred to by the writer. Mr Lamy on the 16th February reported to the President of the Police Committee that he had now been able to obtain a number of ex A.R.P. capes which were being used to make up leggings. Mr Lamy added "Although not ideal, these leggings will afford some protection. Only eight men are without leggings."

George Robins lived at Sunnyside Cottage, Ruette Braye, and ran a poultry farm. He described himself as 'self supporting'. As a result of receiving a telephone call, A/PC 24 Basil Le Page called at Sunnyside Cottage during the lunch hour on the 22nd February and George told him, "Last Sunday morning I noticed one fowl short and again this morning another was missing. I found the feathers by the fowl house and a Belgian coin. I value the fowls at 25/- each. Do you think I should have a Policeman with me for a couple of nights because I still have 62 head of poultry and I would be very glad to have someone with me, watching."

The Constable saw the feathers near the fowl house and noticed how easily entry could be gained to the property from the adjacent fields. There were no marks on the ground and neither the Constable nor George Robins had any suspicions of who might be responsible for the thefts. The next night another chicken was stolen and George reported the theft to the Station, again requesting a Policeman to keep watch with him for a couple of nights. Mr Lamy agreed and A/PC 35 Frank Langford kept observation during the night of the 24th and 25th February but no further losses occurred.

On the 25th February, thirteen-year-old Edgar Mechem called for his chum, Louis Ogier, on his way to school at La Haye du Puits. Louis showed him a bullet that another boy at school had given him.

Edgar later told A/PC 30 de Carteret "While I was there we decided to make a fire and throw the bullet on. This we did and hid behind a shed, we waited but nothing happened. As we went towards the fire, which was out, suddenly the bullet went off and hit me in the knee. I carried on to school and was then taken to the Emergency hospital where I was attended to by Doctor Wilson, who cleaned up the wound and bandaged me up."

The Constable, on investigation, established that the bullet was a live cartridge with a wooden plug, as used by the military for practice. Edgar had been struck on the knee by the plug.

The Germans generally took hygiene very seriously and did everything possible to prevent the outbreak and spread of disease. During the latter part of February 1943 there was a small outbreak of typhus detected amongst foreign workers. The German Doctor in charge, Dr Deschauer, informed Dr Symons, the Health Services officer and they agreed that, provided all necessary precautions were taken, there was little danger to civilians. However, the foreign workers affected were kept under strict guard and in the George Street - Allez Street area, where they were billeted, considerable quantities of lime was spread around the streets.

The Germans took every precaution to ensure that the disease did not spread, including the banning of all dances in the Island. The Bailiff issued a directive on the 26th February to all dance organisers and sent the Acting Inspector a copy, with the request that the Police ensure that the Order was complied with.

"In order to minimize the danger of infection at the present time, it is ordered that, as from this day and until further notice, no dancing whatsoever be held in the Island."

The Organisers notified included:-
Mr W.de Carteret, Hirzel House
Mrs Wellington, Sunnycroft, Grange.
Mrs Cumber, Rouge Huis Avenue.
Mr R.Martel, Les Landes, Vale.
Miss Jolly, Terlaboh, St Clair Hill.
Mr P.Renouf, Highland Estate, St Martin.
Mr S.J.Masterman, Elsarth, Route Militaire.
Mr D.J.Honey, Westbourne Place, Vale.
Mrs F.Hobbs and Miss Farnham, Houmet Lane, L'Islet.
Godfrey Gifford Esq., Berkeley House, Hauteville.
Mr A.K.Jory, Home from Home Restaurant.

No public or Press announcement was made, other than to say that a dance competition had been cancelled due to unforeseen circumstances. As there had been no spread of the disease, the ban on dances was lifted after a month.

Benjamin Brunt, who was known to many Islanders as Doctor Brunt, came to the Island in June 1940 and failed to leave before the Germans arrived. He set himself up in practice as a masseur and osteopath, with consulting rooms at 5 Smith Street. He claimed to be a Chiropractic Doctor and that he had practised for many years in America, treating well known Hollywood film stars. During the three years he had been in Guernsey he had worked up an extensive practice.

**Benjamin Brunt.**

On the 26th February a Miss Barbara Barnes, who frequented with the Germans and had become pregnant, was admitted to the Emergency Hospital in a serious condition. Mr Lamy was informed of the circumstances and went to Dr Brunt's home at Holmleigh, Coutanchez, and arrested him for 'using an instrument with intent to cause an abortion on Barbara Barnes aged 17.' After making a statement Brunt was placed in the prison.

The following morning Mr Lamy received a telephone message from Matron Hall of the Emergency Hospital, informing him that Barbara Barnes had died at 4.35am. Brunt was then charged with the girl's murder. The subsequent trial in the Royal Court, lasted three days. Benjamin Brunt was sentenced to three years imprisonment.

Mr Lamy often used one of the Police motorcycles to check on the Auxiliary Constables on their patrols. At 2.45pm on the 9th March he was riding a motorcycle up Allez Street. As he approached the junction with Union Street he had to pull out to pass three military vehicles parked on the righthand side of the road. As he passed the last vehicle, he collided with a car driven by a German. Mr Lamy was unhurt. There was no damage to the car but the motorcycle's front forks were badly bent and the front mudguard damaged. It was taken to Green's, of Smith Street, for repair. A report of the accident was entered in the Occurrence Book and in the margin was written, in Mr Lamy's handwriting - 'Not for press'.

Three weeks after Mr Langmead had been deported to Germany, his house at Les Cornus was broken into. His son Ronald, who lodged opposite, was called by a neighbour who had noticed that one of the windows had been smashed. Ronald reported the matter to the Station and A/PC 24 Basil Le Page was sent to investigate.

Ronald told him "I am in charge of the keys of my parent's house. Last night I left about 6.00pm and everything was intact. Today a neighbour called me about 1.00pm saying that the rear window was smashed, so I entered the house, but could find nothing missing except the back door key, which had been left in the lock on the inside. I will nail up the back door as I expect them to return."

The Constable found that entry had been gained by undoing the window catch through the broken glass. He found no mark and Ronald Langmead had no suspicions as to who might have broken in. The matter was duly recorded in the Occurrence Book.

Stanley Tuck, a brother of Ex-PC Frank Tuck, was employed by the German firm of Bauleitung as a motor mechanic. During the late afternoon of the 22nd March 1943 he was a passenger in the rear of a lorry and was hanging over the side trying to trace a noise in the back axle. As they drove down the Grange, Stanley Tuck's head hit a lamp standard.

There were three other men in the lorry's cab and one of them, Wilfred Ferbrache, realised that something was wrong. The driver stopped and they saw that Stanley had a cut at the base of his skull but there was very little blood.

They immediately drove to the Town Hospital where it was quickly established that twenty-one-year-old Stanley Tuck was dead. Wilfred Ferbrache ran to the Police Station to report the fatal accident.

Later Sergeant Dyson and PC Marsh examined the three lamp standards on the south side of the Grange, from Grange Court to St John's Street but could find no indication or sign as to which one caused Stanley's death.

**A.P. Delaney.**

Whilst patrolling the High Street around midnight on the 23rd March 1943, A/PC 19 Stewart and A/PC 42 Le Sauvage walked down North Pier Steps trying doors in the vicinity of the air raid shelter under Boots the Chemist. They found the door of the store under Hipps Ltd. unlocked and inside on a table was a wireless set.

Acting Inspector Lamy was later to recall the incident:-

"We had quite a large number of people in the Island who apparently thought more of the Germans than they did of their own people. These could be divided into two categories - open collaborators and writers of anonymous letters. In the first category there was an

Irishman, A.P.Delaney, employed by the Billeting staff. He knew the Island fairly well and was able to take the Germans to the right places, to get the stuff they required. He was formerly manager of Hipps Ltd., a clothing shop in the Town. Beneath this shop was a store.

One night two Police officers found the door open and the only thing in the store was a wireless set. All wireless sets had been confiscated by the Germans, therefore this set was brought to the Police Station and the fact recorded in the Occurrence Book. I felt that although he was a collaborator he was still British and I wanted to give him a chance, but as this incident had been recorded in the Occurrence Book there was always the possibility that the Germans might see it, so I sent for him and showed him the set. He asked where I got it. I told him and said that I would take no action for 24 hours in order to give him an opportunity of thinking out a decent story to cover this matter. He thanked me very much and went off.

Less than ten minutes after he had left my office I received a telephone message from the German Police stating that I had a wireless set in the Police Station. I strongly denied this and they eventually said 'I know you have got a set. Mr Delaney is here and has just told us about it.' So you can see from that, he was even more of a collaborator than I first thought him."

On the 24th March an announcement appeared in the *Evening Press* regarding artillery practice that was to take place during the two following days. Between 7.30am and 3.00pm on the Thursday and 6.00pm and 7.00pm on the Friday, civilians were ordered to leave parts of St Peter Port and some country parishes while Artillery practice took place in an easterly direction.

The country areas included the Emergency Hospital, which meant that more than 90 ambulance cases had to be moved. Moreover many employees lost a day's pay and were put to considerable inconvenience.

In St Peter Port the danger area was the eastern part of the Town and extended from the Longstore in the north, to Havilland Street in the west and Les Val de Terres in the south.

The danger area included the Police Station so Mr Lamy made arrangements for the Station to be locked up and the duties performed from 'The Hollies' in the Grange. At 7.45am a German officer on a motorcycle combination saw the Acting Deputy Inspector at 'The Hollies' and ordered him to ensure that a least two Police officers were on patrol in the evacuated area to prevent house breaking. Mr Banneville informed the Acting Inspector, who immediately ordered that the Station be reopened.

Everyone waited for the firing with considerable apprehension since many feared that the vibration was going to cause immense damage to the Town, particularly the hilly areas. A few heavy salvos were fired, but on the whole it was best described by one resident, as "a fiasco."

On the 25th March, A/PC 36 Solway while on cycle patrol, stopped at a house at Landes du Marche to have his supper. While there, his 3 speed Hercules bicycle was stolen, together with his Police cap and leggings. Later that night, with the Camp Commander he visited the foreign workers' camp at Le Blanc Bois and searched the camp. He found a number of cycles which he was sure belonged to civilians, but did not find his own.

A/PC 10 Sebire and A/PC 31 Mansfield were on patrol a few days later in Trinity Square, and saw a foreigner park a cycle against the wall near Knight's Cafe. The cycle looked remarkably like Constable Solway's which still had not been found, so they questioned the cyclist.

The cyclist, Martin Josse, said that he had purchased it from Mr L.E.Fossey, of L'Islet, and produced a receipt for the cycle dated 12th September 1942.

Mr Fossey was interviewed, "Yes I sold the cycle for 200 reichmarks, to Josse, on the 12th September last. I bought the cycle from the auctioneer, Mr J Leech, at the auction room in Braye Road for the sum of £18/10/- plus tax. I did not fix any sales stamps on the receipt as I thought it was not necessary." The Constable told Mr Fossey that it was necessary and that he would probably be warned for court in the near future. There was still no sign of Constable Solway's cycle.

On the 1st of April Constable Le Cocq responded to a call from the Bailiff and went to Le Vallon, St Martin where he saw Albert Jones who was employed by Mr Carey. He told the Constable:- "Yesterday about 4.00pm I was working on the estate when I saw five Germans dressed in green, cutting branches off trees. I asked them if they had a permit, one said 'Yes'. Later my son said they had cut down a pine. I reported the matter to the Bailiff."

The PC examined the area where the trees had been cut, one which was a pine tree, which he estimated must have been at least 25' high. There were several other branches cut near by. The Feldgendarmerie were notified and they promised to visit the Bailiff's estate during the afternoon.

On really dark nights cyclists found that there was always a real danger of accidents with other cyclists or pedestrians. Only a very small amount of light was permitted. To conform with the German regulations, the whole of the inside of the area of the glass was smoked, then a small circle of not more than half an inch in diameter in the middle, was rubbed clear. This made it almost impossible for a cyclist to see his way with such an apology for a light, its only purpose was for the cyclist to be seen by other road users and then only at the last moment.

On the 4th April, Constable Sebire was cycling down the Lower Rohais approaching the junction with Castel Hill, on his way to his 11.00pm point at Castel Church, when he collided with another cyclist. Bill Sebire later recalled:-

"I was cycling on my right side of the road near the yellow line and the other cyclist seemed to come down from the Castel Hill at a terrific speed, I did not remember any more.

I felt him rubbing my face, but when I came to he was gone, I do not know whether it was a German or civilian cyclist, it happened so suddenly. Later PCs Langlois, Le Page and Le Tissier, who were on their way home off duty, helped me. They did not see anything of the collision. I sustained a bruised right leg and a slightly sprained right hand. My cycle was badly buckled near the front forks. Later the front lamp from the other cycle involved in the accident was found in the road."

The Constable reported back to the Station and was put on foot patrol in the Town for the rest of his shift.

Sergeant Bull who went to La Moye sub Post Office to investigate a break-in on the 8th April, was told by Mrs Elsie Ferbrache, who lived in the adjoining house:- "Some time during the night I heard a noise of breaking glass, but did not awaken my husband because we are always hearing noises around here."

The sub Post Office which also served as a grocery and general provision store was owned by Harold Robin, who had been deported to Germany. In his absence, Doris Tuck of La Blanche Carriere, Vale, was left in charge.

The premises had been locked up the previous evening by Doris Tuck and the shop door was seen to be open at 7.30am the next morning by a neighbour who lived opposite.

Sergeant Bull established that the premises had been entered by forcing the lock on the front door. The shop was in total disorder, coffee and dried beans strewn on the floor and drawers pulled open and ransacked. Some German coins and Reichmarks had been taken from the till, but the safe had not been touched. Miss Tuck gave the Sergeant a description of what was missing, which included beans, cooking fat, butter, coffee, sugar, soap powder and tablets of soap.

No footprints were visible but a clasp knife with 'SS Pradel' marked on the blade had been left on the counter. A/PC 19 Stewart, who accompanied Sergeant Bull, searched all the empty houses and bracken in the area, without finding any of the missing goods. The incident was recorded in the Occurrence Book and became just another of the many break-ins which were never solved.

At a meeting held at Grange Lodge on the 7th April, between Colonel Knackfuss, Major Kratzer, the Bailiff, Jurat John Leale, J.E.L.Martel and R.H.Johns, the Labour officer, the subject of the availability of labour to work for the German Forces was raised. Jurat Leale told the meeting that at present over two thousand civilians were working directly for the Germans. The Colonel said that the German Forces had to find more labour and looked to the States to help them. He suggested that it might be possible to cut down shop staffs and the number of shops and introduce longer shop hours. He then quoted remarks made by Jurat James Carey in the Royal Court the previous week and which were reported in the Press:-

"When you see all these young fellows hanging about town, the theatres still go on and nobody apparently worrying how we produce our food, I wonder what is to happen."

Jurat Leale, who was clearly embarrassed by the remark, said that he had already written to Jurat Carey asking him to supply the names of the men concerned. Immediately after the meeting he contacted Mr Lamy and requested him to have any men seen 'standing about', questioned as to their employment.

The Police questioned men in the queue waiting to go into the Brunt trial. All stated they were employed by the Germans on night shifts and produced night passes as proof. Similar replies were received when theatre and picture queues were interrogated. The findings were reported to John Leale who passed them on to Colonel Knackfuss.

During March A/PC 42 Walter Le Sauvage resigned, leaving the Force seven officers below its authorised strength. On the 19th April an advertisement appeared in the Press:-

ISLAND POLICE

'Applications are invited for the position of Auxiliary Police Constable from men between 20 and 35 years of age, of good physique, education and appearance. Minimum height 5ft 8inches, in possession of cycle with dynamo. Knowledge of French an asset. Pay 50/- rising 60/- weekly plus allowances. Applicants to give full particulars stating date and place of birth, height and qualifications etc.'

The Controlling Committee at its meeting on the 19th April reviewed their decision, made early in the Occupation, to cut the pay of salaried and waged staff. They were very conscious of the increase in prices in the shops that had taken place since the Occupation and the need to offer an adequate living wage particularly as there was now a shortage of workers.

The Committee resolved that the 'uncut' portion of salaries which had been £100, should be increased to £150, a rise of 19/- a week. The new rates became operative on 15th April.

The post of Commandant of the Special Constabulary had become vacant when Colonel R.W.Randall was deported. The Police Committee decided to recommend to the Bailiff that Captain Cowley, who had been an Inspector of the

Special Constabulary since its inauguration in 1939, be appointed as Acting Commandant. The Bailiff was pleased to agree.

A/PC 28 Bill Boalch was on the High Street beat on the 22nd April, when a lorry driven by a German marine came down the High Street and stopped at the entrance of the Arcade. A Naval officer got out of the passenger side of the cab and instructed the driver to drive into the Arcade. Constable Boalch pointed out to the driver that no traffic was permitted to drive through the Arcade because of the cellars under the pavement. The German officer told the driver to drive on and started to walk down the Arcade. When he realised that the lorry was not following he began shouting and gesticulating at the marine.

The marine told him what the Constable had said, but the officer again ordered him to drive on. Constable Boalch stood in the entrance of the Arcade and tried to stop the lorry but the driver forced him to get out of the way to avoid being knocked down.

On the 24th April A/PC 25 Ernest Le Prevost reported that Cyril Cook, a labourer, of 2 Eloi Cottages, L'Islet, had told him:-

"The next door neighbours insulted my wife this afternoon, I want action taken against them."

His wife, Mrs Mary Cook explained:-

"I was playing with my little daughter in the road at about 4.15pm, when three O.T's. who are billeted on my neighbour, beckoned to me by signs from the upstairs bedroom to come and get some washing. When I went inside the front door, Mr and Mrs John Le Caer, the owners, stopped me and said 'their house was not a knocking shop' I asked them what they thought I was ? Mr Le Caer said, 'I don't know what you are'."

The Constable went to see Mr and Mrs John Le Caer, who said:-

"We saw Mrs Cook from our front window making signs to the O.T.'s upstairs. She came to the front door and was about to go upstairs, so we barred her way and told her that we would not allow that in our house. We have nothing against her, but we will not allow any women to go up to the men's rooms."

One of the O.T's. who could speak French, explained that Mrs Cook did the washing for the three OT's and that she had taken their washing that morning. The Constable, not knowing quite what to do, warned all parties to keep the peace and left.

**PC H.P. Smith.**

On the 24th April 1943 news was received of the death of thirty-nine-year-old ex-Police Constable Herbert Percival Smith in Augsberg prison camp, near Munich, in Germany. Exactly one year previously, he, together with sixteen colleagues, had been found guilty by a German Military Court of plundering military food stores and was sentenced to four years' hard labour. His widow Irene, and their three children had been deported to Germany the previous February and were in an internment camp.

At the time it was reported that ex PC Smith had died of a heart attack. Later it was learnt that after being held in a number of prison camps, he and three of his former colleagues, Jack Harper, Charlie Friend and Frank Tuck, were held in the labour camp at Neuoffingen, the headquarters of which was Augsberg prison. The majority of the camp inmates were French political prisoners.

After the war representations were made to the British Red Cross Society regarding the brutal treatment he had received at the hands of the German guards. A report sent to the Red Cross Society, in July 1945, made detailed allegations:-

"The brutal treatment meted out to us and the circumstance surrounding the murder of one of our number, PC 18 Smith, a Welshman by birth, needs investigation. Smith leaves a wife and three children and we are convinced that Mrs Smith is entitled to compensation for his loss.

Smith was tortured and left to die at Augsberg prison in April 1943. The details of Smith's treatment could probably be better told verbally. .....and he was deprived of food and clothes when it was terribly cold, beaten with a shovel and pick-axe in the stomach. This 'pick-axe in the stomach' treatment produced some kind of stomach or kidney disorder which confined him to bed. He was at the camp in this condition for some time on restricted food and even this he could not keep down.

He was made to get out of bed and walk to see the doctor with a man each side of him, too weak to walk alone. He was periodically carried from his bed whilst in fever and placed under a cold shower bath. This treatment was to cool down his temperature. He was constantly berated by the Camp Commander. Later he was taken to Augsberg Prison and left to die in a cell and refused treatment by the doctor there. We have a witness, a French aviation man, who was a prisoner with him when he died and in whom Smith confided on his death bed.

We have in our possession, a letter concerning the murder of Smith from the French political prisoner who was with him when he died. He accuses the Commander, the Workmaster and the Doctor of the murder of Smith!"

Further evidence of his treatment came in July 1946, when a letter was received by the Inspector, from a former inmate of Augsberg, Gottfried Fambach. He wrote:-

"On the 6th March 1943, the former Police Constable Herbert Percival Smith was admitted sick, in the prison in Augsberg. He was previously in the prisoners of war camp at Neuoffingen and became ill due to lack of nourishment and ill treatment. He was locked up in solitary confinement in a cell of the prison and received no medical nor other special treatment. He must have suffered terribly, as he died on the 5th April 1943. No one was allowed to help or assist him. A letter which arrived a few days before, from his wife, was not delivered to him.

In his pocket book there was still a photograph of his family, I think it was a woman and two or three children. I was a political prisoner myself and cleaned his cell. He then requested me to inform you whenever I had the opportunity. On the 3rd June 1945, I was liberated from the Dachau concentration camp by the American troops and have notified the American Military Government on several occasions. However, I have never heard whether your Authorities or the family have been informed. His last greetings were for his dear ones and his fatherland."

A/PC 16 Hall was on patrol in Doyle Road, at 10.25pm on the 26th April when he stopped two foreigners and a local woman whom he knew only as White. When asked for her permit to be out in the streets after curfew, she said, "I do not need one, I am married to this man." The Constable then asked for her identity card. "I have nothing to do with you now, I come under the Feldgendarmerie," she replied.

When asked to accompany the Constable to the Police Station, she refused. The two men with her became abusive and a scuffle ensued. Later they agreed to go with the Constable to the Feldgendarmerie headquarters. On the way they met two German Police who took particulars of the woman's husband who had a permit until 1.00am the following morning. The woman and her husband were then allowed to go home, but she refused to give her name, saying, "I am always being stopped by you people, but you cannot do anything against me." When Constable Hall reported the matter to Sergeant Pugh, he said that the woman and her husband had given the Police trouble on a previous occasion.

In the spring of 1943 the news of Allied successes brought hope to the many Islanders who had kept their wireless sets and to the countless others who by one means or another were kept informed of the good news. Since Montgomery's victory at El Alamein, the news from North Africa had all been good. In Russia the fortunes of war had turned with the German surrender at Stalingrad. Closer to home the waters around the Channel Islands were proving more and more dangerous for German shipping. The R.A.F. mounted regular attacks on sea traffic, with considerable success.

The Germans too, were becoming progressively more concerned and reacted by publishing a Notice in the Press on the 30th April announcing a cut in rations.

"Notice.

On the Channel Islands, as well as in all the territories occupied by German troops, the German Army has secured the current supply of foodstuffs and all necessities of life for the civil population. The British Military Command, however, disregarding the fact that the population of the Channel Islands are their own countrymen are attempting in every way to jeopardise the continuous supply to the Islands by incessant nuisance raids.

If in consequence of these raids the rations of the Island population have now to be decreased, the population can thank for this their countrymen on the other side of the channel. Churchill and his supporters will not achieve any military success from such nuisance. But it characterises their notorious lack of scruples that they do not refrain from exposing their own fellow-countrymen to sufferings that could be avoided.

The population of the islands, however may at least know the culprits..

DER OBERBEFEHLSHABER DER ARMEE."

The same day Colonel Knackfuss wrote to the Bailiff:-

"Reduction of food rations for the English civilian population of the Channel Islands on account of the disturbance of shipping by enemy attacks.

The Commander in Chief of the Army, has after the attacks directed against supply ships, ordered a reduction of the food rations for the English civilian population.

By superior orders, the following reductions are immediately to be effected in the rations of the English population of the Channel Islands:-

1. The bread ration for all English subjects from 21 years of age and over is reduced to 175 grams per day.
2. The meat ration for all English subjects from 21 onwards is reduced to 60 grams a week.
3. The fat ration for all English subjects from 21 onwards is reduced to 150 grams a month.
4. The cheese ration for all English subjects from 21 onwards is reduced to 150 grams a month.

The extra rations (for instance for heavy workers) remain as before.

Following groups of persons are exempted from the reductions:-
1. All non English subjects including Irish.
2. All expectant and nursing mothers.
3. All sick persons, if and as soon as a medical certificate has been approved by the Feldkommandantur.
4. All invalids in hospitals.
5. All employees and workmen employed direct by German Departments as well as those employed for the Germans under Billeting Service on the part of the States, in both cases including the members of their families belonging to their household."

The Controlling Committee reacted to the news with consternation and alarm. They viewed the cuts to the rations of Islanders as a punishment and a reprisal. Sir Abraham Laine said that it should be pointed out to the German Authorities that the Controlling Committee might be obliged to resign if they were forced to carry out the order.

As a result of representations made, Colonel Knackfuss again wrote to the Bailiff on the 3rd May:-

"In amendment to my letter of the 30th April, the bread rations for the civilian population are fixed as follows, until further notice:

1. Heavy workers male over 21.
Previously 2718 grams = 6lb.
Now 2175 grams = 4lb 12oz
2. Heavy workers, female over 21.
Previously 2377 grams = 5lb 4oz.
Now 1930 grams - 4lb 3oz.
3. Normal consumers over 21.
Previously 2036 grams = 4lb 8oz
Now 1630 grams = roughly 3lb 10oz.

The cheese ration is to be fixed at 150 grams monthly. The other food rations as in the previous allotment."

The Bailiff quickly replied saying that:-

"As there appears to be no economic reason for the immediate putting into force of your Order, we must assume that it is in the nature of a reprisal. It is my bounden duty therefore to ask that your Order should be withdrawn as being contrary to International Law."

On the 7th May the Bailiff again wrote to Colonel Knackfuss, saying that it was his duty to apply immediately to the International Red Cross Organisation for help.

"I am appealing to that Organisation and I request that my letter be forwarded immediately. Further, as I regard it as absolutely essential that personal contact be made with the Red Cross Organisation at this stage, I am ready to send a delegation of responsible Island officials to Geneva if it is found impracticable for the Red Cross to send representatives here. I should be obliged, therefore, if you would ascertain whether the necessary facilities would be granted.

Furthermore, I feel that the time has come when my duty to the inhabitants of Guernsey and Sark compels me to demand an investigation of our position by the Protecting Power, namely Switzerland. I am therefore enclosing an appeal to the Minister of State accredited to your Government in Berlin, which I request you forward to him with the least possible delay.

In view of the immediate and disastrous effects of this Order, I must ask that it be suspended, at all events until we have heard the result of our appeals to the

Swiss Minister and to the Red Cross Organisation. Should this Organisation grant us the help asked for, then there would be no economic reason at all for the enforcement of your Order."

The Bailiff also enclosed a report from Dr A.N.Symons, the Health Services officer, setting out the food situation, purely from a medical point of view. The daily ration allowed by the German Order, he assessed, resulted in only 1,556 calories a day. He quoted the fact that a 12 stone man doing light work requires 3,500 calories a day, therefore, he calculated another 1,900 calories are required.

The letter to the International Red Cross and the appeal to the Swiss Minister, bore no result, if indeed they ever reached their intended destinations. Major Kratzer was on record as saying that he would pass the letters on to his superior, "but could not guarantee that the latter would forward them." The cut in the bread ration was instituted by the Germans on the 7th May and the cuts in other rations were quietly forgotten. However the Germans did not miss an opportunity to emphasise that it was the local population that was being punished, when Dr Kratzer wrote to the President of the Controlling Committee:-

"Re: Meat rations for German Civilians.

The meat rations allotted to German civilians are to be issued even when a general distribution of meat is not possible. The necessary amount is to be drawn from the Island's own meat production."

# Chapter 24

# THE POLICE DON'T STUDY ME, WHY SHOULD I STUDY THEM.

"This is a great day for 'Bob the Bobby' who celebrates the completion of 21 years' unblemished and faithful service to Guernsey, the land of his birth, in the Island Police Force."

So read the the tribute in *The Star,* commemorating twenty one years of Police service by Sergeant R.W.Kimber on the 1st May 1943. The article continued:-

"He has done all that one expects a copper to do - from chasing boys scrumping apples in an orchard to arresting a house-breaker who has hoarded in his home stolen loot and sufficient money to make a Policeman's eyes pop out of his head!

Sergeant Kimber has had a very interesting career and testimony to his fine character cannot be better illustrated than by the fact that he commands the confidence and respect of his superiors and public alike, he has always been extremely popular with both.

Prior to joining the Force on 1st May 1922 he has to his credit the equally fine record of 21 years' service in the Royal Marine Artillery, the last nine of which had been as a full corporal.

**PC R.W. Kimber outside the Royal Hotel in 1922.**

Bob Kimber served in many world famous destroyers, battleships and cruisers, HMS Minotaur, London, Hood, Collingwood, King Edward VII, Commonwealth, Duke of Edinburgh and the largest ship he served with was the battleship Warspite, where he ended his naval career. His 21 years service with the Marines covered the reign of 3 sovereigns, Queen Victoria, King Edward VII and King George V.

By rights, today should be the signal for Copper No 7 to retire from the Force to enjoy his well earned retirement, but Bob the Bobby will not yet assign himself to armchair comfort as he has been persuaded to continue in uniform for the duration of the war."

Sergeant Kimber was the second longest serving member of the Force, only Ted Pill had served longer. His wife and two sons had evacuated to Stockport, but he had received Red Cross messages to say that they were all fit and well. Despite his age, Bob Kimber and his wife were destined for yet another career before they finally retired.

On the 3rd May Acting Inspector Lamy was called to Grange Lodge to see Inspector Hertig, who expressed concern at the amount of pilfering of growing crops taking place. The German Inspector described a system which was operating in Jersey, whereby civilians assisted by patrolling certain areas at night. He suggested that a similar arrangement could operate in Guernsey in order to assist the Police and night passes could be provided for certain suitably approved local men.

Mr Lamy agreed that it was possible and that he would arrange for some of the Special Constables to carry out night patrols. He pointed out that the northern part of the Island was the area where most of the overnight thieving occurred, due in his view to the location of four Organisation Todt camps there. Pilfering was going on in other parts of the Island, but it was not so widespread.

As soon as he left Grange Lodge, he contacted Sergeant F.Mallett, of the Northern Section of the Special Constabulary and arranged with him for 23 Special Constables to carry out night patrols. He also arranged for a number of growers to accompany them, because it seemed to him, only reasonable that they should assist in protecting their own property.

The Acting Inspector wrote to the President of the Police Committee informing him of the discussion he had had with the German Inspector and of the action he had taken. He added:-

"That later in the year when crops mature, Specials will probably have to be employed all over the Island. But as they will only be permitted to patrol in the company of a Police officer, the Force must be kept up to strength. At present we are two below minimum working strength and seven below full working strength. We should be at full strength in order to combat this present epidemic of pilfering. We depend upon the fields and greenhouses for our food and we must safeguard it.

The candidates before the Committee are a very poor bunch and quite frankly, there is not one man I would select. It is useless to put any man in uniform and expect to make him a Policeman. The right type of man either will not apply, or does not exist. There is no doubt that the present conditions available to men in German employ and the recent bread ration reduction, will not help matters. We must have more men now, but I am afraid the Committee will have difficulty in finding suitable candidates."

Despite Mr Lamy's pessimism, three further recruits commenced duty on the 10th May:-

| | |
|---|---|
| A/PC 15 George Alfred Smith, 35, | 2, Route des Coutures, St Martin. |
| A/PC 42 Albert William Hallett, 21, | St Peters Valley, Ruette Braye. |
| A/PC 35 Arthur Thomas Le Page, 25, | Hillside, La Turquie, Vale. |

On Saturday the 15th May, Mr Lamy was in his office, when the telephone rang and an officer from the Feldgendarmerie took delight in informing him that one of his men, A/PC 25 Ernest Le Prevost had been caught the previous evening listening to Winston Churchill on his wireless. Ernest, who lived at Downsview, Marais Lane in the Vale, with his wife and four children, was one of many Islanders who had failed to surrender their wireless sets.

The Feldgendarmerie officer said that the Constable had been placed in prison and would be tried by the Germans. Mr Lamy immediately suspended him and informed the President of the Police Committee. Le Prevost was tried by a German Court on the 25th May and sentenced to 14 months' imprisonment. He was later deported to France to serve his sentence.

Ernest Le Prevost later recalled the circumstances of his arrest:-

"During May 1943 someone wrote and told the Germans I had a wireless and many people used to come and listen in when high personages were speaking. So they waited until 9.0pm Friday 14th May when Winston Churchill was speaking from America. Raymond came running in and said 'Daddy, there are a lot of Germans around the house'. So foolishly I got hold of the radio and went to place it in its hiding place in the bedroom, but a Jerry was there at the window. Another followed me in and said

'Ah ze wireless!'

I said 'Yes, did you come purposely for that?' '

'Yes, where is ze ozzer one?'

'That's bad enough' I responded, 'without having two'

Ten days or so before I had two, but the other one was gone.

'Ve vill see'.

With that he ordered the others to search the house.

My little supper was on the table, for I had just arrived from Police duty. After the search, with no supper, I was taken to H.M.Prison, with the order:-

'I will give you until 9 o'clock tomorrow morning to make a list of all the names of ze people who came to listen to ze wirelesses'.

If only they had known it would have been a big list.

Next morning, at 8.00am I was given ersatz coffee without milk or sugar. I asked the Jerry warder,

'Nix essen ?' (no food)

He replied in traditional German fashion - 'Nix essen !'

Dear me, I thought, they mean to starve me into making that list out.

I decided during the night not make a stout refusal, such as,'I will not give you any names', instead I said 'I have no names to give you'. To my surprise at dinner time, they brought me some macaroni soup, my it went down well. After several days of questioning, I was made to sign my name on some typewritten sheets, without the contents being translated to me.

I was tried by the German 'People's Court', in our Police Court and sentenced to fourteen months' imprisonment in France. We left Guernsey a few nights later, eight foreign workers and I. These included five French, two Algerians and a Russian. So commenced my holidays, Nazi fashion."

As a result of his arrest and deportation, Ernest's wife and family were almost destitute so on quite a number of occasions, his former colleagues had a whip round to help his wife and four children.

Mr Lamy was concerned at the situation that might arise in the event of an Allied invasion of the Island or the much talked of second front taking place on the adjoining French coast. He foresaw the likelihood of having to bring all the Force to the Station and accommodating them there for a period of time.

He wrote to John Loveridge, the Secretary of the Essential Commodities Committee, enquiring whether the Committee could make available 'Iron Rations' for emergency feeding.

John Loveridge replied on the 18th May:-

"It has been decided, after consideration, in the light of available supplies of long keeping foods to provide you with the following for 42 men as emergency supplies:-

| | |
|---|---|
| 112 tins liver paste (Weight approximately 3 ozs each) | 21 lb. |
| 21 tins tunny fish (Weight approximately 1 lb each) | 21 lb. |
| 42 tins beans (Weight approximately 2 lb each) | 84 lb. |
| 126 pkts. rusks (Weight approximately 1 lb each) | 126 lb. |
| 2 tins jam (Weight approximately 11 lb each) | 22 lb. |
| 2 boxes x 100 saccharine tablets | |
| 7 pints of cooking oil. | |

In addition, in order that the members of the Force may make a beverage, a stock of carrot tea can be purchased by you from any grocer. The supplies from this department will be released to you on application to our stores at Messrs Young and Company's premises, Esplanade.

It is, of course well understood that these food supplies will be kept under lock and key under your supervision at the Police Station and will only be drawn in case of definite emergency and then only to the extent actually required. I am also enclosing herewith a permit authorising you to purchase one dozen candles to be used in the event of the electricity supply failing."

A/PC 37 Leonard Tucker was on patrol in St Andrew on the 18th May, when he was approached by Mrs W.Moullin, of Newlands Cottage, Monnaie. She told the Constable:-

"There is a long time now that I have been having trouble with my husband, he is always insulting me and my children, I do everything possible for him, cook his meals and he never eats anything. He eats all my bread and the children's, he only allows me one and a half slices of bread for a meal and says I don't go out to work so I don't want anything to eat. He eats the children's rusks and drinks their milk.

The other day he exchanged 1 lb of the children's sugar for a packet of cigarettes. His mother lives next door, she encourages him. She came into my house this morning and started an argument and hit me across the face. I make the dinner out of what is available such as cabbage etc, he calls it rubbish and throws it at me. I have 6 children and with him in the house I can't feed them as he eats all our food."

The Constable listened sympathetically to Mrs Moullin and said he would arrange for her to see the Inspector.

The V.D.Clinic at 33 Hauteville was a regular source of trouble. On the 20th May a call was received from the night nurse, Mrs Whitehead, stating that there had been a disorderly crowd of foreigners outside the premises for about 20 minutes, trying to force their way into the clinic. One of the windows was broken with a stone. A/PC 16 Hall and A/PC 32 Salmon were sent to investigate and reported that they had patrolled the Hauteville area and that all was quiet.

Some time after midnight on the 31st May, Frank Browning of the Bouillon, St Andrew, telephoned the Station saying he had just caught three foreigners stealing potatoes from his field alongside his house.

Sergeant Pugh sent A/PC 21 Le Tissier and A/PC 18 Pill in the Police van. They met Bonamy Brouard of Meadow View who told them that after he had seen three foreigners cross over his property, he caught them lifting Frank Browning's potatoes. He took them to Mr Browning's, who telephoned the Station.

Mr Browning told the Constables:-

"Mr Brouard came to my place at about 12.15am and told me he had caught three foreigners stealing my potatoes and they had 40 lb in their possession and there were quite a lot left on the ground."

The Constables saw where the potatoes had been pulled up. A/PC Frank Pill weighed the potatoes and confirmed that there were 40 lb, he also found 3 empty sacks. Mr Browning complained that he had lost about 4 perches of potatoes in the previous week.

The two Frenchmen and a Belgian were taken to the Station, where all the necessary forms were completed. The foreigners were then taken to the Schute Kommand, Milestone Terrace, Les Banques. After A/PC 21 Le Tissier had informed the officer in charge of the details of the arrests, he was given instructions to take the men to the O.T. prison at Rue Sauvage.

During the summer months, with the fine light evenings, more and more young girls were seen out with German boyfriends, often after curfew. A/PC 26 Parlett was on patrol in Trinity Square when he saw Betty ...... of Park Lane sitting on a bench, in the company of a German sailor, at 11.10pm.

Betty, a sixteen-year-old domestic servant, when asked for her identity card, told the Constable, "I left it home in me handbag." The A/PC escorted her to her home and on arrival, her mother exclaimed:- "Take her to prison, I can't do anything with her." The Constable warned Betty for Court on the 4th June.

Probably the largest fishing boat working out of Guernsey during the Occupation was the 'Sunrise', GU 120, a thirty-foot motor boat, owned by the Quinain brothers. On the 9th June they spent the day fishing in the waters north of Herm. At about 5.30pm when they were north east of Amfrocque rock, approximately 6 or 7 miles from land, the fishing boat was blown to pieces by a mine. Two members of the crew, Archibald Sebire and Herbert Dunn, were drowned. The Quinain brothers, both strong swimmers, were rescued by another fisherman, Dan Domaille, who was fishing a mile away.

When the brothers, Jack and Harry, were later seen by Acting Deputy Inspector Banneville, at their home in Candie Road they told him:-

"We left Guernsey this morning at approximately 9.00am and went to the fishing ground north of Amfrocque. We left the fishing ground at approximately 5.30pm and we were making our way home. We saw a long line of corks which we thought was lost fishing gear, there were about 20 corks, we drew alongside and Harry picked them up with the boat hook.

Just after taking the weight of the line there was a terrible explosion which blew the boat to pieces. We saw nothing of Herbert Dunn, but Archie Sebire came up at the same time as us, Jack swam towards him with a piece of wood, Archie tried to hang on, which he did for some time, but let go. Jack tried to hold him up for some time, but Archie seemed to lose consciousness and disappeared."

Mr Banneville arranged for the relatives of the missing men to be informed. He also notified the Harbourmaster, Captain Franklin, and Captain Obermeyer, the German Harbourmaster.

Sergeant Bob Kimber and PC 9 Reg Marsh went to Wolborough House in the Petit Bouet as a result of a telephone message received at the Station on the 12th June. There they saw Miss Nora Salmon, who told them:-

"I have been keeping company with a German sailor from about 2 years ago until last Christmas, but I have not been with him since. He has followed me around quite a lot. Tonight at 10pm he came to my house and when he saw me in an upstairs window, he shouted for me to go downstairs, but I would not. He then fired his revolver up at my window and said 'that is the first one' then he fired another one at the back door. Before he went away he hit Harold Simon several times with his fist."

The Sergeant notified the Feldgendarmerie who arrived shortly afterwards and took charge. Norma Salmon told the Germans that the sailor's name was Hermann Sommer. The bullet from the second shot was still in the door. PC Marsh found the bullet case and handed it to the Feldgendarmerie. Miss Salmon told the Feldgendarmerie that she did not want any action taken. Although the Germans wanted Harold Simon found immediately, it was not until next day Reg Marsh found him at his home. He told the Constable:-

"Last evening from about 7.00pm I was in the company of a German sailor Hermann Sommer. We had been drinking quite a lot. Just before 10 o'clock he suggested going to Miss Salmon's house and insisted I should accompany him.

On arrival he shouted out for Miss Salmon to come downstairs and when she would not, he fired a shot from his revolver up at the window and then one at the door. I could see that there was going to be some trouble so I made to go away, but he came after me and hit me several times about the face causing me to fall to the ground. He then went away and I went to telephone for the Police."

The statement was handed over to the Feldgendarmerie and as usual no more was heard.

At its meeting of the 15th June, the Police Committee received an application from Mr Lamy for an increase in pay. After careful consideration the Committee agreed that in view of his long hours, great responsibility and good service rendered, that his weekly pay be increased from £6 to £7 a week for so long as he retains his present position.

On the 6th July the Controlling Committee considered the recommendation. The President said that he thought that the increase should be by way of a bonus, but the States Supervisor pointed out that Acting Inspector Langmead had received a salary of £7 weekly and it was thought that the present occupant of the office should receive a similar salary.

The increase was approved.

On the 21st June A/PC 11 Vanden Bergh was sent by the Station Sergeant to Mon Plaisir to report to Sergeant Major Oeser. The Sergeant Major told the Constable:-

"I am handing over this eighteen-year-old man, Patrick Burns, to you for having been found hiding a sack containing potatoes stolen from Mon Plaisir Estate, St Peter Port. This is a civilian case."

The sack containing 16 lb of potatoes, valued 4/8d. Later that day the Constable saw Mrs Burns, she told him:-

"I am very sorry that my son Patrick has got himself into trouble like this, he has never caused me anxiety before. He has always done his best to help me, I have always told him never to take that which does not belong to him. I do not know what possessed him to do this offence and cause this trouble."

As the stolen potatoes were the property of the Magistrate, Jurat Quertier Le Pelley, the Acting Inspector decided that it would be appropriate for him to see and admonish Patrick Burns.

At 2.45am A/PC 42 Bert Hallett was taken by a Feldgendarmerie officer, to 39 States Houses, Old Mill and instructed to take the particulars of those present at an all-night party. The party, which the Germans claimed was an illegal dance, was being held at the home of Mrs Emiline Le Cras. The Constable took the names, addresses, date of birth and identity card numbers of the fourteen persons present and later a copy was sent to the Feldgendarmerie office.

During the Occupation, the curfew restricted normal social activities, so people held all night parties in their homes. Friends would arrive about 10 minutes before the curfew hour, bringing with them some item of food or drink and the festivities would often continue until the morning. One member of the Controlling Committee, Raymond Falla, who was responsible for Agriculture, was a frequent party goer.

His wife and family had been evacuated, so rather than be lonely, he moved in with a friend, W.G.Hubert, who lived at 'Sefton', Doyle Road. Raymond had a reputation for enjoying a good party and was popular with the ladies. He recalled, years later, that some of the best overnight parties were held at the Emergency Hospital where the nurses were great fun. When the party was over the visitors would bed down for the rest of the night in one of the wards.

There was one occasion when he attempted to return home after the curfew hour, only to be caught in Doyle Road by a German patrol. The Germans seeking to achieve the maximum embarrassment, passed the matter over to the Guernsey Authorities. In due course forty-year-old R.O.Falla was convicted by the Magistrate and fined £1. Years later he admitted to being unmercifully ragged by colleagues and friends, about being the only member of the Controlling Committee to be convicted during the Occupation.

A/PC 38 Robilliard and A/PC 19 Stewart were on patrol in Les Amballes, at 11.30pm on 29th June 1943 when they they met two girls with German soldiers. They were asked for their identity cards but refused to produce them, saying that they were German O.T,'s. The Constables knew that they were both local and followed them to Cordier Hill where one of the girls admitted that she was Joan Richings, a cinema usherette, of Cordier Hill, and produced her identity card. The other girl identified herself as Ethel Gardner, a houseworker, of Park Lane.

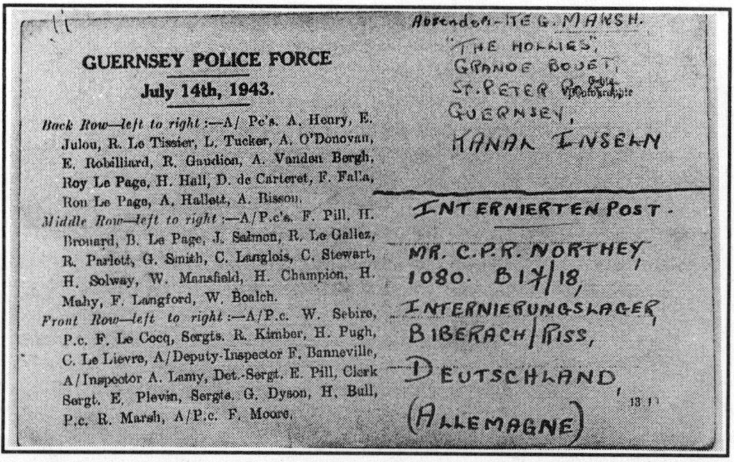

GUERNSEY POLICE FORCE

July 14th, 1943.

*Back Row—left to right* :—A/ Pc's. A. Henry, E. Julou, R. Le Tissier, L. Tucker, A. O'Donovan, E. Robilliard, R. Gaudion, A. Vanden Bergh, Roy Le Page, H. Hall, D. de Carteret, F. Falla, Ron Le Page, A. Hallett, A. Bisson.

*Middle Row—left to right* :—A/P.c's. F. Pill, H. Brouard, B. Le Page, J. Salmon, R. Le Gallez, R. Parlott, G. Smith, C. Langlois, C. Stewart, H. Solway, W. Mansfield, H. Champion, H. Mahy, F. Langford, W. Boalch.

*Front Row—left to right* :—A/P.c. W. Sebire, P.c. F. Le Cocq, Sergts. R. Kimber, H. Pugh, C. Le Lievre, A/Deputy-Inspector F. Banneville, A/Inspector A. Lamy, Det.-Sergt. E. Pill, Clerk Sergt. E. Plevin, Sergts. G. Dyson, H. Bull, P.c. R. Marsh, A/P.c. F. Moore.

Absender:- REG. MARSH.
"THE HOLLIES",
GRANDE BOUET,
ST. PETER PORT,
GUERNSEY,
KANAL INSELN

INTERNIERTEN POST.

MR. C.P.R. NORTHEY,
1080. B17/18,
INTERNIERUNGSLAGER,
BIBERACH/RISS,
DEUTSCHLAND,
(ALLEMAGNE)

**Postcard of the 1943 Police Force sent by PC R. Marsh to former A/PC C.P.R. Northey at Biberach Deportation camp in Germany.**

Constable Robilliard warned both girls for Court the next day. When they failed to appear the Magistrate ordered that they be brought to Court. Jurat Le Pelley then fined them 2/6 each for not appearing in Court when instructed to do so.

Steve Piquet ran a second-hand shop in Fountain Street, which the Police viewed as a cover for his black market activities. At 2.45pm on the 10th July, A/PC 36 Solway visited the shop and found Cornelis van der Watering, attempting to sell Steve Picquet a quantity of valuable jewellery. The Constable took possession of the jewellery and brought Watering to the Station.

Mr Lamy interviewed the thirty-seven-year-old dutchman, who was the engineer on motor vessel 'Corona'.

"I questioned Watering and he identified items of jewellery which he stated he had purchased in Jersey from a second hand shop at 51 Bath Street, St Helier. Other articles he said he purchased from a Jersey man in Tom Jones' Weighbridge Cafe, St Helier.

Watering claimed that he had paid 4,970 reichmarks for these articles. I asked Mr Percy Kimber, jeweller, of Pollet Street, to come to my office and he valued the collection at £325.

Later that day I went to the office of the Feldkommandantur, Grange Lodge and sent the details of the jewellery to Centenier Laurie of the Jersey Police with a request that enquiries be made in that Island to ascertain if any of the articles had been reported missing. I also requested a speedy reply as the M.V.Corona was due to leave port the next evening."

As I had not received a reply from the Police in Jersey and the M.V. Corona was sailing at 9.30pm on the 11th July for St Malo, at 7.45pm I handed all the jewellery and other items back to Cornelis van der Watering.

At 8.00pm the following day I received a message from Grange Lodge to say that enquiries had been made in Jersey and the jewellery had not been stolen".

A/PC 11 Vanden Bergh reported that on the 22nd July he saw Mrs Lilian Champion, the wife of Constable Champion, at the Fish Market. She said:-

"My daughter Hilda Champion was bitten by a dog belonging to Steve Piquet, of 3 Allez Street. The wound has opened again and is badly discharging matter. This is the fourth child that has been bitten by the same dog."

The Constable explained to Sergeant Pugh that the reason for Mrs Champion reporting the matter was because the stitches had been taken out of her daughter's leg and the wound had reopened. Mrs Champion had settled the doctor's fee for attending to the dog bite and wanted to know how she stood regarding paying the second bill. Sergeant Pugh entered the report in the Occurrence Book. In the margin - in thick blue pencil, Mr Lamy wrote, "PS Pugh, why enter this civil matter?"

Sergeant Dyson was on duty in the Station at 11.00pm on the 25th July when he received a telephone call from William Blake, of Bukit Estate, Coutanchez, reporting that there was trouble with a German officer.

The Sergeant immediately set off in the Police van and collected Sergeant Major Oeser from Mon Plaisir on the way. When they arrived at the Estate they saw a German officer together with Mr William Roberts and Mr Frank Cooper, who said:-

"I do not know what exactly has happened, but I heard a commotion outside my house, I went out to see, it was about 10.45pm and outside I saw a German officer feeling the tyres of his bicycle. Then I found out that he had been trying to molest Miss Lambert.

In German, I understood him to say 'he did not know his way to Town', I offered to show him the way, then he wanted to throw a brick through Miss

Lambert's window, but I managed to discourage him. I understood him to say, 'the madame is an enemy of mine'. Eventually, with the help of Mr Roberts, who had just returned home, we encouraged him to go away."

Miss Helen Lambert, aged 37, of Dunedin, Bukit Estate, Coutanchez, told the Constable:-

"It was between 10.30 and 10.45pm, I had just returned from gathering rabbit's food. After I had put my cycle away, I went inside and was kneeling by the fireplace placing a few sticks on the fire to boil a drop of tea for me and my mother, who is old and an invalid, when I heard someone come inside the kitchen. I took no notice as I thought it was someone I knew, when suddenly I felt arms around my neck. I got up and turning around I saw it was a German officer. He caught hold of me and kissed me. Before I could stop him, he tried to throw me on the floor.

He put his hands up my clothes and eventually I broke free. He chased me around the table and then I ran outside. He threw a chair at me and I ran out of the passage. He was chattering all the time in German. He followed me outside and chased me around the house, so I had to find shelter in the fields. I do not know this man at all, I have never seen him before. We are only two women in the house, my mother and myself, he has frightened my mother very much."

Sergeant Major Oeser attempted to detain the German officer, who had obviously been drinking, but as he did not seem to be able to deal with him on his own, Sergeant Dyson telephoned Mon Plaisir and asked for help to be sent.

While at the Bukit Estate, the Sergeant Major handed over to Sergeant Dyson, an Algerian O.T.worker, Mahamed Merouani, who was found in the street after leaving a neighbouring house. "Take him back with you", he said, "and put him in your prison, he was in the streets after curfew. Ask him what he was doing in the woman's house and send us a report in the morning. Let him go in the morning."

Merouani told the Sergeant:- "I know her and the children well, the children were crying in the street, so I took them home to their mother, as I came away I was stopped." Merouani was held overnight in the prison and released in the morning.

The mounting wave of thefts from farms and fields during the hours of darkness was causing concern not only to the Police but also to both the Island and German Authorities. One of the measures being taken with the approval of the Germans, was overnight observation, often by two Auxiliary policemen and a farmer.

A/PC 19 Stewart and A/PC 27 Champion were keeping observation at Bill Mauger's farm at Les Osmonds, St Sampson, where seven cows were tethered in a field near the cycling grounds. Bill Mauger's two sons, Herbert and William, also took turns at keeping watch. Just after 3.00am on the 1st August, two men were seen entering the field and they commenced to milk the cows.

Leaving A/PC Bert Champion and William Mauger at the observation point, Charlie Stewart and Herbert Mauger quietly made their way to within a few yards of the men milking the cows. By this time Bert Champion was closing in on them from the opposite direction. They must have heard something or someone, because they started to make off down the field. The Policemen and the Mauger brothers gave chase and finally caught the men when they fell headlong into a four-foot-deep ditch.

Constable Stewart went into the ditch to arrest them and a fierce struggle ensued, both men resisting vigorously. Eventually one man was detained but the other proved impossible to hold. A/PC Stewart lost his torch in the ditch and as it was a dark night, it was impossible to see who the men were. Herbert Mauger suggested they might be Russians from the nearby flak battery. The man detained was bare footed, had no identity disc as normally worn by German soldiers and would not speak.

The Constables took him to a bungalow near by where a German officer from the flak battery lived. He detailed a guard to take the Constables and the Mauger brothers to the guard room at La Marette, St Sampson. The under officer in charge told them that the man was a soldier from the Capelles area and ordered the Constables to be at the guard room at 10.00am the next day, when they would be supplied with the particulars of the soldier.

The milk in two buckets had all been spilt in the ditch. The buckets, a pair of rubber beach shoes and a forage cap were found afterwards and taken to the Police Station.

Duly at 10.00am the next day Constables Stewart and Champion called at the guard room and were taken to the command post of the Flak Battery. There an officer telephoned the unit to which the soldier belonged and spoke to a Lieutenant who would not divulge the soldier's name or his number. He did, however, say that there were four soldiers involved in the incident and that he would only give the information to the Feldgendarmerie. As the Constables realised that the information was not going to be forthcoming and that the men were being protected, they left and nothing further was heard from the German Authorities.

At the meeting of the Police Committee on the 3rd August a further Auxiliary Policeman was appointed.

**A/PC W.G.O'Toole.**

A/PC 25 William George O'Toole, 22. The Haven, Route Isabelle.

The new Constable, whose nickname was 'Shush', was issued with a uniform, which included a tunic that was too long for him. He took it to a friend of his to make the necessary alterations for him. The lady measured the tunic on him and decided what amount needed to be cut off the length. She carefully measured the amount to be cut off and proceeded to cut one side at a time. When she had completed the second cut it was realised that she had cut one side twice and the other not at all. 'Shush' O'Toole had one of the shortest tunics in the Force !

The Acting Inspector was approached by a deputation of Sergeants who complained that there was not enough differential in the money being paid to Auxiliary Police Constables and themselves.

Mr Lamy promised the deputation that he would raise the matter with the Police Committee. He explained to the Committee that as a result of an increased cycle allowance the money the Constables actually received was in fact, on occasions, more than some Sergeants. He added that he had heard that some of the men were actually boasting that they were taking home more money and this, in his view, was bad for discipline. He concluded by saying that "I am in sympathy with the Sergeants, but under present conditions I cannot see how things can be altered."

The Committee fully discussed the matter and felt that some of the points raised were correct and there was not sufficient difference between the Sergeants' and Auxiliary Constables pay. Also it was felt that PCs Le Cocq and Marsh, who were the only remaining pre war Constables, were receiving less per week than many of the Auxiliaries.

The Committee decided to recommend to the Controlling Committee that an increase in the form of a War Bonus should be granted. Acting Deputy Inspector £1 a week, Sergeants 10/- a week and PCs Le Cocq and Marsh 5/- a week.

The Board of Administration considered the matter and suggested that the Acting Deputy Inspector should receive an increase of 10/- a week while the Sergeants, and the two Constables should receive 5/- per week.

On the 20th August the Controlling Committee discussed the conflicting recommendations. On Mr Martel's suggestion it was decided that the President of the Police Committee should be asked whether it would be practicable to pay cycle allowances once a month and entirely separately from wages.

The Police Committee reconsidered the whole matter of a review of wages and changed their recommendation, so that the Acting Deputy Inspector would be granted an increase of 10/- a week, Sergeant Plevin and the PCs Le Cocq and Marsh, an increase of 2/6 and that all the Acting Sergeants pay be advanced by one increment, of 2/6.

The matter was not considered again by the Controlling Committee until their meeting on the 5th November, when it was finally agreed to approve the latest recommendations by the Police Committee.

A/PC 42 Hallett, who was due on duty at 6.00am on the 5th August, failed to report. A/PC 27 Champion was sent to his home in St Peter's Valley, to find out what was wrong. Hallett told Constable Champion:-

"I am not coming on duty and am going to see about a job today. The Police don't study me, why should I study them. I will see the Inspector later."

Sergeant Kimber wrote a report in the Occurrence Book and in the margin, in red pencil, with the Acting Inspector's initials was "A/PC to see me at 12 noon, 5/8/43."

Mr Lamy saw Hallett and as he could give no satisfactory explanation, dismissed him forthwith and ordered him to return his clothing and equipment by 10.00am on the 6th August.

On the 13th August the Acting Attorney General, Mr Martel, received a letter from the Tribunal of Feldkommandantur 515 stating that former PC 19 Archibald Tardif, who had been sentenced to eighteen months imprisonment for theft of German stores, had had his sentence suspended on the 28th July 1943. After his release, he had been transferred to an internment camp at Le Grande Caserne, St Denis, France.

There had been comparatively few escapes from the Island since the Occupation. Officially and unofficially the Guernsey Authorities had frowned on any attempts to leave the Island. A.J.Sherwill, in September 1940, had publicly stated that "to attempt to get away is a crime against the local population". That was still the official view, largely because any departures or attempts could only result in further restrictions.

On Saturday the 14th August a party of seven Islanders, including A.J.Bougourd and J.T.D.Hubert, managed to slip away from Bordeaux Harbour in an eighteen-foot dinghy and reach England 14 hours later. Some of the escapees had mingled with the bathers and sunbathers at Bordeaux and so managed to leave unobserved by German guards.

As a result Colonel Knackfuss decreed that there would be:-

1. Cessation of fishing for the time being.

2. Prohibition of beaches to all civilians except those civilians holding permits for the collection of seaweed.

The ban on fishing lasted until the second week in September and when it was lifted, new permits were only issued to those whom the Germans described as 'reliable professional fishermen without relatives in England'.

The escapers had left at the height of the mackerel and longnose season. Every boat at that time was catching 200 to 300 mackerel a day. As a result of the new restrictions, the supply of fish was reduced by more than half, just when the food was needed.

# Chapter 25

# THE NUMBERS OF ROBBERIES GREW TO EPIDEMIC PROPORTIONS

Civilians were not the only Islanders who enjoyed the 'all-night-parties'. On occasions members of the Police Force were also to be found enjoying themselves. One such party was held at a house in the Baissieres on the 28th August, when six Auxiliary Policemen, who should have been on patrol, were caught joining in the festivities.

All six, A/PCs Champion, Tucker, Parlett, Boalch, Mansfield and Mahy, were immediately suspended by Mr Lamy and charged with:-

1. Disobedience of orders.
2. Neglect of duty.

They all appeared before a special meeting of the Police Committee at the Police office on the 1st September and were found guilty. A/PC.31 Mansfield was fined 15/-. A/PCs Champion, Tucker, Mahy, Boalch and Parlett were all fined 10/-. Reg Parlett offered to resign and this was accepted.

A member of the Force later commented:-"Parlett, who tried to be big, as usual, offered to resign and this was gladly accepted as I think they were waiting for an excuse to get rid of him."

The Constable remained suspended until the 5th September when his resignation became effective. The remaining Constables return to duty immediately.

At about 3.30am on the 28th August, Mrs Foster, of Mont Morin, St Sampson, heard a hissing sound in their bedroom. She woke her husband Eddie, who also heard the noise. It came from a glass object on their bed which he tried to throw out the open window, but before he could do so, it exploded. Mrs Foster called a neighbour, who telephoned the Police Station.

The German Police, who regularly patrolled the area, arrived within a few minutes and they quickly established that the explosion had been caused by a tear gas bomb that had been thrown through their bedroom window. Constables George Smith and Basil Le Page were sent to the house and by the time they arrived Eddie Foster's eyes were completely closed. An ambulance took him to the Emergency Hospital where he was attended by Dr Collings.

The Constables searched the bedroom and found a fuse and pieces of glass, some of which Mrs Foster put in a matchbox and kept for many years. The German barrier gate was about ten feet from the Foster's house and a guard must have been there when the tear gas bomb was thrown through the open window, but no one ever discovered who was responsible.

Mr Lamy reported the incident to the Feldgendarmerie and was told that another tear gas bomb had been thrown through a window at The Laurels, an O.T. house in Bulwer Avenue.

The next day Mrs Foster and her mother set off to cycle to the Emergency Hospital to see Eddie but on the way Mrs Foster's sight gradually failed. She thought that a mist or fog had descended, when in fact it was a bright summers day. She too became a patient in the hospital but fortunately both she and her husband recovered their sight within a few days.

A cycle was stolen from outside the Britannia Arms in Trinity Square on the 19th July 1943. Early in September Frank William Langford was seen riding the cycle. Sergeant Pill interviewed eighteen-year-old Langford at his home at 73 Mount Durand, where he found two cycles, one of which was the stolen one. Frank's father was A/PC.35 Langford, who at the time was in the Emergency Hospital.

The Acting Inspector and Sergeant Pill visited the Constable in hospital and he admitted taking the cycle. Mr Lamy immediately suspended him. When charged with stealing the cycle, the property of Stanley Le Lievre, valued at £7-10-0, Langford pleaded guilty. He was dismissed from the Force on the 3rd October 1943.

At his Royal Court trial on the 20th November, Frank Langford was represented by Advocate W H Langlois. Langford, said he had taken the cycle from Bullion Lane because there was no number on it and his own cycle had no light.

Acting Inspector Lamy told the Court that:- "Langford's record as a Policeman has been satisfactory, with one minor disciplinary offence." Advocate Langlois pleaded that Langford had borne an exemplary character, his good name and character had gone and this was a greater punishment than the Court could give him. The Bailiff, in passing a sentence of six months hard labour, stressed the fact that the man had been a guardian of the peace and in his view, was not fit to be in the force.

The Commer van, No 1947, that was requisitioned by the Bailiff for Police use in August 1942, never proved entirely satisfactory. The engine was suspect and required constant attention and repair, it was heavy on petrol and the tyres were worn. New tyres were not available and consequently the van was often out of commission because of punctures. It was owned by F.C.Ware of the Meat Market and when requisitioned, had been valued at £136. It was returned to its owner on the 22nd August 1943 and was valued at £75. The owner was paid the difference and shortly afterwards it was purchased by the Germans for £70.

Mr Lamy wrote to the President of the Police Committee:-

"I have been able to secure, on requisition, motor van No 1695. This van is almost new, having only completed 13,000 miles, tyres as new and painted plain blue and similar make and H.P. as 1947."

On the 27th of August a notice appeared on the Station Notice Board, listing 16 men who were detailed to attend the next series of First Aid lectures. It was pointed out that anyone failing the examination would be required to sit again at his own expense. The notice also identified three men, Constables's Brouard, Solway and Salmon, who were required to attend at their own expense, having failed the previous examination.

With the departure of Ambrose Sherwill to Germany, J.E.L Martel had again taken over the duties of Acting Attorney General. W.H.Langlois was the only Advocate left to represent Islanders who appeared before the Courts. When, for any reason, Mr Martel was unavailable, then Advocate Langlois had to perform the duties of Attorney General in his place.

As Mr Martel planned to take a few days' holiday, it was necessary to make other arrangement. On the 28th August the Royal Court passed an Ordinance permitting two Ecrivains, A.Guilbert and J.W.Ozanne, the like powers possessed by the Advocates to appear before the Police and Petty Debts Courts.

The Police Committee at their meeting on the 13th September 1943 received a report from the Acting Inspector regarding the adoption of 'An Island Police Discipline Code'. Up to that time, no written 'Code' had been applied. Previous Inspectors had been guided by the custom and practice of English Forces, particularly the Metropolitan Constabulary. Following considerable discussion and after a number of alterations had been made, the 'Code of Discipline'* was adopted.

The Committee wished the 'Code of Discipline' be registered as an Ordinance. Mr J.E.L.Martel discussed the matter with the Bailiff who did not consider it was necessary to register the new Code. He did believe however, that an additional clause should be inserted into the Order-in-Council of 1938 governing the powers of the Police Committee, to enable it to levy fines for disciplinary offences. The question that no one asked was whether the fines that had previously been imposed on members of the Force over the years were legal!

On the 16th September 1943 the Feldkommandantur received an anonymous letter.

"As I and others have to pay heavy fines for our carter licence and abide to rules, such as having our books always ready for examination, I think it is time you saw into some of those smaller houses who pay no licence at all and beside break the law by selling rationed goods.

**Miss Julia Brichta, later Mrs Barry.**

Mrs Barry, (Julia Brichta), a Hungarian Jew, just married for a business affair to escape your jurisdiction on Jews, carries on a very large bartering trade at her house in Mill Street over Le Bruns the hairdresser. She sells butter, sugar, white flour, honey, ham, eggs and sausages. Butter 30 rm. sugar 50 rm a pound. Mr Deene was found out but she is as bad or worse - has a lot of her things hidden in her rooms.

Another one we all know is Miss E.M.Gosselin, 46 Victoria Road. She, beside bartering in a very large way, canvasses house to house for it. She was heard in a market queue asking a person if she would like some pork and call at her place to get some at 45rm a pound.

I have told the States about her before but nothing is done, just allowed to carry on whilst we have to pay and obey the law. She is selling tea at £5 a quarter pound - flour, sugar, butter, cigarettes, tobacco - gets eggs, milk first and everything we are not allowed to have. I have bought tea at £5 a quarter myself from her. I went to see if all reports were true in what she had.

We cannot do all this in our shops and have to pay rents and taxes, but they can hide all in private houses and live on all the fat of the land while we hardly live sometimes and get customers who won't come to our shops but go to these houses where they are not seen and pay high prices for things, we cannot because we must put prices in the windows.

Yours truly sir, Fair play for all."

*An Island Police Discipline Code, see Appendix 4.

The Germans also received an undated post card regarding Mrs Barry:-

"We advise you to keep a watch on the Black Market activities of Mrs Barry nee Julia Brichta, of 35 Mansell Street, above ladies' hairdresser"

There is no record of what action the Germans took in respect to Mrs Barry, but another anonymous letter they received on the 1st October clearly indicates that they did take the letter seriously.

'Ville au Roi 30.9.43

Sir, Thank you for having acted about Mrs Barry and her Black Marketing and Barter, but she is now bragging she has caught you out. Your men could find nothing - but she gave the Gendarme smokes and other things for himself. Let your men at least do their duty and punish her as well as others - as she really deserves it if ever anybody does. Look under her floor boards and in her piano and you will find sugar - cheese - soap - bacon - German bread - butter which she sells 25 rm a pound.

When she married Barry she paid him £100 for his name and had only a few shilling left. Now she has over £500 in the bank and brags about her good business. Now she has sold and exchanged heaps of things to Lucas, fish market, she has told us often - and told us she gets all her things from O.T. and German sailors to barter with. She is truly a bad tongued Jew and a awful cheat'.

What action was taken, if any, was not recorded.

One of the great characters of St Peter Port, both pre-war and during the Occupation was without doubt, Charlie Duncombe. He was an American negro, who was born in Key West, Florida, in 1880. He arrived in Guernsey in 1907, supposedly by jumping off a passing merchant ship and swimming ashore. His wife and children had been evacuated and Charlie, who lived at 36 Pedvin Street, soon became lonely. He quickly developed a friendship with Miss Odette Bourgonniere, who was almost forty years his junior. Odette moved into 36 Pedvin Street and by the summer of 1943 she and Charlie were the parents of two children.

**Charlie Duncombe.**

On the early evening of the 17th of September 1943, Charlie Duncombe called at the Police Station and complained to Sergeant Le Lievre, that Odette had chucked a pair of wooden soled shoes, which he had paid £2 for, on the fire. He added:-

"This afternoon at about 5.00pm she smashed a photograph of my wife and children. Some time ago she also burnt two cushions I bought for her. She also smashed crockery deliberately at different times. .... All that she does, she does to hurt me."

Sergeant Le Lievre was well aware, as was every Police officer, that the Charlie and Odette regularly complained about each other to the Police. Public disputes between the two were a common occurrence. The incident was, as usual, recorded in the Occurrence Book and taken no further. The Sergeant knew that would not be the last he or his colleagues heard from Charlie Duncombe or his lady friend.

Another of Guernsey's characters was Eric John Stephen Piquet - 'Steve Piquet'. Born in Masterton, New Zealand, in 1892, he came to Guernsey in 1902. During the first war he served in the British Army as a Sergeant Physical Training Instructor and his interest in boxing had led him to become a local promoter. He ran a second-hand shop at 6 Fountain Street. When the Germans arrived he lived at Les Sablons, L'Eree. Soon he moved to Victoria Road and then to Allez Street.

**Steve Piquet.**

On Friday the 17th September Steve Piquet appeared in the Police Court on a charge of failing to forward to the Essential Clothing Committee all clothing and footwear coupons received in respect of sales during August 1943. In Court he verbally took on, Mr W D M Lovell, the Controller of Clothing and Footwear.

Steve asked Mr Lovell:- "Did you receive a telephone message from me to the effect that, as my assistant was on holiday, would it be alright to send the return in later? Your reply was, - Yes it would be okay."

Mr Lovell answered "No, I received no phone call."

Steve Piquet erupted, shouting:- "Liar, there that's plain English, it's no use saying anything, give me the sentence and save time."

The Magistrate imposed a fine of £7.10.0 or 6 weeks in prison. Steve Piquet had to be forcibly removed from the Court by Acting Deputy Inspector Banneville, who during the scuffle received a stomach injury.

On the following Monday Steve Piquet again appeared in Court, this time charged with assaulting a Police officer. The case was unique, as Ecrivain Mr A.Guilbert, appeared in Court for the first time, representing the defendant. On behalf of Piquet, he pleaded guilty and told the Magistrate that his client was very repentant. He acknowledged that Piquet's temper was not of the sweetest. The Magistrate commented:- "I see no excuse for the way he attacked the Police officer. I find it a very serious matter. I sentence Piquet to two months hard labour."

On the 21st September the Feldgendarmerie arrested twenty-eight-year-old Arthur Penney at his home in the Ruettes Brayes, for being in possession of a wireless set. At the time of his arrest Penney had in his house a box containing a large amount of English silver coins, also another package containing a large quantity of cash in notes. When Penney was arrested the house was locked up and the keys were held by the Feldgendarmerie.

At 5.00pm the next day, an officer of the Feldgendarmerie went to the Police Station and reported that earlier that afternoon he had accompanied Penney to his house, where it was found that all the cash was missing, together with all his private papers.

Arthur Penney became ill whilst in German custody and was transferred to the Town Hospital for treatment. On the 30th September the keys of the house were handed over to the Acting Inspector by the Feldgendarmerie and on Penney's instructions passed on to Mrs E.Tostevin, of Belle Vue, Vazon.

Mr Lamy later recalled:- "At 4.45pm on the 30th September I visited 1 Ruettes Brayes, accompanied by Mrs Tostevin and from my observations came to the conclusion that the house could only have been entered with a key. Enquiries were made by Sergeant Pill, but without result. Arthur Penney informed me that he had lost, £245 in English and Guernsey £1 and 10/- notes and £300 in silver coins. Also missing was a 7lb chest of Le Riches Afternoon Tea."

Later that evening Arthur Penney was removed to the Emergency Hospital and operated upon, but died four days later.

Early in September the Germans caught Leonard Stephens at St Peter Port harbour carrying vegetables in his van which had only been authorised for the collection of swill. Stephens had previously been caught and warned by the Feldgendarmerie. When questioned by the Germans he admitted that he often carried vegetables to his father's shop. When asked where he obtained the petrol he admitted that two States sewerage cart drivers, E.G.Duquemin and his brother E.W.Duquemin had sold him petrol.

The Germans punished Stephens for the unauthorised use of his motor vehicle and 'requested' the President of the Controlling Committee to withdraw the van from circulation, collect all the registration documents and send them to the Feldkommandantur. The States were required to prosecute Stephens for the illegal drawing of petrol and to report back to Major Kratzer on the action taken.

Mr Lamy interviewed Ernest Duquemin and learnt that the petrol had come from his uncle's garage in the Vale. His uncle had evacuated in 1940. The petrol consumption of the two sewerage carts driven by the Duquemin brothers were checked and found to be satisfactory and Mr Lamy satisfied himself that there was no pilfering of supplies. The only infringement the Acting Inspector could establish, was that no sales tax had been charged when Duquemin sold the two gallons of petrol to Leonard Stephens. Mr Lamy reported to John Leale that Duquemin was being charged with the minor offence.

At the beginning of October a party was held at the 'Home from Home' Restaurant during which the partygoers sang with gusto, 'We are going to hang out the washing on the Seigfried Line'. After they had sung it they thought no more about it. However, when the time came to go home they found their exit barred by incensed and infuriated German sailors. The angry situation was only defused by the appearance of the Feldgendarmerie who required all the partygoers to produce their identity cards.

Eight partygoers who did not have their cards with them were locked up in the prison for the night. All the others had to report at the Geheim Feldpolizei headquarters at Havelet the next morning. They were severely crossexamined about the activities at the party before their identity cards were returned and they were allowed to go.

The Germans took the matter seriously and Major Kratzer wrote to the President of the Controlling Committee ordering that the 'Home from Home' Restaurant be closed daily at 7.00pm. He added that it could no longer be used for private parties.

He also wrote to the Bailiff banning dances in the Island, saying that the unpleasant incident which took place at the restaurant, "leads me to recommend that dancing parties should no longer be permitted. Already in consideration of the heavy toll of blood exacted on both sides by this war, such parties had better not to take place at the moment."

The Bailiff wrote to Mr Lamy:-

"I enclose a copy of a letter which has been received from the Feldkommandantur, ordering the closing of the 'Home from Home' restaurant daily at 7.00pm and that it shall no longer be used for private parties (dances and the like). I shall be obliged if you will instruct the members of the Police to see the instructions of the Feldkommandantur are duly carried out and also to keep a strict vigilance on that restaurant."

A few weeks later the Bailiff wrote to a number of the organizers of dances, but not to the 'Home from Home' restaurant, informing them that:-

"After discussion with the appropriate German Authorities and in view of representations made to me on behalf of the young people of the Island, I am now at liberty to grant permission for the continuation of dancing in the Island.

The German Authorities, however, request me to ask you for a written assurance that no incident objectionable to the occupying forces shall take place at your dances and on receipt from you of this assurance you will receive from me permission to hold dances.

I may add that exception has been taken by German soldiers in the past to dance bands which can be heard at some distance from dance halls, dancing being prohibited in Germany. You should therefore satisfy yourself that bands at dances do not play more loudly than necessary."

Sergeant Le Lievre, the Duty Sergeant, was concerned when A/PC 25 O'Toole failed to report for duty at 2.00pm on the 17th October. Sergeant Dyson, accompanied by PC Le Cocq, went to O'Toole's address and saw the Constable who, in the Sergeant's words, "deliberately refused to come on duty". He was offered the opportunity of taking a day's leave which was due to him to think it over, but he refused. Sergeant Le Lievre reported the matter to the Acting Inspector who warned the Constable as to his future conduct.

Albecq House, Albecq, Castel, was used as a junior school. At about 3.30pm on Monday the 18th of October, while the children were playing in the garden an explosion occurred in some trees. The mistress immediately called the children into school and noticed that two of them, Valerie Le Cheminant, aged 8, and Ernest De Garis, aged 9, were injured. She telephoned the St John Ambulance and notified the Police Station. PC Le Cocq arrived just as the ambulance was leaving with the two injured children. The Constable spoke to several of the children but could not obtain a clear description of what had happened.

Nearby a German demolition party was at work. With the officer in charge of that party, PC Le Cocq searched the district and found that an explosion had occurred in a tree in the school garden.

The top of the tree was blackened by the explosion. The surrounding trees were all filled with shrapnel, under the tree the officer found the fuse from the missile.

When the Constable visited the two children in the Emergency Hospital, Matron Hall said that neither child had been seriously injured. Valerie had a flesh wound on the chest about 3" long which had been stitched and Ernest De Garis had been x-rayed to see if any shrapnel was left in his leg wound.

Nine-year-old Margaret Jehan later told the Constable:- "We were playing in the yard when the explosion occurred in the corner by the gate. Valerie Le Cheminant was playing with us and she started to bleed. A lot of stones seemed to fall around us."

Beryl Le Ray, aged 8, said "It was like a ball of fire in the corner, a lot of smoke came up and dirt fell around us."

At the beginning of November Ossie Brackley, who had been dismissed from the Force in May 1942 on German instructions, enquired if he could rejoin. Mr Lamy consulted Inspector Zachau, who raised no objection and Ossie rejoined the Force on the 8th November 1943.

By this time in the Occupation the only fuel available to civilians was wood. Trees regularly disappeared despite it being an offence to fell them without permission. PC Reg Marsh was informed that two men were sawing down a tree in Le Val des Terres and upon investigation caught them in the act.

Thomas Pinny, of Cornet Street, and William Duport, of Fountain Street, both un-employed were cutting up a tree when PC Marsh approached them. Tom Pinny said, "About 3 or 4 months ago the Germans, who were working on the tunnel, gave me permission to saw up some branches which they had sawn down from trees, I thought I could do the same here."

William Duport claimed that, "I have never been here before at any time sawing trees, this morning is the very first time."

The Constable told them that they would be charged, but later Mr Lamy, being aware that they were unemployed, decided that a caution would be appropriate in their case.

On the night of the 23rd/24th October a naval action took place in the Channel and HMS Charybdis, a light cruiser, was torpedoed and sunk by German E-boats. Three weeks later bodies, which were in a very decomposed condition, were washed up on beaches in Guernsey, Jersey and France.

Early on the morning of the 13th November 1943, John Fallaize looked over the sea wall at Douit du Moulin, St Peter, and saw a body floating in the sea. He telephoned the Police Station and then returned and pulled the body up the beach.

As a result of the telephone call Sergeant Pugh, together with a member of the Feldgendarmerie, went to Douit du Moulin and saw on the beach the body of a man. The body was decomposed and around the waist was a belt with the name, James Maidment. The Sergeant telephoned the St John Ambulance.

The body had just been lifted into the ambulance, when someone told Sergeant Pugh that a second body was lying on the beach about a quarter of a mile away. Both bodies were taken to the Town Hospital mortuary. Papers found on the second body gave the name of Clifford Ernest Roberts, a British Royal Marine.

Over the next three days eighteen bodies were found on the beaches in the Island and one in Sark. All the bodies were very decomposed and the task of removing them from the beaches was a very unpleasant one. Each body had to be searched to establish the identity and an inventory made of the effects found.

A raft belonging to the Charybdis was found by Albert Brewer at Portinfer. Sergeant Kimber informed the German Naval authorities, who took charge of it.

On the 17th of November the nineteen sailors and marines from HMS Charybdis were buried at the Foulon Cemetery. Thousands of Islanders turned out to honour the British servicemen who had given their lives for their country. The crowds packed the sloping banks overlooking the graves. Over seven hundred wreaths, including floral tributes from members of the Police Force and the Special Constabulary, were spread out on the grass.

After the ceremony the Bailiff wrote to the Acting Inspector:-

"I wish to thank you and through you, the members of the Police Force for the admirable arrangements which were made in connection with the burial of the Naval ratings on Wednesday last. Everything possible was done to make that solemn occasion a most fitting one and I appreciate the efficient manner in which you all carried out your duties."

As the Island approached the shortest day of the year, the numbers of robberies grew to epidemic proportions. Members of the public were wary of getting involved due to the fact that the vast majority of the overnight thefts were carried out by Germans and O.T. workers, many of them armed and prepared to use violence.

A director of *The Star*, Mr J.P. Blaikie Webster, of La Colombelle, Ruettes Brayes, who had had his premises raided and lost poultry and vegetables, offered a £10 reward for the arrest and imprisonment of the persons concerned. As a result, *The Star* highlighted the problem. A reporter wrote:-

"During a talk yesterday with Police officials, I regret to say I was given numerous incidences where residents in the neighbourhood of rifled premises have been actually aware as to what was taking place but failed to raise a finger to aid either their neighbours, or the Police or to assist the capture of the culprits.

Unbelievable as it may seem, there are those among us who have actually admitted that they have sat in the safety of their homes and watched the thieves enter nearby premises, listened to the ransacking of neighbours' goods and subsequently seen the burglars depart with their booty and they have not uttered a cry or taken a step to notify the authorities as to what was happening.

It appears that besides the fear of personal violence being offered by the thieves, if interrupted, there is the almost greater terror of the possibility of having to appear in Court and give evidence for the prosecution. To avoid this apparently some people would sit back and watch any crime committed. The only feeling being entertained in their narrow minds, meanwhile, being one of relief, that it is not they themselves who are the sufferers.

It should hardly be necessary in a civilised community to point out the very essential need of co-operation between the Police and the public in order to enable the one to do their duty to the other, yet it would seen that such collaboration is badly lacking in Guernsey today. Householders who take proper precautions in the way of locking up their premises and the contents thereof have little to fear, it is those who are careless about those things who tempt an observant wastrel into or to continue along the path of crime.

Often it may be only one individual or a small gang at the most who made these nocturnal raids, but so long as the perpetrators are at large the whole Island is in a state of apprehension. Therefore, though it must appear to be stressing the obvious to the majority of Islanders, *The Star* endorses the request of the Police for the co-operation of the public in an effort to trap all criminals and ensure security for all. If any suspicion of something wrong is entertained, let an alarm of some sort be raised for the Island's sake as well as your own, that is, after all, your plain duty to your fellow men."

In view of the upsurge in crime, efforts were again made to recruit further Police officers to fill the growing number of vacancies. The problem was that there were not sufficient applications from suitable candidates. In November, the Police sub Committee considered an application from Arthur Stewart, whose brother, A/PC 19 Charles Stewart had been in the Force for eighteen months.

The Committee heard that Arthur Stewart had been convicted of a number of traffic offences. As it was felt that they were of a very minor nature and as there was an urgent need for Policemen, the Committee duly appointed:-

A/PC 26 Arthur George Stewart, 34, 2 Fernbank, Amherst.

After serving for only a few days Constable Stewart informed the Acting Inspector on the 2nd December 1943, that he had been instructed by the Germans, to report to the O.T. prison the next day to serve a sentence of three weeks imprisonment, imposed by a Military court for a traffic offence the previous August. The Acting Inspector immediately suspended the Constable.

The matter was reported to the next meeting of the Police Committee, who were told that the traffic offence had occurred while he was working for the

Germans and which was only dealt with after he had become a member of the Force. The Committee also heard that there was another offence of alleged stealing, which concerned the Dairy where he had worked at one time. The matter had not been taken to Court at the request of the management. In all the circumstances the Police Committee decided not to reinstate Stewart.

In the meantime time A/PC 33 Roy Le Page had resigned on the 21st November and returned to farming and A/PC 25 O'Toole left the Force on being convicted by a Military Court. He was sentenced to 14 days imprisonment for maligning the Germans. A/PC 35 Arthur Thomas Le Page had also left the Force and was replaced by his namesake Edwin James Le Page. The sub Committee, who were now prepared to appoint almost anyone who was prepared to apply, appointed three more Auxiliary Police officers who commenced duty on the 9th December:-

| | |
|---|---|
| A/PC 35 Edwin James Le Page, 29, | Le Groignet, Kings Mills. |
| A/PC 33 Roy Frederick Thoume, 23, | Les Blanches, St Martin. |
| A/PC 26 Edwin Henry Butt, 38, | Woodleigh, Les Croutes. |

# Chapter 26

# FLOUR SWEEPINGS

On Sunday the 12th December a telephone call was received at the Station stating that the Essential Commodities flour store at Vauvert School, had been forcibly entered during the night and a quantity of flour had been stolen. Sergeant Le Lievre and A/PC 19 Stewart went to the store and soon established that three 220 lb sacks were missing.

There was evidence that the thieves had left by climbing a 7 ft wall in the playground, crossing a yard, then climbing a shed, crossing another yard, before reaching Havilland Street. On the ground near the shed and on the roof was evidence that a quantity of macaroni had been taken.

Later that morning the Acting Inspector visited the premises with the Secretary of the Essential Commodities Committee, Mr John Loveridge who told him that no macaroni was stored there. Mr Lamy quickly formed the opinion that it was very unlikely that such a large quantity of flour could have been carried over the route taken by the thieves and he instructed Acting Deputy Inspector Banneville and Sergeant Pill to search the homes of all seventeen men employed at the store.

Five men were found to have small quantities of flour in their homes, mainly sweepings from the holds of boats or from split sacks. Edward de la Mare, of Hillside, Vauvert, had a small quantity of flour in a tin, which he claimed were sweepings. He considered that he had done nothing wrong because Charles Lewis, the Committee's lorry driver, periodically took a bag of flour sweepings to Deputy F.T.Hill-Cottingham, the States Flour Controller, and that a sack was being delivered that morning.

**Deputy F.T. Hill-Cottingham.**

The Acting Deputy Inspector immediately interviewed Charles Lewis. On his lorry, Mr Banneville found two bags of flour, one weighing about 20 lb and the other 70 lb. Mr Lewis said the sacks contained sweepings and he was delivering them to Mr Hill-Cottingham's house in Village de Putron. The Acting Deputy Inspector had both the sacks taken to the Police Station.

Mr Lamy examined the contents of the two sacks. Both contained flour which was free from dirt, but the larger one had a number of pieces of string, with labels and seals attached.

The following Monday morning, Mr Hill-Cottingham called at the Station and told Mr Lamy that he would like to explain about the bags of flour sweepings. He was told that the matter was still the subject of a Police enquiry and Mr Banneville cautioned him. Mr Hill-Cottingham explained that the transaction was quite in order. An instruction had been given to Charles Lewis to deliver sweepings, similar deliveries had taken place in the past. Sweepings, Mr Hill-Cottingham, explained was "the flour which percolated through the sacks or had been contaminated by vermin. This is swept up and sold to paperhangers, book binders and other trades having a use for it."

When Mr Hill-Cottingham examined the contents of the sacks, he considered that the larger one was sweepings but the smaller sack contained pure flour. He told Mr Lamy that he had asked Mr Lewis to deliver a sample, but this would only be about one or two pounds and it should have been delivered to him at the Ladies' College and not at his home. Mr Hill-Cottingham said he used the sweepings as a mash for his poultry.

From statements taken by the Acting Deputy Inspector, it was apparent that at least three deliveries had been made to Mr Hill-Cottingham's home in 1943. An examination was made of the records at the Ladies' College, which revealed only one delivery. Mr Lamy sent samples of the contents of each sack to Mr Allerton, the States Analyst. He also arranged for two bakers, Mr H.H.Plummer, of Allez Street, and Mr Palmer, of Grand Bouet to bake loaves with some of the flour. When baked all appeared to be in good condition.

Mr Lamy attended a meeting of the Controlling Committee on the 20th December when the matter of a prosecution against Mr Hill-Cottingham was considered. He presented his report and when asked his opinion, said:-

"Under the circumstances I cannot see where criminal proceedings could be instituted against Mr Hill-Cottingham concerning the current transaction. He ordered sweepings and would have received what he and the storeman considered sweepings in the large bag. The smaller bag, he states is good flour and that he had given no instructions for it to be delivered. I think the explanation is one of three things, firstly, the driver intended it for himself, secondly, he intended to do Mr Hill-Cottingham a good turn by delivering it to him, or thirdly he misunderstood his instructions concerning the sample flour and was afraid to admit it for fear of incriminating Mr Hill-Cottingham.

Charles Lewis is a very unreliable witness, he is nervous and appears to be hiding something, although I have always know him as a most honest and reliable man. If it is decided to proceed against Mr Hill-Cottingham, I respectfully suggest that he be brought before the Royal Court when the prosecution would be in the hands of the Acting Attorney General."

The Committee, after a long discussion, decided that there was no alternative but to ask the Acting Attorney General to institute proceedings against Mr Hill-Cottingham. It was further decided that the Vice-President, Sir Abraham Laine, should write to Mr Hill-Cottingham asking him to remain away from duty for the time being. Should he decline to absent himself from duty, the Committee decided to use its powers to enforce this. Two days later one of the Committee clerks, Mr Ken Lewis, delivered the letter to Mr Hill-Cottingham at his home in Village de Putron. He did not return to duty.

Due to the illness of Jurat John Leale the meeting of the Controlling Committee on the 3rd January 1944 was held at his home, 'Ormond', St Sampson. It was reported that Mr Hill-Cottingham had suggested that an enquiry into the whole 'matter' be instituted and that he would be prepared to accept the decision reached.

The Acting Attorney General, Mr Martel, gave details of the evidence which he thought would be given to the Court and stated that, in his opinion, a prosecution would fail. Considerable discussion ensued on the choice between a prosecution or an enquiry, but as it was found impossible to decide on a satisfactory independent Chairman of a Commission of Enquiry, it was resolved that there was no alternative but to prosecute Mr Hill-Cottingham. It was also agreed that the States should be informed.

On the 5th January, before the business of the States began, the Bailiff announced that he had received notice of a question from Deputy Ira C.Ozanne, adding that he was somewhat surprised at the nature of the enquiry.

"In view of the rumours circulating throughout the Island respecting flour transactions in which Deputy Hill-Cottingham is reported to be concerned, can the President of the Controlling Committee inform the States what action has been taken."

Jurat Leale replied:- "On receiving a report from the Acting Inspector of Police in regard to the matter referred to, the Controlling Committee requested Deputy Hill-Cottingham to refrain from the discharge of his duties at the Ladies' College for the time being and the request had been complied with." He added that as legal proceedings in the Royal Court had been started, he could say no more, but he was grateful to Deputy Ozanne for the opportunity of making a statement.

The Royal Court trial of Deputy F.T.Hill-Cottingham took place on Saturday 8th January before the Bailiff and eight Jurats. Mr Hill-Cottingham who was a sixty-five-year-old retired engineer with wide experience in the Federated Malay States and had been a States Deputy since 1932, pleaded not guilty. He conducted his own defence to a charge of having endeavoured to obtain from a flour depot of the Essential Commodities Committee situated at Vauvert School, St Peter Port, rationed food for household consumption namely 56 lb or thereabouts of flour.

The Jurats unanimously found him guilty. He was fined £200 or three months' imprisonment.

In his summing up, the Bailiff admonished Mr Hill-Cottingham not only for having misused his official position and committing a grave breach of trust, but also for undermining public confidence.

"There should on no occasion," said the Bailiff, "be cause for suspicion in the public mind. If the accused found the sweepings useful for feeding his fowls, what right had he above any other member of the public to turn them to his own use, without even consulting the Committee to whom he, as official flour controller, was responsible."

As a consequence of his conviction Deputy F.T.Hill-Cottingham resigned as a People's Deputy. He also, through his counsel, Advocate W.H.Langlois, applied to the Royal Court for leave to appeal to the Privy Council against his conviction.

The Court unanimously decided that it was bound by an Order in Council passed on October 9th 1580, that laid down that no appeal could be made against condemnation, in a matter of a quasi-criminal nature. Leave to appeal was accordingly refused.

The only outstanding matter in relation to the 'Flour Sweepings' case was whether other persons concerned would be prosecuted. At a meeting of the Controlling Committee, J.E.L. Martel gave details of the cases and said, that he thought it would be unfair to prosecute these persons as in view of the fact that Mr Hill-Cottingham had been found guilty, the Court would be bound to return a guilty verdict. In view of that advice it was resolved that there should be no prosecutions in the five other cases.

A steady stream of cases of Islanders found in the streets after curfew were taken to Court. At 11.55pm on the 27th November A/PC 36 Solway and A/PC 12 Mahy found Miss Joan ....., aged 23, in the company of a German officer at

Baubigny. When questioned she replied:- "I am with this German officer, you can let me off." When warned for court, she replied:- "I might not be there."

A persistent offender of curfew regulations was Mrs Margery Le Cheminant. She was seen in the company of a German officer in St Clements Road, at 1.00am on the 12th December by Acting Deputy Inspector Banneville. When questioned she replied "I have been to a party". She was warned to attend Court at 10.15am the next day. Mrs Le Cheminant failed to attend and was, on the Court's orders, brought to Court on the 15th December. The Magistrate, said that in view of the fact that it was her third appearance for being out after curfew, he would fine her £2 or fourteen days imprisonment. For failing to attend Court he fined Mrs Le Cheminant 5/- or two days' in prison.

The German censor allowed reports of curfew offences to appear in the press, but any reference to Germans accompanying the offenders was censored.

PC Francois Le Cocq was on his way home late at night about a week before Christmas, when he stopped a young girl who was out after curfew. After cautioning the girl, he let her go owing to her youth. At 12.20am on Christmas day, he again stopped Nora ........, aged 15, of Ville Baudu, who was wheeling her cycle at Les Banques near the Fruit Export sheds. He questioned her as to her whereabouts that evening. She said that she had been to a party at an O.T. house at 18 Rougeval Road, St Peter Port.

PC Le Cocq later recalled:-

"I went to this address and in a bedroom, the door of which was locked, I found Phyllis ......, aged 14, of Pont Allaire. She had appeared to have slipped on a dress and had no shoes on. In bed, dressed in pyjamas, was Goudeseune Willy, a Belgian O.T. worker. Phyllis admitted being on the bed with this man, but denied having been intimate with him. I took both girls back to the Police Station. Acting on instructions from the Inspector they were placed in the Town Hospital."

As a result, Nora ........ was fined £1 or eight days' imprisonment for being out after curfew and her mother was required to pay bail of £2 for the future good conduct of her daughter. Phyllis's mother was also required to pay £2 bail for allowing her daughter to be exposed to dangers, contrary to the provisions of the Law for the Protection of Children and Young Persons.

Due to ill health, fifty-five-year-old A/PC 13 Henry Brouard was discharged from the Force on the 31st December. He quickly obtained employment with Mackay and Co., as a barman at the Caves de Bordeaux.

Ex PC Peter Bretel who had been convicted by the Military Tribunal in April 1942, of stealing wood from the German wood store and sentenced to four weeks' imprisonment, died on the 21st January. Since the trial he had been employed as an attendant in the States Market and still had hopes of being reinstated as a Policeman when the war was over. Mr A.J.Sherwill was on record as having advised the Police Committee "that the offences were not of such a serious character as to preclude his eventual reinstatement in the Police Force."

Forty-seven-year-old Peter Bretel was cycling along the Banques, on his way home from work, when he collapsed in the road. The St John Ambulance took him home but despite medical attention he died shortly afterwards.

At the beginning of 1944 the States made an assessment of the property that had been taken over by the Germans. Mr Lamy was requested to supply various information and in due course it was revelled that the Germans had requisitioned 2,443 dwellings, 42 hotels, 29 garages and 104 other business premises. Over 2000 vergees of farm land and 160 vergees of glass had also been occupied or demolished. 200 houses had been demolished by the German military authorities. Many other properties that had been requisitioned, then released were left in a damaged and dilapidated state.

Sergeant Bull met the States Import Controller, W.G.Hubert, at the New Jetty, White Rock, who told him:-

"We have a ship here unloading granulated sugar. At about 3.30pm on the 28th January, a checker called me saying he had found an aluminium canister in a bag of sugar. The bag had been opened and about half a cwt of sugar missing. The sugar was taken from the lorry as the bag was intact when it left the hold of the ship.

The German harbour Police, who were on duty opposite the ship, saw two men hanging around the lorry as it was being loaded and they said that the lorry driver and his mate should know who stole the sugar as they also saw these two men."

Mr Fredrick Spurdle, a checker, told the Sergeant:-

"The bag containing the sugar was tied when it left the hold of the ship, about 10 minutes later I found it untied on the lorry and I did not see anyone touch the bag."

Captain Franklin, the Harbourmaster, commented:- "I cannot prove it, but I feel sure it was the two Dutchman who took the sugar, I believe they work on the cranes."

Sidney Jegou, the lorry driver, was interviewed and told the Sergeant:- "I was on the lorry when it was being loaded with sugar. Two broken bags came up, I did not touch any of the sugar, I did not see anyone take any, I did not see any Dutchman around the lorry, I have not seen that canister before."

John Carre, a labourer, said, "I was on the lorry with Sidney Jegou, I saw two half bags of sugar and one broken bag, I did not have any nor did I see anyone touch the sugar."

One of the German Harbour Policemen insisted that the two men knew the two men who were believed to have taken the sugar. The Sergeant then went to the Crown Hotel where he saw Captain Obermeyer, the German Harbourmaster, who requested that the canister, which was of foreign manufacture and contained a small amount of sugar, be handed over to him. Captain Obermeyer took the names of the lorry driver and his mate and said that further enquiries would be made by the Feldgendarmerie.

At 10.00pm on the 3rd February Constable Le Cocq was stopped by a civilian, who told him that a German Marine had just smashed a window in the Smith Street Post Office. He added that the Marine was shouting and appeared to be drunk. As the Constable walked up Smith Street, Mrs Mabel Robin, who lived above the Gas Company premises, told him:-

"At about 10.00 pm I was looking out of my window when I saw a Marine coming up Smith Street, I heard him singing and striking each window as he went past, until he got to the Post Office. As he passed it, he punched his fist through the glass. He then carried on up the street."

The Constable reported the incident to the Station Sergeant, then with two other Constables he set off to find the German Marine. They found him outside the O.G.H.Hotel, the German Soldatenheime, obviously drunk and shouting at the top of his voice. He had lost his forage cap and was bleeding from a cut on the hand. The Feldgendarmerie were called and whilst being removed to prison, the Marine broke the glass in the rear window of the Police van. The Feldgendarmerie requested that a report on the cost of the replacing the broken windows, be submitted to them.

As a result of a message received at the Station, Sergeant Pill and A/PC 24 Basil Le Page, went to New Haven, Rue des Francais where they saw Frederick Ogier. The sixty-year-old farmer-grower told them that between 6.30pm on the 2nd of February and 7.30am on the 3rd, a sixteen-year-old cow had been taken from his stable. Mr Ogier showed the officers the stable. Sergeant Pill could not see any droppings and asked the farmer why. He explained that the cow must have been taken early.

They searched the yard and found fresh hoof marks leading to the Rue des Francais. The lane was searched but no droppings could be found. Mr Ogier told the Sergeant:-

"At 7.30am today I went into the stable to milk, when I found the top part of the double doors open, the bolt having been released from outside, but the lower half closed. I then noticed that my cow, aged 16 years was missing, even the rope gone, I heard nothing unusual during the night."

The Sergeant enquired why an old cow should have been taken instead of a heifer and Ogier said:- "I supposed it being the biggest, they took it."

As a result of certain information being obtained by PC Le Cocq, the Acting Deputy Inspector interviewed Frederick Ogier at the Police Station on the 13th February. Mr Banneville later recalled:-

"I told him I was making enquiries about the cow which he had reported stolen. I told him that from information received, the statement which he had made to Sergeant Pill was untrue. I cautioned him and read a statement to him by another person. He said 'I told lies to Sergeant Pill because I was frightened'. I asked him if he wished to make a statement, he said 'Yes, what I am going to say now is the truth'."

Frederick Ogier then explained:-

"During the later part on January 1944 Mr Champion came to my house and asked me if I had an animal for sale. I said I did not want to sell any because I was afraid. I eventually agreed to sell the cow to him. He saw the animal in the stable and paid me £25 in Reichmarks. We decided that I would leave the cow in a field at Carteret, Cobo. I cannot remember the date but one morning I put the cow with another cow and a heifer in a field at Carteret. In the late afternoon I fetched one cow and the heifer and left the other cow in the field. I did not see it taken but was given 5lb of meat. He had not personally informed the Police of the loss of the cow, but asked someone else to do so."

After Frederick Ogier had left the cow in the field, Herbert Champion arrived during the evening in a Civil Transport lorry driven by Rex Ozard, who later explained:-

"At about 9.00am on the 2nd February Mr Champion of the Police Force came to me at Civil Transport and asked me if I could do half an hour's carting. He said he had some furniture to move. I agreed and arranged to meet him at the top of Mont Arrive. I met him there at 6.00pm and went towards Cobo and when we got to Carteret, Champion said 'here in the field' and it was then I realised it was not furniture I had to fetch. He said 'back into the field'. We loaded a cow and Champion instructed me to go to a field at Bailiffs Cross off the main road."

The cow was dropped off in a field at La Ruette, St Andrew, belonging to Fred Le Messurier Hawkins, who told Mr Banneville:-

"On Wednesday, I think the 2nd February 1944, Mr Champion brought a cow here to be slaughtered, arrangements had been made between me and him to slaughter it a few days before. I slaughtered the animal at about 7.00pm. Mr Champion assisted me, I cut the meat in pieces for him. The meat was taken away in a van driven by Michael West. She weighed about 3 cwt, I received a portion of the meat for my trouble. I have not slaughtered any before for him."

Michael West, of Toronto Lodge, Foulon, told Mr Banneville:-

"Some time ago, I am not certain at all of the date, I was at Mr Hawkins's house. Mr Champion was there, I was asked by Mr Champion to do a carting job. I agreed and one morning I went to Mr Hawkins, and Mr Champion loaded some meat. I carted it from Mr Hawkins's premises to the Bouet. Mr Champion paid me four Reichmarks."

As a result A/PC H.S.F.Champion was seen by the Acting Inspector and admitted his involvement in the illegal sale and slaughter of the cow. Herbert Champion explained to Mr Lamy that he was suffering hard times with nine children, the youngest being 11 months and the eldest 14 years. Rather than see his family go hungry he had been driven to obtain food for them. His wife was about to enter hospital for a serious operation.

On the 21st February A/PC 27 Herbert Champion offered his resignation and it was accepted.

On the 28th February, Herbert Champion, with Frederick Le Messurier Hawkins and Frederick Ogier, appeared before the Royal Court, charged with being concerned in the illegal slaughtering of a cow and the sale of the meat.

In fact no meat was sold. The older Champion children were sent out with parcels of meat, which were given to many friends and relations. One of their 'friends' thought they had not received as much as they thought they should have had and reported the matter to the Police.

All three pleaded guilty and were represented by Advocate W.H.Langlois.

The Bailiff said Champion was the chief culprit and as a Police officer since 1940, had to set an example. If Champion's family had been in difficulty there were lawful remedies he should have sought and assistance would have been forthcoming from organisations catering for such cases.

Frederick Ogier was fined £65 and Fred Hawkins £87. Herbert Champion was fined £120 and given a 6 months' prison sentence, with hard labour. The sentence was, however, deferred until 1st May, in view of his wife's operation.

In the meantime Herbert Champion obtained employment working for the German firm of Marine Hafenbaumt at the Piette Hotel.

H.J.Blampied, H.M's Sheriff, wrote to the President of the Controlling Committee on the 25th April:-

Re - H.S.F.Champion.

On the 26th February last this man was before the Royal Court, when he was sentenced to pay fines amounting to £120 plus an imprisonment of six months at hard labour, the fines being payable on the 1st May next and his imprisonment also to start on the 1st May next.

This man has reported to me today that he is now employed by the German Authorities who will not release him for the time being to undergo his imprisonment. He informs me that the Department is making representations on his behalf to the Feldkommandantur. Would you be good enough to enquire through the Feldkommandantur at what date they will release him."

The contents of the letter was passed to Major Kratzer, who requested precise information as to the department where Herbert Champion was employed. This was supplied and Ex A/PC 27 Champion was released by the Germans and served four months of his prison sentence.

A/PC 14 Ronald Le Page resigned from the Force and on the 21st February two more Auxiliary Policemen were appointed:-

A/PC 13 Josiah Le Poidevin, 51, 2 Olten Villa, Sandy Hook.

A/PC 14 Edwin Percy Peadon, 39, Milton Villa, Les Croutes.

On the 9th March A/PC 26 Ted Butt saw Mrs Hilda Gallienne at her home, at Les Houets, Torteval, regarding an incident the previous evening. She told the Constable:-

"Last night, at 11.00pm two soldiers knocked on the door and asked for the socks which my daughter was mending for Uffz Martz. My daughter passed them through the window, but they would not go away. They said that if we did not open the door they would shoot. They then fired several shots in the air. They then fired a shot through the lock of the front door and one through the front bedroom window.

My daughter let them in and they stayed until 1.30am. They were both drunk. One is named Franz Vinstent and they belong to the battery near the West End cottage."

The Constable inspected the bullet holes in the window and ceiling and the front door lock which was damaged. The wash house at the back of the house had also been damaged and a number of tiles broken. He collected three revolver shell cases which he took to the Station. A report was sent to the Feldgendarmerie.

On the 10th March, two members of the Feldgendarmerie accompanied by a female interpreter, brought Thomas Howard to the Station. They told PC 9 Marsh was in charge of the Station:-

"This man Howard told us of a man named Le Maitre whom he said had plenty of black market butter and flour. Le Maitre's house has been searched and nothing found, the man was even eating dry bread. Howard, we believe, may be trying to make trouble. Put him in the prison and bring him to the 'Hollies' at 9.00am, tomorrow morning."

Thomas Howard was placed in prison and duly delivered to the 'Hollies', in the Grange, the next morning.

Shooting, accidental and in the furtherance of crime was becoming commonplace in the Island. A/PC24 Le Page, on instructions from the Station, went with a member of the Feldgendarmerie to Kingston, Varendes, St Andrews, which was owned by James M.Robins. There he saw nineteen-year-old Frank Roger, of Havilland Vale, Les Hubits, who told him:-

"At about 3.30pm today I was standing chatting to Mrs Robins at the rear porch doorway here, when a bullet came through the glass of the roof and hit me above the left knee. It didn't hurt me and I am able to walk and ride my cycle."

The Constable examined Frank's leg, which appeared to be only slightly injured and advised him to go to the St John Ambulance Station for treatment. The Feldgendarmerie officer made enquiries at the gun positions in the district to try and find out who had fired the bullet and why, but without success.

On the 21st March the Acting Inspector instructed PC Marsh to collect two members of the Feldgendarmerie and go to 44 States Houses, Old Mill, St Martin, where there was trouble with Russians. Upon arrival, the Constable saw two Russian soldiers, in evening dress, lying in the road about 30 feet apart, their faces covered in blood.

At the home of Mrs Bougourd, 44 States Houses, the Constable spoke to John E.Smith, who said:-

"I have all my meals here at Mrs Bougourd's house. I was just sitting down to the table to have a bowl of soup, when two Russian soldiers, who were drunk, came in through the back door and started knocking pictures and vases off the piano and smashing them. One of them kicked the piano, I tried to stop them and one of them hit me. Later two more soldiers which I think were also Russians came in and persuaded the others to leave the house."

The Constable noticed that Smith's left cheek was swollen and his left ear skinned and badly bruised. Other people present corroborated Smith's story. The Feldgendarmerie took one Russian away in a flak lorry and the other was taken, in the Police van, to the military prison. The Feldgendarmerie required a report of the incident to be sent to them in the morning.

Sergeant Harry Pugh and A/PC 36 Solway were on patrol in Mansell Street, at around midnight, when they heard voices. They came from the bottom of Victoria Road, where A/PC 35 Le Page was speaking to a German soldier and Miss Betty Peters.

As Sergeant Pugh and Constable Solway approached the group, Betty Peters, who was under the influence of drink, was trying to convince Constable Le Page that she was a German. A/PC Solway, who knew the girl, asked her to produce her identity card but she refused, saying in German, "I do not care about you".

A German soldier, passing by on patrol, was asked by Miss Peters to take her home. The soldier told the Police officers to, "Get out of it," or words to that effect and accompanied Betty Peters towards Mount Durand, where she lived. Sergeant Pugh and A/PC Solway after waiting a few minutes followed, and caught up with them. The German pointed his rifle at the chest of each Police officer in turn and they decided to take no further action at that time and returned to Trinity Square.

However on the 24th March Miss Peters, of 22 Mount Durand, appeared in Court charged with being found in the streets after curfew, failing to produce her identity card and failing to notify the registrar of a change of address. The Court was told that she had previous convictions for failing to produce an identity card and for not notifying a change of address.

The Magistrate fined her £1 or 8 days' imprisonment for being out after curfew and 5/- or two days on each other charge. Miss Peters stated that she had no money and went to prison.

# Chapter 27

## 'WE ARE OLD ZACHAU'S ARMY'.

Acting Deputy Inspector Fred Banneville entered the Emergency Hospital on the 18th of April to undergo an operation for a hernia. This had been originally caused by a fall during a cold spell some years previously, when the ground was covered in ice but was worsened by a kick he received when forceably removing Steve Piquet from Court. The operation was successfully performed and he remained in hospital for a month and returned to duty in June.

Whilst on patrol in the Commercial Arcade on the 20th April, A/PC 15 George Smith, met a German officer, near Lihou's Restaurant, riding a bicycle. The Constable put up his hand and said, "Radfahren Verboten." The cyclist replied, "officer", pointing to his shoulder straps and attempted to ride on.

Constable Smith put his hand on the handlebars of the cycle and stopped the officer. Putting one foot on the ground, the German struck the Constable on the right ear with the back of his hand and demanded to see his identity card. The officer shouted at the Constable in German, then remounted and cycled on through the Arcade.

Mr J.Hist, was passing and witnessed the whole incident. He went to the Station with A/PC Smith and told PC Le Cocq, who was in charge of the Station, that the officer was a Lieutenant who was dressed in a green uniform with plain silver braid on his shoulders and was wearing riding breeches. Mr Hist, who understood German, heard the officer call the Constable 'An English Swine!'

On the 22nd April Major Kratzer wrote to Jurat John Leale regarding a private party held to celebrate the engagement of Eileen Lander and Frank Hubert, at the home of Miss Mary Massy-Dawson, at Elmwood, Castel Hill. The Feldgendarmerie had interrupted the party at which thirty-five guests were present. They found a quantity of food, including roast pork, milk, bread and butter as well as forty bottles of wine, ten of liqueurs and cognac and five bottles of champagne.

Major Kratzer demanded to know if the foodstuffs were issued in compliance with rationing regulations, whether the wine and spirits were obtained in accordance with the regulations and if the rationing requirements in respect of electricity had been observed. He also pointed out that 'arrangements' whereby "persons receive and are supplied with food and accommodation on a commercial basis, outside the approved restaurants and hotels, cannot be tolerated under the present wartime conditions. Legislation which may exist in the matter should be reinstated."

Mr Leale passed the matter over to the Acting Inspector for investigation. He soon learnt that one of the guests had been Raymond Falla, a member of the Controlling Committee. He had supplied a part of a pig carcase, which under the Slaughtering of Pig Regulations, he was allowed to retain and salt for his own use.

The permit for the slaughter of the pig, Mr Lamy ascertained, had been issued on the 21st January and the pig slaughtered on the 28th January. Half the carcase was passed to the Essential Commodities Committee for inclusion in the Island's general meat reserve.

The bread, butter and milk were contributed by guests from their individual weekly rations. The wines and spirits, many of which were half bottles and only partly full, were brought by guests from their own pre-occupation stocks.

Mr Lamy satisfied himself that the supply of electricity to the house was regulated on precisely the same basis as that of any other private household. Miss Massy-Dawson had not previously exceeded her ration and he could find no evidence that the regulations had been infringed as a result of the party. In fact pre-war candles had been used after the 11.00pm curfew.

All guests had previously reported to the Registrar General their absence from home on the night of the party, in compliance with the directions given by the German Authorities notice No.7 dated 14th June 1941.

The Acting Inspector concluded that he could not see how the party could be viewed as commercial or that any contravention of regulations had taken place.

Major Kratzer, however, took a different view. He insisted that the party was to be treated as a commercial venture and that steps had to be taken to enforce his view of the Law. A further, more detailed report was submitted by the President of the Controlling Committee and Miss Massy-Dawson received a 'suitable' letter. Mary Massy-Dawson was, understandably, not happy and replied:-

"I must thank you for your letter of yesterday's date. I had not noticed any orders in the local paper, forbidding parties in private houses and fail to see why mine should be so singled out."

There the matter rested.

A/PC 28 Boalch, who lived at Sausmarez Mill, was off duty and out of uniform, when on the 30th April he spotted three Germans milking cows owned by Stan Mauger, at Les Hubits Farm. The Constable immediately telephoned the Station and A/PC 19 Stewart and A/PC 38 Robilliard were sent to meet their colleague in Blanches Pierres Lane.

The three Constables made their way towards the field where the Germans were milking the cows. When they were about 8 yards from the entrance, they saw the Germans leaving by the far end of the field. The Germans had also seen the Constables and immediately started to run, two inside the field and the other along the lane.

Constables Robilliard and Stewart gave chase across the field and Boalch in the lane. When Bill Boalch was about 6 feet away from the German he was chasing, the soldier turned around and attacked him with his bayonet. The Constable drew back and the soldier started running again. At La Bellieuse near, St Martin's Church, A/PC Stewart caught up with the same soldier who was still brandishing his bayonet. Again he turned around and this time attacked the Constable viciously.

Charles Stewart grappled with him, brought him to the ground and tried to disarm him. Constables Boalch and Robilliard went to assist him and at the same time the other two soldiers who had been running ahead of their colleague returned and joined in the struggle. During the resulting melee the soldier with the bayonet, had the left side of his face rubbed in the road by one of the Policemen.

Each soldier had a satchel hooked to his clothing and in the struggle the milk spilled from the satchels. The soldier with the bayonet lunged at Constable Robilliard and the bayonet would have gone through his shoulder had he not grabbed the soldier's arm. Instead he received a bad cut on the left forehand nearly cutting off one of his fingers.

The soldiers ran off, chased by Constables Robilliard and Stewart, in the direction of Les Merriennes, where they turned off into a private lane. The slower of the three soldiers, who was lagging behind his two companions, picked up some stones and threw them at the Constables, hitting Stewart on the left ankle. At that point the Constables finally gave up the chase.

The three soldiers were dressed in green uniforms with a broad bright yellow band on their shoulder straps. As far as the Constables could make out, one was a Gefreiter (lance Corporal), one an Ober Gefreiter (Corporal) and was wearing a revolver and the other an ordinary private soldier.

During the struggle Constable Robilliard managed to acquire the Gefreiter's forage cap, which had a small chromium star on the front. It was taken to the Station and later handed over to a member of the Feldgendarmerie, who went to Fort George to make enquiries.

On the 2nd May the Germans informed Mr Lamy that the three men who milked Stan Mauger's cows, had been caught. The soldier with the bayonet whose face was rubbed in the road, developed gravel rash and was easily identified. What action was taken by the German Military Authorities is not recorded.

It was not always young girls who were caught in the streets after curfew, occasionally it was men who were apprehended in the company of Germans. At 12.30am on the 6th May, Constable's Hall and Butt found twenty-two-year-old Fred Harris and forty-seven-year-old Stanley Le Marquand at the bottom of Victoria Road. Both men were in the company of a German soldier and said that the soldier had promised to see them home. They told the Constables that they had been to a party at Le Marquand's home. Both were warned for Court on the 8th of May.

Neither was it only young girls. At 11.40pm on the 20th May 1944 Constable Stewart found Mrs Dulcie Martel, a thirty-six-year-old widow of Amherst, in the company of a German lieutenant at Four Cabot, St Andrew. The Constable asked her for her identity card, which she failed to produce.

Mrs Martel was warned for Court on the 22nd May.

Notification was received by the Acting Inspector on the 13th May that five Islanders involved in production and distribution of an underground news sheet, called G.U.N.S., the Guernsey Underground News Service, had been sentenced to terms of imprisonment by a German Military Court and that details had to be entered in the Island Police register.

Charles Machon, a printer, was the originator of G.U.N.S. When the Germans confiscated all wireless sets in June 1942. He and four colleagues, Cecil Duquemin, Frank W.Falla, Ernest Legg and Joe Gillingham regularly listened to the B.B.C evening news on illegally retained wireless sets and took down the main details in shorthand. A master copy, averaging over 500 words was produced, then copies were made and surreptitiously distributed on a daily basis to those they believed could be trusted.

On the 11th February 1944 A/PC 32 Jack Salmon and A/PC 10 Bill Sebire were on night patrol in Trinity Square when they noticed Peter Doyle, a thirty-year-old Irish citizen, with a small party of Germans. As it was well past curfew, the Constables approached 'Paddy' Doyle, but when he and the Germans realised they had been spotted, they went up Bouillon Steps. The Constables were prevented from following by two armed Germans who barred their way. Jack Salmon later recalled:-

**Peter Doyle.**

"They went up over the steps out of our way. The Jerries would not let us up the steps, so we doubled back up Upper Mansell Street, up Mount Durand and down Bouillon Steps from Mount Durand. The Jerries stopped us down there as well. That was the night they arrested Charles Machon and Cecil Duquemin. We knew who the civilian was, an Irishman, 'Paddy' Doyle, but we could not touch him, as we could not get to him. We had to go off with our tails between our legs and that was it. We knew though."

'Paddy' Doyle was on his way to point out to the Germans where Cecil Duquemin and Charles Machon lived in Victoria Road. First they went to No 54 and arrested Cecil Duquemin and then 'Paddy' directed them to No 74 where Charles Machon lived. With their arrest, the existence of G.U.N.S. came to an end. Charles Machon had thought Peter Doyle was a friend and trusted him enough to give him a daily copy of the news sheet, little realising that he would pass them on to the Germans.

Later Frank Falla, Ernest Legg and Joe Gillingham were also arrested for their part in the underground news sheet.

The German Military Court sentenced Cecil Duquemin to 23 months for 'Spreading seditious information, non delivery of wireless set and listening in common to prohibited broadcast on one occasion'. Charles Machon received a sentence of 25 months for 'Making and spreading leaflets, spreading seditious information and listening in common to prohibited broadcasting on one occasion'.

**Charles Machon.**

Joseph Gillingham was sentenced to 10 months for 'Failing to deliver a wireless set and continually listening in common to prohibited broadcasts. Frank Falla to 16 months for 'Spreading seditious information and failing to deliver a wireless set' and Ernest Legg 20 months. All were deported to the continent to serve their sentences. Regrettably Charles Machon and Joseph Gillingham failed to survive their imprisonment.

A/PC 35 Le Page was patrolling through the Commercial Arcade, when at 6.15am, he heard 'groaning'. While he attempted to locate the source, a German under officer pointed out a woman who had her hand jammed in a window above the Income Tax Office in Fountain Street. Another German soldier, who was with the under officer, managed to gain access through an unoccupied house next door and climbed on to the roof. He reached the room where Miss Alice Audoire, the caretaker of the Income Tax Office, was trapped. The German opened the window and released Miss Audoire, who was in agony.

Miss Audoire, whose hand was blue and badly bruised but not broken, told the Constable that she had been trapped since 5.00am. "I got out of bed to open the office windows and the sash broke and the window jammed my fingers. These windows are very large and heavy."

Mrs Julia Barry was finally caught and convicted by a German Court for her black market activities. She was deported to France on the 5th May. On the 15th May her flat at 35 Mill Street was taken over by the States Billeting officer and certain of her personal effects collected and passed to the States Supervisor for safe keeping. Later the States Supervisor acknowledged receipt of one dressing case together with contents un-examined and one envelope, containing two Bank Pass books.

The Prevot of Sark, Philip Guille, arrived at the Station at 7.30pm on the 8th May and handed over two prisoners to the Acting Inspector. John F.Perree, aged 19, and Thomas P.Le Feuvre, also 19, both from Sark, were charged with stealing and receiving poultry, the property of Mrs Eugenia Baker of the Sark Post Office.

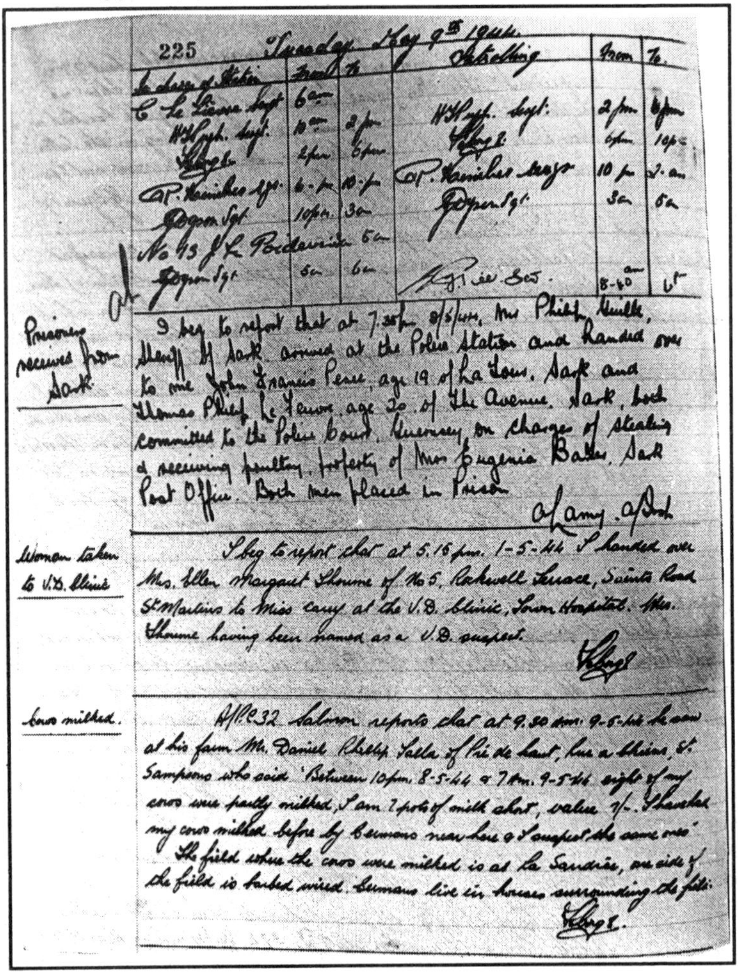

225 Tuesday May 9th 1944.

| In charge of Station | From | To | Patrolling | From | To |
|---|---|---|---|---|---|
| C. Le Lievre Sergt | 6am | | [illegible] Sergt. | 2pm | 6pm |
| [illegible] Sergt. | 10am | 2pm | [illegible] | 6pm | 10pm |
| [illegible] | 2pm | 6pm | A.P. [illegible] | 10pm | 3am |
| A.P. [illegible] Sgt. | 6pm | 10pm | [illegible] Sgt. | 3am | 6am |
| [illegible] Sgt. | 10pm | 3am | | | |
| No 43 J. L. [illegible] | | 6am | | | |
| [illegible] Sgt. | 6am | 6am | [illegible] | 8-40am | 6pm |

Prisoners received from Sark.

I beg to report that at 7.30pm 8/5/44, Mr Philip Guille, Sheriff of Sark arrived at the Police Station and handed over to me John Francis Perree, age 19 of La Tour, Sark and Thomas Philip Le Feuvre, age 20, of The Avenue, Sark, both committed to the Police Court, Guernsey, on charge of stealing & receiving poultry, property of Mrs Eugenia Baker, Sark Post Office. Both men placed in Prison.

[illegible] A/Insp.

Woman taken to V.D. Clinic

I beg to report that at 5.15pm. 1-5-44 I handed over Mrs. Ellen Margaret [illegible] of No 5, [illegible] Terrace, Saints Road St Martins to Miss [illegible] at the V.D. Clinic, Town Hospital. Mrs. [illegible] having been named as a V.D. suspect.

[illegible]

Cows milked.

A/PC 32 Salmon reports that at 9.30am. 9-5-44 he saw at his farm Mr. Daniel Philip [illegible] of [illegible], [illegible], St. Sampsons who said "Between 10pm. 8-5-44 & 7am. 9-5-44 eight of my cows were partly milked, I am 7 pots of milk short, value 7/-. I have had my cows milked before by Germans near here & I suspect the same ones"

The field where the cows were milked is at La [illegible], one side of the field is barbed wired. Germans live in houses surrounding the field.

[illegible]

**A page from the Occurrence Book of Tuesday 9th May 1944.**

In Court both men pleaded guilty and expressed regret for their action and promised to repay the value of the stolen poultry. The Magistrate said that because of their good character, he would not sentence them to a term of imprisonment, but would require the £10.10.0. compensation to be paid and a fine of £5 each, or one month's imprisonment. A further month's imprisonment was suspended if they took the Oath to be of good behaviour for two years. The two men took the Oath and returned to Sark the next day.

At 11.50pm on the 20th May, A/PC 19 Stewart was on patrol in Queens Road and opposite the junction with Belmont Road, saw a young woman accompanied by a German soldier. He stopped and asked the woman if she was a local civilian. She became cheeky and told the Constable to "mind your own bloody business". When asked to produce her identity card she said:- "I haven't got it with me, you can come down home with me to my house and you can see it."

The Constable went with the young woman to her home and she produced her foreign and local identity cards. When he was about to take particulars from them, she snatched them away tearing them in doing so. Constable Stewart was able to read Elizabeth Ann Kilby, born in Switzerland, 33 Hauteville. He was not quite sure of the surname Kilby, but he knew it started with a K. She ran into her house and did not come out again.

Three days later the Constable saw Elizabeth Ann Kilchenmann at the German Marine office. When asked to produce her identity card, it was in two halves but quite readable. It showed that she was born at Schaffhausen, in Switzerland. The last address was 23 Hauteville, but she admitted writing it in herself. Her registered address at the Greffe, was Amherst House, Amherst. She said that she was now living at 101 Mount Durand. Constable Stewart warned her for Court on the 24th May. She was charged with being out after curfew without permission, her identity card being in an improper state and of not notifying her change of address. Miss Kilchenmann was fined £1, 2/6 and 2/6, respectively.

The Germans introduced a system of instant fines for Islanders they found on the streets breaking their regulations. A/PC 24 Basil Le Page was on duty in Trinity Square at 11.00pm on the 26th May, when he was stopped by a member of the Feldgendarmerie who had detained Reg G.Lanyon, of 33 The Pollet. The German told the Constable:-

"This man must bring you two Reichmarks to your Station at 9.00am tomorrow. If after 9.00am make it 10 Reichmarks. He was riding a cycle without a light."

The two Reichmarks 'fine' was paid by Reg Lanyon at 8.55am the following morning and a receipt given.

During the days leading up to the D.Day landings the Allied airforce paid particular attention to the Radar installation at Fort George. At 5.10pm on the 27th May twenty-four 'Typhoons' came out of the sun and dived down on the Fort, with cannons blazing. The installation and many houses in Fort Road and the adjoining area were damaged. Soon after the raid Sergeant Plevin accompanied a Feldgendarmerie officer to the area and inspected the damage caused to several houses. He was not, however, allowed near the Radar installation. Everywhere there was shrapnel and empty cannon shell cases which had been ejected by the Allied planes. There were even some complete belts of 20mm cannon shells.

Many houses in Fort Road had holes in the roofs, broken windows, smashed chimney pots and damaged ceilings. One house, Leacrest, had a burst water tank and was completely flooded.

After the air raid the Germans worked feverishly re-positioning Anti Aircraft guns in and around Fort George, which had hurriedly been brought from other parts of the Island.

In the days that followed, more and heavier raids took place on Fort George. Major damage was caused to civilian property in the vicinity and some of the craters were six feet deep and twelve feet across. Two 500 lb bombs which fell in a field near Fort Road, failed to explode and were detonated by the Germans. Other bombs lay undetected for more than forty years before they were discovered.

Mr Lamy inspected many of the houses and reported the damage to the States Supervisor and Inspector Zachau. In respect of a house in Colborne Road, Les Godains, he reported:-

'Owned by Ambrose Robin, Rouge Huis Avenue, occupied by Harry Goodwin.

4 Dresden china gold painted plates valued at £15 smashed; 21 front windows, front doors and frame smashed; plaster in ceiling over front door, front room ceiling down; side window and 6 rear windows smashed; rear door smashed; bathroom muraline glass window smashed; kitchen, window smashed, ceiling down; west gable, rear room, 2 windows smashed, ceiling down, lavatory window ground floor, muraline glass smashed, dressing room muraline window smashed, landing, plaster on walls down; east gable, wall plaster down, 8 windows smashed; west gable, bedroom 2 windows smashed, all walls and ceiling damaged; garage, 2 windows and doors smashed; all tiles on roof shifted.'

The Acting Inspector, in his report, listed seventy properties which were similarly affected by the bombing raids.

When Sergeant Dyson was on duty at Fort Road at 4.00pm on the 1st June, he noticed a strong smell of gas coming from a house known as Llangroyd. The Sergeant reported:-

"Thinking that there might be a leak as a result of an air raid, I knocked at the door but received no answer, I entered the house through the front window on the ground floor with the idea of shutting the gas off at the meter. Subsequently I found the meter in the cupboard between the front door and the kitchen.

The meter was disconnected and both pipes were re-connected with a piece of cycle inner tubing. I called in Sergeant Pill who witnessed this. When we returned to the house at about 5.20pm, accompanied by Mr Robin, a Gas Company employee, the tenant of the house was already there. When we went to the cupboard, the meter had been re-connected. I could not find any trace of the cycle tubing and Mr Robin stated that the connections on the meter were quite tight.

I saw the tenant, Mr Fredrick Mollet, aged 50, a gardener, and informed him of what I had seen. He said, 'I do not know anything about it at all, all I know is I shut the gas off at the meter at 2pm and went off to work, my wife left as well. The meter was connected then and it was still connected when I returned at about 5.15pm.'

When I entered this house at first with Sergeant Pill I turned a gas ring on and we could hear a good force of gas coming through, this was at 4.15pm."

On Friday the 9th June Frederick Mollet was fined £10 or one month's imprisonment by the Acting Magistrate, Jurat Sir Abraham Laine, for stealing a quantity of gas.

One of the few civilian casualties of the Allied air raids was A/PC 30 Thoume who failed to parade at 10.00pm on the 3rd June. A/PC 36 Solway reported that he had seen Roy Thoume, who said he had been injured in an air raid earlier that evening. He was not seriously injured and returned to duty, two days later.

Many people living in the vicinity of Fort Road, evacuated to safer parts of the Island. Later it was agreed that the States would defray the costs of removal as if the evacuation had been compulsory.

In the early hours of the 6th June 1944 many Islanders were awakened by the sound of wave after wave of planes. Before daybreak almost all Islanders knew that the Allied invasion of Europe had started.

At 3.20am Sergeant Bob Kimber, the Station Sergeant, was informed by a German soldier, who came into the Station, that there was a General Alarm on and that all Police officers were to be called out and Grange Lodge was to be informed when all were present.

A plan had previously been worked out regarding a general mobilisation of the Force in such circumstances, based on the use of the telephone. However, as soon as the General Alarm was declared all civilian telephones in the Island went dead.

Sergeant Kimber immediately sent a Constable to inform the Acting Inspector of the situation. Mr Lamy later recalled the events of the night:-

"In the early hours of D-day, about 3.30 am, I was awakened at home by a Police officer and told that I had to get all the men to the station and report to the German headquarters when this had been completed. All the phones had been cut off so our mobilisation plans went by the board, it meant a personal call in each case. However, we were all in by 5 am, with the exception of the Acting Deputy Inspector and A/PC 16 Hall, who were sick.

I went up to German headquarters, at Grange Lodge, to report. When I arrived I found the front door was locked and I was admitted through a french window into one of the rooms. The German military staff were all congregated round a table on which was a map of the Cherbourg peninsular. The room was lit by candles and aircraft were droning overhead the whole time. Of course I guessed what was happening and from the map I had some idea of the locality. However, that was all the information I gained.

Nothing further happened and I was told to keep all the men together until later when I would receive further instructions. Later in the day I was instructed that the men had to be assembled at the Police Station twice a day - 10.00am and 4.00pm and I had to report to their headquarters at those times."

At about 7.30am on D.Day Mrs Hilda Malbon, an experienced member of the St.John Ambulance Brigade, was upstairs in her bedroom, dressing, when she heard an explosion and saw earth thrown up in the garden at the back of the house.

"My husband, George, called me, he was downstairs. I said 'alright I am coming' He said 'come down'. I hurried down stairs and saw him in the back kitchen crawling into the house. By the time I had reached him he had managed to pull himself upright. I attended to his wounds which were in the stomach and right leg. With the help of a neighbour, we carried him upstairs to bed, where he died at about 8.00am."

The death of George Malbon was reported to the Police and Sergeant Dyson went to 5 Rue Flere, Vale, where he saw the body in a bedroom. Doctors W.R.Cambridge and W.B.Fox confirmed that he had died from wounds suffered when an anti-aircraft shell exploded in the back garden of a neighbouring house. The sergeant noticed holes where the shrapnel had penetrated the lavatory and a pool of blood between the lavatory and kitchen door. George Malbon, thankfully was the only civilian casualty in Guernsey on D.Day.

During the morning A/PC 22 Le Gallez accompanied by a member of the Feldgendarmerie, went to Le Varclin and in a field at Le Varclin Farm, saw where an un-exploded shell had buried itself in a hole, about 3 feet deep. The owner of the farm, Mr T.A.Daff, had evacuated to England and it was not known who was in charge of the property. The Feldgendarmerie made arrangements for the unexploded shell to be removed.

An immediate result of the Allied invasion of Normandy, was that armed German troops in full battle order were to be seen everywhere. Policemen on their patrols were constantly being checked by sentries and road blocks were set up at every point imaginable. In the roads near Government House the Germans placed big coils of rusty barbed wire against walls and hooks were placed on the wall on the opposite side of the road, so the coils could quickly be run across the road to act as a temporary barricade or road block.

Major Heine in Jersey immediately issued a Proclamation to the people of Jersey.

"Germany's Enemy is on the point of attacking French soil. I expect the population of Jersey to keep its head, to remain calm and refrain from any acts of sabotage and from hostile acts against the German forces, even should the fighting spread to Jersey.

At the first signs of unrest or trouble I will close the streets to every traffic and will secure hostages. Attacks against the German forces will be punished by death".

Whilst the local administration became aware of the Jersey Proclamation and of the threat to secure hostages, no such declaration was made in Guernsey.

The curfew was, however, immediately tightened, being brought forward to 9.00pm and all entertainments were cancelled. Island schools were temporarily closed. Evening football matches were cancelled and Beau Sejour and Cambridge Park were shut for all games.

At a meeting held in Jurat Leale's office, on the 19th June, at which the Acting Inspector was present, it was decided that as there were no telephone communications it was necessary to place the Police Force on an emergency footing. That evening all members of the Force were paraded at the Station at 6.00pm and from then on were quartered in the large room on the top floor.

Mr Lamy recalled later:-

"As you may depend, the men made themselves quite at home and one of them brought along a piano accordion. The German official to whom I had to report twice a day was named Inspector Zachau. Each time I returned from reporting I saw the men and told them to carry on. They made up a song to the tune of 'O God our help in ages past'. I forget the whole of the song, but the first line was 'We are old Zachau's army' and they burst out on every occasion they were told to carry on. You can well imagine how far their voices carried when they were singing lustily - it was heard quite a distance away and at times quite a crowd would stop and listen, including German soldiers, but we had no repercussions as they probably did not understand sufficient English."

Probably this enforced 'togetherness' did more to bring about a pride in belonging to the Force, than any amount of training could have produced. When the telephones were reconnected on the 3rd July and men returned to normal duties, they had moulded themselves into a Police Force, with esprit de corps. One wag suggested that it was because of the cooking of Constable Bill Sebire, who took over those duties during their stay at the Station.

Allied air raids continued, almost on a daily basis in the weeks following D.Day. The harbour was a prime target and in particular a small U-Boat which presented an obvious danger to Allied shipping involved in the invasion. What the Allies did not know was that the submarine had previously been damaged and could not submerge.

In an air raid on the 14th June three ships were hit and one, the S.S.Karel, was still burning the following morning. Some of the harbour cranes and buildings on the New Jetty were damaged. The U-Boat was continually moved around the harbour. A/PC Alec O'Donovan took delight in tracking its movements and on the 15th he noticed that it had been brought around to the near side of the New Jetty.

Another Islander, who was observing the movements of the U-Boat was Ken Lewis, a clerk in Controlling Committee's office. He recorded in his diary on Monday 19th June:-

"When the bombs dropped, one dropped right where the submarine had been but two hours previously."

Then on the 21st he noted:-

"Last night some bombs had been dropped and one dropped not more than 15 feet from the submarine which was in the harbour. She comes in at night and goes around to one of the bays behind the Fort in the day."

Probably the largest and certainly the most devastating bomb that was dropped by the Allied air force during the Occupation, was in a raid by Typhoon bombers of the Royal Canadian Air Force on the harbour on the 19th June. Shops and offices in Town did not open until 10.00am, so fortunately there were not many people around when at 8.40am the Typhoon bombers launched their attack.

One bomb, which exploded just above the surface of the Old Harbour, converted the streets of St Peter Port into an apparent battlefield. The sea front from Woolworth's to the Crown Hotel suffered considerable damage and some of the buildings appeared as if they had received direct hits.

Every available Policeman was detailed to patrol the devastated area and to assist in any way they could. As people began to arrive for work soon after 9.00am. they were confronted by a sea of glass. The High Street, Smith Street and part of the Pollet were a mass of splintered glass. Market Street, the Bordage mostly the lower half, Mansell Street, Mill Street, as far as Warry's Clothing shop and Clark's secondhand store had all been damaged. Underfoot the glass was so thickly carpeted that it was impossible to walk about without hearing the crackle of it splintering.

Soon there was a small army of employees and volunteer helpers busily engaged in sweeping the remains of shop windows into heaps in the gutter. Carpenters quickly arrived to secure premises with any material that was available. Shop owners were to be seen recovering some of their scarce stock from the road way. By the late afternoon most of the glass had been removed and St Peter Port had taken on the appearance of a barricaded city.

Whilst on patrol in St Julian's Avenue on the 23rd June, two Feldgendarmerie officers informed A/PC 22 Le Gallez that Paul Botto had escaped from the O.T.Prison on the South Esplanade. They described him as being 5 foot 4 inches in height, broad shoulders, bright face and born in Turin, Italy, in 1909.

Botto had been at large for eight days and had stolen a civilian cycle. He had no identification papers. The Germans instructed that all foreigners were to be stopped and questioned and those failing to produce the necessary papers, taken to the Feldgendarmerie headquarters. The Constable was told that a photograph and further particulars would be sent to the Police Station by the Feldgendarmerie in the morning.

Despite every Policeman being aware of the search for Paul Botto and having been shown his photograph, no sign of him was seen until the Station received a report from Mrs George Le Tissier, of Les Houmets, Castel, that someone was sleeping in her stable without permission.

Sergeant Bull accompanied by A/PC 19 Stewart immediately went to the stable and at 11.15pm on the 1st July, found Botto, bedded down for the night. He had no identity card nor any other papers. The two Police officers took him in the van and placed him in prison. When he was arrested there was a lady's cycle in the stable, which Paul Botto claimed to be his property. It was left in the care of Mrs Le Tissier.

As a result of a telephone call to the Station, A/PC19 Stewart saw James Diamond at his home in Ivy Castle Lane on the 25th June. Mr Diamond told the Constable:-

"At about 6.30am this morning I was disturbed by banging which appeared to be coming from the unoccupied cottage next to me, I went to the front but saw nothing unusual, but I could hear someone upstairs. I went back to my house to get my coat. On my return I saw a man outside the cottage and stood against the wall, was a door. I asked this man what he was doing, he said 'I am getting rabbit food'. I asked him his name, he did not answer and he took his cycle and went away. I took the number of his cycle B239."

Later Constable Stewart saw Henry Ash of Ashleigh, Grand Bouet, who was the owner of the unoccupied property. He said:-

"There is some time now that somebody has been taking the windows away from my cottage and there are none left now. At the time of the evacuation the cottage was in decent order, but now it is in a very poor state."

Later the Constable saw George Toms at his home in Victoria Avenue, St Sampson. He said:-

"About a week ago I went to the Castle Lane to an old house and took two doors which were hanging from their hinges. I went again this morning soon after

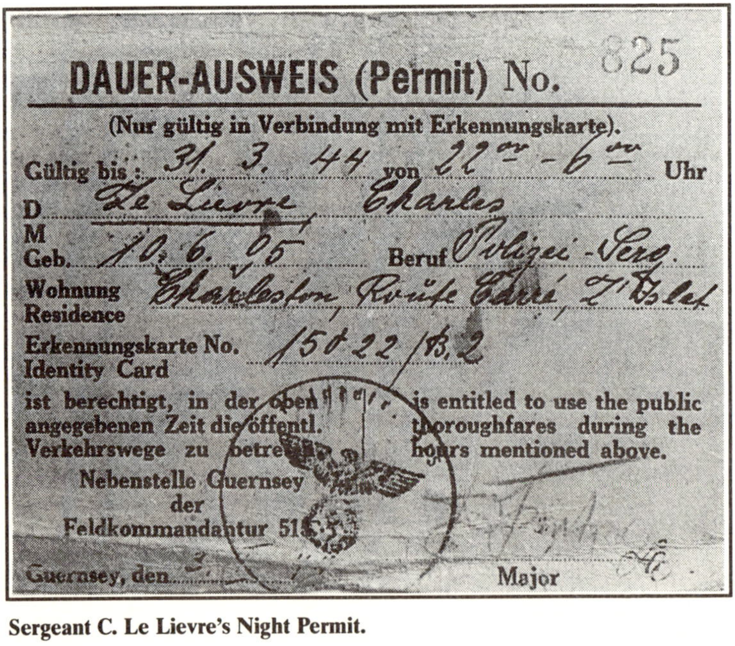

DAUER-AUSWEIS (Permit) No. 825

(Nur gültig in Verbindung mit Erkennungskarte).

Gültig bis: 31. 3. 44 von 22°° - 6°° Uhr

D. Le Lievre Charles

M.

Geb. 10. 6. 05 Beruf Polizei-Serg.

Wohnung / Residence Charleston, Route Carré, L'Islet

Erkennungskarte No. / Identity Card 15022/132

ist berechtigt, in der oben angegebenen Zeit die öffentl. Verkehrswege zu betreten. / is entitled to use the public thoroughfares during the hours mentioned above.

Nebenstelle Guernsey der Feldkommandantur 515

Guernsey, den ............ Major

**Sergeant C. Le Lievre's Night Permit.**

6.00am and was about to take another, which I had taken from upstairs and had placed outside the front door of the cottage, when I saw a man who asked me what I was doing. I said 'I am looking for rabbit food'. He asked me my name but I ignored him and rode off on my cycle. I have not taken any other timber or anything else from that house."

George Toms was building a shed. He had cut up one of the doors and nailed it to the side of the shed, the other door in his possession had not been damaged. Mr Ash valued the doors at 12/6 each. All concerned were warned for court on the 26th June.

In Court George Toms was charged with stealing three doors. He pleaded guilty to taking two doors but not to the third which he said he had left at the house. The Acting Attorney General asked for a fine of £5, but the Magistrate took a lenient view as it was Toms's first offence and fined him £3 or three weeks imprisonment.

# Chapter 28

# THE SMELL OF NEW BREAD

Early on the morning of the 3rd July, Emra de Beaucamp telephoned the Station and started to tell a long story to Sergeant Harry Pugh. The Station Sergeant could not make head nor tale of what de Beaucamp was saying, so he sent A/PC40 O'Donovan to investigate.

Accompanied by a member of the Feldgendarmerie, the Constable saw Emra de Beaucamp at Forest Post Office, who explained:-

"At 10.45pm last night a German soldier called at my shop for tomatoes. I said I did not have any but as he persisted I gathered up a few that I had about and gave them to him. As this man was leaving another soldier walked in, opened the passage door and started to go upstairs, I ran after him and called him back. He spoke, but I could not understand him. He then proceeded outside with the first soldier who had called him. They were joined by a third and an argument arose between them which eventually led to a fight.

While this was going on I locked the door and proceeded upstairs and watched from the landing window. While I was doing this a shot was fired at me, one of the soldiers then got onto the roof by means of a 'horse' that I use for sawing logs. He got through a window and entered a bedroom in which my daughter occupied a bed, I struggled with him and eventually got him outside. I would know two of the three soldiers again. As far as I can remember all this occupied about 1 hour. None of the men were drunk, although the one who entered the bedroom had been drinking. My wife and daughter remained up all night, they were too nervous to go upstairs."

Eileen de Beaucamp, their nineteen-year-old daughter, said:-

"I know the soldier who entered my bedroom, by sight, I have served him in the shop a number of times. One day last week he caught me by the arms across the counter and tried to draw me towards him, I managed to get away. I have never walked out with or mixed with soldiers."

The shot that was fired broke a pane of glass, passed through a wooden partition and both sides of a wardrobe. The Constable found the empty cartridge case, a revolver type, and handed it to the German Feldgendarmerie.

Mr De Beaucamp, the German and Constable O'Donovan later visited Le Manoir, where an identification parade was held. De Beaucamp was able to pick out one of the men, a Georgian soldier. They then went to Le Bourg, where other soldiers were stationed, but the other men could not be found. The Germans promised to carry on with their enquiries and detained the Georgian soldier.

When Constable Stewart came on duty at 2.00pm on the 6th July he was sent to the Guernsey Railway Company's Engineering Works, at Red Lion, where he spoke to William Mates, who told him:-

"Yesterday afternoon between 3.30pm and 5.00pm and today between 10.00am and 11.20am, fifteen to twenty German soldiers arrived in a large camouflaged lorry to move iron girders from Mr J.D.Germain's yard adjoining this property.

On each occasion they climbed into yachts that are stored here in the yard and ripped woodwork from them and took it away in their lorry. A large sailing yacht has drawers and interior woodwork stacked on its deck, presumably to be taken away by the soldiers on their next visit."

The yard had about twenty-five boats in it, which were placed there about twelve months previously when they had to be removed from the Castle Emplacement. One boat, the Isle of Herm, had floor boards, seats and other interior woodwork ripped out, presumably by the German soldiers.

The Bailiff's yacht had lost its mahogany doors, much of the panelling, some of the seats and flooring. The interior of the yacht was strewn with broken glass. The matter was reported to the President of the Controlling Committee with a request that a copy be passed on to the German Authorities.

Whilst there were an ever increasing number of thefts of growing crops from fields, not all the reported losses were quite as they seemed. Anyone suffering a loss of potatoes was able to receive some compensation in the form of an enhanced ration. Mr Lamy was well aware of the ruse and along with other officers, became very proficient in detecting attempts of registering 'arranged' robberies. Police officers were well aware that German soldiers were not the only people in the Island who wore heavy military-type boots !

A/PC 35 Le Page called on Mrs Emily Robert on the 7th July as a result of telephone complaint she had made earlier in the day. She told the Constable:-

"Last night my field was entered and practically all my patch of potatoes was dug up. I have no idea of the value. I suspect German troops."

The patch was situated beyond La Pomare, in St Peter and the whole area had been tampered with and footprints were those of military boots.

The report was recorded in the Occurrence Book and in the margin, written in red pencil and signed by A.Lamy, was "What has been taken? What is left in ground? Impossible to take this amount during one night. A/PC to visit this site again and submit correct report."

What was the result of the Constable's second visit is not recorded but clearly the Acting Inspector had his suspicions.

A/PC 24 Basil Le Page, on the 11th July, saw George Le Quesne at his home at Seawood House, Colborne Road, who told him:-

"Recently I had the key of my house, Villa Fevre, Fort Road, returned to me. Since then someone has dismantled and taken away my shed from the rear of the house. It is a wood sectional shed, measuring approximately 12 feet by 10 feet and valued £35."

Later at the Oberlands, St Martin, the Constable saw W.F.Adams, who said:-

"I was working in a house at Fort Road this morning and between 9.00am and 10.00am some German soldiers with yellow markings about an inch wide on their shoulder straps, came with a motor lorry from the Town direction and took away the shed that some of the soldiers had just dismantled. They drove away in the direction of Morley Chapel."

The Constable made other inquiries in the district but without result until he noticed some parts of a shed at a house in Rue de Putron. He fetched Mr Le Quesne who identified them as part of his sectional shed. The Feldgendarmerie were called and later the shed was returned to Mr Le.Quesne.

The Bailiff lived at Le Vallon, St Martin. On his estate were many trees which, because of the shortage of fuel, attracted the attention of thieves. A/PC Basil Le

Page called at Le Vallon on the 11th July and saw John W. Gallienne, the Bailiff's head gardener, who told him:-

"Between 8.30pm last night and 8.00am this morning someone stole at least half a ton of ash wood, the property of the Bailiff. The wood had been prepared for removal by my staff. There were limbs and split trunks, too heavy for one man to carry alone, I have no idea who could have taken it."

The Constable and John Gallienne combed the area looking for wheel marks or other signs as to how the wood was carried away, but none could be found. As the remaining wood would not be removed until next day the Acting Inspector arranged that two Constables should keep observation that night. This was done, but without result.

Mrs Dorothy Lanyon telephoned the Station at 9.30pm on the 22nd July, saying that she had been assaulted by her husband. A/PC40 O'Donovan went to her home at Ingleside, Bouillon Steps, where she told the Constable:-

"I have had trouble before, I used to do washing for the Germans. He made the excuse then that that was the cause of the trouble, so I gave it up. I only washed for them so that we could get extra bread. He soon missed the bread and pleaded with me to start again. He does not always sleep at home, I believe he spends some nights at Jack Holbeck's. He tells me that Holbeck needs company. He wants a separation but would sooner I left of my own free will. I am now pregnant and he is responsible."

The Constable saw her husband, Ernest Lanyon, a shop assistant, who refused to make a statement. Later at the Police Station he admitted striking his wife with his open hand and punching her in the face. He was put in the Police cells at 10.20pm as it was felt that it would not be safe to let him return to his wife. While at the Station, Ernest Lanyon was insolent to Constable Stewart.

In Court, Ernest Lanyon pleaded guilty to striking his wife and was bound over by the Magistrate to keep the peace for twelve months. He said that he struck his wife as she spent money which was entrusted to him. Lanyon had told the Police that he wanted a separation despite having been married for less than a year.

When an air raid took place there was a standing arrangement that all members of the Force communicated with the Station to find out if they were needed. One such occasion was at 8.45pm on the 24th July when an Allied air attack on the shipping took place. The Occurrence Book recorded that all Police Sergeants and Constables communicated with the Station by telephone promptly, A/PC Henry attended in person.

On the 26th July A/PC 19 Stewart was on patrol in Church Square when at 6.45pm he saw smoke belching from a four storey building in Market Hill. The Constable immediately sent A/PC 38 Robilliard to telephone the Fire Brigade and the Police Station. When the Fire Brigade arrived at 7.00pm. they found the seat of the fire to be in the cellar under the shop, which was tenanted by Stroobant and Symes Limited. The cellar was filled with cardboard containers and dummies which had caught alight.

Fortunately little damage was done to the property other than by the water that the Fire Brigade pumped into the building. Constable Stewart went and informed Major T.Scott, who managed the property for the owners, Walter Properties Limited, of the fire. His only comment was:- "The property is insured."

After the fire had been extinguished, Constable Robilliard, recalled having seen William Lucas, the manager of Stroobant and Symes Limited, hurrying in the direction of the steps at the bottom of Cornet Street at 6.35pm. The Constable called on him at his home and asked him to explain his movements earlier in the evening. Mr Lucas explained:-

"I left the shop at about 6.00pm the 26th July, everything was then in order. I went to the Sarnian Club and left there again at 6.30pm. Then I called back at the shop to get a packet of cigarettes and left again about 6.35pm. I went to Pats, in Fountain Street. I was called from there by Mr Percy Domaille, of the Brighton Hotel, who told me that my shop was on fire."

On Friday the 28th July, twenty-four-year-old sportsman, Graham Buckingham, of Glategny Esplanade, was sentenced by a German Military Court to two years' imprisonment for theft. As he was being taken under armed guard to the harbour on his way to serve his sentence in France, he bent down pretending to tie his shoe lace. When the guard was about ten yards ahead of him, he turned and ran for it, easily outpacing the guard who fortunately did not shoot.

Graham Buckingham, later recalling the events, said:-

"My suitcases, which I had been swinging belligerently all the way down, with the intention of hitting the guard, I threw up a side street near by. I ran through the Canichers around to the Vauxlaurens, up behind Candie, down Gibauderie, through the Croutes and on to Saints."

The Germans made great efforts to find Graham, including questioning and threatening his parents. On the 3rd August they issued a notice and a photograph, which they required to be published in *The Star* on two occasions.

'Buckingham is still at large on this Island, he is holding himself in concealment. The public are reminded again of the strict prohibition against administering any aid whatsoever to fugitives. All those giving him food, shelter or any kind of help will find themselves exposed to severe penalty. With the purpose of avoiding adverse measures the public are expected to fully co-operate in the arrest of the delinquent. All observations concerning his whereabouts and all information leading up to his seizure must be announced immediately to the Standortkommandantur or to the Inspector of the Guernsey Police.'

Graham Buckingham successfully evaded capture by the Germans for many months, but when he was staying with relatives at Milton Lodge, Rue Poudreuse, he fell on a bottle and badly gashed his hand. As the injury required immediate medical treatment, he was taken to the Emergency Hospital where he was arrested by the Germans. Whilst being treated in hospital, where he stayed for four weeks, he was guarded night and day by Auxiliary Policemen.

A/PC 32 Salmon remembers being on guard one evening, when Graham kept complaining that he had not had his evening meal. Jack Salmon went out of the room and down the corridor to find a nurse. This had been a ploy by Graham as he planned to get out of the window and escape down the drainpipe. For some reason he he did not go through with the plan, and Jack recalls; "We never left him alone again."

Later Graham Buckingham was transferred to the Prison where he remained until the Island was liberated.

Another Buckingham who was in the news, although not related to Graham, was Adolphos Buckingham, of Coinrosel, Ville au Roi. A/PC 38 Robilliard and A/PC 35 Le Page were sent to the Ville au Roi at 1.45am on the 14th August. On arrival, Mr Buckingham greeted them, saying:- "A shell has burst in my house."

The two Constables found the remains of an exploded 4 inch shell at the top of the stairs. The Feldgendarmerie were notified and immediately attended. After they had examined the scene, they announced:- "It was British."

The damage to the house included a 4 inch hole in the flat roof of the bathroom and part of an interior wall was blown out. Two bathroom windows were smashed, three windows at the front of house blown out, the bathroom door completely ripped off its hinges and debris was littered all over the house.

The shell which damaged Mr Buckingham's house was one of a number of shells that landed in and around the Town when the Royal Navy was shelling the harbour.

At 2.00am Sergeant Bob Kimber had received a call from the Germans, requesting Police attendance at Boots in the High Street. A/PC 14 Peadon and A/PC 13 Le Poidevin went to North Pier Steps, where water was rushing out of Boots and Hipps and into the Crown Hotel. The water was also pouring into Delas, the ladies clothing shop below the Boots Library.

A/PC 36 Solway and A/PC 28 Boalch had been detailed to work No 4 beat in Town. Bill Boalch later recalled:-

"We walked around the Market and Trinity Square until 11.45pm, then when we were making our way back to the Station we heard some gunfire. At the Town Church we met a German Marine, so we stopped and spoke to him. He asked us to go and have a drink. A/PC Solway said 'We are going up to the Mignot Plateau to see what is going on'. He told the Marine that we would go back later.

We left the Plateau at 12.30am and arrived back at the Station at 12.35am. 'Solly' told Sergeant Kimber where we had been. He said 'I thought that's where you were'. We left the Station again at 12.45am and as we were going down the High Street, we met this Marine again and went to his house at 1.10am. We left there at 2.20am and reported to the Station."

A/PC 36 Solway recalled what happened when they met the German Marine for the second time:-

"His name was Walter and he said 'Come with me and I will give you a drink for the English victory'. Bill Boalch and I went to his house near the Town Church and there I had three drinks. We then left and went along the Quay, where we found that a shell had entered Hipp's, the men's clothing shop.

After we returned to the Station, the time was about 2.30pm, we were he told to get down to Boots and help there. As I went through Hipp's shop water was pouring all over the place so I came out and helped to find the stopcock in the street.

It was then that I was taken queer and went to sit down for a bit. After a while I thought I would go to Jack Holbeck's place in the Pollet, so I was out of the way, but with the intention of reporting to the Station at 6.00am."

Bill Boalch also recalled the events of the night:-

"At about 3.15am I reported back to the Station to tell Sergeant Kimber that the Germans wanted Mr Butterworth, the manager of Boots, to come and open the shop so as the main water could be shut off. At about 3.30am I was back at Boots but did not see Solly.

At 4.05am I was in the Waterworks van coming up the Pollet, when I saw someone lying on the footpath near Collins sweet shop. The driver, the Water board distribution foreman, stopped the van and we both got out and found that it was Solly. I picked him up, but only got him to Grut's doorway before he was sick and his legs gave way, causing him to sit on the ground. I left him there as he said he would be alright."

Mr A.F.Butterworth, the manager of Boots was collected from his home in King's Road and in the darkness inspected his premises. He found that a shell had penetrated the roof and had gone through the ceiling of the Boots library, then smashed a wooden partition at the top of the stairs and shattered a big bookcase. Books had been strewn all over the floor and were damaged by water. The shell had then hit the floor, but had not gone through because underneath the floor was a thick metal plate. The unexploded shell had then ricocheted upwards and hit the ceiling, before dropping on to the floor, where it came to rest.

The shell had also damaged the ceiling in Delas below and severed a water main within the building. The water caused all the electrical fittings to short. The 4 inch shell was British and weighed 50 lb. The Germans quickly removed it.

Constable Ted Peadon later recalled that at about 5.00am:-

"When I rejoined Constable Le Poidevin in the Pollet, he pointed out Solway in a sitting position in Mr Grut's doorway. He roused and went a little way down the High Street, but returned and went down the Pollet, where we heard him knock at a door and call out 'Jack'. Later as we passed down the Pollet, Solway was nowhere to be seen."

Bill Boalch continued his account:-

"I was told by Ted Peadon that Solway was at Holbeck's shop in the Pollet. ..... I was asked by Sergeant Kimber where Solway was and he told me to go and fetch him. I did so arriving back at the Station at 6.12am with Solway."

Constable Solway told the Sergeant he was sorry, but the drink had made him feel queer.

Sergeant Kimber wrote out a report for the Acting Inspector:-

"I beg to report A/PC 36 Solway for being drunk whilst on duty at 6.10am on the 14th August 1944."

Mr Lamy asked the Acting Deputy Inspector to see Jack Holbeck, who said:-

"At about 5.10am on the 14th August 1944, I heard someone knocking on my door. I opened the window and looked out, I couldn't make out who it was. I went downstairs and opened the door, Police Constable Solway stumbled in. He was under the influence of drink. He was so bad I could not make sense. I told him to go away as he was on duty, I tried to give him a drink, a strong cup of tea to sober him up, but he refused to take it."

Mr Banneville, whilst at Jack Holbeck's shop, noticed a bicycle with a Policeman's cape. The Acting Deputy Inspector later recalled:-

"I asked Holbeck what this cycle and cape were doing there, he said 'It belongs to Solway, he is upstairs in my kitchen'. I went into the kitchen and there saw A/PC Solway sitting on a chair partly dressed, he was sober. I spoke to him, he said, 'I am sorry, I told Sergeant Kimber I was sorry, I had three drinks I think, from a German as I was excited and these bowled me out. I wasn't what you would call drunk. I came here to get out of the way. Mr Holbeck did not supply me with any drink at all'. In my opinion Solway was recovering from the effects of drink."

Mr Lamy saw Constable Solway and suspended him from duty. The next day the Constable was seen by the President of the Police Committee and was fined 30/- for being drunk whilst on duty.

Another shell from the British Naval bombardment of St Peter Port harbour landed in Victoria Road. The next morning A/PC 21 Le Tissier saw Frank Semore, of 5 Victoria Crescent, who told him:-

"At about 1.40am this morning I heard an unusual noise. I got out of bed and on looking through the window, I noticed that a shell had pierced the cement in front of the basement window."

The shell had grazed the bay window of 4 Victoria Crescent, also the house opposite, before finally burying itself in the cement floor. The Constable informed the Feldgendarmerie who on arrival said they would get the unexploded shell removed.

Constable Le Tissier then visited Mrs Daphne M.Duquemin, of 88 Victoria Road, directly opposite 5 Victoria Crescent, who told him:-

"During the night I heard the breaking of glass and when I got up this morning I found that three windows in my front room had been smashed. I found pieces of cement in my front room."

Later that morning A/PC15 Smith visited Henry Le Poidevin at his home at 94 Mount Durand, who said:-

"During the firing last night a shell dropped in my back garden."

The A/PC was shown the hole made by the unexploded shell and informed the Feldgendarmerie. When they arrived they immediately started enlarging the hole made by the shell. After spending a considerable time digging they had still not recovered the shell. They told the Constable that they would return to their headquarters and consult their officers about further digging.

How many of the shells failed to explode, is unknown, but it would seem that the Allied naval action was not as successful as it might have been. As one former Policeman surmised years later, "There may still be a number of unexploded British 50 lb 4 inch shells buried deep in and around St Peter Port."

As the Allied success continued in Normandy, the Germans in the Channel Islands became more and more cut off from the French mainland and from essential supplies. The last cargo of supplies arrived in St Peter Port Harbour on the 7th August 1944.

As Henry Charles Le Poidevin, an unemployed 18-year-old labourer, walked past the bakehouse of Butler and Langlois in Victoria Road, the smell of newly-baked bread whet his appetite. After he told his friend Ernest Lanyon, who lived close by at Ingleside, Bouillon Steps, of the tempting aroma, they decided to break into the bakehouse. They climbed onto the roof of the building and Henry got into the bakehouse through the skylight. He gathered up an armfuls of loaves and passed them through the skylight to Ernest. They collected 130 loaves, which they put in a blanket and carried them to Ernest Lanyon's house where they hid them in the roof.

The next morning, the 17th August, Charles Butler, opened up his premises at 23 Victoria Road, found nothing wrong with the locks but was horrified to find a large part of his newly-baked bread missing. The Police were called and at 8.30am A/PC 20 Julou visited the bakehouse. He later recalled:-

"I examined the premises and found that entry had been gained by scaling a wall about 7 feet high at the rear of the premises in Petites Fontaines Lane and entering by a skylight which had been left open for ventilation. The skylight was immediately above the oven. There was a drop of about 5 feet from the skylight to the top of the oven and a further drop of about 7 feet to the floor. This could easily be climbed by stepping on the fittings of the oven. The bread was stored in the same room as the oven.

In the gutter on the roof I found a 2 lb loaf. Barbed wire surmounted the wall in Petites Fontaines Lane, but this was easily negotiable."

Sergeant Harry Bull was at home, at 2 Victoria Terrace, when at about 1.15pm Stanley Butler, of 20 Victoria Road, called to see him. He told the Sergeant that he suspected Ernest Lanyon, of having broken into his father's bakehouse. He told the Sergeant:-

"Although Lanyon's house has been searched by the Police this morning, I feel sure that the bread is still in the house."

Together they went to Lanyon's house where Sergeant Bull questioned both men, who strenuously denied breaking into the bakehouse and claimed that they had both been at No 5 Tower Hill, Lanyon's brother, where they had spent all the previous night playing cards. The Sergeant searched the house and although he could smell new bread in the loft he could not find any.

He took Lanyon downstairs and asked Stanley Butler to see that he did not leave the house. He then returned to the loft alone and began a thorough search. He noticed a cane dressing table standing against the brick wall. He moved the table slightly and found that a hole had been made in the brickwork. This hole led into another loft and looking through, the Sergeant saw three galvanised tubs full of bread.

Henry Le Poidevin made a full statement admitting the theft. Sergeant Bull arrested both men and took them and the bread to the Police Station.

In the Royal Court, on Saturday 16th September, Ernest Lanyon and Henry Le Poidevin were both sentenced to 4 months hard labour. When Acting Inspector Lamy gave details of Lanyon's record to the Court it emerged that he had previously been found guilty of being found on enclosed premises and fined, in addition to which a deferred sentence had also been imposed. That deferred sentence expired just 90 minutes before the offence of stealing the bread from the bakehouse was committed.

On the instructions of Jurat Pierre de Putron, the Food Controller, the recovered bread was delivered to the Matron of the Town Hospital. A receipt was obtained for Station records.

Despite the Allied military successes in Europe, many young girls and women were still regularly seen in the company of Germans. One local wrote in his diary:-

"It was annoying to see so many members of the female population fraternising with German soldiers, a large number of women from 15 years of age upwards were always to be seen around the roads with Germans, even some married women were often seen about, despite the fact that many of them still had their husbands living in Guernsey. One also had to be very careful who one spoke to as some of these girls or women had no scruples about telling the Germans what you said, especially if it was detrimental to the Third Reich."

Another entry in the Diary, recorded the local feeling against the 'Jerry bags', at the time:-

"It was threatened that after the Occupation, girls who had been going about with the Germans would have their hair cut off and Owen Lewis, who works in the Post Office, told me that postcards have been sent out to some girls and on them is put 'You are No. .... on the list for a haircut, signed the G.U.B. (Guernsey Underground Barbers)' Joyce ........ the dancer was No. 1 on the list. She had had a baby from the Germans."

A/PC 37 Tucker and A/PC 32 Salmon were on duty in the High Street at 10.30pm on the 19th August when they saw Miss Annie Le Cheminant, a nineteen-year-old house worker, of 4 Sir William Place, coming up the Pollet, in the company of two German officers.

The two Constables told her to stop, but she took no notice and carried on down the High Street. They followed her up Market Street where she was again told to stop. Miss Le Cheminant still took no notice, but carried on down Fountain Street and along the North Plantation, where she was eventually stopped and asked to produce her identity card.

She explained "It has the wrong address, I have not had time to change it." The Constables then escorted her to the Police Station in company of the two German officers. Miss Le Cheminant was asked by the Station Sergeant why she did not stop when told to by the Constables, she replied:- "The German officers told me to carry on and take no notice." She was warned for Court on the 21st of August and taken home in the Police van.

Annie was fined £1 or eight days' imprisonment for being out on the streets during curfew and 2/6 or 1 day's imprisonment for failing to notify a change of address.

The German Military Command notified the Acting Inspector that they were aware that milk was still being sold unlawfully by producers to soldiers and civilians. In view of the food situation they considered it intolerable and required that civilian 'contraventions of this Order be punished by imprisonment'.

During the evening of the 22nd August, A/PC 16 Hall kept observation on Melrose Villa, La Mare, St Peter, a farmhouse occupied by Walter T. Langlois.

At 7.10pm a German soldier entered the house carrying two mess tins and a gallon jug. He came out five minutes later with the mess tins and jug full of milk. At 7.20pm a second soldier entered the farm carrying two mess tins and he also came out with them full of milk.

The next evening the Constable again kept watch, this time accompanied by Wilson Falla, the States Milk Inspector. At 7.15pm a German soldier, one of the visitors the previous night, entered the farm. As he left with the milk, A/PC Hall approached him and took him back to the farmhouse where they saw Walter Langlois, who explained:-

"These soldiers have been coming here for about a week or a fortnight and I give them three pots of milk each, I charge them 1 mark for a litre, they come here about 4 times a week."

The soldier had purchased, 1 pot of full cream and 2 pots of watered milk. A sample of watered milk was taken by Mr Falla. In the room there were two more pots of full cream and four pots of watered milk, which the Milk Inspector ordered should be taken to the States Dairy in the morning. The Constable charged Walter Langlois with failing to send all the milk to the dairy and for selling a rationed commodity to an unauthorised person on two occasions. Walter Langlois was warned for court on the 29th August.

The funeral of forty-year-old labourer Bertie Jehan, of Les Crabbes, St Saviours, on the 28th August was attended by the Bailiff, Jurat John Leale, and many of the leading members of the Island community. Among the dozens of wreaths was one, 'With the deepest sympathy of the Bailiff and people of Guernsey'. Traffic arrangements at the Church and en route to the Cemetery were under Police supervision. A German officer from the company stationed near to Bertie Jehan's home took part in the church service.

On the night of the 23rd August a considerable quantity of potatoes had been stolen from Bertie Jehan's smallholding. Bertie and his son decided to keep watch the next night from a greenhouse on the potato plot. At about 1.30am his son heard someone digging in the potato patch and went to investigate. They saw a German and gave chase as he ran off down the lane. Bertie Jehan was gaining on the intruder when he turned and fired two shots, both of which missed, but a third shot, fired from about four yards, hit Bertie in the stomach. As he lay there he told his son that he thought that he was going to die. Bertie was taken back to his home, where he died about an hour later.

Sergeant Le Lievre and A/PC 21 Le Tissier arrived at the scene with two Feldgendarmerie officers shortly after Bertie Jehan died.

The Sergeant checked the area and found two bags containing about 60 lb of potatoes.

At the inquest, the Coroner returned a verdict of murder or manslaughter by some person unknown.

For once the Germans took the matter of the death of Bertie Jehan very seriously and set about trying to identify the killer. Whilst they were carrying out their investigations two further incidents took place.

On the 1st September Frederick Jehan, a farmer, of 'Le Chene' Forest, noticed two Georgian soldiers in a lane near his house. He next saw them in his greenhouse stealing tobacco leaves that had been placed there to dry. When the soldiers realised that they had been spotted, they ran out of the greenhouse and drew their pistols and pointed them at Mr Jehan. He heard the striker in the pistol fall, but no shot was fired. The Georgians then ran off.

Two days later Percy Mechem, of 'Carteret Farm' Cobo, arrived home and found a German soldier in the passage of his house. The soldier asked where he could obtain some tobacco. As he walked past him, Mr Mechem noticed part of a bread loaf protruding from a bag he was carrying. Quickly checking, Percy realised that a half loaf had been stolen from his kitchen cupboard. He shouted to the soldier to come back and when he did not, gave chase and caught up with him. The German drew his pistol and said something in German which Mr Mechem did not understand. The soldier then ran off behind some greenhouses and disappeared.

At a meeting between the Bailiff, Lt.General von Schmettow and Colonel von Helldorff at La Corbinerie on the 6th September, the matter of 'threatening of civilians with revolvers' was discussed.

The Bailiff handed the General a translation of a letter which he had received from the Acting Inspector, reporting the two cases of civilians being threatened with revolvers by members of the German Forces. He requested that an order be given to the troops that such actions were forbidden. The General said that such an order was already in force and that the strictest possible measures would be taken to punish any offenders who were caught.

General von Schmettow added that investigations were still proceeding in the hope of discovering the murderer or murderers of Bertie Jehan. Already more than 5000 army boots had been examined since footprints on the scene of the crime showed nails missing from the soles of the boots. Also the revolver bullet which had been recovered, was of a special type. More than 100 revolvers had been examined but unfortunately the culprit had not been found. The General promised that the investigation would continue.

At a meeting between the Bailiff and Colonel von Heldorff on the 19th September, Bertie Jehan's murder was again discussed. The Colonel said that although investigations were continuing, he regretted very much that the murderer had not yet been found. The soldiers who had threatened civilians with a revolver had been caught and were being severely punished. In addition, all pistols had been taken from Russian units and orders had been given that no German soldier with the exception of the Feldgendarmerie, was allowed to enter any civilian house.

# Chapter 29

## WAR CRIMINALS AND QUISLINGS

Since the Germans had ordered the surrender of all civilian wireless sets in June 1942, many people had mastered the art of making crystal sets. The major difficulty was the provision of headphones. Soon telephone hand sets were disappearing from wherever they could be found. During the evening of the 1st September A/PC 17 Henry called at the Royal Hotel and saw the manager, James Mentha. He told the Constable:-

"Between 7.00 and 7.30 this evening someone entered the public telephone room ..... and cut the receiver from the instrument and have taken it away. I have no suspicions."

The Constable inspected the telephone and found that the receiver had been cut away with a sharp instrument. Mr Mentha said that no one had left the hotel during the half hour period. A search was made but no sign of the receiver was found. The Constable commented to the manager:- "At least someone will be receiving the B.B.C. news first hand."

As the blockade of the Island became totally effective after the fall of St Malo, the use of electricity was severely restricted. From the 20th August 1944 the lighting ration was reduced to 1½ units per household per week. The ration for businesses was cancelled. The use of electricity during the night was completely banned.

On the 4th September Edward Roland, a horse driver, appeared in the Police Court, charged with using an electric light at Hirzel Street on the 31st August at 11.15pm. The Magistrate, Jurat Le Pelley, had heard many original and inventive reasons put forward in mitigation, but admitted that he had heard a new and highly original one when the defendant said:-

"I switched the light off when I left the premises to go home. The switch must have been knocked on by the horse's tail."

The Magistrate said that he thought it a good 'tail', but still fined Edward Roland 5/-.

**Quertier Le Pelley.**

Many people, including the members of the Controlling Committee were sure that the Occupation was nearing the end. They were sure that Hitler would not allow 20,000 men and a vast store of military equipment be cut off in the Channel Islands. It seemed obvious that the men and equipment were needed by the Germans in their fight against the Allies in France.

The Controlling Committee began to give serious consideration to a number of 'problems' that liberation would bring, including the exchange of Reichmarks for Sterling, the treatment of 'War Criminals and Quislings' and control of Foreign workers and prisoners in the two camps at Les Naftiaux and Rue Sauvage. The Acting Inspector was invited to meet and advise the Controlling Committee.

Arrangements were made for Reichmarks to be exchanged during the three days following the Island's liberation at the rate of 2/- for each Reichmark. Only persons holding local Identity Cards would be permitted to change Reichmarks into sterling and persons wishing to exchange amounts in excess of £50 would be given a receipt for the Reichmarks, for redemption at a later date. That information would then be given to the Income Tax Authority.

The President of the Controlling Committee believed that on arrival in the Island of Allied troops, they would be asked whether there were any 'War Criminals' who should be detained and brought to justice. He did not himself believe that there were any cases which would come under that category. The President considered that the Allies would also ask whether there were any local 'Quislings'. He said there was the case of Mr Timmer. In his view, a Committee of Enquiry should be set up to report on the activities of Mr Timmer and of Timmer Limited.

**Gerrit Timmer.**

Mr Percy Dorey pointed out that much could be said in favour of Mr Timmer and that many other growers' activities were as serious as his. However, the Controlling Committee decided that the States of Deliberation should be advised that an enquiry would be instituted into the activities of both Mr Timmer and Timmer Limited.

The President said that officials of the Feldkommandantur had endeavoured to ascertain from Raymond Falla, H.R.Bichard and L.A.Guillemette the attitude of the local administration, should they appoint Mr J.P.Blaikie-Webster, a Director of The Star, as President of the Controlling Committee in his place. This matter appeared, to him, to be too serious to ignore. Mr Johns agreed especially in view of certain articles that had appeared in *The Star*.

After consideration, it was decided that the case should be reported to the Allied authorities for their advice.

With regard to the two camps of foreign nationals the Committee anticipated the possibility of immediate trouble between these men and the Germans which might result in bloodshed. It was considered that to avoid trouble immediately after the end of the Occupation, these camps should be visited and the men given a good meal and told they were free to leave the camp. They should also be told that any case of misbehaviour would be punished.

The Acting Inspector advised the Committee that in his view a large group of men would be difficult to control, but if they were liberated they would break up into small groups and would not be so dangerous.

The Committee, however, decided to advise the Bailiff that these men should be left under the control of the German Authorities, pending the arrival of the Allied forces. The President hoped that an opportunity would arise for them to discover the Germans' point of view on the matter.

One morning, early in September, sixty-year-old widow Mrs Kate Baldwin, was walking up Smith Street when she collapsed. A/PC 23 Langlois, went to assist and walked and supported her to the Town Hospital. Kate Baldwin apologised for being a nuisance, saying:- "It was only weakness through the lack of food."

The German Order that milk, potatoes, vegetables and other food were not to be sold to military persons was almost impossible to police. Many farmers and growers would sooner sell some of their produce to Germans than have it stolen. Despite regular warnings and a number of Police Court cases the practice was widespread.

As a result of 'information received', observation was kept on 'Hillcott', a house situated at Calais, St Martin, occupied by Daniel Mahy, a fifty-year-old postman. A/PC 37 Tucker and A/PC 16 Hall spent three days on observation duty, from 5.30pm to 9.00pm each day. During the period they observed between 12 and 18 soldiers leave the house with vegetables, each night.

At 8.45pm on the third evening the Constables approached two German Marines as they left the house with a trailer. It contained two sacks in which the Constables found vegetables and potatoes, The Marines were asked to return to the house, where Mr Mahy admitted selling the items. At the Constables' request, Mr Mahy refunded the Marines their 15 Reichmarks for 30 lb of potatoes and 5 Reichmarks for the vegetables, which included onions, carrots, sugar beet and beans.

After searching Mahy's house and outbuildings, with his consent, the Constables found 5 cwt of potatoes. They also discovered four sacks of apples, also a quantity of onions, beans and tomatoes. Mr Mahy claimed that the apples were from his own trees, which he had been forced to pick as they were being stolen. Some of the vegetables Mahy admitted buying to sell again. He said, "I have 14 sacks of potatoes in Mr Perrin's shed to be sent to the States Potato Board depot." When the shed was searched by the Constables they could only find 12 sacks.

The next day Constable Tucker returned with the Potato Inspector. Together they visited Mr Perrin's shed at Vue de la Normandie, Calais, where Mr Mahy's potatoes were stored. Mr Piddock, after measuring all the land planted by Mr Mahy with potatoes, found a shortage of approximately 1 cwt from a perch recently dug. It was this quantity that Mr Mahy admitted selling to the Germans.

Daniel Mahy appeared in Court on the 23rd September and was fined £40 with the alternative of four months in prison.

During September the Allies had launched a propaganda operation aimed at bringing about the early surrender of the German forces in the Islands. Early in the month there were strong rumours that a message had been dropped by parachute from an Allied plane, addressed to General von Schmettow. This was later confirmed to the Bailiff by Colonel von Helldorff, who said the message only contained instructions to get in touch with the Allies by telephone. He added that with the cables broken, such communication was therefore impossible.

During the first two weeks of September, almost every night, Allied planes dropped tens of thousands of leaflets in German.

PC Le Cocq reported that on the 13th September a container of leaflets was dropped by an aircraft. The container failed to explode and crashed into a corrugated iron roof of a shed, breaking a pulper inside.

Ken Lewis wrote in his diary:- "About 10.00 o'clock I heard a plane over the Island and the searchlights were on, I went out and heard the explosions from the leaflet containers, they sounded fairly close to home. I got up early and went all around the lanes looking for leaflets. I went half way through the Steam Mill Lanes and then came back. I later heard that the lower parts of the Lanes were full of leaflets. However, Mr Froome gave me one."

On the 19th of September he again referred to the leaflets in his diary:- "Soon after I was in bed this evening I heard a plane and got up and was just out of bed when the flak opened fire. There were a number of searchlights on and the firing lasted several minutes. The plane then went off but did not drop any leaflets, later at about 10.45pm she came back over the north of the Island and the searchlights were again in action." Ken Lewis later added:- "The leaflets last night were dropped near 'Paradis' in the Vale. I had one given me."

On the 22nd September Ken Lewis recorded in his diary:-

This afternoon there was some excitement as a boat flying a white flag was seen a short distance off St Martin's point. We rushed up to our highest window at work and saw it with our telescope. We could easily distinguish the white flag and there was another flag in the stern. People that were closer said it was a blue flag with a white star on it. This was probably an American flag. The ship, which was a torpedo boat of sorts, kept flashing a signal and eventually a German launch went out and returned about an hour later. The other vessel then went off. There were a number of German officers at the end of White Rock. Several cars including the General's staff car with three staff officers later came off the White Rock. There was a rumour of course that British and American staff officers had landed but that was untrue. Something has happened but no one knows at present."

Acting Inspector Lamy met Jurat John Leale in the street on the Saturday morning and asked him whether there was any truth in the rumours that were circulating in the Island about a meeting between an American warship and a German boat from St Peter Port harbour. Jurat Leale said that he would be meeting Colonel von Helldorff later and that the question would be asked. He promised to keep the Acting Inspector informed.

At the meeting John Leale asked the Colonel whether he could tell him anything of interest to the local community regarding the rumoured meeting. Von Heldorff said nothing had happened at the meeting except that the Americans asked some silly questions which had nothing at all to do with the civilian population. In reply to a further question he said that quite definitely fighting would not ensue in the Island because of the German replies to the American questions. "The Germans", he said, "did not intend to discuss their position with the Americans. Discussion with the British would be a different matter."

On the 24th September Victor Carey, the Bailiff, reported to the Acting Inspector that between 7.30pm the previous evening and 7.45am that morning, someone had fired a shot through his sitting room window. Mr Lamy and Sergeant Le Lievre visited the Bailiff's home and saw the hole in the window and some small splinters of glass in the room, but no trace could be found of the bullet. They carefully searched the area to see if there was any other damage or evidence of intruders, but found none.

Later John Gallienne, the Bailiff's head gardener, telephoned to say that he had found what he thought was a bullet. Sergeant Le Lievre returned to Le

Vallon with a member of the Feldgendarmerie, and were handed a small ball bearing, which was probably fired from a catapult.

On the 30th September 1944 Anthony Eden, the British Foreign Secretary, related a story that he had heard, to the Prime Minister, Winston Churchill, regarding the betrayal of some of the soldiers who raided the Island during the early part of the war. The Prime Minister was extremely concerned and raised the matter with the Home Secretary, Herbert Morrison.

When further such stories reached the Prime Minister he instructed the Foreign Office to make enquiries into allegations concerning the betrayal by a Guernsey Police Constable of a British soldier who had taken part in a raid on the Channel Islands.

The Foreign Office checked the story and found that it was without foundation. They checked all men missing from raids during the early part of the Occupation, examined Prisoner of War lists and found that no men were unaccounted for, and therefore concluded that the story was false. They assumed that the story probably related to the landing in Guernsey made by Lieutenants Symes and Nicolle.

On the 11th October Anthony Eden was shown a copy of the proposed reply to the Prime Minister and said he was glad the story was unfounded. The reply was passed on to the Prime Minister and that was the end of the matter.

Captain Ernest Cowley, the seventy-four-year-old Commandant of the Special Constabulary, carried out his last duty on the 6th September when he supervised the Western Patrol. Later that day he entered the Emergency Hospital, where he died on the 9th October. Captain Cowley joined the Special Constabulary at its inaugural meeting on the 22nd March 1939 and was appointed Commandant when Colonel R.W.Randell was deported in 1942.

During the Great War Captain Cowley was appointed Recruiting officer and in that capacity was responsible for enrolling a total of almost five thousand Guernseymen into the Army. He often recalled with pride that the Commanding officer of one Regiment said to him:- "Bring me as many Guernseymen as you can. They make the finest soldiers we get." And his reply was :- "The Guernseyman is known as 'a donkey'. He will go anywhere and do anything but you cannot drive him."

At his funeral, the Bailiff, Acting Inspector Lamy, the President of the Police Committee and the Acting Advocate General, were pall bearers. All members of the uniformed Police, who were not on duty, were present as well as more than one hundred Special Constables.

With the shortage of fuel, wood of every description was being appropriated to all means possible. When on patrol in the Lower Rohais, A/PC 14 Ted Peadon was approached by Lewis Foote, of Ashburton, Lower Rohais, who told him:-

"Someone has stolen a wooden gate belonging to my uncle, Mr George Foote, of Meadow Grove, St Peter Port. It had been unhinged and yesterday I went to fix it and found that it was gone."

The Constable visited the field from which the gate was missing at Les Varientes, St Andrew. Lewis Foot said the value of the gate was about £3 and had no suspicions as to who might have stolen it.

On the 3rd November A/PC 36 Solway was sent to see Thomas Ounsworth at his home at 'Beau Sejour' in the Vale Road St Sampson. The Constable arrived at 10.35pm and was told by Tom:-

"My pal William Enticott, who lives with me, left home this afternoon at about 12.30pm today to go ormering and I have not seen him since. He said he was going with Mr Fred Noyon in his boat. He did not take any food with him, I was expecting him home about 7pm, I did not worry about him until I saw it was gone curfew. So I phoned the Police Station to find out if anything had happened to him."

At 11.15pm the same evening the Constable visited Captain Fredrick W. Noyon's house at West View, Vale Avenue, Vale. He knocked, but there was no one at home. The Constable noticed that the dining room was laid out with everything ready for the Captain's meal, but nothing appeared to have been touched. He then went to see Steven Noyon, Captain Noyon's nephew and he told him:-

"I saw my uncle Fred, with whom I go fishing, at about 11.00am today and I asked him if he was going fishing. He said, 'no we will go tomorrow morning at 9.00 o'clock, Saturday'. I then left St Sampson's pier and came away home. I am surprised he went out on Friday as of late he has not been feeling all that well."

A/PC Solway returned to the Station and reported the absence of Captain Noyon to Sergeant Le Lievre. He recorded the details in the Occurrence Book and added that there had been no report from the German Police at St Sampson of a boat missing.

What was not recorded and could not be recorded was that the escape of Captain Fred Noyon, together with Bill Enticott, was carefully organised and had received official approval.

Acting Inspector Bert Lamy later recalled:-

"Towards the end of 1944 food stocks and medical supplies were at their lowest ebb. We had practically nothing to eat. Hospitals had almost exhausted their supplies and it was impossible to obtain any from the Continent. Patients were only served with one meal a day and other meals had to be provided by their friends and relatives, about the only thing that could be supplied were various kinds of vegetables. Only the most severe operations could be performed in order to conserve supplies. It then became apparent that some drastic action was necessary and it was arranged that someone would get away from the Island and give a true report of the conditions.

The man chosen was an ex-Mercantile Captain, who was then acting as a fisherman and he made the arrangements. There were only a few of us in the scheme because it was risky to trust too many. It was agreed that at a meeting of the States one member would ask the President of the Board of Health and the President of the Essential Commodities Committee for a true state of the Island stocks. Statements were made in detail and the matter stated publicly at a meeting of the States. I attended that day and Captain Noyon, who was to take the information, was also present.

As soon as possible after the meeting, he went to his boat and fooled the Germans, who always accompanied fishermen on the expeditions and set out. It was all arranged that if everything went well the following day a relative of his would come to me and report him and his boat, missing. He was duly reported missing and of course the facts had to be reported to the German Authorities, but he got safely away and eventually the first Red Cross supplies were sent to us."

A small group, which included Deputy C.H.Cross who had been deported in 1942 but for medical reasons, was allowed to return to the Island, carefully planned Fred Noyon's escape. On the 21st October Deputy Cross had given Sir Abraham Laine, the President of the Essential Commodities Committee, notice that he wished to ask a question at the States meeting on the 1st November. He asked;-

"Will you kindly give me approximate information as to how long the following commodities will last according to present rationing, in this Island of Guernsey.

Flour, meat, coffee, cocoa, sugar, tea, salt, fats, jam, cheese, soap, coal, coke, wood fuel, paraffin oil, electric lighting, gas, footwear for children and adults, clothing for children and adults, also medical and surgical requisites."

At the States meeting Sir Abraham Laine gave the answers to the questions in great detail.

The stock of flour and wheat at the 21st of October was 424 tons, but Sir Abraham added that since that date the Germans had requisitioned 150 tons for their own use. Based on the present ration Sir Abraham said the stock would only last until the 12th December.

Deputy Cross was informed that there was no stock of meat in the cold store. There was 17 tons of sugar, 18 tons butter, 9 tons of cheese and 26 tons of macaroni. The stock of tea was nil and none had been issued since February 1941. The last issue of jam had been in July 1944 and cocoa had run out in September.

There was no stock of coal or coke and only 80 tons of logs. Civilian stocks of petrol were completely exhausted. Paraffin stock amounted to a mere 950 gallons. Electricity supply was severely rationed and only available for 11 hours a day and would cease by about Christmas time. Gas, which was on for 4 hours a day, would last until the end of December.

Household soap had run out in August 1944 and the stock of soap powder was a mere 23 cwts. What stock there was of footwear was likely to run out by the end of November and there was no stock of leather for shoe repairs. The stock of clothing was very limited and was likely to be exhausted shortly.

The position of the more important medical supplies, Deputy Cross was told, was very bad. Catgut, which was essential in important operations, would run out within the month. Cotton wool gave out a long time ago. The stock of important drugs was no-existent. Medicines for the treatment of influenza were finished. The only area where any stocks existed were anaesthetics and insulin.

Captain Fred Noyon and Bill Enticott left the Island during the afternoon of Friday the 3rd November under the cover of a mist. Old Fred's boat, the Littlewood, was spotted by an American warship off the French coast. They were towed into Cherbourg harbour, where an accident caused considerable damage to the Littlewood. Just over a week later Captain Noyon and Bill Enticott arrived in England, where they handed over their vital information to the British Authorities.

Also at the States meeting on the 1st November Deputy C.W.Arnold was elected to the Police Committee in place of Colonel R.W.Randall, who had been deported more than a year previously. The only other change on the Committee was that W.E.Poat, who was in very much improved health, took over from Hubert Brock as Vice-President.

On the 8th November the Acting Inspector wrote to the President of the Police Committee:-

"I beg to report that in the near future I can visualise the Police will be unable to function with any degree of efficiency as the stocks of essentials run out. The stealing of foodstuffs and wood is on the increase and as these commodities get scarcer and the weather colder, it is reasonable to expect increased stealing.

The stock of civilian petrol is exhausted and we are dependant on a monthly allocation from the German Authorities. Bicycle tyres are unobtainable, boot leather practically exhausted, food and fuel rapidly dwindling.

Bearing these facts in mind, it will be seen that Police will be unable to adequately patrol the country from Headquarters situated in St Peter Port. I have given the matter serious consideration and would respectfully suggest that two sub-stations be set up, one in the Capelles district to serve the Northern part of the Island and another in the neighbourhood of Le Gron, St Saviours, to serve the West and South West portions, the remainder of the Island would be served from St Peter Port. This would necessitate the Police Committee renting one or two rooms in each district for the duration of the present conditions.

The scheme could be adopted without engaging extra men. One Sergeant and nine men would be necessary at each sub-station. My idea would be to keep the men in their own locality, this would save tyres, footwear and enable each to have his meals at home. This arrangement would not be considered under normal circumstances, as it is unwise to have Police officers working in their own locality. The Sergeant would be responsible for the discipline of his sub-station and would be expected to split his duties accordingly.

The advantage of this scheme would be that we will be in a position to continue the country patrols and in the case of enquiries, will save endless time by having a man near the district instead of having to walk from Town. There are also disadvantages but these are technical, concerning supervision and reports, but they can be overcome.

If the Committee approve these suggestions, I would respectfully suggest that the Sergeants in charge of the sub-stations be given a weekly allowance to cover their extra responsibilities while so acting. Also suitable accommodation be found in the districts stated and the telephone installed at each place. It would be fully understood that these arrangements would cease as soon as possible after the Occupation."

The Police Committee carefully considered the proposals and at their meeting on the 30th November authorised the opening of two sub-stations. It was agreed that PCs Le Cocq and Marsh be utilised for Station duties in Town and that their pay be increased by 3/6 per week.

At 11.00pm on the 17th November A/PC 34 Raymond Gaudion was on cycle patrol at Pleinmont, when his light went out. He continued along the right hand side of the road, in the complete darkness but unbeknown to him, a German was riding in the opposite direction, also without lights. Inevitably they collided and while the German was uninjured, the Constable suffered an injury to his left hand. Dr B.S.Collins put him on accident insurance and the Constable returned to duty after a few days.

Constables Le Cocq and Hall called on forty-two-year-old Mrs Louise Le Cheminant at her home, Holly Tree, Grande Rue, St Martin, regarding a routine matter. The two Constables found the front door was ajar, they rang the bell and walked in and immediately noticed the very strong smell of gas. Behind a curtain near the front door they found that the gas main had been reconnected with a cycle inner tube, bypassing the gas meter. PC Le Cocq telephoned the Gas Company and one of their foremen came and disconnected the installation.

Mrs Le Cheminant told the Constables:-

"Last night about 8.30pm having no fuel with which to cook dinner, I put the hose on the pipes to obtain a supply of gas, last night was the first time I did it."

On the 4th December Mrs Le Cheminant appeared in Court and admitted the offence. The Acting Attorney General told the Court that she had been before the Court previously on a similar charge and had on that occasion been given the benefit of the doubt. "This", he said, "should have been a lesson to her". The Magistrate fined Mrs Le Cheminant £10 or two months imprisonment. He warned her that if it happened again he would have no option other than to send her to prison.

On the 24th November former Auxiliary Police Constable John Lovell appeared in Court charged with breaking and entering a store at St Julian's Avenue and stealing a quantity of boxwood. The Acting Inspector, prosecuting, told the Magistrate that enquiries were still being made and asked for the defendant to be remanded in custody for one week. The Magistrate agreed. One week later he was committed for trial before the Royal Court.

When PC Le Cocq searched Lovell's home at St Julian's Cottage, he discovered that both the gas and electricity installations had been tampered with. Former A/PC 12 Lovell pleaded guilty to maliciously or fraudulently abstracting electricity and gas. He was fined £10 or two months imprisonment on each charge.

On the 16th December Lovell was tried before the Royal Court for stealing 10 tons of wood, valued £50, from Geo. Munro Ltd and breaking and entering Mr H.H.Plummer's bakehouse at Allez Street and stealing 330 lb of flour, 95 lb bread, 4 lb of sugar beet and a sack, together valued at £9.10.3½. He was sentenced to 18 months' imprisonment with hard labour.

During the conclusion of the case the Acting Attorney General referred to the "smart work" of PC Le Cocq. He had been going up the Vauvert when he noticed a queue of people at a wood store. He was suspicious and questioned John Lovell, who said that the wood came from a demolished vinery in St Andrew's. Later he admitted to the Constable that it was stolen. When subsequently searching Lovell's house, PC Le Cocq noticed quantities of flour, which he established had also been stolen. The Bailiff also commended PC Le Cocq and added that "The Court must make the game not worth the candle."

# Chapter 30

# RED CROSS TEA

Since the escape from the Island of Captain Fred Noyon and Bill Enticott, hope had been rising that the International Red Cross would send a relief ship with urgently needed food supplies. Rumour upon rumour persistently circulated around the Island bringing alternately hope and despair to Islanders. On the 9th December a notice appeared in the *Evening Press* reporting that the Bailiff had been informed by the German Authorities that an International Red Cross ship had sailed from Portugal for the Channel Islands the previous day.

A hastily arranged meeting was held in the Victoria Road School Room for helpers who were to receive and distribute the Red Cross food parcels. Most of those attending were St John Ambulance members. Acting Deputy Inspector Banneville was present, on Mr Lamy's instructions, so that the Police would be aware of the arrangements being made.

The overall responsibility for the receipt and distribution of the Red Cross parcels was given to John Loveridge, the Secretary to the Essential Commodities Committee. In creating detailed plans, he consulted Mr Lamy and between them the role that the Police Force was to play was clearly established and defined.

The Germans were to be responsible for unloading the Red Cross parcels from the ship which would be berthed at the London Berth and transporting them to St George's Hall. They proposed to use their light railway which ran from White Rock around Salerie Corner and then into the Piette timber yard. The Germans planned to build a platform as an annex to the main entrance, in the timber yard, with the railway running parallel to the platform.

During the transfer of the parcels from the ship to St George's Hall it was agreed that two uniformed members of the Police Force would be detailed for patrol duties on the main road entrance and two in the Piette timber yard. A night guard would be provided by staff from the Essential Commodities Committee and a member of the Special Constabulary.

During the distribution of the parcels to the various retailers who would issue them to the general public, four Police officers would patrol the area of St George's Hall.

John Loveridge stressed to the Acting Inspector that:-

"This is one of the most important tasks which has been entrusted to the Committee and every person concerned is expected to do his utmost to ensure that the work is carried out rapidly and efficiently so as to reflect credit on the organisation. The work will be carried out under the critical eye of the public, the German Authorities and most important of all, probably the International Red Cross Commissioner."

The arrangements and organisation were complete, all that was missing was the Red Cross ship. The whole Island awaited the arrival of the relief supplies. All conversations were inevitably about the possible arrival of the Red Cross parcels. Police officers were expected by the public to know all the details and every member of the Force was constantly being stopped and questioned on the subject.

Repeatedly rumours circulated that the Red Cross ship had sailed and would arrive in a few days. Then rumour had it that the vessel had been seen off the Casquets, then off the Hanois lighthouse. Another report said it was in the Little Russel.

When Islanders heard on their crystal sets, the B.B.C. reporting that a Swedish ship had left Lisbon with food, soap and medical supplies, many people really believed that help was at last, at hand. The only question was whether relief would arrive in time for Christmas. If it did it would be the best possible Christmas present Islanders could receive.

On the 14th December Herr Schneberger of the Platzkommandantur received a letter from a 'G.A.Tippett', no address given, stating:-

"Just to let you know that Mr R.Mallett from the Potato Office, warned his friend Mr Ferbrache, a grower, to hide his potatoes. Why should he have 2 tons of potatoes and barter them for sacks of wheat. He has got a lot of things stored in the loft of his house, also a wireless set.

They also get plenty of German oil for light.

Mr Ferbrache,
Highland Estate,
St Martin."

The Germans sent the letter to the Bailiff for further action and report. The Acting Attorney General received a copy, which he sent to Mr Lamy, requesting, "Please investigate and report".

Sergeant Pill was put in charge of enquiry and a search at the Greffe soon revealed that there was no person in the Island named G.A.Tippett. Mr R.Mallett, whom the Sergeant regarded as a trusted States official, denied the allegation made in the letter. His house in Grande Rue, St Martin, was searched but nothing incriminating found.

He also saw Henry Ferbrache, of Highlands Estate, Rue des Grons and searched his premises. In the pantry he found about 1 lb of wheat, 3 lb of flour and 200 lb of potatoes, which he did not consider excessive for a family of three. Neither could he find any sign of a crystal set.

Sergeant Pill made enquiries at the Potato Board and ascertained that Henry Ferbrache had planted 1 vergee 4 perches of potatoes and returned in all 21 cwt to the depot. This return was regarded by the Potato Board as very satisfactory.

On the 22nd December the Acting Inspector replied to the Bailiff enclosing three copies of his report which rejected the allegations and exonerated Mr Mallett and Mr Ferbrache.

During early December, because of the acute food shortage, the Controlling Committee ruled that all States employees should not work more than six hours per day. This caused the Acting Inspector considerable problems in arranging shifts to cover the complete twenty-four hours. With the advent of the Sub-Stations which would be in operation throughout the day and night, the reduction in hours meant that additional Sergeants would be required to provide sufficient supervision.

Mr Lamy wrote to the President of the Police Committee on the 19th December suggesting that in order to overcome the problem, the intermediate rank of Corporal be created. He further suggested that Constables Le Cocq and Marsh be promoted Corporals. The Committee agreed and promoted the two remaining PCs from the pre Occupation Force, as from the 25th December 1944. The creation of the new rank required the approval of the Royal Court to an

Ordinance amending the Schedule laid down in the Order-in-Council of 1938. However, it was not an entirely new rank, as Arthur Langmead had held the rank of Corporal for more than two years, before being appointed Sergeant in August 1926.

On the 15th December the Platzkommandantur wrote to the Bailiff concerning the appointment of additional men for Police duties. The Germans were, like the Civil Administration, very concerned at the dramatic rise in robberies and thefts. They believed that the only way to control the situation was to recruit more Police and to increase the number of patrols, particularly in the country districts. The Bailiff passed the letter on to the Acting Inspector for action. Mr Lamy, however, was not as fully convinced, as to the solution, as were the Germans. He was aware that the vast majority of incidents were being caused by German troops, over whom the local Police had no jurisdiction.

However, the letter was reported to the Police Committee at its meeting on the 20th December and it was agreed to enlarge the Force as the Germans requested. The situation was not helped by the resignations of two Auxiliary Constables, A/PC 15 Alfred Smith and A/PC 19 Charles Stewart.

On the 27th December a notice appeared in the *Evening Press*:-

"ISLAND POLICE

A number of men of good character, minimum height 5'8", sound physique, between the ages of 20 and 45 years are required for patrol duties.

Applications will be welcomed from members of the Special Constabulary. Pay 50/- plus 2/6 clothing allowance weekly. Applications giving date and place of birth, height, qualifications, whether in possession of cycle etc., to be forwarded to Police Office not later than 29th December 1944."

Christmas Day arrived, but the Red Cross ship did not. Sergeant Harry Pugh was in charge of the Station from 6.00am until 2.00pm. As he munched his meagre sandwiches during his two-hour meal break, taken in order not to exceed the six hours' work decreed by the Controlling Committee, he reflected that if the Red Cross supplies did not arrive very soon, Islanders would be dying of starvation by early February.

When newly promoted Corporal Francois Le Cocq took over from him at 2.00pm he cycled home to Kessingland Cottage, in Grand Bouet, where he lived alone, his wife having evacuated. On his way home he collected his Christmas lunch from Mrs Moore, who was in charge of the newly-opened Communal Cooking and Feeding Centre in Grand Bouet. It consisted of a quart of stew, comprising meat, macaroni, potatoes, onions and other vegetables.

Crimes reported to the Station during Christmas Day included the loss of a pig, valued at £5, from a sty at Les Messuriers, Forest, - the loss by William Fitzgerald of 3 cwts of potatoes and 60 lb of onions from Les Domaines, St Saviour - cows, belonging to William Clark, of La Hougue, Castel, being milked in his stable overnight and the loss of parsnips stored in his shed.

On Boxing Day morning Mrs Vester Vigezzi of The Hollies, St Peter Port, was caught riding a pedal cycle through the Commercial Arcade. When stopped she said, "I was only riding until I met a Policeman." Asked to produce her identity card, she announced:- "I left it at home."

When warned for Court at 10.15am on the 27th December she announced:- "I think I will call and see Mr Lamy on my way up." The incident was recorded in the Occurrence Book. Apparently Mrs Vigezzi did call and see Mr Lamy, as he had written in the margin, against the report "Cautioned". Perhaps the Christmas spirit was taken into consideration.

Wednesday 27th December was one of the coldest days of the year. Islanders woke up to a freezing hard morning with at least a quarter of an inch of ice on the ponds. Many people found their hand pumps frozen and had to use precious fuel to boil water to thaw the pipes.

Dramatic news came during the morning when the International Red Cross Ship, the 'S.S.Vega' was sighted off Pleinmont. Almost instantaneously the whole Island knew of its arrival and hundreds of people flocked to the Esplanade to welcome the Swedish ship to the Island. Many other people went to Jerbourg to admire the S.S.Vega as it steamed towards St Peter Port harbour.

Sergeant Bob Kimber, who lived at 'Chefoo' on the Jerbourg Road and had came off duty at 6.00am, was awoken by the crowds on their way to Jerbourg Point to catch a sighting of the S.S.Vega. He dressed in his uniform and went down towards La Bouvee and from the garden of Les Faitieres, saw the outline of the S.S.Vega through the mist, accompanied by a German patrol boat.

Back at the Station the Acting Inspector was making arrangements for the Town patrols to be strengthened and other officers to control the crowds, which were growing larger by the minute. A few minutes after Sergeant Harry Pugh came on duty at 2.00pm, staff from the Controlling Committee offices rushed into the Station and told him how, through their office telescope, they had seen the S.S.Vega steaming towards the mouth of the harbour and drop anchor behind the Castle.

There she stayed tantalisingly throughout the afternoon, until just after 5.30pm., when at last she weighed anchor and eased her way into St Peter Port Harbour.

The public were not allowed on to the White Rock, it was restricted to Germans and permit-holders only, but every window, every roof which had sight of the London berth where the S.S.Vega was due to dock, was packed with people. Every available vantage point was filled with Islanders who wanted to welcome the S.S.Vega.

**The Red Cross ship, the Vega, alongside London Berth.**

As she slowly entered the harbour on that moonlit winter's evening, all eyes were strained to catch a glimpse of the ship that was going to save the Island from starvation. As she turned towards the London berth and tied up, cheering broke out from the thousands of joyful Islanders who wanted to witness and be part of that historic moment.

Back at the Station, Sergeant Pugh was preparing to hand over to Sergeant Harry Bull when they heard the cheering. They realised that the Red Cross supplies had at last arrived.

During the next few days the arrangements for unloading and storage of the 42,400 parcels went entirely according to the plan devised by John Loveridge. The Police detailed to patrol the area did so without difficulty or incident.

German soldiers and foreign workers manhandled the crates of parcels from the S.S. Vega and loaded them on to the trucks of the German light railway, which transported them to St George's Hall. Each train load, which consisted of ten trucks, was accompanied by two German armed guards and one St John Ambulance man. Gradually the task of stacking the food parcels in the hall proceeded, until it was completed on Saturday morning the 30th December. The S.S. Vega left for Jersey at lunch time. There were no crowds to see her leave, all eyes and thoughts were now on St George's Hall.

Inevitably there was some pilfering of the Red Cross parcels, but as John Loveridge reported to the President of Essential Commodities Committee:-

"In regard to pilferages, I am perfectly satisfied from my own observations during the supervision of the discharge, that these shortages have not taken place during discharge, as with all the precautions taken this would have been absolutely impossible."

In all 70 parcels were pilfered, 56 New Zealand and 14 Canadian. Of the 19,411 packets of cigarettes which arrived on the S.S. Vega, 30 packets were missing when checked.

During Saturday, sufficient parcels were transferred to retail shops throughout the Island to enable every Islander to collect one on Sunday 31st December. Whilst the parcels were in the charge of the retailers they were responsible for their safety. They were forbidden to leave the parcels unattended at any time. George Lewis, the Auxiliary Policeman who had been dismissed on German instructions in 1942, volunteered to do a turn of guard duty, from 6.15 to 9.30pm on Saturday the 30th December outside Luff's shop in St Martin.

Every Islander received a Red Cross parcel, babies, the sick, hospital patients and even those unfortunates who were in prison. The biggest distribution was at Le Riche's High Street shop where over three thousand parcels were distributed. It was a very happy end to 1944.

There were, however, certain conditions imposed by the International Red Cross. The food parcels were provided for the benefit of each member of the civilian population, no German could receive one or even some of the contents. They were to be given out free of charge and no one was allowed to sell any of the contents.

Some of the parcels came from Canada and others were from New Zealand. The Canadian parcel was in a square box and weighed 11 lb, while the New Zealand one was oblong and only weighed 10.1/4 lb The Red Cross parcels from Canada contained:

| | | | |
|---|---|---|---|
| 5oz chocolate, | 12oz biscuits, | 3oz sardines, | 16oz milk powder, |
| 6oz prunes, | 8oz salmon, | 12oz corned beef, | 7oz raisins, |
| 8oz sugar, | 4oz tea, | 4oz cheese, | 16oz marmalade, |
| 16oz butter, | 10oz spam, | 3oz soap, | 1oz pepper and salt. |

The New Zealand Parcels contained:

| | | |
|---|---|---|
| 4oz tea, | 16oz corned mutton, | 12oz lamb and green peas, |
| 6oz chocolate, | 16oz butter, | 16oz coffee and milk, |
| 6oz sugar, | 7oz peas, | 14oz jam, |
| 16oz honey, | 12oz cheese | 6oz raisins. |

On the 28th December a conference was held at 'Rozel', Mount Durand, attended by the Bailiffs of Guernsey and Jersey, Colonel Iselin and Monsieur Callais of the International Red Cross, John Leale, Admiral Huffmeier and other German and Island representatives, to discuss future Red Cross shipments to the Channel Islands. A further meeting was held the following day.

Dr B.S.Collings, who had attended both meetings as the representative of the British Red Cross, called at the Station and told Mr Lamy that they had made a great deal of progress and that further supplies were assured on a monthly basis. He said that Colonel Iselin had informed the meeting that negotiations were afoot between the British and German Governments for supplying the Islands, possibly directly from England, with a shipment of coal. The Bailiff of Jersey, A.M.Coutanche, had commented that no problem was more acute in the Islands than that of fuel.

Another subject discussed was the possibility of evacuating people suffering from ailments which might respond to medical treatment which was not at present available in the Islands. It was suggested that if a hospital ship were sent for this purpose, a neutral doctor would accompany it and would make the final decision in each individual case.

At around 9.55pm on New Year's Day, Corporal R.Marsh received three telephone calls from members of the public, reporting that windows were being smashed in the Contree Mansell area of the Town. One caller said that the windows were being smashed by a German.

Acting Deputy Inspector, who was in the Station when the calls were received, went with A/PC 36 Solway and A/PC 35 Le Page to investigate. When they reached the Commercial Arcade, they met a German Marine who was running in their direction. Mr Banneville, who challenged the Marine, later recalled:- "He responded by threatening me with what I first thought was a revolver. I closed with him and he then made a violent attack with his dagger. He also attacked Solway and Le Page. I then advised these officers to stand clear.

We followed the Marine up High Street and when at the top, he attacked a civilian who was accompanied by a woman. This civilian turned out to be a German citizen. A German soldier who passed by, was asked to assist in the arrest of this Marine but would not have anything to do with it.

Accompanied by Solway and this German citizen, we followed him down the Pollet Street and near No.39 he made a dash for the Harbour. When nearing the harbour entrance this German subject requested the sentry to stop the Marine. He was detained by the sentry. I noticed that his right hand was badly cut and he was taken to the guard house where his hand was dressed. Two naval officers arrived and then the Feldgendarmerie arrived. A/PCs Boalch and Le Poidevin, who I had sent up to Contree Mansell, saw the man in the guard house and identified the man seen by them in Market Street. I was instructed to report to Captain Obermayer's office at 11.00am the 7th January 1945."

The Acting Deputy Inspector and Constable Solway examined properties from Mount Durand to Market Street and found that 16 shop windows had been damaged by the use of a sharp pointed instrument. At Mrs Emily Kibble's home at 1 Mount Durand, blood was found on the windowsill. Four plate glass windows had been smashed at 9 Mansell Street and were all stained with blood. No 4 Market Street also had blood on the window. The damage was later estimated to be £257.16.0. The Germans dealt with the Marine but no record exists to indicate the punishment imposed.

As a result of the advertisement in the Press, the Police sub-Committee interviewed candidates for Auxiliary Policemen and fifteen were appointed on the 3rd January 1945:-

| | |
|---|---|
| A/PC 42 Ronald Edward Archenoul, 20, | Steam Mill Lanes, St Martin. |
| A/PC 43 John Edward Aubert, 34, | 14 Rougeval, St Peter Port |
| A/PC 44 Arthur Russell Bailey, 19, | Kings Mill, Castel. |

| | |
|---|---|
| A/PC 45 Ronald Walter Bourgaize, 19, | 2 Beverley Cottages, La Fosse, St Martin. |
| A/PC 46 Albert George Bichard, 30, | 5 Dracena Way, St Martin. |
| A/PC 47 George Edward Bougourd, 24, | Hillside Cottage, Castel Hill, St Andrew. |
| A/PC 48 Harold Frederick Kendall, 31, | Fermoy, Bosq Lane, St Peter Port. |
| A/PC 49 Walter Belmore Wood Lovell, 40, | St Elmo, Coronation Road, St Peter Port. |
| A/PC 50 Charles Nicholls, 22, | Les Choffings, St Saviour. |
| A/PC 51 Emile George Perrott, 23, | La Ruette Farm, St Saviour. |
| A/PC 52 Ronald Henry Pagnier, 20, | La Fosse, St Martin. |
| A/PC 53 Arthur George Stephen Reeve, 35, | 20 Pedvin Street, St Peter Port. |
| A/PC 54 Sidney John Torode, 27, | Rosc Cottage, Grandes Rocques, Castel. |
| A/PC 55 Clifford Henry Tickner, 48, | Rosyth, Saltpans, St Sampson. |
| A/PC Osmond Stevens, 34, | Rue Sauvage, St Sampson. |

The fifteen new recruits commenced duty on the 6th January and fourteen of them were sworn in at a sitting of the Royal Court on Saturday 13th January. Osmond Stevens however did not survive long enough to be sworn in as an Auxiliary Policeman.

On the 10th January a notice appeared in the Press:-

"ISLAND POLICE.
NOTICE.

In order to meet present conditions, the Island has been sub divided into three Police districts with a Station in each district. The boundaries are roughly as follows;

Town. Town side of a line Red Lion to L'Aumone Cross Road, Castel, thence Rectory Hill, Bailiff's Cross Road to Jerbourg. Station: St James Chambers. Telephone 570.

North. North of a line Albecq to Red Lion. Station: Roman Catholic School, L'Islet. Telephone 4208

South. South of a line Albecq to Jerbourg. Station: Junction of Les Blicqs and Chemin du Roi, Forest. Telephone 5393

It will greatly assist if persons requiring Police assistance will apply at their local Station.

A.P.Lamy, Acting Inspector."

Sergeant Charles Le Lievre was placed in charge of the North sub Station and Sergeant Harry Dyson the South sub Station.

The new recruits were issued with night passes and a request was made to the Secretary of the Essential Commodities Committee for cycle dynamos for three new Auxiliaries, Reeve Aubert and Bougourd. An application was also made on behalf of Sergeant Plevin. Four permits were issued.

In *The Star* on the 10th January one of the new recruits was given headline recognition.

"From Bass to Bobbie.

'Hank' Reeve the well-known bass-slapping musician, is to take a hand at slapping law breakers, for he has enlisted into the ranks of the Island Police Force.

'Hank' is well fitted for the job as he is a jujitsu expert and conducted a wrestling class when he was in the Army.

So prospective law breakers should take this advice 'Watch your step', or you may get tied up in knots, by one who knows how to do it"

On the 13th January, Charles Lewis, an employee of the Essential Commodities Committee, found two empty Red Cross cartons at the back of the stage, in the Artistes room, at St George's Hall. The find was reported to John Loveridge, who immediately reported the matter to the Police. Acting Deputy Inspector Banneville was sent to investigate and was shown one Canadian Red Cross carton and one invalid carton, both empty.

The parcels concerned were two that had been exchanged and had been left open near the office. Mr Banneville questioned the night watchman, Red Cross representatives, Special Constables and Police officers who had been an duty at the Hall since the 3rd January.

The Acting Deputy Inspector wrote a full report which was forwarded to the Bailiff and the President of the Essential Commodities Committee. He suggested that:-

"It would appear that too many persons have access to the premises. I would respectfully suggest that the doors leading to the yard be kept locked, except when vehicles are loading or unloading and a Constable should be on duty in the vestibule to admit authorised persons and that all persons be searched by him before leaving. This would make the stocks as secure as possible, but of course could not prevent anyone stealing and consuming the goods on the premises."

The Bailiff read his copy of the report and wrote to the President of the Controlling Committee:-

"I have been greatly disturbed by a letter from the Acting Inspector of Police, dated the 17th instant, enclosing a report from Acting Deputy Inspector Banneville, with regard to the pilfering of Red Cross parcels, soap and I believe, tobacco from St George's Hall. I have carefully read the report and it appears to me that there should be a tightening up all round of the guarding and checking of these parcels in the Hall. As I personally gave a receipt as Bailiff of the Island to the Red Cross Commissioner for these parcels the public will naturally hold me responsible for their delivery to them.

Under these circumstances I feel quite sure that you will do everything possible to ensure that these parcels are not tampered with in any way and that they are properly safeguarded. One or more members of the Island Police Force should undoubtedly be on the premises day and night to see that everything is carried on in the proper manner and I trust that no recurrence of a like nature will occur and that those responsible may be brought to justice."

The President of the Essential Commodities asked his Secretary if he had any comments. John Loveridge most certainly did and he expressed them very strongly in a three-page letter to his President:-

"I cannot agree with the views of the Police. In my opinion the thefts took place during the night time watches which comprise our night guard, one or two Special Constables, a uniformed Policeman and two or more Red Cross representatives. It is almost impossible for anyone to tamper with cases or parcels without authority during the hours of daylight..... It was suggested and first agreed by the Police that a trap should be set during the night but the Police did not deem it expedient for this to be done."

He questioned virtually ever aspect of the Police report in considerable detail. As a conclusion he wrote:-

"As we have been taken severely to task by the Bailiff in regard to these thefts and the Bailiff is acting on the strength of the Police report, I would call for an amending report from the Police." John Loveridge went on to suggest:- "I recommend as suggested by the Inspector that a uniformed Constable be on duty

24 hours a day in the vestibule to admit authorised persons and to be searched by him before leaving."

As a consequence arrangements were made to allow only persons with a pass, issued by Louis Guillemette and signed by John Leale, into St George's Hall. Corporal Le Cocq was positioned in the vestibule and detailed to admit only persons with official passes and to search everyone leaving the Hall.

Corporal Le Cocq was inspecting every pass and only letting those in with the necessary authority, when John Leale appeared with Louis Guillemette.

"Your pass please sir." requested the Corporal.

John Leale, swallowed hard, obviously trying to control himself, turned to his Secretary and said:

"You had better go back to the office and get two passes for us."

Louis Guillemette quickly returned with two passes he had made out and handed them to John Leale for him to sign. Then he turned and presented them to Corporal Le Cocq, who said:

"Thank you Sir." and stood aside and let them in.

Francois Le Cocq, years later, admitted that it was just pure cussedness on his part, as he believed, although wrongly, that John Leale and Louis Guillemette were the ones who had originally complained about the lack of security.

One of the conditions that the International Red Cross imposed on the free distribution of Red Cross parcels was that no one was allowed to sell any of the contents.

On the 19th January, seventy-one-year-old Philip Anley, of Blenheim, Doyle Road, sold a quarter-pound packet of tea from his Red Cross parcel at Messrs Stroobant & Symes, Church Hill, for 40 Reichmarks. The Police were immediately informed by the manager, Mr Lucas, and as a result Anley appeared in Court on the 23rd January. He was found guilty and fined £10 or two months' imprisonment. The Court also directed that his action should be reported to the Bailiff's Red Cross Supplies Committee with a view to debarring him from receiving further Red Cross parcels.

The Committee decided that Anley would not for the time being be allocated Red Cross parcels and his grocer was informed accordingly.

On the 28th January Mr P.F.Anley wrote to the Committee:-

"Re Red Cross Tea.

I regret that the Committee have thought fit to deal so drastically with me, as under the present food shortage the consequences may be serious. I am old and underweight considerably now and even the butter allowance has been cut down to 2 oz, presumably because of the Red Cross Parcels from which I am debarred.

I did not intentionally take the Red Cross tea, as I had other tea to dispose of. I was in a hurry and took it as it was a quarter pound already weighed out. I can prove to the Red Cross Committee that I have Lipton's tea if they will grant me an interview."

The President of the Bailiff's Red Cross Supplies Committee, John Leale replied:-

"This matter has been considered by my Committee and it has been decided to adhere to the previous decision. "

However on the 13th February the Committee decided that Mr Anley should no longer be debarred from receiving Red Cross parcels.

On hearing the Committee's decision Mr Anley wrote:-

"I wish to convey my heartfelt thanks to the Bailiff's Red Cross Supplies Committee for their kindness in allowing me again to receive the Red Cross Parcels and Supplies, the value of which is inestimable".

As far as the rank and file German soldiers and foreign workers were concerned the food situation was desperate. The civilians had the Red Cross food parcels but the troops and foreign workers still had only their very meagre rations. Inevitably there was an upsurge of crime and in many cases it was accompanied by physical violence.

At 8.45pm on the 18th January A/PC 29 Frank Falla was on patrol at the Bridge, near a States Potato depot, at the Stone Workers Hall. He later recalled:-

"On entering Commercial Road I noticed a hand-cart near the Hall. I returned to the Bridge and met George Symons, the butcher, and told him about it. We both went down to investigate and tried the door of the Hall. At the same time two German Marines ran out of the porch. We both gave chase, Symons overtook one and he and the German fell to the ground. The other Marine managed to get away. We both tried to detain the German. At the same time Norman Collenette, of Bunker Hill, L'Ancresse came on the scene. At my request he went and telephoned the Police Station.

Then a German soldier came from the North Cinema direction and spoke to the German on the ground and asked me what was the matter. The soldier immediately used his bayonet on both Symons and myself. Symons received a gash on the back of his head. Symons managed to take the bayonet away from the soldier. The Feldgendarmerie arrived after being telephoned for by the Police Sub-Station at L'Islet. Mr Symons was taken to a house nearby where his injury was dressed. The only blow I received was a kick on the knee from one of the Marines. They took the number of the soldier from off the bayonet. The bayonet and hand-cart are in the charge of the Feldgendarmerie at Braye Road."

Forty-five-year-old George Symons, of 'Benbow', the Bridge, also recalled the events that night:-

"At about 8.45pm, after coming from the cinema, I saw Constable Falla on the Bridge, on duty. He requested me to accompany him to investigate at the store at the Stone Workers Hall, having seen a hand-truck in Commercial Road against the wall. I accompanied him and we went as far as the corner, we did not hear anything. As we were passing the Hall on our return, A/Pc Falla tried the door and two German Marines ran out from the foyer. We immediately gave chase, I caught one of them outside Le Maitre's shop on the Bridge.

As soon as I had this man, Constable Falla arrived, we tried to detain the Marine, in doing so we all fell to the ground. While on the ground I took the Marine's bayonet to prevent him using it and hid it in my clothing. Then a civilian passed by and Constable Falla asked him to telephone the Police. In the meantime another Marine arrived, he looked on for a few seconds and then drew his bayonet and hit me over the head with it and cut the back of my head. I felt dazed and went to a friend to have my wound bathed. After that I went back to the Bridge but nobody was about."

Nothing more was heard of the incident from the German Authorities.

Earlier that day A/PC Roy Thoume had gone to see Frank Browning at Le Bouillon Farm in St Andrew, in response to a telephone call received at the Les Blicqs sub-Station.

When the Constable arrived at around 7.40am, he found thirty-three-year-old Frank lying on the floor, with his right leg doubled up underneath him. His left leg and ankle was covered in blood from a bullet wound in his ankle.

By the time a member of the Feldgendarmerie arrived it was daylight. A search outside revealed a soldier's cap and an eighteen-inch-long poker. Just inside the barn door they found a sack containing a few apples. The Feldgendarmerie took possession of the cap and poker.

Frank Browning told the Constable:-

"At about 7.15am I heard a noise coming from our barn which adjoins our house. I called my father and brother and told them to go to the barn via the door leading from the house, while I went outside to catch whoever might be there as they came down the outside steps. I went up the steps and when I reached the top, a soldier with an overcoat, pointed a rifle at my chest. I pushed it down and he fired, the bullet entered my left leg just above my ankle. I fell down the steps and in doing so I believe I have broken my right leg. My father and brother carried me into the house."

Frank Browning's father, Frank Browning senior, told A/PC Roy Thoume:-

"When my son called me, I went through the bedroom door which leads into the barn. As I opened the door I saw a flash and heard the report of a rifle. It came from a soldier standing by the door at the top of the steps. I went into the barn and then another soldier came down from the loft above and fired his revolver through the door at the top of the steps. He ran down the steps with the other soldier, then they ran up the path by our haystack and I could not hear them any more."

Kenneth Browning, Frank's brother, told the Constable:-

"When I was called by my brother, I followed my father and reached the barn just as the soldier who had come down from the loft, fired his revolver. I ran out behind him as he went down the steps. At the bottom of the steps I found my brother who was on the ground groaning, my father by then was alongside of him. We picked him up carefully and carried him inside the house. I then went and telephoned for the St John Ambulance and the local Police."

A/PC Roy Thoume searched the area and established that entry to the barn had been made by a ladder obtained from a nearby stable. With it the two Germans had reached a barred window. The bars had been forced and entry made through the window. Once inside it was possible to open the barn door. By the design of sole and heel footprints found at the bottom of the ladder and also on a footpath leading to the fields, it appeared to the Constable that one of the men was wearing rubber Wellington boots.

Frank Browning was taken by the St John Ambulance to the Emergency Hospital at Castel where he was attended to by Dr Gibson. It was found that besides the bullet wound in his left leg he had also suffered a compound fracture of his right leg.

**Fred W. Bush in greatcoat and other St John Ambulance men supervising the unloading of Red Cross Flour at Braggs Store on the Glategny Esplanade.**

# Chapter 31

# "DOUBTFUL SUICIDE"

On the 22nd January 1945 a German Notice appeared in 'La Gazette Officielle':-
"In view of the serious food situation which justifies public claims even on private sources to which the owners were fully entitled and in further view of the distribution of free gifts by the International Red Cross and the promise of further supplies which can be accepted in decency only where there are no private sources of any size, it is hereby ordered as follows:-

1. Where a household, business or concern of any kind will hold a considerable quantity of tinned food, not more than altogether 3 tins or jars of tinned or potted meat, fowl, fish or fat and not more than 10 tins or jars of ripe fruit or vegetables may be retained per head of that household etc. Any excess must be distributed by the owner to civilians in less fortunate circumstances or offered to the soup kitchens.

The tins contained in the Red Cross parcels, as well as any home-made fruit or vegetables preserves are excluded from the provisions of this order and will not be counted as allowance.

Institutions, invalids requiring special diet, may retain stores in excess of the above figures and may, through their doctors, appeal to the Platzkommandantur, Guernsey, for the retention of any excess stores they may still have and require.

2. Similarly not more than 5 lb of flour and 2 lb of sugar may be retained for every member of a household, etc: any excess to be distributed as above.
3. Anyone contravening this order will be punished according to Par.22 of the Order for the Protection of the Occupying Authority and the stores in excess of the provisions of this order will be confiscated.
4. This order shall come into force on February 1st 1945."

As a result of this order the German Feldgendarmerie searched private houses and commercial premises and took away any food or drink that they considered excessive. The food seized by the Germans was kept for their own use. Many of the Feldgendarmerie took the view that now Islanders had Red Cross parcels, any other stock of food was excessive. In fact very few people possessed any reserve of food, it had long since been eaten.

The searches were looked upon by Islanders as legalized armed robbery.

On the 23rd of January A.C.Richings, the States Controller of Petroleum supplies, responded to a letter from the Platzkommandantur requesting details of the estimated consumption for the month of February 1945. A copy was forwarded to Mr Lamy. The Police were allocated 40 gallons for their four vehicles, three motorcycles and the Commer van.

The Bailiff was allocated 5 gallons for his Standard 9. His other cars, a Humber 20 and an Austin 18, were laid up for the duration. Most doctors received an allocation of 12 gallons and the St John Ambulance 60 gallons. The

Glasshouse Utilisation Board received 32 gallons, while Timmer Limited were allocated 54 gallons for February 1945.

At 8.00pm on the 23rd January the German Harbourmaster, Captain Obermeyer called at the Police Station and reported that two fishermen and a Frenchman were missing. The fishermen were Thomas John Le Page, and his brother John William Le Page, both of 2 Gas Lane, St Peter Port. Acting Deputy Inspector Banneville accompanied Captain Obermeyer and another German officer to the Le Page brothers' home which they thoroughly searched. Enquiries were made in the neighbourhood, but no further light could be shed on the brothers' disappearance.

Fred Banneville knew more of the escape than he dare reveal to the German Harbourmaster. The brothers had been 'recruited' by the acting French Consul, Monsieur P.L.V.Lambert, to take important information to the Allies. The escape plan was known and approved by members of the Controlling Committee.

Arrangements were made for a French electrical engineer who had worked on a number of the German long range battery installations to accompany the brothers. His first-hand knowledge was greater than any plan could provide. Tom and Jack obtained permission for the Frenchman to accompany them on some of their previous fishing expeditions in order to allay the fears of the Germans. The brothers also took plans of the German fortifications and details of the deteriorating food position.

When they left St Peter Port harbour they sailed around to the east of Herm before setting course for the French coast. After being at sea for only four and a half hours they were picked up by the Americans and soon the information they had taken with them, was in the hands of the British Authorities.

Another of the many anonymous letters that were being written during the closing days of the Occupation was received by the manager of the Dairy on the 27th January:-

"Why is Mr A. Mahy, of Windmill Vineries, Ville au Roi, permitted to receive full cream milk daily from Douglas Ozanne, of Ruettes Brayes Farm. As I understand this is strictly forbidden. I do not see why this is allowed to go on when I and many others have forgotten the taste of good milk. Trusting you will see into this immediately, if not I shall, but I thought you the right one to inform."

The Acting Inspector was passed the anonymous letter and he sent A/PC 12 Mahy to see Douglas Ozanne at his farm. He told the Constable:-

"I have never supplied Mr Mahy with full cream milk. Two or three times a week he brings his dinner here to cook in our Esse cooker and as he wraps it up to and fro, I suppose people think he is fetching milk."

A/PC 26 Ted Butt was sent to interview Alfred J.Mahy, of Windmill Vineries. He told the Constable:-

"I have never had full cream milk from Mr Ozanne, I get my ration from Mr Torode at the Ville au Roi. The only business I do with Mr Ozanne is when he grazes his cattle on my land and pays me with manure."

No further action was taken.

Former Police Sergeant Alf Howlett reported to A/PC 13 Le Poidevin that one of his greenhouses had been entered during the night of 30th January 1945 and about 20 head of broccoli stolen. Alf said that he suspected German soldiers. The Constable inspected the greenhouse and concluded that entry must have been made with a key. None of the glass was broken and the locks were undamaged. He discovered footprints in the greenhouse, with studded soles and narrow heel tips, similar to boots worn by German soldiers.

Alf Howlett had returned to the Island on the 8th January 1944, after serving his prison sentence on the continent, and now worked full time on his smallholding. His wife, Annie, who was deported to Germany in February 1943, had returned to the Island on the 25th April 1944.

Food shortages daily became more desperate as far as the Germans and the foreign workers were concerned. The inevitable result was that the level of crime escalated. In the fields, the main target, at that time of year was parsnips. On farms and in private houses food of any description was always at risk, particularly Red Cross parcels.

The daily log of crimes reported and entered in the Occurrence Book continued to expand. On the 30th January 1945, some of the crimes listed in the Occurrence Book at the Town Station included:-

Breaking and entering dwelling house,
Breaking and entering shop,
Breaking and entering house, jewellery and food stuff stolen alleged,
Breaking and entering house, food stuff stolen alleged,
Stables entered, oats stolen,
Greenhouse entered, wood stolen,
Greenhouse entered, leeks stolen,
Two women sawing branches from trees,
Larceny of dog alleged,
Larceny of wood from stables,
Breaking and entering,
Rabbit stolen.

The two Sub Stations had an even longer lists of crimes, mainly concerned with food and fuel. Many crimes, however, went unreported because the public generally accepted that the Police could do little other than record the incident.

The item 'Two women sawing branches from trees', was reported by A/PC 39 Moore. At 5.30pm the Constable saw Douglas Ozanne, of Ruettes Brayes Farm in one of his fields at Steam Mill Lanes, who told him:-

"About half an hour ago, I was in my field here when I saw two women sawing branches off my trees in the next field. I at once phoned the Police and detained the women until you arrived. The value of the wood is 10/-."

The two women, Mrs Germine Potter and Miss Amy Greening, both of Mount Durand, admitted sawing off branches. They appeared in Court on the 31st January and were each fined ten shillings.

The 'Larceny of dog alleged', was a 'possible' crime reported by A/PC 43 Aubert. At 3.15pm he saw George Saumarez De Lisle of Doyle Road, who told him:-

"During the morning of the 25th January I lost my fox terrier dog which goes by the name of Bols. It was white with black and red patches."

A neighbour, Mrs Mary Peck, of Doyle Road, said:-

"I saw the dog on Friday or Saturday last in the French Halles, it was being led by a German soldier, I know the dog very well. I would not know the soldier again."

As nothing more was heard of the dog there can be little doubt as to its fate.

Towards the end of the Occupation everyone had become only too familiar with the activities of thieves. Red Cross parcels, bicycles, potatoes, chickens and even cats and dogs were all targets of petty thieving. Sometimes the Germans and the foreign workers would offer to buy a dog or cat and only if the owner refused did they steal them. By the end of the Occupation, the cat population of the Island had been virtually wiped out.

Mrs Emily Kibble had moved into 1 Mount Durand just before Christmas 1944, while Eric Kibble was still serving a nine-month prison sentence for being found in possession of a wireless set. Towards the end of his sentence he was allowed a certain amount of freedom and two days before he was due to be released, he broke into a German store at Granville House, Mount Durand, and stole a large quantity of tinned food. He was caught and sentenced by the Germans to a further two years' imprisonment. Mrs Kibble, whose home was searched, later explained:-

"The Germans found all kinds of foodstuffs. On the 6th January 1945 I was sentenced to three months' imprisonment by a military court. At the time there was a waiting list for prison and I was told to arrive at the prison at 5.00pm on February 12th. This was later postponed for a week."

In the Police Court on the 31st January two boys, aged 10 and 12 years, were convicted of breaking and entering Mrs Kibble's house and stealing tins of prunes, sardines, fruit, beans, soup, salmon and marmalade from her Red Cross parcel. After the Magistrate heard the evidence each boy was sentenced to 8 strokes of the birch.

The same day Mrs Kibble wrote to John Loveridge, the Secretary of the Essential Commodities Committee:-

"I have been informed by Mr Mahy, of the Bailiff's Red Cross Supplies Committee to put my case to you as regards the part of my Red Cross parcel having been stolen and other food stuffs as well. The Police have had the case in hand and the two boys who broken into my place, has been dealt with by the Police. They have eaten all the food they taken and the empty tins have been found.

I asked the Police if I could have my food replaced that was taken from the Red Cross. Sergeant Pill told me to see Mr Mahy. And then I was told by Mr Mahy to put my case to you.

These are missing from the Red Cross parcel.

Tin butter, tin salmon, tin marmalade, tin sardines, packet prunes.

I remain, yours faithfully, Mrs E.C.Kibble. Thanking you.

P.S. Also taken pre-war 1 tin beans, 2 tins fruit, 1 tin tomato soup."

Mrs Kibble's request was turned down.

As 12-year-old Michael Gilmour, of La Rocque, Cobo, was going to school on the 20th February he found a handbag and some ladies clothing at the top of the beach opposite the old Inn, at Vazon, near the German watch tower. He took them to school, where he handed them to his teacher, Mrs Robinson, who immediately telephoned the Police Station.

The Acting Deputy Inspector went to Castel School, at Albecq House and was handed the handbag and clothing found by Michael Gilmour. The handbag, contained an identity card belonging to Mrs Kibble, ration books, a small bottle labelled poison, which was empty. There was also a pair of rubber boots, a blue rubber coat and a grey skirt.

The details of the find were recorded in the Occurrence Book. In the margin, Mr Lamy wrote - "Doubtful suicide".

At 10.40am the next day the Station received a telephone call from the German Military Court at Escalonia, Mount Durand, saying that Mrs Emily Kibble had failed to report to the Court to start her prison sentence and that she was to be found and placed in prison.

The Acting Deputy Inspector, accompanied by Constable Solway, went to her home and found the door open. Some of the furniture had been removed and no one was there. Later he went to Vazon where, with a German Sergeant Major, he searched the rocks in the vicinity of where the clothing was found, but without result.

On the 31st January the President of the Controlling Committee received a letter from Herr. Schneberger:-

"Re Motorcycle Pol No 90.

On the 21st October 1944 the 'Velocette' motorcycle Police No 90 was found buried 20 yards east of the corner Rue des Marettes - Icart Road, by a member of the Forces. The owner of the motorcycle was found to be Noel Bonnel, who evacuated to England in June 1940.

According to the owner's brother Rex Bonnel, of 1, Glenfield, Jerbourg Road, the latter, together with his brother, had buried the motorcycle. The motorcycle had not been left either to him or to any other person in custody. He had therefore not felt bound to report the motorcycle in accordance with the Feldkommandantur's order of 12th June 1942.

The motorcycle has been confiscated without indemnity, in favour of the Wehrmacht, in lieu of the sentence which cannot be imposed."

At the beginning of the Occupation Rex Bonnel lived with his parents and sister at Le Douit Cottage, Saints Bay Road. His brother Noel was away from the Island, serving in the British army. Rex and his brother both owned motorcycles. Rex had declared his to the Germans when required to do so, but had kept quiet about his brother's.

Before the family moved to 1 Glenfield, Jerbourg Road, Noel's motorcycle was secreted in a hole dug into the bank alongside Le Douit Cottage. Before it was hidden, it was well oiled and greased. The bank was partly refilled, except for a small air vent along the top. A quantity of tomato staging was piled against the bank so that the motorcycle wouldn't be seen.

The Russell family moved into Le Douit Cottage and when they became short of fuel they used the tomato staging and the motorcycle was exposed. The Germans quickly traced its ownership to Noel Bonnel and Rex Bonnel was ordered to report to Grange Lodge. They wanted to know why he had not declared it and who it actually belonged to, since the original owner was not in the Island.

Rex told them "It is not my motorcycle and I don't see that you can charge me with anything."

"We shall see", was the pointed response.

Fortunately the Germans accepted Rex's story and merely confiscated the motorcycle.

Around the same time that the motorcycle was discovered Rex had another brush with the Germans. He kept a number of rabbits. The garden of 1 Glenfield was very narrow, which made it easily accessible to any German who was on a nightly thieving mission. In order to provide some protection, Rex ran a wire around the boundary hedge and attached it to a bell in his bedroom window.

Each morning he removed the wire and replaced it again before dark. One morning when he was dismantling the system, some German troops on manoeuvres came through the garden and noticed the rabbits. Rex said to his father, "Sure as hell they are going to be around here tonight."

It was about three o'clock in the morning when the bell rang and the family dog started to bark. There were three or four Germans in the garden and when Rex shouted at them, they ran away taking some of the rabbits with them. About half an hour later Rex again heard the sound of tramping feet around the side of the house.

He went out and was confronted by a German who stuck a revolver in his stomach and ordered, "Raus, Raus, Raus", so he had to get back into the house. The Germans then went into the neighbouring garden and Rex watched them searching the ground with a flashlight. Clearly they had dropped something on their first visit which they must have felt could be incriminating and had come back to look for it. In the meantime Rex's father telephoned the Police Station and they in turn informed the Feldgendarmerie.

About half an hour or so after the thieving party had left, the Feldgendarmerie arrived, knocked on the door and asked Rex what all the fuss was about. He told the Germans that thieves had taken some of his rabbits and one of them asked "Was it a tall one and a little one, if it was, we met them up the road."

The following morning Rex found his missing rabbits in a box that had been left at the side of the house. It was one of the rare occasions during the Occupation when livestock stolen by the Germans, was returned to its owner and in this case - alive.

After the Island was liberated the arena of the pre-war North Show and Battle of Flowers at Port Soif, was used as a 'graveyard' for captured German tanks, armoured vehicles, guns and other equipment. Rex Bonnel went there and after spending several hours searching, retrieved his brother's 'Velocette' motorcycle, still in working order.

A/PC 28 Bill Boalch, who was working from the West Sub-Station, had a busy morning on the 6th February. Three overnight break-ins had been reported and he was detailed to investigate each occurrence. First he visited Basil Le Huray, of 'Esperance', Forest, whose stable had been broken into, he suspected by Russian troops stationed in the district. The bottom half of the stable door had been literally torn away but fortunately the inside of the door had been barricaded with bars which were nailed in position and these had prevented any further access being gained.

Then Bill Boalch visited Frank H.Tourtel, of Thornhill, Forest who told him:-

"This morning at 2.45am I heard someone downstairs. I got up and saw a light in my conservatory at the back of the house. I came down and on opening the dining room door which leads to the conservatory, I heard a door shut. I went outside and was just in time to see the figure of a man jump over the hedge into the road. I could not see how he was dressed. Entry was gained by removing a pain of glass from the roof of the conservatory."

The Constable could find no marks from boots. Frank Tourtel confirmed that nothing appeared to have been taken.

The Constable's third call of the morning was at the Forest Post Office, at L'Epinel, where Mrs Aimee de Beaucamp told him:-

"This morning at about 4.20am I heard a crash of glass. I awakened my husband, who went downstairs and found a pane of glass in the shop smashed. Whoever it was could not get in and there is nothing missing."

The lock box was broken, but a bolt on the inside of the door had prevented it being forced. A shutter on the inside of the window saved entry being made that way. There were no footprints. Two sheds were broken into, but nothing was missing.

Sergeant Dyson, who was in charge of the sub Station, got in touch with the Sergeant Major at Avondale, Forest, and informed him of the three attempted break-ins. The Sergeant suggested that the Germans should do something to control the Russian troops from prowling around the area at night. The German Sergeant Major agreed that, for the time being, two Auxiliary Policemen would patrol with his men from 11.00pm till 5.00am.

Dr Collings who had attended another meeting at 'Rozel', Mount Durand, on 7th February, between representatives of the International Red Cross, Colonel von Helldorff and Victor Carey, later told Mr Lamy that the S.S.Vega had had a very rough passage back to Lisbon after her first trip to the Channel Islands.

Repairs had been necessary and these had taken more than a fortnight to complete. As a consequence the Vega's second visit had been delayed. Dr Collings, said that the British Red Cross had purchased 8 tons of soap in Portugal, which it had been hoped would be shipped on the second visit of the Vega. The Portuguese Government had, however, declined to allow the soap to leave the country.

The subject of the possible evacuation of invalids, the meeting had been told, was still under discussion between the German and British Governments, but the real difficulty was finding a suitable ship. Only Swedish ships were acceptable and very few were available. 300 applications for evacuation, including next of kin, had been received so far and more were expected.

At 7.00am, on the 11th February, one of the recently recruited Auxiliary Policemen, A/PC 42 Ronald Archenoul, failed to parade for early turn. A/PC Sebire who was sent by Corporal Le Cocq to check, found Archenoul still in bed at 10.00am. He told Bill Sebire:-

"My alarm failed to go off at 6am, I woke at 7am."

He was asked by Constable Sebire why he had not reported at all.

Archenoul replied "My boots are leaking, I will see the Inspector tomorrow."

At 11.00am the next day he saw the Mr Lamy, who dismissed him.

The German Police were officially and unofficially searching private houses and confiscating considerable quantities of food. Ken Lewis wrote in his diary:-

"The Germans are searching houses for food and making lists of stores and collecting them later. People such as Alan Mackay, Victor Creasey and Madame M. Pommier, had good hauls, the Germans took away two lorry loads from Pommier."

William Leckey, of the White Horse Inn, L'Ancresse, called at the North Sub Station and reported to Sergeant Charles Le Lievre, that:-

"The Feldgendarmerie came to my house on Friday 9th February and said 'We wish to search your house, we are the Feldgendarmerie'. I gave them every assistance, as I had nothing to hide. They found about 18 lb of flour, made from gleanings, on top of a wardrobe, it was quite open, not hidden. One of them said 'This is black market' and added 'We will confiscate this, the bags will be returned to you through the civil Police'.

I told them how I had obtained the flour and how I exchanged some clothing for it and the Gendarme said 'It is forbidden'. I did not think it was. My wife is very ill and has been under Dr Gibson ever since she had her last operation in May 1944. Now I have nothing left for her and I wish to protest. This flour is not black market."

When Acting Inspector Lamy saw the item recorded in the Sub Station's Occurrence Book, he instructed that the matter be reported to the President of the Controlling Committee.

Mr W.Breton, of Homelea, Landes du Marche, had a similar experience to tell Sergeant Le Lievre. After hearing that other complaints had been referred to the President of the Controlling Committee, he decided to write to John Leale direct. In a letter dated the 12th February, he wrote:-

"Whilst grinding wheat, sweet corn and oats by hand grinder recently, I had a visit from the German Feldgendarmerie who informed me that I was not allowed to grind wheat without a licence. I informed them that I was not aware of this especially as I was not using oil or petrol of any description. Nevertheless they took away all the cereals which I had in hand, amounting to about 105 lb and belonging to ten families.

I have visited the Feldgendarmerie at Braye Road, who took away the cereals and at Birnham Court, but I still have not received any other reason for their retaining the cereals except that I need a licence to grind them.

I have made local enquiries and I have not been able to find out that I needed a licence. I shall be obliged if, as President of the Controlling Committee, you will take the matter up with the proper authorities, as in view of the present position regarding bread, the people to whom the cereals belong would like return of same."

There is no record of Jurat John Leale having been able to help Mr Breton and his customers.

However, John Leale, the Bailiff and the Acting Attorney General, did hold a meeting with Colonel von Helldorff on the subject of 'Searching of houses by German Police'. Mr Leale said that he was disturbed because it had been reported that the German Police told a man who had only 1 cwt of beans that he was to set them aside and they would be collected. Mr Leale added:-

"In such days as the ones through which we were living, 1 cwt. of such goods as beans or sweet corn could not be considered unreasonable for a family. People had a right to know where they stood."

Mr Martel said that there was some nervousness lest Germans masquerading as Police should go to people's houses. The Colonel said that the Feldgendarmerie could always be identified by their metal breast plates and the German Agricultural Auxiliary Police by their yellow armbands inscribed 'Hilfspolizei'.

**Advocate J.E.L. Martel.**

The Bailiff said he had understood that goods confiscated would be handed over to the civilian authorities. He asked for an assurance that this would be done. Mr Martel said that goods had been confiscated which were never mentioned in the German Order of the 20th January 1945. He instanced alcohol and soap.

Colonel Von Helldorff said that the Order had been issued without his knowledge, whereupon Mr Martel presented him with a copy. The Colonel, after glancing at it, remarked that he would have a new order drawn up to cover the points raised.

On the 19th February the new Order was issued in La Gazette Officielle:-

"NOTICE.

Re: Restricting civilian alcohol and soap supplies.

The welfare of the community no longer permits single well-to-do members to hoard supplies of soap, wine and spirits exceeding their actual needs.

The Notice of January 20th 1945 re handing over excess tinned foods is therefore extended to include soap, wine and spirits. All supplies exceeding 5 litres of spirits and 10 litres of wine including champagne, per household, as well as supplies of soap exceeding 2 tablets per head of the household, will be confiscated in favour of hospitals and institutions."

# Chapter 32

# HEIL TO OUR BELOVED FUHRER!

Eighty-nine-year-old widow Mrs Sarah Warr of Richmond Corner, St Sampson, told A/PC 30 De Carteret when he visited her on the 15th February:-

"Last Saturday, some time, a German soldier came into my house while I was peeling my ration of potatoes and took six of them. He said he was hungry. I told him, 'So am I'. He then went away. Today another one came, I think it was about 11.00am, he was a different one to the other, but I did not let him come in, I shut the door. I am living alone and they frighten me. I cannot describe either of them. The one who came today went to Mr Poat across the road."

The Constable went to see Wilfred Poat, but as he was not at home, he spoke to his gardener, Henry Thoumine, who told him:-

"At about 11.00am this morning a German soldier came here and walked straight into the house without permission and asked the maid for food. The maid called me to chase him away, this I did, although he was inclined to be obstinate. He asked me for vegetables, I refused him and he went away. This man comes around the neighbourhood practically every week begging for food. I would recognise him if I saw him again. He is medium height, middle age and has a long moustache. I don't know where he is billeted."

The Constable spoke to Mrs Frossard, the wife of Rev. E.L.Frossard, the Rector of St Sampson, who had also had this German begging at her house. Mrs Frossard's neighbour had also been approached by the same German, begging for food. No one knew where he was billeted.

A/PC 48 Harold Kendall, one of the new recruits, was on patrol at La Vallette on the 19th February, when he was approached by James Collenette, who was working on the gardens. He told the Constable:-

"Last Saturday, at about 4.00pm I came to these gardens and saw Mr Duncombe and another man sawing down a tree about 20' high. I told them it was forbidden to take the wood away, the other man said 'Other people do it'. Later they loaded the wood into a cart and went off with it."

The Constable after inspecting the remains of the tree saw Charlie Duncombe at his home in Pedvin Street. He told him that he was making enquiries concerning the sawing down of a tree at Vallette Gardens. Charlie, who was now 64, explained:-

"On Saturday I went to the top of the Belvedere with Mr Legg and sawed off a branch from a tree which fell and rolled over the cliff into the gardens where we cut it up and that is what Mr Collenette saw me doing."

The Constable then saw Albert Legg, who told him:-

"Charlie Duncombe called for me at my home on Saturday at 3.00pm, to go and help him. I did not know what for until we got to the gardens. We then sawed down a tree, Mr Collenette came and told us it was forbidden to remove wood."

No action was taken.

At 1.00pm on Thursday 22nd February, A/PCs Henry and Reeve went to 1 Rockville, Hauteville, where they met Mrs Alistine Bonny, of 43 Hauteville. She told them:-

"Every morning, at about 7.30 to 8.00, I used to hear Mr Sigwart sifting coke, but this morning this did not wake me. About 10.30am there was still no appearance, so I thought they must be having a rest, as Mr Sigwart was a tired man. But as time progressed and I saw nothing of them I began to get nervous. At about a quarter to twelve I noticed that the blackouts were still up. I rang the bell to attract Mr Sigwart to answer the door. When I received no reply I conjectured something was wrong. The back door was banged on with a hammer, but this did not draw any reply. I then decided to ring the Police."

Constable 'Hank' Reeve tried all the doors to the house, but found them locked. Constable Bert Henry borrowed a ladder and managed to get into the house. The A/PCs went down the stairs to the ground floor. There, 'Hank' Reeve later recalled:-

"I went into the dining room at the back of the house. It was very dark and I fell over something just inside the door. I lit my lighter and discovered it was the body of Mrs Marie Sigwart."

The two Constables then went up the stairs to the first floor where in the bath they found the fully clothed body of John Sigwart with a piece of material around his neck. The bath was about a quarter full of water. Constable Henry telephoned the Police Station and informed Sergeant Kimber of what they had found.

Acting Inspector Lamy and Acting Deputy Inspector Banneville immediately went to Hauteville and took charge of the investigation. Mr Lamy later recalled:-

"When I arrived, everything was in darkness. On the floor was the body of Mrs Marie Sigwart, who was 74, lying face downwards. She appeared to have been strangled as a piece of material was tied tightly round her neck and she showed no signs of having struggled. Her dentures were under the sideboard.

Seventy-seven-year-old Mr Sigwart, a retired jeweller and watch maker, was found lying in the bath on his back with a slight incline to the left. He was fully clothed. His left foot was dry but the whole of his body was wet. He had two handkerchiefs tied around his neck, one tight the other loose."

In a recess in the drawing room, was a cabinet which has been forced open. In the bedroom on the first floor, a cupboard and a chest of drawers had been ransacked. A ladies nightdress was lying on the couch in the sitting room. In the front bedroom on the 2nd floor a cabin trunk had been rummaged through and its contents disarranged.

The bodies were examined by Doctors Collings and Bisson and then removed to the Town Mortuary by the St John Ambulance Brigade.

Later that day Constable Henry had the gruesome task of going to the mortuary and searching the bodies. He removed a gold wedding ring, a gold brooch, a pair of gold earrings and the material that was tied around Mrs Sigwart's neck. From Mr Sigwart's he removed four studs, nine coins, a handkerchief and a piece of material from around his neck.

At the inquest, the Coroner heard from a neighbour that he had heard heavy footsteps on the stairs of the Sigwarts' house at about 11.30pm. "They were", said Charles Loaring, "fairly fast. I thought this rather unusual because the footsteps were louder than I was accustomed to hear, secondly because it was so late."

Another witness, Miss Marie Bougeard, told the Court that:-

"I called for a clock at about 6.00pm on Wednesday. Mr Sigwart told me it was not ready. He asked me to go in, but I told him that I was going up the road. Then he said that he would see me on Sunday at Church. I passed the house at about ten minutes to nine and noticed a light in the hall and a bicycle inside the gate on the right going up the steps. The gate was closed."

The evidence of the heavy footsteps and the bicycle parked on the steps, together with the protracted inquest, - it was twice adjourned, - caused intense local speculation. Was it murder by some person, so far unknown?

At the final session of the inquest, held on the 5th March, the Coroner, Jurat Quertier Le Pelley, recorded a verdict of death due to strangulation in respect of Mrs Sigwart and suicide by drowning in the case of her husband.

On Friday 23rd February, fifty-nine-year-old Albert Le Page, a grower, of Mont De Jour, Portinfer, was charged with stealing a telephone pole from near his home. He was also charged with causing wilful damage to two telephone poles, lines and insulators at the same time and place. He pleaded guilty to the first charge, but not guilty to the second.

Acting Inspector Lamy told the Court that during inquiries Albert Le Page denied the theft, but blocks found on his premises were identified as being part of the pole. Two other poles in the same vicinity had also been sawn down, although it could not be proved to be the action of the accused. The damage was estimated to be £10. Le Page was sentenced to fourteen days' imprisonment and ordered to pay the costs of the damage.

On the 25th February the Island's electricity finally ran out. Ken Lewis wrote in his diary:-

"We stayed up to 10.06pm and saw the light go out. We put on all the switches and all the lights went out together, probably never to come on again till after the end of the Occupation. Mum did some ironing last night to take the last chance of using the electric iron."

The Station Sergeant was often to be observed writing up the Occurrence Book by the light of a candle. As soon as the entry had been made the candle was snuffed out as the supply of candles were almost non existent and had to be kept for emergencies. The consequence was that fewer and shorter reports were entered in the Occurrence Book during the hours of darkness.

John Mahy, a seventy-four-year-old farmer, lived at Avondale, Landes du Marche. On Sunday afternoon, the 25th February he had delivered his milk to the dairy. When he returned home at 3.30pm, he was surprised to see the back door unlocked and wide open. When he saw two carrier bags in the passage he assumed that his wife had returned early from chapel.

He later recalled:-

"I went along the passage and when I got abreast the front room door, I glanced inside and shouted 'are you there' thinking my wife must have been upstairs. As soon as I called out, a German soldier came out of the front room. He was wearing a mask made of some black material, which covered his nose and mouth. Pointing a revolver at me, he said 'no speak or I shoot'. At the same time another soldier came from behind and caught my throat with his two hands and tried to strangle me. He had come from the kitchen and when he released me, drew his bayonet.

The soldier with a revolver closed on me and tried to get me down on the floor, but I managed to struggle to the outside door. Then I was tripped and fell on to the floor. One sat on me while the other soldier tied my hands at the wrists and my legs at the ankles, with pieces of clothing.

Then they lifted me up and put me on a chair. The soldier with the revolver, stood guard over me and again said, 'no speak or I shoot'.

The other man was ransacking the house and finding what food he could. He brought it near to where I had been sat, ready to take away. I saw four carrier bags and a sack containing the contents of the last two Red Cross parcels received on the 15th of this month. They also took 40 lb of potatoes, a fruit pudding, half a gross of Farmers matches, 3 candles, apples and beans. When they had finished one soldier left carrying two carrier bags and the other, two bags and a sack.

When I thought they had gone I got up and hopped to the door, but they were still in the yard, they saw me, came back and bound me to the chair with a length of wireless aerial cable. They cut the telephone flex and used that to tie my legs to the legs of the table. A towel was used to gag me. They then went and searched the shed adjoining the house and took three fully grown rabbits.

After a time I was able to free myself and hop out of the house and reached the road where I managed to attract the attention of someone passing who freed my hands and feet. I asked him to notify the Police.

So I was left without any food except for a few potatoes, not very nice at my age of seventy-four."

A/PC 20 Julou responded to Mr Mahy's call for assistance. The Constable found no sign of force having been used to gain entry and concluded that the farm house had been entered with a duplicate key. He traced footprints from the house across fields to the States Houses at Pont Valliant where German soldiers were billeted. John Mahy told the Constable that the Germans were dressed in green and wore peaked caps, but he could not identify them again. The Feldgendarmerie were notified.

A/PC 40 O'Donovan was on duty in the North sub Station when Albert Guilbert, a sixty-two-year-old grower, reported that he had been assaulted by a German soldier.

He told the Constable that an hour earlier, on hearing a noise in his fowl house, he had gone outside to investigate. He said:-

"On approaching the fowlhouse, I saw a German soldier leaving. I tried to stop him, but he struck me in the mouth. He got away with two fowls, these I value at £2. I think the soldier may come from Les Vardes."

Albert Guilbert's mouth was still bleeding when he reported the incident at the Station. Mr Guilbert, who was accompanied by a friend, then went to the Feldgendarmerie at Braye Road to report the attack to them.

On the 29th February 1945 Vice-Admiral Huffmeier issued a proclamation on his appointment as Commander in Chief of the German Forces in the Channel Islands.

"New Commander in Chief of the Channel Islands.

On the 28th February 1945, at 12 0'clook noon, I have taken over from Generalleutnant Graf von Schmettow, who has been recalled to the Fatherland for reasons of health, the duties of Commander in Chief of the Channel Islands and Commandant of the Fortress of Guernsey. I know only one aim; to hold out until final victory. I believe in the mission of our Fuehrer and our people. I will serve them with unflinching faithfulness.

Heil to our beloved Fuhrer !

Huffmeier, Vice-Admiral and Befehlshaber Kanalinseln."

Although the appointment of the former Captain of the battleship Scharnhorst was never published in either the Evening Press or The Star, news quickly spread around the Island. The proclamation was published in the German Newspaper 'Deutsche Guernsey Zeitung', which was printed on the Guernsey Press premises.

The Vice-Admiral, a dedicated Nazi, engineered General von Schmettow's removal from command. It was certainly not, as was officially suggested, for health reasons. His appointment was bad news for the Island.

General von Schmettow had ruled the Islands with reasonable benevolence and certainly without the excesses which had been seen in parts of occupied Europe. Huffmeier's declared intention was not to surrender, but fight to the death. However Acting Inspector Lamy believed that in the event of surrender the Vice-Admiral would order the destruction of all German arms and ammunition supplies. He was aware that the harbour and other installations had been prepared for demolition and that explosives were already in place.

Corporal Le Cocq called, as a result of an urgent telephone request, on Brian P. Ogier at his home at Les Gigands, St Sampson, at 4.00pm on the 28th February. Brian Ogier told the Corporal:-

"A few minutes ago I was with Tom Jolly when we saw some Germans stealing our broccoli. With Tom I ran down and shouted at the Germans. When we got near I saw that there were three soldiers below the rank of under officers, two of them had bayonets and the other an automatic. This last one drew the weapon, pulled back the breech to load it and pointed it at me so as to cover his comrades' retreat to the road. One soldier that was amongst the broccoli, drew his bayonet and kept me back till the third got into the road with the broccoli.

The German with the automatic waited till the others were in the road, then they made off through the lane that leads to the Sauvagees. On following them through the lane we met two soldiers, who had met the other three farther down. Tom told one of them what had happened, all this soldier said was, 'Be careful what you say' and walked off."

Corporal Le Cocq informed the Feldgendarmerie at Braye Road and they immediately sent two of their policemen to Les Gigands. The Corporal and the members of the Feldgendarmerie patrolled the district and at about 5.00pm they saw Nicholas Blampied of 'Baubigny', St Sampson who told them:-

"About ten minutes ago I found three soldiers in my broccoli patch, they had cut about 40 broccoli and with three sacks on their shoulders, made off towards the main Baubigny Road."

The patrol of the district continued for some time but no trace was found of the three soldiers.

Not only was there a spate of robberies of Red Cross parcels, each of which was reported to the Police and investigated, but a considerable number of Islanders complained that some of the contents were missing or in poor or bad condition. What Islanders thought the Police could do to rectify the matter is difficult to understand. Others complained to the Secretary of the Essential Commodities Committee. One such complainant was the Bailiff, who in a hand written note, wrote:-

"Dear Mr Loveridge,

Both pieces of cheese in my parcel and my sister-in-law's were found to be bad and my chauffeur has these with him. Can they be exchanged or can anything be done ? And if so by whom ? Would you kindly tell him if there is anything to be done under the circumstances and he will do it.

I am sorry to give you the trouble.

Yours truly,

Victor G.Carey."  March 4th 1945

**The Bailiff, Victor G.Carey.**

Clearly a difficult decision for a Civil Servant to make when approached by the Bailiff. In normal circumstances any Civil Servant would have taken the request as a 'command' and replaced the two items without delay or question. John Loveridge knew that there were a considerable number of Islanders with an equally justifiable claim to have their defective food replaced.

The shrewd young Civil Servant, who was himself to become the Island's Bailiff some twenty years later, sent a reply, which astutely passed the decision back to the Bailiff.

"The Bailiff,
The Royal Court,
Guernsey. 5th March 1945
Sir,
I have the honour to acknowledge the receipt of your letter of the 4th instant in regard to the packets of cheese contained in the Red Cross parcels of yourself and Mrs Fanshawe Swete, which items are bad and which you have sent me under separate cover. We have been and are still being inundated with similar queries in regard not only to damaged items but also shortages in the parcels.
We are therefore drawing up a list of such queries which will be submitted to you for favour of ruling.
I have the honour to be,
Sir,
Your obedient Servant,
J.Loveridge,
Secretary."

On the 7th March Acting Deputy Inspector Banneville, accompanied by two members of the Feldgendarmerie, went to see Wycliffe Greenway, of Bramber, Saints Road, at his field at La Fosse, who told him:-

"When I took my calves in just before 6.00pm this evening, 3 German soldiers who I have often seen near my stables, were there again. They told me they had just caught 2 Georgians stealing my beetroots. I placed the sack of roots in my stable and went home for tea. On my return to the stable about 7.00pm I found one of my calves, 'Greenway's Beauty', aged 6 months' was missing. On my way to call the Police, I met one of the German soldiers I had seen near the stables, with a package on his cycle with blood showing through the wrapping. I stopped him and shouted for help, a German officer came and I told him I suspected this soldier of having my animal. The officer took the man away. I would know the men if I saw them again."

While the Constable was interviewing Greenway, a soldier passed by and Mr Greenway identified him as one of the men whom he had seen earlier. The man's particulars were taken by the German Feldgendarmerie and as a result of further inquiries, two further soldiers from Les Hubits were arrested. The cycle the German was riding and the parcel he was carrying were taken away by German Police. The parcel was found to contain parts of the animal's hindquarters.

The recovered meat was taken by Mr Greenway to the cold store. Later more of the hindquarters of the missing animal was found by A/PC 16 Harold Hall when he was making enquiries about a missing goat at Les Dunes, Vazon.

A/PC25 Ossie Brackley was sent to the Elm Grove Bakery at 3.30am on the 10th March as a result of a telephone call being received at the Station. He was met by the night-watchman, Thomas Rose, who told him:-

"At about 3.00am I was in the bakehouse when I heard a noise outside and saw someone flash a light towards the window. From the light I could see someone was coming towards the door, I shouted 'who is there' and someone answered but I could not understand because I could not make out if it was Germans or civilians.

I opened the door and went outside where I noticed two soldiers, one of them told me to go back into the bakehouse. As I turned to go he drew his revolver and ordered me to stand with my back towards him in the alleyway leading towards the back door. I was told not to move or make a noise. I then heard the other soldier go into the bakehouse and then he went to the bottom of the garden twice, the other soldier never moved from near me until his partner whistled. The soldier then left me and ran towards the bottom of the garden. I ran inside and telephoned and met Mr Cherry."

Samuel Cherry, the proprietor of the Elm Grove Bakery, who lived on the premises, told the Constable:-

"I was awakened by a noise and came downstairs to see what was the matter. When Rose told me what had happened I telephoned the Feldgendarmerie and they said they could do nothing before daylight. I have checked the loaves and find twenty-two, 2 lb loaves have been taken, also one sack of flour weighing 140 lb."

Constable Brackley also telephoned the Feldgendarmerie, but received the same answer as Mr Cherry.

A written report was sent to the Feldgendarmerie and the President of the Controlling Committee was also informed.

The Germans realised, with the possible exception of Admiral Huffmeier, that the war was rapidly drawing to a close and they became more co-operative and reasonable with all the States officials and members of the Police Force. At a meeting held on the 11th March the air of new-found co-operation is clear from an extract of the minutes:-

"Kapitaenleutnant Reich said that the Festungskommandant wished to thank the Local Administration for the way in which their work had been carried out in the past and hoped it would continue to be done in a like manner. Jurat Leale said the Island Administration had no intention of changing their methods. Kapitaenleutnant Reich said that, although they knew the Allied Forces at present on German soil were taking up an attitude very different from that adopted here by the German Forces, they also had no intention of altering their policy here. He added that especially on the Eastern Front it is known that the German population is not being treated as one would expect between cultivated peoples. Even on the Western Front Administration Offices and Courts Martial have been set up and the death penalty has been pronounced against children. The German Forces in the Island intended to continue to behave like decent soldiers.

Kapitaenleutnant Reich recalled, that Jurat Leale had some time previously called attention to a few cases of bad behaviour on the part of the troops. Jurat Leale here interrupted to say that he again had a case to report and Kapitaenleutnant Reich said that he knew of this case and that the two soldiers, who a few weeks previously had fired upon a civilian on whose property they were stealing, had been very severely punished, their sentences being three years and two months and one year respectively. He assured the local representatives that all cases would be severely dealt with if the culprits were caught. The German Authorities on their part expect the Civil Administration to deal in like manner if civilian cases occurred."

Sergeant Harry Dyson's home at Mont Mado, Les Hubits, was broken into while he was on duty and his Red Cross parcel stolen. On the 10th March 1945 the Acting Inspector wrote to the Secretary of the Bailiff's Red Cross Supplies Committee requesting a replacement parcel.

Mr Lamy wrote that in view of the fact that Sergeant Dyson lived alone, his wife and family having been evacuated and was on duty helping to protect other people's property, could an exception be made in this case and a replacement parcel issued.

After consideration the Committee resolved that no exception could be made.

The Committee felt that as soon as it was known that replacement Red Cross parcels were being issued then the number of 'reported break-ins' would escalate. They felt it was necessary to take a tough line. Even the Bailiff had refused himself and his sister-in-law, replacement cheese.

Members of the Force were finding it almost impossible to maintain a reasonable standard of personal presentation. On the 18th March A/PC 10 Bill Sebire wrote a brief note to Mr Loveridge:-

"Dear Mr Loveridge.

Can you help me?

I would like a stick of shaving soap, also a tin of boot polish and oblige.

Yours truly, W.K.Sebire Tel 1503".

Mr Loveridge replied on the 20th March:-

"In reply to your note received today, I regret that we only received an insignificant number of shaving sticks through the International Red Cross and that it is impossible until further and more adequate supplies are received to make an issue.

In regard to boot polish, stocks have been exhausted for some considerable time and here again I regret I cannot assist you."

The food situation as far as the German forces were concerned had become desperate. They did not receive any supplies from the Red Cross and the stocks of food in the Island were fast running out. Towards the end of March the Germans intensified their search of local properties for what they called 'excessive' stocks of food and drink. On the 27th March 1945 Herr Schneberger issued eight different Orders requisitioning stocks of roots, tinned food, wine, spirits and soap for the troops.

Mr Hocart, of Les Domaines, St Saviour had his entire stock of 300 kg carrots and 1200 kg swedes confiscated.

Messrs A.B.Le Cornu, Les Lohiers, St Saviour had 400 kg swedes, 75 kg parsnips and 25 kg carrots confiscated.

Mr McCathie, whose address was given as 'Guernsey' had 24 bottles of port out of a stock of 60 bottles confiscated.

Mr V.Creasey of Brock Road, had 108 tins of soup and 19 tins of vegetables confiscated.

Mr A.M.Mackay, of Doyle Road, lost 156 tins of soup, 14 tins of vegetables, 16 tins of fish, 77 bottles of cognac, 43 bottles of whisky, 12 bottles of vodka, 24 bottles of cointreau, 144 bottles of claret and 30 pieces of soap.

The Royal Hotel was searched and as a result had 29 tins of milk, 332 tins of vegetables, 71 kg of peas, 28 kg of beans, 41 kg of sugar, 25 kg of macaroni, 41 tins of fruit, 490 pieces of palmolive soap, 72 candles, 12 bottles of champagne and 297 bottles of spirits confiscated.

Mr Bricard, of Ville au Roi, had 20 tins of vegetables, 21 tins of butter, 192 tins of milk, 15 kg of pepper, 10 tins of fruit, 42 bottles of spirits, 199 bottle of wine, 50 bottles of champagne and 170 bottles of cider confiscated.

Mr Goasdoue, of Sous L'Eglise Farm, St Saviour had 990 kg of carrots and 510 kg of parsnips seized by the Germans.

Despite assurance given to the civilian Authorities, these searches were carried out by armed Germans, who took everything they wanted for their own use. No thought was given to the promise that had been made by Colonel Helldorff that any excess supplies seized would be passed over to the hospitals. In the meantime Admiral Huffmeier had removed Colonel Helldorff from his command.

On the 26th March sixty-five-year-old Fred Bougourd left his home in Vara Road at about 6.30am and went to work at nearby Les Hubits Farm, where he was employed as a horseman by Stan Mauger. When he arrived he thought he saw the cowman near the stable window and went to speak to him, but then realised it was a German.

Fred was attacked by the German who hit him on the head with a pickaxe handle and, when he fell to the ground, continually kicked him in the chest. When his employer found Fred, he immediately telephoned the Police Station. A/PC 24 Le Page was sent to the farm and spoke to Fred Bougourd, who complained of bad pains in his chest. The Constable advised him to go and see a doctor.

The Constable noticed that a window had been opened and found a large sack near by. It appeared that the German was attempting to steal a four-day-old calf which was inside the stable. Fred Bougourd was not able to give a description of the soldier.

Mr Lamy reported the incident to the President of the Controlling Committee who in turn informed the German Authorities.

Corporal Le Cocq was on duty in the Station at 1.00am on the 27th March when he received a telephone call from Mrs Gertrude Bougourd, of Sunnyside, Le Varclin, reporting that there were German soldiers in her garden. The Corporal tried to contact the Feldgendarmerie by telephone but could not get an answer. So he set off with A/PC Aubert to St Martin in the Police van. On his way up Hauteville he saw two German Policemen who said they could not assist him, as they were enquiring into an attempt that had been made to enter a military food store.

Corporal Le Cocq and A/PC Aubert arrived in Le Varclin and were met by Mrs Bougourd who told them:-

"I telephoned the Station as I saw 3 or 4 Germans in my garden, I rang a hand bell and telephoned you, I am here alone."

The Policemen found that the side gates had been forced open and that three sheds in the garden had been entered. They secured the sheds and patrolled around the district.

Constable Johnny Aubert then noticed a movement in the field opposite. They hid for a time and saw German soldiers come out of the field and turn down Le Varclin. When the two Policemen gave chase, the Germans scattered and dropped two sacks, a French broom and an axe, which led the Corporal to believe that they were after cattle. Francois Le Cocq chased one man down Le Varclin towards Calais, but was kept at a distance by the German firing at him with his automatic pistol. The German eventually disappeared over the cliffs towards Fermain Bay.

A/PC Aubert later confirmed that he had seen four men, one an under officer. "I grappled with one man, who was a flak man and was masked. This man struggled free and made off across the field into the grounds of Les Preaux."

The Constable followed the German and when he jumped over a hedge into Sausmarez Road, within 20 yards of a German guard, he vigorously blew his whistle. The soldier then jumped back into the field and ran off in the direction of the Hermitage.

On his way back to the Station, Corporal Le Cocq reported the incident to the German Authorities at Birnham Court. They asked for a full report to be submitted to them in the morning.

The two sacks, which contained cabbages cut from the rear of the Hawthorns in Sausmarez Road, the axe and the French broom were taken to the Station.

Whilst firearms were being regularly used by the Germans in their thieving missions, many other thefts were attempted or accomplished without their use.

A/PC 37 Tucker reported that on the 28th March William Flambard, of the Baissieres, St Peter Port, told him:

"Between 10.00pm last night and 8.00am this morning someone broke into my kitchen and stolen my ration of Red Cross soap and my back door key. They couldn't get into any of the other rooms because all the rooms were locked."

The Constable noticed that the window where the entry was made, was on the gable of the house only 12 feet from the main Baissieres Road. A hole had been bored through the window sash and a wire put through and the catch pulled up. No marks of any description had been left and Mr Flambard had no suspicions.

Half an hour later the Constable saw Mr E. Girard, of Etibots Farm, The Baissieres, who informed him:-

"Between 10.00pm last night and 6.00am this morning someone has broken into my conservatory at the back of the house and has taken about 100 brown paper bags and half a pint of haricot beans. They haven't taken anything else because they couldn't get into any of the other rooms."

A/PC Tucker then inspected the conservatory and found that entry to the house had been attempted by removing a pane of glass from the door to get the key inside. However, the thieves had failed to unlock the door, so they had forced off the box staple. The window sash showed signs of having been drilled, in the same manner as Mr Flambard's but on this occasion the thieves had been unsuccessful.

# Chapter 33

# UNCONDITIONAL SURRENDER

John De Garis, a forty-five-year-old farmer, of Sea View Farm, Castel had for some time been having his cows milked at night. For about ten nights he and his friend Bonamy Martel, a thirty-four-year-old farmer, of Kings Mills, Castel, had kept watch on his stables, accompanied by a sergeant from the Feldgendarmerie. For three nights no watch was kept but it was restarted when John De Garis was again robbed. Just before 10.00pm on the 31st March 1945, Bonamy Martel and the German sergeant went into the stable and settled down for the night. While the German slept, Bonamy took the first watch. He later recalled:-

"At 2 o'clock I heard a faint step in the yard. I was about one foot from the window and I saw a face looking through the window. I could see it was a soldier. I called the Feldwebel (sergeant) who got up with a jerk, making some noise. The soldier looking through the window bolted. I could see another in the yard, he also ran away. The Feldwebel also saw them running away. We looked around the farm but could not find them, so we returned to the stable.

The Feldwebel took over watch. About 4.30am we were just having some food, when without warning the stable door opened and two soldiers walked in. One was carrying a container, which was larger than a bucket. We both got out from the straw where we were hiding, the Feldwebel flashed his torch, drew his revolver and challenged the intruders. One of the soldiers was standing in the centre of the stable with his hands above his head, the Feldwebel told me to take charge of this one and look for his card. He then gave me a piece of iron pipe in case the soldier tried to get away. He then went two or three paces forward, again challenging the other soldier.

I then saw the straw move against the wall behind the Feldwebel. I shouted 'look out' and at the same time they both charged, one at me, the other at the Feldwebel's back. I hit the one who came for me with the iron bar, he put up his hands to save the blow. I then grabbed at his pocket and took his card.

I was then in the doorway, I saw the Feldwebel on his side, the soldier on top of him, I then heard a shot followed by two others in quick succession. I then had my soldier on the ground, sitting on top of him. I expected to see the Feldwebel come and help me, instead of that I saw the other soldier run out of the stable with a revolver in his hand and a mask on his face. He came to within one foot of my head, pointed the revolver at me and was about to fire when I struck the revolver out of his hand with the iron bar.

He picked up the revolver, put it against my chest and pulled the trigger. There was only a click. He took the bar and hit me on the back of the head. By then I was losing strength. He loaded the revolver and put it against my chest again. I pushed his hand upwards and with the other hand snatched the revolver away and threw it in the fowlhouse.

He went behind me and caught hold of my shoulder and pulled me back. During that time I shouted for help. The soldier under me managed to get up and the other one came at me with a knife as sharp as a razor and stuck it in my throat. I caught hold of his wrist and pulled out the knife, in so doing my throat was again cut.

John De Garis then arrived. One soldier had me held by the head, the other just about to finish me off with the knife. From that time both John De Garis and I grappled with the soldier. I banged the soldier's head against a wall, he was losing blood and trying to run away. I caught him again and banged his head against the house door and then chased him into the next yard.

Mrs Nora De Garis was there, she tried to help by using the hay fork, Mrs Helen De Garis, senior, was helping her son. Mrs Nora De Garis attempted to hit the soldier, but missed and hit my hand. I felt too faint to continue and collapsed in the doorway. The soldier then bolted.

John De Garis came out into the yard streaming with blood from a cut throat. Mr Bichard, who lives opposite, was called, he fetched help from a nearby battery. We then found the Feldwebel lying dead in the stable with three shots near or through the heart. A soldier dressed my wound. They phoned the German doctor and Feldgendarmerie. They arrived and took charge. I went with them on enquiries until 11.00am. The German doctor inserted three stitches in my throat and dressed my head injuries. We then went to the battery at the Courtil Jardin, where the soldier who had shot the Feldwebel was arrested."

John De Garis also remembered the night clearly:-

"At about 4.30am I heard three shots fired from the direction of the stable. I got up immediately and opened the window and called out. I then heard Bonamy Martel calling for help. Both my wife and I rushed outside. When I arrived I found two soldiers on the top of Bonamy, who was then on the ground. He and I tried to each hold a soldier, one had a knife and was trying to cut Bonamy's throat. Finally the one I was struggling with threw me to the ground, caught hold of my throat, I thought he was trying to throttle me. I then became weak and found that I was bleeding freely from the throat.

My mother and my wife came out and with a broom and hay fork tried to beat off the soldiers. Both soldiers ran away, one towards the stables and the other towards the garden. We called Mr Bichard, who lives opposite. He went to a nearby battery for help. My cut throat was attended to, first by a soldier and then by a German doctor who took me by car to the Emergency Hospital. I don't remember the time I arrived."

John De Garis received a cut four or five inches long on the left side of his throat, which required three stitches. He also had an abrasion under his left eye, a scratched face and a bruised left knee.

Bonamy Martel received a large cut on the head, two cuts to the throat, one about three to four inches long and the other smaller, as well as abrasions on his face and hands.

Mrs Helen De Garis, senior, later recalled:-

"I knew my son had the Feldgendarmerie to keep observation in the stable. At about 4.30am to a quarter to five, Sunday morning I heard three shots fired from the direction of the stable. I got up and went to the window and heard Mr Martel calling for help. I went outside, my son and daughter-in-law arrived. One soldier was striking Mr Martel, the other striking my son. My son then fell to the ground, I had a broom so I hit the soldier.

I could hear fighting in the next yard. After some time my son, who was bleeding a great deal, collapsed. The soldier then ran away. We all went into the house and I locked the door. A few minutes later I looked through the window and saw both soldiers by the stable, I could see what I thought was a large bucket in the yard and we then called Mr Bichard, who fetched help."

Nora De Garis junior, recalled:-

"At about 4.30am on the 1st April, I heard two shots fired from the direction of our stable. I ran to the window and heard Mr Martel calling for help. My husband was with me, we both ran downstairs and outside. When I arrived I saw Mr Martel fighting with a soldier, my husband, who was a little ahead of me was fighting with another soldier. I picked up a fork and tried to help Mr Martel who was bleeding from his throat and head. After a time the soldier ran away and we got both the men inside the house where they collapsed. They were later attended by a soldier and later a German doctor took my husband to the Emergency Hospital."

The local Police learned of the incident only as a result of the enquiries made by the Feldgendarmerie. Sergeant Plevin, who was detailed to investigate, saw John De Garis at the Emergency Hospital and took a statement from him. Later he saw Bonamy Martel at his home.

The Sergeant inspected the stable and yard at Sea View Farm, where the attempted murder of the two farmers had taken place and saw large patches of dried blood for a distance of about 50-60 yards. The metal pipe used by Bonamy Martel was collected by the Sergeant and taken to the Police Station. Sergeant Plevin was informed by a German captain that one of the two soldiers involved was still at large. The twenty three year old soldier, Michael Churodse, a Georgian stationed at the Grantez Mill, Castel was, the captain warned, armed with a rifle and ammunition.

Acting Inspector Lamy, recalling the events, commented:-

"Later the same day the soldier who had shot the German policeman was arrested, the second man was never found, although they knew his name. It has been suggested that the arrested man, knowing his friend had lost his identity card, had killed him and disposed of the body, leaving no trace, believing the story that 'dead men tell no tales'. However, he was tried, sentenced to death and executed within three days of the happening."

On the 3rd April A/PC 25 Ossie Brackley called to see Mrs Alice Brown, of 6 Allez Street, after the Station had received an urgent telephone. Mrs Brown told the Constable:-

"At about 2.45pm today I heard heavy footsteps on my stairs and I thought that it was the man who lives in the top storey. Then my door opened and a German soldier entered and asked if I had any potatoes or vegetables, I said 'no' and he ordered me to stand in the corner of the kitchen. He had a pistol, his coat collar was turned up and he tried to hide part of his face. He then opened all the drawers and cupboards and took all of the food I had left, which was a tin cheese, half a tin corned beef, a loaf and half a pound of butter.

I told him I was hungry and that was all the food I had in the house and that I would inform the Police. He then said he was also hungry and that I would have some bread in two days. He was tall and wearing blue uniform."

All the cupboards and drawers had been ransacked and there was no other food in the house. The details of the incident were recorded in the Occurrence Book by Sergeant Bull, but he realised that there was virtually no likelihood of the items being recovered or the thief being caught. The Acting Inspector sent a letter to the President of the Controlling Committee informing him of the theft.

The food situation was now so desperate for the Germans that they were driven to drastic action. On the 5th April they issued a Notice to their troops, which was also published in The Star.

"NOTICE.

In Order to prevent thefts from fields more effectively than heretofore, guards and patrols, beginning April 5th 1945, 8.00pm have the following orders:-

*During the day* to prevent every theft from fields and glasshouses by arresting such thieves and to make immediate use of their firearms, if they should try to escape.

*During the night*, on principle, *not to call*, but to shoot sharp, aiming at every person committing larceny (i.e. stooping and taking vegetables or potatoes, or breaking into a glasshouse).

*Der Festungskommandant.*"

All through the day and early evenings Germans were going house to house, begging for food. Numerous complaints were received at both the Sub Stations as well as the main Police Station.

A/PC 30 De Carteret on patrol in St Sampson, saw John Robin, of Glenview, Les Effards, who reported:-

"Between 10.30am and 11.00am this morning two German soldiers dressed in green uniforms came to my house and forced their way into my kitchen and asked my wife for food. My wife told them she had nothing to give them, one of them, a short one, searched the kitchen and scullery. The other a tall man with a bandaged left hand, searched the shed outside. They then went away without taking anything."

Shortly afterwards the Constable was approached by Mrs Elaine Robin, of 'Penrose' St Sampson, who told him:-

"At about 11.00am this morning two German soldiers, one tall and the other short, passed me as I was going to deliver my milk. I saw them turn into my gateway, so I rode back. One of my workmen was talking to them in the cart road leading to the back of my house. They had asked him for food, but he said he had none to give them. They said they were starving. The tall one had his hand bandaged and they both went away in the direction of Baubigny.

Constable De Carteret then saw Miss Irene Brochet, of Hilden, Les Effards, a housekeeper, who told him:-

"At about 11.50 this morning I went into the greenhouse at the back of the house and when I came back a few minutes later, my mother told me that two German soldiers had opened the scullery door and come into the house. She was in the room adjoining the scullery and she came into the scullery just in time to see the taller of the two, who had his left hand bandaged, take about 3 ounces of local tobacco, belonging to Stephen Crabbe, out of a tin on a shelf near the window. They then went away, I ran into the road and caught them up and asked for the tobacco back. They denied having taken any. A German officer came along on a cycle at that moment and I told him. He brought the tall one back to my house and searched him, but found no tobacco. The shorter German went on towards Baubigny."

The Constable reported the three incidents to the Sub Station Sergeant who informed the Feldgendarmerie at Braye Road. They said they would take over the investigation.

In response to a call to the West Sub Station, A/PC 16 Hall visited Frederick W.Torode at Epinel, in the Forest. He told the Constable:-

"Between 9.40pm last night and 7.30am this morning my two pigs were stolen from my sty. I have recovered one of them. I found it wandering around near

Basil Le Huray's farm at Les Caches, Forest. Russian soldiers have been cutting down trees on my farm since Wednesday last, they are from Le Bourg. The missing pig weighed about 150 lb."

The Constable saw that the sty door had been wrenched away from its fastenings. In a field at the rear of the farm he found a pool of blood where the missing pig had obviously been slaughtered. He also discovered a few splashes of blood on the grass leading to the road. On the road the trail of blood ended, suggesting that a vehicle had been used to cart the carcase away.

The Feldgendarmerie were informed. They searched the area and found four Russian soldiers with the carcase of a pig at La Corbiere.

There is nothing in the records to indicate whether the carcase was the missing pig and if it was whether it was returned to the farmer.

While at Sausmarez Manor at lunch time on the 10th April, on a routine matter, A/PC 43 Johnny Aubert heard someone shouting, "stop him, stop him". He saw a German soldier being chased by a civilian across the field from the direction of Luff's Corner and joined in the chase. The soldier, realising that he was being caught, fell on the grass. Whilst running away he had dropped his spoils, which were items from a Red Cross parcel, including tins of Nestles milk, corned beef and coffee. There were also some biscuits and a tin of chocolate which the soldier had partially eaten as he ran.

Later the Red Cross items were returned to Mrs Simon by Constable Mansfield, who obtained a signature in his note book as a receipt.

Mrs Rita Chalmers, who lived at Murray Villa in Steam Mill Lanes, was woken up at about 1.30am on Thursday the 12th April, by a scream, followed by a moan. It seemed to come from the direction of Sunnyside Cottage, about 60 yards from her house. She noted the time and listened carefully, but heard no other sound and soon fell off to sleep again.

At about 2.00am Mr T.G.Heggs heard noises which sounded to him as if someone was tapping on corrugated iron. He got up and looked outside but could see nothing, so went back to bed. He was sure that the noise had not been made by the wind and it appeared to come from the direction of Sunnyside Cottage.

Later that day, at about noon, Stan Mauger, of Les Hubits Farm called at Sunnyside Cottage, to collect some eggs from George Robins. George was a sixty-two-year-old poultry farmer, who had traded with locals and Germans during the Occupation. During the previous few months, due to the constant raids on their poultry, he and his wife Lil had made it a rule that they never left their premises unoccupied at any time.

Mr Mauger could not get an answer to his knocking and noticed that the blackout curtains were still drawn. After shouting in a loud voice, "Is there anyone home?", he opened the back door and saw, in the semi darkness, Mr Robins lying faced downwards in a pool of blood in the kitchen. Mr Mauger fetched a relative of the Robins', Mr

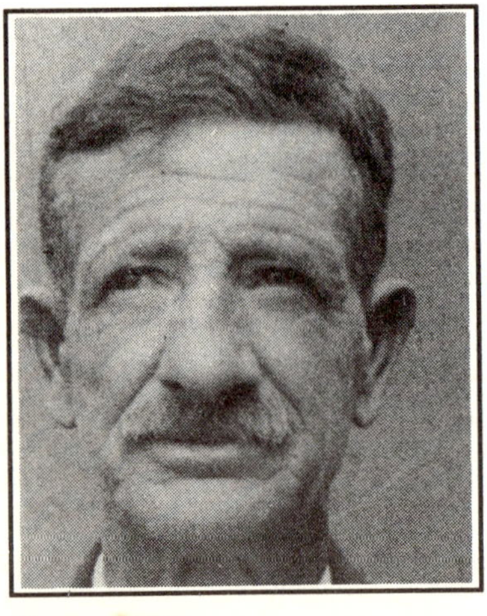

**George Robins.**

R.J.M.Tapp, who was a male nurse. He entered the house and after seeing the body of Mr Robins also found Mrs Lily Robins, laying dead in the corner of the kitchen. He immediately telephoned Sergeant Dyson at the Police Sub Station at Les Blicqs.

The Sergeant, accompanied by A/PC 21 Le Tissier, went to the cottage in Steam Mill Lanes and saw the two badly injured bodies lying in large pools of blood. The kitchen and the rest of the house was in total disorder. In consequence of what he had seen, the Sergeant immediately sent Constable Le Tissier to notify the Acting Inspector and the Feldgendarmerie at Birnham Court.

When the Acting Inspector arrived he saw both the bodies lying on the floor in the kitchen, each had severe head and throat injuries. Mr Robins had 12 head wounds and his throat had been cut. Mrs Robins had six head wounds and her throat was also cut. Both were fully dressed. Dr Collings gave it as his opinion that the head wounds had been caused by a fairly heavy sharp instrument, such as a bayonet.

A careful search was made for the weapon, but nothing was found at the time. The house had been ransacked and the contents of two Canadian Red Cross parcels, which Mr Robins had collected the previous day, were missing. Five Rhode Island Red chickens were also missing. The head of one fowl, which had been severed on the premises, was found in an outhouse.

Mr Tapp told the Acting Inspector that he saw George Robins on Wednesday evening when he called concerning a chicken run. Mr and Mrs Robins were, in his view, both of a friendly disposition and not the type of people to make enemies. They were careful with the Red Cross food and did not eat it ravenously.

A careful search of the house was made and a bread bin appeared to have been rifled and a box thought to have contained money was empty. A map of Europe was lying on a table with blood stains on it, this had been carefully re-folded. The only food found in the house was about 4 lb of flour, some milk and a few small items.

Mr Lamy later recalled:-

"The German Police who arrived with other officials, were of the opinion that the crime had been committed by a Georgian soldier, basing their deductions on the method of attack.

A large number of Georgians had been absorbed into the German Army and there were many detachments in the neighbourhood. However, the troops close to this particular house were German. Later we were lucky to find the weapon which caused the head wounds. It had been stolen from a nearby farm and had been thrown away in a field.

About three weeks later the war finished. We took up the enquiry and searched the house and grounds occupied by the German troops. After digging we found a guard book which contained the names of the persons who were in that house that night. We made enquiries amongst the German troops and felt pretty certain that the people we were after had been quartered in that house. However, the British Authorities had then commenced sending German soldiers to prisoner of war camps and it so happened that this particular detachment with the four men had been sent away. I made repeated requests to the Prisoner of War department to trace these men but unfortunately in the chaos nothing happened."

An inquest was held on Friday the 13th April when a verdict of "Wilful murder by some person or persons unknown" was returned in each case.

At 5.30am on the 14th April, eighty-two-year-old John Hotton, of 'Kelso', Les Vauxlaurens, was awakened by the sound of breaking glass. He got out of bed and with a lighted candle, went into his hall, where he saw two German soldiers. One of them knocked the candle from his hand. At gun point he was pushed into a bedroom with his housekeeper, Mrs Smith, where one German covered them while the other searched the house. Their Red Cross parcels and the remaining part of a steamed pudding were taken and before leaving, the Germans cut the telephone wires. John Hotton and Mrs Smith had to wait for daylight and the end of the curfew, before they could report the robbery to the Police.

Later that morning at about 11.30, Wilfred Ozanne, aged 76, of 'Lindhurst', Les Varendes, was working in his greenhouse when he noticed a soldier in his bedroom. As he went into his house he met the soldier in the hall carrying a bag. Mr Ozanne asked what it contained and the German caught hold of him and unceremoniously threw him outside.

Mr Ozanne immediately asked a neighbour to telephone for the Police. When they arrived they sent for Dr Collings, who treated Mr Ozanne for fractured ribs. Later he discovered that the thief had taken a tin of cheese and a loaf of bread. The Police established that the soldier concerned was attached to a flak unit and had been stealing in the neighbourhood for a considerable time. A full description of the man was given to the Feldgendarmerie.

Many of the new recruits engaged at the beginning of January 1945 were still working in civilian clothes with only an armband for identity. On the 16th April the Acting Inspector wrote to the President of the Police Committee, saying that he was now in a position place three of the men in uniform. He suggested that uniforms in the Town area was the priority and put forward the names of A/PCs Aubert, Kendall and Reeve, "if the uniforms can be fitted". He added that quite a number of the January intake of new Auxiliary officers "give good promise and should make very efficient Policemen". His prediction proved accurate as one of the recruits, A/PC 44 Arthur Bailey, was to become Chief officer of the Force.

**A/PC Arthur Bailey.**

On the same day the Acting Inspector also sent a second letter to his President, concerning 'wood fuel at the Police Station'. He reported that A/PC 24 Basil Le Page, had approached his uncle, Jurat John Roussel, who had agreed to supply the Station with enough wood for the remainder of the winter at a nominal cost of £4.10.0. The Acting Inspector suggested that a letter thanking the Jurat should be sent by the President.

At 12.45pm on the 24th April John Carre, of Sunnyside, Le Blicqs, St Andrew, called at the West Sub Station and told Sergeant Dyson:-

"I staked my cows out in my field at 9.00am this morning and at 11.30am when I went to shift them I found one missing, together with the chain and stake. In my opinion she was taken about half an hour after I had put her there because there is very little grass eaten."

Sergeant Dyson went with John Carre and visited the field next to the New Cemetery at Chemin Le Roi Lane. Although the field was only about 300 yards from the Sub Station neither that part of the lane nor the field could be seen from there. Outside the gate of the field which led on to the Chemin Le Roi Lane the Sergeant noticed a military type footprint which appeared to have been made quite recently. These footprints led to and from the field in an easterly direction.

The next afternoon A/PC 46 Bichard saw Miss Sylvia Gallienne at Sunnyside Farm, who told him:-

"At 9.30am on Tuesday 24th April I was walking through Chemin Le Roi Lane near the Cemetery, when I saw a man pulling the stake of a cow tethered in a field next to the Cemetery. The cow seemed stubborn. I was walking towards Les Blicqs, I could see him kicking the animal. He passed me in the lane afterwards leading the animal towards Aeroplane Vinery. I do not know him but would recognise him again. He was dressed in medium grey flannels, grey cap, brown coat, black boots, height about 5'8", clean shaven and a full face. I could not say near about his age."

Later the Constable spoke to Harold White, of Oxford, Les Cornus, St Martin, who told him:-

"At about 9.30am Tuesday morning I met a man in Chemin le Roi, leading a cow. He seemed to have trouble in leading it, but I took no notice at the time. I cannot give any description because I was cycling at the time."

The Constable made enquiries around the district and of people who regularly passed along the Forest Road during the hours between 9.00am and 10.30am, but without result.

The cow, which was owned by John Carre, was called 'Opal V. of Sunnyside' and was born on the 1st July 1939. It was fawn and white with a registered number 42242. Sergeant Dyson informed the Feldgendarmerie of the loss of the cow and provided them with details of the animal.

On Saturday the 5th May, Victor Gontier, of Glengall, Les Landes, Forest was charged before the Police Court Magistrate, Jurat Quertier Le Pelley with stealing a cow, valued at £60, the property of John Carre. Mr Gontier admitted the theft and due to the seriousness of the charge, evidence was taken in writing for sentence by the Royal Court.

In consequence of complaint by neighbours, A/PC 23 Cliff Langlois called to see eighty-year-old Mrs Mary Lihou at her home in the Grand Bouet, at 12 noon on the 27th April. She told him that her husband, Stephen, had assaulted her, but that she did not want him charged as he was mental. "I would like to have him put in the mental home because I cannot put up with this any longer. He knocks me about something awful, look at the state of my arms, where he has been hitting me this morning."

The Constable then saw her husband, seventy-eight-year-old Stephen Lihou, who said:-

"Do not believe her, she is mad. The marks on her arms were made by trying to stop her from hitting me. Do not take any notice of her, her father was hanged out the back of the Island as a felon. She was with him for a long time, you know she is really my sister".

Constable Langlois examined Mrs Lihou's arms, both of which were bruised and skinned from wrist to elbow on both arms. The A/PC was convinced that Stephen Lihou was mental. Dr Collings was asked to examine Mr Lihou and on his instructions he was placed in the Town Hospital.

A/PC 18 Frank Pill called at La Colombelle, Ruettes Brayes, the home of Mr Blaikie Webster, at 11.15am on the 27th April as a result of an insistent telephone call received at the Station. Mr Blaikie Webster told the Constable:-

"When I came down this morning at about 6.45am, I found that someone had entered my house. They have stolen tea, sugar, chocolate, salt, soap, prunes, coffee, milk, jam, candles, matches, cheese. Also 1 fountain pen, 1 lighter. They also took some rhubarb. Also my black dog, age about 7 years, but they did not take my bread. I had the Feldgendarmerie up here this morning and they said it was done by German soldiers."

Entry had been made by breaking a glass pane and then lifting up the casement fasteners. Before leaving, Mr Blaikie Webster asked the Constable to tell the Acting Inspector that he would like the loan of a police whistle.

The Acting Inspector took no action on the request.

Many members of the Force were constantly occupied in responding to reports of break-ins and robberies.

A/PC 14 Ted Peadon was responding to one such report when he called to see Richard W.Summers, of Orange Lodge, Water Lanes, on the 29th April, who told him:-

"At about 2.30pm today someone knocked on my front door and on going out, I saw two German soldiers who asked for cabbage and potatoes. As I went indoors by the back door, one of the soldiers put his foot against the door preventing me from closing the door. I ran upstairs to my bedroom, where they threatened me with a revolver and a bayonet. They then pushed me down and tied my hands behind my back, also my feet with compressed brown paper string. They then tied a piece of old flannel round my mouth.

They then took the following articles:- 1 gold dipped watchchain, 6 eggs, 15 lb potatoes, a tin salmon, a tin of apples, half a tin of lamb and green peas, 10 Red Cross cigarettes, a piece of toilet soap and 2 rations of washing soap, also a chopper.

While they were still in the house, Alfred Help, of 16 Norman Terrace, Amherst, St Peter Port, rang my front door bell, which probably disturbed them and they made off. On going into the road they threatened Help with a revolver. I do not know where they came from, but I would recognise them again."

Richard Summers managed to free his hands and sounded a gong to attract attention. By the time help arrived the soldiers had disappeared.

Constable Peadon, who was accompanied by a member of the Feldgendarmerie, saw that the contents of a chest of drawers in the bedroom had been strewn about by the German soldiers in their search for valuables. The Feldgendarmerie took over the investigation of the case.

At midday on the 1st May the Bailiff's head gardener, John Gallienne, reported:-

"At about 7.30pm last evening, I noticed that someone had broken open the door of the stable in which the fowls are kept. I believe that four large laying fowls out of six were gone. I believe it was Germans as they are always about the place. I value the loss at £4.0.0."

A/PC 14 Peadon was sent to investigate the Bailiff's loss. The chain and padlock which secured the door had been forced. No foot marks or traces of any kind could be seen. The break-in became just another statistic.

On the 2nd May, the Acting Inspector provided the President of the Controlling Committee with statistics relating to the number of reported cases of thefts of foodstuffs there had been during the Occupation. He wrote:-

"Between the 23rd and 29th of April 1945, 235 cases of vegetables being stolen have been reported to the Police. That is a considerable increase on last week's total. Also during the past week 6 horned cattle and 4 pigs have been reported stolen.

Cases of foodstuffs reported stolen to the Police for the period of the Occupation from 1942 to the 29th April 1945 are:-

1942 1,693 cases
1943 2,570 cases
1944 2,945 cases
1945 2,054 cases up to the 29th April."

On a later occasion he listed the number of Black Market charges during the Occupation years:-

1941 8 cases
1942 41 cases
1943 58 cases
1944 101 cases
1945 13 cases
Total 221 cases.

Everyone realised that the end of the war in Europe was only a matter of days away. The President of the Controlling Committee, John Leale, kept the Acting Inspector fully informed on the constantly changing situation in the Island. The burning question was whether Vice-Admiral Huffmeier would choose to fight on or surrender. Huffmeier's speech to his troops at the Regal cinema on the 1st May had been a defiant one in which he reaffirmed his loyalty to the Fuehrer.

A message from Adolf Hitler had been received by the Fortress Commandants of Dunkirk, the Channel Islands, Lorient, Saint Nazaire, La Rochelle, Crete and the East Aegean Islands.

"In the serious hour of fight for the fate of Germany, the Fuhrer remembers his soldiers in the Atlantic Fortresses and the advanced bastions of the Aegean Sea and expects of them that they will continue to fulfil their duties with an exemplary soldierly attitude."

Vice-Admiral Huffmeier signalled back:-

"On behalf of my officers and men I thank the Fuhrer for his remembrance even at this hour. We shall be faithful to him as he is always to us. Our way is clear. Only our Fuhrer's Germany. Heil to our beloved Fuhrer."

John Leale told Mr Lamy that in the early hours of the 2nd of May the German forces in Alderney were requested by 'flash' signals from the Cotentin peninsula, to immediately start negotiations for surrender. Vice-Admiral Huffmeier had ordered the request be answered by the signal "Antwort Uberflussig" - 'Reply Superfluous'.

Bert Lamy was surreptitiously listening to the B.B.C. news on his crystal set at home - it was contained in an electric light joint box - when he heard the news of Hitler's death in Berlin. Later that day the *Evening Press* carried a brief announcement on the front page which read:-

"DEATH OF THE FUHRER.

The Fuhrer has fallen in the capital of the Reich in the battle against Bolshevism. His successor is Gross-Admiral Doenitz."

The Acting Inspector normally ignored the front page of the *Press* and *The Star*, as only being German propaganda, however, this was a report he was only too willing to accept. He now believed for the first time, with the appointment of Admiral Doenitz, that liberation could be achieved without the need for the

**J.P. Blaikie-Webster.**

Allies to storm the Island. He, like many in Guernsey, prayed that Huffmeier would be dissuaded from defending the Island to the last man.

After having his Red Cross parcel stolen on the 27th April, Mr Blaikie Webster applied to the Bailiff's Red Cross Supplies Committee for a replacement. When the Committee met on the 5th May the Secretary reported his application. The Secretary reported that he had referred Mr J.P.Blaikie Webster to the published notice governing the replacement of Red Cross parcels. Mr Blaikie Webster had retorted that he considered the Committee's action wrong and not in accordance with the ideals of the Red Cross. He wished to protest very strongly and would report the matter to the British Government and to the Canadian and New Zealand Red Cross societies as soon as the Occupation ended. The Committee decided to take no further action and await events.

The Town Police Station and the two sub Stations continued to be inundated with reports of break-ins and thefts. Potatoes had become the main target.

At 8.00pm on the 6th May A/PC 20 Julou saw at Marette de Bas, St Sampson, Nicholas Falla, a grower, who informed him:-

"During curfew last night one of my greenhouses was entered and 5 perch of potatoes cleared. This crop had just been requisitioned by the Germans. I have no suspicions."

Constable Julou found that entry had been gained by forcing the door, probably using shoulder pressure. Footprints of various sizes, all of a military pattern, were around the area of the dug potatoes. Nicholas Falla said that German troops were stationed near by.

The next day A/PC 13 Le Poidevin went to see Herbert Morton, of La Canurie, Vale, who had telephoned the sub Station. He told the Constable:-

"A few weeks ago the German Military requisitioned three of my greenhouses planted in potatoes. Today the Germans started laying mines all over the ground amongst the potatoes".

Constable Le Poidevin, accompanied by a member of the Feldgendarmerie, saw Germans laying the mines and the Gendarme said:-

"Everything is in order, they have had permission from the Admiral."

During the afternoon of the 7th May, Frederick Heaume, of Les Houards, Forest, went to the West Sub Station and told A/PC Arthur Bailey:-

"In consequence of the local Police informing the German Police about the theft of my heifer, I accompanied members of the German Police through a mined area between the Gouffre and La Corbiere and identified the skin of my heifer. The head and four legs were also there. This part of the beach was being used as a slaughtering place for stolen animals. I noticed several hides and skins and bones of numerous animals. We also found a bath full of meat and two buckets of dripping. Two other large baths were blackened on the outside, apparently by being used as a means of cooking the meat. Axes, knives, hammers, sharpening stones and a large fork were also found. The Feldgendarmerie told me not to tell anyone, but I thought it my duty to tell the Police."

Everyone, the whole Island, had a feeling of expectancy, waiting for the war and the Occupation to be over. Everyone with a crystal set, and there were probably well over a thousand in the Island, was listening to the B.B.C. for the news that was so long in coming.

The President of the Controlling Committee, Jurat John Leale, was preparing a report that he wanted to make to the States of Deliberation as soon as possible after liberation. Ken Lewis, a clerk with the Controlling Committee, recorded in his diary how he and and another clerk, Shelia Luscombe, worked long hours typing out the very long report. Ken took part of the report home and spent the evening of the 7th May typing it so that it would be ready for presentation whenever needed.

**Jurat John Leale.**

John Leale also discussed with the Acting Inspector the arrangements necessary when the British troops landed. He said:-

"Lamy, I have a beautiful speech ready for when our troops come in, but I bet I will forget it and just say - Thank God you have come."

During the Sunday and Monday the Germans were busy destroying many of their records which they did not want to fall into either the Allies, or Guernsey Authorities, hands. Military files were taken out on a minesweeper and dumped in the Hurd Deep and the Russel. A number of trips were made and a considerable number of files were consigned to the waves.

On Monday afternoon Sergeant Dyson at the West Sub Station was informed that the Germans were blocking the airport with obstacles, to prevent planes landing. They were also reported to be connecting up the explosive charges on posts in the fields. It looked very much to Sergeant Dyson as if the Germans intended to resist. Later that evening the obstacles were removed and the charges disconnected.

Listeners to the B.B.C. heard the announcement that everyone had been waiting for, that Tuesday the 8th May was going to be V.E. Day, Victory in Europe Day. Britain was going to celebrate, but was Guernsey, that was the question on every lip.

Mr Lamy later recalled:-

"That same night the German troops in Guernsey were out in force manning guns, tanks and anti-tank guns. They were fully booted and spurred, more than they had ever been during the whole of the period of the Occupation. It looked then as if we had had a reasonably quiet period throughout the Occupation and now it was coming to a showdown and probably fighting.

However, the next morning at 10.00am I was in the Police Station, feeling rather miserable and looking out of the window, I noticed a German Staff car draw up outside the Royal Court building and two German officers go in. Later

I saw John Leale, with his head down looking rather serious in the street below my window.

I suspected the worst and literally ran over to Mr Leale's office to hear it. When I got there he was all smiles and came across and shook my hand and said - 'The Germans have informed the Bailiff that the war so far as we are concerned is over at 3.00pm this afternoon and that we can fly our flags'. Of course that put a different complexion on it. Flags went out immediately and so did hundreds of other flags which people were carrying and the Town was packed.

There was very little demonstration, the people were too stunned to demonstrate. They were walking about the Town carrying flags and the German soldiers walking about the Town going about their normal duties - neither one side taking notice of the other."

After the Bailiff had seen the two German officers, *The Star* issued a small 'Special Edition' that brought the news for which all Islanders had been waiting:-

"THE WAR IS OVER FOR GUERNSEY
German Officers Inform Bailiff of Surrender
HISTORIC STATES MEETING AT MID-DAY TO-DAY

At 10.30 this morning '*The Star*' was officially informed by Mr Louis Guillemette, Secretary to Jurat John Leale, President to the Controlling Committee of the States of Guernsey, that the war, so far as Guernsey was concerned, had ended.

People of Guernsey can today at 3 o'clock, if they are able to do so, listen to the speech made over the British radio by Prime Minister Winston Churchill. Immediately after that hour flags can be flown in Guernsey as a sign of rejoicing.

At 10.00am today Korvetten Kapitan Reich and Baron von Aufsess called on the Bailiff at his Chambers at the Royal Court House. Jurat John Leale, President of the Controlling Committee, and his Secretary, Mr Louis Guillemette, were also present. Kapitan Reich said that the war was over in the Channel Islands as well as elsewhere. He said that Mr Churchill, the British Prime Minister, was making a speech at 3 o'clock this afternoon and that the German authorities had no objection to the hoisting of flags after the speech.

On receipt of this news the Bailiff convened an extra-special States Meeting to be held at mid-day today where the full details of this momentous news was conveyed to members of the States."

Winston Churchill, the Prime Minister, broadcast at 3.00pm. The whole Island was openly listening on crystal sets which until that moment had remained hidden:-

"Hostilities will end officially at one minute past midnight tonight, Tuesday the 8th May, but in the interest of saving lives, the 'Cease Fire' began yesterday to be sounded all along the fronts and our dear Channel Islands are also to be freed today."

'Our dear Channel Islands are also to be freed today.' There is not a Guernseyman, who listened to Churchill's broadcast, who cannot tell of the excitement and pride that they felt when they heard those never-to-be-forgotten words. It was, for every Guernseyman, not a moment in history, but 'The' moment in history.

Acting Inspector Lamy later recalled the situation:-

"I was then in a very difficult position because although the Germans said the war was over so far as we were concerned at 3 o'clock, it did not terminate until midnight. We had no Allied troops in the Island and I was responsible for law and order. Shortly after 3 o'clock I had a telephone message from the German Authorities stating that the position had now changed. Instead of me asking them - they had to ask me certain things. I had heard several guns firing and the message from German Headquarters asking why they were firing. I told them I did not know and it was their business to see that they did not fire and requested them to put the German Police on the enquiry. However, it transpired that they were only emptying the rounds left in the barrels.

I had only one incident which might have proved ugly. A number of locals living near a German battery had gone out and pulled down the German flag, hoisting the Union Jack. The Germans in turn promptly pulled down the Union Jack and hoisted the German swastika again. This went on for a short while and the Germans notified me of it. I was afraid that any German, finger trigger conscious, might pull a gun thereby starting something we could never cope with. I sent a couple of Police officers down to tell the locals that there was very little we could do. We would have British troops in the next day and to wait a little while thereby saving loss of blood. Fortunately they saw sense and thus no further trouble arose. The Germans were confined to their billets that night and everything passed off peacefully."

At 1.00pm on the 8th May A/PC 32 Salmon met Wilfred Hamill, of 'Beauregard', Hauteville, who told the Constable:-

"At about 12.30pm today I was near the bottom of the 'Star Steps', South Esplanade, when two German soldiers in plain uniforms asked me for a cigarette. I sold them one each and while giving them change they struck me and knocked me down. When I recovered I found they had stolen about 300Rm. and £60 in English notes which I had in my hand. They also took my 2 lb loaf of bread which I had in my bag. The money belongs to a Spaniard. I would not recognise them again."

Wilfred Hamill had an abrasion over the right eye, cuts to both hands and was suffering from shock. The matter was reported to Corporal Le Cocq, who entered it in the Occurrence Book.

Corporal Le Cocq instructed A/PC 36 Solway and A/PC 23 Langlois to go immediately to 10 Victoria Road, where he had just been informed that a shooting incident had taken place.

On arrival at 7.15pm, the two Constables saw Henry McCulloch, a tailor, who told them:-

"About 15 minutes ago I was threatened by Peter Doyle over something that happened some time ago. Doyle said he would get me, or if he did not, his pals would. He then drew a revolver. I closed with him and we went into the road and then I ran away. By what I am told Doyle fired three shots at me. I did not hear the shots because I am deaf."

Mrs Helena Flambe, of Flora Villa, Brock Road, told the Constables:-

"Peter Doyle came into the shop and said 'I want you'. He then produced a revolver, which he said was German. Mac then closed with him and finally they got into the road. Then Doyle fired three shots at Mac. Luckily they all missed."

When Peter Doyle was brought to the Station, he said: "I am not saying anything." He was clearly under the influence of drink and was behaving very abusively. Sergeants Le Lievre and Dyson, with some difficulty, placed him in prison. Later Doyle's house was searched by Cpl Le Cocq, A/PC 23 Langlois and A/PC 36 Solway. A case and a box both containing revolver bullets were found in the house.

Whilst at the house, Cpl Le Cocq stopped three German sailors who were about to leave and searched them. One was found to be in possession of a bag of flour, a tin of ham, six rusks, a tin of oats and a small tin of fat. Mrs Doyle was seen to hand some money to one of the German sailors. The ammunition and food were taken to the Station.

At 45 minutes past midnight on the 9th May Sergeant Bull received a telephone call from the Prison Gaoler, who reported:-

"Peter Doyle has escaped from prison, it appears that he has had help from outside."

Sergeant Bull immediately sent A/PCs 14 Peadon and 39 Moore to Doyle's home, at Harcourt, Route Charles, where he was found and returned to prison. Peter Doyle said:-

"I got out because I was cold and wanted some blankets, it is a secret as to how I got out."

Two hours later the Police were back at Doyle's home, this time in response to a telephone call from his wife, Margaret. She told A/PC 25 Brackley:-

"I was awakened at about 2.30am when I heard a noise at the back of the house as if someone was trying to get in. There was more than one person as I heard voices. When I opened the window I heard someone run away."

The Constable, who was accompanied by A/PC 43 Aubert, searched the vicinity without result.

John Leale, the President of the Controlling Committee, wrote to the Bailiff on the 8th May:-

"Now that the Occupation of the Island is over, I wish to place in your hands, for submission to the States at the earliest possible date, this my resignation from the Presidency of the Controlling Committee. At the same time I would ask for the opportunity to lay before the States a report of the Committee's work. This report will, I am afraid, from its nature, be of a lengthy character."

During the early morning of the 8th May, the destroyers, H.M.S. Bulldog and H.M.S. Beagle, sailed from Plymouth and made a rendezvous with a German minesweeper at 2.00pm, off the south coast of Guernsey.

Admiral Huffmeier sent as his envoy a young naval officer, Kapitanleutnant Zimmermann, who went aboard the Bulldog. He had only been authorized by the Admiral to discuss armistice terms and was quickly sent packing with the message that the surrender was to be unconditional and that a properly accredited representative, with full powers, must attend a further rendezvous at midnight.

On leaving, he 'announced' that as the German surrender did not officially take effect until one minute past midnight, the presence of Allied ships would be looked upon as a hostile act by Admiral Huffmeier. He warned that if the Royal Navy did not withdraw, they would be fired upon by the German long range batteries.

The Royal Navy retired to a safe distance to await the time of the second rendezvous. When Major General Heine arrived aboard H.M.S. Bulldog at midnight, the two British warships sailed into the Little Russel. At 7.14am, on the 9th May 1945, the unconditional surrender of the German garrison in Guernsey was signed on the quarter-deck of H.M.S. Bulldog and Guernsey's Occupation was officially over.

# Chapter 34

# THANK GOD YOU HAVE COME

Acting Inspector Lamy hardly slept that night, he just lay awake thinking over the events of the day and planning how the Force was going to cope with the coming day. He probably had less than three hours' sleep and at 6.00am collected the Acting Attorney General, J.E.L.Martel, from his home in Rouge Huis Avenue. Together they went down to the harbour to await the arrival of the first British troops. A German guard was still posted at the Weighbridge preventing the ever growing crowd from flooding on to the White Rock. As they passed the guard they saw the Swastika flag being hoisted on the German patrol boats for the last time.

Mr Lamy later recalled:-

"A patrol boat went out to H.M.S. Bulldog, which was lying just outside the harbour. After about half an hour it came back, now under the command of Lieutenant Rex Ferbrache, a Guernseyman. The boat came alongside and Colonel Power and Lieutenant-Colonel Stoneham came ashore. Mr Martel and I greeted them and a party of about twenty troops. They were the only troops we had in Guernsey at that particular time.

**Lt. Commander R.E. Ferbrache arrives aboard a German naval craft to be greeted by Acting Inspector A.P.Lamy.**

I took Colonel Power first to the Royal Hotel, so he could establish a headquarters and then down to John Leale, the President of the Controlling Committee. I knocked and John Leale came to the door in his pyjamas. He looked flabbergasted when he saw us, then he exclaimed 'Thank God you have come'. I laughed, he said 'What are you laughing at?' - I said 'Don't you remember?' - 'Yes', he said 'I do'.

**Lt. Colonel H.R. Power, on the gangplank, being welcomed ashore by A/Inspector A.P. Lamy on Liberation morning. In background are Advocate J.E.L. Martel and Sergeant H.J. Bull.**

After that I took Colonel Power up to Grange Lodge, which was the Civil Headquarters of the German occupying troops. He then took over the office and as far as I was concerned, my responsibilities were finished as far as the Germans were concerned."

**The Liberation Force outside the States Office.**

When the first contingent of troops arrived at the inner west berth of the New Jetty, they were met by, not only Mr Lamy and Mr Martel, but also by Sergeant Bull, Sergeant Plevin and Acting Deputy Inspector Banneville. As the German boat, now flying the White Ensign, docked, someone on deck called out "Hello, Sergeant Bull!" It was Guernseyman Sergeant 'Nobby' Hamon. As the troop of soldiers were marched down the White Rock to the Royal Hotel by Captain Hill, the crowd of celebrating Islanders mobbed them.

In attempting to clear the way for Colonel Power and the Police car, driven by Sergeant Bull, through the massed crowds at the Weighbridge, Deputy Inspector Banneville's efforts earned him a severely sprained hand.

Over on the other side of the Harbour, at 9.30am, A/PC 20 Julou saw Frank Grant at the slaughter house. Frank, a slaughterman, told the Constable:-

"Between 4.45pm last night and 9.00am this morning, someone entered the slaughter house and has stolen a calf and half of another, clean meat and twelve plucks, the property of the States. I cannot estimate their value. I have no suspicions."

The Constable examined the premises and found that the entry had been made by scaling a 10ft wall at the rear of the building. The thieves must have entered the meat store by getting a hand between the bars which were only 3 inches apart and sliding the pin from the door. The half of the calf which was not taken was left on the floor, it had been cut with a knife. A report was entered in the Occurrence Book.

Another 200 British troops arrived during the early afternoon and Acting Inspector Lamy was there to welcome them. The party included the 20th Civil Affairs Unit. Later in the day Colonel Power, the Chief Civil Affairs officer for the Channel Islands, held a meeting at the Royal Court House attended by the Bailiff, John Leale, and others including the Acting Inspector.

**Lt. Colonel H.R.Power and John Leale arriving for Flag raising ceremony on Liberation day.**

The Colonel explained that the Military were occupying the Island only in order to assist the Civil Administration. He gave details of supplies which were due to arrive later in the week. He informed the meeting that the officer commanding the military forces in the Channel Islands was Brigadier Snow and the powers under the Defence Regulations would be vested in him.

The Colonel told the meeting that all prisoners who had not offended against local laws would be released immediately. Foreign labourers employed by the Organisation Todt were to be classed as prisoners-of-war. Arrangements had been made to deal with French prisoners, who would be evacuated. With regard to public safety, the Colonel stated that five experienced Police officers would be sent to assist the local Police, if necessary.

Whilst Guernsey celebrated as it had never celebrated before, members of the Island Police Force were on almost continuous duty throughout the day.

However, some managed to join in the festivities. Francois Le Cocq was observed wearing an outsized paper hat and posing for photographs outside the Police Station.

**Corporal F. Le Cocq, Jimmy and Henri Travers with the *Star* newspaper announcing liberation on May 8th.**

A/PC 16 Harold Hall was on duty outside the Royal Hotel when he saw a grey Austin saloon, registration number 4958, which had been reported stolen earlier that evening. Driving the car, which belonged to Gerrit Jan Timmer, was Walter Mahy, a twenty-one-year-old labourer of Springhurst, Forest. Francis Tanguy, of Hillview, Forest, was in the passenger seat.

Mr Timmer, of Suntrap, Forest, had reported to the Town Station that at about 7.30pm two men, one of whom he recognised as Walter Mahy, were on their way to Town in his car. The car had been taken from a shed at Timmer's Vineries, L'Epinel, Forest.

When the Constable stopped the car outside the Royal Hotel and questioned the driver, Walter Mahy said:-

"I stole the car from a shed at Timmer's Vineries at 7.30pm. I knew it was Timmer's. I just wanted to go to Town with my chum Tanguy. I intended to return the car as soon as we arrived back at the Forest."

**A/PC F.J. Moore, A/PC A.H. Henry, A/PC B. Le Page, Sgt. H.T. Pugh and Cpl. F. Le Cocq outside the Police Station on Liberation day.**

Francis Tanguy added:-

"We decided to take Timmer's car because he is a Quisling."

Years later Walter Mahy explained:- "When I drove down St Julian's Avenue I wanted to turn right but the place was packed out. This policeman came up to me and looked at the number and said 'This is Mr Timmer's car'. Later the Police took us home in the car and returned it to its owner. We heard nothing more."

At 9.00pm that evening Corporal Francois Le Cocq, who was in charge of the Station, received a telephone message from Major W.R.F.Clark requesting the attendance of a Policeman. Sergeant Bull took charge of the station and Corporal Le Cocq went in the Police van to La Houguette, Castel, where Major Clark told him:-

"Some minutes ago, at about 8.45pm, this young fellow came into our house in a state of collapse and abject terror and asked to be given over to the British troops or the local Police. We gave him food and drink and he has recovered somewhat."

**Crowds at the Weighbridge on Liberation day.**

The man, who was in German uniform and claimed to be a Pole named Bronilous Musznski, stationed at Beaucamps. He seemed to be afraid but when the Corporal told him he was taking him to Town, his demeanour changed. Musznski told Francois le Cocq:-

"I am 23 years old and have been in the army 2 years. I have been friendly with civilians and with two friends visited them today. On our return we were accosted by a Sergeant who told us we were under arrest and asked for our papers, proving we were Polish nationals. We were then ordered into a hut and told to hurry. My friends were in first and from what I heard I thought they were being ill treated, so I ran away. They chased me and I went into a civilian's house and asked to be handed to the Police or Tommies. They told me that an officer lived here, so I came here."

For his protection, Bronilous Musznski was placed in the Prison.

As a consequence of the Island's liberation, the role of the Police Force change dramatically. The constant stream of reports of break-ins and thefts which had occupied their time and efforts in the recent past almost disappeared. Instead of reports of Germans stealing food, furniture and other household goods, now the reports were of them giving away and disposing of furniture to locals.

A/PC 55 Clifford Tickner, whilst he was in charge of the L'Islet Sub Station, received a telephone message from Corporal Le Cocq, saying that Germans stationed at Delancey were disposing of furniture to local people living in the vicinity. The Constable immediately went to the Feldgendarmerie at Braye Road, but was unable to get any assistance or any German to accompany him to Delancey. He later reported to Corporal Le Cocq that he had patrolled the Delancey area for a time but had seen 'no untoward happenings'.

Later A/PC 12 Mahy, accompanied by Vernon Le Maitre, the Billeting officer, and Stafford Ogier, a Custodian of Property, interviewed twenty-four-year-old John Richards, of Granite Lodge, Vale, who told them:-

"I worked for a German soldier at Delancey. He gave me permission to remove a piano from his billet to my house. I also have his cycle. Those are the only things I have. I did not know that I was doing wrong."

Richards was instructed to deliver the piano to Stafford Ogier, at Les Gigands, Baubigny, the next day. The cycle was delivered to Vernon Le Maitre, at Brookdale, Summerfield Road.

The Constable, still accompanied by the two States officials, then visited Henry Clarke at 'Hure Mare', near Les Maresquets, Vale. He was questioned regarding furniture taken from German billets, that was in his possession. He explained to the Constable:-

"I have two armchairs and a gramophone which were given me at 6 The Grange, St Peter Port."

The Constable instructed Mr Clark to hand over the articles to the Custodian's office at Les Gigands.

On the 10th May A/PC de Carteret saw Cecil Le Huray at his home at 2 Primrose Vinery, Belgrave. He told the Constable:-

"On the 6th May my employer, Edward Dorey, Oatlands, St Sampson, billeted nine Germans in this house. They had two rooms and I had the other two. There was an officer in charge of them and they did guard over the vinery. On Tuesday the 8th May, I went to Town early, my son followed later. He forgot to lock our kitchen door. When I arrived home later my son told me that our Germans had had a party, with other Germans. I did not notice anything wrong that night but next morning the 9th May I found that one of my cupboards had been ransacked and half a tea set and six silver tea spoons, the property of my mother, evacuated to England, were missing. Also a quantity of cutlery, four slices of bread and a tin of salmon which had belonged to me were missing. I suspect the Marines who were billeted here. I would know them if I saw them but I don't know where they are now."

The presence in the Island of a considerable number of foreign workers was causing concern. By their nationality they were allies, but were being classed as prisoners of war by the British military authorities. They had come to Guernsey to work for the Organisation Todt and were housed in camps around the Island. In some ways the civilian authorities were waiting for the balloon to go up in respect of these foreign workers.

At 7.20pm on Sunday the 13th May a telephone call was received by Sergeant Pugh, from Miss Mary Roberts, sating that foreign labourers from the O.T. Camp Ursula, at Rue Sauvage, St Sampson, were on the march to Town. Mary, who was nicknamed, 'machinegun Mary' by the Police because of her stutter, said they had just passed her home at Le Ramee and were proceeding down the Coutanchez.

Corporal Le Cocq and A/PC 28 Boalch immediately set off in the Police car and met the men, about 200 strong, marching in an orderly manner along Pitronnerie Road. The Corporal got out of the car and signalled the column of men to halt, which they did. He then spoke to their leaders, one from each nationality, and as a result, gave permission for two of them to go and see Monsieur P.L.V.Lambert, the French Consul. He arranged to take the three other leaders back to their camp in the Police car. He told the remainder of the men that if they went back to camp he would listen to their grievances.

Corporal Le Cocq reported:-

"They all returned to the camp, where I heard their complaints which were,

A. Objection to having German guards over them.

B. Objection to being considered collaborators.

C. Complaint regarding an Algerian who had been assaulted.

D. Scarcity of food in the camp.

There were various other minor complaints. I contacted military authorities who dealt with the complaints. I remained in the camp and I was present when a distribution of bread and meat was issued to the camp people at 12.30am. Arrangements were made for a representative to leave the camp each morning to contact military authorities. The men agreed to make their own arrangements for the distribution of foodstuffs within the camp."

Acting Inspector Lamy congratulated Corporal Le Cocq and described it as 'Good work'.

Years later Francois Le Cocq commented:-

"I had a very good rapport with many of the Frenchmen as I spoke the language. That is why I was able to sort out the trouble with the Rue Sauvage camp. It was a case of keep the peace, keep things quiet. A lot of the foreign workers were forced labourers, but many were prisoners from jails who were given the choice of staying in prison or coming to the Island to work for the Germans."

The next evening Sergeant Bull was in charge of the Station, when at 8.15pm, L/Corporal Donaldson, of the British Military Police brought in a Georgian soldier, named Gogatischwiei, in civilian clothes. The Military Policeman informed the Sergeant that the Georgian had been found in the Commercial Arcade armed with an automatic pistol. He was placed in H.M.Prison and the pistol retained by the Military.

Earlier that day the Rt.Hon. Herbert Morrison, the British Home Secretary, had arrived in the Island on a short visit. At 3.00pm he addressed the States and afterwards made a short speech to the crowd outside the Royal Court.

Before addressing the States, Herbert Morrison had a briefing from the Bailiff, Brigadier Snow and members of the Controlling Committee. At one point the Acting Inspector, Mr Lamy, was called in to acquaint the Home Secretary with the situation in regard to the Police Force.

Mr Morrison said the welfare of the Channel Islands had never been absent from his mind nor from that of the British Government, particularly since 'D' day. "The Islands," he said "could have been taken by force, but this would have meant smashing them up. As it was thought to be only a matter of weeks, it was better to wait. We were anxious to feed our fellow countrymen but not feed the Germans. After receiving sufficient assurances regarding assistance from the International Red Cross, food had been sent to the Island."

The Bailiff said that the Germans had threatened on occasions but, on the whole, had governed in accordance with International Law. They had all been courteous with the exception of Admiral Huffmeier, who had refused to see him, always sending his Second-in-Command.

Mr Lamy told the Home Secretary:-

"During the last two months thieving had been terrific, but the soldiers were possibly hungrier than the civilian population. There had been stealing during the whole of the Occupation, but not to the same extent as during recent weeks. There had also been no violence until recently. In one case, a man who had been defending his potatoes had been shot dead. The Germans had given assurances that they would do their utmost to discover the criminal but had apparently been unsuccessful.

Another man who entered his house to find soldiers there, was gagged and bound and all his food stolen. Recently a man and his wife had had their throats cut and their heads battered in. There were Georgians living in the vicinity and the Feldgendarmerie were of the opinion that the crime had been committed by them and not by Germans." Mr Lamy continued, "I was not quite satisfied and have asked that the guard opposite the house should remain in the Island. In recent weeks fire-arms had also been used as threats by thieves."

Mr Leale told Mr Morrison, that if no Red Cross supplies had arrived he believed that half the population would have died.

The Home Secretary asked whether there had been any collaboration. He pointed out that co-operation was necessary for the good of the Island, but collaboration meant assisting the Germans in occupying and continuing the Occupation.

Mr Leale replied that some persons had made considerable sums of money through selling goods to the Germans, but he thought that in these cases the prime consideration was the making of money and not assisting the Germans.

In a reply to a further question, the Bailiff said :-

"A large number of young women and a few of the older ones had associated with the troops and that approximately 200 babies had been born, of whom German soldiers were reputed to be their fathers. In most cases the approach was by the women and not by the soldiers."

Mr Martel reported that the sentences imposed by the German Courts-Martial were generally fair. Mr Sherwill had attended several trials and had stated that the sentences were fair, all cases being thoroughly investigated. Some of the more recent sentences had been heavier, especially in the case of failure to surrender wireless sets. The Germans had taken over half the local prison for civilian and military prisoners and the conditions there were not good.

The Home Secretary said he was grateful to the Bailiff and the Administration for the way they had carried on. He thanked them for acting on the assumption that deliverance would come and thought they had done their job very well.

A/PC 40 Alec O'Donovan and A/PC 50 Charles Nicholls arrived at 'Suntrap', Forest, the home of Gerrit Jan Timmer, at 12.30am on the 15th May in response to an urgent telephone call. He told the Constables:-

"At about 11.00pm a stone crashed through the glass roof of my sun lounge breaking a large pane of glass. I ran outside and I was able to see four youths making off in the direction of my packing sheds. I pursued them across my garden and was in time to prevent them pulling down my flag. They ran away when they heard me. I do not know who they were.

I consider that the Rev. J.H.Finey, of the Forest is helping this hooliganism against me. At 6.00pm on the 10th May I received a telephone message from him asking me to take down my flags, that I refused to do. On Sunday last, he made direct reference to me from the pulpit. If this goes on I feel I shall have to appeal for Police protection."

The Constables drove around the immediate neighbourhood in the Police car, but did not see or hear anything unusual.

The resentment of the public against Gerrit Timmer manifested itself in a number of ways. One such was noticed by the Rev Finey's daughter, when she returned to the Island some time after the end of the Occupation. She recalled:-

"I can remember seeing 'Timmer is a Quisling' in black on the stone wall on the road leading to Le Gouffre, just past what is now the States houses."

At a meeting of the Controlling Committee held on the 15th May the President reminded members that Mr J.P.Blaikie-Webster had had a Red Cross parcel stolen and that the Bailiff's Red Cross Supplies Committee, in accordance with their policy, had refused to replace the parcel. Mr Blaikie-Webster had informed Mr Guillemette, the Secretary, that he proposed to report the matter to the British Authorities.

If he did, the President wondered whether the Military Authorities should be made aware of certain matters concerning Mr Blaikie-Webster. After consideration it was agreed that should any accusation be made by Mr Blaikie-Webster, no action should be taken apart from justifying the action complained of. It was also agreed that no steps should be taken, for the present, regarding the decision of the Committee of 5th September 1944 to bring to the British Authorities' attention certain matters regarding Mr Blaikie-Webster and Messrs Timmer Ltd.

Peter Doyle had another 'brush' with the Police on the 15th May when he failed to produce his identity card at the request of A/PC 39 Moore. Doyle said:-

"I have not got one, I have lost it"

When Peter Doyle appeared in the Police Court he was charged with the possession of ammunition without the authority of the Police in contravention of Fire Arms Law. A second charge was that on the 8th May 1945, while drunk, he behaved in a disorderly manner at Victoria Road. Further that when required by a Police officer, he failed to produce his identity card. The Magistrate, Jurat Quertier le Pelley, fined him £2 on the first charge and in default of payment, 14 days' imprisonment. The second offence resulted in a fine of £1 or eight days and for failing to produce his identity card, a fine of 5/-.

Peter Doyle was later described by a member of the Occupation Police Force as:-

"A typical Irishman who was not to be trusted. A rough and tough Irishman, which ever way the wind blew, he went. A man who had his price and would sell his mother to the Germans if the price was right. He was a menace, there is no doubt about it.

He was one of those troublesome ones who quickly left the Island after liberation, - he was pressured out. The sort of thing, - you can have it this way or you can have it that way, but if I was you I would, because if you don't ..... .

All sorts of things were done at that time which would make the legal powers shudder, but they worked. The 'Ways and Means Act' was used in a lot of cases to keep things quict."

Shortly after the Island was liberated, Mrs Emily Kibble reappeared from the dead. Her disappearance in February, which had been described by the Acting Inspector as a 'Doubtful Suicide' had been a hoax to deceive the Geheim Feldpolizei, the German Secret Police, and prevent her from going to prison.

While she was waiting to serve her prison sentence Mrs Kibble had become friendly with Rene Bessin, who helped her stage a 'suicide'. She disposed of all her possessions, furniture, household goods and clothing. Instead of reporting at the prison, Emily went to the Southview Hotel, Rene Bessin's home at Petit Bot. The same evening Rene took the clothes she had been wearing, her identity card, ration book and handbag and left them on a rock, on the beach between Albecq and Cobo.

When they were found the next day by schoolboy, Michael Gilmour, most people believed that she had committed suicide.

Mrs Kibble lived, with her Sealyham dog, 'Queenie', at Southview for the next thirteen weeks, before re-appearing on liberation day. Rene Bessin had shared his meagre rations and Red Cross parcels with her during her period of hiding. She had been confined to a small room in a part of the hotel that was not being used, only occasionally going into the back yard for fresh air.

On one occasion she narrowly escaped being detected. A local girl, who had previously worked at the hotel, informed the Germans, who were never really convinced that Mrs Kibble had committed suicide, that she might be hiding at

Southview. A local Policeman who was sent to investigate but did not look too energetically and Emily was not discovered.

When Mrs Kibble applied for her Red Cross parcels which she had missed due to her 'disappearance', she was refused. Eric Kibble in the meantime, had returned from Alderney, where he had been sent by the Germans to serve his sentence, and applied to the Bailiff's Red Cross Supplies Committee, requesting them to reconsider their decision. He wrote saying that he felt morally bound to repay, in kind, Mr Bessin, who had fed Emily during her seclusion. After Sir Abraham Laine, a member of the Committee, had pointed out that had Mrs Kibble served her sentence she would have received her parcels, it was agreed that she should be given two Red Cross parcels.

On the 9th July 1945 Emily signed a declaration, stating:-

"I, Emily Berry, nee Mellor, do hereby declare that I am the wife of William Berry who is residing in England and that I erroneously described myself as Emily Kibble on my Identity Registration Form on the 26th October 1940."

**Mrs Emily Berry known as Mrs Kibble.**

During the immediate post war years Mrs Berry ran, 'Kyston', a successful guest house, on the Glategny Esplanade.

The Bailiff did not reply to Jurat John Leale's letter, tendering his resignation as President of the Controlling Committee, until the 18th May. He then wrote:-

"I beg to acknowledge the receipt of your letter of the 8th instant, requesting me to submit to the States as soon as possible your resignation as President of the Controlling Committee.

I have also received from Colonel H.R.Power, Chief Civil Affairs officer, a letter regarding your resignation and I cannot do better than to enclose a copy of it for your information. I agree with Colonel Power that under present conditions it is inadvisable for you to relinquish the Presidency of the Controlling Committee.

I have said it before and I say it again, that during the whole time you have presided over that Committee you have had the full confidence of the States and myself, as well as that of the inhabitants of the Island. I would further remind you that about two years ago you acquainted me with your intention to resign as soon as the Occupation was at an end and suggested that I should form a Committee to recommend to the States as to what modification, if any, of our pre-occupation administration was desirable in post-occupation days.

Although at your request neither you nor any of your colleagues were invited to serve on this Committee, I believe you know that we came to certain important conclusions and I hope to present these to the States at an early date.

Obviously your resignation and the States decisions as to the future, are only different aspects of the same problem. In view, therefore, of the representations of Colonel Power and the Committee's recommendations I am taking the responsibility of withholding your resignation for the time being. I am convening a meeting of the States for next Wednesday the 23rd instant for the purpose of receiving your report on the activities of the Controlling Committee during the past five years."

At the meeting of the Police Committee held on the 22nd May 1945, it was unanimously resolved that:-

"The Committee desires to place on record their appreciation of Acting Inspector Lamy's devotion to duty and excellent work during the trying times of the Occupation period and requests the President to convey a copy of this decision to the President of the Controlling Committee with the recommendations that the Inspector be confirmed in his appointment in the event of Inspector Sculpher not resuming duty."

When the Controlling Committee met a few days later, the resolution passed by the Police Committee was reported and endorsed. With regard to the question of Inspector Sculpher resuming his duties the Committee felt it was a matter which should be dealt with by the Police Committee when the full facts were known. John Leale later wrote to the President of the Committee in regard to the future of Inspector Sculpher.

"....to the best of this Committee's knowledge Inspector Sculpher was suspended by the Germans, who considered that he had been dilatory in his duties. It is, therefore, a matter for the Police Committee to decide, whether this is so or otherwise, when the full facts are known and to act according to its findings.

Should it be decided that Inspector Sculpher is not to be re-engaged, the question of his dismissal will have to be submitted to the Appointments Board and that body asked to appoint his successor."

The signs of discontent amongst Islanders that had been anticipated by the Bailiff and others, began to manifest themselves in small but inevitable ways. The Reverend E.L.Frossard, the Rector of St Sampson, telephoned the L'Islet sub Station on the 1st June and informed Sergeant Le Lievre that he had seen, written in chalk on Le Maitre's garage in Grandes Maisons Road, 'Down with Leale and up with wages.'

Sergeant Charles Le Lievre immediately went to Grandes Maisons Road, where he found that the slogan had been rubbed out by Charles Roger, who lived opposite.

A few days later A/PC 55.Tickner noticed on the door of Mr A.Potter's store in Grandes Maisons Road, in black paint 'Food to buy, no money to buy it'. It was later painted out by Mr Potter.

Inevitably the subject of collaborators and quislings was raised by the general public. They knew, in their view, of many cases and they wanted to see something done about them. An office was established at the Channel Islands Hotel and anyone could make a report in respect of the activities of fellow Islanders during the Occupation. A number of accusations and claims were submitted. Whether any action resulted is not recorded, neither does any record of the 'reports' submitted appear to exist.

There was considerable feeling on the matter and letters were published in the press. Lt-Col E. Lawson, of Val au Bourg, Saints, had a letter published, headed:-

" Quislings.

There are some matters of great interest connected with the late Occupation on which many of us would like to hear comments. Can you tell us whether the German criminals who were caught, were ever punished. Of course the vast majority of German thieves were never caught but some of the many thieves were caught.

Then about our Quislings, there are very few of them, I am thankful to say, but there were some we know about. The wretched girls and still more miserable married women who cohabited with the Germans, we can leave to the relatives they have disgraced, but what about the informers, those loathsome people, male and female, who for money or for spite, sent their fellows to German prisons or death. Can nothing be done about them. All are not known but many are."

A further letter appeared in the press on the 4th June, from Mrs Margaret Guille, again headed:-

"Quislings.

I agree with your correspondent Colonel Lawson in his attack on Quislings, wretched girls and informers. But just as despicable, if not more so, is the type of person who during the Occupation made fast friends with Germans, entertaining them in their homes at all times of the day and night and supplied them with foodstuffs and who are now smilingly welcoming our troops into their homes, only to exploit them for food, cigarettes etc.

Fritz is gone but Tommy is here - and one uniform seems the same to them as another."

The War Crimes Branch of the Treasury Solicitor's Department were taking an interest in the subject of possible War Criminals in the Island. On the 2nd June the officer in charge, P.H.B.Kent, wrote to the Bailiff:-

"I have the honour to advise that the Treasury Solicitor was given a general instruction by H.M.Government in December 1942 in relation to the collection of material for the preparation of charges against War Criminals.

1. Up to date we have filed two cases with the United Nations War Crimes Commission in relation to the deportations in September 1942 and February 1943. The persons charged are as follows:-

(i) The first accused is or are a person or persons in high authority in Germany who was or were responsible for the issue of the order that certain British subjects in the Channel Islands, in or about the month of February 1943, should be deported to Germany.

(ii) The second accused is Colonel Knackfuss, Feld Kommandant of the Channel Islands in the month of February 1943, who directed that such order should be carried out.

(iii) General Muller, Commanding the Force of Occupation in the Channel Islands in February 1943.

(iv) Subordinate officers, non-commissioned officers and men who carried out the said order.

2. We shall be greatly obliged if you can furnish us with any information which would lead to the identification of the first accused, namely the person or persons in high authority in Germany responsible for the issue of the Order. Any names of subordinate officers, non-commissioned officers and men who carried out the order, who are fourthly accused, would be helpful. We realise of course that such orders may have been carried out with great consideration and that the offence so far as subordinates are concerned is technical and under orders, though 'superior orders' is not accepted as a defence.

Our information as regards the first deportation was derived in the first instance from the *Evening Press*. We have since secured affidavits from Mr Charles Roche, of Jersey, and Colonel Brousson. Information as regards the second deportation was secured from Colonel Brousson and Group Captain C.R.J.Randall. It is not quite clear whether there were two separate deportations for different reasons, or whether the second deportation was in the nature of completion of the original Order. There is also no information as to the grounds on which the deportations took place.

It is thought that you will be in a position to furnish material assistance in determining these outstanding questions and we shall be greatly obliged if you will communicate to us as soon as possible.

We shall also welcome information as to the steps being taken now to furnish information in relation to any other war crimes which have been committed. You will appreciate that it is of importance at the present juncture that all available information, supported if possible by affidavits, should be sent to this department as soon as possible, so that charges may be prepared and submitted to the United Nations War Crimes Commission as a preliminary to the further steps leading to prosecutions.

In the event of the matter of investigation being in the hands of some other authority other than yourself, you will perhaps advise them of our requirements. As regards the deportations, however, it seems to me that you will be able to furnish particulars which may be of special use.

3. We have been in touch with the Home Office who agree to our direct communication with yourself in this matter."

The Bailiff responded on the 5th June:-

"I am in receipt of your letter of the 2nd instant. Major F.F.Haddock, of the Judge Advocate's Department, has already approached me with a view to obtaining an affidavit on matters concerning War Crimes and I have referred him to Jurat Leale as being the one able to give most information. Major Haddock was at the War Office on the 1st June where he saw Brigadier Shapcott who asked him to obtain this affidavit.

The Brigadier, I understand, also has other affidavits taken from Islanders which were obtained by this officer. Unless I hear to the contrary I will allow Jurat Leale to make an affidavit setting out the full circumstances of the deportations with relevant documents as exhibits. He will hand this to Major Haddock who will forward it to his department. At the same time I will forward a copy to you. I have acquainted Mr Leale with the terms of your letter so that he may pay particular attention to the points you raise.

If the reference to section 3 refers to Alderney I understand that a full investigation has taken place and a detailed report by Major Haddock has been given to Brigadier Shapcott."

Early in July 1945 a conference was held at the Home Office in London regarding War Crimes and Collaboration. J.E.L Martel and Colonel Bill Arnold represented Guernsey. Jersey sent their Attorney General, Duret Aubin, and Sir Frank Newsome and J.B.Howard represented the Home Office.

The subjects discussed included :-

1. Women who associated with Germans
2. People who entertained Germans as guests.
3. Profiteers.
4. Information givers.
5. Contractors who worked for Germans.

After a long discussion it was agreed that no action could be taken regards women who associated with the Germans or people who entertained them as guests. Profiteers would be dealt with by financial legalisation. With regards to the last two items it was agreed that these could be dealt with under United Kingdom Treason Act.

On the 7th June their Majesties the King and Queen visited Guernsey and received a rapturous reception. A/PC 48 Harold Kendall drove their Majesties on their tour of the Island and the Queen thanked him very much for a lovely drive. Before they left, Harold was given a pound note as a gift from the King and Queen. He treasured that note and nothing and no one ever persuaded him to spend it.

The Royal visit presented Acting Inspector Lamy, for the first time, with the task of organising such an event. No one on the Force had any experience of a Royal visit, but they rose to the occasion and despite the arrival of the Royal party being put back twenty-four hours, everything went off entirely according to plan.

Mr Lamy issued a memo stating:-

"All leave will be suspended, some men will be required to perform long tours of duty, this is unavoidable, but time will be made up later.

Every effort must be made to smarten up uniforms, trousers are to be pressed.

Dress;- serge jackets, helmets, medals will be worn.

Auxiliaries in civilian clothes may have a new armlet on application to the office.

A full dress rehearsal is to be held on Monday 4th June.

I hope every man will do his best to make the 6th June 1945 a success from the Police standpoint."

The Royal visit was an outstanding occasion and the Acting Inspector was justly proud of his men.

In the Royal Court on the 9th June 1945 Peter Vermeulen, of Sunbursa, Bailiffs Cross, was convicted of having, without a licence, on the 24th April, slaughtered a cow, belonging to John Carre, a farmer, of Sunnyside, Les Blicqs. Also of slaughtering a cow other than in the public slaughterhouse or in an authorised place, obtaining rationed foodstuff for consumption and suppling Victor Gontier and several unknown persons foodstuffs.

Peter Vermeulen was sentenced to six months' imprisonment with hard labour and fined £100, or a further three months in default, with £12.12.0 costs. The Court also recommended that he be deported.

Peter Maria Vermeulen was born in Vught, Holland, in 1922 and came to the Island as a Todt worker in August 1941. He was due to work for the Germans in Alderney as an interpreter, but was warned by a fellow countryman not to go. He managed to remain in Guernsey, working for a time as a docker at St Peter Port harbour. He also worked as a carpenter for the O.T. firm of Boerch. Later he married a local girl, Miss Bettie Domaille, and together they developed an enterprise selling sugar beet syrup from a cottage at St Clair Hill, rented from J.E.L.Martel, the Acting Attorney General.

**Peter Vermeulen.**

Their enterprise was so successful that by the end of 1944 they were able to purchase their own home, Sunbursa, in St Andrew.

When Victor Gontier admitted stealing the cow from John Carre, the Police soon had sufficient evidence to charge Peter Vermeulen with slaughtering the animal.

Peter Vermeulen purchased the cow for 1404 Reichmarks and slaughtered it in his garage. Peter Vermeulen later said:-

"When I knew the Police were around I cut the hide up into big pieces and put them in the cesspool inside my garage."

On the 20th December 1945 the Home Secretary, Chuter Ede, signed a Deportation Order which was effected on the 13th February 1946, when Sergeant Dyson accompanied Peter Vermeulen on the mailboat to England. Mrs Bettie Vermeulen and their son also left the Island, voluntarily.

In 1950, after the Lieutenant Governor had been consulted and raised no objection, the Deportation Order was revoked and Peter Vermeulen and his family returned to Guernsey.

# Chapter 35

## I BEG TO APPLY TO BE REINSTATED.

The Police Force at the time of the liberation of the Island comprised:-

Acting Inspector Albert Peter Lamy, 42.
Acting Deputy Inspector Frederick James Banneville, 48.
Detective Sergeant Edward James De Jersey Pill, 51.
Clerk Sergeant Ernest William Plevin, 34.
Sergeant Charles Le Lievre, 49.
Sergeant George Henry Lewis Dyson, 39.
Sergeant Henry John Bull, 43.
Sergeant Robert William Kimber, 61.
Sergeant Henry Thomas Pugh, 45.
Corporal Francois Le Cocq, 30.
Corporal Reginald Percy George Marsh, 29.
A/PC 10 William Kelly Sebire, 56.
A/PC 11 Albert James Vanden Bergh, 60.
A/PC 12 Henry William Mahy, 34.
A/PC 13 Josiah Le Poidevin, 52.
A/PC 14 Edwin Percy Peadon, 40.
A/PC 16 Harold Hall, 41.
A/PC 17 Albert Hill Henry, 51.
A/PC 18 Frank Herbert Cecil Pill, 41.
A/PC 20 Emile Edgar Julou, 24.
A/PC 21 Roland Wilfred Le Tissier, 28.
A/PC 22 Reginald George Le Gallez, 23.
A/PC 23 Clifford Charles Langlois, 31.
A/PC 24 Basil Le Page, 32.
A/PC 25 Oswald Harry Brackley, 39.
A/PC 26 Edwin Henry Butt, 39.
A/PC 28 William James Boalch, 27.
A/PC 29 Frank Henry Falla, 47.
A/PC 30 Daniel George De Carteret, 35.
A/PC 31 Wilfred John Mansfield, 25.
A/PC 32 John William Salmon, 25.
A/PC 33 Roy Frederick Thoume, 25,
A/PC 34 Raymond Philip Gaudion, 23.
A/PC 35 Edwin James Le Page, 31.
A/PC 36 Henry Thomas Solway, 36.
A/PC 37 Leonard George Tucker, 23.
A/PC 38 Edwal Arthur Robilliard, 22,
A/PC 39 Frederick John Moore, 58.
A/PC 40 Alexander Charles O'Donovan, 41.
A/PC 41 Alfred John Bisson, 46.

A/PC 43 John Edward Aubert, 34.
A/PC 44 Arthur Russell Bailey, 19.
A/PC 45 Ronald Walter Bourgaize, 19.
A/PC 46 Albert George Bichard, 30.
A/PC 47 George Edward Bougourd, 24.
A/PC 48 Harold Frederick Kendall, 31.
A/PC 49 Walter Belmore Wood Lovell, 40.
A/PC 50 Charles Nicholls, 22.
A/PC 51 Emile George Perrott, 23.
A/PC 52 Ronald Henry Pagnier, 20.
A/PC 53 Arthur George Stephen Reeve, 35.
A/PC 54 Sidney John Torode, 27.
A/PC 55 Clifford Henry Tickner, 48.

It was not long before former members of the Force were writing to the Acting Inspector and the President of the Police Committee, enquiring if their positions were still available to them. Former PC 10 Cyril Eley, PC 8 Ted Sparrow and PC 29 John Grainger, who had been recalled to the Colours in September 1939, made application to return to the ranks of the Force. John Grainger wrote on the 10th June 1945:-

"I expect you will be surprised to hear from me after all these years. I am hoping that you and all the boys are keeping in the best of spirits. As for myself, I am discharged from the Royal Navy and waiting for the word to come home.

I would like to come back again into the Force, that's if my place is still vacant. At present I am staying with friends, with my two daughters. You will know that my wife is still on the Island. Give my regards to the boys and hoping to see them again."

Mrs Kathleen Grainger had not evacuated, although her two daughters had left with their school. In 1940 she had been employed as a grocer's assistant, but later in the Occupation was required to work for the Germans, first at Chez Nous, on the Esplanade, and later doing housework at Morley Chapel.

Mr Lamy replied to John Grainger confirming that his position was still open for him when he returned. He added "There are very few old faces left."

Before long John Grainger was back in uniform as PC 19. and later Cyril Eley, PC 15, and Ted Sparrow, PC 14, were also to return to the Force. Cyril Eley went on to become Chief Officer.

On the 28th June 1945 Arthur Langmead wrote to the President of the Police Committee:

"Re-instatement in Police.

I beg to inform you that I have arrived in England from Germany and have applied for the necessary permit to return to Guernsey. As I expect this will be granted shortly I would be glad if you would kindly place this application before the Police Committee for my suspension to be withdrawn and for my re-instatement in the Police Force.

The Office records will show that I was suspended on the 30th July 1942, by the Germans. This was because of an anonymous letter received by them making allegations against me which were untrue, but which occupied them until December in trying to prove. The subsequent sentence imposed on me was without any trial and was a sequel to various incidents which occurred during the period I was in charge. On three occasions I was threatened by the Feldgendarmerie officer and his satellite Oeser.

Most of the members of the Committee now serving will remember the difficult period when the Force had to be rebuilt. It was just complete when I was suspended. Advocate J.E.L.Martel will bear out the long hours and hard work that was being undertaken in collaboration with his department during this period.

Finally, sir, reference to the Police Register will show that my service was of consistent and steady progress which was acknowledged by the Police Committee. Constable 1922, Corporal 1924, Sergeant 1926, Clerk Sergeant 1930, obtained certificate New Scotland Yard 1933, Deputy Inspector 1938.

I submit, sir, that this record is worthy of every consideration and that I should be given the opportunity of continuing my service. I would welcome an opportunity of an interview with the Committee."

The anonymous letter that Arthur Langmead referred to was one written by an Auxiliary Constable to the Germans. Many years later a member of the Force at the time Inspector Langmead was suspended from the Force, commented:- "Mr Langmead did not last long as unfortunately he had to discipline one of the Auxiliary Constables over some little matter and this Auxiliary Constable, A/PC Petit, took spite out on him by writing a letter to the Germans."

At the meeting of the Police Committee on the 11th July, at which A.C.Bichard was appointed President in the place of C.E.Agnew, Mr Langmead's letter was considered. Before coming to a decision they decided to seek the advice of Mr Ambrose Sherwill, who had recently returned to the Island and had again taken up his post as Attorney General.

The Police Committee met on the 23rd when they again considered Mr Langmead's application. The President, Mr A.C.Bichard, reported that he had consulted Mr Sherwill who suggested the Committee consider four matters:-

1. The Committee's attitude towards Mr Langmead's re-instatement.
2. Were there any other known cases of stealing or receiving.
3. The effect on the remainder of the Force should he be re-instated.
4. Mr Langmead's position differed from other men, in that he was Deputy Inspector and in charge of these men.

After a lengthy discussion the Committee unanimously decided that Mr A.J.Langmead could not be re-instated in the Police Force. The Committee fully appreciated Mr Langmead's excellent service in the past and asked the President to approach the President of the Board of Administration with a view to his re-employment in another States Department and that Mr Langmead be informed accordingly.

The President, Mr Bichard, wrote to Mr Langmead, who had now returned to the Island, at Enid House, Les Cornus, St Martin:-

"With further reference to your letter of the 28th June. I beg to inform you that the matter was further considered at a meeting of the Committee held on 23rd July, when it was decided that owing to your sentence and subsequent imprisonment for receiving, you could not be re-instated in the Police Force.

The Committee fully appreciates your excellent record and services rendered in the past and are in touch with the Board of Administration with the possibility of you being transferred to some other States Department, thus enabling you to continue your service in States employ."

After making an unsuccessful application for reconsideration through an Advocate, Arthur Langmead reluctantly accepted a position with the States Housing Authority.

Inspector W.R.Sculpher who had been deported with his wife in September 1943, was in the Biberach Internment Camp in Germany when it was liberated by French troops on the 23rd April 1945. Although free, the internees had to wait until the 2nd June when they were flown by the R.A.F. to Hendon. From there they were transferred to the Reception Centre at Stanmore before being finally free to join their relatives and friends in England.

In Biberach, Mr Sculpher had been President of the Camp Tribunal which dealt with all cases of infringement of the Camp rules. The Camp had its own Police Force, who were identified by white armbands. Arthur J.Langmead was the Inspector and Ex.A/PC 35 Roy Northey, Deputy Inspector. Arthur's father, Jack Langmead, a former Police Sergeant who retired in 1937 and Ex.A/PC 27 Geoff Scraton, were Sergeants.

On the 11th June former Inspector W.R.Sculpher sent a telegram and a letter to Jurat John Leale enquiring whether he could resume his duties as Police Inspector.

John Leale felt embarrassed at receiving the enquiry and sought to avoid giving a direct answer by passing Mr Sculpher's letter to the Bailiff. He replied to the former Inspector, at 90 Beresford Road, Hornsey:-

"Thank you for your telegram and letter. I have passed the matter on to the Bailiff. During the Occupation I have not regarded it as my province to deal with matters of law and order when I could possibly avoid doing so. The Bailiff is the appropriate person. I will pass this letter of yours to him.

You say nothing about your health or that of Mrs Sculpher, but I conclude that you have safely weathered the storm of camp life in Germany."

The Bailiff passed the letter to the Police Committee and their view was that they still regarded Mr Sculpher as the Inspector. He in the Committee's view, had not been dismissed, had not committed any crime and had not been charged with any offence.

On the 31st of July 1945 Mr Sculpher and his wife returned to the Island and after contacting Mr A.C.Bichard, the President of the Police Committee, he was invited to attend a meeting of the Committee on the 7th August. After Mr Sculpher reassured the Committee that he wished to resume his duties as Inspector, the President informed the Bailiff:-

"I have the honour to inform you that at the meeting of the Police Committee held on the 7th August 1945, the position of Inspector Sculpher was discussed. It was unanimously decided that he would resume duty forthwith."

The Committee put the emphasis on 'resume duty', rather than on reinstatement. They took the view that his absence from duty had been entirely the result of German action. The Committee also requested the Board of Administration, who were responsible for staffing matters, to pay Inspector Sculpher the salary due to him whilst suspended by the German Authorities.

Mr Lamy was confirmed as Deputy Inspector and Acting Deputy Inspector Banneville kept his position and title for the time being. The Committee were not sure how to deal with the situation and finally resolved to have two Deputy Inspectors. This was justified, the Committee felt, because of the urgent need to provide the Force with additional training.

Of the former Police officers who had been convicted by the German Military Court in 1942, two, PC's H.P.Smith and P.J.F.Bretel, were now dead. Of the other fifteen deported from the Island, only Sergeant Alf Howlett had returned to Guernsey permanently. After the Occupation he obtained employment as a commissioner at the Gaumont Cinema. PC Eugene Le Lievre, PC 'Snip' Piesing, PC Alf Le Gallez had all returned to Guernsey on the completion of their sentences, but were deported to internment camps along with other Islanders in February 1943.

PC Archie Tardif had been transferred to an internment camp when he completed his term of imprisonment. PC Bill Burton managed to escape from prison but the others, PC Frank Whare, Sergeant Fred Duquemin, PC Tom Gaudion, PC Charlie Friend, Sergeant Jack Harper, PC Bill Quin, PC Kingston Bailey, PC Frank Tuck and PC Fred Short remained in prison until the advancing Allied Forces liberated them. Some had suffered more harshly than others.

Bill Burton, who had been sentenced to 3 years by the German Military Court, was taken to France on the 13th June 1942 and imprisoned at Caen before being moved to Penitentiaire de Villeneuve, St. Georges, where, by feigning illness, he managed to remain until August 1944. He later recalled:-

"When I managed to escape from prison, I joined the French Maquis until the liberation of Paris. I then made my way to Granville and from there on to Cherbourg, where I got in touch with the R.A.F. who sent me to England."

In July 1945, Bill Burton wrote to the President of the Police Committee, from Rothwell, near Leeds:-

"I beg to apply to be reinstated in the States Police Force. I was a member of the said Force from 31st March 1924 to 5th March 1942, when I was arrested by the Nazis, for offences committed against them. I was sentenced as you know, sir, to three years' penal servitude. I committed no offences against our civil population.

I would deem it a favour, sir, if you would place this application before your Committee and hope for an early reply."

He also wrote to Mr Lamy asking him:- "If I could resume my duties as promised us while we were serving our term in the local prison."

Frank Whare, another former Police officer who had served the greater part of his sentence at Penitentiare de Villeneuve, St. Georges, penned a letter to the President of the Police Committee on the 29th July:-

"Being desirous in the near future of returning home, may I be permitted to write to you for advice. To be as brief as possible, may I respectfully ask if there is any prospect of re-instatement. It is unnecessary for me to go into details of the circumstances of my dismissal, except to say that it was due to enemy Occupation.

It is true that I was indicted before the Royal Court on a charge, of which I was entirely innocent, although I signed an admission to the Feldgendarmerie. This signature was obtained by them, by their threat to arrest my wife for interrogation, which I wished to avoid at all costs. In support of this I may say, that when I was interviewed at Fort George by PS.Banneville, I told him I was not guilty and that the German statement was not true, but I asked him not to take it down in writing. I repeated this to Inspector Langmead when he interviewed me a few days later and it was only in consequence of a letter from the German Authorities, shown to me by Inspector Langmead, that I finally pleaded guilty, with the result that everyone knows.

This letter, I was informed, was to be filed for future reference. I now feel branded as a criminal for an offence of which I knew nothing at all, which has been my hardest blow after a hitherto clean record and which I will go to any length to erase.

I need not enlarge on my past years of service or character, details of which are accessible to you, but would ask that you and your Committee consider them in my favour in coming to a decision."

The President of the Police Committee replied to Frank Whare on the 3rd August:-

"Referring to your letter dated the 29th July, concerning your re-instatement in this Force.

I beg to inform you that the matter was recently before the Committee, when it was decided that no men convicted of stealing or receiving could be re-employed on the Force."

A similar letter was sent to Bill Burton.

Both Frank and Bill accepted the decision of the Police Committee. Frank Whare obtained employment as a stoker at the States Dairy while Bill Burton was given a job by a friend who was a grower.

Jack Harper, Charlie Friend and Frank Tuck were freed from Augsberg Prison by the Americans on V.E.Day. They had all been subjected to brutal treatment during their period in prison and had been forced to work on track laying and repairs to German railways.

After their release, Frank Tuck and Jack Harper stayed with the Americans at Landsberg, while they regained their strength and weight. Frank suffered an accident, falling from a truck and breaking his arm and was sent to an American military hospital at Rheims for three weeks before being flown to Lyneham in Wiltshire on the 21st June 1945.

From there he made his way to Glasgow, where his mother lived. Later he spend a considerable period in a Liverpool hospital, recovering from his treatment at the hands of the Germans. While there he met a nurse, whom he married and they set up home in Liverpool. For a time he drove an ambulance for the local authority.

Jack Harper stayed on with the Americans for four months during which time he was made an honorary U.S.Army Staff Sergeant and placed in charge of a food warehouse. Eventually he was taken to Brussels where he was interrogated by the British Consul, regarding his treatment by the Germans.

Frank Tuck later recalled their imprisonment and treatment:-

"When I was released I was frail, Jack Harper was even worse, he was immobile and so was Charlie Friend, I was just able to walk. The Americans rescued us and they were very careful, they would not let us eat too much at first. They fed us up.

The treatment meted out by the Germans to Sergeant Harper was extended over a long period. He was beaten with a pick and shovel, kicked and trampled on, deprived of food and clothes, even at umpteen degrees below zero. He was chained to a tree in the snow for six hours or longer with no food, chained to a post all night with no supper. He was stabbed in the buttocks till the blood trickled through his trousers, made to lift 2 cwt bags of cement and railway sleepers and beaten whilst doing so. Tripped and made to fall whilst carrying these sleepers, then they were thrown onto his chest. He was made to sit down in the mud and snow for several hours at a time and pronged with a fork. His clothes were taken away when it was terribly cold and he was placed under cold showers and left to dry without a towel and was constantly tormented and jeered.

A fact which can be regarded as relevant is that when we were released at Augsberg the Americans said that they had not seen anyone in worse condition than Harper.

My own treatment, though not as bad as that of Harper, or Smith who died, came within the category of brutality and pre-meditated torture, I had been kicked and knocked down and beaten with a pick axe handle and flogged with a butt of a rifle and on one occasion I can remember being so weak that I could hardly walk through having been beaten across the kidneys, but I was chased to work just the same.

I look back on those days with horror and I shudder at the thought of them."

After being interrogated, Jack Harper was flown by the R.A.F. to London. He subsequently returned to Guernsey. Of his return home he later commented:-

"I was regarded with coldness during my stay in Guernsey, couldn't get a job, so I decided to quit and went to London where I secured a job. During that time I received some correspondence from my son, Morris, who incidentally was an American soldier, and to get away from it all I decided to join him in Buffalo, New York.

I came to America on the 16th December 1946. I secured a job on the 6th January 1947 at Buffalo and worked in the Chevrolet motor car plant."

Charlie Friend was also in a very bad state. After his release, he spent a long period in Frenchay Hospital, Bristol, recuperating, before he returned to Guernsey. He obtained employment with Hubert's as a carpenter.

Kingston Bailey had served his sentence, first at Penitentiaire de Villeneuve, St. Georges, then at Bernau and Swabmunchen in Germany. He was told by the camp Commandant that he was being released and transferred to an internment camp to join other Channel Islanders, but instead was sent to the notorious Dachau concentration camp, arriving there on the 19th December 1944. Ex Constable Bailey remained at Dachau until the end of February 1945 when he was unexpectedly transferred to Laufen internment camp.

Kingston Bailey, along with other deportees including ex Constables, Tom Gaudion, Eugene Le Lievre, Alf Le Gallez, Snip Piesing and Bill Quin, were all released and repatriated to England in May 1945.

After he returned to Guernsey, Kingston tried his hand at many trades, including a time as a wholesale merchant. Tom Gaudion who had a part time growing business of his own prior to the Occupation, became a full time tomato grower when he returned to the Island. Alf Le Gallez became a bus driver for Guernsey Railways and eventually died at the wheel as a result of a heart attack. Archie Tardif obtained employment as a hall porter at the Royal Hotel. 'Snip' Piesing expanded his part-time activity to become a poultry farmer, while Bill Quin took a job with Stan Taylor as a cycle mechanic at Grande Rue, St Martin. Eugene Le Lievre was employed overseas for a time before returning to Guernsey.

Ex Sergeant Fred Duquemin served the main part of his sentence at Siegburg in Germany. He was not released and sent to an interment camp like other former colleagues who had completed their sentences. Fred's two-and-a-half-year sentence turned into three years. When the Americans crossed the Rhine and started threatening Siegburg, he and another 20 prisoners in his working party were moved eastwards. After a time the lorry they were travelling in, broke down and they were lodged in a local prison whilst the guards searched for another lorry. However the Yanks beat them to it when on the 27th March a U.S. tank drew up outside the prison and Fred Duquemin was liberated.

He and his fellow prisoners, Frenchmen, Dutchmen, Poles and Russians, had been employed filling in bomb craters at nearby airfields. Fred Duquemin had not spoken English to anybody for eighteen months.

Fred was looked after by the Americans for a couple of days and within a week, was flown by the R.A.F. to Thetford in East Anglia. He was quickly reunited with his wife and family, who had been evacuated to England in June 1940.

Three years of captivity affected Fred in many ways. His twelve-year-old daughter recalled how her father had changed:-

"You did not have to hear that he had suffered, you could see. His skin was literally hanging in folds. If a dog barked, his head would turn sharply. He could not walk past a cigarette end without picking it up, he kept a tin in his pocket. If a bell rang or there was a sharp noise, he was looking over his shoulder. If there was food, he ate it, if it was there, the safest place for it was in his stomach, because it might not be there later."

Fred Duquemin returned to Guernsey with his family and obtained employment at the airport, along with another of his former colleagues, Fred Short. However, he remained for the rest of his life extremely bitter about the treatment he and his former colleagues received at the hands of the local establishment.

Fred Short, who had been sentenced to three years and three months hard labour, left Guernsey on the 13th June 1942 with his colleagues. On their way to Caen prison they stopped at Granville prison for about an hour while their escorts had lunch. They were left in the charge of the French gaoler, who with the help of his family supplied Fred and his fellow prisoners with food and cider. He was allowed to go to the toilet, which was across a yard. When he came out, he saw that the main gate of the prison was open and could see people walking up and down the main street.

Fred walked down past the prison warders' office window, he was sure they saw him and said nothing, out of the prison gate and into the street. Walking along the pavement approaching him was none other than Raymond Falla, a member of Guernsey's Controlling Committee, who made many trips to Granville during the Occupation buying supplies for the Island. He greeted Fred and asked:-

"What are you doing here ?"

Fred explained that he had just walked out of the prison and asked:-

"Can you give me some German money. I have friends in St Malo and other places that I can get to. If you give me some money I can make good my escape."

Raymond Falla refused, saying:-

"No I am not giving you any German money. The trouble I would get into if it was found that I had given Fred Short money. All the good work I am doing getting supplies for Guernsey would go out of the window."

It wasn't very long before the French warders came out looking for Fred and asked "What are you doing here?"

Fred Short, then and ever since, interpreted the question as 'Why have you not run away.' The French warders seemed rather surprised and disappointed that he had not escaped when he had the chance. Often over the next three years Fred was to regret that he had not escaped when he had the opportunity. Fred has never forgiven Raymond Falla for refusing to assist him that day in Granville.

In 1943 Fred was held in a labour camp in Southern Bavaria and was one of four hundred prisoners digging a canal. As a result of the heavy work and the lack of medical attention, his hands and feet were in a very bad state. He later recalled:-

"The inside of my hands and soles of my feet had become like raw meat, blisters had been appearing and breaking for quite some time and had more or less become major wounds. This also applied to the majority of prisoners. I applied for medical aid but this was refused. One morning I deliberately failed to answer my name at role call. The guards entered my hut and I informed them that I required medical treatment. I was then knocked to the floor and kicked, then dragged out of the hut and placed in the detention block.

Later that morning I was taken before the camp commandant, a staunch Nazi. I showed him the state of my hands and when about to show him the state of my feet he knocked me to the floor. On regaining my feet he spat in my face. I was sentenced to one week solitary detention with the dark cell treatment, this meant one hour's daylight per day, the other twenty-three in total darkness. My diet was black bread and water daily with a bowl of weak soup every third day.

After serving this sentence I was again taken before the camp commandant and through an interpreter I informed him that the Geneva Convention was all against the treatment I was receiving and as a British subject I wished to go before a higher authority. I was again returned to the detention block and after several days I was again brought before the camp commandant who asked me whether I still wanted to see a higher authority. I replied I still wished to do so. He then informed me that it will of course mean a German Court where I would be tried for my political views and opposition to Hitler's Third Reich and inciting other prisoners in the camp to do likewise. He told me that he was going to write a full report to the appropriate authority and did I know that if found guilty the penalty was death. I was put back in detention where I remained for a further three weeks."

Fred Short was sent to Munich, where he was to be tried by a People's Court. The journey to Munich was broken by a stay at Augsberg, where he was invited by the commandant, to join the International Army. Fred later recalled the 'invitation':-

"The International Army consisted of people who were Dutch, Russian, British and others who threw their lot in with the Germans and joined their army. I was given documents which I refused to sign and promised good food and all the good things in life if I joined. In fact for two days running I was made to parade with a contingent of the International Army in order to try and encourage me to change my mind, but I didn't."

Fred Short was tried before a People's Court and sentenced to be detained in custody for as long as the Authorities deemed necessary - life imprisonment. Fortunately he only learnt the details of the sentence when he and a Dutch naval officer, who was also a prisoner, inspected their files after they were liberated. After the trial he was sent to a prison at Diez-Lahn, near Frankfurt, where he served the rest of his time, until liberated.

When he was freed by the Americans in March 1945, Fred Short was the only British subject in the prison. He had been held at the top of a three-storey block in solitary confinement. He weighed only 5 stone 10 pounds and was unable to walk up or down stairs unaided. He was in such bad shape that he was transferred to an American hospital in Metz, Alsace-Lorraine, where he remained for three months. He was then taken to a American convalescent hospital at Epinal, a former French officers college, in north western France, where he stayed until October. Fred was so well looked after by the Americans that when he left hospital he weighed more than 9 stone.

He was flown from Paris by the R.A.F. to Hendon. After spending a few days at a reception centre, Fred caught the train from Paddington to Pembroke where he was reunited with his wife and family. For a time he took a job as a club steward before returning to Guernsey in September 1946.

Even then his troubles were not over as he was unable to obtain possession of his home in Steam Mill Lanes, as the couple living there refused to move out. They would not even allow him in to view his own property. He had to obtain a Court Order, with a three month stay of eviction, before he was finally able to return to his home. Only then did he find out just how badly damaged it had been by the Germans who had been billeted there.

While he was imprisoned on the Continent some of his furniture was stolen and the rest had been sold for a mere £65. Fred and his wife had to set about restoring and refurbishing their home. All that there was left was an inventory which had been taken immediately after his deportation, by I.C. Fuzzey Ltd., and a grant of a £100 from the States.

Another who came back from imprisonment on the Continent, was Ernest Le Prevost, who as A/PC 25 had been sentenced by the Germans in 1943 for possessing a wireless set. After being shipped to St Malo he landed up at Troyes prison in August 1943. He remained there for eight months, before being transferred with 100 other prisoners of all European nationalities, to Dijon. The journey took seventeen hours during which time they were chained, in pairs, hand and foot. He remained in Dijon for five months before the advancing Allies forced the Germans to move him to a Merchant Navy camp near Bremen.

After nine months at Bremen, the camp was liberated by the Guards Armoured Division on the 27th April 1945. After spells at Luneburg and Brussels he was flown to Hendon on the 18th May. He returned to Guernsey in July 1945 and joined his father in the building firm of E.Le Prevost and Son.

Amongst the many hundreds of Islanders who returned from Biberach and Laufen deportation camps were widow Mrs Elda Brouard and Mrs Elisabet Duquemin, both Jews. Of the six Jews identified by the Germans, during the Occupation, they and Frau Annie Wranowsky, of Sark were the fortunate ones. The other three, Therese Steiner, Auguste Spitz and Marianne Grunfeld, all died in the gas chambers of Auschwitz. Annie Wranowsky, became Mrs Mason when she married her eighty-six-year-old employer in August 1945.

**Annie Wranowsky.**

An Islander who had evacuated in 1940 and who had not returned was Mr E.J.Brache. He owned a house known as Amulree, at L'Ancresse. In September 1945 he wrote to Miss Milbower, of La Moye, Vale, requesting her to retrieve a chest he had buried in his garden before he evacuated. Miss Milbower, fearful of what might happen to her if she was discovered retrieving the chest, asked Inspector Sculpher for his advice. He accompanied her to the house and dug as instructed, in a flower bed opposite the entrance steps and recovered the chest intact with its contents of household silver.

Herbert Champion after serving his prison sentence for illegality purchasing and slaughtering a cow, worked with his wife on her stall in the fish market. With a view to fishing commercially, he purchased a 16ft fishing boat, the 'Joy', for the sum of £25.

Bert Champion explained:-

"My wife had the rental of a fish stall in the Guernsey fish market and it was our hope that I should do fishing and Mrs Champion to sell the same in the fish market, so supplying the public and giving us the means to live comfortable with our 9 children, whose ages ranged at that time from 16 years down to 3 years."

In November 1944 he obtained permission from the German Authorities to go ormering in Saints Bay. With Dennis W. Carre and Gerald Lesbirel he anchored in the Bay and began to collect ormers. After a time they returned to the boat and found her fast by the keel. They waited for her to re-float, by which time a strong easterly wind had blown up and a fair swell was running. Bert Champion recalled the events:-

"On the boat re-floating we boarded her and began to haul in the anchor. It was noticeable that the anchor dragged, then held, dragged again but finally came away smartly into the hands of Dennis Carre, who fell backwards and just saved himself from falling overboard. It was at this moment that the boat was caught broadside to the wind and hit a small rock, making a six-inch hole in the port side below the water line.

She began to fill. Being that we were in about 2 ft of water we jumped overboard and getting on shore, pulled the boat high and dry and tied her down. After making our way back to St Peter Port by land, we reported the accident to the then German Harbourmaster, Captain Obermayer. We asked for his permission to return by boat to Saints Bay next day to patch up and tow the 'Joy' to St Peter Port harbour. He refused permission. I told Captain Obermayer that I had 9 children, fishing was my living and everything I had was in the boat.

It was no use, we were forbidden to go to Saints Bay by sea. I asked permission to go to the bay by land and salvage the engine and anything else we could save. This could not be done, I was told, as it was impossible to go over the cliffs owing to mines. He did not understand how we had managed to come up the cliffs without coming into contact with mines. And so this was the end of the 'Joy', I have not seen anything of her since."

On the 11th July 1945 Herbert Champion wrote to the Authorities making a claim for compensation for the total loss of the boat and equipment. The "Joy" was in very good condition, had a 2½hp engine, new foot boards, mast, sail, paddles, rowlocks, anchor and numerous fishing items. The whole being valued by Herbert Champion at £60

He added that it was beyond his means to make good the loss of the motor boat. The little savings he possessed had been used in purchasing the boat, making her sea worthy and buying fishing equipment.

The claim was assessed and the report submitted by the assessor read:-

"The applicant was attached to the Island Police and later imprisoned for illegally slaughtering a cow. He then purchased the boat 'Joy' for the sum of £25 with a view to fishing commercially. In November 1944, after collecting Ormers, he and his friends wrecked the boat and it is doubtful if the German Authorities had any responsibility in its ultimate loss. Applicant is now in regular employment as a fish salesman and as he cannot be regarded as a professional fisherman as he has never been registered with the authorities, I am unable to make any recommendation in his favour."

Bert Champion received no compensation.

When Robert Mahy returned to the Island he found that his B.S.A. motorcycle, that he had left in the care of Green's of Smith Street, had been requisitioned in April 1941, for use by the Police Force. It was returned to him after Bill Green had valued it at £14. The machine had been valued at the time of it being requisitioned at £43. The difference of £29 was paid to Mr Mahy by the States. He signed a full discharge stating that he had no further claim on the States of Guernsey in connection with the motorcycle.

Mrs Julia Barry, who had been deported to the Continent on the 5th May 1944 as a result of her conviction for Black Market activities by a German Court, returned to the Island on the 5th July 1945. She had been held in a number of prisons including Jersey, St Malo and Rennes, before finishing up in Ravensbruch concentration camp, north of Berlin.

In April 1945 Mrs Barry was one of twelve British subjects who were released by the Germans to the Red Cross authorities and transferred to Sweden. After spending five weeks in Sweden and putting on two stone in weight, she was flown to Glasgow, before finally returning to Guernsey.

After her deportation from the Island, her flat at 35 Mill Street had been taken over by the States Billeting officer. Some of her personal effects had been collected and passed to the States Supervisor for safe keeping. These included a dressing case and two bank pass books. On her return these items were returned to her.

Soon afterwards she wrote to the States Supervisor:-

"35 Mill Street,
30th August 1945

Sir,

My name is Mrs Julia Barry and I came back from the German concentration camp not long ago. Although the German Military authorities told the States Billeting officer that I will be shot, they passed my bank books, jewellery and latchkey, to you to look after them.

When I came home, I was happy to know, that I was not robbed by the Germans as thousands of others and I shall find my clothing to put on.

But I had a great shock when the Billeting officer told me at my arrival, that he has given away all my clothing. So I didn't gain anything by the Germans' generosity. I am ruined all the same. What right of disposal had the States representative to give away my things, I don't know. My husband who was here all the time and asked for my house and belongings, was refused saying, he will look after my home.

Instead of giving him my house, he gave it to a girl of 20, whose parents are living in town, but there she couldn't do the same, as she did in my home. She with her German friends finished what the Billeting officer left. This girl burned and sold most of my furniture, beddings, curtains etc. and made a good income from them.

My loss is £200 and I'm very poor. For the same reason, as I was in the concentration camp and condemned to death, the French women had high decorations. And what have I ? An empty house, without a chair to sit on, no tables - four she sold - and not a blanket or sheet to sleep there. I am still in the Red Lion, where the Billeting officer put me. It is very sad to know, that for all I have done, I didn't deserve to find my own house un-touched.

But I appeal Sir to your love of justice and leave the jurisdiction in your hand. I am sure I shall be not disappointed.

I remain Sir, Yours obediently, Mrs Barry.

Mrs Barry, who as Miss Julia Brichta had married Jeremiah Barry in April 1942 to obtain Irish citizenship and paid him £100 for the privilege, never lived with him as husband and wife. Jeremiah had continued to live at 3 Burnt Lane, St Peter Port, while his wife had resided in Mill Street. Not long after returning to Guernsey Mrs Barry went to live in London. Later when Jeremiah wanted a divorce so that he could marry and settle down, Mrs Barry made him pay all the costs, which far exceeded the hundred pounds she paid him for his name and nationality in 1942.

# Chapter 36

# SENSATIONAL POLICE ENQUIRY REPORT

Many of the men who had joined the Force as Auxiliary Policemen during the Occupation were now giving carefully consideration to their future. Some joined so that they had a job and had never envisaged themselves as peacetime Policemen. Others were content to stay with the Force until a better job came along. Only a few of the Auxiliaries had joined with a view of making a career in the Force.

It was not long before resignations were being submitted and men were leaving the Force. Some wished to return to their old jobs or trades at the earliest opportunity, others left the Force because they were attracted by the higher pay and better working conditions that could be obtained elsewhere.

Three men resigned from the Force in June and a further three in July. Whilst the Police Committee was content to reduce the size of the Force from its Occupation strength, fifty-three men, they were concerned that some of the men that were leaving had the potential of becoming first rate peace time officers.

On the 5th June the Controlling Committee ordered that all States employees, including Policemen, who were earning less than £3.10.0 should receive an increased of 10/- a week. This increase benefited the Auxiliary Constables but did nothing for the Sergeants and Corporals. At that time Sergeants' weekly pay started at £3.10.0, rising by four increments to £4.0.0. Corporals were paid a flat rate of £3.11.0. With the added bicycle allowance, some Constables were drawing considerably more per week than either Sergeants or Corporals.

The Police Committee on the 24th July, drew the attention of the Controlling Committee to the disparity in rates of pay and requested them to authorise an appropriate increase. The matter was passed to the Board of Administration for their consideration. No action resulted until the Sergeants requested that the Police Committee receive a deputation at their meeting on the 17th September. Sergeants C.Le Lievre and H.G.Dyson were nominated to represent their colleagues.

At the same time the Auxiliary Policemen also presented Inspector Sculpher with a 'round robin' signed by twenty-two Constables. It read:-

"We, members of the Auxiliary Police Force, humbly beg of you to give our exact position regarding:

1. Termination of our service, approximate date.
2. Whether, if having the necessary qualification, we would become members of the regular Police Force.
3. The qualifications necessary.
4. Conditions and rate of pay.

Sir this humble request becomes necessary owing to the fact that many are losing chances of better positions, through not knowing the above details."

The Police Committee considered the representations made by members of the Force, but put off any decision regarding pay levels until its October meeting.

They did, however, decide that Auxiliaries could become regular members of the Force, if Inspector Sculpher was satisfied with their performance. He was also given authority to weed out those he did not feel would qualify as regulars.

In the meantime there had been a steady stream of resignations. By the middle of October 1945, twenty-three Auxiliary officers had left the Force.

A/PC 10 William Kelly Sebire
A/PC 12 Henry William Mahy
A/PC 13 Josiah Le Poidevin
A/PC 14 Edwin Percy Peadon
A/PC 18 Frank H.C. Pill
A/PC 22 Reginald George Le Gallez
A/PC 28 William James Boalch
A/PC 31 Wilfred John Mansfield
A/PC 33 Roy Frederick Thoume
A/PC 34 Raymond Philip Gaudion
A/PC 35 Edwin James Le Page
A/PC 37 Leonard George Tucker
A/PC 38 Edwal A Robilliard
A/PC 41 Alfred John Bisson
A/PC 45 Ronald Walter Bourgaize
A/PC 46 Albert George Bichard
A/PC 47 George Edward Bougourd
A/PC 48 Harold Frederick Kendall
A/PC 49 Walter Belmore Wood Lovell
A/PC 50 Charles Nicholls
A/PC 51 Emile George Perrott
A/PC 54 Sidney John Torode,
A/PC 55 Clifford Henry Tickner

Another member of the Force to leave was Sergeant Bob Kimber, who was finally allowed to retire, at the age of 62, on the 12th August 1945, after twenty-three years' service in Police uniform. Twice he had been asked to stay on for a further year after reaching the official retirement age. Colleagues had a whip round and collected £6-7-0 with which they bought a retirement gift for 'Sergeant Bob'.

Retirement was to be short lived, as it was not long before Bob Kimber was appointed Prison Gaoler. His wife was later employed as the Prison Matron. They remained there for nine years, before Bob Kimber retired for the last time.

As a result of Bob Kimber's retirement, Corporal Francois Le Cocq was appointed Sergeant on the 4th September 1945. Corporal Reg Marsh was later that month promoted to the rank of Acting Sergeant. Reg went on to reach the rank of Inspector, while Le Cocq became Chief Inspector. They both retired after distinguished Police careers.

By the middle of October when no action had been taken to rectify the problem of low pay, Inspector Sculpher again wrote to the President of the Police Committee drawing his attention to the abnormal number of resignations. He wrote:-

"Police work is specialised and I fear is not fully appreciated. Those who have resigned have done so of their own volition to adopt more congenial work, but I am constrained to think that the chief cause can be found as stated in the application to resign by A/PC Langlois. This man states he can command £4.10.0 weekly for 48 hours, with regular hours and meals, no night work, every Saturday afternoon off and Sunday free. Despite these considerations I do not think he would leave if the promised increase in pay was forthcoming. He has told me that the most he can obtain in the Police Force is £3.10.0 weekly. I have told him that an increase is promised. He counters this by saying 'How much and when?"

I am convinced that more resignations are contemplated, and respectfully ask that this matter may be discussed and, if thought desirable, that representation be made to the Committee responsible that there is serious unrest in the Police Force and that the men should be told how much increase of pay is proposed and the date it can be expected."

The matter of pay was considered at the meeting of the Police Committee on the 22nd October and the Inspector was asked to prepare an amended budget based on new rates of pay for Sergeants and Constables. These were:-

Sergeants £5.15.0 rising by 8 increments of 2/6 to £6.15.0
Constables £4.0.0 rising by 12 increments of 2/6 to £5.10.0

These proposals raised the budgeted cost of Police salaries and wages from £9,390 to £10,018 for the financial year 1946. This included the cost of Inspector Sculpher's salary of £670 and Mr Lamy's of £500.

The Inspector also reported that he had transferred fourteen men to the Regular Force and that the remaining five were, in his opinion, unsuitable for transfer.

Those transferred to the regular Force were:-

PC 16 Harold Hall
PC 20 Emile Edgar Julou
PC 21 Roland W. Le Tissier
PC 23 Clifford C. Langlois
PC 24 Basil Le Page
PC 25 Oswald Harry Brackley
PC 30 Daniel George De Carteret
PC 32 John William Salmon
PC 36 Henry Thomas Solway
PC 40 Alexander Charles O'Donovan
PC 43 John Edward Aubert
PC 44 Arthur Russell Bailey
PC 52 Ronald Henry Pagnier
PC 53 Arthur George Stephen Reeve

Listed by Inspector Sculpher as unsuitable, mainly on the grounds of age, were:-

A/PC 11 Albert James Vanden Bergh
A/PC 17 Albert Hill Henry,
A/PC 26 Edwin Henry Butt
A/PC 29 Frank Henry Falla,
A/PC 39 Frederick John Moore

When deportee Roy Northey, formerly A/PC 35, returned from Germany with his wife and family on the 20th July, he did not apply to rejoin the Force. Whilst in Germany he had written to Mr Lamy enquiring what his position would be on his return to Guernsey. The Acting Inspector had replied that as he had only been engaged on a temporary basis, he could give him no guarantee as to his future employment. Roy later recalled:-

"I knew that when I was taken on as an Auxiliary it was only temporary and going on what the strength of the Force was before the war and what it was when I was deported, which was many more, I thought they would be getting rid of people rather than take on more. So I went back to my old job, working for Mr Poat.

Then one day, after I had been back a little while, I was in town and I saw Sergeant Dyson. He greeted me, saying:-

'When are you coming back to see us again. We have got a job for you up there'.

I said 'you have got more than enough.'

'You come and see the Inspector, you will be alright'.

So I went up and saw Mr Sculpher. He was quite happy for me to start back on the force.

Roy Northey applied to rejoin the Force on the 29th of October and was sworn in on the 10th November 1945 as Police Constable 18. He was promoted Sergeant in 1950 and retired from the Force on Liberation Day 1967.

**Constables Roy Northey and Arthur Bailey.**

Shortly after Roy Northey rejoined the Force consideration was given by the Board of Administration as to whether deportees in States employ should receive pay for the period of their internment. Roy Northey applied as he had been in the States employment at the time, although only on a temporary basis.

The Board of Administration had compiled a list of States Servants who had been deported and who might qualify for payment. Seventy-four employees were identified, 14 of whom were permanent, including Ambrose Sherwill, Inspector Sculpher and A.J.Langmead and 32 waged, including Sergeants F.Duquemin, J.Harper and A.Howlett, Constables T.Gaudion, H.Smith, W.Quin, F.Short, A.Tardif, K.Bailey, F.Whare, H.Piesing, E.Le Lievre, A.Le Gallez, W.Burton, F.Tuck and C.Friend. Classified as temporary employees were C.P.R.Northey, G.Scraton and E.Le Prevost.

After considerable consideration and consultations between various States Committees and exchanges of letter with Government offices in London, it was agreed that permanent and salaried staff, but not temporary employees should receive half pay for the time they were interned in Germany. However, the former Sergeants and Constables were excluded.

Roy Northey continued to press his claim. At one point the Police Committee agreed to pay him and asked the States Supervisor to 'arrange accordingly'. However, the Supervisor referred the matter back to the Board of Administration, who decided that:-

"the nature of the service of Mr Northey with the States, does not render him eligible for benefit in respect of deportee's pay."

Later however, he was granted seniority for his length of service which was dated from the time he originally joined the Force in 1942.

Probably the longest ever serving member of the Police Committee's staff was Mrs Elsie Kenny. Elsie was the Station cleaner, a position she had held since the late twenties. Every morning and evening she cleaned the Station and the Inspector's office above, often doing many little extras, such as sewing, washing and ironing for the Sergeants and Constables who had been left on their own when their families evacuated. Elsie worked right through the Occupation and the post war years, until retiring at the age of seventy in 1965. When she retired she was still cleaning the whole of the new Police Station in St James, on her own. Just before her hundredth birthday she recalled:-

"I loved my job, I was part of a big happy family and we used to have fun." She added:- "During the Occupation my wages never reached a pound a week."

A former Police Sergeant said of her:-

"She was a great character, very popular and well liked. She would do anything she could to help you, she did far more than you would expect a cleaner to do. She was a mothering sort of person to members of the force."

In December 1945 a list of Occupation Honours was announced. Amongst those honoured by King George VI, was Albert Peter Lamy who received the British Empire Medal for services during the enemy Occupation of the Island. The Bailiff, Victor Carey, and Jurat John Leale, President of the Controlling Committee, both received knighthoods, while Deputy Johns was awarded the O.B.E. Both L.A. Guillemette and J.H. Loveridge received the M.B.E. The Police Force was particularly proud of the honour conferred on Mr Lamy, as indeed were the general public.

On the 10th August, a few days after Inspector Sculpher returned to duty, Advocate J.E.L.Martel, still a member of the Controlling Committee although back in private practice, raised the matter of the Inspector's reinstatement. He referred to the fact that ex-Deputy Inspector Langmead had not been reinstated by the Police Committee, although Mr Sculpher had been. He suggested that an investigation should be held into the circumstances which resulted in both men being suspended by the German authorities during their occupation of the Island.

He recalled that in Mr Sculpher's case the Germans had ordered suspension, but in Mr Langmead's case he had been convicted by a German Court. Advocate Martel expressed the opinion that no cognisance should be taken of the German conviction and that in the public interest an enquiry should be held.

After debating the matter, the Committee agreed with Advocate Martel and it was decided that a letter be forwarded to the Police Committee suggesting that an investigation should take place.

As a consequence of that discussion, the Bailiff set up a Committee of Investigation. However, prior to the Committee's appointment, Inspector Sculpher was, in September 1945, invited to resign. On his refusal, the Bailiff appointed a three-man Committee on the 27th October, with a mandate:-

> "To enquire into the circumstances leading up to and surrounding the offences committed during 1941 and 1942 by certain members of the Island Police force, with a view to determining whether and if so, to what extent, the state of indiscipline and loss of sense of public duty revealed thereby can fairly and properly be attributed to the lack of supervision or other defect in the

control of the force. And to report accordingly with such recommendations and suggestions as the Committee of Investigations may think proper in the circumstances."

The existence of the Committee of Investigation was made public by an announcement in La Gazette Officielle on the 30th October. The members appointed were, Chairman, C.W.Bickmore of the Home Office and who had been Chief Financial adviser to the Liberation Force Commander. Commander S.B.Mainguy and Major F.Barritt Hills, manager of the States Electricity Department.

Many of the Police officers who had been convicted by the German Military Court and the Royal Court in 1942, welcomed the announcement of an Inquiry and made representation to the Chairman, Mr C.W.Bickmore, to be heard. Their pleas were ignored.

The Committee held eight meetings, at one of which Major Cotton, the head of the Public Security section of 20 Civil Affairs unit and a professional policeman, attended to describe to the Committee, the duties of the head of a Police Force. The Committee did not find it necessary to hear any witnesses because, as they later reported:-

"We have not found it necessary, in view of the quantity of documentary evidence which is available and the length of time which has elapsed since the date of these unfortunate occurrences to call any witnesses before us. We have examined the German file of statements and correspondence and transcript of proceedings before the Police Court and the Royal Court, the minutes of the Police Committee and the files of the daily press. We have paid two visits to the Police Station in order to ascertain the Station routine and inspect the accommodation."

The Committee went on to explain:-

"The use of material afforded by the German records, repellent though it may appear at first sight when we are dealing with the conduct of a British Force, is in this instance unavoidable: they are a first hand record of the investigation of the offences alleged and in the circumstance of a wholesale disorganisation of the Force and of the restrictions on the freedom of action of the constituted authorities by reason of the Occupation, almost the only coherent record available. But in any event, after making due allowance for the military origin and authoritarian tone of these records, the investigations appear to have been conducted by the occupying authorities in an objective spirit."

The Committee of Investigation reported to the Bailiff on the 23rd of November 1945, less than a month after it had been appointed.

The conclusions of the Bickmore Committee were:-

"1. The trials before the Military Court and the Royal Court in April and June 1942 exhibit a demoralized Police Force.
2. This demoralization proceeded from inadequate training, poor organisation and defective supervision and control.
3. The officer in charge, Inspector Sculpher, must be held responsible for these defects.
4. The action of the Police Committee in permitting Inspector Sculpher to resume duties without ordering an investigation to be held into his responsibility for the demoralization of the Force under his command, was imprudent."

The Committee recommended:-

"1. That the agreement of Inspector Sculpher be terminated forthwith for failure to command and maintain discipline in the Police Force and to train the members thereof in the execution of their duties.

2. That a successor be obtained from England, if possible on an agreement for a tour of duty not exceeding three years.

3. That after an initial period when his assistance would be required by the new head of the Force, Deputy Inspector Lamy should be attached for not less than six months and perhaps longer to a Force on the mainland, in order to enable him to secure professional training and experience."

The Report stated that the The Committee of Investigation had considered the possibility of finding a successor to Mr Sculpher from the ranks of the Force.

"We agree with the decision of the Police Committee, arrived at in consultation with the Attorney General, that it is impossible to consider the re-employment of Mr A.J.Langmead. In any event we do not think he would be suitable for the job of putting the Force on a proper footing. We recognise the justice of the tribute paid to acting Inspector Lamy's services by the Police Committee, but we do not think that he has the requisite professional qualifications or experience to ensure that the Island gets value, in present circumstances for the money spent on the Police Force."

After the Bailiff received the report of the Committee of Investigation, he forwarded a copy to the Inspector for his observations. On the 4th of December Mr Sculpher replied.

"I have the honour to report that I have read the Report of the Committee and regret that they should have considered it unnecessary to call witnesses, or at least to give me an opportunity of explaining points of procedure that differ from those obtaining in England. Instead it appears that the Committee have confined their attention to German documents, a report submitted by Mr Poat and a statement by Major Cotton.

I have always been anxious that an enquiry should be held and for that reason, while away from the Island, refrained from communication with anyone in authority in the Island, nor have I discussed the subject since returning, preferring that if an inquiry was held no word of mine should influence any person.

In 1930 I took charge of the Island Police and until the Occupation I do not think that any reasonable person could complain of the work, discipline and training of the Force. From the records it can be seen that there were occasional lapses of discipline by the men. These were dealt with firmly, but fairly.

Soon after the Occupation I realised that the Germans distrusted me. I decided that my action should be strictly correct. The language question and different methods of procedure obtaining in England and Germany caused some friction with under officers and the Feldgendarmerie.

On one occasion I refused to comply with a request by a member of the Geheim Feldpolizei. He should have met me to conduct an enquiry in the afternoon, but came to my home at 9.30pm when it was too dark to see and then under the influence of drink. My refusal was reported to Fuerst Von Oettingen and from that time I was a marked man.

Indeed, this same German told me that it had been his lot to arrest a Chief of Police in Belgium. I guessed what he meant and from that point was ultra careful not to offend.

I was continually submitting reports of offences obviously caused by Germans, but the German Police would not co-operate with me, nor did they report to me the result of their enquiries. On one occasion Fuerst von Oettingen complained to you, sir, of my conduct."

The Inspector went on to respond to the Report in detail and concluded:-

"I have always taken a keen interest in my work which has always come first and have never consciously neglected anything. I sincerely regret that the Police Force should have become so demoralized and fully realise that whatever happened to the Force, I was in command and must accept responsibility.

This serious lapse by the men under my charge has seriously shaken me and in the circumstances I feel that I cannot carry out the duties with the confidence demanded and to your satisfaction. Therefore I respectfully wish to tender my resignation."

Mr Sculpher's resignation was not accepted.

On receipt of Inspector Sculpher's reply, the Bailiff forwarded a copy to Mr C.W.Bickmore for his observations. When a reply was received that had been agreed by the other two members of the Committee of Investigation, the Bailiff wrote to the President of the Board of Administration asking him to consult the President of the Police Committee with a view to taking 'appropriate action'.

When the two Presidents discussed the 'Bickmore Report' and its recommendations, they agreed that the matter was one which called for a decision by the full Board of Administration after hearing the views of the Police Committee.

The Police Committee met on the 27th December and again on 11th January 1946 to consider their response. Then on the 15th they met jointly with the Board of Administration. On the 17th January the Police Committee unanimously adopted recommendations 1, 2 and 3 of Committee of Investigation. The Board of Administration met on the 22nd January and also unanimously adopted the recommendations.

The same day, the President of the Board of Administration, Deputy R.H.Johns, wrote to Inspector W.R.Sculpher:-

"Dear Sir, 22nd January 1946.

I have to inform you that the Board of Administration have considered documents sent to them by the Bailiff, including:

1. Report of the Committee of Investigation which the Bailiff set up to investigate the Police irregularities during 1941-42.

2. Your observations on the Report.

3. A second letter from Mr C.W.Bickmore, with the contents of which the other members of the Committee of Investigation are in agreement, giving his comments on your observations on the Report and after consultation with the Police Committee, have adopted the following recommendation of the Committee of Investigation appointed by the Bailiff, namely:-

'That the agreement of Inspector Sculpher be terminated forthwith for failure to command and maintain discipline in the Police Force and to train the members thereof in the execution of their duties.'

I must ask you, therefore, to regard this letter as terminating your agreement with the Board of Administration as from this date.

Regarding payment of salary during your period of internment in Germany and up to the date on which you resumed duty, the Board's decision is that you shall receive two thirds of what you would have received had you been deported while functioning as Police Inspector.

I am authorised to enclose herewith an extract from a letter from H.M.Attorney General commenting on the findings of the Committee of Investigation, which bears testimony to the quality of your work in one branch of your duties as Police Inspector.

Yours faithfully,
R.H.Johns,
President,
Board of Administration."

The extract from the letter of the Attorney General, A.J.Sherwill, dated the 26th November 1945 referred to by Deputy Johns:-

"I cannot in justice refrain from making it clear that as regards that aspect of the Inspector's activities with which I have been intimately acquainted since his appointment - namely, the collection and presentation of evidence in and the conduct of, criminal and quasi-criminal matters - it is my considered opinion that his great experience and knowledge of criminal law and his integrity, ability, restraint and deep seated sense of fairness to accused persons, have been of enormous assistance to my predecessor and myself."

In the Occurrence Book for the 22nd January 1946 Mr Sculpher wrote:-

"I visited at 10.55pm". This was signed, "W.R.Sculpher, Inspector".

At 11.15pm on the 22nd January PC 44 Arthur Bailey was on patrol in Fountain Street, when he found the door leading to the Market Halles, opposite Barclay's Bank, open. The Constable entered the market and found that nothing appeared to have been disturbed and neither was there any sign of damage. He inspected the lock and came to the conclusion that it had been turned without the doors being properly closed. On return to the Station he informed Sergeant Pugh, who recorded the incident in the Occurrence Book.

The next morning Inspector Sculpher, as was his practice, inspected the Occurrence Book and at the end of the report by Constable Bailey, counter signed with the initials, 'W.S' in red pencil. Those were the last two entries that Mr Sculpher was to make in the Occurrence Book.

Later that day an entry was made by Mr Lamy:-

"I beg to report that Mr W.R.Sculpher terminated his employment as Police Inspector as from 12 midnight on the 23rd January 1946. Mr A.C.Bichard, President of the Police Committee, called and informed me that I was to carry on in his stead for the time being. A.Lamy, Acting Inspector."

Albert Peter Lamy again took command of the Force and other than for the period when he was seconded to the Southampton Borough Force, from September 1947 to September 1948, remained Chief officer until he retired on the 30th April 1965.

In 1942 Bert Lamy had taken control of the Force at a time of crisis and restored confidence not only of the men but also with the general public. He had an outstanding memory for faces and facts and a sense of sequence in narrating events. He had the ability to set the scene of a charge when he was outlining it in Court. A former Police officer and colleague summed Bert Lamy up as "A friend and good companion to all the Police force".

The dismissal of Inspector Sculpher was published in the *Evening Press* on the 1st February, under the front page headline of 'Sensational Police Enquiry Report'.

William Sculpher, now ex Inspector, packed his bags and belongings and with his wife, Sarah, made a dignified departure from the Island and went to live with his brother at West Acre, King's Lynn. He, in his view and in the view of many Islanders, had been sacked by the Guernsey Establishment, just as he had been removed by the German Military authorities from his post in 1942, without ever being formally charged with any offence and not having had the right to defend himself or of being legally represented. He left Guernsey a stunned and broken man.

Immediately there was a wave of sympathy for the ex Inspector, at the way he had been treated. Many Islanders wrote to him offering support in any action he took to clear his name.

Support not only came from Islanders, but also from former colleagues. Mr Sherwill had expressed his respect for Mr Sculpher and on the 4th February, in Court, the Magistrate, Mr H.J.Casey, said:-

"Before we begin the business of the day I want to say one or two words. Since the last sitting of this Court, there has appeared in the local press, the report of the Committee that sat to investigate the administration of the Police in this Island. On that report I refrain from making any comment, but I do want to say a word about Inspector Sculpher, who from that report it is clear, is going to leave us.

Inspector Sculpher prosecuted in this Court. He was particularly fitted to do so because he had a vast experience of crime and he had a good knowledge of criminal law and particularly of the law of evidence. What fitted him more than all to act as prosecutor in this Court was his scrupulous sense of justice and his consistent fairness to the unfortunate man who was in the dock. He never pressed for a conviction and never sought in any way to introduce into a case any presumptive or any inadmissible evidence but always pressed his case fairly and did his best to maintain the highest standards of British Justice.

I only hope that his successor will possess these qualities and these qualifications to which I have referred."

On the 6th March 1946, a tribute to Mr Sculpher appeared in the *Evening Press* from Lord de Saumarez:-

"He seemed to represent the very backbone of England - that was what fellow captives said about him when he was a deportee. Praise indeed which it gives me much pleasure to record and one can but wish that such high integrity, courage and devotion to human principles in the face of the enemy shall not go unrewarded."

The support Mr Sculpher received from the general public in Guernsey encouraged him to petition his Majesty's Secretary of State for Home Affairs requesting that a fresh inquiry be held. Many letters of support for Mr Sculpher's petition were sent to the Home Office by Islanders.

After due consideration the Home Office advised the Board of Administration, through official channels, that:-

"The manner in which the inquiry was conducted by the Committee of Investigation, left much to be desired in that, in particular, a great reliance was placed upon German documents to which Committee had access and the possibility of prejudice in such documents against the Inspector had not been checked by recourse to such witnesses as were available and being the Inspector was never given the opportunity, at any time before the Committee reached its conclusions, to testify on his own behalf, or to examine or make representations personally or through Council with regards the evidence on which the Committee relied, but never the less at this stage it is inexpedient that a fresh inquiry should be held or set on foot."

At its meeting on the 19th December 1946, the Board of Administration resolved:-

"The Board hereby resolves after mature consideration to withdraw the notice of dismissal on 22nd January 1946. The Board further resolves subject to the agreement of Inspector Sculpher, that his services shall be regarded as having been terminated by notice properly given by him, expiring on the 30th September 1946, which will then render him eligible for a pension."

William Sculpher, through his legal advisers, accepted the Board of Administration's proposal as regards his resignation and pension, but asked that suitable publicity be given to the to the agreement. Deputy Johns made a full statement in the States of Deliberation, which was greeted with applause. One member, Douzaine Delegate Ira C.Ozanne, said he was glad to hear something about 'that blot' and added :-

"I think that the whole question has been a scandal and that Mr Sculpher had not even been allowed to defend himself".

The withdrawal of the dismissal notice and acceptance of Inspector Sculpher's resignation meant that the need to hold a further inquiry was avoided.

Mr Sculpher received a cheque for his back pay and his pension.

He sent a message to his many friends in Guernsey who supported his petition to the Home Secretary:-

"Your faith in me has been a tremendous help, a real inspiration, I can never thank you enough."

So ended a distinguished and eventful Police career, which had started on the 11th July 1904 in the Metropolitan Police. It had brought him to the Island in 1930 to serve the Guernsey Establishment, the Establishment that was, in his view and the view of many Islanders, the cause of his demise.

# Chapter 37

# POSTSCRIPT

In September 1950 Ex Constable Frank Tuck, who was living in Liverpool, approached Silverman and Livermore, a firm of Solicitors in the City, to represent him and other ex Guernsey Police officers in an attempt to have their convictions set aside and their names cleared.

Previously, on the 26th July, Frank had written to the Home Secretary on his and ex-Constable Kingston Bailey's behalf, seeking advice on how to proceed with an application for compensation for loss of office. Officials at the Home Office carefully analysed his letter and identified the main arguments in support of his claim:-

1. The thefts of food from German stores were the outcome of their patriotic resolve to hinder the occupying authorities.
2. The offences against the civilian stores were committed in error.
3. The entire Police Force was involved but that some escaped because of their colleagues' silence.
4. That their plea at the German Military trial, that they were motivated by hunger, was the alternative to being found guilty of sabotage, the penalty for which was death.
5. That they were unable to make a proper defence at their trial before the Royal Court because of the threat contained in a letter from the German Commandant.
6. The proceedings of the Committee of Inquiry of 1945 were unsatisfactory in as much as the Committee did not hear witnesses and based their findings on the evidence contained in German documents.

Mr Marks, a Home Office official, took the view that there appeared to be some substance in points 4 and 5, as it would, in the circumstances have been impossible for all the evidence for the defence to be produced and at the same time avoid the intervention of the German Authorities. As regards point 6, he wrote, "The Home Office have already expressed the view that the manner in which the Inquiry was conducted is open to considerable objection."

Despite having carefully considered Frank Tuck's letter and having expressed 'a certain amount of sympathy' the reply sent, was that the Secretary of State was unable to advise him.

In view of what Frank felt was an unhelpful reply, he instructed solicitors Silverman and Livermore to write to the Home Office asking them to reconsider their attitude. The Solicitors drew attention to the fact that the Home Office intervened on behalf of Ex Inspector Sculpher and asked for similar assistance to be afforded to Mr Tuck.

Mr Marks's response was:-

"In view of Mr Tuck's conviction by the Royal Court - quite apart from the findings of the Committee of Enquiry - it would have been improper for the

Insular Authorities to re-employ him as a Police officer. This being so and since there can be no question of interfering with the findings of the Civil Court as the only appeal against such findings is to the Privy Council, there would not appear to be any action the Home Office should take."

In November of that year Frank Tuck returned to Guernsey and announced to the Press that he and his fellow ex-policemen were planning to petition the Home Secretary to obtain a review of the judgement and sentences passed by the German Military Court and the Royal Court in 1942.

Frank told the Press:- "We all hoped that the Committee set up by the Bailiff after the end of the Occupation would give us the opportunity to have our cases reopened. We were disappointed that we were not allowed to give evidence or to be legally represented. Now", Frank said "we want the British Government to review the case so we can all be completely vindicated."

All the former policemen, with the exception of H.P.Smith who died in Augsberg Prison and Peter Bretel, who died of a heart attack, pooled their life savings and engaged the distinguished British lawyer, E.C.Goldrein, of the firm Silverman and Livermore.

Eric Goldrein came to the Island and took dozens of statements, running to more than 50,000 words, from the men concerned and from many other independent witnesses. Before returning to Liverpool, he commented:

"I am satisfied that the German and civilian trials, which led to the conviction of these men, were a mockery of justice and I am placing the whole of the facts before the Home Secretary.

I am satisfied beyond any reasonable doubt that the taking of food in these circumstances by Police officers, who up till then had borne exemplary characters and have since, was regarded by them as an act of sabotage against the occupying power. The most important factor in the matter is that they were unable to plead sabotage in their own defence at the German trial because sabotage was punishable by death and it was wholly for that reason that they made such a poor showing in cross examination in the German court.

The most terrible feature of the case is the way in which evidence against them was obtained by the Germans in the first instance. The brutality by the Germans against them was not disclosed at the trial, but it was quite clear that threats of every kind were used against them. There was duress and physical assault of all kinds, that included threats of instant death and a very violent assault which in fact incapacitated some of the men completely. It included such assaults as brutal kicking in the course of which one of them was permanently injured. It was indisputable that the statements were written in German and that the accused men had no means or opportunity of checking them. They were presented with statements made by their fellow Police officers in order to extort statements from them.

The whole circumstances in which the so called evidence was obtained would be completely unacceptable to normal British justice. When the trial was held, a Swastika flag was hung in the background and even at the civilian trial there were many Germans present and the same limitations were therefore placed on any defence they might otherwise have had."

On the 14th November 1951, eight ex-police officers, ex-Sergeants Alf Howlett, Jack Harper, ex-Constables Kingston Bailey, Frank Tuck, Charlie Friend, Bill Quin, Fred Short and Frank Whare who appeared in the civilian case, were granted special leave by the Privy Council to appeal against their conviction before the Royal Court on 1st June 1942. The other seven men, who only appeared in the Military Trial, could not be included in the appeal as the Privy Council had no jurisdiction in regard to the German Military Court.

Due to financial and legal difficulties, it was not until October 1955 that their appeal was heard before the Judicial Committee of the Privy Council.

During the intervening period the Home Office became concerned about the position that would arise if the appeal succeeded. Sir Leslie Brass, of the Home Office, recorded:-

"As the dismissals were on account of the convictions by the German Court and before the trials by the Royal Court, the success of the Appeal should in logic not affect the dismissals; but it will doubtless be contended that the convictions by the German Court are equally unsatisfactory. Further Frank Gahan Q.C. seems inclined to think that convictions by a German Court could not be recognised in any way, but this seems to me to be a bit unreal in relation to a time when the Island was in German Occupation. It would however seem to follow, on Gahan's view that the convictions by the German Court afforded no ground for the dismissals and as I suppose that the men were dismissed by the appropriate Committee unheard, it will doubtless be contended that a grave injustice has been perpetrated."

Another aspect which caused Sir Leslie some concern was whether during the German Occupation the Royal Court ceased to be His Majesty's Court. The view that the Home Office appeared to favour was that the Courts did not necessarily cease to be the King's Courts merely because of the temporary occupation by the enemy. In fact the Germans had allowed the Courts to function freely and to administer laws which had been made by His Majesty in Council. It was believed that, as the civil government had been maintained, then the Island could not be considered conquered, only occupied.

The Privy Council appeal was heard before Viscount Symons, Lord Oaksey and Lord Morton. Mr Geoffrey Bing QC and Mr Mark Smith represented the former Police officers and Mr Frank Gahan QC, Mr William Arnold, Her Majesties Attorney General for Guernsey and Mr Geoffrey Le Quesne appeared for the Crown.

Mr Bing, addressing their Lordships, said:-

"Some of the appellants had long periods of service in the Guernsey Police, two of them, Howlett and Harper, were Sergeants. In the first place they were arrested by the German authorities, questioned and then tried by them for offences against German property. Afterwards, at the request of the Germans and on the basis of the information collected by the Germans, they were tried in the Royal Court and sentenced to various terms of imprisonment.

In some ways this case is unique in that the appellants were never in fact called upon to serve a day of their sentence imposed by the Royal Court, but the convictions stood recorded and the appellants case is that they were engaged in patriotic and proper activities and that it is wrong that they should be penalised by having a conviction recorded against them which was a result of their merely doing their duty by their Country in the very difficult circumstances of the German Occupation."

Mr Bing continued:- "The former Police officers claimed that their trial before the Royal Court was held under pressure of the German authorities, they said that in the circumstances no fair trial took place and they could not put forward any real defence. This was that the acts complained of form part of a series of acts in support of the British Crown and in resistance to the German occupiers of Guernsey.

These men were of good conduct with nothing recorded against them. When they were arrested by the Germans in 1942 they were kept in custody and interrogated. Records of the German trial have largely disappeared but from the few records available it seems that the form of interrogation was to obtain a statement from one person and then go to another, confront him with it and on that basis obtain a confession from him. The German trial was reported in the newspapers, but for some reason or other the Germans afterwards became extremely reticent about the proceedings. Portions of the original text of confessions which the men were alleged to have made were sent to the Island authorities who subsequently took statements with the object of confirming what the men were alleged to have said to the Germans."

Mr Bing added:- "The actual non-German premises alleged to have been entered were five in number, the first of them being the Essential Commodities store at Trinity Square, St. Peter Port. Four entries were alleged to be made in November 1941, five of the appellants being concerned.

In May 1942 Doctor Biel, the German Judge Advocate, wrote to the Acting Attorney General saying: 'In the event of the accused denying the admissions made by them to the Feldgendarmerie, please advise me immediately as in this case the Chief of Tribunal will take up the proceedings even as regards the thefts committed even at the expense of the English traders'.

Some of the appellants were shown a copy of Doctor Biel's letter by the Island Police and changed their pleas from not guilty to guilty to avoid the risk of being tried again by the German military court. There was no doubt that the men had been taking great quantities of German property, their defence was that the non-German property was taken by mistake and that they would never have taken anything from the civilian population. In my submission," continued Mr Bing, "the Germans were very anxious to prove that the Police were taking things not from the Germans, but indiscriminately, therefore they had to put pressure on the Court and this letter was the method by which they put it on."

Viscount Symons inquired of Mr Bing:- "Are you asking us to say that a Court has a duty to do nothing to prejudice the activities of patriots engaged in the struggle against an enemy and where it has accepted a plea of guilty, then in the interests of the prisoner, at a later date its judgement is to be revised." His Lordship suggested that there was nothing like that in the history of law.

Mr Bing replied:- "The whole concept of resistance was a new one, previously, it was a direct distinction between competence and non-competence, but now they were dealing with an acknowledged legal position in which the ordinary individual was entitled to take part and should be protected in taking part, in resistance against an enemy."

Mr Frank Gahan QC, for the Crown, said, "A number of suggestions had been put forward regarding the background of the case which the Crown did not accept. There was, in his submission, no suggestion from beginning to end that the Germans were exercising any pressure on the Royal Court. What happened was that statements were made to the Germans showing that certain civilian stores had been entered. So far as the Crown was aware these statements were transmitted to the proper official of the Island of Guernsey and he said he would investigate the matter."

Mr Gahan continued "In our submission there is nothing to show on the record other than that the Court was dealing with the allegations in the ordinary Court of Justice in the way that the Court would have dealt with any other such allegations. The Crown did not accept a suggestion that the men were engaged in any systematic sabotage. The Crown's submission was that this was petty thieving and not part of any deeply laid plan for embarrassing the enemy. The quantities concerned were all trifling and the Crown did not accept the suggestion that they were intended for the benefit of the people of the Island who were short of food.

One of the charges concerned the alleged theft of eighty-six bottles of port, but taking them could not possibly be an impediment to the Germans because they were sold to a local hotel who wanted them for sale over the counter."

Mr Gahan commented:- "It was unfortunate that each of the men refused an offer of having counsel to represent him."

After three days hearing the case, their Lordships retired and considered the case privately for about fifteen minutes. Viscount Symons then announced that the mens' appeal would be dismissed except in one case. The appeal of Quin, Short and Friend against their conviction of breaking and entering the stores belonging to Bucktrouts Ltd and stealing spirits and wine was allowed. Having regard to the fact that they were convicted in other cases their sentences would not be reduced. There was no order as to costs.

Later Lord Oaksey delivered the reasons for the decision of the Judicial Committee of the Privy Council. He said:-

"The main grounds of appeal are, first that by reason of the German Occupation the appellants were unable to put forward to their trials their real defence, namely that the offences alleged to have been committed by them were really acts of sabotage; that the true nature of these acts was sufficiently indicated to the Court and that the Court should therefore have entered pleas of 'not guilty', notwithstanding that the first seven appellants pleaded guilty; and secondly that the appellants' admissions or confessions were induced by the production of a letter from the German authorities which stated that if they denied the admissions made by them to the German authorities, the German chief of Tribunal would take up proceedings against them in respect of the thefts committed at the expense of the 'English traders'.

Their Lordships are of opinion, that the first ground of appeal is not one of which in view of the course taken at the trial an appellate Court can take cognisance. The remedy, if any, of the appellants is to pray that in this behalf the prerogative of mercy may be exercised in their favour. In regard to it, their Lordships must not be understood to assent to the proposition that if such a plea had been advanced and proved before the Royal Court that Court ought to have entertained it. This is a matter upon which they express no opinion.

As to the second contention of the appellants their Lordships are however of the opinion that in the case of those appellants who contended that their confessions had been induced by the production of the letter from the German authorities and who did not subsequently admit before the Royal Court that they had committed the thefts, the convictions must be quashed.

It was, in their Lordships' opinion, the duty of the prosecution to produce to the Court the letter on which the appellants relied and if that had been done, it would have been the duty of the Court to consider whether the appellants' plea should be withdrawn and the evidence of those who denied the truth of their confession should be accepted.

In the case of the appellant Howlett, who relied upon this letter, their Lordships are of the opinion that there had been no miscarriage of justice since it was clear from Howlett's statement on 18th May 1942, which was proved before the Royal Court, that he had in fact broken and entered and stolen from the Essential Commodities Store and his only defence was that he thought it was a German store.

But in the case against the appellants Friend, Short and Quin, relating to Bucktrout's store, Short and Quin both denied in evidence before the Royal Court that they had ever entered the store and said that they had only confessed to doing so because they were shown the letter from the German authorities and

Friend said he only admitted the charge 'to make his statement check with other statements made'.

In the case against Burton and the appellants Friend and Whare, the appellant Whare also relied upon the letter of the German authorities but when called as a witness against Burton admitted on oath that he had committed the thefts in question and in the case against Harper he, though he pleaded not guilty to a charge of receiving the goods stolen by Burton, Whare and Friend, had already admitted in evidence that he received the goods in question and knew they came from Le Lievre's store.

Their Lordships are therefore of the opinion that only in the case of the appellants Friend, Short and Quin and only in the case of one of the charges against these appellants is there any ground for saying that there may have been a miscarriage of justice. Their Lordships humbly advised Her Majesty that the convictions of those appellants in the case against them in respect of breaking and entering and stealing from Bucktrout's store should be quashed. But these appellants were properly convicted on other charges and their Lordships see no reason for advising Her Majesty that their sentences should have been less severe than they were. They have already humbly advised Her Majesty that the other appeals should be dismissed."

The ex-Police Officers went on to petition the Queen for a pardon, in a further attempt to clear their names, but without success.

Many people held the view that the British Judicial system was just not equipped to deal with the situation which arose in Guernsey during the German Occupation. As a result, seventeen members of the Island Police Force were in their view and that of many other people, denied natural justice. They all paid a heavy price, Bert Smith with his life and the others with their health, reputations and livelihoods.

# Appendix 1.

Police action taken under various Laws and Ordinances during 1929.

Charges and Summons cases included:-

57 cases of drunkenness and black list offences.
6 cases of drunk in charge of vehicles.
9 cases of housebreaking and burglary.
45 cases of larceny.
20 cases of assault.
7 cases of disorderly conduct.
3 cases of false pretences.
3 cases of homeless and destitute.
2 cases of carrying a gun without licence.
17 cases of wilful damage.
4 cases of riding bicycles without lights.
5 cases of riding bicycles unlicenced.
3 cases of riding bicycles with no reflector.
4 cases of riding bicycles in a prohibited area.
2 cases of riding bicycles holding on to vehicles.
9 cases of riding motor vehicles with no silencers.
3 cases of using unlicenced motor vehicles.
21 cases of using motor vehicles with no lights.
2 cases of causing obstruction.
4 cases of driving to the common danger.
6 cases of exceeding the speed limit.
1 case of bigamy.
3 cases under the Children's Act.

In addition there were 90 road accidents which the Police attended. 18 persons were reported missing, 22 put in hospital and 4 rescued from drowning. 6 soldiers were arrested for the military authorities and 6 sailors who missed their ship were 'seen off'. 43 inquests were held and 374 aliens registered on entering the Island. The public reported 714 article as being lost of which 265 were found and returned to their owners. 334 articles were handed in to the Police station of which 120 were eventually returned to the finder as they had been unclaimed. 12 evictions or as they were then called, ejectments, were effected by Order of the Court. 158 public vehicles were examined.

# Appendix 2.

**Estimated Police Budget for 1931.**

| | | | |
|---|---|---|---|
| **PAY.** | | | |
| Inspector | | 353- 0- 0 | |
| Sergeants | 7 @ 75/- | 1,365- 0- 0 | |
| Constables | 1 @ 57/6 | 149-10- 0 | |
| | 25 @ 55/- | 3,575- 0- 0 | |
| | | | £5,442-10- 0 |
| **UNIFORM.** | | | |
| Trousers fine | 33 @ 21/6 | 35- 9- 6 | |
| Trousers coarse | 33 @ 20/6 | 33-16- 6 | |
| Serges | 18 @ 26/6 | 23-17- 0 | |
| Tunics | 20 @ 38/6 | 38-10- 0 | |
| Capes | 10 @ 34/6 | 17- 5- 0 | |
| Chevrons | 10 @ 3/6 | 1-15- 0 | |
| Helmets | 33 @ 9/6 | 15-13- 6 | |
| Great coats | 5 @ 52/6 | 13- 2- 6 | |
| Gloves | 33 @ 3/- | 4-19- 0 | |
| Overalls | 20 @ 10/6 | 20-10- 0 | |
| Boots | 33 @ 24/- | 40-15- 0 | |
| Boots allowance 1/- weekly | | 84-16- 0 | |
| | | | £330- 9- 0 |
| **CYCLES.** | | | |
| Allowance for pedal and motor cycles | | | £100- 0- 0 |
| **OFFICE.** | | | |
| Post and telephone | | 46- 0- 0 | |
| Printing and stationery | | 30- 0- 0 | |
| Rent and cleaning | | 68- 0- 0 | |
| Fuel and light | | 40- 0- 0 | |
| Medical attendance | | 60- 0- 0 | |
| Prison charges | | 90- 0- 0 | |
| Conveyance of prisoners | | 35- 0- 0 | |
| Photographs | | 30- 0- 0 | |
| Accident insurance | | 25- 0- 0 | |
| Office furniture | | 20- 0- 0 | |
| Sundries and petty cash | | 98- 1- 0 | |
| | | | £542- 1- 0 |
| **TRAFFIC CONTROL** | | | |
| Signs, supply and upkeep | | 70- 0- 0 | |
| White lines, paint and upkeep | | 150- 0- 0 | |
| Police car insurance and tax | | 16- 0- 0 | |
| Police car petrol and tyres | | 36- 0- 0 | |
| Police car repairs | | 15- 0- 0 | |
| | | | £287- 0- 0 |
| **TOTAL** | | | £6,702- 0- 0 |
| Less income | | | 700- 0- 0 |
| **NET EXPENDITURE.** | | | £6,002- 0- 0 |

Police Accounts.

| | 1938 | 1939 | 1940 | 1941 | 1942 |
|---|---|---|---|---|---|
| Salaries and wages. | 6187 2 5 | 6458 7 5 | 5533 19 9 | 4770 15 7½ | 6620 17 3 |
| Uniforms | 396 1 11 | 372 3 4 | 222 9 1 | 101 9 5 | 505 16 9 |
| Postage & telephone | 53 6 5 | 60 1 0 | 58 9 7 | 34 16 8 | 62 9 8 |
| Printing and stationery | 61 13 8 | 87 19 3 | 43 16 3 | 20 7 6 | 42 18 3 |
| Sundries and petty expenses | 43 11 9 | 56 17 1 | 84 3 7 | 16 17 10 | 79 14 4½ |
| Cleaning | 36 12 8 | 37 19 11 | 40 7 6 | 44 9 10 | 41 17 1 |
| Fuel light and heat | 48 17 9 | 64 0 8 | 58 11 8 | 33 10 10 | 40 18 0 |
| Rent | 42 0 0 | 42 0 0 | 42 0 0 | 54 0 0 | 42 0 0 |
| Medical attendance | 72 2 0 | 96 5 11 | 57 8 3 | 39 9 10 | 62 8 0 |
| Prison charge | 53 3 4 | 54 6 6 | 46 9 0 | 48 18 0 | 40 17 0 |
| States insurance | 59 17 2 | 37 17 8 | 55 9 7 | 77 12 378 | 13 9 ½ |
| Photographs and black list | 16 9 0 | 11 19 0 | 2 19 0 | | |
| Public vehicles | 2 9 11 | 1 5 9 | 14 6 | | |
| War bonus | | | 36 18 10 | | |
| Traffic control | 931 5 7 | 763 1 10 | 667 8 7 | 197 4 2½ | 379 13 5 |
| | 8004 13 7 | 8144 5 4 | 6951 5 2 | 5439 12 0 | 7998 3 7 |
| Special Constabulary | | 233 6 8 | 761 16 9 | 1390 0 2 | 309 17 6 |
| Gross cost | | 8377 12 0 | 7713 1 11 | 6829 12 2 | 8038 1 1 |
| **INCOME.** | | | | | |
| Forced sale of police car | | | | | 155 0 0 |
| Prison charges | 5 13 6 | 5 18 6 | 1 10 0 | | |
| St P.P. harbour service | 600 0 0 | 600 0 0 | 300 0 0 | | |
| States insurance received | 30 7 4 | 8 5 10 | 23 17 10 | 40 9 7 | 39 17 6 |
| Driving tests | 105 12 3 | 105 2 6 | 45 0 5 | 9 5 10 | 9 13 4 |
| Public vehicles licences and permits | 145 8 0 | 220 10 6 | 135 8 0 | | |
| Other recoverables | 18 11 0 | 30 12 5 | 14 5 6½ | 7 5 1 | 63 7 3 |
| Police services to E.C.C. | | 12 5 0 | 81 18 4 | | |
| Police services to public assistance authority | 6 0 0 | | | | |
| Total income | 911 12 1 | 982 4 9 | 602 0 1½ | 57 0 6 | 267 18 1 |
| Net cost | | | | | |
| Magistrate's salary | 400 0 0 | 400 0 0 | 242 14 8 | 164 0 0 | 155 0 0 |

| POLICE ACCOUNTS. | 1943 | 1944 | 1945 | 1946 |
|---|---|---|---|---|
| Salaries and wages | 6901 6 10½ | 7450 9 10½ | 11780 9 10 | 10634 11 0 |
| Uniforms | 360 17 11 | 610 9 4 | 264 17 6 | 1025 6 7 |
| Postage & telephone | 78 2 0 | 79 6 5 | 89 4 5 | 123 5 3½ |
| Printing and stationery | 38 14 5 | 23 6 4 | 81 1 5 | 355 8 1 |
| Sundries and petty expenses | 109 3 8½ | 154 19 4 | 53 4 3½ | 258 17 11½ |
| Cleaning | 48 6 0 | 49 14 8 | 56 17 1 | 93 15 6½ |
| Fuel light and heat | 67 1 9 | 59 15 9 | 65 11 0 | 79 2 5 |
| Rent | 42 0 0 | 44 12 6 | 78 5 0 | 44 12 0 |
| Medical attendance | 72 6 9 | 71 2 3 | 68 4 6 | 50 5 6 |
| Prison charge | 40 4 0 | 41 4 0 | 35 15 6 | 52 3 0 |
| States insurance | 73 16 1½ | 69 0 11 | 73 10 10 | 31 17 10 |
| Photographs and black list | | | | 60 8 0 |
| Public vehicles | | | 1 5 0 | 26 5 0 |
| War bonus | | | | |
| Traffic control | 585 18 1 | 627 6 7 | 688 15 9 | 954 8 11 |
| Legal expenses | | | | 159 1 6 |
| Advertising | | | | 98 15 6 |
| | 8417 17 7½ | 9281 7 11½ | 13265 2 1½ | 14048 4 1½ |
| Special Constabulary | | | | |

**INCOME**

| | 1943 | 1944 | 1945 | 1946 |
|---|---|---|---|---|
| Prison fee | | | | 1 8 6 |
| St P.P. harbour service | | | | |
| States insurance received | 35 14 4 | 31 9 5 | 33 17 1 | 3 12 6 |
| Driving tests | 12 5 0 | 4 17 6 | 216 6 7 | 278 10 0 |
| Public vehicles licences and permits | | | 105 1 0 | 161 6 6 |
| Salaries recovered | | | | 259 18 4 |
| Other recoverables | 16 8 8 | 24 17 9 | 24 16 9 | 47 6 3 |
| Insurance reports | | | | 5 5 0 |
| Police services to E.C.C. | | | | |
| Sale of cycle | | 8 0 0 | | |
| Refund of insurance | | | 10 7 4 | |
| Total income | 64 8 0 | 69 4 8 | 390 8 9 | 757 7 1 |
| Magistrate's salary | 159 0 0 | 164 0 0 | 330 7 8 | 545 0 0 |

# Appendix 3.

New recruit Examination 29th April 1933.

Arithmetic.

1. Bring £71-11-3 to threepences.
2. The sum of the two numbers is 1,150 and their difference is 250. What are the numbers.
3. How many times must 72 be added to 835 to give 1,411.
4. The total score of three cricketers is 110. If A and B together make 70 runs and B and C together make 65 runs, how many runs do each make.

5. A man's yearly income is £543-10s and his daily expenditure is £1-1-6d. How much does he save in a leap year.
6. A postman's weekly wage is £1-15s. He is fined 1/6 every time he is late. He receives £21-18-6 at the end of 13 weeks. How many times was he late.
7. How long will nine tons of coal last for ten fires if each consumes 18 lb per day.
8. If 'A' can do in four hours the same piece of work which 'B' could do in five hours and 'C' in 12 hours. How long will it take if they all work together.

Essay.

Write a short essay on either of the following subjects :-
1. Describe your experience at a race meeting.
2. What is your opinion of 'cruelty to animals'.
3. You are called to a scene of a collision between two motor vehicles and a person has been seriously injured. Make a report stating what action you took.

Dictation - A selected piece.
Reading - From a book that was passed around.

The result was:-

| | Dictation | Arithmetic | Composition | Reading | Total |
|---|---|---|---|---|---|
| Gale | 27 | 21 | 15 | Good | 63 |
| Piesing | 21 | 21 | 15 | Good | 57 |
| Laffin | 24 | 20 | 10 | Impediment | 54 |
| Bougourd | 27 | 16 | 10 | Good | 53 |
| Robinson | 0 | 11 | 10 | Good | 1 |
| Possible marks | 30 | 21 | 30 | 81 | |

Inspector Sculpher's assessment of the examination was :-
"Except in the case of Robinson, whom I regard as a failure, it will be seen that in two subjects all the remaining four are fairly good. In composition all are very week, while Laffin has an impediment, but this is not very serious although when excited it might be worse.
In weight and height, Bougourd is an easy first, 5'10«" and 13 stone. Gale and Piesing are practically level but on the light side. Laffin should weigh more than 10 stone 9 lb for 6'1".
Subject to the doctor's report Bougourd, Piesing and Gale appear suitable candidates, but I am doubtful regarding Laffin".

# Appendix 4.

POLICE DISCIPLINE CODE.

DEFAULTERS.

Any member of the Force commits an offence against discipline if he is guilty of:-

1. Discreditable Conduct, that is to say, if he acts in a disorderly manner or any manner prejudicial to discipline or likely to bring discredit on the reputation of the Force or of the Police Service.

2. Insubordinate or oppressive conduct, that is to say, if he:-

   a. is insubordinate by word, act, or demeanour, or,
   b. is guilty of oppressive or tyrannical conduct towards an inferior in rank, or,
   c. uses obscene, abusive or insulting language to any other member of the Force, or,
   d. wilfully or negligently makes any false complaint or statement against any member of the Force, or,

e. assaults any other member of the Force, or,
f. overholds any complaint or report against any member of the Force.

3. Disobedience to Orders, that is to say, if he disobeys, or without good and sufficient cause omits or neglects to carry out any lawful order, written or otherwise.

4. Neglect of Duty, that is to say, if he:-

a. neglects, or without good and sufficient cause omits, promptly and diligently to attend to or carry out anything which is his duty as a Constable, or,
b. idles or gossips while on duty, or,
c. fails to work his beat in accordance with orders, or leaves his beat, point, or other place of duty to which he has been ordered, without due permission or sufficient cause, or,
d. by carelessness or neglect permits a prisoner to escape, or,
e. fails, when knowing where any offender is to be found, to report the same, or to make due exertions for making him amenable to justice,or
f. fails to report any matter which it is his duty to report, or,
g. fails to report anything which he knows concerning a criminal charge, or fails to disclose any evidence which he, or any person within his knowledge, can give for or against any prisoner or defendant to a criminal charge, or,
h. omits to make any necessary entry in any official document or book.

5. Falsehood or prevarication, that is to say, if he:-

a. knowingly makes or signs any false statement in any official document or book, or,
b. wilfully or negligently makes any false, misleading or inaccurate statement, or,
c. without good and sufficient cause destroys or mutilates any official document or record, or alters or erases any entry therein.

6. Breach of Confidence, that is to say, if he:-

a. divulges any matter which it is his duty to keep secret, or,
b. gives notice directly or indirectly, to any person against whom any warrant or summons has been or is about to be issued, except in the lawful execution of such warrant or service of such summons, or,
c. without proper authority communicates to the public, Press, or to any unauthorised person, any matter connected with the Force, or,
d. without proper authority shows to any person outside the Force any book or written or printed document the property of the Police Committee, or,
e. makes any anonymous communication to the Police Committee or any superior officer, or,
f canvasses the Police Committee with regard to any matter concerning the Force, or,
g. signs or circulates any petition or statement with regard to any matter concerning the Force, except through the proper channel of correspondence to the Police Committee, or in accordance with the constitution of the Police Federation, or,
h. calls, attends any unauthorised meeting to discuss any matter concerning the Force.

7. Corrupt Practice, that is to say, if he:-

a. receives any bribe, or,
b. fails to account for or to make a prompt and true return of any money or property received by him in his official capacity, or,

c. directly or indirectly solicits or receives any gratuity, present, subscription or testimonial, without the consent of the Police ommittee, or,

d. places himself under pecuniary obligation to any publican, beer retailer, spirit grocer, or any person who holds a licence concerning the granting or renewal of which the police may have to report or give evidence, or,

e. improperly uses his character and position as a member of the Force for his private advantage, or,

f. in his capacity as a member of the Force, writes, signs or gives without the sanction of the Police Committee, ant testimonial of character or other recommendation with the object of obtaining employment for any person or of supporting an application for the grant of a licence of any kind, or,

g. without the sanction of the Police Committee, supports an application for the grant of a licence of any kind.

8. Unlawful or unnecessary exercise of authority, that is to say, if he:-

   a. without good and sufficient cause makes any unlawful or unnecessary arrest, or,

   b. uses any unnecessary violence to any prisoner or other person with whom he may be brought into contact in the execution of his duty, or

   c. is uncivil to any member of the public.

9. Malingering, that is to say, if he feigns or exaggerates any sickness or injury with a view to evading duty.

10. Absent without leave or being late for duty, that is to say, if he without reasonable excuse is absent without leave from, or is, late for, parade, Court or any other duty.

11. Uncleanliness, that is to say, if he while on duty is improperly dressed or is dirty or untidy in his person, clothing, or appointments.

12. Damage to clothing or other articles supplied, that is to say, if he:-

    a. wilfully or by carelessness causes any waste, loss or damage to any article of clothing or appointment, or to any book, document, or other property of the Police Committee, served out to him or used by him or entrusted to his care, or,

    b. fails to report any loss or damage as above, however caused.

13. Drunkenness, that is to say, if he, while on or off duty, is unfit for duty through drink.

14. Drinking on duty or soliciting drink, that is to say, if he:-

    a. without the consent of his superior officer, drinks, or receives from any person, any intoxicating liquor while he is on duty, or,

    b. demands or endeavours to persuade any other person to give him, or to purchase or obtain for him, any intoxicating liquor while he is on duty.

15. Entering licenced premises, etc. while on duty, that is to say, if he enters, while on duty, any premises licensed under the Liquor Licensing Laws, or any other premises where liquors are stored or distributed, when his presence there is not required in the execution of his duty.

16. If he lends money to any superior or borrows from or accepts any present from any inferior in rank.

17. Any member of the Force also commits an offence against discipline and will be liable to punishment, if he is quilty of an offence which is punishable on conviction whether summarily or on indictment.

Any offence against discipline may be punished by:-

(i) dismissal
(ii) being required to resign (as an alternative to dismissal)
(iii) reduction in rank.
(iv) eduction in rate of pay.
(v) fine.
(vi) reprimand.
(vii) caution.

Every punishment, except a simple caution, will be entered on the defaulter's conduct sheet.

When a Police officer is considered to be guilty of any irregularity or misconduct, it is the duty of the officer cognisant of the facts to bring the case to the notice of the Station officer before going off duty and to inform the accused that he intends to do so. Report of the circumstances is also to be made to the patrolling or other superior officer if opportunity occurs.

This does not imply that Police are necessarily to be reported for trifling irregularities, which can often be dealt with by immediate verbal reprimand. Repeated acts of negligence, however, although in themselves trifling, must not be overlooked.

Except for trifling irregularities, the accused will be required to submit a written report in explanation, of his conduct or of the accusation made against him. The Station officer will obtain statements from the officer making the complaint and from all witnesses and will ensure that every necessary immediate enquiry is made. The accused officer may be sent for at once if the course appears necessary, but generally should make his report on the conclusion of his tour of duty. The Station officer will enter brief particulars in the Occurrence Book and submit reports through the Deputy Inspector to the Inspector.

# Index